The Public Sector in Hong Kong

The Public Sector in Hong Kong

Second Edition

Ian Scott

Hong Kong University Press
The University of Hong Kong
Pokfulam Road
Hong Kong
https://hkupress.hku.hk

© 2023 Ian Scott

ISBN 978-988-8754-03-8 (*Paperback*)

All rights reserved. No portion of this publication may be reproduced or transmitted in any form or by any means, electronic or mechanical, including photocopying, recording, or any information storage or retrieval system, without prior permission in writing from the publisher.

British Library Cataloguing-in-Publication Data
A catalogue record for this book is available from the British Library.

Digitally printed

For Christopher and Lindsay

Contents

List of Figures	viii
List of Tables	ix
Abbreviations and Acronyms	x
Preface to the Second Edition	xii
Preface to the First Edition	xiv
1. The Public Sector: An Overview	1

Part I: Accountability

2. The Constitutional Framework	37
3. Accountability and Organisational Change	75

Part II: The Public Sector and Its Problems

4. The Civil Service: Structure and Functions	103
5. The Civil Service: Personnel Policies and Integrity Management	137
6. Government and Public Bodies	167

Part III: Policy Formulation and Implementation

7. Policy and the Budgetary Cycle	203
8. The Policy Process	236
9. Policy Implementation	266
10. The Chinese Government's Influence on Policy	296

Part IV: The Government and the People

11. Efficiency, Responsiveness, and Transparency	327
12. Rights, Complaints, and Redress	357
13. The Public Sector in Its Political Setting	391
Selected Bibliography	413
Index	437

Figures

Figure 1.1:	The Public Sector	3
Figure 1.2:	Government, Market, and Society	5
Figure 4.1:	The Government Secretariat 2018	108
Figure 7.1:	Public Expenditure as a Percentage of GDP	209
Figure 7.2:	Growth of Government Recurrent Expenditure 1997–2020	210
Figure 7.3:	Estimated Government Revenue 2022–2023	214
Figure 7.4:	Estimated Government Expenditure 2022–2023	218
Figure 11.1:	Are You Satisfied with the Performance of the HKSAR Government? 1997–2020	333
Figure 12.1:	Complaints and Enquiries to the Ombudsman 2016–2021	377

Tables

Table 2.1:	Composition of the Legislative Council 1991–2021	51
Table 2.2:	Judicial Review: Applications for Leave to Apply and Findings against the Government	67
Table 4.1:	The Organisation of Government: Evolving Principles	104
Table 4.2:	Bureaus and Departments in the Hong Kong Government	111
Table 4.3:	Strength of the Twelve Largest Departments 2020	112
Table 4.4:	Administrative Officers: Grade Structure and Establishment 2021	114
Table 4.5:	Establishment and Strength of the Civil Service 1997–2021	130
Table 5.1:	The Civil Service by Gender and Terms of Appointment 2020	143
Table 5.2:	Civil Service Pay Scales	149
Table 6.1:	The Organisation of the Public Sector	177
Table 7.1:	The Budgetary Cycle	222
Table 7.2:	The Medium Range Forecast	223
Table 7.3:	Police Force: Analysis of Financial Provision 2021–2022 and 2022–2023	229
Table 7.4:	Social Welfare Department: Analysis of Financial Provision 2021–2022 and 2022–2023	229
Table 7.5:	Total Public Expenditure: Year-on-Year Change 2021–2022 and 2022–2023	232
Table 7.6:	Total Public Expenditure by Percentage by Policy Area Group	234
Table 9.1:	A Typology of Policy Implementation Styles	272
Table 12.1:	Substantiated and Reportable Allegations against the Police 2015–2021	384

Abbreviations and Acronyms

BLDC	Basic Law Drafting Committee
CAPO	Complaints Against Police Office
CEPA	Closer Economic Partnership Arrangement
CFA	Court of Final Appeal
Chinese Government	The Central Government of the People's Republic of China
CSB	Civil Service Bureau
CSSA	Comprehensive Social Security Assistance
CSTDI	Civil Service Training and Development Institute
DAB	Democratic Alliance for Betterment and Progress of Hong Kong
EOC	Equal Opportunities Commission
EPP	Enhanced Productivity Programme
Hansard	Official Proceedings of the Legislative Council of Hong Kong
HKFP	Hong Kong Free Press
HKFTU	Hong Kong Federation of Trade Unions
Hong Kong Government	Government of the Hong Kong Special Administrative Region
HKSAR	Hong Kong Special Administrative Region
HKUPOP	Hong Kong University Public Opinion Poll
HZMB	Hong Kong–Zhuhai–Macau Bridge
ICAC	Independent Commission Against Corruption
ICC	Integrated Call Centre
IPCC	Independent Police Complaints Council
KCRC	Kowloon Canton Railway Corporation
KPI	Key Performance Indicators

MPS	Master Pay Scale
MRF	Medium Range Forecast
MTRC	Mass Transit Railway Corporation
NPC	National People's Congress
NPCSC	National People's Congress Standing Committee
OECD	Organisation for Economic Cooperation and Development
PLC	Provisional Legislative Council
PCO	Office of the Privacy Commissioner
POAS	Principal Officials Accountability System
POBO	Prevention of Bribery Ordinance
PORI	Public Opinion Research Institute
PRC	People's Republic of China
PRD	Pearl River Delta
PSC	Public Service Commission
RAE	Resource Allocation Exercise
RTHK	Radio Television Hong Kong
SAR	(Hong Kong) Special Administrative Region
SARS	Severe Acute Respiratory Syndrome
SCMP	South China Morning Post
SCCSS	Standing Commission on Civil Service Salaries and Conditions of Service
SQW	Service Quality Wing (Hong Kong Police Force)
UGC	University Grants Committee

The Hong Kong dollar is pegged to the US dollar at 7.8 dollars to 1 US$. Unless otherwise stated, all amounts are expressed in Hong Kong dollars.

Preface to the Second Edition

Since the first edition of this book was published, the Hong Kong government has been confronted with the erosion and decline of its proclaimed core values. Its commitment to the protection of civil liberties, the rule of law, fairness, political neutrality, and its traditionally hallowed virtues of effective implementation, high performance, and efficiency have all come under stress or have been seriously questioned or compromised. In the course of a tumultuous decade, the government has been caught between widespread and persistent opposition to the existing political order and the growing influence of the Chinese government on policy and practice, culminating in the passage of the national security law in June 2020. While the legislation probably signals the end of an era, its effects on public sector performance cannot yet be fully determined. What is clear is that the Hong Kong government has lost much of the autonomy that was promised in the Sino-British agreement and the Basic Law. How the Hong Kong government has attempted to deal with diverse pressures in the critical areas of public management, policy formulation and implementation, civil liberties, and complaint-handling processes provides the focus for this edition.

This book is based on primary sources such as constitutional documents, Legislative Council debates, the annual reports of government departments and statutory bodies, the reports of oversight institutions, and the findings of commissions of inquiry; the secondary literature, particularly that relating to politics and public administration in Hong Kong; and interviews and surveys of civil servants. Since the promulgation of the national security law, however, the amount of primary material has declined. At the time of writing, for example, the quarterly personnel statistics have not been updated since June 2020, some government departments have not produced annual reports in the past year, and it is no longer possible to conduct interviews and surveys of civil servants. In the absence of such information, discussion of the effects of the national security law on the public sector is necessarily restricted to those organisational and policy areas, such as the police force, the courts, and educational establishments, that have been directly and publicly impacted by the law.

Preface to the Second Edition

In addition to updating and revising material on the public sector as far as I am able, I have also included a new chapter on the influence of the Chinese government on policy in Hong Kong and incorporated some research findings on integrity management across the public service and in the police force, corruption prevention and the role of the Independent Commission against Corruption (ICAC), and on coordination and innovation. I am grateful to the Hong Kong Research Grant Council and to Ting Gong, who was the principal investigator on three of those projects (Project Nos. CityU11603219 and 11605917 and City University of Hong Kong Project No. 7005144). I have also collaborated with Ting Gong on research relating to the ICAC and on coordination and innovation and have greatly benefited from her support and her able and meticulous scholarship. On integrity management projects on the civil service and, separately, on the police force, I greatly appreciate the research efforts of my former colleagues, Brian Brewer and Joan Y. H. Leung. I am grateful also to Hanyu Xiao and John Bacon-Shone for their valuable advice and work on the corruption surveys. On all of these projects, we were fortunate to have excellent research support from Hang Chow, Sha Xinlei, and Sunny Y. L. Yang. I would like, especially, to acknowledge Sunny Yang's highly efficient work in formatting chapters and creating the figures and tables for this book. Without her efforts, revising the book would have been a much lengthier exercise.

I am also grateful to many people who have contributed in different ways to this revised edition: the civil servants and academics, too numerous to mention individually, who have provided information and insights on how the public sector works; my colleagues in the Department of Public Policy at the City University of Hong Kong who have been a constant source of new research and interesting ideas; Ian Thynne, who made useful comments and suggestions on some of the draft material; the Public Opinion Research Institute for permission to publish Figure 11.1; and for the support of the staff at Hong Kong University Press.

My wife, Terry, showed remarkable tolerance of the shortcomings of an often-distracted spouse, and my children, Christopher and Lindsay, once again helped with some of the practical issues of putting a manuscript together. I am indebted also to Huw Whitwell for resolving some potentially major computer problems. Any mistakes are, of course, my own responsibility.

Ian Scott
February 2022

Preface to the First Edition

Since the retrocession to China in 1997, the public sector in Hong Kong has experienced major problems and undergone significant changes. External pressures, internal civil service reform measures, and a political climate very different from that of colonial times have contributed to uncertainty and a loss of direction, to increases in the workloads of civil servants but to relatively little achievement in the resolution of perennial policy issues. Externally, the government—previously seemingly immune from budgetary shortfalls—has been beset by periodic economic downturns that have seen it move into deficit with all the difficult political decisions that entails. It has also faced pressure from the sovereign power. Although the degree to which the Chinese government intervenes in Hong Kong affairs varies, often depending on its assessment of the national importance of the issue, it has been most clearly evident in the restrictions which it has placed on the pace of democratic development, in its interpretation of the Basic Law, and in its support for local political parties and groups sympathetic to its position. While this has influenced the political context in which the public sector works, there has been relatively little intervention in the affairs of the civil service and other public sector organisations.

Internal reform measures have added to the turbulence. The immediate post-1997 emphases on greater managerial efficiencies and downsizing of the civil service have now been scaled back but they have left a legacy of organisational and personnel problems. The executive's accompanying attempt to assert greater control over the civil service in the name of accountability has yet to be fully worked through and may well cause more disruption if the lines of command of the recent political appointments are not clearly delineated. The extension of the "accountability system" within the government suffers from the fundamental contradiction that the executive itself is appointed by the Chinese government and is not directly accountable to the people of Hong Kong. Despite the buffeting that the civil service has experienced from efforts to introduce more managerial practices and greater political control, the administrative culture of the civil service has proved to be remarkably resilient. It still possesses high administrative capacity in carrying out the routine implementation of policies which have long been accepted by the community. Where it faces difficulties is in formulating and implementing new policies. Its low policymaking capacity stands in marked contrast to its administrative performance and there is a substantial backlog of issues that have been addressed but have subsequently been abandoned or delayed.

The principal reason for policy shortcomings has been the rise of civil society and the difficulty which the government has experienced in developing effective channels of communication with grass-roots organisations and in meeting their demands, *inter alia*, for universal suffrage and a directly elected Chief Executive. Hong Kong's institutional framework allows for few mediating institutions between the government and the people. Political parties are weak because they cannot win office and are unable, in consequence, to aggregate demands or build credible policy platforms. They can provide no surety that, even if they win control of the relatively powerless legislature, their platforms will be translated into policy. For its part, the government makes policy, but it has no mandate from the people to do so. Its policy agenda cannot be taken as a package which has been supported by the electorate and it is, as a result, required to find elaborate justifications for its proposals. It claims to act in the best public interest; to consult on major new initiatives; and to be as efficient, responsive, and responsible as possible. Some of those claims may be partially true. But when faced with a sceptical population, most of whom want a democratically legitimated government, they cut no ice. Each new proposal comes before an often-recalcitrant legislature and a highly critical public who are increasingly versed in the art of ensuring that policies of which they do not approve do not succeed.

This book is an attempt to explain how the public sector has fared in this new political and economic environment. It seeks to describe the constitutional, organisational and policy problems that have confronted the public sector, to analyse how the government has tried to deal with those problems, and to suggest possible ways in which its difficulties might be minimised or resolved. The research on which this book is based stems from a long-standing interest in public administration in Hong Kong. In 2005, some of the research findings were contained in a book, *Public Administration in Hong Kong: Regime Change and its Impact on the Public Sector* (Singapore Marshall Cavendish), comparing public administration in the colonial period with that after the handover. Two years later, the book was out of print and Marshall Cavendish were no longer engaged in academic publishing. I am grateful to Colin Day, the publisher of Hong Kong University Press, who was interested in the suggestion that the Press might bring out a new and revised book which would draw on the original work but which would focus more on post-1997 problems.

I have been fortunate to be able to undertake research in a congenial and stimulating environment. It has been my privilege and pleasure to teach at the graduate level in both the Department of Politics and Public Administration at the University of Hong Kong and the Department of Public and Social Administration at the City University of Hong Kong. I have borrowed liberally from the excellent research on politics and public administration that has been conducted by members of staff in both institutions. I am grateful, too, to the graduate students of both departments, many of whom work in the civil service or other parts of the public sector and whose dissertations have been a rich source of information. Both departments are blessed with exceptional support staff and they have been unfailingly helpful and resourceful when unexpected problems arose.

Many serving and former civil servants and other public sector employees have helped to update material for this book and to provide me with a perspective on the problems that they face. I am especially grateful to those who agreed to be interviewed and to members of staff in the Civil Service Bureau who answered my written queries.

I would like to thank also Brian Brewer, John Burns, Elaine Chan, Hon Chan, Joseph C. W. Chan, Janet Cheng, Anthony B. L. Cheung, Peter T. Y. Cheung, Linda Chow, Tamara Dent and members of the Asia Research Centre at Murdoch University, Mark Hallyar, Adrienne LaGrange, Peter Lai Hing-ling, Danny Lam, Kanas Lau, Eliza Lee, James Lee, Joan Leung, Paul Morris, Margaret Ng, Martin Painter, Jon Quah, Vanessa So, Dorothy Tam, Ian Thynne, Gavin Ure, and H. K. Wong. This book required help from many different people and I am grateful for all the assistance I have received.

Finally, I have to thank my wife, Terry Lui, who not only provided critical comments but also proofread all the chapters. My son, Christopher, helped to solve most of my computer problems and standardised the tables and my daughter, Lindsay, checked the referencing and proved a stern critic of style and consistency. Needless to say, responsibility for all the remaining mistakes is my own.

Ian Scott
January 2009

1
The Public Sector
An Overview

The public sector may be defined as those government agencies and related organisations that are funded by revenue raised from taxes, fees, or the sale of state-owned assets.[1] The agencies include bureaus, departments, the judiciary and funded statutory bodies, and fully or partly subsidised organisations such as publicly owned corporations, social welfare agencies, schools, and universities. They do not include private companies or voluntary associations. In Hong Kong, the civil service consists of 13 policy bureaus and almost 70 departments.[2] At the end of March 2021, the bureaus and department employed around 178,000 people, approximately 4.6% of the Hong Kong labour force.[3] The 70 "related organisations", which range from small tribunals to large statutory bodies and public corporations, such as the Hospital Authority and the Airport Authority, employ at least as many people as the civil service. The Hospital Authority alone employs 88,000 people.[4] Most tertiary institutions and many welfare organisations are also largely funded by the taxpayer.

Government and the Public Sector

The Issue of Autonomy

In recent decades, relationships between governments and their public sectors have become much more complex. Two factors have contributed to this complexity. The first is that many governments have given executive agencies outside the civil

---

1. In Hong Kong, the sale of land, which is owned by the government, has been an important source of revenue. The conventional definitional of the public sector as those organisations funded through taxation has been amended accordingly. See Wegrich, K. (2007). Public sector. In M. Bevir (Ed.), *Encyclopedia of governance* (Vol. II, pp. 776–777). Thousand Oaks: Sage.
2. Hong Kong Government (2018, 1 July). *Organisation chart of the Government of the Hong Kong Special Administrative Region.* https://www.gov.hk/en/about/govdirectory/govchart/index.htm. See Figure 4.1.
3. Legislative Council Panel on Public Service (2021, 17 May). An overview of the civil service: establishment, strength, retirement, age profile and gender profile. LC Paper No. CB(4) 986/20-21(03). The figures are for people in position (the "strength") rather than the number of funded posts ("the establishment"), which in March 2021 was approximately 192,000.
4. Hong Kong Hospital Authority. (2021). *About us.* https://www.ha.org.hk/visitor/ha_visitor_index.asp?Content_ID=10008&Lang=ENG&Dimension=100&Parent_ID=10004

service a greater degree of autonomy. The second is that the delivery of public goods and services has become much more of a partnership between government, the private sector, and voluntary social organisations.

In Western countries, governments have widely adopted private sector practices, leading to a distinction between "core government", comprising important centralised functions such as finance, security, and overall policymaking responsibility, and decentralised government agencies or other public sector organisations which are often concerned with the delivery of social policies such as education and welfare. Underlying decentralisation is the notion that, if public sector organisations are given autonomy from central control, they may better utilise private sector methods to provide more efficient services.

Figure 1.1 shows a possible relationship between core government and the public sector, assuming that some power has been divested to decentralised public sector organisations. The autonomy from core government that these bodies can exercise will depend on their functions, level of public funding, perceptions of their need for independence, and often on the political circumstances that led to their creation. In many cases, autonomy is limited to the performance of very specific functions. For example, regulatory agencies, fully funded by the government, may be set up to control, say, the stock market or to protect consumers from inferior or dangerous products. These agencies have autonomy because they can administer existing legislation independently, but they do not make the ultimate decisions on what that legislation should be. Similarly, central banks may be given autonomy to determine interest rates, but they may need to work closely with government and legislatures to coordinate economic policy. The funding of a service often determines the organisation's autonomy. The greater the funding, the more likely it is that the government will insist on close scrutiny of the organisation. Some agencies, however, such as an Audit Commission or an Ombudsman, are set up as fully funded, oversight bodies. In these cases, the organisation's function to act as a check on government requires independence. Many governments also own public corporations that generate revenue and are intended to make profits. Public corporations usually have greater autonomy than other public bodies although there are normally provisions for ultimate central government control.

In Hong Kong, unlike many developed countries, devolution of responsibilities sometimes has little to do with the merits of private sector practices.[5] It is not always about the supposed private sector virtues of efficiency, productivity, and less hierarchical structures but more frequently about political convenience. The Hong Kong civil service has long taken pride in its efficiency and is not always convinced that public bodies with some degree of autonomy are equally efficient. When those bodies are established outside direct government control, the government normally retains a watching brief over their policies through the appointment of chief

---

5. Cheung, A. B. L. (2016). NPM in Asian countries. In T. Christensen & P. Lægreid (Eds.), *The Ashgate research companion to new public management* (pp. 132–144). New York: Routledge.

Figure 1.1 *The Public Sector*

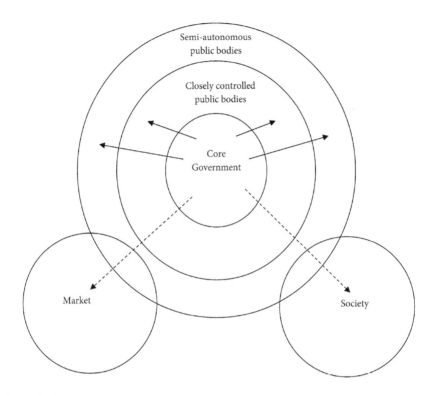

Source: Author.

executives and membership on the board. Public bodies are expected to act within the parameters of government policy. The government has argued, for example, that it has the right to intervene in tertiary institutions to ensure that government policy is implemented.[6] And, although the publicly owned transport companies, the Mass Transit Railway Corporation (MTRC) and the Kowloon-Canton Railway Corporation (KCRC), were operating independently on commercial principles, the government had no compunction about initiating a long-term lease of all KCRC assets to the MTRC.[7] The autonomy of oversight organisations is usually respected. The ICAC, the Audit Commission, and the Ombudsman have all been able to fulfil their functions without overt interference.

---

6. Yeung, S. K., & Lee, J. P. (2007). *Report of the Commission of Inquiry on allegations relating to the Hong Kong Institute of Education* (p. 101). Hong Kong: Government Logistics Department.
7. Yeung, R. (2008). *Moving millions: The commercial success and political controversies of Hong Kong's railways* (Ch. 11, Epilogue). Hong Kong: Hong Kong University Press.

The Functions of the Public Sector

The principal function of the public sector is to provide goods and services[8] for the community. These goods and services could potentially cover the whole range of human needs and desires from education to childcare to medical services to clean air to a safe environment. But there are always questions about how demands should be met. Should the public sector provide most of the desired goods and services? What role should the market and the private sector play? Should voluntary organisations be involved in the provision of more services? Figure 1.2 illustrates a possible relationship between government, market, and society. Public goods and services provided by the government alone fall within the unshaded area marked "government" while the shaded areas represent partnerships between the government and market and government and voluntary organisations to deliver public goods and services jointly. Figure 1.2 could be redrawn to show a smaller government and a larger market and/or society. Services could be divested from government to the private sector or voluntary organisations, and government could be reduced to core functions. Alternatively, Figure 1.2 could be redrawn to show a dominant government providing most goods and services with a smaller role for the market and societal organisations.

For many years in Hong Kong, the government's philosophy was "big market, small government".[9] In line with this principle, most public goods and services should be provided by the private sector or by voluntary associations. Historically, public expenditure as a percentage of Gross Domestic Product (GDP) has suggested as much. Until recently, it has been below 20%; the public expenditure percentage in most developed countries is often over twice as much.[10] The Basic Law, Hong Kong's constitution, specifies that government should "keep the budget commensurate with the growth rate of its gross domestic product".[11] That would seem to imply a commitment to a small public sector and the notion that government should not intervene directly in the market or society.

But that is a misleading impression. "Small government" in Hong Kong certainly does not mean limited government. The government is ubiquitous. In 2019, there was approximately one civil servant for every 42 citizens, one of the highest ratios in Asia and even higher if the employees of fully or largely funded public

---

8. Public goods and services are commonly defined as those goods and services that are provided by governments because the market cannot allocate them efficiently. See Srinivasan, K. (2007). Public goods. In M. Bevir (Ed.) op. cit., pp. 765–766.
9. Tsang, D. Y. K. (2006, 18 September). Big market, small government. https://www.ceo.gov.hk/archive/2012/eng/press/oped.htm
10. Wong, W., & Yuen, R. (2012). Economic policy. In W. M. Lam, P. L. T. Lui, & W. Wong (Eds.), *Contemporary Hong Kong government and politics* (2nd ed., p. 257). Hong Kong: Hong Kong University Press.
11. *The Basic Law of the Hong Kong Special Administrative Region of the People's Republic of China* (2020). Article 107. https://www.basiclaw.gov.hk/en/basiclaw/index.html

Figure 1.2 *Government, Market, and Society*

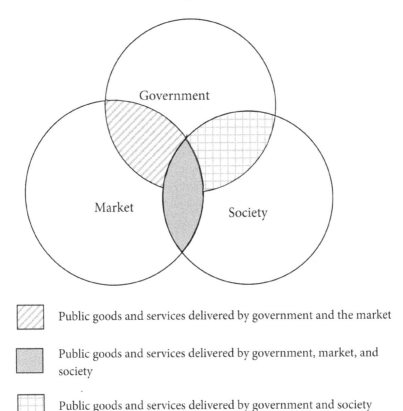

	Public goods and services delivered by government and the market
	Public goods and services delivered by government, market, and society
	Public goods and services delivered by government and society

Source: Author.

sector organisations are included.[12] The government frequently intervenes in the economy not only to provide services but also to regulate. It plays a critical role in the delivery of public housing, education, health, and social welfare services, and has a 35,000-strong police force that attempts to maintain public order. In 2017, in her first policy address as Chief Executive, Carrie Lam said that the government should take on a role as a facilitator, which required the recruitment of more civil servants.[13] Over the past decade, the government has paid increasingly less attention to the constitutional requirement and long-standing principle that expenditure should not exceed the rate of growth of GDP. By 2020, the government was

---

12. OECD Data (2020). *General government spending*. https://data.oecd.org/gga/general-government-spending.htm
13. Lam, C. (2017). *We connect for hope and happiness* (para 9). https://www.policyaddress.gov.hk/2017/eng/pdf/PA2017.pdf

budgeting for the largest deficit in Hong Kong's history and said that it expected to be in deficit for the next five years; public expenditure as a percentage of GDP was forecast to rise to over 26% (see Chapter 7).[14]

How, then, should we characterise the role of the government in relation to the private sector and society? We might see the Hong Kong government as a developmental or capitalist government rather than as one which is essentially a behind-the-scenes facilitator.[15] In that sense, the government ideally acts to preserve the long-term interests of capitalism but does not necessarily always serve the short-term interests of capitalists.[16] It may, for example, regulate the labour market rather than permit firms to pay low wages in unsafe working conditions. It may provide social services to satisfy citizens' needs even if this means that funding comes in part from company taxation. In its efforts to maintain the capitalist system, the Hong Kong government often seeks to lead rather than simply to facilitate, but to do so successfully requires a degree of relative autonomy from the market, society, and the Chinese government.

The relative autonomy of the Hong Kong government has been shrinking over the past two decades. Its ability to introduce new policies has been significantly constrained by almost continual opposition from many civil society organisations, such as political parties, unions, and a multitude of specific interest groups.[17] Many of these organisations did not believe that the public interest could be fully addressed under the existing political system and they looked for more democratic solutions. The Chinese government, too, had an agenda that it wished to see implemented. This resulted in measures promoting greater integration with the Mainland, interventions on matters within the Hong Kong government's jurisdiction, and public expenditure in line with Beijing's policies (see Chapter 10).[18] For many Hong Kong people, the high degree of autonomy promised to the post-1997 government in the Joint Declaration and the Basic Law was undermined.[19] Increasingly, the Hong Kong government was caught between two conflicting forces: democrats who wanted greater autonomy, even independence from China, more democracy, and a stop to the erosion of civil liberties, and a Chinese government that wanted more rapid integration of the Hong Kong Special Administrative Region (HKSAR) into

---

14. Financial Secretary (2020a). *The 2020–21 budget* (para 168, Appendix B). https://www.budget.gov.hk/2020/eng/budget33.html
15. Lee, E. W. Y. (1998). The political economy of public sector reform in Hong Kong: The case of a colonial-developmental state. *International Review of Administrative Sciences, 64*(4), 625–641; Scott, I. (1989). Administration in a small capitalist state. *Public Administration and Development, 9*(2), 85–199.
16. To paraphrase Miliband, it acts on behalf of capitalists but not necessarily at their behest. Miliband, R. (1977). *Marxism and politics* (p. 74). Oxford: Oxford University Press.
17. Chan, J., & Chan, E. (2017). Hong Kong 2007–2017: A backlash in civil society. *Asia Pacific Journal of Public Administration, 39*(2), 132–152.
18. Scott, I. (2017). One country, two systems: The end of a legitimating ideology? *Asia Pacific Journal of Public Administration, 39*(2), 83–99.
19. *Joint Declaration of the Government of the United Kingdom of Great Britain and Northern Ireland and the Government of the People's Republic of China on the question of Hong Kong* (1984). https://www.refworld.org/docid/3ae6b525c.html

China and an end to the protests that rocked the polity.[20] The Chinese government's enactment of national security legislation for Hong Kong in 2020 represented what it thought was a final solution to the impasse.

In the following pages, the Hong Kong public sector is analysed in the context of its political, economic, and social environment. The purpose of the book is twofold:

- to describe and analyse how the public sector works and to examine its relationships with the polity, society, and the market; and
- to assess its attempts to overcome problems of accountability, autonomy, and legitimacy; its reduced capacity to formulate and implement policy; and the continuing pressure to deliver goods and services efficiently and in response to expressed needs.

The Colonial Inheritance

Over the period 1841 to 1997, when Hong Kong was a British colony, the government acquired organisational and policymaking characteristics and relationships with the public that were designed to maintain political stability and to perpetuate colonial rule. In 1984, the Sino-British agreement preserved many of these features in the post-handover political system. They were incorporated in the Basic Law, which became the constitution of the HKSAR after the resumption of Chinese sovereignty in 1997. The present structure of the government and the public sector consequently owes much to its colonial origins. Although the political and economic environment has changed considerably since 1997, the structure of the civil service retains the form and functions that were characteristic of colonial administration. Public bodies, many created in the last two decades before the handover, have remained in place.

Organisational Characteristics

The principal organisational characteristics of colonial administration were:

- centralised government;
- hierarchically organised departments;
- "small" government and fiscal frugality;
- recruitment by merit, political neutrality, commitment to the rule of law; and
- "clean" government.

---

20. Cheung, T. (2020, 13 January). Beijing's top official in Hong Kong pledges deeper integration. *SCMP*. https://www.scmp.com/news/hong-kong/politics/article/3045777/beijings-top-official-hong-kong-pledges-deeper-integration

Centralised Government

Centralised government was a feature of colonial administration from the outset. Initially, centralisation met the need to maintain political control, to allocate scarce resources, and to administer a small area. With the acquisition of the New Territories on lease in 1899 and with the creation of the Urban Council, some decentralisation of authority was permitted.[21] But these bodies had only limited autonomy: their funding came directly from the government and their policies were ultimately subject to its approval. Partly because of the centralised nature of government, the emergence of public bodies was a relatively late development. Even with the eventual establishment of many statutory bodies, such as the Hospital Authority, the government often strongly influenced their policies and practices.

Hierarchically Organised Departments

Consistent with centralised government, the departments were organised on strongly hierarchical lines. The Police Force was established as a paramilitary body and other uniformed services—Correctional Services, Customs, Fire Services, and Immigration—were set up with a similar emphasis on strict discipline and obedience to orders. Within the non-disciplined departments, organisational structures were also strongly hierarchical. Departments consequently tended to develop independently from each other and to focus on top-down implementation rather than on horizontal coordination. While such a system was appropriate for maintaining political control, it was not entirely suitable when the government under an active Governor, Sir Murray MacLehose (1971–1981) attempted to expand education, housing, health, and welfare provision. In 1973, the McKinsey consultants recommended structural changes which have remained the basic structural form of the civil service ever since.[22] The Government Secretariat was reorganised into specific policy branches (later called bureaus) with responsibility for a cluster of related departments. Headed by a senior civil servant usually from the administrative grade, the branches were responsible for formulating policy which was then expected to be implemented by the departments. In practice, this politics/administration dichotomy did not always work smoothly and some departments, such as the Police Force, retained a good deal of autonomy.

---

21. Wesley-Smith, P. (1980). *Unequal treaty: China, Great Britain and Hong Kong's New Territories*. Hong Kong: Oxford University Press.
22. McKinsey and Company (1973). *The machinery of government: A new framework for expanding services* (pp. 14–17). Hong Kong: mimeo.

Small Government and Fiscal Frugality

Until the 1950s, when a public housing programme was introduced, the colonial government was small and provided only minimal services. Its role was to maintain law and order and support the growth of a capitalist economy. There was pressure from both the British government and from local entrepreneurs to ensure that there were no budget deficits and that public expenditure was carefully scrutinised. Taxes were kept low. As the economy prospered, government revenue from company tax and the sale of land grew substantially. The government began to accumulate large surpluses. Although "small government" remained an important formal objective, the government eventually became large, complex, and differentiated with a major impact on the market and society. Expanded social services, increasingly delivered by the government or by subvented organisations, were seen as an important means of reducing the legitimacy deficit. By 1997, to meet this expanding role, the civil service establishment had risen to 190,000.[23]

Recruitment by Merit, Political Neutrality, and Commitment to the Rule of Law

British expatriates occupied all the senior positions in the colonial administration until after the Second World War. The government then adopted a policy of localisation whereby an expatriate would be employed only when there was no qualified local candidate. Localisation was nonetheless very slow. Even in the 1980s, most directorate-level positions and senior positions in the Police Force were still held by expatriates. Thereafter, with the impending transfer of sovereignty, localisation was accelerated so that, by 1997, only 1,200 or so expatriates remained in the civil service. Appointments and promotions based on the merit principle are monitored by a Public Service Commission which was established in 1950 and continued to function after the handover.[24]

The concept of political neutrality was inherited from Britain where it meant that senior civil servants would give advice to ministers without fear or favour and would implement impartially any course of action which the minister decided to take. In the fused Hong Kong system of government, most senior positions were held by civil servants, taking the final political decision as well as advising themselves on the most appropriate measures. The concept of political neutrality was adapted accordingly to mean that civil servants would take decisions in the public interest and that they were accountable to the public to act impartially in taking

---

23. Civil Service Branch (1997). *Civil service personnel statistics 1997* (p. 12). Hong Kong: Civil Service Branch.
24. Public Service Commission (2021). *Annual report 2020* (p. 1). https://www.psc.gov.hk/eng/ann_rep/files/20rep.pdf

decisions.[25] Political neutrality survived the handover, but its original meaning was fundamentally undermined by those who believed that civil servants' loyalty to political office holders should override any notion of accountability to a wider public.[26] The *Civil Service Code*, introduced in 2009, states that "[c]ivil servants shall serve the Chief Executive and the Government of the day with total loyalty and to the best of their ability, no matter what their own political beliefs are".[27] In August 2019, after thousands of civil servants demonstrated against its strong-arm tactics towards protesters and questioned its interpretation of political neutrality,[28] the government stressed the provision in the code, emphasising that political neutrality meant loyalty to the government.[29]

The colonial government frequently claimed that the rule of law was the cornerstone of good governance. In practice, the tightly knit relationship between the executive, the Legislative Council, the civil service, and the judicial system meant that the courts were not always as independent as the government claimed. After the Tiananmen Square incident in Beijing in June 1989 and the subsequent enactment of a Bill of Rights, the maintenance of the rule of law became something of a mantra for those who feared that the Chinese government would violate their civil liberties after 1997.[30] The government also set up statutory bodies that protected individual rights. These included the Equal Opportunities Commission, the Privacy Commissioner, and an ombudsman with strengthened powers, all of which continued to function after the transfer of sovereignty.

Clean Government

Corruption was a perennial problem in the colonial administration. By the 1960s, it was particularly prevalent in the Police Force where syndicates operated to extract bribes from drug traffickers, prostitutes, nightclub owners, taxi drivers, and small businesses. In 1970, the government passed a more stringent corruption law, the *Prevention of Bribery Ordinance*, although it was still administered by the police.[31] After a public scandal when a senior police officer, Peter Godber, who had been charged with corruption offences, managed to escape from Hong Kong, the

---

25. Scott, I. (1996). Civil service neutrality in Hong Kong. In H. K. Asmeron & E. P. Reis (Eds.), *Democratization and bureaucratic neutrality* (pp. 277–293). Basingstoke: Macmillan.
26. Cheung, J. (2003, 17 October). Civil service neutrality is a British thing: State leader. *SCMP*.
27. Civil Service Bureau (2009). *The Civil Service Code* (Section 3.7). https://www.csb.gov.hk/english/admin/conduct/files/CSCode_e.pdf#page=3
28. Chung, K., Su, X., & Lum, A. (2019, 3 August). Hong Kong civil servants embarrass the government with protest against the extradition bill and determination to "stand together as citizens." *SCMP*. https://www.scmp.com/news/hong-kong/politics/article/3021276/hong-kong-civil-servants-embarrass-government-protest
29. Hong Kong Government (2019, 3 August). Civil service neutrality restated. https://www.news.gov.hk/eng/2019/08/20190803/20190803_205232_873.html
30. Jones, C. A. G. (2015). *Lost in China: Law, culture and identity in post-1997 Hong Kong* (pp. 63–65). Cambridge: Cambridge University Press.
31. McWalters, I., Fitzpatrick, D., & Bruce, A. (2015). *Bribery and corruption law in Hong Kong* (3rd ed., pp. 18–21). Singapore: LexisNexis.

governor decided that the ordinance should be administered by an independent commission and set up the Independent Commission Against Corruption (ICAC), which began work in 1974.[32] The commission soon proved to be extremely effective in reducing corruption in the civil service to minimal levels. By the 1990s, it was receiving more complaints about private sector corruption than about public sector corruption. It has remained an important feature of the post-1997 system.

Colonial Policy Formulation and Implementation

The significant features of the colonial system of policy formulation and implementation were:

- minimal basic functions provided by the government,
- social policy provision by non-government organisations,
- policy formulation within very restricted circles, and
- top-down policy implementation focused on outcomes rather than process.

Minimal Basic Functions

In 1980, the economist Milton Friedman wrote that the Hong Kong government was the closest in the world to meeting Adam Smith's prescriptions for the appropriate functions of government in a capitalist system.[33] Smith believed that government should only be concerned with law and order, the administration of justice, and some public works. Friedman added a fourth responsibility: that of protecting those who could not protect themselves.[34] The description does not entirely fit Hong Kong since, by 1980, the government was providing some 40% of the population with public housing,[35] had expanded its education, health, and welfare programmes, and had built three new towns in the New Territories. But Friedman's description does convey something of the ethos of the Hong Kong government. From the earliest times, government and business believed that it was better to stick to minimal functions and not to become involved in social policy provision which would require raising taxes and a different organisational structure.

---

32. See Lethbridge, H. J. (1985). *Hard graft in Hong Kong: Scandal, corruption and the ICAC*. Hong Kong: Oxford University Press; Manion, M. (2004). *Corruption by design: Building clean government in Mainland China and Hong Kong* (pp. 27–83). Cambridge, MA: Harvard University Press; Scott, I., & Gong, T. (2019) *Corruption prevention and governance in Hong Kong* (pp. 27–34). Abingdon: Routledge.
33. Friedman, M. (1980). *Free to Choose* (pp. 47–49, 54–55). Harmondsworth: Penguin.
34. Ibid., p. 53.
35. Hong Kong Government (1981). *Hong Kong 1980* (p. 91). Hong Kong: Government Printer.

Social Services Provision

Until the 1950s, the colonial government thought that social services should be provided by voluntary organisations. It gave land and grants to churches and charitable organisations but only slowly began to deliver social services directly.[36] When it did become more directly involved, organisational reforms were necessary to speed up decision-making and to introduce more planning.[37] While the changes improved performance, they did not resolve the problem of lateral coordination between strong departments or policy issues about which the government and the society sometimes held opposing views. The education curriculum was a constant source of concern. Health care financing began to become problematic in the 1980s. And welfare policy was politically contentious, caught between the belief, entrenched in policy, that the able-bodied should work and the views of social workers and unions that the government had the means to fund more comprehensive social security benefits.

Policy Formulation within Restricted Circles

The colonial government's policymaking was conducted in-house in the Government Secretariat. Policies would usually be devised after an extended conversation conducted by memorandum between the most senior civil servants. Some consultation would then take place with committees of prominent figures appointed by the administration. Green papers with a clear indication of the government's preferred position were then sometimes distributed to the public for comment. Subsequently, a white paper containing the definitive policy would be issued, the policy would be approved by the Executive Council, and, if necessary, legislation would be passed by the Legislative Council. This style of top-down policy initiation, followed by varying degrees of consultation, has continued into the post-handover era although the government has been much less able than its colonial predecessor to insist that its proposals should be implemented.

Top-Down Policy Implementation

The colonial government saw policy implementation as a matter of targets that had to be met on time and within budget. It was not particularly concerned with the process of how these targets were achieved. Those opposed to its proposals were regarded as obstacles to implementation. The government was sensitive to matters that might involve traditional Chinese customs and practices, but it was also prepared to act quite forcefully when objectives had been set and there were deadlines

---

36. Sinn, E. (1989). *Power and charity: The early history of the Tung Wah Hospital, Hong Kong* (p. 13). Hong Kong: Oxford University Press.
37. McKinsey and Company (1973) op. cit.

to be met. In constructing public housing and building the new towns, for example, squatters were moved off the land to make way for the new estates. Colonial government attitudes towards policy implementation focused on the efficient and cost-effective achievement of the objective. The public was expected to be grateful recipients of whatever benefits were provided.

The Colonial Government and the Legitimation of Power

A major feature of the colonial government's relationship with the people was a continuing legitimacy deficit that occasionally escalated into a crisis. Attempts were made to reduce this deficit by claims that government was based on the rule of the most able, on a "tripod of consents", and on good performance. In the 1990s, it also attempted to make the civil service more user-friendly and argued, against the evidence, that the government was accountable.

The government suffered from a continuing legitimacy deficit because, as a colonial regime, it had difficulty in generating consent for its rule. In common with colonies elsewhere, it would have preferred to rule with the support of traditional elites. But in Hong Kong, when the occupation took place in 1841, there were hardly any people, let alone traditional leaders. For the next 40 years or so, there were no institutional means of expressing the views of a public who were seen as sojourners who would return to China or migrate elsewhere.[38] Thereafter, the government, through the boards of the District Watch Committee and the Tung Wah and Po Leung Kuk charitable organisations, consulted Chinese elites on some matters affecting the people. The implicit bargain was that in exchange for direct government access, the elites would maintain social order.[39]

The system worked well enough until the communist takeover in China in 1949. Within six years, there was a fourfold population increase as migrants streamed into Hong Kong. New social problems, particularly the housing shortage, meant that advice from charitable organisations was no longer as relevant as it had been. There were riots in 1956, which left 59 people dead, and again in 1966 and 1967.[40] In 1966, the government appointed a commission to investigate the riots, which found that there was a "gap" between the government and the public, resentment of the police, and the need for labour reform and improvements in social services.[41]

Much of the next decade was devoted to bridging the gap, reducing the legitimacy deficit, and generating more support for the system without introducing

---

38. Sinn, E. (2013). *Pacific crossing, California gold, Chinese migration and the making of Hong Kong* (p. 9). Hong Kong: Hong Kong University Press.
39. Lethbridge, H. J. (1978). *Hong Kong: Stability and change* (p. 117). Hong Kong: Oxford University Press.
40. Hong Kong Government (1956). *Report on the riots in Kowloon and Tsuen Wan October 10th to 12th 1956 with covering despatch dated 23rd December 1956 from the Governor of Hong Kong to the Secretary of State for the Colonies* (p. ii). Hong Kong: mimeo.
41. Commission of Inquiry (1967). *Kowloon disturbances 1966: Report of the Commission of Inquiry*. Hong Kong: Government Printer.

elections. A variety of methods were employed. The government's rationale for colonial rule was that it was based on the consent of the local people, of Britain, and of China.[42] This was a myth. Consent could not be expressed through elections or any other mechanism, the consent of Britain was that of a colonising power, and the Chinese government had said that it would take Hong Kong back when the time was appropriate.

A more powerful argument was that the government deserved to rule because it had performed well. It claimed credit for Hong Kong's economic prosperity, which saw GDP growth rates, for example, running at 12% per annum between 1976 and 1981.[43] It also argued that it deserved to govern because it gave the people what they wanted and delivered goods and services efficiently and cost-effectively. Education, health, and housing services had been in short supply so that their rapid expansion in the 1970s satisfied unmet demand and gave some credence to the argument that good performance generated support for the system. Once those basic needs had been satisfied, however, it became more difficult to use the same means to reduce the legitimacy deficit.

In the 1990s, the government was faced with the problem that it could not change the political system to increase its legitimacy. The last Governor, Chris Patten, did expand the franchise for the 1995 election, but the political system had been set in stone by the Joint Declaration and the Basic Law and could not easily be changed to accommodate growing democratic sentiment. What the government did instead was to provide the civil service with a more human face. Performance pledges stressed service to the customer, offices were painted, and the Police Force was reformed.[44] The civil service benefited from changed public perceptions. It was seen to be less distant than in the past, to be more efficient, and to be staffed by competent, well-educated officers.

In the final years of colonial rule, the government made another attempt to present itself as an accountable government. In 1995, it published a booklet entitled "Serving the Community", arguing that accountability was "the fundamental principle which drives the public sector".[45] Civil servants were accountable in three respects. They were answerable to the Legislative Council, the Audit Commission, the ICAC, and the Commissioner for Administrative Complaints (later called the Ombudsman); they were required to keep the community informed of government's decisions and actions; and they were expected to provide, "within reason", access to information about these decisions and actions.[46] After 1997, the government

---

42. See Miners, N. (1975). *The government and politics of Hong Kong* (1st ed., p. viii). Hong Kong: Oxford University Press.
43. Hong Kong Government (1982). *Hong Kong 1981* (p. 35). Hong Kong: Government Printer.
44. Cheung, A. B. L. (1996). Performance pledges—Power to the consumer or a quagmire in public service legitimation? *International Journal of Public Administration 19*(2), 233–260.
45. Hong Kong Government (1995). *Serving the community* (p. 21). Hong Kong: Government Printer.
46. Ibid., pp. 21–22.

continued to subscribe to this version of accountability; no progress was made in resolving the problem of the legitimacy deficit.

The Public Sector after 1997

The principal features of the public sector in the post-handover period have been:

- government attempts to increase political control over the civil service,
- reduced policy capacity and coordination in a disarticulated system, and
- continuing evidence of major legitimacy problems.

Political Control and the Civil Service

The structure of the government and the public sector has remained largely unchanged since the handover. The formal binary division between policy bureaus and departments responsible for implementation has remained. Initially, most senior civil servants retained their positions as policy secretaries. The civil service was promised conditions of service no less favourable than before 1997 (Basic Law, Article 100) and statutory bodies have generally operated much as they did before the handover. However, there was a significant shift in power dynamics when the Chief Executive and the Chinese government sought to increase their political control over the civil service. Externally, interactions between the civil service and legislature also underwent major changes. Before 1997, the government had worked closely with other major institutions; after the handover, it became much more disarticulated with the executive, legislature, and the civil service often acting independently and sometimes in an uncoordinated manner.[47]

Soon after the handover, the government strengthened its already highly centralised structure by abolishing the elected Urban and Regional Councils and bringing the departments which served those councils back into the mainstream of government. Its rationale was that Hong Kong did not need this middle tier between the government and the District Councils.[48] The post-1997 government was circumspect about creating new public bodies[49] although some were established in the information technology and innovation fields. The government was constrained at times by economic circumstances, at others by fears that new agencies would become too autonomous, and generally by the prevalent belief, especially among senior civil servants, that most matters were better managed by a centralised administration.

---

47. Scott, I. (2000). The disarticulation of Hong Kong's post-handover political system. *The China Journal, 43*, 29–53.
48. Constitutional Affairs Bureau (1998, June). *Review of district organizations: Consultation document* (pp. vi–vii). Hong Kong: Printing Department.
49. Civil Service Bureau (1999). *Civil service reform: Consultation document: Civil service into the 21st century*. Hong Kong: Printing Department.

In 1999, the Chief Executive, Tung Chee Hwa, launched a reform programme that was intended to improve efficiency in the civil service and to change some of the fundamental assumptions on which it was based.[50] There had been some evidence of inefficiencies, including a public housing corruption scandal and the chaotic opening of a new airport, for which the civil service bore some responsibility.[51] Tung believed that the civil service should be more like the private sector with more civil servants on contracts and performance pay. If the reforms had been fully implemented, they would have undermined the colonial principle that the civil service should be based on a permanent establishment with fixed salary scales and would have weakened the civil service as a political force. But the government was only partially able to implement its proposals. New recruitment and appointment rules were introduced, making it more difficult for recruits to obtain permanent positions (see pp. 142–144). On other issues, there was resistance from the civil service associations and inherent problems in implementing proposals such as performance pay.

Where the government did succeed, at least initially, was in downsizing the civil service. The difficult economic circumstances resulting from the Asian financial crisis fuelled the long-standing pressure from business groups and the Legislative Council to reduce the size of the civil service and to cut salaries. The government froze recruitment and began a process that resulted in lowering salaries for all civil servants to June 1997 dollar levels. At the same time, the civil service establishment was cut. Some civil servants were transferred to other public sector organisations, and the number of artisans and labourers, who had formed a large part of the colonial civil service, was significantly reduced.[52] In some departments, notably in the Housing Department, where estate management was contracted out, the establishment dropped sharply. Voluntary retirement schemes also contributed to smaller numbers. The civil service establishment declined from a high of 190,503 in 1997/1998 to a low point in the post-handover period of 159,401 in 2007/2008.[53] Thereafter, the size of the civil service gradually increased again until, by March 2021, its establishment had reached 1997/1998 levels.[54]

The reform proposals may have had the underlying objective of increasing political control over the civil service. A more fragmented civil service on contract terms might have led, as in other countries, to greater direct political influence on how the civil service operated. Perhaps with this in mind, Tung devised and introduced the Principal Officials Accountability System (POAS) in 2002, increasing

---

50. Painter, M. (2012). Hong Kong. In K. Verhoest, S. Van Thiel, G. Bouckaert, & P. Lægreid (Eds.), *Government agencies: Practices and lessons from 30 countries* (pp. 342–352). Basingstoke: Palgrave Macmillan.
51. Burns, J. P. (2004). *Government capacity and the Hong Kong civil service* (pp. 163, 166–167). Hong Kong: Oxford University Press.
52. Civil Service Branch (1997), op. cit., p. 16; Civil Service Bureau (2008), op. cit., p. 36.
53. Civil Service Branch (1997), op. cit., p. 12; Civil Service Bureau (2008), op. cit., Table 1.1.
54. Legislative Council Panel on Public Service (2021, 17 May). *An overview of the civil service: Establishment, strength, retirement, age profile and gender profile* (p. 2). LC Paper No. CB(4) 986/20-21(03).

the powers of the Chief Executive. Until then, principal officials, serving as policy secretaries, had with one exception, all been senior civil servants. They could be moved from one position to another in the civil service, but they could not be dismissed. Under the new system, principal officials became political appointees on contract, could be drawn from outside the civil service, and could be dismissed by the Chief Executive. They were accountable but only to the Chief Executive and to the Chinese government, which had to agree to their appointments. Their accountability to the Legislative Council remained as weak as it had been before the change.

In 2005, the new Chief Executive, Donald Tsang, announced that the number of political appointments would be increased to include a "small number of positions dedicated to political affairs".[55] Every head of a bureau, the politically appointed principal officials (policy secretaries), was to have an under secretary and a political assistant reporting to them who would assist in the formulation of policy, coordination with other bureaus and with the Legislative Council, provide political input, help with media relations, networking, preparing political speeches, and making suitable social and political appointments.[56] Civil servants opposed the changes, fearing that lines of command would become distorted and that they would be serving two masters.

The government succeeded in asserting more political control, but civil servants doubted whether this was an improvement. In semi-structured interviews conducted with 28 senior civil servants between 2009 and 2012, a study found that 80% agreed or strongly agreed that they had a duty to act in the public interest even if this conflicted with the views of their principal official (policy secretary); 48% agreed or strongly agreed with the statement that political interference was "a disturbing feature of government administration in Hong Kong"; and 58% agreed or strongly agreed that the effectiveness of the public service would be increased if civil servants had more say in policymaking.[57] *The Civil Service Code* of 2009 strongly affirmed that political appointees should not interfere with the line operations of departments.[58] But policy was another matter. The POAS meant that administrative-grade civil servants lost their traditional monopoly on policy formulation. Some members of the administrative grade became politically appointed directors of bureaus, but the grade itself lost its traditional monopoly over policy formulation. The often strongly held views of the Chinese government and its local Liaison Office in Hong Kong also diminished the autonomy of senior civil servants and reduced their influence on policy.

---

55. Tsang, D. Y. K. (2005). *Strong governance for the people* [2005–2006 policy address] (para. 25). https://www.policyaddress.gov.hk/05-06/eng/pdf/speech.pdf
56. Constitutional Affairs Bureau (2006). *Consultation document on further development of the political appointment system* (pp. 28–30). https://www.legco.gov.hk/yr05-06/english/panels/ca/papers/ca0731cb2-consultation-e.pdf
57. Burns, J. P., & Li, W. (2015). The impact of external change on civil service values in post-colonial Hong Kong. *The China Quarterly, 222*, 522–546.
58. Civil Service Bureau (2009). *The Civil Service Code*, op. cit., Section 6.

Reduced Policy Capacity and Coordination

Post-handover policy formulation and implementation were adversely affected by:

- economic problems,
- political problems, and
- policy coordination and the disarticulated system.

Economic Problems

On 2 July 1997, the day after the Chief Executive, Tung Chee Hwa, assumed office, the Thai government decided to float the baht, an event which probably triggered the Asian financial crisis.[59] As the Hong Kong economy began to slow, property prices plummeted and negative equity and unemployment began to rise. In 2003, an outbreak of atypical pneumonia, SARS, killed nearly 300 people and seriously affected many businesses. Unemployment reached a record 8.7% and bankruptcies increased from 600 cases in 1997 to 24,922 cases in 2003.[60] The huge surpluses of colonial days were gone and the budgetary deficit was seemingly spiralling out of control. The government understandably blamed external factors for the territory's problems. Critics maintained that the major reason was poor governance.[61] The government's credibility in managing economic affairs had been undermined.

Political Problems

Economic failures were compounded by political volatility. Immediately after the handover, the Chinese government dissolved the Legislative Council and reconstituted it without the democratic parties. When new elections were held under a more restricted franchise in 1998, there was a substantial increase in turnout over all previous Legislative Council elections and some democratic candidates were returned to the council. In 2003, the government decided to introduce legislation to enact Article 23 of the Basic Law, which required that the HKSAR should enact legislation "on its own" to prohibit "any act of treason, secession, sedition, subversion against the Central People's Government" (see Chapter 2). The proposed legislation sparked concerns about civil liberties, eventually resulting in a demonstration of an estimated 500,000 people on 1 July 2003.[62] A majority in the Legislative Council refused to support the legislation and it was withdrawn. Tung resigned in 2005, but this did little to improve the government's capacity to introduce new policies, which

---

59. Jao, Y. C. (2001). *The Asian financial crisis and the ordeal of Hong Kong* (p. 4). Westport, CT: Quorum Books.
60. Hong Kong Government (2004). *Hong Kong 2003* (p. 99). Hong Kong: Printing Department.
61. Goodstadt, L. (2013). *Poverty in the midst of affluence: How Hong Kong mismanaged its prosperity* (pp. 3–4, 224). Hong Kong: Hong Kong University Press.
62. Cheng, J. Y. S. (Ed.) (2005). *The July 1 protest rally: Interpreting a historic event* (Ch. 1, 2). Hong Kong: City University of Hong Kong Press; Lee, J., & Mo, C. (2003, 2 July). 500,000 march through the streets. *SCMP*.

were severely constrained after the demonstration, or to resolve the impasse over constitutional reform.

After the economy improved, the government was able to take new initiatives but it could not always implement them effectively, given its low credibility, the prospect of filibusters in the Legislative Council, and the review of administrative decisions by judicial review. The consultative system, based on public consultation documents, advisory committees, and occasional surveys, proved to be an inadequate guide to public opinion. The 2003 demonstration, for example, came as a surprise to the government, which thought that the consultation document on the legislation with some amendments, had won public approval.[63] Meanwhile, civil society organisations proliferated and often took their grievances to the streets.[64] The government found it difficult to deal with these new groups and coalitions, which were often created after a policy had been announced. On some issues, such as the introduction of a goods and services tax in 2006[65] and changes in the education curriculum in 2012,[66] the government proposed new measures and then backed down. On other matters, even when there was widespread opposition, the government refused to concede. On the high-speed rail link to Guangdong and the Hong Kong–Zhuhai–Macau Bridge (HZMB), both of which were strongly supported by Beijing, the government pressed on despite the great expense, scarcely proven benefits, and repeated demonstrations against the projects (see pp. 312–315).[67] Other issues requiring fundamental reform or more funding, such as health care financing, public housing and welfare, and rising poverty levels, simply festered.

The government did not have a consistent strategy on policy implementation and it soon developed a siege mentality. It tried to adopt civic engagement with the pressure groups opposed to its proposals, but that initiative soon died.[68] It feared that public attacks on new major policy reforms might further erode its support and perhaps provoke even wider unrest. Efforts were concentrated on making efficiency gains to existing social policies, leaving unanswered the question of meeting expanding demand. While the government was able to proceed with caution on social policies, it could not do so when the Chinese government was directly involved, particularly on constitutional and security issues.

---

63. Hong Kong Government (2002). *Proposals to implement Article 23 of the Basic Law*. Hong Kong: Security Bureau.
64. Ma, N. (2007). *Political development in Hong Kong: State, political society, and civil society* (Appendix 5). Hong Kong: Hong Kong University Press.
65. Financial Services and the Treasury Bureau (2007). *Public consultation on tax reform: Final report* (p. 12). https://www.taxreform.gov.hk/eng/pdf/finalreport.pdf
66. Morris, P., & Vickers, E. (2015). Schooling, politics and the construction of identity in Hong Kong: The 2012 "moral and national education" crises in historical perspective. *Comparative Education, 51*(3), 305–326.
67. Cheung, C. Y. (2014). Hong Kong's systemic crisis of governance and the revolt of the post-80s youth—The anti-express rail campaign. In J. Y. S Cheng (Ed.), *New trends of political participation in Hong Kong* (pp. 417–447). Hong Kong: City University of Hong Kong Press.
68. Lee, E. W. Y., Chan, E. Y. M., Chan, J. C. W., Cheung, P. T. Y., Lam, W. F., & Lam, W. M. (Eds.) (2013). *Public policymaking in Hong Kong: Civic engagement and state-society relations in a semi-democracy*. London: Routledge.

Social policy neglect resulted in growing inequality, declining social mobility, and a growing number of people living below the poverty line. A Commission on Poverty was created in 2005, but it made little progress and was revamped in 2013 when the poverty line was officially defined as household income below 50% of median income.[69] The government tried various means to reduce poverty, but they stopped far short of significant tax reform and the redistribution of income by providing more and better services.[70] By 2016, the number below the poverty line was 1.3 million. In the same year, the Gini coefficient rose to 0.539, which was the highest level of income inequality for 40 years.[71] In 2018, Oxfam found that the monthly income of the top 10% of wealthy households was 44 times that of poor households and predicted that more people would fall below the poverty line.[72] It noted that health care and welfare expenditure fell below that of all OECD members, except Britain, and that the government, given its significant reserves, could afford to spend much more.[73]

Policy Coordination and the Disarticulated System

Post-handover policy coordination suffered from the hierarchical departmental structures inherited from the colonial government. With them came the problem that a lack of horizontal coordination creates for some kinds of policy implementation. Other problems stemmed from the emergence of a more disarticulated political system and the introduction of the POAS.[74] Departments did not coordinate easily with each other, which was less important in a colonial regime with minimal functions than when more complex social policy problems had to be addressed. Coordination between the civil service and other institutions also became more difficult. The Basic Law was not intended to create a separation of powers, but political institutions began to act more as unconnected bodies than they had done under colonial rule.

After the dissolution of the Provisional Legislative Council in 1997 and the 1998 election, the Legislative Council gradually became polarised into pro-establishment/pro-Beijing and democratic members. The electoral system is half composed of functional constituencies, many with small electorates, and half composed of directly elected seats on a list proportional representation system (see Chapter

---

69. Wong, J. S. C. (2017). The role of government in poverty alleviation in Hong Kong: Part 1—Dynamics of policy attention, choice and change. *Asia Pacific Journal of Public Administration, 39*(4), 238–257.
70. Wong, J. S. C. (2018). The role of government in poverty alleviation in Hong Kong: Part II—Diversity of instrument choice. *Asia Pacific Journal of Public Administration, 40*(1), 23–42.
71. Census and Statistics Department (2016). *Hong Kong 2016 population by-census—Thematic report: Household income* (pp. 11–12). https://www.censtatd.gov.hk/hkstat/sub/sp459.jsp?productCode=B1120096
72. Oxfam (2018). *Hong Kong inequality report* (pp. 8, 12). https://www.oxfam.org.hk/en/f/news_and_publication/16372/Oxfam_inequality%20report_Eng_FINAL.pdf
73. Ibid., p. 8.
74. Fong, B. C. H. (2014). Executive-legislative disconnection in post-colonial Hong Kong. *China Perspectives, 1*, 5–14; Scott (2000) op. cit.

2, Table 2.1). This configuration ensured a perpetual pro-establishment majority in the chamber although the democrats were not without resources. They used filibusters to delay government proposals and, since they also had over one-third of the seats, employed their veto power over constitutional issues. In 2016 and 2017, however, the courts disqualified six democratic members for failure to take their oath of allegiance properly[75] with the consequence that the democrats lost their veto power. In December 2017, the Legislative Council amended its rules of procedure to prevent the use of the filibuster in most cases.[76] In their efforts to hold the government to account, activists have also resorted to seeking judicial review to challenge government decisions (see pp. 65–69).

The POAS also contributed to the problem of policy coordination. The Chief Secretary for Administration and the Financial Secretary lost their control over final decisions on public expenditure and, with it, important means of policy coordination. Under the POAS, they were equal in status to their fellow principal officials. Budget changes (the "envelope system") gave policy secretaries the power to allocate funds among the departments under their purview (see p. 222). This tended to discourage programme coordination with other bureaus, reinforcing beliefs in the self-sufficiency of the bureau and its departments. In 2005, when Donald Tsang Yam-kuen became Chief Executive, he returned some financial control powers to the Chief Secretary and the Financial Secretary although the "envelope system" remained in force.

Horizontal policy coordination was always going to be difficult within a structure which strongly emphasised vertical coordination within the departments. But the difficulty was compounded by the disarticulation of the political and bureaucratic institutions, the fractious politics of the post-handover environment, and by political attempts to exert more control over the civil service. Bringing the Legislative Council in line by disqualifying members and eliminating filibusters did not result in a smoother policy process: the issues were taken up by protesters on the streets.

The Legitimation of Power after 1997

The post-1997 government did little to reduce its legitimacy deficit and gradually saw it spiral into a crisis that reflected not only deep discontent with government policy but wider disaffection with the entire political system and increasing "mainlandisation". Conflict between opposing views on how power should be legitimated and exercised centred on:

---

75. Kong, T. G. (2018, 31 January). Disqualified: How the government compromised on Hong Kong's only free and fair election. *HKFP*. https://www.hongkongfp.com/2018/01/31/disqualified-hong-kong-govt-compromised-citys-free-fair-elections/
76. Hansard, 13–15 December 2017.

- the introduction of universal suffrage and the protection of civil liberties, and
- problems of governance in a polarised polity.

According to Beetham, the legitimation of power consists of three elements: express consent, legal authority, and moral authority.[77] Express consent is most easily obtained through free and fair democratic elections. Non-democratic regimes may reduce their legitimacy deficit by reliance on a legitimating ideology, by good performance, and by other ameliorating measures and ensure long periods of stability in the process. However, attaining performance legitimacy is a delicate business and can easily be undermined by unexpected events and economic downturns. Legal authority is usually achieved through a constitution and laws that are seen to be fair and just and equally applicable to everyone. If legal authority is to bolster legitimacy, it should also reflect how the people wish to see their political affairs arranged, the accountability of the government, and the protection of civil liberties. Moral authority is the assessment of whether the actions of a regime are compatible with the principles of expressed consent and legal authority. A loss of moral authority occurs when people "make the link . . . between the 'bad' and the 'wrong'".[78]

Conflict over the Introduction of Universal Suffrage and the Protection of Civil Liberties

The post-handover system suffered from weaknesses in each of these elements of legitimacy. Consent could not be achieved through elections that were biased in favour of pro-establishment candidates. Legal authority was founded on the Basic Law, imposed after a drafting process dominated by the Chinese government (see pp. 39–40) but was never approved by the Hong Kong people. The moral authority of the government gradually declined. Accountability was called into question by the increasing role played by the Chinese government in the decision-making process. Protesters took to the streets and unaddressed policy problems compounded public discontent.

The Basic Law did contain two possibilities for progress towards ensuring consent through more democratic elections. The first was that it provided for a review of the provisions for the 2007 and 2008 Chief Executive and Legislative Council elections, raising the prospect of a faster pace of democratic reform. In 2004, the Chinese and Hong Kong governments closed the door on this possibility. The Hong Kong government's task force laid down nine conditions so restrictive that they left no alternative but the maintenance of the status quo.[79] The Standing Committee of the National People's Congress (NPCSC) said that Hong Kong had

---

77. Beetham, D. (2013). *The legitimation of power* (2nd ed., pp. 15–19). Basingstoke: Macmillan.
78. Ibid., p. 216.
79. Constitutional Development Task Force (2004). *The second report of the constitutional development task force: Issues of principle in the Basic Law relating to constitutional development* (pp. 37–39). https://www.legco.gov.hk/yr03-04/english/panels/ca/papers/ca0416cb2-report2-e.pdf

little experience with democracy and that there should be no change to the current arrangements.[80] In 2005, the democratic members used their veto to prevent the government from obtaining the two-thirds majority it needed to make some minor increases in the size of the Legislative Council and the Chief Executive Election Committee.[81] The size of the Legislative Council and the electoral committee were slightly expanded for the 2012 elections, but there was no change in the structure of power relationships.

The second possibility for constitutional reform lay in Basic Law provisions stipulating that both the Chief Executive and the Legislative Council should ultimately be elected by universal suffrage (Articles 45 and 68). In 2007, Tsang said that his foremost objective was to seek a consensus on constitutional reform. The government issued a green paper canvassing for views[82] but found that there was "no mainstream view" on Legislative Council elections under universal suffrage.[83] On Chief Executive elections, however, a clear majority favoured the introduction of universal suffrage no later than 2017.[84] The NPCSC then announced that the Chief Executive and the Legislative Council might be elected by universal suffrage in 2017 and 2020 respectively, but that there would be no change to the arrangements for the 2012 Chief Executive election.[85]

In 2014, two Chinese government documents signalled a stronger central government line on autonomy and universal suffrage. In June, a State Council document on "one country, two systems" declared that Hong Kong's autonomy was determined by the Chinese government and that there was no such thing as residual power.[86] It replaced the previous promise of "Hong Kong people ruling Hong Kong" with "Hong Kong people administering Hong Kong" under the direction of the central leadership. A NPCSC decision on 31 August outlined the Chinese views on universal suffrage.[87] It accepted that Hong Kong people wanted universal suffrage but placed restrictive conditions on its implementation. A nominating committee for the Chief Executive election was to choose two or three candidates who would need the endorsement of at least half of the committee. Candidates would be required to

---

80. Hong Kong Government (2013). *Methods for selecting the Chief Executive in 2017 and for forming the Legislative Council in 2016* (Appendix II). https://www.legco.gov.hk/yr13-14/english/panels/ca/papers/ca1209-cdoc20131204-e.pdf
81. Hansard, 21 December 2005, 3313–3559.
82. Hong Kong Government (2007). *Green paper on constitutional development*. Hong Kong: Government Logistics Department.
83. Hong Kong Government (2007). *Report on consultation on green paper on constitutional development* (p. 33). Hong Kong: Government Logistics Department.
84. Ibid., pp. 55–58.
85. Hong Kong Government (2013) op. cit., Appendix I.
86. State Council of the People's Republic of China (2014, 15 March). *The practice of the one country, two systems policy in the Hong Kong Special Administrative Region*. http://english.www.gov.cn/archive/white_paper/2014/08/23/content_281474982986578.htm
87. Standing Committee of the National People's Congress (2014, 1 September). *NPC Standing Committee decision on Hong Kong 2017 election framework*. http://be.china-embassy.org/eng/sghd/201409/t20140901_2076170.htm

"love the country and love Hong Kong", effectively excluding democratic candidates from contesting the election. The documents provoked huge demonstrations calling for proper universal suffrage and the resignation of the Chief Executive.

The Chinese government's decision had been anticipated by the democrats who came together in an alliance aimed at achieving universal suffrage under free and fair conditions. The pan-democrats were joined by the Occupy Central with Love and Peace movement, created in 2013, which advocated a peaceful civil disobedience campaign to take possession of public space. A third group of "localists" was composed largely of young protesters, often students, who had been involved in many previous demonstrations. They were divided into Scholarism, which had successfully fought against the introduction of the "moral and education" curriculum, and the more radical People Power. People Power did not accept that protests should always be peaceful and was often involved in confrontations with the police. What the groups had in common was the belief that the Mainland government was encroaching on Hong Kong's autonomy and civil liberties, that there should be universal suffrage, and that the public should nominate candidates for the Chief Executive election. Together with some unionists, the groups made up the Umbrella Movement which occupied parts of Hong Kong Island and Kowloon for 79 days between 26 September and 15 December 2014.[88]

The government did not attempt to remove the protesters but condemned their actions as violations of the rule of law. There were claims that the police were using excessive force. On 28 September, the police used tear gas for the first time since 2005, which increased public sympathy for the protesters and undermined a long-running and successful community policing programme. The demonstrations, at times estimated to be over 100,000 strong, were difficult to contain. Although the Umbrella Movement eventually petered out, it changed the political landscape. It challenged the government's view that it had the consent of the people and it created a substantial pool of young activists who continued to take to the streets on issues that went beyond elections to the nature of governance in Hong Kong.

The Legislative Council considered the Chinese government's proposal on universal suffrage in June 2015.[89] The motion was lost by 28 votes to eight because many pro-establishment members were not present, but it would have been defeated anyway because the pan-democrats would have exercised their veto. After the occupation, the localists formed political groups to contest the 2016 Legislative Council elections, but six localist candidates were banned from running because the Electoral Affairs Commission found that they did not sincerely believe that Hong

---

88. Bush, R. C. (2016). *Hong Kong in the shadow of China: Living with the Leviathan* (Ch. 5). Washington, DC: Brookings Institution Press; Ma, N. (2019). From political acquiescence to civil disobedience. In N. Ma & E. W. Cheng (Eds.), *The Umbrella Movement: Civil resistance and contentious space in Hong Kong* (pp. 27–49). Amsterdam: Amsterdam University Press.
89. Hansard, 17, 18 June 2015, 13239–13372, 13379–13467.

Kong was an inalienable part of China.[90] The NPCSC issued a ruling disqualifying two elected members on a case that was still *sub judice* in Hong Kong, provoking further protests.[91]

In June 2019, when the government introduced an amendment to the *Fugitive Offenders Ordinance*, which was designed to facilitate extradition of fugitives from Taiwan, mainland China, and Macau, another long-lasting storm of protests caused even worse damage to regime and government legitimacy than the Umbrella Movement.[92] The proposed legislation was perceived as a major threat to civil liberties, raising the spectre of Hong Kong residents facing charges in China (see p. 259). The Extradition Bill provoked huge demonstrations—some estimated in the millions—focusing on the protection of civil liberties. Even after the proposal was eventually retracted in September 2019, protests continued as civil liberties and calls for greater democracy became part of a single platform.[93] The protesters made five demands: withdrawal of the Extradition Bill,[94] a commission of inquiry into alleged police brutality,[95] retracting the classification of protesters as "rioters",[96] amnesty for arrested protesters,[97] and universal suffrage for both the Chief Executive and Legislative Council elections.[98] Aside from withdrawing the bill, the government did nothing to assuage these demands. Pitched confrontations between police and protesters took place virtually every weekend and public holiday. The protesters caused considerable damage to railway stations, shopping malls and universities. By January 2020, almost 7,000 of them had been arrested.[99] The police used tear gas and rubber bullets to try to stop the protests and were widely criticised for alleged

---

90. Ng, J., Cheung, T., & Fung, O. (2016, 2 August). Protests shut down electoral commission briefing as Hong Kong Indigenous' Edward Leung disqualified from Legco election. *SCMP*. https://www.scmp.com/news/hong-kong/politics/article/1998201/hong-kong-indigenous-edward-leung-disqualified-legislative
91. Grundy, T. (2016, 6 November). "There is no more one country, two systems": Thousands rally against Beijing's intervention in oath row. *HKFP*. https://www.hongkongfp.com/2016/11/06/there-is-no-more-one-country-two-systems-thousands-rally-against-beijings-intervention-in-oath-row/; Kong (2018), op. cit.
92. Chan, H. (2019, 23 December). Explainer: Hong Kong's five demands—Withdrawal of the extradition bill. *HKFP*. https://www.hongkongfp.com/2019/12/23/explainer-hong-kongs-five-demands-withdrawal-extradition-bill/
93. Bulard, M. (2019, September). What's really behind Hong Kong's protests. *Le Monde diplomatique*, https://mondediplo.com/2019/09/02hong-kong; Lee, F. L. F., Tang, G. K. Y., Yuen, S., & Cheng, E. W. (2020). Five demands (and not quite) beyond: Claim making and ideology in Hong Kong's anti-extradition bill movement. *Communist and Post-Communist Studies*, 53(4), 22–40.
94. Chan (2019) op. cit.
95. Chan, H. (2019, 24 December). Explainer: Hong Kong's five demands—An independent investigation into police behaviour. *HKFP*. https://www.hongkongfp.com/2019/12/24/explainer-hong-kongs-five-demands-independent-investigation-police-behaviour/
96. Cheng, K. (2019, 28 December). Explainer: Hong Kong's five demands—Halt the characterization of protests as "riots." *HKFP*. https://www.hongkongfp.com/2019/12/28/explainer-hong-kongs-five-demands-halt-characterisation-protests-riots/
97. Cheng, K. (2019, 25 December). Explainer: Hong Kong's five demands—Amnesty for all arrested protesters. *HKFP*. https://www.hongkongfp.com/2019/12/25/explainer-hong-kongs-five-demands-amnesty-arrested-protesters/
98. Chan, H. (2019, 26 December). Explainer: Hong Kong's five demands—Universal suffrage. *HKFP*. https://www.hongkongfp.com/2019/12/26/explainer-hong-kongs-five-demands-universal-suffrage/
99. Hansard, 8 January 2020, 3987.

excessive use of force, selective enforcement, and incompetence.[100] Many protesters, and some police officers, were hospitalised. By early 2020, the protests had slowed although there were still occasional violent confrontations involving multiple arrests. The COVID-19 outbreak achieved what the police could not, removing protesters from the streets but leaving lasting damage to the legitimacy of the government and the reputation of the force.

In June 2020, the National People's Congress enacted a national security law for Hong Kong that created broadly defined offences of secession, subversion, terrorism, and collusion with a foreign country to subvert national security.[101] The vague nature of the offences and the establishment of new security agencies to investigate and enforce them intensified fears about violations of civil liberties and sparked widespread international condemnation. Hong Kong's public sector was also directly affected by the law, particularly the Police Force, the Judiciary, and the school system, which was required to make changes to the curriculum (see pp. 320–321). The Police Force subsequently arrested many localist and pan-democratic leaders.

Election laws were also subsequently changed. On 11 November 2020, the National People's Congress decided that any Hong Kong legislator who had advocated or supported "Hong Kong independence"; refused to recognise China's sovereignty or exercise of sovereignty over Hong Kong; sought foreign or overseas forces to interfere in Hong Kong affairs; and otherwise endangered national security would be immediately disqualified and required to relinquish their seat.[102] In March 2021, the NPC adopted a decision to improve the electoral system which led to reductions in the number of directly elected and functional constituency seats and the election of 40 of 90 members by an Election Committee (see Table 2.1).[103] Another committee, composed of the Chief Secretary for Administration, two other secretaries and three non-official members, was given the power to vet all Legislative Council candidates to ensure that they were "patriots".[104] When the election was held in

---

100. Amnesty International (2020). *Hong Kong: Missing truth, missing justice. The case and international legal framework for the establishment of a commission of inquiry into the 2019 protests* (pp. 5–6). London: Amnesty International.
101. Government of the People's Republic of China (2020). *The Law of the People's Republic of China on safeguarding national security in the Hong Kong Special Administrative Region*. https://www.elegislation.gov.hk/fwddoc/hk/a406/eng_translation_(a406)_en.pdf
102. NPC Observer (2020, 11 November). NPCSC clarifies "allegiance" requirements for Hong Kong legislators, disqualifies pro-democracy legislators. https://npcobserver.com/2020/11/11/npcsc-clarifies-allegiance-requirements-for-hong-kong-legislators-disqualifies-pro-democracy-legislators
103. NPC Observer (2021, 11 March). Decision of the National People's Congress on improving the electoral system of the Hong Kong Special Administrative Region. https://npcobserver.com/2021/03/11/2021-npc-session-npcs-hong-kong-electoral-overhaul-decision-explained/; see also State Council Information Office of the People's Republic of China (2021, 20 December). *Hong Kong democratic progress under the framework of one country, two systems* (Ch. V). http://english.scio.gov.cn/node_8027477.html
104. Hong Kong Government (2021, 6 July). *Chief Executive appoints Candidate Eligibility Review Committee members* [Press release]. https://www.info.gov.hk/gia/general/202107/06/P2021070600318.htm

The Public Sector: An Overview

December 2021, a Legislative Council composed almost entirely of "patriots" was duly elected.[105]

Why did the Hong Kong government not do more to address the protesters' demands and perhaps stave off the introduction of the national security law? First, its room for manoeuvre was severely circumscribed. The Police Force was adamantly opposed to a commission into its alleged brutality, to reclassifying "rioters" as protesters, and to granting amnesty to those who had been arrested. It was backed by the Chinese government, which had already made its position on demands for democracy very clear.

Second, the Hong Kong government misinterpreted the problem, apparently believing that the protests stemmed from "deep-seated" social issues rather than political concerns.[106] None of the demands, however, were about social issues and, even if they had been, the government was not prepared to devote sufficient resources to fix the problems. After August 2019, when the pro-China media began to explain the cause of the protests as foreign incitement and pro-establishment/pro-Beijing political figures stepped up their claims that the protesters had been brainwashed by the liberal studies programme in the secondary schools,[107] the government's explanation of events gradually changed to an acceptance of these arguments. There was little or no credible evidence to support any of these explanations but, in the absence of any basis for negotiation with protesters who were often described as "leaderless", there was no alternative but to deploy police on the streets to control them.

The failure to identify the problem properly led to a fundamental political mistake. The government believed that it had public backing in its efforts to control the protests. It could easily have postponed the November 2019 District Council elections on the grounds that the protests had caused too much disruption. Instead, the government believed that the elections would affirm its actions and return a pro-establishment majority in all 18 district councils. The councils have no executive powers, but they were elected, unlike the Legislative Council and the Chief Executive, on a first-past-the-post system, largely on universal suffrage. The democratic camp took its opportunity, suspended the protests, and campaigned vigorously. They won 392 of 452 seats and took control of 17 of the 18 district councils on a record 71% turnout; only 47% had voted in the previous elections.[108]

---

105. Pang, J. & Pomfret, J. (2021, 20 December). Turnout hits record low for Hong Kong's 'patriots-only' election. *Reuters*. https://www.reuters.com/world/china/hong-kong-votes-overhauled-patriots-only-election-2021-12-19/
106. Hansard, 13 November 2019, 1465.
107. Lam, J.& Chiu, P. (2019, 3 July). Former Hong Kong leader Tung Chee Hwa blames liberal studies at secondary schools for encouraging violent protests among young people. *SCMP*. https://www.scmp.com/news/hong-kong/politics/article/3017180/former-hong-kong-leader-tung-chee-hwa-blames-liberal; McLaughlin, T. (2021, 9 September). How China weaponized the press. *The Atlantic*. https://www.theatlantic.com/international/archive/2021/09/hong-kong-china-media-newspaper/620005/
108. Registration and Electoral Office (2019). *Voter turnout rate – District Council election 2019*. https://www.elections.gov.hk/dc2019/eng/turnout.html

Pan-democratic candidates won close to 60% of the vote.[109] The results were a massive vote of no confidence in the government and its handling of the protests. They raised more legitimacy questions about the governance system and about how the public sector could continue to function effectively in a polarised polity.

Problems of Governance in a Polarised Polity

Governments use power to implement decisions and policies and to achieve outcomes through the public sector. In polarised polities, this becomes much more difficult because those holding political power may not enjoy the unequivocal support of the bureaucracy and because a significant proportion of the population may choose not to comply with the government's orders. Both issues were germane in the Hong Kong situation.

After 2012, the government's ability to command unquestioning loyalty from its employees began to decline as increasing numbers of civil servants sympathised with the protesters and opposed government policies. The attempt to introduce a "moral and national" education policy was opposed by many teachers, some of whom were employed in government schools.[110] Pro-establishment politicians thought that some teachers were inciting their students to participate in demonstrations and the Secretary for Education threatened to dismiss school principals if they supported teachers under investigation for protesting.[111] Relations between government and the civil service continued to deteriorate during Leung Chun-ying's tenure as Chief Executive. Civil servants from many different departments joined the numerous rallies calling for the unpopular Leung's resignation.

Dissent within the civil service intensified during the 2019 protests. In July 2019, 100 administrative grade officers submitted a petition to Carrie Lam calling on her to appoint an independent inquiry into the causes of the unrest.[112] Thousands of other civil servants demonstrated on the streets, demanding that the Extradition Bill be withdrawn.[113] By January 2020, 41 civil servants and at least 80 teachers had

---

109. Cheng, K. (2019c, 25 March). Hong Kong District Council election: Democrats take control of 17 out of 18 councils in landslide victory. *HKFP*. https://www.hongkongfp.com/2019/11/25/hong-kong-district-/council-election-democrats-take-control-17-18-councils-landslide-victory/
110. Morris & Vickers (2015) op. cit.
111. Cheng, K. (2019d, 30 December). Hong Kong education chief warns principals may be fired if they support teachers for protesting. *HKFP*. https://www.hongkongfp.com/2019/12/30/hong-kong-education-chief-warns-, principals-may-fired-support-teachers-investigation-protests/
112. Lum, A., Ting, V., & Cheung, E. (2019, 26 July). One in seven of Hong Kong's elite civil servants call on Carrie Lam to hold independent inquiry into extradition bill unrest but police remain firmly opposed. *SCMP*. https://www.scmp.com/news/hong-kong/politics/article/3020206/one-seven-hong-kongs-elite-civil-servants-call-carrie-lam.
113. Chung, Xu, & Lum (2019) op. cit.; Tse, H., & Mak, M. C. F. (2022). Value dynamics in support to social movement: Hong Kong civil servants in the anti-extradition bill movement. *Social Transformations in Chinese Societies*. https://doi.org/10.1108/STICS-04-2021-0007.

been arrested for their part in the protests.[114] There were calls for strikes in support of the protesters.

To address the situation and in the context of the promulgation of the national security law, the government decided to require all serving civil servants, new appointees and non-civil service staff to take an oath or sign a declaration to

> uphold the Basic Law of the Hong Kong Special Administrative Region, bear allegiance to the Hong Kong Special Administrative Region of the People's Republic of China, be dedicated to my duties and be responsible to the Government of the Hong Kong Special Administrative Region.[115]

The government said that the oath would "enable civil servants to have clearer awareness of the responsibilities and requirements entailed by their official position."[116] The requirement came into effect in mid-January 2021 when government employees were given four weeks to take the oath, sign the declaration or risk being dismissed, retired in the public interest or have their probationary status terminated. At the end of the period, 129 civil servants (113 civilian grade civil servants and 16 disciplinary service personnel), who neglected or refused to sign the declaration or take the oath, were given a further seven days to present reasons for their neglect or refusal.[117] None of the explanations offered were accepted. Of the non-civil service staff, 535 neglected or refused to sign the declaration and were dismissed or resigned.[118] In a letter to all civil servants in July 2020, the Secretary for the Civil Service said that civil servants had a duty "to be allegiant to the . . . HKSAR and the HKSAR Government under the framework of the Basic Law and the *Civil Service Code*."[119] It is interesting that this wording differs from the "be responsible" used in the oath but it may make little difference in practice. Civil servants already have an obligation under the *Civil Service Code* to serve the government with "total loyalty"[120] and the Secretary is under pressure from members of the Legislative Council Panel on Public Service to interpret the vague term "be responsible" broadly and to implement it stringently.[121] For the government, Panel

---

114. *China Daily* (2020, 13 January). CE backs disciplinary action for wayward teachers, civil servants. https://www.chinadaily.com.cn/a/202001/13/WS5e1c2bb7a310128217270931.html
115. Civil Service Bureau (2021, 6 December). Oath-taking/declaration requirement for civil servants. https://www.csb.gov.hk/english/admin/oathserving/2769.html
116. Secretary for the Civil Service (2020, 15 July). Upholding the Basic Law and pledging allegiance to the HKSAR: proposal on oath-taking/signing the declaration by civil servants. https://www.csb.gov.hk/english/letter/2744.html.
117. Legislative Council Panel on Public Service (2022, 9 February). Policy measures of the Civil Service Bureau in 2021 policy address (p.3). LC Paper No. CB(4)57/2022(01); Legislative Council Panel on Public Service (2021, 19 April). Update on implementation of the requirement for civil servants to take oath or sign declaration. LC Paper No. CB(4)773/20-21(04).
118. Legislative Council Panel on Public Service (2022, 9 February) op. cit.
119. Secretary for the Civil Service (2020, 15 July) op. cit.
120. Civil Service Bureau (2009) op. cit., Section 3.7.
121. Legislative Council Panel on Public Service (2021, 19 April). Minutes of meeting (pp. 7–14). LC Paper No. CB(4)1310/20-21.

on Public Service members, and civil servants themselves, the oath may be little more than another means to quell dissent in the civil service.

Prolonged protests, strikes, and violence de-legitimate governments and bring into focus the question of whether perceived unjust laws should be obeyed. The Hong Kong protesters repeatedly disobeyed police orders that many demonstrations were illegal, ignored a government order that wearing face masks to protect against tear gas and avoid facial recognition techniques was also illegal, engaged in violent confrontations with the police, broke into the Legislative Council, and vandalised many Mainland-owned businesses. The government thought that this behaviour would be condemned by a majority of citizens. But the actions of the protesters were weighed against the methods used by the police and the failure of the government to respond effectively to the crisis.

The pan-democrats' victory in the District Council elections and several surveys show the decline in confidence in the government and the Police Force in particular. A Public Opinion Research Institute (PORI) poll conducted monthly between June 2019 and February 2020 found that over 70% of respondents were dissatisfied with the performance of the government with the figure rising to 82% in February 2020.[122] Over the same period, respondents who distrusted the Hong Kong government ranged between 60% and 76%.[123] A Bauhinia Foundation poll conducted in October/November 2019 found that all aspects of the implementation of the rule of law—including equality before the law, judicial independence and autonomy, open government, maintaining law and order, and preventing government abuse of powers—showed a very significant drop in public satisfaction compared with that of the previous two years.[124] Satisfaction with police performance declined rapidly. Between June and November 2019, a PORI poll showed a fall from 50%, already the lowest level since 1997, to 27%.[125]

These figures provide overwhelming evidence of the decline of legitimacy in the Hong Kong government. For the public sector and the work that it does to provide goods and services, this presents fundamental challenges. How does a government instruct a civil service, riven within itself, to do what it wants it to do? And how does it ensure that the law is obeyed when public confidence in its performance has reached such low levels?

---

122. PORI (2020). Are you satisfied with the performance of the Hong Kong government? https://www.pori.hk/pop-poll/hksarg/h001.
123. Ibid. Do you trust the Hong Kong government? https://www.pori.hk/pop-poll/hksarg/k001
124. Bauhinia Foundation (2019). *Public perceptions towards the rule of law in Hong Kong—An opinion survey* (conducted for the Bauhinia Foundation by the Hong Kong Institute of Asia Pacific Studies, The Chinese University of Hong Kong). http://www.bauhinia.org/index.php/english/research/106
125. PORI (2021, 8 June). POP releases popularity figures of Hong Kong disciplinary forces and the PLA Hong Kong garrison. https://www.pori.hk/press-release-en/2021-06-08-pm.html?lang=en

Analysing Systemic Problems in the Public Sector

From this overview of relationships between Hong Kong's public sector and its volatile, contentious polity, three major problems that provide the central themes for this book may be identified:

- The problem of ensuring that politicians and public sector employees are accountable.
- The problem of formulating and implementing policies.
- The problem of legitimating the use of power.

Each problem strains relationships within the public sector itself and between the public sector and the political system, market, and society. When there is a smooth working relationship between the political officeholders and the civil service, when needs can be identified and appropriate solutions devised, when policies can be formulated and implemented with the support of elected politicians, business, and civil society, then government and the public sector can deliver goods and services efficiently and can respond effectively to future problems. But these relationships have increasingly deteriorated in post-handover Hong Kong to the detriment of public sector performance. To analyse why this is so, each problem needs to be analysed in its conceptual context.

Accountability

How politicians and civil servants are held accountable for the way they exercise power is a central consideration in any political system. Accountability includes both the external constitutional measures and internal bureaucratic controls that are required to ensure that power is exercised legally, appropriately, and in the public interest.[126] It is necessary to distinguish also between answerability, the willingness of a government to explain its actions, and political responsibility, where a government accepts the consequences of its mistakes resulting, possibly, in the resignation of office holders or the government itself.[127]

Constitutions, written or unwritten, usually determine how accountability issues are handled, but the Basic Law is only specific about the accountability of the Chief Executive who, after election by a small and unrepresentative committee,[128] is then confirmed by the Chinese government to whom he or she is accountable (Article 43). The principal officials are selected by the Chief Executive and cannot be removed by the Legislative Council. The government, similarly, is answerable

---

126. Thynne, I., & Goldring, J. (1987). *Accountability and control: Government officials and the exercise of power* (p. 11). Sydney: Law Book Company.
127. Ibid., pp. 7–9; Bovens, M. (1988). *The quest for responsibility: Accountability and citizenship in complex organisations* (pp. 26–28). Cambridge: Cambridge University Press; Burns (2004) op. cit., pp. 157–158.
128. Young, S. N. M., & Cullen, R. (2010). *Electing Hong Kong's Chief Executive*. Hong Kong: Hong Kong University Press.

but not accountable to the council (Article 64). Neither the council nor the public can vote the government out of office. While civil servants are held accountable for their actions through the internal hierarchy and oversight institutions, their political masters have no mandate from the people.

Problem Identification, Policy Formulation, and Implementation

Identifying a policy problem, formulating a solution, and then implementing it is a rational process fraught with difficulties in normal times but verging on the impossible when the autonomy of a government is compromised, when resources are tight, or when political unrest presents a serious constraint. If a government is not relatively autonomous from society or external forces, then it is not in control of its own policy agenda and loses the right to decide on the items which should receive priority. If resources are tight, then its choices may be limited. If choices have to be made in an atmosphere of contentious politics and with only passing reference to popular demands, then the government is likely to encounter opposition in implementation.

Because these issues were all relevant in post-1997 Hong Kong, the government suffered from weakened policy capacity,[129] especially over the last decade of protests and as the Chinese government increasingly insisted that Hong Kong's policy agenda should complement its own. If the colonial government had often underestimated its capacity to introduce new policies,[130] the post-1997 government initially often overestimated its ability to do so. The subsequent policy failures undermined its credibility and resulted in a government reluctant to introduce new policies for fear of further failure or the political consequences.[131] Policy problems increased in an atmosphere of rising discontent.

Legitimacy

For the exercise of power to be fully legitimate, three conditions are required: conformity to established rules, the justifiability of laws by reference to the shared beliefs of rulers and ruled, and the express consent of the people.[132] It follows that if these conditions are absent, the way power is exercised is compromised.

Constant and widespread friction between a government and its people is often symptomatic of more intractable difficulties than simple discontent with particular policies. Any individual or group may be dissatisfied or disadvantaged by a specific

---

129. Cheung, A. B. L. (2007b). Policy capacity in post-1997 Hong Kong: Constrained institutions facing a crowded and differentiated polity. *Asia Pacific Journal of Public Administration, 29*(1), 51–75.
130. Ure, G. (2012). *Governors, politics and the Colonial Office: Public policy in Hong Kong, 1918–58* (pp. 219–220). Hong Kong: Hong Kong University Press.
131. Scott, I. (2007). Legitimacy, governance and public policy in post-handover Hong Kong. *Asia Pacific Journal of Public Administration 29*(1), 29–49.
132. Beetham (2013) op. cit., pp. 15–18.

policy decision but may benefit from government action on another issue. In many political systems, these compensatory rewards even up the policy ledger and serve to relieve pressure on the government. If this does not happen, or if the policy issue assumes such significance that compensatory rewards are unimportant, there may be constitutional remedies to rectify the situation. In democratic systems, for example, the government may be removed at the next election. In Hong Kong, where the government is not elected, cannot be removed, and has no mandate from the public, it is scarcely surprising that majority views have often been expressed in protests on the streets. Discontent with particular policies or decisions may be representative of more systemic problems faced by the polity. If citizens do not believe that the power relationships under which they live are legally valid and morally justifiable and if they do not give their consent to that relationship, then the regime will suffer from a legitimacy deficit. If it does nothing to correct or reduce that deficit, then it can face a crisis of legitimacy in which its authority to rule is seriously called into question.

Both before and after 1997, the Hong Kong government faced the need to reduce its legitimacy deficit. But the legitimacy problem remains. The government cannot demonstrate that it has the consent of the people. Opinion polls and the 2019 District Council election results strongly suggest that it has not. The government has yet to show that it can improve major social policies to resolve contentious problems. And fundamental constitutional issues have divided the polity.

These related problem areas—accountability, policy formulation and implementation, and legitimacy—present a major challenge for the government to devise and implement policies in the public interest. Those problems, and attempts to resolve them, provide the framework for the remainder of this book.

Part 1 (Chapters 2 and 3) considers issues relating to the political accountability of public officials: the constitutional and legal framework, the effect of the introduction of the POAS, and the political system established under the Basic Law.

Part 2 (Chapters 4–6) focuses on bureaucratic accountability, the values and structure of the civil service, reform initiatives, and public bodies outside the civil service.

Part 3 (Chapters 7–10) analyses the policymaking system. These chapters focus on the budgetary process and policy formulation and the policy process and implementation in the context of greater integration with mainland China.

Part 4 (Chapters 11–13) focuses on the relationship between government and the people and attempts to reduce the legitimacy deficit. The book concludes with an analysis of changing public sector values in a contentious political setting.

Part I

Accountability

2
The Constitutional Framework

Constitutions are supposed to be definitive, legally binding accounts of the rules and principles that govern polities. They describe the powers and functions of the major executive, legislative, judicial and administrative institutions and delineate relationships between them. They provide the authority for government decisions and help to legitimate how power is exercised. They usually specify the procedures by which executive authorities are to be held accountable. Sometimes, they reflect the aspirations and values of the people and help to protect their civil liberties from possible encroachments by the state.

While Hong Kong's Basic Law has most of the features of a constitution, it also has three peculiar characteristics resulting from the resumption of Chinese sovereignty and the legacy of the colonial political order. First, a constitution normally implies sovereignty and assumes that the ultimate source of legal authority is vested in the jurisdiction and that the powers of the political and administrative institutions that compose the state are not constrained by any external body. Since Hong Kong is part of China, sovereignty rests with the Chinese state. The source of formal legal authority is the constitution of the People's Republic of China (PRC) rather than the Basic Law. The Basic Law specifies that the political arrangements that apply in Hong Kong will be distinctly different from the rest of China and that it will enjoy "a high degree of autonomy" based on the concept of "one country, two systems."[1] But power is not entirely vested in the Hong Kong authorities. The Chinese government retains responsibility for foreign affairs, defence, and the right to interpret and amend the Basic Law. In 2020, it also enacted national security legislation for Hong Kong which, under the Basic Law, the Hong Kong Legislative Council should do on its own (Article 23). Hong Kong courts have the power to determine whether a local ordinance is consistent with the Basic Law.

How the Basic Law has been interpreted reflects the dynamics of power relationships between the PRC and the HKSAR and the increasing efforts of the Chinese government to integrate Hong Kong into the Mainland. While the Basic

---

1. Fong, B. C. H. (2017). One country, two nationalisms: Centre-periphery relations between Mainland China and Hong Kong. *Modern China, 43*(5), 523–556; Scott, I. (2017). One country, two systems: The end of a legitimating ideology? *Asia Pacific Journal of Public Administration, 39*(2), 83–99.

Law is a formal description of how political institutions are expected to work, practice has deviated from the expectations of both the Chinese government and the Hong Kong people. Some provisions have enabled the sovereign power to impose its views on how the polity should be run, others have resulted in an impasse, and still others have led in unintended directions.

Second, the Basic Law is fundamentally different in a formal constitutional sense from the colonial political order. The colonial constitution was largely unwritten. Legal authority stemmed from the *Royal Instructions* and the *Letters Patent*, supplemented by unwritten conventions. How the executive authorities interpreted those conventions enabled significant constitutional changes to be made without major amendments to written constitutional documents. The Basic Law, by contrast, is a written constitution that has only been in force for a relatively short time. In the many constitutional disputes that have occurred since 1997, the different interpretations of the Basic Law reflect deep disagreements over Hong Kong's political arrangements.

Third, although there were fundamental differences between the largely unwritten colonial constitution and the written Basic Law, it was expected that there would be continuity in how the central institutions of government performed. The Basic Law drafters deliberately drew on the central features of colonial rule in constructing the new political order. Xu Jiatun, the Chinese government's representative in Hong Kong in the 1980s, noted, for example, that "when we are designing the Basic Law ... we ought to place emphasis ... and utilise the British system of administration".[2] The Basic Law drafters were particularly attracted to the centralisation of power in the executive authorities; a weak and, until 1985, entirely unelected Legislative Council; and the informal, but very influential, participation of business and professional elites in the exercise of power. The Chinese government wanted to promote political stability in Hong Kong after 1997 and colonial practice seemed to offer a successful model.

But what the Basic Law drafters took from the colonial constitution was its pre-1984 legacy. The political effects of the transition to Chinese sovereignty and the economic effects of increasing affluence on popular aspirations, especially demands for a more democratic and representative government, were largely ignored. The Basic Law centralised power in the office of the Chief Executive; the Legislative Council remained weak; and functional constituencies, disproportionately favouring business and professional elites, became an entrenched feature of the electoral system.

Does the Basic Law establish a framework for political accountability and to what extent is the government held accountable for its actions? Does the Basic Law provide legitimate authority for the exercise of power? The first section of the chapter describes and analyses the powers and accountability of the major

---

2. Xu, J. (1993). *Xu Jiatun Xianggang hu yi lu* [The Hong Kong memoirs of Xu Jiatun] (Vol. 2, p. 183). Hong Kong: United Daily News.

institutions. The second section focuses on the political dynamics associated with the Basic Law and the attempts of activists to improve or maintain the accountability of the government in three major areas: efforts to introduce universal suffrage in the Chief Executive and the Legislative Council elections; potential threats to civil liberties posed by attempts to legislate Article 23 and an Extradition Bill; and judicial independence, the rule of law, judicial review, and the interpretation of the Basic Law. Section three analyses the erosion of the high degree of autonomy of the HKSAR provided for in the Basic Law, particularly after the Chinese government's decision to pass a national security law for Hong Kong. The chapter concludes with an analysis of how these developments have affected the accountability of the government and the public sector.

Accountability and the Basic Law

The preamble to the Basic Law notes that the principle of "one country, two systems" will govern the relationship between the PRC and Hong Kong and that the socialist system and policies will not be practised in the HKSAR.[3] National laws, except for those concerning foreign affairs and defence, are not to be applied in Hong Kong, and the capitalist system and way of life is to be retained for 50 years. Specific provisions protect the rights of citizens, the legal system, the economy, education, science, culture, religion, and labour and social services and follow the wording of the Joint Declaration between Britain and China signed in 1984.[4] What was not agreed between the British and Chinese governments at that time—and what has caused continuing controversy—are the provisions governing the elections of the Chief Executive and the Legislative Council and the pace at which more representative and accountable government would be introduced. The Chinese government's views on the Chief Executive, the principal officials, and Legislative Council elections are outlined in a single brief paragraph in the Joint Declaration and say little except that only local inhabitants may hold office, that the Chief Executive may be selected or elected and appointed by the Central People's government, and that the Legislative Council shall be constituted by elections.[5]

The political vacuum created by the absence of firm guiding principles on the composition, powers, and functions of the central institutions in the Joint Declaration left open the possibility that the Basic Law might eventually lead to a more democratic Hong Kong. The Chinese government had promised a future of "Hong Kong people ruling Hong Kong", and there was some expectation that this

---

3. *The Basic Law of the Hong Kong Special Administrative Region of the People's Republic of China* (2020). Preamble. https://www.basiclaw.gov.hk/en/basiclaw/index.html
4. *Joint Declaration of the Government of the United Kingdom of Great Britain and Northern Ireland and the Government of the People's Republic of China on the question of Hong Kong* (1984). https://www.refworld.org/docid/3ae6b525c.html Para1
5. Ibid., Annex 1, p. 1.

might allow some choice about whom those rulers should be. But the consultation process quickly dashed that hope. The Chinese government set up two committees to draft the Basic Law. The first, the Basic Law Drafting Committee (BLDC), had primary responsibility for producing the Basic Law and was composed largely of Mainland drafters and conservative Hong Kong political figures.[6] The 59 members were primarily drawn from the Mainland although 23 did come from Hong Kong. Of those, only two, Martin Lee Chu-ming and Szeto Wah, were democrats, but both resigned from the committee and were subsequently expelled after they expressed support for the Tiananmen Square demonstrations in 1989. A second committee, the Consultative Committee, was supposed to feed Hong Kong views into the drafting process. But it soon became clear that this committee had little power, was controlled by the Chinese drafters, was not representative of public opinion,[7] and was intended to serve simply to legitimate and endorse the decisions of the BLDC.

The Basic Law was promulgated in 1990 without a referendum or any other form of ratification to determine whether it was acceptable to the Hong Kong people. The Chinese government took the view that Hong Kong people were Chinese, that Hong Kong was Chinese territory, and that the National People's Congress (NPC) had the authority to pass the legislation. The British government did not insist on any form of popular endorsement, preferring to avoid further difficulties during the transitional period. Consequently, the Basic Law began life with two serious impediments: it had not received the approval of the people and it was based on political practices that, even in 1990, let alone 1997, were outdated and inappropriate for an increasingly participative and highly political society. The formal powers of the major institutions more closely resemble a written version of the colonial constitution rather than the more democratic polity that some had wanted.

The Chief Executive

The Chinese government does not see the Chief Executive as accountable to, or representative of, the Hong Kong people. Rather, just as the Governor was the representative of the British Crown, the Chinese government regards the Chief Executive as its appointee in charge of Hong Kong affairs. He or she is armed with most of the formal autocratic powers previously vested in the Governor. Under Article 48, the Chief Executive has the power to decide on government policies and to issue executive orders; to sign bills passed by the Legislative Council; to nominate the principal officials for appointment by the Chinese government; to appoint and remove judges of courts at all levels; to appoint or remove the holders of public office following legal procedures; to implement directives from the Chinese government in

---

6. Ghai, Y. (1999). *Hong Kong's new constitutional order: The resumption of Chinese sovereignty and the Basic Law* (2nd ed., pp. 57–64). Hong Kong: Hong Kong University Press.
7. Chu, Y. Y. (2000). The failure of the united front policy: The involvement of business in the drafting of Hong Kong's Basic Law. *Asian Perspective, 24*(2), 173–198.

matters provided in the Basic Law; to conduct external affairs authorised by the central authorities; to approve motions regarding revenues and expenditure to the Legislative Council; to decide whether government officials should testify or give evidence to legislative committees; and to handle petitions and complaints and to grant pardons. The Chief Executive can also return bills to the Legislative Council for further consideration (Article 49) and may dissolve it under certain circumstances (Article 50).

These are formidable powers and are largely untrammelled because there is no provision to make the Chief Executive accountable to the public or to any institution other than the Chinese government. The Executive Council is appointed by the Chief Executive and is described as "an organ for assisting the Chief Executive in policy-making" (Article 54). The Chief Executive must consult it "before making important policy decisions, introducing bills to the Legislative Council, making subordinate legislation or dissolving the Legislative Council" (Article 56) but is under no obligation to follow its advice. The Chief Executive is accountable to the "Central People's Government and the Hong Kong Special Administrative Region" (Article 43). But it has never been clear what this means. It cannot be the government since the Chief Executive is head of the government. Nor can it be the Legislative Council since it cannot remove the Chief Executive without repeatedly voting down the budget (Article 52(3)) or beginning a tortuous impeachment process. Nor can it be the vast majority of Hong Kong people since they cannot vote for the Chief Executive. Formally, the Chief Executive holds autocratic powers and is only minimally accountable. However, the power of the office holder has been substantially reduced by citizens' unwillingness to accept what they perceive to be unjust laws and by the increasing intervention of the Chinese government in Hong Kong affairs.

To remove the Chief Executive without the support of the Chinese government is virtually impossible. There is a convoluted impeachment process (Article 73(9)), but the three attempts to impeach a Chief Executive all failed at the first hurdle. In 2012, Legislative Councillors tabled a motion charging Donald Tsang with serious dereliction of duty, but Tsang's term in office expired before the motion could be debated.[8] In 2017, an impeachment motion charged C. Y. Leung with a breach of law and/or dereliction of duty after he improperly interfered in a Legislative Council probe into his business affairs.[9] In 2019, Legislative Councillors tried to impeach Carrie Lam for "disregarding mainstream opposing views and unrelentingly pushing through a highly controversial bill".[10] Both motions were defeated. If they had succeeded, an investigative committee chaired by the Chief Justice would have considered the issue. If there was sufficient evidence to support the charge, a

---

8. Scott, I. (2014). Political scandals and the accountability of the Chief Executive in Hong Kong. *Asian Survey*, 54(5), 966–986.
9. Hansard, 7, 8 June 2017, 9272–9474.
10. Hansard, 5 December 2019, 2859–3025.

two-thirds majority of the Legislative Council would still be required for impeachment. Even then, the Chinese government decides whether the Chief Executive should be removed.

The Legislative Council

The Basic Law establishes an "executive-led" system. It follows that the Legislative Council's powers are relatively weak in relation to the executive. The Basic Law drafters wanted to dampen political participation and to reduce its legislative autonomy to prevent the development of a counterpoint to executive authority. Article 64 specifies that the government is accountable to the Legislative Council, but it is a very weak form of accountability. The government shall "present regular policy addresses to the Council; it shall answer questions raised by members of the Council; and it shall obtain approval from the Council for taxation and public expenditure". The council can "examine and approve" the budget (Article 73) but risks dissolution and elections if it is not passed. The intention of the Basic Law is to create a debating chamber that will dutifully endorse the bills brought to it by the government. Bills introduced by the government require a simple majority to pass whereas motions, bills, or amendments to government bills introduced by Councillors require a majority of each of two groups of members, those from the geographical, directly elected constituencies and those from the functional constituencies (Annex II).

The Judiciary

The judicial system was intended to function independently as it had done before the handover (Articles 19, 81). Judges are appointed by the Chief Executive on advice from an independent commission (Article 88) and can only be removed by the Chief Executive on advice from a tribunal of not less than three local judges. What was expected to provide reassurance on the rule of law after 1997 has proved more problematic than initially anticipated.

Even before the handover, there was a dispute over the composition of the Court of Final Appeal. The Chinese and British governments agreed in 1991 that only one overseas judge should sit in judgement on a case, but legislators argued that this was in contravention of the Basic Law.[11] The issue remained unresolved until 1995 when the Legislative Council finally passed a bill which provided for a Court of Final Appeal in which a case would be heard by four local judges and one overseas judge. Subsequently, the Judiciary faced the problem of ensuring that Hong Kong laws were not in conflict with the Basic Law, a task that was made more difficult by the

---

11. Gittings, D. (2016). *Introduction to the Basic Law* (2nd ed., pp. 189–190). Hong Kong: Hong Kong University Press.

overriding constitutional power of the Standing Committee of the NPC (NPCSC) to interpret the Basic Law (Article 158) and by challenges to administrative decisions by judicial review. Pressure from the Chinese government and the democrats, compounded by the national security law, has had serious implications for the rule of law, judicial independence, and the future of judicial review.

Under Article 44 of the national security law, the Chief Executive has the power to create a pool of designated judges to hear cases. Under Article 46, a panel of three judges sit in judgement and the Secretary for Justice may issue a certificate stating that a case can be heard without a jury. In February 2021, before the first national security case came to trial, the Secretary issued a certificate in the case of *Tong Ying Kit v Secretary for Justice* arguing that the safety of jurors might be in danger and that there was "a real risk that the due administration of justice might be impaired."[12] The stringent conditions for granting bail have also caused public concern. Article 42(2) of the National Security Law provides that judges should be satisfied that the accused will not commit an act endangering national security if released on bail. But it was not entirely clear what conditions need to be met to satisfy the judges. There have been some contradictory rulings and concerns about those facing long periods in remand before their cases come to trial. When the issue reached the CFA in *HKSAR v Lai Chee Ying*, the court found that Article 42(2) does create a presumption against bail.[13] The High Court's decision to grant bail to Lai, the founder of the pro-democracy newspaper *Apple Daily*, was overturned. In December 2021, the CFA further extended the presumption against bail to cases brought under other laws if there were national security implications.[14] It has been argued that this presumption against bail ensures that those charged under the national security law remain in prison for long periods as a means of punishing the government's political opponents without bringing them to a fair trial.[15]

Even before the promulgation and implementation of the national security law, the integrity of the courts and the legal system had come under attack. In an important speech at the opening of the 2020 legal year, in the context of these attacks, the Chief Justice, Geoffrey Ma Tao-li, sought to explain how the law operated.[16] He spoke at some length about what he described as a central characteristic of the way in which justice should be dispensed, the requirements of a fair trial. One element

---

12. Department of Justice (2021, May). Summary of judgment: *Tong Ying Kit v Secretary for Justice*. HCAL 473/2021; [2021] HKCFI 1397.
13. *HKSAR v Lai Chee Ying* [2021] HKCFA 3.
14. Ho, K. (2021,15 December). Stringent national security bail threshold applicable to other offences, Hong Kong's top court rules. https://hongkongfp.com/2021/12/15/stringent-national-security-bail-threshold-applicable-to-other-offences-hong-kongs-top-court-rules/
15. Chan, J. M. M. (2021). Judicial responses to the national security law: *HKSAR v Lai Chee Ying*. *Hong Kong Law Journal*, 51(1), 1–14; Cohen, J. A. (2022). Hong Kong's transformed criminal justice system: Instrument of fear. *Academia Sinica Law Journal*, 2022 special issue, 1–20; Wong, L., Kellogg, T. E., & Lai, E. Y. H. (2021, 28 June). Hong Kong's national security law and the right to fair trial: A GCAL briefing paper. https://www.law.georgetown.edu/law-asia/wp-content/uploads/sites/31/2021/06/HongKongNSLRightToFairTrial.pdf
16. Hong Kong Government (2020). CJ's speech at ceremonial opening of the legal year 2020 (13 January). https://www.info.gov.hk/gia/general/202001/13/P2020011300622.htm

of a fair trial was that any person charged with a criminal offence should be "entitled to be tried without delay".[17] The Chief Justice also said that it was important to maintain judicial independence and to realise that it was the duty of judges to reach decisions based on the law and nothing else.[18] Since 2019, perceptions of the fairness of the judicial system and the impartiality of the courts have declined substantially.[19] It may be difficult to recover the high regard in which the judicial system and the rule of law were once held and to re-gain public acceptance that the principles of which the Chief Justice spoke are being observed in practice.

The Civil Service

The Basic Law provides that the civil service should exercise its powers and functions much as it did under colonial rule and that its personnel system should remain largely unchanged. In 1995, the Preliminary Working Committee (PWC), which was responsible for overseeing the transition from the Chinese side, released a working paper on the civil service, the only one of 26 papers that was made public. The paper notes that:

> The Chinese government attaches great importance to the stability of the Hong Kong civil service... and ... regards Hong Kong's 180,000 civil servants as a huge wealth, a source of strength for the realization of "Hong Kong people governing Hong Kong" after 1997.[20]

The PWC followed the Basic Law on issues of recruitment, management, and conditions of service, adding the provisions that those who wanted to leave should submit their resignations as soon as possible, that public servants would not be held responsible for their decisions under the colonial government, and that the principle of political neutrality would continue to be observed.[21] The British government wanted to exit Hong Kong without domestic unrest and this required a stable civil service. Both sides consequently gave the civil service strong public support, lauding its efficiency and stressing its continuity with the past.

The Basic Law makes specific mention that "public servants ... including the police department ... may all remain in employment and retain their seniority with pay, allowances, benefits and conditions of service no less favourable than before" (Article 100). Expatriates are prevented from holding the most senior positions which are reserved for "only Chinese citizens among permanent residents of the

---

17. Ibid.
18. Ibid.
19. PORI (2022). The rule of law, fairness of the judicial system, impartiality of the courts -combined charts. https://www.pori.hk/pop-poll/rule-law-indicators-en/g-combined.html?lang=en
20. Preliminary Working Committee (1995, 8 December). *Some views of the Preliminary Working Committee of the HKSAR preparatory committee on maintaining the stability of the Hong Kong civil service and its system.* Hong Kong: mimeo.
21. Ibid.

Region with no right of abode in foreign countries" (Article 101). Under Article 103, the management of the civil service, recruitment on grounds of merit, conditions of employment, assessment, discipline, and pay and conditions of service are to remain unchanged. Shortly after the handover, the government introduced the *Public Service (Administration) Order* which provided more detail on appointment procedures, dismissal, discipline, and delegation, drawing on the colonial civil service regulations.

In the transitional period, the Hong Kong government created independent statutory bodies and strengthened others to assuage citizens' fears about civil liberties and arbitrary administration (see Chapter 12). A *Bill of Rights Ordinance* was passed in 1991 and incorporated the provisions of the International Covenant on Civil and Political Rights into Hong Kong law.[22] The Chinese government objected strongly, arguing that the Basic Law (Article 39) already provided that the covenant should apply in Hong Kong. In the 1990s, the Hong Kong government also tried to strengthen citizens' rights by creating statutory bodies to protect civil liberties. Despite the formal legal protections offered by these organisations, civil liberties have remained a highly sensitive issue, triggering large demonstrations over the attempt to enact security laws in 2003, the failed Extradition Bill in 2019, and the Chinese government's decision to enact national security legislation in 2020.

Deficiencies in the Basic Law

The Basic Law drafters wanted the political executive to be able to make policy authoritatively. They had no intention of setting up a system of checks and balances; the polity was supposed to be "executive-led" and other institutions were expected to remain subordinate to the executive.[23] Yet a system that was meant to be unified and centralised soon became disarticulated. The principal institutions began to function separately, often with inadequate coordination, and not always harmoniously. The Chief Executive presided over a fragmented policymaking environment, resulting in unsatisfactory compromises, changes in direction, retractions, and poor implementation.[24]

An important, but unintentional, weakness in the Basic Law was that the relationships between the central institutions were inadequately described and could function within their prescribed powers without necessarily interacting in a coherent and unified way. For example, immediately after 1997, senior civil servants were less diligent in providing Legislative Council members with information

---

22. Gittings (2016) op. cit., pp. 274–285.
23. Lo, P. Y., & Chen, A. H. Y. (2018). The judicial perspective of separation of powers in the Hong Kong Special Administrative Region of the People's Republic of China. *Journal of International and Comparative Law*, 5(2), 337–362.
24. See Goodstadt, L. F. (2018). *A city mismanaged: Hong Kong's struggle for survival*. Hong Kong: Hong Kong University Press.

on bills or appearing in person, partly, it seems, because they felt that they were protected against undue legislative interference in policymaking by the Basic Law. Legislative Councillors of all political persuasions complained that the government seemed unaccountable.[25] Civil servants themselves were concerned that the pollical executive often seemed to have different policies in mind from those that had been carefully formulated in the policy bureaus. Proposals were sometimes nullified by ill-considered alternatives or vetoes.

The unintended consequences were caused as much by how post-1997 politics developed as they were by the lack of specific provisions on governing relationships between the central institutions in the Basic Law. But the absence of those provisions meant that there were uncertain areas in resolving differences between the executive authorities, Legislative Council, and the Judiciary, which left the impression of a government at war within itself. The friction between the Chief Executive and the democrats in the Legislative Council intensified to the point where Carrie Lam in 2019 was greeted with such a torrent of abuse that she was unable to deliver the annual policy address. The government and the Judiciary have been at loggerheads for years over many of the courts' findings in judicial review cases. Politics and constitutional practice in post-1997 Hong Kong are light years away from the model from which the Basic Law is derived, the pre-1984 unwritten colonial constitution in which power was vested in a centralised, unified, and omniscient government supported by a compliant legislature and an uncontroversial judiciary.

The Basic Law was intentionally designed to discourage the development of political parties.[26] The Chinese government did not want to see a mass democratic party in Hong Kong. However, in 1992, it sanctioned the creation of the Democratic Alliance for Betterment of Hong Kong (DAB), which challenged the electoral dominance of the democrats in the directly elected seats in the legislature. Despite finding favour with Beijing, only one party member was chosen in Tung Chee Hwa's post-1997 Executive Council and the absence of a governing party in the Legislative Council initially caused some problems.[27] Eventually, the growing rift between the pro-establishment/pro-Beijing groups and the democrats gave the government the support it needed.

The party system in Hong Kong has always been fragmented, partly because the electoral system was deliberately designed to prevent the democrats from obtaining a majority and partly because the government has already been selected and

---

25. Scott, I. (2000). The disarticulation of Hong Kong's post-handover political system. *The China Journal, 43,* 29–53.
26. Ma, N. (2012). Political parties and elections. In W. M. Lam, P. L. T. Lui, & W. Wong (Eds.), *Contemporary Hong Kong government and politics* (expanded 2nd ed., pp. 159–177). Hong Kong: Hong Kong University Press.
27. Constitutional Development Task Force (2004). *The second report of the Constitutional Development Task Force: Issues of principle in the Basic Law* (p. 20). https://www.legco.gov.hk/yr03-04/english/panels/ca/papers/ca0416cb2-report2-e.pdf

elections are not about winning power.[28] Neither the Hong Kong nor the Chinese government have wanted to breathe life into political parties by reforming the electoral system. The weakness of political parties has major consequences for how demands are expressed. If parties are powerless, their utility diminishes and the public looks elsewhere to express its views. This helps to explain the rapid rise of civil society after 1997 and the emergence of many different interest groups, also often fragmented and sometimes opposed to each other, but also on occasions able to work together in coalitions outside the formal political institutions. The street protest became institutionalised as a way of voicing grievances.

The restricted role of political parties has contributed to the disarticulation of the system. The major protests in 2003, 2014, and 2019–2020 saw pressure groups and civil society organisations rather than political parties take the lead. They have mobilised the population on constitutional issues such as universal suffrage and civil liberties as well as on specific policy issues. The government has been unable to devise appropriate, accurate, or credible consultative mechanisms to assess public opinion. Decisions have often been made with insufficient knowledge of their political implications.

Because the Basic Law was introduced without the consent of the people and did not entirely reflect their beliefs, it has become a matter of debate and controversy rather than an unchallenged source of authoritative decisions. In 2004, Qiao Xiaoyang, a former Chairman of the NPC's Law Committee, noted that "[t]here has not been a single day in which it [the Basic Law] has not been subject to queries, distortions and even vilifications".[29] The "queries, distortions and vilifications" are symptomatic of a legitimacy deficit and reflect the deep-seated differences over how power is exercised. In 2004, Qiao thought that there was an emerging consensus on how political development might take place. By 2018, his comments on the Basic Law focused instead on "the hierarchy of the relationship between China and Hong Kong".[30] He said that he was "deeply saddened by the emergence of radical forces advocating Hong Kong independence" which the Chinese people would never tolerate.[31] The Basic Law has not been the only cause of political discontent, but it has contributed to a polarised polity by crystallising issues on which there is profound disagreement within the community.

---

28. Carey, J. M. (2017). Electoral formula and fragmentation in Hong Kong. *Journal of East Asian Studies, 17*(2), 215–231.
29. Qiao, X. (2004, 29 April). Striving in a pragmatic spirit to find the right path to political development. *SCMP*.
30. Qiao, X. (2018, 27 April). Opposing China's socialist system flouts Hong Kong's Basic Law. *SCMP*. https://www.scmp.com/comment/insight-opinion/article/2143642/opposing-chinas-socialist-system-flouts-hong-kongs-basic-law
31. Ibid.

The Political Dynamics of the Basic Law

In addition to these systemic deficiencies, there has been prolonged contention over some of the Basic Law's specific provisions. In this section, politics in three critically contentious areas—universal suffrage, civil liberties, and judicial independence—are considered. As a backdrop to these controversies, the increasing mainlandisation of Hong Kong has driven both protests over violations of civil liberties and those focusing on universal suffrage.

Universal Suffrage

Demands for universal suffrage have been a perennial theme of post-1997 politics. Articles 45 and 68 state that the "ultimate aim" is to hold elections under universal suffrage for the Chief Executive and the Legislative Council. But there was no timetable for implementation and any chance of progress was seriously adversely affected by the decisions to disqualify or arrest localist and pan-democratic candidates and elected members.

Chief Executive Elections

The first Chief Executive was elected by a carefully selected election committee of 400 members, subsequently increased to 800 in 1998 and to 1,200 in 2012.[32] The composition of the election committee has meant that it has always been highly unlikely that a democrat could win the nomination. Even if that did happen, the Chinese government, under Article 45, need not appoint the nominee. Since 2002 when, despite his widespread unpopularity, Tung Chee Hwa was returned unopposed, the election of the Chief Executive has been contentious. In the following year, a Democratic Party Legislative Councillor, Albert Ho Chun-yan, proposed that the Basic Law should be amended to allow the Chief Executive and the Legislative Council to be elected by universal suffrage, but the motion was defeated by the functional constituency members.[33] The Chinese and Hong Kong governments were constitutionally required to consider whether the provisions for the 2007 and 2008 Chief Executive and Legislative Council elections should be amended. Polls showed that a majority favoured universal suffrage for both elections.[34] In April 2004, the Hong Kong government's Constitutional Task Force produced a paper that placed so many conditions on universal suffrage that it became impossible.[35] The NPCSC then confirmed that the Chief Executive would not be elected by universal suffrage

---

32. *The Basic Law* (2020) op. cit., Annex 1; Young, S. N. M., & Cullen, R. (2010). *Electing Hong Kong's Chief Executive* (p. 18). Hong Kong: Hong Kong University Press.
33. Hansard, 21 May 2003, 6699–6762.
34. Constitutional Development Task Force (2004) op. cit., p. 17.
35. Ibid., p. 39.

in 2007.[36] In December 2007, the State Council conceded that the Chief Executive might be elected by universal suffrage in 2017.[37]

Despite the highly restricted franchise, elections for the Chief Executive in 2007, 2012, and 2017 all resulted in contests with a democratic candidate running for office in 2007 and 2012. The size of the election committee was increased to 1,200 in 2010, but it remained unrepresentative and strongly favoured pro-Beijing candidates. Its four sectors, each comprising 300 members, drew heavily on small functional organisations (sectors 1–3) and Legislative Council members, delegates to the NPC and the Chinese People's Political Consultative Committee, elected District Council members, and the Heung Yee Kuk (sector 4). The Chinese authorities usually made clear well in advance who they wanted to see elected.[38] Nonetheless, candidates campaigned on platforms, held debates, and sought public support as well as from the election committee.

Between 2007 and August 2014, there was much political positioning and debate on the arrangements for the election of the Chief Executive. The Chinese government and the pro-establishment camp accepted that universal suffrage was desirable but noted the provision in the Basic Law that a "broadly representative" nominating committee would select which candidates could run (Article 45). The democrats argued that this subverted the meaning of universal suffrage and that nominations should be as open as possible.[39] The State Council's document in 2014 on one country two systems,[40] which asserted greater central government control over Hong Kong, raised the political temperature. Shortly after publication of the document, Occupy Central, a civil disobedience movement, organised an informal referendum with over 792,000 voters expressing their opinion on three proposals for nominating candidates.[41] The winning proposal from the Alliance for True Democracy stated that candidates should be nominated by 35,000 registered voters and should come from a party obtaining 5% of the vote in the last Legislative Council election. The Hong Kong government dismissed the referendum as having no force in law and a former leading Beijing official said that it was "meaningless".[42]

---

36. NPCSC (2004). *Decision of the Standing Committee of the National People's Congress on issues relating to the methods for selecting the Chief Executive of the Hong Kong Special Administrative Region in 2007 and for forming the Legislative Council of the HKSAR in 2008*. http://www.npc.gov.cn/zgrdw/englishnpc/Law/2007-12/12/content_1383886.htm
37. State Council of the People's Republic of China (2014, 15 March). *The practice of the one country, two systems policy in the Hong Kong Special Administrative Region* (Annex II). http://english.www.gov.cn/archive/white_paper/20as below14/08/23/content_281474982986578.htm
38. Lo, S. S. H. (2017). Factionalism and Chinese-style democracy: The 2017 Chief Executive election. *Asia Pacific Journal of Public Administration*, 39(2), 100–119.
39. Lau, E. (2014, 18 April). Beijing must keep its word on universal suffrage. *SCMP*. https://www.scmp.com/comment/insight-opinion/article/1486036/beijing-must-keep-its-word-universal-suffrage
40. State Council of the People's Republic of China (2014, 15 March) op. cit.
41. Chan, K. M. (2015). Occupying Central. *SUR International Journal on Human Rights*, 12, Issue 21, 1–7.
42. BBC (2014, 30 June). Hong Kong's democracy "referendum" draws nearly 800,000. https://www.bbc.com/news/world-asia-china-28076566

On 1 July, an estimated 500,000 people rallied in favour of universal suffrage; the police claimed the demonstration was illegal and arrested 500 people.

The NPCSC announced its decision on electing the Chief Executive on 31 August 2014.[43] A nominating committee was to choose two or three candidates who had to be endorsed by at least half the committee. The committee would also decide on whether a candidate loved the country and loved Hong Kong. The requirement was obviously aimed at excluding democratic candidates. Occupy Central had already said that, if the NPCSC did not propose a democratic solution, its members would blockade roads and occupy public spaces. A student strike against the Standing Committee's decision, led by Scholarism and the Hong Kong Federation of Students, started on 22 September and was followed by a protest outside government headquarters. On 28 September, Occupy Central announced that its civil disobedience campaign had begun. Throughout the 79-day subsequent occupation, the protesters stayed firmly committed to their demands: the resignation of the Chief Executive, C. Y. Leung, and the election of the Chief Executive by universal suffrage. After the occupation, the Legislative Council rejected the Chinese government's proposals for universal suffrage, leaving the method of electing the Chief Executive unchanged.[44] Universal suffrage remained a fundamental demand of those seeking to change the political order and was one of the five demands made by the 2019–2020 protesters.

Elections to the Legislative Council

Table 2.1 shows the evolution of the Legislative Council, essentially a story of stalemate between democrats fighting for universal suffrage and fair elections, and the fears of the Hong Kong and Chinese governments that democrats might win control of the council.

Since 1991, when directly elected seats were first introduced, electoral support for democratic parties has been sufficiently strong that they would have won a majority in the Legislative Council if elections had been held on a "first-past-the-post" system. Since 2004, the only change to the composition of the council was in 2010, when the Democratic Party voted with the government to add five seats to both the directly elected and the functional constituencies for the 2012 elections.

Elections for directly elected seats take place under a proportional, multi-member list system, which increases the chance of winning a seat with a relatively low percentage of the vote. The system affects the public accountability of members because constituents do not have a single member representing them. The public tends instead to take its grievances to complaint-handling institutions. Functional constituency seats have many business and professional members, who generally

---

43. NPCSC (2014, 1 September). Full text: Standing Committee decision on Hong Kong 2017 election framework. http://be.china-embassy.org/eng/sghd/201409/t20140901_2076170.htm
44. Hansard, 17, 18 June 2015, 13239–13372, 13379–13467.

Table 2.1 *Composition of the Legislative Council 1991–2021*

Year	Officials	Appointed	Directly elected	Functional Constituencies	Election Committee	Total
1991	3	18	18	21	–	60
1995	–	–	20	30	10	60
1998	–	–	20	30	10	60
2000	–	–	24	30	6	60
2004	–	–	30	30	–	60
2008	–	–	30	30	–	60
2012	–	–	35	35	–	70
2016	–	–	35	35	–	70
2021	–	–	20	30	40	90

Sources: The Basic Law, op. cit, Annex II; Legislative Council (2021). Election brief. https://www.elections.gov.hk/legco2021/eng/brief.html

support the government and are sometimes returned unopposed in seats with very small electorates.[45] It is not always clear who is being represented, especially when companies, which have votes in some constituencies, are illegally or corruptly registered, or when people have no connection with the functional area.[46] The electoral system consequently has always produced a Legislative Council that is not entirely representative of, or accountable to, the public. After the promulgation of the national security law and the radical changes to the electoral rules that followed, it became much less so.

On 30 July 2020, returning officers disqualified 12 pro-democracy candidates from running in the Legislative Council elections seemingly based largely on the supposition that, if elected, they would not uphold the Basic Law or pledge allegiance to the HKSAR.[47] On the same day, the Constitutional and Mainland Affairs Bureau issued a press release, noting that the returning officers' decision was in conformity with the *Legislative Council Ordinance* and that "there was no question of political censorship, restriction of the freedom of speech or deprivation of the right to stand for election as alleged by some members of the community".[48] The election,

---

45. Gittings (2016) op. cit., pp. 124–151; Wong, S. H. W. (2015) *Electoral politics in post-1997 Hong Kong: Protest, patronage and the media* (pp. 54–56). Singapore: Springer.
46. Electoral Affairs Commission (2017). *Report on the 2016 Legislative Council election* (p. 26). https://www.eac.hk/en/legco/2016lce_detailreport.htm; Scott, I., & Gong, T. (2019). *Corruption prevention and governance in Hong Kong* (pp. 177–178). Abingdon: Routledge.
47. Ho, K., Grundy, T., & Jennifer Creery, J. (2020, 31 July). Hong Kong bans Joshua Wong and 11 other pro-democracy figures from legislative election. *HKFP*. https://hongkongfp.com/2020/07/30/breaking-hong-kong-bans-8-pro-democracy-figures-from-legislative-election/
48. Constitutional and Mainland Affairs Bureau (2020, 30 July). HKSAR government supports returning officers' decision to invalidate certain nominations for Legislative Council election. *Press release*, https://www.info.gov.hk/gia/general/202007/30/P2020073000481.htm

which had originally been scheduled for September 2020, was then postponed until December 2021.[49] In the interim, in November 2020, the National People's Congress announced that any Hong Kong legislator advocating independence, refusing to recognise China's right to exercise sovereignty over Hong Kong, consorting with foreign forces to interfere in Hong Kong affairs, or otherwise endangering national security would be disqualified and required to relinquish their seats.[50] On this basis, democratic representation in the legislature was virtually eliminated. Many democrats were also arrested under the national security law. In January 2021 alone, 53 party leaders, former legislators and activists were arrested on the grounds that they had organised a "primary" to select candidates to run in the election.[51]

Given the impact of the arrests, that all candidates had to be "patriots", and that, even if elected, they could have been immediately disqualified from taking their seats, it was highly unlikely that pan-democratic parties and groups would have fielded candidates in the election. In March 2021, an NPC decision to "improve" the electoral system further reduced that possibility.[52] The legislature was to be expanded to 90 members, the Election Committee was to be increased in size to 1,500 members, and a review committee for vetting candidates was to be established in accordance with previously enacted laws and decisions relating to national security. Fewer than 5,000 people were eligible to vote for members of the Election Committee which favoured pro-establishment parties and groups at the expense of the democrats. The review committee, composed of three top officials and three non-officials with strong links with the Mainland Chinese and Hong Kong governments,[53] was charged with ensuring that all candidates were patriotic. It was decided that the legislature would be composed of 20 directly elected seats (down from 35 in the previous election), 30 functional constituencies (down from 35) with 40 members elected by the Election Committee.[54] In May, the new rules passed the Legislative Council by 40 votes to 2.[55]

The Hong Kong government hoped that the public would see the changes as fair and necessary and that the electoral system itself would be endorsed by a large

---

49. Hong Kong government (2020). *Legco elections postponed for a year* [Press release]. https://www.info.gov.hk/gia/general/202007/31/P2020073100898.htm#:~:text=The%20Hong%20Kong%20Special%20Administrative,a%20year%20to%20September%205%2C, 31 July.
50. NPC Observer (2020, 11 November). NPCSC clarifies "allegiance" requirements for Hong Kong legislators, disqualifies pro-democracy legislators. https://npcobserver.com/2020/11/11/npcsc-clarifies-allegiance-requirements-for-hong-kong-legislators-disqualifies-pro-democracy-legislators
51. BBC (2021, 6 January). National security law: Hong Kong rounds up 53 pro-democracy activists. https://www.bbc.com/news/world-asia-china-55555299
52. NPC Observer (2021, 11 March). Decision of the National People's Congress on improving the electoral system of the Hong Kong Special Administrative Region. https://npcobserver.com/2021/03/11/2021-npc-session-npcs-hong-kong-electoral-overhaul-decision-explained/
53. Hong Kong Government (2021, 6 July). Chief Executive appoints Candidate Eligibility Review Committee members. Press release. https://www.info.gov.hk/gia/general/202107/06/P2021070600318.htm
54. Ho, K. (2021, 30 March). Beijing unanimously approves election overhaul, reducing democratic representation. *HKFP*. https://hongkongfp.com/2021/03/30/breaking-beijing-unanimously-approves-hong-kong-election-overhaul-reducing-democratic-representation/
55. Hansard, 27 May 2021, p. 6583.

turnout.[56] The Chief Executive urged the public to vote[57] and the government provided free public transport on polling day. The results were a foregone conclusion. Where there was a contest, it was usually simply to determine which pro-establishment candidate would be elected; only one person thought to be a democrat was elected. A 30% turnout, the lowest on record for a Legislative Council election and 28% below that of the 2016 election, did not suggest that there was much enthusiasm among voters for the new system.[58] The Chief Executive argued that a low turnout might still be a sign of support for the new measures because people were satisfied with how government was performing.[59] However, a public opinion poll, taken just before the election, showed satisfaction levels with the performance of government at only 25%.[60] The new system achieved the aim of ensuring a more compliant legislature in tune with government, but it offered no real choice to voters and further reduced the accountability of Legislative Councillors to the electorate.

Civil Liberties

Hong Kong people have been highly suspicious of measures perceived to threaten their civil liberties and have scant regard for government assurances that their concerns are unfounded. Attempts to introduce legislation thought to be inimical to civil liberties have provoked massive demonstrations. In 2003, the government tried to pass national security legislation by enacting Article 23 of the Basic Law and in 2019, it tabled an extradition bill that raised the spectre that Hong Kong residents might be transported to mainland China for trial, a fear that was probably generated by the abduction of five booksellers in 2015 (see p. 58). In both cases, the government had to withdraw the proposed legislation. However, on 21 May 2020, the Chinese government announced that it had decided to legislate a national security law for Hong Kong, triggering more protests and international condemnation.

Article 23

In September 2002, the Hong Kong government released a consultation paper on legislation to deal with subversion, treason, sedition, and the theft of state secrets

---

56. McLoughlin, T. (2021, 21 December). Why authoritarian regimes bother with elections. *The Atlantic*. https://www.theatlantic.com/international/archive/2021/12/hong-kong-stunt-election-democracy/621071/
57. CGTN (2021, 19 December). Carrie Lam calls on people to vote for Hong Kong's peace, stability. https://news.cgtn.com/news/2021-12-19/Carrie-Lam-calls-on-people-to-vote-for-HK-s-long-term-peace-stability-167cwtk2V2g/index.html
58. Smith. M. (2021, 20 December). Low turnout the true measure of voter sentiment. *Australian Financial Review*. https://www.afr.com/world/asia/low-turnout-the-true-measure-of-hong-kong-voter-sentiment-20211220-p59iyn
59. Lau, C. (2021, 8 December). Hong Kong elections: city leader Carrie Lam says low voter turnout 'does not mean anything', may indicate good governance. *SCMP*. https://www.scmp.com/news/hong-kong/politics/article/3158944/hong-kong-elections-city-leader-carrie-lam-says-low-voter
60. PORI (2021, 9–14 December). People's satisfaction with the HKSAR government. https://www.pori.hk/pop-poll/government-en/h001.html?lang=en

under Article 23 of the Basic Law.[61] Predictably, there was strong support for the proposed measures from the Chinese government and united front groups in Hong Kong. Equally predictably, civil liberties groups, journalists, democratic parties, some legislators, and the Bar Association were outraged.

Article 23 states that:

> The Hong Kong Special Administrative Region shall enact laws on its own to prohibit any act of treason, secession, sedition, subversion against the Central People's Government, or theft of state secrets, to prohibit foreign political organizations or bodies from conducting political activities in the Region, and to prohibit political organizations or bodies of the Region from establishing ties with foreign political organizations or bodies.

The government thought that there might be opposition to the new offences of secession and subversion[62] and proceeded cautiously. Under existing laws, Hong Kong had provisions to deal with treason and sedition but none to cover secession or subversion. The consultation document stated that these offences would be precisely defined.[63] Theft of state secrets, which particularly alarmed journalists, was to be covered by the *Official Secrets Ordinance* with the addition of the offence of unauthorised access to, or disclosure of, protected information.[64] On secession and subversion, the government proposed a new offence: to withdraw a part of the PRC from its sovereignty, "to intimidate" its government or to attempt to overthrow it.[65]

The consultation was widely criticised on three grounds. The first was that it was too vague. The Bar Association, for example, claimed that the offences were "not clearly and tightly defined". It thought that secession was adequately covered under existing legislation and that "subversion was not an offence known to the common law".[66] Bankers and entrepreneurs, too, expressed concern that the proposed laws might restrict the free flow of information.[67] There were calls from respected community figures for a white bill containing the proposed legislation before the consultation ended. The government argued that the principles had to be accepted first.

A second major concern related to freedom of expression and whether the Chinese government would continue to tolerate groups in Hong Kong who were opposed to it. The Falun Gong and the Hong Kong Alliance in Support of the Patriotic Democratic Movement in China were believed to be particularly vulnerable. Tung had already labelled Falun Gong an "evil cult"[68] and the Bar Association

---

61. Security Bureau (2002). *Proposals to implement Article 23 of the Basic Law: Consultation document.* https://www.info.gov.hk/archive/consult/2002/bl23-e.pdf
62. Fu, H. (2001). The national security factor: Putting Article 23 of the Basic Law in perspective. In S. Y. S. Tsang (Ed.), *Judicial independence and the rule of law in Hong Kong* (p. 78). Basingstoke: Palgrave.
63. Security Bureau (2002) op. cit., p. 10.
64. Ibid., p. 37.
65. Ibid., p. 30.
66. Hong Kong Bar Association (2002). Response to the consultation document on the proposals to implement Article 23 of the Basic Law. https://www.hkba.org/sites/default/files/20021209-art23.pdf
67. Segal, P. (2002, 19 December). Business: The biggest victim. *Far Eastern Economic Review* (pp. 30–34).
68. Hong Kong Government (2001, 8 February). *Chief Executive's statement about Falun Gong* [Press release]. https://www.info.gov.hk/gia/general/200102/08/0208178.htm

thought that Falun Gong might be proscribed if the legislation was passed.[69] The Secretary for Security said that the alliance would not be banned unless it had a subversive connection or advocated the use of force.[70] Suspicions remained that the legislation was aimed at controlling political groups that the Chinese government perceived to be threats to national security.

A third concern was the equally strong suspicion that the legislation would be detrimental to the freedom of the press.[71] In 1994, a Chinese court sentenced a Hong Kong journalist, Xi Yang, to 12 years in prison for reporting the sale of gold reserves by the Bank of China.[72] Once again, the government attempted to allay the fears of journalists and others. The Secretary for Justice said that Xi Yang's offence had been to refuse to disclose his sources.

The consultation period ended on 24 December 2002. By that time, the government had received 97,097 submissions containing 340,513 signatures.[73] It argued that submissions from organisations, original letters, and pre-printed, standard letters showed strong support for its proposals. But it discounted the signature forms which showed that only 25.5% supported the government while 72.2% were opposed. Some 175,823 signed the forms.[74] Given subsequent events, the signed forms better reflected public opinion than the views expressed by organisations or cyclostyled forms. The government's consultative methods and its analysis of the outcome were widely criticised.[75]

The government did pay some attention to the consultation exercise. It modified the legislation that was eventually presented to the Legislative Council,[76] claiming that there would not be much change to existing practices. It also provided extravagant guarantees that freedom of expression and other civil liberties would be protected; that it respected public opinion; and that the major concerns of the pressure groups had been met. It then set a deadline of 9 July 2003 for the passage of the legislation. Opposition continued to build. Leading lawyers remained critical of the powers given to the police to search homes without a court warrant.[77] Again, the government sought to allay public suspicions. On 3 June, the govern-

---

69. Hong Kong Bar Association (2002) op. cit.
70. Hon, M. S. M. (2002, 25 September). Will it or won't it breach the rules? *SCMP*.
71. Weisenhaus, D. (2005). Article 23 and freedom of the press: A journalistic perspective. In H. Fu, C. J. Petersen, & S. N. M. Young (Eds.), *National security and fundamental freedoms: Hong Kong's Article 23 under scrutiny* (pp. 277–301). Hong Kong: Hong Kong University Press.
72. Cullen, R. (2001). Freedom of the press and the rule of law in Hong Kong. In S. Y. S. Tsang (Ed.) op. cit., pp. 48–72, 159, 175 note 10.
73. Hong Kong Government (2003, 28 January). *Government further clarifies legislative proposals to implement BL23*. [Press release]. https://www.legco.gov.hk/yr02-03/english/panels/se/papers/ajlssecb2-1069-2e-scan.pdf
74. Ibid.
75. Shamdasani, R., & Chan, Q. (2003, 13 January). Fears over analysis of security law views. *SCMP*.
76. Legislative Council (2003, February 13). *Legislative Council brief: National Security (Legislative Provisions) Bill*. Hong Kong: mimeo.
77. Article 23 Concern Group (2003, April). *Why the Blue Bill on National Security (Legislative Provisions) is not good enough*. Hong Kong: The Group; Lee, K. (2003, 28 June). Most people oppose security bill. *SCMP*.

ment introduced further amendments, providing more safeguards for civil liberties and limiting the power to search homes.[78] On 14 June, the legislation reached the Legislative Council's Bills Committee. With only one democratic legislator present, the government passed "an unprecedented motion" to prevent further clause-by-clause debate of the legislation.[79]

The process increased opposition to the bill. A coalition of parties, human rights groups, religious organisations, and trade unions planned a demonstration for 1 July, a holiday celebrating Hong Kong's return to China. The organisers, the Civil Human Rights Front, hoped that 100,000 protesters would attend but, in the event, an estimated 500,000 marched peacefully through the streets.[80] While civil liberties were the central focus of opposition to the legislation, the protest also reflected widespread discontent with government policies.[81] The government made even more concessions but said that the second reading should still go ahead.

The unlikely catalyst for defusing the situation was the pro-establishment Liberal Party chairman, James Tien Pei-chun. Tien paid a hurried visit to Beijing. On his return, he announced his resignation from the Executive Council and urged the government to defer the legislation. He said that the Chinese government wanted the legislation passed although it had no clear preferences on details or the timetable.[82] Without the Liberal Party's support, and the prospect that other legislators might join the democrats in opposing the bill, there was little option but for the Chief Executive to defer the second reading.[83] Even then, further large demonstrations called for his resignation.

In an attempt to bolster his fading support, Tung accepted the resignations of the Financial Secretary and the Secretary for Security, promised to re-open consultation on Article 23, and outlined numerous measures to improve the government's relationship with the people.[84] He then flew off to Beijing to discuss the crisis with China's leaders. The Chinese President, Hu Jintao, reaffirmed his support and thought that the bill would be passed after "earnest and wide-ranging consultation" led to a better understanding of the legislation.[85] But the issue had gone beyond the legislative measures to become symbolic of wider systemic problems and government policies. On 5 September, Tung withdrew the bill.[86]

---

78. Hong Kong Government (2003, 3 June). *Government announces draft amendments to the National Security (Legislative Provisions) Bill* [Press release]. https://www.info.gov.hk/gia/general/200306/03/0603276.htm
79. *SCMP* (2003, 16 June). Scrutiny of bill makes a mockery of the system. Editorial.
80. Cheung, J., & Lee, K. (2003, 2 July). 500000 march through the streets. *SCMP*.
81. Cheng, J. Y. S. (2005). Introduction: Causes and implications of the July 1 protest rally in Hong Kong. In J. Y. S. Cheng (Ed.), *The July 1 Protest Rally: Interpreting a historic event* (pp. 1–26). Hong Kong: City University of Hong Kong Press.
82. Cheung, J. (2003, 2 July). James Tien quits over Article 23. *SCMP*.
83. Hong Kong Government (2003, 7 July). *Chief Executive's transcript on national security law* [Press release]. https://www.info.gov.hk/gia/general/200307/07/0707200.htm
84. Cheung, J. (2003, 18 July). Tung opens door to change. *SCMP*.
85. Armitage, C. (2003, 21 July). Beijing puts Hong Kong on notice. *The Australian*.
86. Cheung, J., Lee, K., & Ma, J. (2003, 6 September). Tung shelves Article 23 legislation. *SCMP*.

Surveys showed that the attempt to legislate Article 23 was perceived to strike at the heart of the rule of law and to endanger guaranteed rights and freedoms.[87] It damaged the credibility of Hong Kong's "high degree of autonomy" because it was widely believed that the bill had only been introduced because the Chinese government wanted it, not because it was necessary. It increased mistrust of the political executive and showed that the government had neither the consent nor the moral authority to introduce such legislation.

The Decline of Civil Liberties

The withdrawal of the legislation was a victory for the protection of civil liberties in Hong Kong and led to many subsequent "ritualistic protests".[88] But it did not prevent the gradual erosion of many rights and freedoms.

There were four major areas in which civil liberties were at greater risk. First, the Hong Kong way of life, which is guaranteed for 50 years under Article 5, was perceived to be under threat from mainlandisation. Popular grievances affected many aspects of life. United front groups have gradually penetrated many Hong Kong institutions, mobilising support for pro-Beijing policies.[89] Mainland business entrepreneurs have taken over some Hong Kong companies and driven up property prices to unaffordable levels. Mainland tourists were alleged to behave badly and to congest shopping malls. Parallel traders from the Mainland, who buy goods in quantity at retail outlets in Hong Kong and resell at a profit in China, affect the supply of goods to local residents. Coupled with growing resentment of mainlandisation, there has been a sharp rise in the number of Hong Kong people who identify themselves as Hong Kongers rather than as Chinese.[90]

Second, the freedom of the press, which is promised in Article 27 of the Basic Law, has been under constant threat. In 2002, the organisation Reporters without Borders ranked Hong Kong 18th in world press freedom. By 2016, it had slipped to 69th of 180 countries and by 2020 fell further to 80th.[91] In 2017, the Hong Kong Journalists Association noted that the Chinese government or Mainland corporations had direct control or stakes in eight of 26 mainstream media outlets.[92] Criticism of the Chinese government in the press has been met with pressure to

---

87. Hong Kong Transition Project (2002). *Accountability & Article 23: Freedom, fairness and accountability in Hong Kong* (p. 57). Hong Kong: The Project.
88. Lee, L. F., & Chan, J. M. (2011). *Media, social mobilisation and mass protests in post-colonial Hong Kong: The power of a critical event* (pp. 11–14). New York: Routledge.
89. Lo, S. S. H., Hung, S. C. F., & Loo, J. H. C. (Eds.) (2019). *China's new united front work in Hong Kong: Penetrative politics and its implications*. London: Palgrave Macmillan.
90. Ping, Y. C., & Kwong, K. M. (2014). Hong Kong identity on the rise. *Asian Survey, 54*(6), 1088–1112.
91. Reporters without Borders (2017). *2016 world press freedom index*. https://rsf.org/en/ranking/2016
92. Hong Kong Journalists Association (2017). *One country, two nightmares: 2016 annual report* (p. 5). https://ifex.org/images/china/hong_kong/2016/07/05/hongkong_annualreport_2016_hkja.pdf

withdraw advertising and the dismissal of critical journalists. There has also been violence and threats. In the worst case in 2014, Kevin Lau, a former editor of *Ming Pao*, a respected centrist newspaper, was brutally attacked with a cleaver by two men, who were subsequently sentenced to 19 years in prison.[93] There was no evident connection with China, but journalists observed that *Ming Pao* had been running potentially embarrassing stories on corruption and human rights on the Mainland.

Third, freedom of association, of assembly, of procession, and demonstration are all protected under Article 27. However, the right to hold a demonstration or procession requires police permission and permits have been granted less freely in recent years. Relations between police and protesters deteriorated sharply during the Umbrella Movement and gradually worsened considerably with a 2016 riot in Mongkok and the repeated 2019 protests, many of which did not have police permission.

Fourth, Article 28 guarantees the freedom of the person of Hong Kong residents. In 2015, five Hong Kong booksellers disappeared and were detained in China for questioning.[94] They sold books, banned in mainland China but legal in Hong Kong, including some about the private lives of Chinese leaders. A bookseller who had a Swedish passport was sentenced to 10 years in China for providing intelligence to foreign entities. The remainder were released in 2016. After his release, one bookseller, Lam Wing-kee, reported that he had been kidnapped at the border, detained for eight months, and forced to make a televised confession.[95] He warned that it could happen to anyone, an already widespread fear that drove millions of protesters to the streets when the government announced in 2019 that it intended to introduce amendments to the *Fugitive Offenders Ordinance*.

The Extradition Bill

There are some similarities in the politics of government-public relationships in the attempts to legislate Article 23 and the introduction of the Extradition Bill. In both cases, the government ignored public opinion and stuck obdurately to its plans until the weight of public pressure forced it to withdraw the legislation. In both cases, the fear of what the legislation entailed was focused on the consequences for civil liberties in Hong Kong. Unlike the 2003 protests, the 2019 protests were the trigger for more prolonged and violent disturbances accompanied by demands for universal suffrage and a commission to investigate the actions of the Police Force.

---

93. Ibid., p. 28.
94. Palmer, A. W. (2018, 3 April). The case of Hong Kong's missing booksellers. *New York Times*. https://www.nytimes.com/2018/04/03/magazine/the-case-of-hong-kongs-missing-booksellers.html
95. Ng, J. Y. (2016, 20 June). All in it together: The bookseller's ordeal in China could happen to any of us. *HKFP*. https://hongkongfp.com/2016/06/20/be-warned-the-booksellers-ordeal-in-china-could-happen-to-any-of-us/

Ostensibly, the need for legislation arose because a Hong Kong resident allegedly murdered his girlfriend in Taiwan and could not be extradited for trial.[96] But there were far wider implications for civil liberties and relations between Hong Kong and mainland China. The proposed amendments to the *Fugitive Offenders Ordinance* were an attempt to resolve the long-standing difficulties between Hong Kong and the PRC over the extradition of suspects. Although the possibility of an extradition agreement had been broached shortly after the handover, no progress had been made. A major stumbling block was that the two legal systems were fundamentally different. Anyone extradited to the PRC, if convicted, was likely to face much stiffer penalties on the Mainland than in Hong Kong, including the death penalty for some offences. One of the government's aims was to try to establish due process to prevent reoccurrences of the booksellers' case and to return suspected criminals to Hong Kong. Neither argument held much water for most people, who believed that the law would be used by the Chinese security forces to extradite political opponents from Hong Kong.

Between the government's announcement in February 2019 of its intention to legislate and its publication of the legislation on 29 March,[97] some concessions were made to the business community, removing nine offences that affected those involved in business in the PRC.[98] But there were no concessions to democrats who organised a demonstration two days after the publication of the amendments, arguing that civil liberties were in jeopardy.[99] When the bill reached the Legislative Council on 3 April, democrats argued that it contravened Articles 2, 4, and 5 of the Basic Law and that the legislation should not be tabled because there was a pending case asking for judicial review on grounds of human rights violations.[100] The proposed legislation contained 37 offences on which suspects could be extradited, provided that the offence would incur a three-year sentence in Hong Kong.[101] The procedure for extradition was to involve three steps: (1) a request to the Chief Executive from any government or territory to issue a certificate to request provisional arrest; (2) a hearing by a judge, who would then decide whether to issue an arrest warrant; (3) a final decision by the Chief Executive to proceed with the arrest and rendition.[102] Under the existing legislation, the Legislative Council was

---

96. Legislative Council Panel on Security (2019, 15 February). Administration's paper on the co-operation between Hong Kong and other places on juridical assistance in criminal matters. CB (2)767/18-19(03). https://www.legco.gov.hk/yr19-20/english/panels/se/papers/se_s.htm#yr1819
97. Meick, E. (2019, 7 May). Hong Kong's proposed extradition bill could extend Beijing's coercive reach: Risks for the United States. *U.S.-China Economic and Security Review Commission.* https://www.uscc.gov/sites/default/files/Research/USCC%20Issue%20Brief_HK%20Extradition%20Bill.pdf
98. Hong Kong Government (2019, 29 March). *Fugitive Offenders and Mutual Legal Assistance in Criminal Matters Legislation (Amendment) Bill.* https://www.legco.gov.hk/yr18-19/english/bills/b201903291.pdf
99. Chan, H. (2019, 31 March). In pictures: 12000 Hongkongers march in protest against "evil" China extradition law, organisers say. *HKFP.* https://hongkongfp.com/2019/03/31/pictures-12000-hongkongers-march-protest-evil-china-extradition-law-organisers-say/
100. Hansard, 3 April 2019, 8420–8446.
101. Hong Kong Government (2019) op. cit., Explanatory memorandum, para.4.
102. Meick, E. (2019) op. cit.

vested with power to issue the certificate but, under the amendments, this would now become the prerogative of the Chief Executive.

The Hong Kong Bar Association was highly critical of the proposed legislation.[103] It asked the government what changes had occurred since 1997 when mainland China was intentionally excluded from extradition agreements because of its human rights record and criminal justice system. It thought that the Chief Executive's new role in issuing certificates removed the Legislative Council's vetting power and that dispensing with judicial authentication of supporting documents was a mistake. The government said that the amendments would "plug loopholes", but the Bar Association said that they would weaken existing legislation and remove essential elements in a fair extradition process. On 6 June, 3,000 lawyers dressed in black staged a silent protest.[104]

The crowds opposing the bill continued to grow. The first demonstration on 31 March attracted about 12,000.[105] By 28 April, an estimated 130,000 took to the streets. On 9 June, half a million were said to be involved in the most violent demonstration to that point. The Legislative Council meeting on the second reading was scheduled for 12 June, but protesters surrounding the chamber led to its postponement. On 15 June, Lam suspended the bill.[106] But the protesters were not mollified, suspecting that the bill would be reintroduced. On 16 June, almost two million protesters were estimated to have marched through the streets demanding the withdrawal of the bill.[107]

The government's handling of the bill, as Lam admitted, had been deficient. There had been insufficient consultation, but the government still pushed on. The demonstrations became increasingly violent. Of the 12 June protest, Amnesty International wrote that "the largely peaceful protesters faced an onslaught of tear gas, guns firing rubber bullets, pepper spray and baton charges from police . . . causing 81 casualties".[108] In later demonstrations, which occurred every weekend

---

103. Hong Kong Bar Association (2019, 2 April). Observation of the Hong Kong Bar Association (HKBA) on the Fugitive Offenders and Mutual Legal Assistance in criminal matters legislation. https://www.hkba.org/sites/default/files/HKBA%20Observations%20on%20FOMLACM%20Bill%202019%20%28Final%29.pdf
104. *SCMP* (2019, 7 June). Hong Kong lawyers hold silent march against controversial Extradition Bill. https://www.scmp.com/video/hong-kong/3013537/hong-kong-lawyers-hold-silent-march-against-controversial-extradition-bill
105. Chan, H. (2019, 31 March) op. cit.
106. Chief Executive (2019, 15 June). *Opening remarks by CE at media session* [Press release]. https://www.info.gov.hk/gia/general/201906/15/P2019061500707.htm
107. *SCMP* Reporters (2019, 17 June). "Nearly 2 million" people take to streets, forcing public apology from Hong Kong leader Carrie Lam as suspension of controversial extradition bill fails to appease protesters. *SCMP*. https://www.scmp.com/news/hong-kong/politics/article/3014737/nearly-2-million-people-take-streets-forcing-public-apology. On measuring the size of the crowd in the 9 and 12 June protests, see Scarr, S., Sharma, M., Hernandez, M., & Tong, V. (2019, 20 June). Measuring the masses: The contentious issue of crowd counting in Hong Kong. *Reuter Graphics*. https://graphics.reuters.com/HONGKONG-EXTRADITION-PROTESTS/0100B01001H/index.html
108. Amnesty International (2020). *Hong Kong: Missing truth, missing justice; the case and international legal framework for the establishment of a commission of inquiry into the 2019 protests* (p. 2). London: Amnesty International.

and public holiday until the end of 2019, the protesters erected barricades across streets, threw rocks at the police, vandalised subway stations and mainland Chinese-owned businesses and those owned by supporters of the government. On 1 July, protesters broke into the Legislative Council and spray-painted slogans, damaged equipment and tore down portraits.[109] The police came under great pressure. Its manpower resources were stretched to the limit, its members and their families were doxed, young constables were ostracised, and there were constant allegations of excessive use of force and brutality. The government strongly supported police action but there was little it could do in the short term to assist police efforts to maintain public order. For their part, the protesters demanded an independent commission to inquire into police conduct. The government said that it would leave any investigations to the Independent Police Complaints Council (IPCC).

In September 2019, to bolster the credibility of the council, the IPCC Chairman invited five overseas experts to form an advisory panel. In November, the panel advised that the IPCC did not have sufficient powers and resources to investigate the protests.[110] A month later, the entire panel resigned, observing that the issue of the inadequate powers and resources of the council had not been resolved.[111] Despite this warning, the IPCC continued to investigate police misconduct and, in May 2020, produced a report which almost entirely exonerated the police.[112] The report was greeted with derision by many who had observed the protests. Among other critics, Hong Kong Watch said that it was "a shocking whitewash which shows that there is no viable mechanism in Hong Kong to ensure accountability for police brutality or police complicity with violence by criminal thugs".[113] Clifford Stott, a former member of the advisory committee, said that the report was "part of a wider set of coordinated announcements designed to deliver the new 'truth.'"[114] The IPPC report accepted the police view that it had to use force to maintain order, concluded that it had not done so excessively, and implied that some protesters were terrorists.[115]

---

109. *The Atlantic* (2019, 2 July). Photos: Hong Kong protesters break into Legislative Council building. https://www.theatlantic.com/photo/2019/07/hong-kong-protesters-break-into-legislative-council-building-photos/593158/
110. Lum, A. (2019, 10 November). Hong Kong police watchdog does not have the powers and resources to cope with scale of protests, say IPCC's expert advisers. *SCMP*. https://www.scmp.com/news/hong-kong/politics/article/3037080/hong-kong-police-watchdog-does-not-have-powers-and
111. AFP (2019, 11 December). Int'l experts to quit Hong Kong investigation into police handling of protests. *HKFP*. https://hongkongfp.com/2019/12/11/breaking-international-experts-quit-hong-kong-investigation-police-handling-protests/
112. Independent Police Complaints Council (2020). *A thematic study by the IPCC on the public order events arising from the Fugitive Offenders Bill since 2019 and the police action in response.* https://www.ipcc.gov.hk/en/public_communications/ipcc_thematic_study_report.html
113. Wong, R. (2020, 15 May). "Absurd, preposterous whitewash": Reactions pour in as Hong Kong police watchdog clears force of wrongdoing. *HKFP*. https://hongkongfp.com/?s=%27absurd%2C+preposterous+whitewash
114. Ibid.
115. Independent Police Complaints Council (2020) op. cit., 163, 174.

It was becoming increasingly clear that the Police Force was not accountable for its actions. Two incidents suggested that its enforcement of the law might be selective. When the protesters broke into and vandalised the Legislative Council, the police were suspected of selective enforcement of the law because they had many ways of stopping the protesters and had observed the intrusion but left soon afterwards.[116] It was thought that the police were trying to sway public opinion against the protesters.

Another, even more serious, case occurred on the evening of 21 July 2019. A group, variously estimated at between 70 and 100,[117] dressed in white shirts and widely thought to include triad members, attacked protesters and other passengers at the Yuen Long railway station.[118] At least 45 people were hospitalised.[119] Despite repeated calls for help, the police confirmed that it had taken 39 minutes before officers were deployed at the station by which time the first attack had ceased.[120] The Commissioner of Police said that it was difficult to deploy manpower sooner because his resources were stretched.[121] Once the police left the scene, the attackers launched a second assault. The Chief Executive said that the attacks were "shocking" and a violation of the rule of law.[122] The Chief Secretary for Administration, Matthew Cheung, was reported to have called the perpetrators "thugs" and said there was "a discrepancy between what the police did and what the public expected."[123] On 22 and 23 July, the police arrested eleven men over the attacks. Two years later, seven of them were convicted on charges of rioting, wounding with intent and conspiracy to wound with intent and sentenced to prison terms ranging from three years and six months to seven years.[124]

---

116. Burns, J. (2019, 26 July). Hong Kong police breed mistrust and uncertainty with selective enforcement of the law. *HKFP*. https://hongkongfp.com/2019/07/26/hong-kong-police-breed-mistrust-uncertainty-selective-law-enforcement/
117. IPCC (2020) op. cit., Ch. 10, p.8. The IPCC estimates the number at 70 but most reports suggest about 100.
118. Choi, A., & Lam, J. (2019, 22 July). Rod-wielding mob dressed in white storms Hong Kong's Yuen Long MTR station, attacks protesters and passers-by. *SCMP*. https://www.scmp.com/video/hong-kong/3019535/rod-wielding-mob-dressed-white-storms-hong-kongs-yuen-long-mtr-station. For a timeline of the events of 21 and 22 July, see Lo, S. S-H, Hung, S. C. H., & Loo, J. H. C. (2021). *The dynamics of peaceful and dynamic protests in Hong Kong: The anti-extradition movement* (pp. 123–124). Singapore: Palgrave Macmillan.
119. Kuo, L. (2019, 22 July). "Where were the police?" Hong Kong outcry after masked thugs launch attack. *The Guardian*. https://www.theguardian.com/world/2019/jul/22/where-were-the-police-hong-kong-outcry-after-masked-thugs-launch-attack
120. Ho, K. (2021, 21 July). Explainer: from "violent attack" to "gang fight" – how the official account of the Yuen Long mob attack changed. *HKFP*. https://hongkongfp.com/2021/07/21/from-violent-attack-to-gang-fight-how-the-official-account-of-the-yuen-long-mob-attack-changed-over-a-year/
121. Hong Kong Government (2019, 22 July). *Transcript of remarks by CE at media session* [Press release]. https://www.info.gov.hk/gia/general/201907/22/P2019072200890.htm
122. Ibid.; Ho, K. (2021, 21 July) op. cit.
123. Chan, H. (2019, 26 July). Hong Kong's chief sec. apologises over handling of Yuen Long attacks, stirring dissent from police. *HKFP*. https://hongkongfp.com/2019/07/26/hong-kongs-chief-sec-apologises-handling-yuen-long-attacks-stirring-dissent-police/
124. Ho, K. (2021, 22 July). 'They had lost their minds': Hong Kong court jails 7 men for 3.5 to 7 years over 2019 mob attacks. *HKFP*. https://hongkongfp.com/2021/07/22/breaking-hong-kong-court-jails-7-men-for-3-5-to-7-years-over-2019-yuen-long-mob-attacks/

In May 2020, the IPCC report presented a very different version of the Yuen Long attacks. Most significantly, it said that "[p]ublic perceptions had been misled … [by] the framing of the incidents inside Yuen Long Station as a one-sided indiscriminate terrorist attack when it had actually started off as a gang fight involving a sizeable number of participants from both sides.[125] The report provided some evidence, however, that the attack had been planned in advance and that Yuen Long residents had been warned to stay indoors on 21 July because of a gathering of 500 triad members.[126] It also raised the issue of collusion between police and triads and gave a long list of reasons for public beliefs that such collusion had occurred, but said that the IPCC had no statutory powers to investigate.[127] No blame was directly levelled at the police for their actions (or lack of them) although the report suggested that police crowd control measures might be improved, that public relations could have been better handled in the aftermath of the attack, and that the emergency call system needed an overhaul.[128] A democratic Legislative Councillor, Lam Cheuk-ting, who was injured in the attack, dismissed the report as " rubbish".[129] Amnesty International said that the report was biased and noted that the IPCC had no powers to resolve the many public complaints about police behaviour.[130]

Because the IPCC had no investigative powers of its own, the report was necessarily based on police evidence. Even before it was released, the police, under a new Commissioner, had made some effort to improve its public image. But it was not until August 2020 that it made a public announcement of its new explanation of events.[131] A senior police officer claimed that the extensive video evidence of what had happened did not present the "full picture" and that there had been a confrontation "between two evenly matched rivals".[132] The police spokesman also claimed that the force had responded to emergency calls within 18 minutes. This appears to relate to the arrival of the quick response team; sufficient police were not deployed to the scene to restore order until more than 30 minutes after the attack had begun.[133] On the same day as the announcement was made, the police arrested thirteen people, including the Legislative Councillor, Lam Cheuk-ting, on

---

125. IPCC (2020) op. cit., Ch10, p. 85.
126. Ibid., pp. 18, 21.
127. IPCC (2020) op. cit. Ch. 10, pp. 114–117.
128. Ibid., pp. 114, 118–121.
129. Pao, J. (2019, 15 May). Police report fails to resolve protest disputes. *Asia Times*. https://asiatimes.com/2020/05/police-report-fails-to-resolve-protest-disputes/
130. Amnesty International (2020, 15 May). Hong Kong: Impotent and biased IPCC report into protests fails to bring justice any closer. https://www.amnesty.org/en/latest/news/2020/05/hong-kong-impotent-and-biased-ipcc-report-into-protests-fails-to-bring-justice-any-closer/
131. Ho, K. (2021, 21 July) op. cit., McLaughlin, T. (2020). How history gets rewritten. *The Atlantic*. https://www.theatlantic.com/international/archive/2020/09/hong-kong-protests-propaganda/616135/
132. *BBC* (2020, 26 August). Yuen Long attack: Hong Kong police accused of 're-writing history'. https://www.bbc.com/news/world-asia-china-53915500
133. Ho, K. (2021, 21 July) op. cit.

suspicion of conspiracy to riot during the Yuen Long attack.[134] The new explanation was widely condemned as an effort to rewrite history[135] and seems to have done little to change public perceptions of the events.[136]

Carrie Lam eventually withdrew the Extradition Bill on 4 September, but the protests continued into 2020. The government had misplayed its hand. The concession was too late. Perceived police brutality remained unaddressed and there was no obvious escape from the government's intransigency and the protesters on the streets.

Full Circle: China Legislates Article 23

On 21 May 2020, the Chinese government announced that it would ask the NPC to legislate a national security law because the Legislative Council had been unable to do so. The legislation was to include measures to prevent sedition, secession, foreign interference, and terrorist activities.[137] Lam said that her government would cooperate fully in the drafting of the proposals and that civil liberties would not be affected.[138] She was unable to deny that Chinese security agencies would be permitted to operate in Hong Kong because she was not aware of the provisions of the legislation.[139]

Once more, the protesters took to the streets. The police responded with tear gas and arrested hundreds of protesters, mostly on charges of illegal assembly.[140] Many activists, legislators, and academics criticised the Chinese government's decision;[141] one legislator saw it as the end of "one country, two systems."[142] A People's Liberation Army spokesperson reportedly said that there were 10,000

---

134. Lam, O. (2020, 26 August). Hong Kong police accused of rewriting history to oppress political dissent. *Global Voices*. https://globalvoices.org/2020/08/27/hong-kong-police-accused-of-rewriting-history-to-oppress-political-dissent/
135. *BBC* (2020, 26 August) op. cit.; Ho, K. (2021, 21 July) op. cit.; Lam (2020, 26 August) op. cit., McLaughlin (2020) op. cit.
136. Cheng, A. (2020, 4 September). Hongkongers won't tolerate any police spin on Yuen Long mob attack. *SCMP*. https://www.scmp.com/comment/opinion/article/3100081/hongkongers-wont-tolerate-any-police-spin-yuen-long-mob-attack
137. Ho, K. (2020, 22 May). "Defenceless" Hong Kong needs state-level law "to prevent, stop and punish" threats to Chinese sovereignty, says Beijing. *HKFP*. https://hongkongfp.com/2020/05/22/defenceless-hong-kong-needs-state-level-law-to-prevent-stop-and-punish-threats-to-chinese-sovereignty-says-beijing/
138. Hong Kong Government (2020, 22 May). *Transcript of remarks by CE at media session*. https://www.info.gov.hk/gia/general/202005/22/P2020052200913.htm
139. Hong Kong Government (2020, 26 May). *Transcript of remarks by CE at media session before the Executive Council today* [Press release]. https://www.info.gov.hk/gia/general/202005/26/P2020052600406.htm
140. Wong, R., & Grundy, T. (2020, 24 May). Police fire tear gas and make 180 arrests as Hongkongers rally against national security law. *HKFP*. https://hongkongfp.com/2020/05/24/breaking-police-fire-tear-gas-as-hongkongers-rally-against-national-security-law/
141. Wong, R. (2020, 22 May). "This is the end of Hong Kong": Reactions pour in as Beijing proposes security law. *HKFP*. https://hongkongfp.com/2020/05/22/this-is-the-end-of-hong-kong-reactions-pour-in-as-beijing-proposes-security-law/
142. Ibid.

troops ready to safeguard sovereignty in Hong Kong.[143] When the legislation was enacted on 30 June, there was an immediate international reaction. The local stock market fell sharply after the United States government said that it would rescind its special trading relationship with Hong Kong. The British government offered the right of residence to the three million Hong Kong residents eligible for British National Overseas passports.[144]

The national security law had a widespread impact on Hong Kong's autonomy, its constitutional order established under the Basic Law, and the consequences for the operation of the common law. But the most immediate concern was that civil liberties were in serious jeopardy.[145] The offences were vaguely worded and the dozens of arrests that followed the enactment of the law often seemed to have only a distant connection with national security. In many cases, the primary characteristic of those arrested was that they were political opponents of the regime (see pp. 406–407). Although the national security law says that civil liberties will be protected, both the Chinese and Hong Kong governments implied that the law would take precedence over civil liberties.[146] The Chinese government said that national security was a paramount concern because of foreign interference in Hong Kong. Lam, while reiterating that Hong Kong's rights and freedoms would still be protected, noted that the International Covenant on Civil and Political Rights, to which Hong Kong is a signatory, recognised that national security was an over-riding concern.[147] In 2021, in the case of *HKSAR v Lai Chee Ying*, the Court of Final Appeal (CFA) accepted that it had "no power to hold any provision of the NSL (national security law) unconstitutional or invalid as incompatible with the BL (Basic Law) or the Hong Kong Bill of Rights."[148] Although the CFA went on to say that it thought that provisions in the national security law were intended to act in tandem with constitutional rights and freedoms, that does not necessarily preclude the executive from deciding that a person exercising a civil liberty may be violating national security.

Judicial Independence, Judicial Review, and the Interpretation of the Basic Law

Articles 18 and 19 of the Basic Law provide that the common law will continue to apply in the HKSAR, which "shall be vested with independent judicial power, including final adjudication". Article 158 then modifies this independence by

---

143. Davidson, H. (2020, 26 May). China's military say it is prepared to protect security in Hong Kong, as protests grow. *The Guardian*. https://www.theguardian.com/world/2020/may/26/chinas-military-says-it-is-prepared-to-protect-security-in-hong-kong-as-protests-grow
144. BBC (2020, 1 July). Hong Kong: UK makes citizenship offer to residents.
145. Government of the People's Republic of China (2020). *The Law of the People's Republic of China on safeguarding national security in the Hong Kong Special Administrative Region*, op. cit.
146. Ibid., Articles 4, 5.
147. Hong Kong Government (2020) op. cit.
148. Hong Kong Lawyer (2021, July) *HKSAR v Lai Chee Ying* [2021] HKCFA 3.

vesting the final power of interpretation in the NPCSC. Hong Kong courts are permitted to review pre-1997 laws, new legislation, and administrative decisions to ensure consistency with the Basic Law. Potentially, this allows some scope to hold the government accountable. For their cases to be heard, applicants must first seek leave to apply for judicial review, which is not always granted. According to the government, judicial review is "the review by a judge of the Court of First Instance of any exercise, or refusal to exercise, any public decision-making powers" and is a means "by which the courts can supervise how Government officials or other public officers exercise their powers or carry out their duties".[149] This differs from an appeal because a judicial review is only concerned with the question of whether an action was lawful or unlawful.

After the handover, democratic activists began to use judicial reviews as a means to seek redress on constitutional matters and to delay the implementation of government policies and decisions. Applications rose to the point where the Legal Aid Department and the CFA acted to reduce the number of reviews.[150] In 2007, over half the applications for legal aid were rejected by the department and, in November 2007, the CFA ruled that cases had to be "arguable", not just "potentially arguable", to bring the case to court.[151] As Table 2.2 shows, applications continued to rise until 2015, but the percentage refused permission to apply also increased substantially. Judicial review as a means of holding the government accountable has declined as a consequence.

An early, and defining, judicial review case concerned the right of abode in Hong Kong. Article 24(3) of the Basic Law provides that persons of Chinese nationality born outside Hong Kong to a Chinese citizen born in Hong Kong or resident in the territory for not less than seven years are entitled to become permanent residents of the HKSAR. The government thought that this provision might lead to a flood of new migrants from the Mainland with detrimental consequences for social services. The Provisional Legislative Council (PLC) then passed legislation requiring any eligible offspring to obtain certificates entitling them to migrate to Hong Kong. Initially, the debate focused on whether the right of abode was an absolute right under the Basic Law or whether it might be qualified by administrative decisions such as a certificate of entitlement.

When the case reached the CFA, the issue acquired greater constitutional significance. In January 1999, in *Ng Ka-ling v Director of Immigration*, the judges unanimously decreed that all Chinese-born children born of a Hong Kong parent had the right of abode. The CFA also stated its views on its constitutional position and that of the NPC in interpreting Hong Kong law. The court saw its role as "acting

---

149. Department of Justice (2019). *The judge over your shoulder: A guide to judicial review for administrators* (3rd ed., p. 1). https://www.doj.gov.hk/en/publications/the_judge_over_your_shoulder.html
150. Hui, P. (2008, 3 March). Judicial review legal aid bids on the rise. *SCMP*. https://www.scmp.com/article/628457/judicial-review-legal-aid-bids-rise
151. *Peter Po Fun Chan v Winnie C.W. Cheung and Another*, FACV10/2007. https://vlex.hk/vid/peter-po-fun-chan-862802310

Table 2.2 *Judicial Review: Applications for Leave to Apply and Findings against the Government*

Date	Number of applications	Leave granted	Leave refused	Applications refused (in per cent)	Findings against the government (in per cent)
2008	147	67	66	49.6	27
2009	144	67	72	51.8	28
2010	134	66	58	46.7	18
2011	103	51	40	44.0	29
2012	161	63	80	55.9	22
2013	182	38	72	65.5	32
2014	168	84	66	44.0	36
2015	259	67	141	67.7	44
2016	228	26	114	81.4	12
2017	1146[1]	16	228	95.0	15
2018	3014[2]	N/A	N/A	N/A	7

Source: Adapted from Department of Justice (2019). *The judge over your shoulder: A guide to judicial review for administrators* (3rd ed., pp. 1–2). https://www.doj.gov.hk/pdf/2019/JOYS_3rd_e.pdf#page=10

Notes:
1. Includes asylum seekers of whom there were 1,006 in 2017. See Legislative Council (2018, 5 December). Judicial review and non-refoulement claims. https://www.legco.gov.hk/research-publications/english/1819issh11-judicial-review-and-non-refoulement-claims-20181205-e.pdf
2. Includes asylum seekers of whom there were 2,851 in 2018.

as a constitutional check on the executive and legislative branches of government to ensure that they act in accordance with the Basic Law".[152] And then it went further:

> It is for the courts of the Region to determine whether an act of the National People's Congress or its Standing Committee is inconsistent with the Basic Law, subject . . . to the provision of the Basic Law itself.[153]

Just over a week after the CFA had released its judgement, four Mainland legal scholars, who had been involved in drafting the Basic Law, attacked the decision.[154] They argued that since the NPC was the institution with the highest authority in the land, the NPCSC, not the CFA, had the right to interpret whether the laws of Hong Kong were consistent with the Basic Law.

---
152. Court of Final Appeal (1999). *Final Appeal No 14 of 1998 (Civil) (Ng Ka Ling v Director of Immigration)* 1 HKC 291, 29 January.
153. Ibid.
154. Xiao, W., & others (2000). Why the Court of Final Appeal was wrong: Comments of the mainland scholars on the judgment of the Court of Final Appeal. In J. M. M. Chan, H. Fu, & Y. Ghai (Eds.), *Hong Kong's constitutional debate: Conflict over interpretation* (pp. 64–68). Hong Kong: Hong Kong University Press.

The Hong Kong government then sought a clarification on the CFA's decision because, as its counsel contended, there was concern that it was setting itself above the sovereign power. The CFA retreated, claiming that it did not question the authority of the NPCSC or its powers under Article 158 to interpret the Basic Law.[155] In April 1999, the government estimated that 1.67 million children might seek right of abode. In May, the Executive Council announced that the CFA's decision would be appealed.[156] The NPCSC then declared that Mainland children who were born after their parents became permanent residents of Hong Kong had no right of abode and that certificates of entitlement to emigrate were valid requirements.[157]

The Chief Executive maintained that the NPCSC decision was "entirely legal and constitutional" and said that the rule of law would never be compromised.[158] Academics, too, argued that the constitutional principles enshrining Hong Kong's autonomy had been upheld.[159] A contrary view was that the government had seriously compromised Hong Kong's autonomy and subverted the legal system. The Chairman of the Bar Association said that the "political will of the government has prevailed over due process" and that "any CFA decision is only final if the government wants it to be".[160] A statement from academics published in the local press criticised the government for putting itself above the law.[161] The right of abode cases reduced credibility in the institutional framework because of the evident conflict between the government and judiciary and increased tensions between belief in the rule of law and judicial independence and government decisions.

Despite their setback on the right of abode issue, Hong Kong courts continued to display independence in their decisions. Although the outcome of most judicial reviews favoured the government (see Table 2.2), the courts found for the applicants in several important cases. Some examples, both in favour and against the government, illustrate the wide range of constitutional issues that have come before the courts through judicial review.

In 1997, the legality and competence of the PLC was challenged because it was not, as the Basic Law provides, established by election. The court dismissed the case, finding that a committee, set up under Chinese law, had the power to make arrangements for the transition.[162] In the same year, the Chief Executive's right to appoint and dismiss civil servants was also unsuccessfully contested.[163] Two years

---

155. *SCMP* (1999, 26 February). Judges say they never intended to question NPC.
156. Hong Kong Government (1999, 19 May). *Speech by Secretary for Security* [Press release].
157. Standing Committee of the NPC (1999). *Interpretation of Articles 22(4) and 24(2)(3) of the Basic Law of the Hong Kong Special Administrative Region of the People's Republic of China*. In Chan, Fu, & Ghai (2000) op. cit., pp. 478–486.
158. Yeung, C. (1999, 27 June). NPC lays down the law. *Sunday Morning Post*.
159. Chen, A. H. Y. (2002). The constitution and the rule of law. In S. K. Lau (Ed.), *The first Tung Chee-hwa Administration* (pp. 84–85). Hong Kong: Chinese University Press.
160. Leong, A. (2003, 14 January). Does the system protect our rights as before? Not as much. *SCMP*; Weng, B. (2001). Judicial independence under the Basic Law. In S. Y. S. Tsang (2001) (Ed.), op. cit., pp. 61–66.
161. Ibid., p. 66.
162. *HKSAR v Ma Wai Kwan and Others*, CAQL 1/1997.
163. *The Association of Expatriate Civil Servants v The Chief Executive of HKSAR*, HCAL 90/1997.

later, an elected Regional Councillor argued that the government's decision to abolish the Regional Council was unconstitutional since it violated his rights under the International Covenant for Civil and Political Rights, which is enshrined in the Basic Law (Article 39).[164] The appeal was dismissed. Several cases have involved ordinances where the court has been asked whether provisions in the Basic Law override new legislation. In the *Catholic Diocese of Hong Kong v Secretary of Justice*, the church argued that, by amending the *Education Ordinance*, the Education Bureau was replacing the previous education system which was guaranteed under the Basic Law.[165] The appeal was dismissed.

Findings that have gone against the government have significantly affected its ability to continue to implement infrastructural, land development, and housing projects and to administer the provisions of some ordinances. In the *Town Planning Board v Society for the Protection of the Harbour*, the court found that there was nothing in the Basic Law that affected the provisions of the *Harbour Protection Ordinance* and found in favour of the society.[166] The government was prevented from reclaiming a large amount of land from the harbour. In 2011, the government experienced an even more serious defeat. In *Chu Yee Wah v Director of Environmental Protection*, the appellant successfully challenged the Director of Environmental Protection's decision to approve the environmental impact assessment reports for the construction of the HZMB.[167] Construction was postponed on the Hong Kong side and, with further delays caused by difficult construction conditions, added nearly two years to the completion date.[168] In other cases, the courts found that some provisions of the *Crimes Ordinance* were discriminatory and that the government's covert surveillance activities under the *Telecommunications Ordinance* were in breach of Article 30 of the Basic Law.[169]

In 2014, the Chinese State Council announced that there was no separation of powers in the Basic Law and that judges in courts at all levels should be administrators and patriots.[170] Judicial independence was caught in the middle of the growing friction between the Chinese and Hong Kong governments and the pan-democrats. As political tension rose and the Umbrella Movement clashed with the Police Force, the number of applications for leave to pursue judicial review increased substantially (see Table 2.2).[171] The Chief Executive, C. Y. Leung, claimed that the remedy

---

164. *Chan Shu Ying v The Chief Executive of the Hong Kong Special Administrative Region*, HCAL151/1999.
165. *Catholic Diocese of Hong Kong v Secretary for Justice*, HCAL157/2005.
166. *Town Planning Board v Society for the Protection of the Harbour*, FACV14/2003.
167. Kwok, D. W. H. (2011). *The Hong Kong-Zhuhai-Macau Bridge: Summary of the case*. Hong Kong: Civic Exchange.
168. Leung, K. (2018, 19 October). World's longest sea-crossing is finally finished but Hong Kong-Zhuhai-Macau bridge has come at a high cost. *SCMP*. https://www.scmp.com/news/hong-kong/transport/article/2169199/decade-deaths-and-delays-worlds-longest-sea-crossing
169. *Leung TC William Roy v Secretary for Justice*, HCAL160/2004; *Leung Kwok Hung and Another v Chief Executive of the HKSAR*, CACV 73/2006.
170. State Council (2014, 15 March) op. cit.
171. Kong, T. G. (2015, 21 April). Overview of legal cases related to the HK Umbrella revolution. https://medium.com/@KongTsungGan/overview-of-legal-cases-related-to-the-hk-umbrella-revolution-7734adecdb0

was being abused, particularly in cases relating to land, housing, and politics[172] and the pro-Beijing media and some academics joined the chorus. In 2015, a former CFA judge, Henry Litton, made a speech, and later published a book, in which he argued that judicial review should not be used to attack government policy.[173] The Chief Justice, Geoffrey Ma Tao-li, defended judicial review, arguing that it often involved issues of fairness, transparency, and access to justice and important matters such as the right of abode, freedom, environmental issues, social welfare, and elections.[174]

After the 2016 Legislative Council elections, six elected radical activists were disqualified for failing to take the oath properly. Of these, Leung Chung-hang and Yau Wai-ching chose to unfurl a banner reading "Hong Kong is not China", pledged their loyalty to the Hong Kong nation, and insulted China.[175] The Legislative Council Secretary-General, who was chairing the session before a president was elected, refused to accept their oaths. When the president was elected, he decided that the two activists should be permitted to retake their oaths although he later reversed his decision. The Chief Executive applied for judicial review, arguing that Leung and Yui should be required to vacate their offices immediately.[176] Before the High Court judge could reach his decision, the NPCSC decided that the two activists should be disqualified and prevented from taking their seats.[177] The judge subsequently said that he had reached the same decision and found that the Legislative Council President had been incorrect in providing an opportunity to retake the oath.[178] The Chief Executive said that the government would "fully implement" the decision and might even launch another attempt to introduce a national security law.[179] Leung and Yau's appeal to the CFA was dismissed. In July 2017, four other elected members were disqualified after both the government and the activists had lodged applications for judicial review.

---

172. Hong Kong Government (2016, 12 January). Judicial reviews must not be abused: CE. https://www.news.gov.hk/en/categories/admin/html/2016/01/20160112_100624.shtml
173. Litton, H. (2019). *Is the Hong Kong judiciary sleepwalking to 2047?* Hong Kong: Sheriff Books.
174. Hong Kong Government (2016, 11 January). CJ's speech at ceremonial opening of the legal year 2016. https://www.hkcfa.hk/filemanager/speech/en/upload/153/press_release_20160111_01en.pdf
175. Cheung, T., Ng, J., & Lau, S. (2016, 12 October). Three rejections and multiple deviations mark Hong Kong Legislative Council swearing-in. *SCMP.* https://www.scmp.com/news/hong-kong/politics/article/2027413/three-rejections-and-four-deviations-mark-hong-kong
176. *Chief Executive of the HKSAR v The President of the Legislative Council and Sixtus Leung Chung Hang and Yau Wai Chung*, HCAL185/2016.
177. Lo, P. Y. (2018). Enforcing an unfortunate, unnecessary and "unquestionably binding" NPCSC interpretation: The Hong Kong judiciary's deconstruction of its construction of the Basic Law. *Hong Kong Law Journal*, 48(2), 399–491.
178. Ng, J., Lau, C., Lam, J., & Cheung, T. (2016, 16 November). Barred Hong Kong localists vow to keep fighting after High Court decision. *SCMP.* https://www.scmp.com/news/hong-kong/politics/article/2046162/hong-kong-court-rules-localist-lawmakers-must-vacate-legco
179. Lam, J., Ng, J., & Cheung, G. (2016, 7 November). Hong Kong will move on controversial security law, C. Y. Leung says, as Beijing bans independence activists from Legco. *SCMP.* https://www.scmp.com/news/hong-kong/politics/article/2043556/beijing-passes-interpretation-hong-kongs-basic-law-legco

The intervention of the NPCSC and the decisions in both cases were widely criticised. The Hong Kong Bar Association said that it gave the impression that the NPCSC was legislating for Hong Kong and "cast doubt on the commitment of the Central People's Government to abide by the principles of 'One Country, Two Systems', 'Hong Kong People Ruling Hong Kong', and 'High Degree of Autonomy'".[180] Legal commentators asked how two very different systems of law could coexist if the NPCSC was going to intervene in cases that were *sub judice*.[181] There was also criticism of the "backsliding" of the Judiciary and its acceptance of the NPCSC's decision as absolutely binding, without trying to see its full implications for the Basic Law.[182] Protesters again took to the streets to demonstrate against the violations of the rule of law and the one country, two systems concept.

Further controversy occurred in October 2019 when the government, employing a scarcely used colonial ordinance, pushed through a regulation banning the use of face masks in protests to try to improve police facial recognition techniques. The protesters largely ignored the regulation, but 24 pan-democrat Legislative Councillors applied for judicial review to overturn it.[183] In November 2019, the High Court decided that the regulation was unconstitutional and in violation of multiple provisions in the Basic Law. The government appealed the decision and, in April 2020, the CFA found that the ban was constitutional if the protest was illegal but was not constitutional if the protest was legal.[184] By that stage, COVID-19 had persuaded most Hong Kong citizens that wearing a face mask was desirable.

In the charged political atmosphere of Hong Kong, where the legitimacy of the constitution is in question, where the sovereign power has strong views on how laws should be made and adjudicated, and where civil society organisations have become increasingly sophisticated in their use of legal avenues, the courts and the rule of law are under mounting stress. The Public Opinion Research Institute has periodically asked a survey question on whether Hong Kong was a society governed by the rule of law.[185] On a scale of 0 to 10, where 10 represented "very much", the surveys found a fall from 7.17 in 1997 to 4.45 in 2020 and a precipitate decline in 2019 from 6.20 to 4.41. Since the survey was conducted, the loss of belief in the integrity of judicial institutions has been further battered by the Chinese government's decision

---

180. Hong Kong Bar Association (2016, 7 November). The Hong Kong Bar Association's statement concerning the interpretation made by the National People's Congress Standing Committee of Article 104 of the Basic Law. https://www.hkba.org/sites/default/files/20161107%20-%20Statement%20re%20NPCSC%20interpretration%20BL104%20%28Eng%20Version-web%29.pdf
181. Chan, J. (2018). A storm of unprecedented ferocity: The shrinking space of the right to political participation, peaceful demonstration and judicial independence in Hong Kong. *International Journal of Constitutional Law*, 16(2), 373–388.
182. Lo, P. Y. (2020). Twilight of the idolised in Hong Kong's legal and judicial cultures. In C. Chan & F. de Londras (Eds.), *China's national security: Endangering Hong Kong's rule of law* (pp. 133–157). Oxford: Hart Publishing.
183. *Kwok Wing Hang and Others v Chief Executive in Council and Another* HCAL 2945/2019.
184. *Leung Kwok Hung v Secretary for Justice and Chief Executive in Council* CACV542/2019.
185. PORI(2020). The rule of law. https://www.pori.hk/pop-poll/rule-of-law-indicator/g002

to legislate a national security law for Hong Kong. Authoritarian rule by law has begun to replace the rule of law.[186]

A High Degree of Autonomy?

There was always the possibility that sovereignty and autonomy would prove mutually irreconcilable. Article 12 of the Basic Law specifies that HKSAR "shall enjoy a high degree of autonomy", but the same clause also states, in apparent contradiction, that it shall "come directly under the Central People's Government". Many provisions, however, emphasise that Hong Kong laws will be made in Hong Kong. Article 18 states that national laws shall not be applied to Hong Kong except for those concerned with foreign affairs and defence. Article 22 explicitly prohibits Mainland central government departments, provinces, autonomous regions, or municipalities from interfering in the affairs of the HKSAR. All Mainland government agencies with offices in Hong Kong are required to abide by local laws. But other important powers are reserved for the Chinese government, including the final say on the electoral system, the appointment of the Chief Executive and principal officials and, critically, the power to interpret what the Basic Law actually means.

Mainland officials created further anxieties by insisting that one country took precedence over two systems.[187] In the face of the strident demands for the popular election of the Chief Executive, in 2014 the State Council redefined what was meant by a high degree of autonomy. A critical passage reads:

> The high degree of autonomy of the HKSAR is not full autonomy, nor a decentralized power. It is the power to run local affairs as authorized by the central leadership. The high degree of autonomy of the HKSAR is subject to the level of central leadership's authorization. There is no such thing called "residual power."[188]

A high degree of autonomy was thus defined as the discretion that the Chinese government would allow the HKSAR and no different from any other local administration in China. In September 2015, a curious incident suggests that this interpretation was shared by the Chief Executive, C. Y. Leung. Leung came to the defence of the head of the Chinese Liaison Office in Hong Kong, Zhang Xiaoming, who implied in a speech on the Basic Law that the Chief Executive's powers were above

---

186. Chan, C. & de Londras, F. (Eds.) (2020). *China's national security: Endangering Hong Kong's rule of law*. Oxford: Hart Publishing; Davis, M. C. (2020). *Making Hong Kong China: The rollback of human rights and the rule of law*. Ann Arbor: Association for Asian Studies.
187. Xiao, W. (2001). *One country, two systems: An account of the drafting of the Hong Kong Basic Law* (p. 2). Beijing: Peking University Press; Eagleton, J. (2014). The mixing of well and river water under "one country, two systems". Nottingham: China Policy Institute, University of Nottingham.
188. State Council (2014, 15 March) op. cit.

the law.[189] The Hong Kong Bar Association issued a rebuttal,[190] and the Chief Justice made a rare public statement,[191] noting that Hong Kong had judicial independence and that no one was above the law. Leung claimed that critics had misinterpreted Zhang's remarks and then added that Hong Kong was "just a local government, without complete administrative and legislative powers".[192] The press release was quickly removed from the government website and attracted little comment. But, if Hong Kong had become "just a local government", one country, two systems had moved some distance from vesting a high degree of autonomy in the HKSAR. The clear message was that the Hong Kong government only exercised authority at the behest of the Chinese government.

The subsequent failure to provide universal suffrage, the erosion of civil liberties, and the declining importance of judicial review all contributed to the perception that the Joint Declaration and the Basic Law were being violated. The 2014 and 2019–2020 protests reflected the view of many localist and pan-democratic activists that there was no longer any alternative but to protest the loss of autonomy on the streets.

From January 2020, the Liaison Office began to play a more openly assertive role in Hong Kong. Wang Zhimin was replaced as head of the Office by Luo Huining, who had no previous experience in Hong Kong. By April, Luo was calling for national security laws to apply in the HKSAR.[193] The Liaison Office also claimed that it was not bound by Article 22 of the Basic Law, which prohibits the interference of Chinese government departments in Hong Kong affairs.[194] Carrie Lam said the Liaison Office had the right to supervise Hong Kong affairs.[195] Changes in the Chinese government's attitude towards Hong Kong were also reflected in the Chinese government's Hong Kong and Macau Affairs Office where Zhang Xiaoming, the head of the office was demoted in favour of Xia Baolong, who was seen as a hardliner.[196]

---

189. *SCMP* (2015, 16 September). Zhang Xiaoming's controversial speech on Hong Kong governance: The full text. https://www.scmp.com/news/hong-kong/politics/article/1858484/zhang-xiaomings-controversial-speech-hong-kong-governance
190. Hong Kong Bar Association (2015, 14 September). Statement of the Hong Kong Bar Association on the speech of Director Zhang Xiaoming at the seminar held on 12 September 2015 marking the 25th anniversary of the promulgation of the Basic Law of the Hong Kong Special Administrative Region. https://www.hkba.org/sites/default/files/20150914%20-%20Press%20Statement%20of%20HKBA%20-%20English.pdf
191. Chief Justice (2015, 16 September). *Transcript of remarks by the Chief Justice* [Press release]. http://www.info.gov.hk/gia/general/201509/16.htm
192. Chief Executive (2015, 15 September). *Gov't respects judicial independence: CE* [Press release]. Personal copy; no longer accessible at www.gov.hk.
193. Richburg, K. B. (2020, 28 April). Hong Kong's autonomy, dying in full view. *The Strategist*.
194. Chan, J. M. M. (2020). A strained interpretation of Article 22 of the Basic Law. *Hong Kong Law Journal*, 50(1), pp. 7–18.
195. Richburg (2020, 28 April) op. cit.
196. Pepper, S. (2020, 22 February). Off with their heads! Beijing names new men to run Hong Kong, but will there be change? *HKFP*. https://hongkongfp.com/2020/02/22/off-heads-beijing-names-new-men-run-hong-kong-affairs-fresh-crackdown-imminent/

The Chinese government's announcement in May 2020 that it would legislate a national security law for Hong Kong was a hammer blow for any notion that some compromise might be found. It posed two critical problems affecting the credibility and consistency of the Basic Law. Article 23 provides that the Hong Kong Legislative Council shall "on its own" legislate national security laws. The Chinese government proposed to overcome this difficulty by adding its measures to Annex III of the Basic Law that concerns national laws which apply in the HKSAR. There were further inconsistencies, however, in the provisions relating to the relative powers of the Chinese government and the Hong Kong authorities. Except for laws relating to foreign affairs and defence, the power to make laws is vested in the government of the HKSAR. Article 22 prevents Chinese institutions from intervening in Hong Kong and the general tenor of the Basic Law is that the Hong Kong government has the right to decide on its own policies. The Chinese government's announcement undermined that premise. Hong Kong's "high degree of autonomy" has been severely tested in recent years. Since 2014, it has been clear that the Chinese government intends to assert more direct control over Hong Kong and to speed up economic and social integration with the Mainland.[197]

Conclusion

When a constitution lacks legitimacy, issues that might otherwise be easily resolved take on a wider and deeper political significance. The legitimacy of the constitution itself becomes part of the controversy. Under these circumstances, the accountability of the government is almost certain to become an issue. If the constitution cannot hold the government to account, then the rift between those in authority and those whom they seek to govern is only likely to grow. In this chapter, the three areas that have been examined in detail—the failure to provide universal suffrage, the erosion of civil liberties, and the challenges to judicial independence and the rule of law—have all weakened the accountability of the government to the people. The absence of universal suffrage means that the Chief Executive is only elected by a "small circle" and that representation in the Legislative Council has been disproportionately biased to business and professional groups through the functional constituency system and, latterly, towards those deemed to be "patriotic". The erosion of civil liberties means an increase in arbitrary power and the loss of freedoms that have been a valued part of the Hong Kong way of life. The threats to judicial independence, the rule of law, and judicial review take away the means of ensuring justice and of holding the government to account. As a result of these developments, a government that was never very accountable has become very much less so.

---

197. Scott, I. (2017) op. cit.

3
Accountability and Organisational Change

Although the Basic Law has been a focus for prolonged disputes on critical questions concerning the accountability of the government, the constitutional debate is only one dimension of the issue. The political and administrative actions of a government and how they affect its accountability are not entirely determined by constitutional interpretation. A constitution may give a government considerable discretion to abolish departments and agencies, to create new ones, to establish new relationships between the political executive and its bureaucracy, and to allow departments varying degrees of autonomy in how they carry out their duties. Any of these measures is likely to raise issues about whether the changes provide the means to hold the government, its departments, or its office holders to account. To judge whether a government or any of its institutional components is politically accountable, the test is not whether the system is representative or democratic but whether external bodies, be they voters, legislatures, or a superior level of government, have the power to impose sanctions on office holders in the event of unsatisfactory performance.[1]

In this chapter, we examine four organisational changes that have significantly affected how the government and its office holders are held to account and how power is exercised:

- the abolition of the Urban and Regional Councils,
- the introduction of the Principal Officials Accountability System (POAS),
- the introduction of the political appointments system, and
- changing concepts of accountability in the Police Force.

The Abolition of the Urban and Regional Councils

The Urban and Regional Councils (the municipal councils) were statutory bodies set up to introduce a measure of local government in Hong Kong. From 1973 onwards, the Urban Council was financially autonomous and could decide on

---

1. Burns, J. P. (2004). *Government capacity and the Hong Kong civil service* (pp. 157–158). Hong Kong: Oxford University Press.

how its resources would be allocated and managed.² The councils provided important services through the departments attached to them—the Urban Services Department and the Regional Services Department—in the areas of food safety and environmental hygiene, arts and cultural services, and sports and recreational services.³ Until 1982, when District Board elections were held for the first time, Urban Council elections were the only means by which Hong Kong citizens could express their views through the ballot. Although elections were contested, they did not attract much interest and turnout was low.

The Basic Law makes no specific mention of the municipal councils. Article 97 does state, however, that district organisations "which are not organs of political power" may be established for consultative purposes or to provide services. In October 1997, Tung Chee Hwa called for a "fresh look at the regional organisations, the Municipal Councils and the District Boards, so as to decide . . . whether the present structure of local representative government will continue to ensure the efficient and responsive delivery of services".⁴ In the following June, the Constitutional Affairs Bureau released a consultation document in which it outlined government concerns over funding arrangements, the fragmentation of responsibilities for food and hygiene, arts and culture, and sports and recreation, the issue of whether there was a need for both district and municipal organisations, and the question of whether the role of the District Boards should be expanded.⁵ The government made quite clear that its preferred option was to dissolve the municipal councils and to transfer their responsibilities to other policy bureaus and the District Boards.⁶

The debate over the future of the municipal councils took place in the context of a decision in December 1997 to slaughter approximately 1.2 million chickens after an outbreak of avian flu. The Urban Services Department and the Regional Services Departments were responsible for the slaughter of the chickens, but it was not carried out properly, leading to many complaints. Some felt that the government's preference for abolishing the municipal councils was "using the chickens to kill the Councils".⁷ The government denied this but claimed strong public support for an enhanced role in food and hygiene matters, probably because of the avian flu crisis.⁸ Its decision to review the municipal councils and the District Boards predated the avian flu crisis, however, and probably reflected longer-standing government concerns about inefficiencies and financial practices in the Urban Services and Regional Services Departments. The Chinese government's decision not to

---

2. Miners, N. (1998). *The government and politics of Hong Kong* (5th ed., pp. 160–163). Hong Kong: Oxford University Press.
3. Constitutional Affairs Bureau (1998). *Review of district organizations: Consultation document* (pp. 1–12). Hong Kong: Printing Department.
4. Tung, C. H. (1997). *Building Hong Kong for a new era* (pp. 49–50). Hong Kong: Printing Department.
5. Constitutional Affairs Bureau (1998) op. cit., pp. vi–vii.
6. Ibid., pp. 33–37.
7. Hansard, 29 July 1998, 1199.
8. Constitutional Affairs Bureau (October 1998). *Review of district organizations: Consultation report* (pp. v, 43). Hong Kong: Printing Department.

recognise the electoral arrangements in place at the retrocession meant that all members of the municipal councils and District Boards were appointed after 1997 and that a review of their composition and functions would probably have been necessary.

An immediate political concern for the government was to deal with claims that the dissolution of the municipal councils would have adverse effects on political development and representation. According to the government's report on the consultation exercise, three arguments were advanced in favour of retaining the councils: that they had decision-making powers and served as a useful training ground for future politicians; that they enabled public participation in the making of local policies through their elected representatives; and that they could effectively supervise the work of the executive departments.[9] The government rejected these views, citing the authority of unnamed "leading social scientists".[10] It maintained that there was sufficient representation and enough public offices to train future politicians and that future democratic development should focus on elections to the Legislative Council.[11] The government was accused of manipulating the results of the consultation exercise, of prejudging the issue, and of unnecessarily shortening the consultation period.[12] In the end, however, its original view prevailed and the municipal councils were abolished. In 2000, the functions undertaken by the Urban Services and Regional Services Departments were transferred to a new Food and Environmental Hygiene Department and a Leisure and Cultural Services Department directly under the control of the Hong Kong government. The 18 District Boards were retained but were renamed District Councils. The government decided that it would reserve the right to appoint up to 102 members to the councils as against 390 who would be elected and 27 *ex officio* members who would be retained. In the previous election in 1994, except for the *ex officio* members, all members of the District Boards had been elected.

The abolition of the municipal councils could be seen as consistent with the continuing dominance of the senior civil service and the strengthening of the existing system. There had been concern even before the handover about possible corruption, overstaffing and poor supervision in the Urban Services and Regional Services Departments. However, the longer-term effect of the abolition of the municipal councils and the changed arrangements for the composition of the District Councils was to eliminate centres of potential opposition to the political executive. Urban and Regional Councillors had a history of criticising the government. In the District Councils, which potentially provided a similar forum, the Chief Executive used his right to appoint over 25% of the members of the councils to nullify the successes of the democratic parties in the November 2003 elections

---

9. Ibid., p. 23.
10. Ibid.
11. Ibid.
12. Hansard, 29 July 1998, 1204.

and to ensure that most of the councils were pro-government in their orientation.[13] Thus, although the changes were sold to the public as means of promoting efficiency, in retrospect, these developments were a step along the road towards greater centralisation of authority in an "executive-led" government with reduced public accountability.

The Principal Officials Accountability System

In 2000, Tung foreshadowed an even more radical change to the political system aimed, supposedly, at establishing "a comprehensive system of public accountability".[14] Public concern over the accountability of the civil service did increase after 1997. Some serious cases where the government or a statutory body failed to implement or explain its decisions properly—for example, the decision not to prosecute a newspaper owner whose paper had inflated its circulation figures, a multimillion dollar scandal about the faulty construction of public housing blocks, the catastrophic opening of the new airport, and the methods used in dealing with the avian flu crisis—all called into question the adequacy of the accountability mechanisms.[15] But the system that was eventually unveiled was motivated more by the Chief Executive's intention to exert more direct political control over the civil service than to enhance accountability.

The central idea was a new system of appointing 14 of the principal officials: the three secretaries (the Chief Secretary, the Financial Secretary, and the Secretary for Justice) and the 11 directors of bureaus, who would serve on contract at the pleasure of the Chief Executive. The conditions of service of the five principal officials mentioned in Article 48(5) of the Basic Law who were all civil servants— the Commissioner of Police, the Director of Audit, the Commissioner against Corruption, the Director of Immigration, and the Commissioner of Customs and Excise—were to remain unchanged.[16] The Chief Executive could nominate suitable candidates, either from within or outside the civil service, for the 14 key principal officials' positions to the Central People's Government and would have the authority to recommend their removal. The 14 principal officials would all be members of the Executive Council where they would be joined by five unofficial members, who included the leaders of the Liberal Party and the DAB. The principal officials would have the responsibility for formulating and explaining policies, canvassing support

---

13. Cheung, J. (2003, 10 December). Democrats in battle to head councils. *SCMP*.
14. Tung, C. H. (2000). *Serving the community, sharing common goals* (p. 38). Hong Kong: Printing Department.
15. Burns (2004) op. cit., pp. 161–167; Loh, C., & Cullen, R. (2002). *Accountability without democracy? The Principal Officials Accountability System in Hong Kong*. Hong Kong: Civic Exchange.
16. Constitutional Affairs Bureau (2002). *Legislative Council Paper: Accountability system for principal officials* (p. 6). Hong Kong: The Bureau. https://www.legco.gov.hk/yr01-02/english/panels/ca/papers/ca0418cb2-paper-e.pdf. The Director of the Chief Executive's Office became a principal official in 2002. Constitutional and Mainland Affairs Bureau (2007). *Report on the further development of the political appointment system* (p. 43). https://www.cmab.gov.hk/doc/issues/report_en.pdf

from the Legislative Council and the public for their policies and would be answerable to the Chief Executive for the success or failure of those policies and would attend meetings of the Legislative Council to answer questions, move bills, and take part in motion debates.[17] The critical difference was that the principal officials, who, with two exceptions, had all previously been permanent and pensionable senior civil servants, were now to be replaced by political appointees who were on contract and, in theory, could be more easily dismissed by the Chief Executive.

The proposed system was further developed in a government paper presented to the Legislative Council in April 2002.[18] The rationale given for the new system was that it would enhance the accountability of the principal officials for policy failures and would enable the Chief Executive to dismiss those who were not performing adequately.[19] As a "comprehensive system of public accountability", however, the proposed system was seriously deficient. The principal officials were only accountable to the Chief Executive, not to the Legislative Council or, in any meaningful sense, to the public. When asked whether a principal official would be dismissed if the Legislative Council were to pass a motion of no confidence in that official, Tung said that "it would be one of my considerations but not the only consideration influencing my final decision".[20] No principal official has ever been dismissed as a result of a direct vote of no confidence by the Legislative Council. To have developed a more accountable system would have required amendments to the Basic Law whereas the changes to the appointment system for principal officials could be accommodated within the existing provisions of the Basic Law (Article 48(5)). But to amend the Basic Law to introduce more accountability would have required the support of the Chinese government and does not, in any case, appear to have been Tung's primary objective.

The new system was also expected:

> to ensure that the Government can better respond to the needs of the community; enhance coordination in policy formulation; strengthen the cooperation between the Executive and the Legislature; ensure effective implementation of policies and provide quality services to the public.[21]

It was not entirely clear how those goals would be achieved. The newly appointed principal officials were required to produce plans for the reorganisation of their bureaus and departments which were intended to improve policy coordination and implementation. Since each bureau could come up with its own plan, there were no immediate benefits in policy coordination and no immediate indications of how these measures would resolve the problems that the government faced in

---

17. Tung, C. H. (2001). *Building on our strengths, investing in our future* (pp. 35–36). Hong Kong: Printing Department.
18. Constitutional Affairs Bureau (2002) op. cit.
19. Ibid., p. 5.
20. Hansard, 17 April 2002, 5499.
21. Constitutional Affairs Bureau (2002) op. cit., p. 6.

implementing policy. The relationship between the executive and the legislature might have been improved if the ways in which the principal officials were accountable to the legislature had been clarified, but the document only suggested that the most senior civil servants in the bureaus, now to be called permanent secretaries, would continue to have a public role and would attend meetings of Legislative Council panels and deal with the media.[22] The civil service was to remain politically neutral, but it also had "a bounden duty . . . to be loyal to the Chief Executive and the principal officials of the day".[23] There were also unresolved questions about the relationship between the principal officials and the Executive Council. The principal officials were all members of the Executive Council, but the council still had members who were not principal officials. It was expected that the principal officials would meet separately from the Executive Council, raising questions about duplication and where the final authority for decisions lay.[24]

The 14 new principal officials, of whom five came from outside the civil service, took office on 1 July 2002.[25] The principal officials who had been civil servants retained their former roles although there were some portfolio changes. Unlike the other principal officials, the Secretary for the Civil Service was required to be drawn from the ranks of senior civil servants and was permitted to return to the civil service.[26]

Almost immediately after the new system came into effect, the accountability of principal officials became an issue. On 25 July 2002, the Hong Kong Stock Exchange (HKEx) released a report establishing the criteria for the delisting of low-priced stocks. On the following day's trading, the market lost HK$10.91 billion in market capitalisation.[27] The controversial proposals in the consultation paper were rapidly withdrawn. Several parties, including the Chief of the HKEx and Chairman of the Securities and Futures Commission (SFC), were involved in drafting and releasing the proposal and had some responsibility for the ensuing debacle.[28] To the extent that the principal officials were involved, the Financial Secretary was absolved because he did not receive a copy of the proposal before it was released.[29] Public attention focused instead on Frederick Ma Si-hang, the Secretary for Financial Services and the Treasury, who had received a copy of the proposal but who had not read it.[30]

---

22. Ibid., p. 11.
23. Secretary for the Civil Service (2002, 18 April). *SCS writes to colleagues on accountability system* [Press release]. https://www.info.gov.hk/gia/general/200204/17/0417284.htm
24. Lau, E. (2003, 10 September). So, just what is the point of Exco? *SCMP*.
25. Hong Kong Government (2002, 24 June). *New team of principal officials appointed* [Press release]. https://www.info.gov.hk/gia/general/200706/23/P200706230083.htm
26. Secretary for the Civil Service (2002, 18 April) op. cit.
27. Kotewall, R. G., & Kwong, G. C. K. (2002). *Report of the panel of inquiry on the penny stocks incident* (p. 100). https://www.info.gov.hk/info/pennystock-e.htm
28. Ibid., pp. 158–161.
29. Ibid., p. 153.
30. Ibid., pp. 158–159.

The summary table of the proposal arrived in Ma's office on 17 July, but he was away from Hong Kong and only became aware of its contents on 26 July.[31] On 31 July, the Financial Secretary announced that there would be an independent inquiry into the incident and the Legislative Council convened a special meeting of its Financial Affairs Panel. According to the inquiry report:

> The Secretary was bombarded with a series of hostile and severe criticisms to which he was unable to acquit himself with either clarity or distinction. It would have required the skills and experience of a much more seasoned bureaucrat to have come out of that barrage relatively unscathed.[32]

Legislative Councillors observed that the Secretary might be regarded as having underperformed his official duties by failing to keep himself informed, that ignorance was just as inexcusable as negligence and that Hong Kong's reputation as a financial centre might have been jeopardised as a consequence of the proposal.[33] In his defence, Ma accepted that "as a principal government official, he was prepared to take a certain degree of responsibility for the whole incident".[34] But he also felt that there were mitigating circumstances. When the investigative panel did not attribute blame directly to any individual, Ma initially took this as vindication of his position. Subsequently, he issued a public apology, a development that the government claimed "demonstrated the force of the accountability system in action".[35]

The investigative panel noted, to the contrary, that major criticism had already been directed at the new system:

> The Penny Stocks Incident quickly developed into a political hot potato. There were criticisms of the role of Government, the SFC and the HKEx [and] the lack of clarity over the division of responsibilities between the FS [Financial Secretary] and the Secretary as well as what the accountability system entailed.[36]

At stake, too, were the circumstances under which a principal official might feel obliged, or be required, to resign. Many legislators felt that Ma's initial refusal to offer an apology and Tung's contention that the incident had nothing to do with accountability made a mockery of claims that the new system was an improvement on past practice.[37] Accountability appeared to mean something much less than resignation or even an apology for poor performance: a requirement, perhaps, to explain lapses in judgment or inadequate performance but not necessarily to relinquish office.

---

31. Legislative Council Panel on Financial Affairs (2002). *Minutes of a special meeting held on 31st July 2002.* Hong Kong: mimeo.
32. Kotewall & Kwong (2002) op. cit., p. 110.
33. Legislative Council Panel on Financial Affairs (2002) op. cit., pp. 8, 14, 17.
34. Ibid., p. 8.
35. Secretary for Constitutional Affairs (2003). *Twelve-month report on implementation of the accountability system for principal officials* (p. 18). https://www.cmab.gov.hk/upload/20040219153857/12mthreport-e.pdf
36. Kotewall & Kwong (2002) op cit., p. 169.
37. Li, A., & Leung, A. (2002, 11 September). "Whitewash" attacked by all sides. *SCMP*.

A second test of the system was occasioned by quite different circumstances: the personal conduct of the Financial Secretary. In January 2003, the Financial Secretary, Antony Leung Kam-chung, purchased a new car, four days after a budget strategy group, of which he was a member, had considered raising first registration tax on cars. On 11 February, the strategy group confirmed that it would raise taxes. On 5 March, at an Executive Council meeting, at which another principal official revealed that he had recently bought a car, Leung failed to disclose his own purchase.[38] On 10 March, following media reports, he apparently offered his resignation to the Chief Executive. Tung then wrote to Leung on 15 March, noting that, although his actions were a breach of the Code for Principal Officials, he had concluded that "your mistake warrants a formal criticism from me but not your resignation".[39] A NPCSC member reportedly said that the matter was "no big deal".[40]

Legislative Councillors thought otherwise. On 17 March, Leung was called before the Legislative Council's Constitutional Affairs Panel and grilled in much the same manner as Ma had been.[41] Leung claimed that the purchase of the car had been a practical necessity and that he had no intention to avoid tax but that he had been guilty of inappropriate behaviour and of an oversight.[42] Democratic legislators focused particularly on the implications of the conflict of interest for integrity and trust in government. The official line was that it had been an honest mistake. There were also comments about inconsistencies in the account of his offer of resignation, a central issue in the subsequent Legislative Council debate calling for the establishment of a select committee to investigate the matter.[43] The motion to establish a select committee was defeated, but the issue further damaged the credibility of the accountability system and the Financial Secretary's own position. The ICAC also conducted a separate investigation into the case, referring the results to the Department of Justice, which eventually decided that there should be no prosecution because it could not be proved that Leung deliberately sought to evade tax.[44] Leung and the Secretary for Security, Regina Ip Suk-yee, eventually did resign in July 2003 following the demonstrations against the government's proposed legislation under Article 23.

After the grilling that Ma and Leung had taken in the Legislative Council's committee, the government changed its strategy. Relying on the pro-establishment

---

38. Cheung, A., & Cheung, J. (2003, 10 March). The Financial Secretary avoids his own tax rise on car purchase. *SCMP*. https://www.scmp.com/article/408768/financial-secretary-avoids-his-own-tax-rise-luxury-car-purchase
39. Tung, C. H. (2003, 15 March). Letter to Antony Leung Kam-chung. https://www.info.gov.hk/gia/general/200303/15/letter_e.pdf
40. Cheung, J., & Cheung, G. (2003, 11 March). Tung admonishes his finance chief. *SCMP*.
41. Legislative Council Panel on Constitutional Affairs (2003). *Minutes of a meeting held on 17th March*. Translated from Chinese. Hong Kong: mimeo.
42. Ibid., p. 1.
43. Ibid., pp. 34–35; Hansard, 9 April 2003, 5529–5593.
44. Hong Kong Government (2003, 15 December). *DPP decides not to prosecute Antony Leung* [Press release]. https://www.info.gov.hk/gia/general/200312/15/1215115.htm

majority in the council to prevent detailed scrutiny of a principal official's performance, it chose instead to circumvent the legislature by setting up committees of inquiry into contentious issues with terms of reference that were not specifically aimed at holding the official to account. If the Chief Executive found evidence in the committee's report warranting dismissal, that recommendation could then be forwarded to the Chinese government's Hong Kong and Macau Affairs office for action. Thus, in 2003, after the SARS epidemic abated, the government launched two inquiries into whether it might have been contained more effectively and whether the Hospital Authority might have been better prepared for the difficulties of treating patients and the protection of its staff, some of whom had succumbed to the disease.

The first inquiry was a panel of experts, set up by the Chief Executive in May 2003. Tung originally appointed Dr Yeoh Eng-kiong, the Secretary of Health, Welfare and Food, to head the inquiry over objections that there might be a conflict of interest. The appointment was rescinded after the July 2003 demonstrations. The Expert Panel, which reported in October 2003, found that Hong Kong had handled the crisis well. No individual was "deemed to be culpable of negligence, lack of diligence or maladministration"[45] and the committee simply made some suggestions for improvements in the event of any future outbreak.[46] The second inquiry was set up by the Hospital Authority to investigate any shortcomings in its handling of the situation. The committee found that "the Government could have acted sooner and with greater clarity to warn the community of the potential risks", and they were critical of the lack of coordination between the Hospital Authority and the Department of Health and the Secretary of Health, Welfare and Food. They did not attach specific blame to individuals.[47]

What the government feared most was the prospect of a select committee set up by the Legislative Council that would investigate the conduct of principal officials and which would, if past practice were any guide, attempt to attribute responsibility for shortcomings. Establishing a select committee had been the democrats' preferred strategy in the Leung case, but that had been defeated by the Liberals and the DAB. In May 2003, however, the DAB voted for a Democratic Party motion on a non-binding resolution to set up a select committee if the government did not itself establish an independent commission of inquiry.[48] While the other inquiries were in the process of collecting evidence, the Legislative Council did nothing to set up a select committee. But once the government-appointed Expert Panel and the

---

45. SARS Expert Committee (2003). *SARS in Hong Kong: From experience to action: Report of the SARS Expert Committee* (p. 159). https://www.sars-expertcom.gov.hk/english/reports/reports/reports_fullrpt.html
46. Ibid.
47. Hospital Authority Review Panel (2003). *Report of the Hospital Authority review panel on the SARS outbreak* (pp. 20, 147, 158). Hong Kong: The Authority. https://repository.vtc.edu.hk/thei-fac-sci-tech-sp/325/
48. Legislative Council House Committee (2003). *Minutes of a meeting held on 10th October 2003* (p. 10). https://www.legco.gov.hk/yr03-04/english/hc/minutes/hc031010.pdf; Yeung, C. (2003, 29 June). Hong Kong's 'accountability' system backfires. *SCMP*.

Hospital Authority Review Panel had reported, there was cross-party concern in the Legislative Council that no officials had been censured for their role in handling the epidemic. In October, despite a reported government offer to set up an independent commission of inquiry, legislators voted instead to set up a select committee.[49] Legislators saw the SARS expert committee's report as a whitewash that had failed to address a central issue and they noted public dissatisfaction over its finding that no one was to blame for the handling of the epidemic.[50]

The Legislative Council's House Committee carefully considered the terms of reference of the select committee to avoid the impression of a witch-hunt. It was eventually decided that the select committee should examine the performance and accountability of the government and the Hospital Authority and their officers at policy-making and management levels concerning their handling of the SARS outbreak. When the committee reported in July 2004, it exonerated the Chief Executive, who had refused to testify because it was "constitutionally inappropriate" in an executive-led government, but was scathing in its criticism of the Secretary for Health, Welfare and Food who, the committee said, did not show "sufficient alertness" in the initial stages of the outbreak, was "confusing and misleading" in his public announcements, did not show the "communication skills expected by the public of a policy secretary" and failed to require the Director of Health to add SARS to the list of notifiable diseases as quickly as he should have done.[51] The secretary apologised to the deceased, family members, and health care workers but initially declined to resign.[52] However, three days after the Select Committee report had been released, he changed his mind and submitted his resignation.[53] This case is the only instance in which the legislature was able to bring about, almost directly, the resignation of a principal official.

In the wake of the SARS outbreak, the government made HK$1 billion available for community projects to restore morale.[54] The American Chamber of Commerce proposed a festival (Harbour Fest) that would feature top-rated world artists with the objectives of making people "feel good" and setting the scene for the development of Hong Kong as a future events centre. A government working party endorsed the project which was to be managed, on the government side, by its investment agency, InvestHK. Critically, no policy secretary was given responsibility for the project, which was plagued with many different problems. It eventually suffered a $100 million loss that had to be underwritten by the government.

---

49. Hallyar, M. R. (2007). Governance and community engagement in managing SARS in Hong Kong. *Asian Journal of Political Science, 15*(1), 39–47.
50. Legislative Council House Committee (2003) op. cit., p. 10.
51. Legislative Council (2004). *Report of the Select Committee into the handling of the Severe Acute Respiratory Syndrome outbreak by the Government and the Hospital Authority* (pp. 251–252). https://www.legco.gov.hk/yr03-04/english/sc/sc_sars/reports/sars_rpt.htm
52. Benitez, M. A. et al. (2004, 6 July). Officials accept responsibility over SARS but won't step down. *SCMP*.
53. Benitez, M. A., & Lee, K. (2004, 8 July). "Dedicated" Yeoh quits over SARS. *SCMP*.
54. Independent Panel of Inquiry (2004). *Report of the independent panel of inquiry on the Harbour Fest* (p. 1). www.gov.hk/en/residents/government/policy/government_reports/reports/docs/harbourfest.pdf

The Director of InvestHK, Mike Rowse, subsequently wrote that "as fast as the bad press gathered speed, so the politicians jumped on the bandwagon and the Ministers ran away".[55] The reconstruction of how the debacle occurred suggests that there was never any clear line of authority determining how the project would be implemented. An independent review panel thought that a major mistake was that, despite the government's financial liability, it devolved all responsibility for the management of the event to the American Chamber of Commerce.[56] The Director of Audit also wrote a critical report on its implementation, noting the need *inter alia* for greater transparency and public accountability.[57] But the government's embarrassment did not end there. It fined Rowse a month's salary for failing to assess the Harbour Fest budget properly. He responded by taking the government to court, successfully won his case, and then wrote a book in which he argued that the Financial Secretary was ultimately responsible for the decision and criticised the POAS for politicising the civil service.[58]

After Tung resigned in 2005, his successor, Donald Tsang Yam-kuen, had to complete the two-year balance of Tung's term. His freedom of action was restricted. If he wanted the Chinese government to support his re-election in 2007, he could not afford the confrontations with civil society that had characterised the Tung administration. Under Tung, principal officials had been encouraged to be entrepreneurial and to cut through red tape. They did not work as a team but rather as high-profile individuals with different agendas and often conflictual relationships, both inside and outside their bureaus and departments. Under Tsang, they were more disciplined and unified. At the cost of inaction on some critical issues, there were no new major policy initiatives.[59] Tsang believed that achieving a consensus on constitutional development was a necessary precondition to making successful policy in contentious areas.[60] Principal officials were limited to introducing non-controversial measures or refining existing policies.

Greater collective responsibility was achieved by two means: reworking the policy hierarchy within government and relying more on senior civil servants to fill the positions of principal officials and top administrative aides. One reason why principal officials under Tung had been relatively independent spirits was that the system introduced in 2002 downgraded the roles of the Chief Secretary of Administration and the Financial Secretary. Principal officials reported directly to Tung, without the previously mediating and authoritative roles played by those officials. Directors of bureaus increasingly took their own initiatives, canvassing their

---

55. Rowse, M. (2009). *No minister and no, minister: The true story of HarbourFest* (p. 35). Hong Kong: Treloar Enterprises.
56. Independent Panel of Inquiry (2004) op. cit., pp. 14–16.
57. Director of Audit (2004). *Report No. 42: Hong Kong Harbour Fest* (p. 61). https://www.aud.gov.hk/pdf_e/e42ch04.pdf
58. Rowse (2009) op. cit., 80–83.
59. Scott, I. (2007). Legitimacy, governance and public policy in post-handover Hong Kong. *Asia Pacific Journal of Public Administration, 29*(1), 29–49.
60. Chief Executive (2007) op. cit.

proposals directly with the Chief Executive. This caused considerable confusion, particularly over the role of the Financial Secretary. Tung partially addressed the issue in June 2003[61] but did not resolve the wider problem of poor policy coordination. In the first substantive statement of his first policy address, Tsang announced that henceforth all heads of bureaus would be required to have their proposals cleared by the Financial Secretary and the Chief Secretary of Administration in the Policy Committee.[62] This was a reversion to the pre-2002 system and had the effect of curbing the enthusiasm of principal officials for announcing proposals that may have been good ideas but which had not been properly costed or approved. When the Chief Secretary for Administration, Rafael Hui Si-yan, completed his term of office in June 2007, Tsang thanked him for his contribution in chairing the Policy Committee and the Star Chamber, which vetted public expenditure, and said that those committees were "now known for their depth, intellectual rigour and remarkable efficiency".[63]

In his first two-year term, Tsang inherited the principal officials who had served under Tung. However, when he was re-elected in 2007, he appointed former civil servants to senior positions, including the Financial Secretary and nine of the 12 principal officials who were policy secretaries. All but one of those officials had been administrative grade officers.[64] Tsang himself had been an administrative officer and Chief Secretary for Administration and he seemed to regard experience within government as more important than entrepreneurial ability in appointments to top positions. His team more resembled the pre-2002 situation when all principal officials, bar two, had been civil servants. The POAS had been designed partly to reduce the power of the senior civil service, but Tsang's new line-up suggested that its pre-eminent position had been reaffirmed.

Under Tsang, the only major controversy over the accountability of principal officials concerned events which had taken place mainly under the Tung administration. In January 2007, the Council of the Hong Kong Institute of Education (HKIEd) (now The Education University of Hong Kong) decided not to renew the term of its President, Professor Paul Morris. Shortly afterwards, HKIEd's Vice-President, Professor Bernard Luk, wrote in an intranet message, widely reported in the local media, that the reason for the decision not to reappoint Professor Morris was that he had refused to support a proposed merger between HKIEd and the Chinese University of Hong Kong. It was also alleged that Professor Morris had been pressured to dismiss staff critical of government policy.

---

61. Chief Executive (2003, 27 June). Responsibilities of the Financial Secretary and the Secretary for Financial Services and the Treasury. https://www.fso.gov.hk/pdf/fs-sfst_e.pdf
62. Tsang, D. Y. K. (2005). *Strong governance for the people* (paras 8–9). https://www.policyaddress.gov.hk/05-06/eng/index.htm
63. Hong Kong Government (2007, 28 June). CE thanks outgoing principal officials. https://www.news.gov.hk/isd/ebulletin/en/category/ontherecord/070628/html/070628en11001.htm
64. Hong Kong Government (2007, 23 June). *New team of principal officials appointed* [Press release]. https://www.info.gov.hk/gia/general/200706/23/P200706230083.htm

Academic autonomy is enshrined in the Basic Law and many felt that, if proven, the actions of the secretary constituted a violation of the right of institutions to run their own affairs.[65] The government then set up a commission of inquiry to investigate three allegations relating to academic autonomy: that the Secretary of Education and Manpower had threatened to cut student numbers at the HKIEd unless the president agreed to a merger with the Chinese University of Hong Kong; that senior government officials had called on the president of HKIEd to dismiss academics who wrote articles critical of government policy; and that the Secretary for Education and Manpower had requested the vice-president of HKIEd to issue a statement condemning a teachers' protest and the Hong Kong Professional Teachers Union which had assisted them.[66] The commission was asked to ascertain whether there had been any improper interference with academic freedom or institutional autonomy.

The commission held hearings for 39 days with evidence presented formally by teams of lawyers and with witnesses cross-examined by opposing counsel. On the issue of threats to reduce the student numbers at the institute, the commission accepted that the Secretary for Education and Manpower, Arthur Li, had probably said that he would "rape" the HKIEd but found that "there was no concerted effort" to force the HKIEd to reduce numbers if it did not agree to the merger.[67] On calling for the dismissal of academics that criticised the government, the commission found that the requests of the Permanent Secretary for Education, Fanny Law Chiu-fun, to Professor Morris to curb the criticisms of government by two academics constituted an improper interference with their academic freedom.[68] It also noted that Law had requested a professor at the HKIEd to sack a staff member who was critical of government policies. On the alleged request from the secretary to the vice-president to issue a statement condemning the student protest and the Hong Kong Professional Teachers' Union, the commission found that it was not established.[69] The commission evidently felt that it had to steer the difficult line between government interference with academic autonomy and the pursuit of public policy.

Tsang's response was very similar to the way Tung had dealt with previous controversies. He observed that the commission's findings cleared the actions of the officials although this was only partially true.[70] The commission did clear the Permanent Secretary on one count of improper interference with academic freedom but found her guilty on another. Law resigned from her new post as ICAC

---

65. Yeung, C. K., & Lee, J. P. (2007). *Report of the commission of inquiry on allegations relating to the Hong Kong Institute of Education* (pp. 98–106). https://www.gov.hk/en/residents/government/policy/government_reports/reports/docs/HKIEd.pdf
66. Ibid., p. 113.
67. Ibid., p. 1.
68. Ibid.
69. Ibid.
70. Chief Executive (2007, 20 July). *CE speaks on the report submitted by the Commission of Inquiry on allegations relating to The Hong Kong Institute of Education* [Press release]. https://www.info.gov.hk/gia/general/200706/20/P200706200264.htm

Commissioner after the commission had reported although she maintained that she had done nothing wrong. Tsang said he had asked her to stay, promising her full support.[71] Li was not reappointed as a principal official but may have intended to step down before the controversy became a public issue. Even though it had appointed the commission, the government was not satisfied with the finding that officials who contacted academics to express critical opinions of their views were improperly interfering with academic freedom. The Secretary for Education and Manpower subsequently asked for a judicial review of the finding.[72]

The accountability of the principal officials serving as policy secretaries declined even further during the Leung and Lam administrations.[73] One reason was the increased polarisation of Hong Kong politics and the consequent disclination of the political executive and the Chinese government to allow any avenues through which the pan-democrats might claim vindication of their repeated charges of poor government performance. Polarisation hardened the line between the majority pro-establishment/pro-Beijing legislators and the minority pan-democrats in the Legislative Council, preventing a repeat of the joint action by the democrats and the DAB in the SARS case which had led to the resignation of the Secretary for Health, Welfare and Food. The Legislative Council had little room to develop into a body that could hold principal officials accountable. The democrats might vent their frustration on the policy secretaries at question time and when the Chief Executive delivered the annual address, but the legislative panels and committees did not allow the detailed scrutiny of performance which might have uncovered grounds for dismissal.

A second related reason for the decline in accountability was that power became increasingly centralised in the Chief Executive.[74] It is the responsibility of the Chief Executive alone to decide whether principal officials have violated norms contained in the Code for Principal Officials, whether they are culpable of negligence or dereliction of duty, or whether their competence in decision-making is in question. The Chief Executive and the Chinese government decide whether they should continue to hold office. As a corollary, until 2020, the Chief Executive may have been less inclined to dismiss a principal official for fear that, in a volatile political climate, this could provide fuel for those opposed to the administration.

Under Leung and Lam, not only was the Legislative Council's ability to oversee the performance of principal officials reduced, but the device of setting up commissions of inquiry to investigate controversial issues was no longer used as frequently. When principal officials left office, it was because they were candidates in Chief

---

71. Ibid.
72. Education Bureau (2007, 17 September). *Education Bureau launches judicial review* [Press release]. https://www.info.gov.hk/gia/general/200709/17/P200709170128.htm
73. Vines, S. (2018, 21 January). Remember "public accountability"? Carrie Lam doesn't. *HKFP*. https://hongkongfp.com/2018/01/21/remember-public-accountability-carrie-lam-doesnt/
74. Lee, E., & Yeung, R. L. K. (2017). The "Principal Officials Accountability System": Its underdevelopment as a system of ministerial government. *Asia Pacific Journal of Public Administration*, 39(2), 120–134.

Executive elections or because they had been dismissed. An exception was Mak Chai-kwong, who resigned in 2012 after 12 days in the post when he was charged with corrupt offences of which he was later acquitted.[75] C. Y. Leung dismissed two of his principal officials in 2015 but did not give the reasons why they had been dismissed.[76] The media focused its attention on the unpopular Secretary of Education, Eddie Ng, asking why he had not been dismissed. Ng's unpopularity stemmed from his attempts to push the unsuccessful national education policy and from other perceived mistakes in office.[77] But he, like most other principal officials under Leung, saw out his term in office, ending with a net approval rating of minus 56%, the least popular of Leung's ministers.[78] Introducing more accountability through the Legislative Council or commissions of inquiry had come to be seen as a sign of weakness.

Under Carrie Lam's beleaguered administration, ministerial changes were used as an attempt to strengthen the government in the face of the challenges from civil society organisations and possibly at the behest of the Chinese government. In April 2020, Lam reshuffled her policy secretaries, bringing in some Beijing loyalists and dismissing four ministers.[79] She was quick to say that the reshuffle had nothing to do with the political unrest and that the changes were aimed at revitalising the economy after the coronavirus outbreak. The Secretary of Mainland and Constitutional Affairs was moved to become Secretary of the Civil Service because of an alleged confusing statement on the status of the Liaison Office under Article 22 of the Basic Law, but it was not clear why other policy secretaries had been dismissed or to what extent the Chinese government had been involved in the decision.

If we look at the POAS from the perspective of the last 20 years, how might it be judged? In 2006, the government has put forward three arguments to justify the system. First, it said that the Chief Executive and the principal officials, although not formally accountable to the public, acted "in a manner which meets the standards of Hong Kong as an open and transparent community".[80] Openness and transparency are important features of good governance, but they are only tangentially related to political accountability and can hardly be said to have characterised the Leung and Lam administrations. Principal officials have shown that they are prepared to be answerable to the Legislative Council for their actions which might be taken as an

---

75. *SCMP* (2012, 13 July). Minister arrested by ICAC resigns. *SCMP*.
76. Cheung, G., & Ng, J. (2015, 23 July). Removal of Tsang Tak-sing from the Hong Kong government is a sign that leftists are out in the cold. *SCMP*.
77. Lee & Yeung (2017) op. cit.; Siu, P. (2017, 21 February). Embattled Hong Kong education minister Eddie Ng says he will retire at end of term. *SCMP*.
78. HKUPOP (2017). HKU POP releases popularity figures of CE, CE-elect and principal officials. https://www.hkupop.hku.hk/english/release/release1472.html
79. Hong Kong Government (2020, 22 April). Government announces appointment and removal of principal officials [Press release]. https://www.info.gov.hk/gia/general/202004/22/P2020042200459.htm
80. Constitutional Affairs Bureau (2006). *Consultation document on further developments of the political appointment system* (p. 4). https://www.legco.gov.hk/yr05-06/english/panels/ca/papers/ca0731cb2-consultation-e.pdf

indication of openness and transparency. But, if answerability is simply to describe what has happened followed by a defence or an apology, it will not mollify those who believe that accountability means that principal officials should resign for poor decisions, inadequate performance, or improper behaviour. When it created the POAS, the government argued that it would make it easier for the Chief Executive to remove principal officials if they were not tenured civil servants, which would, in turn, make the executive more accountable. In practice, this has made very little difference since Chief Executives have only rarely dismissed principal officials who themselves have not offered—at least publicly—to resign on their own accord for policy failures. Thus, despite the government's efforts to put a gloss on the system,[81] the accountability of the executive is no further advanced than when the POAS was first introduced.

A second justification for the POAS was that it opened up positions in the political executive "to individuals inside and outside the civil service, thereby enabling Hong Kong to draw from a wider pool of political talent".[82] This, too, is only tenuously related to political accountability. Tung originally presented the system as more responsive to community needs because the principal officials were not civil servants, could be drawn from a wider spectrum of the community and might be more broadly representative, and would have to pay heed to public opinion if they wished to keep their positions.[83] Civil servants, by contrast, were permanent and pensionable and could presumably more readily ignore public demands. Under Tsang, however, a majority of the principal officials in charge of policy bureaus were former administrative officers. Former civil servants also held many of the principal official positions in the Leung and Lam administrations although some DAB members and other politicians were also appointed (see pp. 301–302). Lam reportedly still complained that the DAB had failed for many years "to nurture and provide talent for the government".[84] The POAS itself only marginally helped to create a wider pool of talent because, even under the pre-2002 system, it was possible to appoint people from the private sector to high-level policy positions.

A third justification of the system was that it strengthened "the foundation of a professional and politically neutral civil service".[85] The government further argued that the clarification of roles would allow civil servants to devote themselves to the implementation of policy. There are two problems with this argument. The first is that it is based on a false politics/administration dichotomy. A separation of roles between the political functions of politicians and the administrative functions of bureaucrats is not practically possible, as many scholars of public administration

---

81. Ibid., Ch. 1; Constitutional and Mainland Affairs Bureau (2006) op. cit., Ch. 2.
82. Constitutional and Mainland Affairs Bureau (2006) op. cit., p. 6.
83. Hansard, 17 April 2002, 5493–5494.
84. *The Standard* (2020, 9 October). Tsang Yok-sing says Carrie Lam not pleased with DAB failings. https://www.thestandard.com.hk/breaking-news/section/4/157096/Tsang-Yok-sing-says-Carrie-Lam-not-pleased-with-DAB-failings
85. Ibid.

have noted.[86] In the Hong Kong context, civil servants often have a definitive role in formulating as well as implementing policy; implementation itself often takes on a political dimension. Second, the idea of a politically neutral civil service has been undermined by the government's insistence that civil servants should be loyal—and interpreting loyalty to mean blind obedience to political orders.

None of the government's justifications for the POAS is convincing. The accountability of principal officials has diminished since the system was introduced, with adverse consequences for relationships between the principal officials and the Legislative Council and the civil service.

The Political Appointments System

In October 2005, Tsang proposed to make a small number of political appointments to the government, promising that they would not undermine the political neutrality of the civil service.[87] In July 2006, the Constitutional Affairs Bureau produced a consultation document that outlined the roles of new positions of under secretaries, holding the rank of deputy directors of bureaus, and political assistants. The justification for the new positions was that the existing layer of 14 political appointees was "too thin" to engage in public communication and liaison; that additional political appointments would be conducive to maintaining the neutrality of the civil service; and that the new positions would serve as a career path for political talents.[88] The Chief Executive's office and the policy bureaus, except for the Civil Service Bureau, were each to have a deputy director and a political assistant. The deputy directors were to report to the principal officials and were to be responsible for political input into policy objectives, coordination with other policy bureaus, attending panel and committee meetings of the Legislative Council, responding to motion debates in the meetings of the council, timetabling and securing the passage of bills, maintaining close contact with the media, political organisations and business and community groups, and deputising for the principal officials in their absence.[89] The political assistants, who were to report to the deputy directors, were to engage in community liaison and prepare statements and speeches for the principal official and the deputy director.[90]

The proposal raised many concerns that had already been posed in other countries about such political appointments: the challenge to the monopoly of civil service policy advice to the minister; the possibility of duplication of work and

---

86. MacDonald, S. H. (2007). Politics-administration dichotomy. In M. Bevir (Ed.), *Encyclopedia of governance* (Vol II, pp. 721–722). Thousand Oaks: Sage.
87. Tsang (2005) op. cit., para 25.
88. Constitutional Affairs Bureau (2006) op. cit., pp. 15–16.
89. Ibid., pp. 28–29.
90. Ibid., p. 30.

unclear lines of authority; and the accountability of the appointees.[91] In Hong Kong, the opposition to the proposal followed similar lines. In 2007, the Constitutional and Mainland Affairs Bureau, as it had become, produced a report on the proposal in which submissions from those opposed to political appointments were also published.[92] There were some trenchant criticisms of its effects on the civil service.[93] Opposition among senior civil servants and civil service unions continued even after its introduction[94] and eventually led to a clearer statement of the roles of senior civil servants and political appointees in the *Civil Service Code*, prohibiting interference in the line functions of the civil service.[95]

Legislators argued that the process of recruiting deputy directors and political assistants should be open and that the Legislative Council should be able to question prospective appointees. This, the bureau firmly rejected, arguing that open recruitment was "not suitable for political appointments ... since it is one of the fundamental principles for political appointees to subscribe to the C(hief) E(xecutive)'s manifesto."[96] Instead, an Appointments Committee, comprising the Chief Executive, the Director of the Chief Executive's Office, Secretaries of Departments, and Directors of Bureaus, was to make the selection decision. The selection process raised once more the question of accountability. Political appointees were accountable to principal officials who were accountable to the Chief Executive, but there was no provision for any external check on the system.

When the eclectic mix of former journalists, academics, DAB members, business people, and civil servants who made up the first batch of deputy directors and political assistants was announced in May 2008, the government was widely criticised for failing to appoint people with appropriate experience. Only three of the initial tranche of 17 appointees had any experience in government and most had none at all.[97] Anson Chan, a former Chief Secretary for Administration, said that the division of responsibility between the political appointees and senior civil servants was not clear and that morale in the civil service might be affected.[98] It was then discovered that five of the eight deputy directors had foreign passports although Tsang had said that the new appointees should be "patriotic".[99] Under the Basic Law, principal officials are not permitted to have right of abode elsewhere.

---

91. Shaw R., & Eichbaum, C. (Eds.) (2018). *Ministers, minders and mandarins: An international study of relationships at the executive summit of parliamentary democracies.* Cheltenham: Edward Elgar.
92. Constitutional and Mainland Affairs Bureau (2006) op. cit.
93. Ibid., pp. 14–15, Annex 1.
94. Scott, I. (2011). *How politicised is the Hong Kong civil service?* (pp. 8-9). CGC working paper series No. 2011/006. Hong Kong: Centre for Governance and Citizenship, The Hong Kong Institute of Education.
95. Civil Service Bureau (2009). *Civil Service Code* (pp. 6–11). https://www.csb.gov.hk/english/admin/conduct/1751.html
96. Ibid., p. 46.
97. Scott (2011) op. cit., pp. 9–10.
98. Wu, E., & Leung, A. (2008, 22 May). Anson Chan attacks new appointments. *SCMP*; Yeung, C. (2008, 30 May). Running the show. *SCMP*.
99. Constitutional and Mainland Affairs Bureau (2006) op. cit., p. 44; Yeung, C. (2008, 30 May). Fresh faces get a harsh dose of political reality. *SCMP*.

Another cross-party criticism was that the government would not disclose the exact salaries of the political appointees to legislators.[100]

The administration initially shrugged off the criticisms, saying that there was no Basic Law requirement that deputy directors and political assistants were not able to hold foreign passports and declined to provide information on individual salaries. But there was growing public feeling that the political appointees should renounce their foreign passports, and there was widening criticism of how the government was handling the issue. Eventually, the five appointees with foreign passports undertook to relinquish them.[101] The Democratic Party tabled a motion in the Legislative Council requiring the government to disclose the criteria for the selection of the political appointees, which was defeated.

The furore over the appointment of deputy directors and political assistants illustrates some of the government's problems with political accountability. If the exercise had been conducted more openly, it is highly probable that the passport issue would have been raised at an earlier stage in the Legislative Council and that complaints about the government's failure to disclose the salaries of appointees could have been resolved. The government's reason for not consulting the legislature fully, that candidates had to subscribe to the Chief Executive's election manifesto, seems an inadequate justification of its actions. The tendency to make critical decisions without sufficient consultation and then to announce them as a *fait accompli* has led to problems both of accountability and of policy implementation.

When the system bedded down, it was evident that the deputy directors were performing many different roles which were not necessarily held in common across the system. In some cases, they were involved in the detailed formulation of public policies; in others, their tasks were mainly related to liaison and dealing with Legislative Council committees.[102] Where detailed consideration of policy was involved, there was overlap with the policy bureaus in the civil service, the possibility of duplication, and the danger that lines of authority would become confused. The political appointments system appears to have further reduced the administrative grade's policymaking and political roles and has been seen as a challenge to traditional civil service values and a potentially disruptive influence on smooth and efficient policymaking.[103]

The Accountability of the Police Force

Accountability issues and police forces are inextricably linked. How the police use their considerable powers, especially the use of force, and how those powers are

---

100. Wu, E., & Fung, F. W. Y. (2008, 31 May). Come clean on aides' pay, say parties. *SCMP*.
101. Leung, A., Wong, A., & Wu, E. (2008, 6 June). New team nationality row "underestimated". *SCMP*.
102. Scott (2011) op. cit., Appendix 1. See also Hansard (2019) 27 March, 7934–7945.
103. Burns, J. P., & Li, W. (2015). The impact of external change on civil service values in post-colonial Hong Kong. *The China Quarterly*, *222*, 522–546.

checked and supervised, are concerns for any political system that claims to protect civil liberties. In Hong Kong, there have been three major accountability issues at the heart of disputes over the role of the Police Force. First, is the Police Force accountable to the Hong Kong government? Second, by what means, if at all, can a police force be held accountable to the public? Third, do methods of resolving complaints against the police hold police officers accountable?

Accountability to the Hong Kong Government

The Police Force has always had a special status and considerable autonomy within the Hong Kong government. It was established in 1844 as a paramilitary unit with primary responsibility for maintaining law and order, a role that it played throughout colonial rule. As by far the largest department in the government—almost one in every five civil servants is a police officer (see Table 4.3)—the force has developed its own rules of conduct under the *Police Force Ordinance*, its own pay scale, which is much more generous than that of other civil servants, and its own complaint-handling agencies. Under the Basic Law, the Commissioner of Police is a principal official of equal status to his notional superior, the Secretary of Security. The *Police Force Ordinance* gives the Commissioner the power to exercise "supreme direction" over the force, subject to the orders and control of the Chief Executive.[104] Although the Chief Executive has the formal legal power to hold the force accountable, in practice, there appear to have been few constraints on police actions until the Chinese government asserted jurisdiction over some of its functions in June 2020.[105]

Apart from periodic attempts to try to rid the force of corruption and occasional reforms to enable it to control unrest more effectively, the government has left the police largely to its own devices. In 1973, the Governor, MacLehose, removed corruption control from police jurisdiction and set up the ICAC. Four years later, the ICAC had been so successful in rooting out corruption that junior police officers mutinied. MacLehose then offered a partial amnesty, placing time limits on ICAC investigations.[106] He probably feared a breakdown in law and order, but his concessions revealed the government's dependence on the police to maintain stability. The ICAC was able to continue its successful corruption prevention programmes and the police soon became a much cleaner organisation.

As 1997 approached, there were political concerns that a paramilitary force would be detrimental to efforts to promote public confidence in the new regime. In 1993, Coopers and Lybrand produced a consultancy report that recommended changes in the top command structure and in relationships between the government

---

104. *Police Force Ordinance*, Cap 232, Section 4.
105. Hui, D. L. H., & Au, R. C. Y. (2014). Police legitimacy and protest policing: A case study of Hong Kong. *Asian Education and Development Studies*, 3(3), 223–234.
106. Scott, I., & Gong, T. (2019). *Corruption prevention and governance in Hong Kong* (pp. 40–42). Abingdon: Routledge.

and the police, implying that this meant changes to police culture.[107] The recommendations were accepted despite some dissent among senior management. The force then developed innovative programmes to support a community policing role. This new initiative was well received by new recruits, less so by middle-ranking and criminal investigation officers.[108] Public satisfaction with police performance gradually increased (see pp. 339–342).[109]

By 2012, however, in the wake of sometimes violent protests, satisfaction with the police began to decline.[110] On 28 September 2014, the police fired tear gas into Umbrella Movement protesters, the first use of teargas in almost a decade. There was a further fall in satisfaction levels and the unintended consequence of mobilising more support for the movement.[111] Protesters then occupied parts of central Hong Kong Island and Kowloon for 79 days. Although the police did not attempt to clear the occupied areas, there were still many violent confrontations. A case in which seven policemen were charged and convicted of assaulting an Umbrella Movement protester illustrates the conflicting political dynamics involved.[112] The judge said that the assault was vicious and sentenced each policeman to two years' imprisonment. Pro-establishment and pro-Beijing groups demonstrated against the sentence. Junior police officers deplored the decision and called for financial support for an appeal. The judge was attacked in the media. On appeal, two officers were permitted to walk free and the other five were given reduced sentences.[113] The Commissioner of Police reportedly approved a campaign for staff unions to raise money for an appeal.[114] The government left the impression that maintaining order, however that was achieved, was its first priority.

From 2014 onwards, there was a gradual increase in violent confrontations between police and protesters, which set the scene for the major disturbances of 2019–2020. During this unrest and despite evidence of the excessive use of force

---

107. To, Y. H. J. (1998). *Changing 'cop culture': Attitudes to discretionary power by patrol officers* (p. 2) [Unpublished master's thesis]. The University of Hong Kong.
108. Brewer, B., Leung, J. Y. H., & Scott, I. (2015). *An assessment of the impact of value-based integrity programmes on the Hong Kong Police Force.* Hong Kong: Department of Public Policy, City University of Hong Kong.
109. Lo, C. W. H., & Cheuk, A. C. Y. (2004). Community policing in Hong Kong: Development, performance and constraints. *Policing: An International Journal of Police Strategies and Management, 27*(1), 97–127.
110. PORI (2021). Satisfaction with the Hong Kong Police Force. https://www.pori.hk/pop-poll/disciplinary-force-en/x001.html?lang=en
111. Ibid.; Ma, N. (2020). Rude awakening: new participants and the Umbrella Movement. In Ma, N. & Cheng, E.W. *The Umbrella Movement: Civil resistance and contentious space in Hong Kong* (rev. ed., p. 86). Amsterdam: University of Amsterdam Press.
112. BBC (2017, 14 February). Hong Kong police officers convicted of beating protester. https://www.bbc.com/news/world-asia-38967605
113. Chan, H. (2019, 26 July). Two Hong Kong cops freed over activist Ken Tsang assault case, five others have jail term reduced. *HKFP.* https://hongkongfp.com/2019/07/26/breaking-2-7-hong-kong-cops-walk-free-winning-court-appeal-ken-tsang-assault-case/
114. Siu, J. & Lee, E. (2017, 17 February). Outrage at two-year prison for Hong Kong policemen who beat up political activist. *SCMP.* https://www.scmp.com/news/hong-kong/law-crime/article/2071703/two-years-jail-seven-policemen-who-beat-occupy-activist-ken

by the police from a wide range of different sources, including the media,[115] the United Nations Human Rights office,[116] human rights organisations,[117] doctors who attended to the victims' injuries,[118] observers of the protests,[119] and videos of police behaviour,[120] the government refused to act on the protesters' demand for a commission of inquiry. Instead, Carrie Lam said that the government would rely on a report from the IPCC. However, in December 2019, its five-member distinguished panel of independent international experts, who had been appointed to assist in the investigation, said that they would "stand aside" because they believed that "a crucial shortfall was evident in the powers, capacity and independent investigative capability of the IPCC."[121] When the IPCC delivered its report in May 2020, it found that "the use of force by the Police in past months has been in reaction to illegal action by the protesters" and attached no blame to police officers for the excessive use of force.[122] The public reaction, and that of many NGOs, was one of anger and incredulity.[123] The report provided a clear indication that the Police Force was not accountable to the government or, it seemed, to any other body.

Value-Based Accountability

Between 1996 and 2014, the Police Force attempted to introduce community policing based on the inculcation of values in all its officers. The idea was that, if values could be internalised through extensive training programmes, then public support for the force would increase and its work would become much easier. In 1996, the Commissioner of Police identified the core values of the force as "integrity and

---

115. Ho, R. (2019, 27 November). The Hong Kongers building a case against the police. https://www.thenation.com/article/archive/hong-kong-police-brutality/
116. United Nations Human Rights Office (2019, 19 November). Press briefing on Hong Kong, China. https://www.ohchr.org/EN/NewsEvents/Pages/DisplayNews.aspx?NewsID=25312&LangID=E
117. Amnesty International (2020). *Hong Kong: Missing truth, missing justice; the case and international legal framework for the establishment of a commission of inquiry into the 2019 protests*. London: Amnesty International; Article 19 (2019, 4 July). Hong Kong: Authorities must uphold the right to protest. https://www.article19.org/resources/hong-kong-authorities-must-uphold-the-right-to-protest/; Human Rights Watch (2020, 7 January). Hong Kong: Create independent investigation of police. https://www.hrw.org/news/2020/01/07/hong-kong-create-independent-investigation-police#:~:text=(New%20York)%20%E2%80%93%20Hong%20Kong,to%20Chief%20Executive%20Carrie%20Lam
118. Chan, H. (2019, 28 August). On the frontlines: the Hong Kong public hospitals making a stand against violence. HKFP. https://hongkongfp.com/2019/08/28/frontlines-hong-kong-public-hospital-doctors-making-stand-police-violence/
119. Purbeck, M. (2019). A report of the 2019 protests. *Asian Affairs, 50*(4), 465–487.
120. BBC (2019). Hong Kong police storm metro after protests. https://www.youtube.com/watch?v=iejjwdxQDYw
121. *Radio Free Asia* (2019, 11 December). International policing experts back away from Hong Kong's complaints probe. https://www.rfa.org/english/news/china/complaints-12112019131554.html. See also pp. 56–57, 369–72.
122. Independent Police Complaints Council (2020). *A thematic study by the IPCC on the public order events arising from the Fugitive Offenders Bill since 2019 and the police action in response* (p. 162). https://www.ipcc.gov.hk/en/public_communications/ipcc_thematic_study_report.html
123. Davidson, H. (2020, 15 May). Anger as Hong Kong watchdog clears police over protest response. *The Guardian*. https://www.theguardian.com/world/2020/may/15/hong-kong-police-watchdog-clears-force-protest-response

honesty; professionalism; fairness, impartiality and compassion in all our dealings; acceptance of responsibility and accountability; respect for the rights of members of the public and of the Force; effective communication both within and outside the Force; dedication to quality service and continuous improvement; and responsiveness to change".[124] The values were designed to promote responsiveness (see pp. 339–342). Training in what the values meant was carried out annually across the force through the Living the Values programme, which annually explored the operational meaning of a particular value and, using workshops, competitions, and videos, involved junior officers in discussions of what they understood by it.[125]

In 2014/2015, our research team conducted focus groups and interviews with junior police officers to assess their reactions to the programme.[126] We concluded that officers might be divided into four groups: cynics, mainly experienced officers who were opposed to community policing; the converted, a few veterans who thought that there might be some value in the new ideas; supporters, young newly recruited officers who saw the workshops as a continuation of what they had learned in Police College; and pragmatists, who applied what they could use from the workshops and discarded what they could not.[127] The tensions between these groups were not seriously felt until the Umbrella Movement when the force claimed that the protesters were attacking it and used tear gas to disperse them. The cynics, who viewed the appropriate role of the Police Force as a paramilitary organisation, shaped its subsequent performance.

The Living the Values programme was well attuned to practical policing issues and its effect on the behaviour of junior police officers on the beat was very much appreciated by the Hong Kong public. Although there were no sanctions on police officers who failed to live up to the values, other than through the defective police complaints mechanism, it provided an avenue for a better and more accountable relationship between the police and the public. But junior police officers needed to acquire more seniority before the values could be properly institutionalised. In the end, community policing was overtaken by events, and the Police Force reverted to its paramilitary colonial frame of reference.

Internal Checks on Police Behaviour

Handling complaints against the police has long been a controversial matter in Hong Kong. The principal reasons for dissatisfaction with the Complaints Against the Police Office (CAPO) are that it is not independent, that members of the force

---

124. Hong Kong Police Force (2011). *Service quality: 17 years of service quality, 1994–2011* (p. 6). Hong Kong: mimeo.
125. Hong Kong Police College (2009). *Community policing in Hong Kong: Engaging the community*. www.police.gov.hk; Hong Kong Police Force (2009). *Ethics and integrity in the Hong Kong Police Force*. Hong Kong: mimeo.
126. Brewer, Leung, & Scott (2015) op. cit.
127. Ibid., pp. 37–41.

are rarely disciplined for unacceptable behaviour as a result of complaints and that the monitoring process conducted by the IPCC is ineffective (see pp. 383–386). Aside from the ICAC, which investigates suspected corruption offences, there are no credible external organisations holding police officers accountable for their behaviour.

None of the possible means of holding the Police Force accountable has worked. Its relationship with the Hong Kong government is unclear although most evidence suggests that the Police Force is largely autonomous. The successful attempt to introduce community policing and hold the police accountable to its own value-based integrity standards was blown away in the increasingly violent confrontations with protesters after 2014. Establishing accountability for unacceptable behaviour through CAPO and the IPCC has also failed and neither organisation has ever enjoyed the ICAC's respect or credibility as a complaint-handling institution. With the promulgation of the Chinese government's national security legislation in June 2020, the Police Force was given powers of arrest over a wide range of vaguely defined issues. It does not seem likely that its accountability to the Hong Kong government, its self-proclaimed values, or responsiveness to the public will increase in the near future.

Conclusion

Political accountability requires that office holders are held accountable for their actions to an external independent oversight body that can impose sanctions upon them. The measures that have been introduced since 1997 have aimed at strengthening the political executive, but there has been very little reciprocity in improving the mechanisms that hold the political executive accountable. The abolition of the municipal councils was regressive because Urban and Regional Council members played a role in providing a measure of electoral accountability to the public. In abolishing the councils, the government in effect claimed that efficiency was more important than accountability. It also rejected the view that elected Urban and Regional Councillors could provide an avenue to advance to the Legislative Council and higher levels of government. Yet the same argument—that the new positions would be a breeding ground for political talents—was later used by the government to justify political appointments that had no electoral legitimacy.

The POAS has had far-reaching implications for the location of power within the government and a significant impact on how policy is formulated and implemented. But on the grounds which it was originally sold to the Legislative Council and the public—that it would make principal officials more politically accountable for their work—it must be judged to have been a singular failure. It has not solved the problem of the disjunction between the Legislative Council and a political executive whose accountability is principally to the Chief Executive and, through that office, to the Chinese government.

The political appointments system raised further questions about the accountability of personnel who did not have to meet the standards of a normal merit appointment to the civil service but who had nonetheless power and influence in policy formulation. The new system was another illustration of the disjunction between the political executive, the bureaucracy, and the Legislative Council. Finally, although the Police Force often acted autonomously within the Hong Kong government, community policing did help to make it more responsive to public needs and to its own values. The protests, however, led to a reversion to its former paramilitary status. In none of the four major areas analysed in this chapter has there been significant improvements in accountability. On the contrary, the accountability of the political executive and of the police has been diminished as a result of organisational change.

Part II

The Public Sector and Its Problems

4
The Civil Service
Structure and Functions

The Basic Law provides only a general framework for the organisation of the Hong Kong civil service and has even less to say about public bodies. Article 48 specifies that the Chief Executive shall lead the government and may appoint judges and holders of public office and Article 62 empowers the government to conduct administrative affairs. Some departments, such as the Police Force, Immigration, and Customs and Excise, are mentioned in the Basic Law and it is stipulated that there shall be a Commission against Corruption and an Audit Commission, but there is no description of the organisation or powers of these bodies. Instead, the Chief Executive may decide, in consultation with the secretaries of bureaus and department heads, how their organisations should be structured. The arrangements may then be formalised in ordinances or executive orders, regulations, and circulars. Most bureaus and departments have been organisationally stable for many years,[1] but refinements, and sometimes substantial changes, are often made as the government takes on new responsibilities, merges bureaus and departments, or introduces new services. The need for reorganisation may also stem from the government's search for improvements in efficiency, effectiveness, and economy.

The underlying principles on which the Hong Kong civil service should be organised have been widely shared by political leaders and the public both before and after 1997. But in the last decade or so some of the basic principles have been undermined or redefined. Table 4.1 shows the principles on which the colonial and immediate post-handover government were supposed to be based and how they have evolved until mid-2020. Practice has sometimes differed substantially from the principles on which it is supposedly based. The Hong Kong government can no longer be described, for example, as small or limited in function although politicians still occasionally make that claim. Political neutrality has been redefined. The administrative grade has been shorn of some of its previous political power. Changing economic conditions and a closer relationship with mainland China have modified the long-standing stress on fiscal frugality. In this chapter, we examine the principles underlying the formal structure and functions of the Hong Kong

---

1. Ho, P. Y. (2004). *The administrative history of the Hong Kong government agencies 1841–2002*. Hong Kong: Hong Kong University Press.

Table 4.1 *The Organisation of Government: Evolving Principles*

Pre-2002	Mid-2020
Government should be centralised and organised hierarchically.	Government remains centralised and organised hierarchically.
Government should be run by an administrative elite selected from the most able candidates available.[1] Political neutrality means that those holding office should act impartially and in the best public interest.[2]	Government should be run by political appointees selected by the Chief Executive. Political neutrality means loyalty to the political executive.[3]
Government should be "small government" and only perform limited functions[4] while focusing on fiscal frugality, efficiency and "value for money".[5]	Government should be "appropriately proactive" and address market failures.[6]
Civil servants should be recruited and promoted on merit and should hold permanent and pensionable terms for their working lives.[7]	Civil servants continue to be recruited on merit. Most have jobs for life.
The civil service should be free of corruption and subject to the rule of law.[8]	The civil service maintains a zero-tolerance policy towards corruption.

Sources:
1. Burns, J. P. (2004). *Government capacity and the Hong Kong civil service* (pp. 105–108). Hong Kong: Oxford University Press.
2. Scott, I. (1996). Civil service neutrality in Hong Kong. In H. K. Asmeron & E.P. Reis (Eds.), *Democratization and bureaucratic neutrality* (pp. 277–293). Basingstoke: Macmillan.
3. Constitutional Affairs Bureau (2002). *Legislative Council paper: Accountability system for principal officials.* https://www.legco.gov.hk/yr01-02/english/panels/ca/papers/ca0418cb2-paper-e.pdf; Constitutional and Mainland Affairs Bureau (2007). *Report on the further development of the political appointment system.* https://www.cmab.gov.hk/doc/issues/report_en.pdf; Civil Service Bureau (2009). *The Civil Service Code* (p. 4). https://www.csb.gov.hk/english/admin/conduct/1751.html
4. Haddon-Cave, P. (1984). The making of some aspects of public policy in Hong Kong. In D. Lethbridge (Ed.), *The business environment in Hong Kong* (2nd ed.). Hong Kong: Oxford University Press; Tsang, D. Y. K. (2005). *Strong governance for the people* (para 72). https://www.policyaddress.gov.hk/05-06/eng/index.htm
5. Finance Branch (1995). *Practitioner's guide: Management of public finances* (p. 31). Hong Kong: Government Printer.
6. Leung, C. Y. (2013). *Seek change, maintain stability, serve the people with pragmatism* (para 20). https://www.policyaddress.gov.hk/2013/eng/index.html
7. Huque, A. S., Lee, G. O. M., & Cheung, A. B. L. (1998). *The civil service in Hong Kong: Continuity and change* (p. 25). Hong Kong: Hong Kong University Press; Chan, A. (2001, 19 April). *Speech by the Chief Secretary of Administration at an Asia Society luncheon* [Press release]. https://www.info.gov.hk/gia/general/200104/19/0419138.htm
8. Scott, I., & Gong, T. (2019). *Corruption prevention and governance in Hong Kong* (pp. 155–160). Abingdon: Routledge.

government and civil service listed in Table 4.1 and analyse how practice has deviated from the first three principles. In Chapter 5, we consider the remaining principles and the government's record in meeting those criteria through its personnel policies.

The Structure of Government

The Colonial System

The formal structure of the Hong Kong government has traditionally been highly centralised. Power has always been concentrated in the hands of a relatively few senior figures, partly because of the political circumstances in which the rulers of Hong Kong have found themselves but also because decentralised government has only occasionally been considered necessary. The civil administration of Hong Kong was promulgated by a despatch from the Colonial Office in June 1843.[2] In September 1843, the offices of Governor and Colonial Secretary were established together with the Judiciary, Finance, Harbour and Lands, and Roads and Public Works Departments. A Police Force and an Audit Commission were created in 1844.[3] For the next 20 years or so, Hong Kong's administration was chaotic and corrupt. In the following 20 years, however, civil service reforms produced a strongly centralised system of hierarchically organised departments. The first cadets (later called administrative officers) were appointed in 1862 and assumed the most senior positions within the civil service.[4] Corruption in the police was addressed later in the 1860s by appointing a cadet as head of the force.[5] And, by the 1880s, public finances were managed more efficiently and systematically.

At the apex of the system was the Governor although he was often dependent on the advice of his Colonial Secretary, who was in charge of the civil service. Power was concentrated in the Colonial Secretariat, staffed mainly by cadets who were responsible for the central functions of finance, policymaking and the regulation of the civil service itself. Responsibility for relations with the public lay with the Secretariat for Chinese Affairs, a separate body, which sought the advice of elite Chinese opinion.[6] When the New Territories were acquired in 1899, there was some devolution of power to the district officer, who consulted local elites on sensitive

---

2. Endacott, G. B. (1964). *An eastern entrepot: A collection of documents illustrating the history of Hong Kong* (pp. 255–259). London: HMSO.
3. Collins, C. (1952). *Public administration in Hong Kong* (p. 51). London: Royal Institute of International Affairs.
4. Miners, N. (1990). The localization of the Hong Kong Police Force, 1841–1947. *Journal of Imperial and Commonwealth History, 18*(3), 298–315.
5. Tsang, S. Y. S. (2007). *Governing Hong Kong: Administrative officers from the nineteenth century to the handover to China, 1862–1997* (pp. 19–20). London: IB Taurus.
6. Hase, P. (2001). The District Office. In E. Sinn (Ed.), *Hong Kong, British crown colony, revisited*. Hong Kong: Centre of Asian Studies, University of Hong Kong; Hayes, J. (1996). *Friends and teachers: Hong Kong and its people 1953–87* (Ch. 8). Hong Kong: Hong Kong University Press.

issues.[7] On Hong Kong Island and in Kowloon, government remained highly centralised.

Over time, the government gradually created more departments, initially concerned with law and order functions but latterly expanded into social services, notably the provision of public housing from the mid-1950s. Before the Second World War, the Colonial Secretariat was able to make and implement incremental decisions but did not have the capacity or the inclination to take on larger and more ambitious policies. After the war and the communist victory in China in 1949, Hong Kong's population quadrupled in four years, creating many additional pressures. Senior officers were overloaded and the Secretariat was becoming clogged up and unable to respond rapidly enough to the problems it faced.[8]

There were various reform proposals, but it was not until 1972 that the Governor decided that the administrative structure should be revamped to deliver social services more effectively. The McKinsey consultants, who were employed to make recommendations, found that the Secretariat was overloaded and over-centralised because the departments could not "actually take many decisions" and that, as a consequence, "large numbers of decisions have to be taken centrally".[9] They devised a new structure in which the policy functions bundled together in the Colonial Secretariat were hived off to six policy branches and two resource branches (finance and the civil service), each of which was headed by a secretary.[10] The policy branches were supposed to formulate policy which the departments under their control were then expected to implement. In practice, as with most politics/administration dichotomies, it did not work entirely to plan and policies were usually made after discussions between the branches and senior departmental officials. Over time, the problem of overlapping and unclear responsibilities led to the creation of more branches and more departments.

Power remained highly centralised, however. The policy secretaries were mostly members of the administrative grade, which aided cohesion and unity of purpose, and they reported directly to the Colonial Secretary (later called the Chief Secretary). Control over expenditure remained firmly in the hands of the Financial Secretary. The newly created Civil Service Branch took over responsibility for the management of the entire civil service. It was expected to administer the personnel management function and to provide for better coordination with the departments and the Public Service Commission than its predecessor, the Establishment Branch, had been able to do.[11] The McKinsey structure, with some modifications resulting from the introduction of the POAS, has remained in place since 1973.

---

7. Hayes (1996) op. cit., pp. 85–107.
8. Colonial Secretariat (1949). *Report on the organization, methods and staff survey* (pp. 73–78). Hong Kong: Legislative Council Sessional Paper. Hong Kong: mimeo.
9. McKinsey and Company (May 1973). *The machinery of government: A new framework for expanding services* (p. 7). Hong Kong: mimeo.
10. Ibid., pp. 16–17.
11. Ibid., p. 12.

The Government Secretariat after 1997

Figure 4.1 shows how the government is presently organised. The Chief Executive has replaced the Governor at the apex of the structure and derives his powers from *The Public Service (Administration) Order* and the *Public Service (Disciplinary) Regulations* which gives him similar authority over the civil service to that formerly exercised by the Governor. Beneath the Chief Executive, the Chief Secretary for Administration is the head of the civil service and the lineal successor to the Colonial Secretary. Slightly beneath the Chief Secretary in the hierarchy are the Financial Secretary and the Secretary for Justice, who replaced the colonial Attorney-General. Initially, the Chief Secretary and the Financial Secretary vetted policy proposals and related increases in public expenditure coming from the bureaus (as the branches were called after the handover) and filtered out those which the government could not afford or did not consider to be a priority. When the POAS came into effect in 2002, this critical function was devalued. The Chief Secretary and the Financial Secretary were downgraded to the level of policy secretaries.[12] This meant that vetos on policy proposals rested with the Chief Executive without the filtering which the Chief Secretary and the Financial Secretary had undertaken in the past. When Donald Tsang succeeded Tung Chee Hwa as Chief Executive in 2005, one of his first acts was to reassert the pre-eminent positions of the Chief Secretary and the Financial Secretary.[13]

By 2002, the Hong Kong civil service was divided into 16 bureaus and nearly 60 departments and agencies which were assigned to each of the bureaus. The bureaus continued to be largely staffed by the administrative grade. In February 2002, members of the grade were also the heads of some 26 operational departments.[14] When the POAS was introduced, the Chief Executive reduced the number of bureaus from 16 to 11, resulting in many mergers and reorganisation of bureaus. There were significant changes concerning the devolution of powers from the Chief Secretary and the Financial Secretary to policy secretaries, the division of responsibility between the Financial Secretary and the Financial Services and Treasury, and the reallocation of permanent secretaries.[15] Policy secretaries were given more financial autonomy through the introduction of an "envelope" system, which was intended to provide them with "clear parameters on the operating resources available to them".[16]

Every new Chief Executive has been intent on changing the organisational structure of bureaus and departments within the rubric of the McKinsey framework.

---

12. Secretary for Constitutional Affairs (2003). *Twelve-month report on implementation of the accountability system for principal officials*. https://www.cmab.gov.hk/upload/20040219153857/12mthreport-e.pdf
13. Tsang, D. Y. K. (2005). *Strong governance for the people* (paras 8–9). https://www.policyaddress.gov.hk/05-06/eng/index.htm
14. Secretary for the Civil Service (2002, 27 February). *Establishment of the AO and EO grades* [Press release]. https://www.info.gov.hk/gia/general/200202/27/0227148.htm
15. Secretary for Constitutional Affairs (2003) op. cit.
16. Ibid.

Figure 4.1 The Government Secretariat 2018

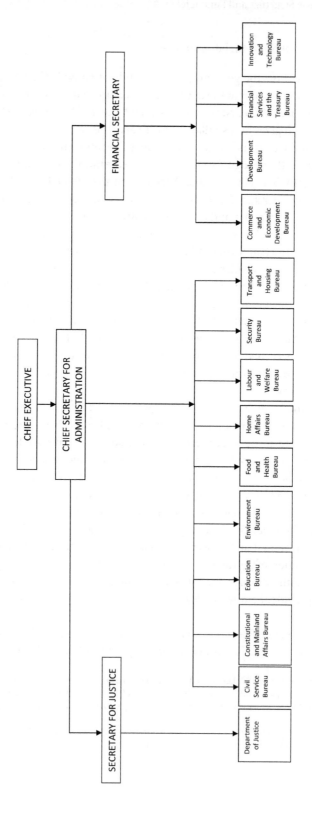

Source: Adapated from https://www.gov.hk/en/about/govdirectory/govchart/docs/chart.pdf.

In June 2007, under Tsang, the number of policy bureaus was increased to 12 and there were reviews of the structures of each of the bureaus.[17] In 2012, C. Y. Leung proposed that a new bureau focusing on innovation and technology be established. Shortly before Leung became Chief Executive, the Legislative Council considered the proposal and voted against it. Leung returned to the proposal in his 2014 policy address[18] and the Legislative Council voted in favour of establishing the bureau. However, the democrats then used filibusters in the Finance Committee to prevent the bureau from receiving funding. They argued that the new bureau would be expensive and would replicate failures in innovation policy that had characterised previous government efforts although they also used the opportunity to express their objections to the arrangements for the 2017 Chief Executive elections.[19] It was not until November 2015 that the Finance Committee was finally able to pass a vote to fund the new bureau.

When Carrie Lam became Chief Executive in 2017, she further strengthened the Innovation and Technology Bureau, bringing the Efficiency Unit (now the Efficiency Office) within its domain, providing $500 million for technological innovation in the civil service and replacing the former Central Policy Unit with the Policy Innovation and Coordination Office.[20] In her 2021 policy address, she outlined a plan to reorganise the bureaus[21] which was further developed in her address to the Legislative Council in January 2022.[22] A new bureau of Culture, Sports and Tourism was to be created and the existing Housing and Transport Bureau (now to be called Transport and Logistics) was to be separated into two bureaus. The functions performed by some bureaus were to be divested and taken over by others to reflect more attention to particular areas. Responsibility for food was to be acquired from the Health Bureau by a retitled Environment and Ecology Bureau; the Home Affairs Bureau was to be re-titled Home Affairs and Youth to allow it to develop comprehensive youth policies; and Innovation and Technology was to become Innovation, Technology and Industry. Functions relating to manpower planning, poverty and retirement protection were to be transferred from other parts of government to the Labour and Welfare Bureau.

There may be many reasons for organisational change. A long-standing belief in the Hong Kong government is that if a policy is deficient, there is likely to be

---

17. Constitutional and Mainland Affairs Bureau (2007). *Legislative Council brief: Reorganisation of policy bureaux of the Government Secretariat*. https://www.cmab.gov.hk/upload/LegCoPaper/LegCoBrief_20070503e.pdf
18. Leung, C. Y. (2014). *Support the needy, let youth flourish, unleash Hong Kong's potential* (para 37). https://www.policyaddress.gov.hk/2014/eng/index.html
19. Hansard, 22 October 2014, 787–832. Hansard 29 October 2014, 995.
20. Lam, C. (2017). *The Chief Executive's 2017 policy address* (para 17). https://www.policyaddress.gov.hk/2017/eng/speech.html
21. Chief Executive (2021). *The Chief Executive's 2021 policy address*. https://www.policyaddress.gov.hk/2021/eng/policy.html
22. Chief Executive (2022, 12 January). Opening remarks by CE at Legco Chief Executive's question and answer session (attachment). https://www.info.gov.hk/gia/general/202201/12/P2022011200312.htm

something wrong with the structure and the way the hierarchy is working. It could be, of course, that there is something wrong with the policy, but it is often politically easier to make minor adjustments to the structure than to introduce amendments to policies. Since the Tung administration, the Hong Kong government has generally made incremental policy changes so most organisational refinements have involved relatively small adjustments. A final consideration is that the introduction of organisational changes with the advent of a new Chief Executive is meant to send a message that a fresh and dynamic administration has taken office.

Departments

Formally, a department is a government body that exercises authority to implement the laws and regulations which fall under its jurisdiction. In 2018, the government listed 65 "departments" under the bureaus (see Table 4.2). But the Hong Kong government also considers some organisations, which are not, strictly speaking, departments, such as the advisory bodies on civil service salaries and the University Grants Committee, to fall under the jurisdiction of bureaus. The confusion over the term reflects the centralising tendency of the government. Bureaus have oversight over the public bodies that fall broadly within their jurisdiction. Although public bodies have varying degrees of autonomy, the government reserves the right to intervene in all cases to ensure that such organisations are properly managed and that they support and implement centrally determined policies and objectives.

Apart from some social services departments, the proportional size of departments within the civil service has remained relatively unchanged since colonial days. Table 4.3 shows the strength of the 12 largest departments in 2020. Compared with the percentage in 1988, as a proportion of the civil service, the disciplined services (Police, Fire Services, Correctional Services, Immigration and Customs) have increased. Customs was not represented in the 12 largest departments in 1988, but much greater cross-border traffic since then has required additional staff. There have also been significant increases in numbers in Immigration and in the Fire Services Department. Health and Housing have declined in both absolute and percentage terms, reflecting the creation of the Hospital Authority, which employed many civil servants from the former Medical and Health Department, and the privatisation of the management of some housing estates.

Since 2008, there has been less change in the proportional size of the departments although the 25% increase in the 2020/2021 Police Force's budget will raise its numbers in 2021 significantly by about 2,500 officers.[23] The Social Welfare

---

23. Financial Secretary (2020b). *The 2020/2021 budget estimates*. Head 122, 591. https://www.budget.gov.hk/2020/eng/pdf/head122.pdf

Table 4.2 *Bureaus and Departments in the Hong Kong Government*

Bureaus	Departments and Agencies
Chief Secretary for Administration	Administration Wing; Human Resources Planning and Poverty Co-ordination Unit; Legal Aid Department
Secretary for Justice	Department of Justice
Financial Secretary	Hong Kong Monetary Authority; Office of the Government Economist
Civil Service Bureau	Joint Secretariat for the Advisory Bodies on Civil Service and Judicial Salaries and Conditions of Service
Constitutional and Mainland Affairs Bureau	Registration and Electoral Office; Offices in the Mainland and Taiwan
Education Bureau	University Grants Committee Secretariat; Working Family and Student Financial Assistance Agency
Environment Bureau	Environmental Protection Department
Food and Health Bureau	Agricultural, Fisheries and Conservation Department; Department of Health; Food and Environmental Hygiene Department; Government Laboratory
Home Affairs Bureau	Home Affairs Department; Information Services Department; Leisure and Cultural Services Department
Labour and Welfare Bureau	Labour Department; Social Welfare Department
Security Bureau	Auxiliary Medical Service; Civil Aid Service; Correctional Services Department; Customs and Excise Department; Fire Services Department; Government Flying Service; Hong Kong Police Force; Immigration Department
Transport and Housing Bureau	Civil Aviation Department; Highways Department; Housing Department; Marine Department; Transport Department
Commerce and Economic Development Bureau	Tourism Commission; Hong Kong Observatory; Intellectual Property Department; Invest Hong Kong; Office of the Telecommunications Authority; Post Office; Radio Television Hong Kong; Television and Licensing Authority; Trade and Industry Department; Hong Kong Economic and Trade Offices (Overseas)
Development Bureau	Architectural Services Department; Buildings Department; Civil Engineering and Development Department; Drainage Services Department; Electrical & Mechanical Services Department; Lands Department; Lands Registry; Planning Department; Water Supplies Department
Financial Services and the Treasury Bureau	Census and Statistics Department; Companies Registry; Government Logistics Department; Government Property Agency; Inland Revenue Department; Official Receiver's Office; Rating and Valuation Department; Treasury
Innovation and Technology Bureau	Innovation and Technology Commission; Office of the Government Chief Information Officer; Efficiency Office

Source: Adapted from https://www.gov.hk/en/about/govdirectory/govchart/docs/chart.pdf.
Note: This structure was in place between 2018 and 2022 when plans were in train to create a new bureau of Culture, Sports and Tourism, to split the Housing and Transport Bureau and to re-title and re-organise the functions of other bureaus (see p. 109).

Table 4.3 *Strength of the Twelve Largest Departments 2020*

Department	Strength	2020 (%)	2008 (%)	1988 (%)
Hong Kong Police Force	33,245	18.7	20.8	17.6
Fire Services	10,695	6.0	6.0	4.0
Food and Environmental Hygiene	10,524	5.9	6.4	-
Leisure and Culture Services	9,516	5.4	4.6	-
Housing	9,131	5.1	4.8	6.5
Immigration	8,817	5.0	4.1	2.8
Customs and Excise	7,112	4.0	3.6	1.9
Correctional Services	6,631	3.7	4.2	3.3
Health	6,526	3.7	3.0	14.5
Social Welfare	6,229	3.5	3.4	1.9
Education	5,446	3.1	3.4	1.9
Post Office	4,866	2.7	3.1	2.5
Others	58,898	33.2	32.5	25.4
Total	177,656	100	100	100

Sources: Calculated from Civil Service Branch (1988). *Civil service personnel statistics 1988* (pp. 10–14). Hong Kong: Government Printer; Civil Service Bureau (2008). Strength of the civil service. https://www.csb.gov.hk; Civil Service Bureau (2020, 31 March). Strength of the civil service. https://www.csb.gov.hk/english/stat/quarterly/541.html

Note: Civil servants in the Leisure and Cultural Services Department and the Food and Hygiene Department were drawn largely from the former Urban Services and Regional Services Departments which together constituted 13.2% of the civil service in 1988.

Department's establishment rose substantially in percentage between 1988 and 2008, but most of the increase in absolute numbers occurred before 1997. Since 2008, the size of the department has increased marginally. The post-1997 government has tended to support increases in the disciplined services and to meet demand for social services by other means, aiming to keep the size of departments concerned with social policy implementation relatively stable.

Although bureaus are charged with policy formulation, they are often unable to develop proposals without the advice and ideas of senior departmental officers. Consequently, there is continual interaction between the bureau and the departments. It might be argued that this is a duplication of resources that could contribute to slower decision-making. The merger of the Education Bureau with the Education Department in 2003 and the Environment Bureau with its department in 2005 was predicated on the belief that the bureaus and departments had overlapping responsibilities.[24] Proponents of separating bureaus and departments, which includes many administrative officers, argue to the contrary that links between bureaus improve coordination and the quality of policymaking. The structure may also lead to tension between the generalists in the bureaus and the specialists in the departments. Departmental officers complain that administrative officers have too little experience in their areas to make sensible proposals and that they are sometimes parachuted into senior departmental positions, adversely affecting their promotion prospects.

Hierarchy: Grades and Ranks

New appointees to the civil service join one of its hundreds of grades. There are two types of grade. Generalist grades, the administrative, executive, and clerical grades, are found throughout the civil service and are managed by the Civil Service Bureau. Specialist grades, such as engineers, accountants, and architects, are mainly located in one or a limited number of departments. Grades are subject to change and mergers, depending on the recommendations of the Civil Service Bureau and the Establishment Subcommittee of the Legislative Council's Finance Committee. Their comparability for pay determination purposes is decided by the Standing Committee on Civil Service Salaries and Conditions of Service.

Grades are subdivided into ranks and new appointees are usually assigned to the lowest rank within the grade. In the Police Force, for example, there are 15 ranks ranging from a single Commissioner of Police at the head of the organisation to constables at the bottom.[25] Depending on qualifications, new recruits may join at the rank of inspector or the rank of constable.[26] A host of other grades also work in the Police Force. There are both police departmental grades, such as translators, interviewers, and traffic wardens and civilian grades, which include administrative officers, executive officers, typists, treasury accountants, clinical psychologists, and many others. The Police Force is one of eight disciplined services falling under the Security Bureau. As a disciplined service, hierarchy is particularly important in issuing orders and ensuring compliance. In such departments, there are more ranks to supervise and monitor the performance of junior officers.

In other grades, collegiality may be a more important quality than compliance with orders. In the administrative grade, for example, there are seven ranks (see Table 4.4) and in the Department of Justice, only three. The function performed by the grade changes the shape of the hierarchy. In the disciplinary services, most

---

24. Education and Manpower Bureau (2002). *Legislative Council brief on the merger of the Education and Manpower Bureau with the Education Department and Education Commission with the Board of Education*, EMBCR 6/2/3321/90 Pt.3 (p.2). https://www.legco.gov.hk/yr02-03/english/bills/brief/b24_brf.pdf
25. Hong Kong Police Force (2021, 31 March). Organization structure: Organization chart of HKPF. https://www.police.gov.hk/ppp_en/01_about_us/os_chart.html
26. Hong Kong Police Force (2020). Recruitment. https://www.police.gov.hk/ppp_en/15_recruit/er.html

Table 4.4 *Administrative Officers: Grade Structure and Establishment 2021*

Rank	No. of Posts
Administrative Officer Staff Grade A1 (D8)	20
Administrative Officer Staff Grade A (D6)	15
Administrative Officer Staff Grade B1 (D4)	29
Administrative Officer Staff Grade B (D3)	64
Administrative Officer Staff Grade C (D2)	219
Senior Administrative Officer	233
Administrative Officer	168
Total	748

Source: Civil Service Bureau (2021). Administrative Officer grade. https://www.csb.gov.hk/english/grade/ao/751.html.

officers are in the junior ranks and the organisational structure is a sharp pyramid that aids the rapid communication of orders down the line of command. In the administrative grade, there is a more even spread of staff within the ranks, reflecting collegiality and potential for flexibility in postings across the civil service.

Most grades are departmental grades. Civil servants in those grades will spend their working careers within the department and are not usually transferred to other departments although they may be seconded to deal with particular situations. The efficient working of the administrative system depends on the knowledge acquired by these civil servants in dealing with the same kinds of problem over long periods of service. The hierarchical structure of the civil service promotes efficiency, ensuring that orders issued at the top are carried out by more junior staff. But there are disadvantages. Many departments do not usually encourage upward communication of information from lower levels of the organisation. The consequences are twofold: senior officers may become overloaded with minor matters requiring decisions or problems may exist for some time before senior officers become aware of them. If senior civil servants are content with the status quo, departments can become moribund and unable to deal with new problems or to seize new opportunities.

Administrative and executive grade officers are usually posted to new positions every two to three years. The rationale for this practice is to provide experience in different aspects of administration across the civil service. But the practice is also important because the officers are expected to have a broader service-wide perspective and knowledge of central government requirements to help promote horizontal coordination. Administrative officers are the conduits through which information on policy passes from the centre to the departments and back from the departments, through the administrative officers, to the centre. Executive officers, for whom there was an establishment of about 3,800 in March 2021, perform similar important tasks in ensuring that the personnel practices devised by the Civil Service Bureau and laws with which the departments must comply, such as the *Protection of*

Data Ordinance, are observed.[27] Without the role played by these generalist grades, the system would be much more disjointed and departments would be much more autonomous and uncoordinated. A top-down, centralised, hierarchical system in an organisation as large as the Hong Kong civil service needs adequate channels of communication to avoid the emergence of administrative practices contrary to the intentions of the centre.

The Administrative Grade

The administrative grade has traditionally been the key policymaking grade within the civil service although its dominance has been increasingly challenged by political appointees and structural changes such as the POAS, by technocrats in specialist departments whose promotion prospects may be adversely affected by appointments from the grade, and by the Chinese government's growing influence on policy. In March 2021, the administrative grade had an establishment of 746 (see Table 4.4), a slight increase over the previous year, but the strength of the grade was only 680.[28] The numbers in post were adversely affected by a wastage rate of 5.2%, mainly retirements and resignations, and a freeze on civil service recruitment.[29] At the directorate level, the highest-ranking and best-paid posts in the civil service, administrative officers held 317 positions.[30] However, the directorate itself has also declined in numbers in post, from an establishment of over 1,500 to a strength of about 1,400.[31] The proportion of administrative officers to directorate-level positions is around the historical average of 19%[32] and administrative officers are still heavily represented in the bureaus. Of the 18 permanent secretaries in the 13 bureaus in 2020, all but one were administrative officers.[33] In 2020, 22 administrative officers were heads of 64 listed government departments, divisions, units, and commissions,[34] a drop from 29 in 2008.[35] Administrative officers usually serve as permanent secretaries in generalist departments, such as Home Affairs and Leisure and Cultural Services, while specialists head technical departments, such as Highways and the Water Supplies Department. Many administrative officers serve

---

27. Civil Service Bureau (2020). Executive officers. https://www.csb.gov.hk/english/grade/eo/431.html
28. Legislative Council Panel on Public Service (2021, 17 May). Minutes of meeting (p. 8). LC Paper No. CB(4)1340/20-21.
29. Ibid.
30. Ibid.
31. Legislative Council Panel on Public Service (2021, 17 May). *An overview of the civil service: establishment, strength, retirement, age profile and gender profile* (p. 2). LC Paper No. CB(4) 986/20-21(03).
32. Burns, J. P. (2004) op. cit., p. 110.
33. Hong Kong Government (2020). Name list of permanent secretaries and heads of government departments. https://www.gov.hk/en/about/govdirectory/pshd.htm
34. Calculated from ibid. and appointment information provided in government press releases. Information on the career service of three officers was not available.
35. Personal communication, Civil Service Bureau, 17 July 2008.

in directorate-level management positions in the departments below the level of head.

The Colonial Period

For much of the colonial period, the administrative grade was an entirely male, expatriate elite usually recruited from among graduates with good degrees from British universities.[36] No Chinese were recruited to the grade until 1948 and localisation was very slow; even by 1968, there were still only 14 Chinese administrative officers.[37] Women were not admitted until 1959 and only then after a fierce debate among the senior officials. By 1997, the grade had expanded to around 500 officers of whom nearly 50% were female. Local officers made up well over 90% of the grade and expatriate recruitment had ceased. New recruits were expected to be intelligent, innovative, concerned with the welfare of the community, and fluent in Cantonese, English, and Putonghua. Salaries were generous and promotion was usually rapid.

Despite the localisation of the grade, its ethos and public esteem remained largely unchanged during the colonial period. Administrative officers were respected for their high levels of integrity, for their meritocratic selection in a highly competitive process, and for their ability to resolve problems. When decisions were made by this closed elite and implemented authoritatively by the departments, the grade had great power and influence within the structure of government. By the 1990s, however, the political environment began to change. The administrative grade slowly retreated from its position of unquestioned pre-eminence and morale within the grade began to decline.[38] The directly elected members of the Legislative Council were more critical of government policies than were their appointed predecessors; the Chinese government was suspicious of an elite that was seen to be working for the British government; some high-profile local Chinese officers, who had been identified with the policies of the last British Governor, left the service for statutory bodies or the private sector; and Articles 61 and 101 of the Basic Law prevented expatriates from holding the most senior positions. By 1997, power remained in the hands of the administrative grade. But their dominance was no longer unquestioned: their political masters sought to exert greater control over the way the civil service worked and how policies were formulated and implemented.

---

36. For a detailed analysis of the composition of the grade, see Burns (2004) op. cit., Ch. 4. For a history of the grade, see . Tsang, S. Y. S. (2007). *Governing Hong Kong: Administrative officers from the nineteenth century to the handover to China, 1862–1997*. London: IB Taurus. See also Coates, A. (1975). *Myself a mandarin*. Hong Kong: Heinemann Educational Books; Hayes (1996) op. cit.; Bray, D. (2001). *Hong Kong metamorphosis*. Hong Kong: Hong Kong University Press; Ho, E. P. (2005). *Times of change: A memoir of Hong Kong's governance 1950–1991*. Hong Kong: Hong Kong University Press.
37. Miners, N. J. (1977). *The government and politics of Hong Kong* (2nd ed., p. 90). Hong Kong: Oxford University Press.
38. Hase (2001) op. cit.

The Administrative Grade after 1997

Until 2002, all but one of the policy secretaries were administrative officers. After the introduction of the POAS in 2002 (see pp. 78–91), the grade's influence on policymaking was reduced. Some administrative officers left the grade to become politically appointed directors of bureaus with responsibility for policy. Within the grade, promotion prospects were adversely affected by Tung's cuts to the directorate-level establishment and the morale of administrative officers declined further.[39] However, in 2005, Tsang (himself a former administrative officer) increased recruitment at the directorate level and restored the diminished powers of the Chief Secretary for Administration and the Financial Secretary.[40]

After the handover, the new regime had three choices on how it would exercise power. The first was to seek democratic legitimation and to move towards the universal suffrage promised in the Basic Law, a course of action to which the Tung administration and the Chinese government were adamantly opposed. A second option was continued rule by the senior civil service. Before the handover, the Chinese government gave assurances that the civil service would function much as it had done in the past and the Basic Law provided that conditions of service would remain unchanged. In 1997, the Chief Secretary, the Financial Secretary, and the serving policy secretaries, who were administrative grade officers, were all reappointed as principal officials; only the newly created position of Secretary for Justice went to an outsider.

The third option, which emerged as Tung's and the Chinese government's preferred choice, was to exert more political control over the civil service. Despite the assurances of the Chinese government that the system of governance would continue after 1997, there was an undercurrent of opposition to the continuing pre-eminence and power of senior members of the administrative grade. Members of Tung's appointed Executive Council, pro-China united front groups and some entrepreneurs were amongst those who saw the civil service as an obstruction to the implementation of policy goals and as a relic of colonial rule and privilege. There was friction between senior civil servants and the Executive Council, some councillors seeking to reverse proposals even after they had been carefully vetted in the civil service.

The Chinese government was equally suspicious of the administrative grade. Anson Chan On-sang, the Chief Secretary for Administration, for example, was personally warned by the Chinese leadership to support the Chief Executive.[41] In 2002, Qian Qichen, the Vice-Premier, reportedly said that the Chinese government questioned the loyalty of senior civil servants who had been appointed by

---

39. Yeung, C. (2002, 26 August). Reality check for civil service elite. *SCMP*.
40. Civil Service Bureau (2005, November). Note for Establishment Sub-Committee of the Finance Committee. ECI (2005–2006). https://www.legco.gov.hk/yr05-06/english/fc/esc/papers/ei05-08e.pdf
41. Hon, S.M. (2000, 27 September). Support Tung, Qian tells Anson. *SCMP* (2000, 27 September). Anson's reprimand. Editorial.

the colonial administration.[42] At the fifth anniversary of the handover, the Chinese President, Jiang Zemin, in a comment taken to be an attack on senior government officials' commitment to Tung's policies, said:

> Civil servants at all levels, especially ranking officials, should conscientiously submit to and support the leadership of the chief executive, work with one heart and strive to achieve fresh success.[43]

All this came with a barrage of hostile criticism for the policy failures of the post-1997 government. Rather than the rational, far-sighted, competent officials, who were held in high public esteem at the handover, civil servants, and particularly the administrative grade, were now portrayed as overpaid, underachieving spendthrifts who, rather than the Chief Executive, were responsible for the decline of Hong Kong. Indeed, seemingly so intense was the feeling against civil servants that the Chief Executive himself felt compelled to note that civil servants were not responsible for Hong Kong's growing fiscal deficit.[44]

Initially, the centralising measures taken by the post-handover administration—the abolition of the municipal councils and some civil service personnel reforms—did not affect the continuing dominance of the administrative grade. Once the POAS was implemented in 2002, however, there were significant implications for administrative officers. The scheme created political support for the Chief Executive at the director of bureau level because the new appointees were dependent on him for their continuation in office. In the process, the positions of Chief Secretary for Administration and the Financial Secretary were downgraded to that of directors of bureaus. Vetos on policy proposals rested with the Chief Executive without the same degree of filtering which the Chief Secretary for Administration and the Financial Secretary had undertaken in the past. The glue that held the system together and enabled a centralised governmental structure to work effectively had been removed.

After the introduction of the POAS, the administrative grade atrophied in the face of challenges that affected their promotion opportunities, conflicted with their beliefs about how government should be run, and raised the possibility of disputes with political appointees. Administrative officers still held a large proportion of directorate-level positions, but their influence on policy was declining. By 2018–2019, the annual wastage rate of administrative officers had reached 4.1% and, since many were leaving for non-retirement reasons, this caused "concern over talent retention".[45] For the public as well, the position lost some of its previous

---

42. Lague, D. (2002, 25 July). Standing up to the boss. *Far Eastern Economic Review*, 22–23.
43. Ibid., 23.
44. Tung, C. H. (2003). *Capitalising on our advantages, revitalising our economy* (p. 22). Hong Kong: Printing Department.
45. Legislative Council Secretariat Research Office (2019). Recruitment and turnover of civil servants (p. 2). https://www.legco.gov.hk/research-publications/english/1920issh10-recruitment-and-turnover-of-civil-servants-20191111-e.pdf

lustre. Applications for the position of administrative officer, which was once the prized job for every fresh graduate, declined sharply although there were still 15,000 applicants for 48 positions in 2018/2019.[46] The figures should be seen in the context of a civil service in which resignations were rising and vacancies were proving more difficult to fill.[47]

The key problem facing the administrative grade is that it stands for rational impartial administration by generalists within a civil service that is increasingly technocratic and politicised. Specialists have long felt that the dominant role of generalists has outlived its usefulness. In November 2003, for example, the Chairman of the Hong Kong Senior Government Officers Association, Peter Chan Pak-fong, an engineer, reportedly said that the generalist approach inherited from the colonial era no longer suited the needs of a knowledge-based society and that lay people should not be allowed to lead experts.[48] The increasing percentage of recruits holding specialist qualifications and the percentage of administrative officers holding the highest positions has created an imbalance between generalists and specialists. By April 2020, there were suggestions that the Chief Executive's removal of two directors of bureaus and the transfer of a third, in the context of continuing hostility from the Chinese government towards the grade, may mark its demise.[49] In the same month, the former Director of Immigration replaced a former administrative officer as Secretary for Constitutional and Administrative Affairs. In June 2021, the retiring Chief Secretary for Administration, a position traditionally held by an administrative officer, was replaced by a former Deputy Commissioner of Police and Security of Security, John Lee Ka-chiu. His position as Security of Security was then assumed by the Police Commissioner. If this represents the decline of the administrative grade, then there will be a power vacuum that does not bode well for the stability of the civil service.

Political Neutrality

Successive administrations have been faced with the problem that the values inculcated into administrative officers have not been seen to be appropriate for achieving the objectives of the post-1997 regime. At the heart of the clash between the values of the old system and those of the new political elite is the concept of political neutrality. Under colonialism, drawing on British practice, political neutrality was taken to mean impartiality in decision-making in the best public interest. Since administrative officers were themselves exercising power under colonial rule, the

---

46. Ibid.
47. Ibid.
48. Cheung, J. (2003, 3 November). Colonial civil service system attacked. *SCMP*.
49. Burns, J. (2020). Restoring impartiality: Are Hong Kong's administrative officers on the way out? *HKFP*. https://hongkongfp.com/2020/04/26/restoring-impartiality-are-hong-kongs-administrative-officers-on-the-way-out/

concept did not carry with it the same notion of impartial policy advice to a political executive. After 1997, the Hong Kong application of the concept was slightly reinterpreted to bring it closer to its original meaning. Political neutrality meant the right of senior civil servants "to speak truth to power", to advise the political decision-makers on appropriate courses of action and then to implement to the best of their ability whatever was decided.

In her valedictory address in 2001, the outgoing Chief Secretary, Anson Chan, defended this conception of political neutrality:

> [Civil servants] know they can tender advice without fear or favour, safe in the knowledge that even the most unwelcome advice would not lead to blighted career prospects or unpleasant postings out of earshot of those who may not like what you have to say . . . I believe passionately in the notion of a politically neutral civil service.[50]

Increasingly, political neutrality was supplanted by the expectation that civil servants should, above all, be loyal to the government and unquestioningly obedient to political appointees, a requirement that did not sit well with many Hong Kong civil servants. A Chinese State Councillor reportedly said that political neutrality was an outdated British idea in the context of another councillor's remark that civil servants should be patriotic and uphold the Basic Law.[51] In 2009, the government promulgated the *Civil Service Code*, which states that political neutrality means:

> Civil servants shall serve the Chief Executive and the Government of the day with total loyalty and to the best of their ability, no matter what their political beliefs are.[52]

There was acknowledgement that implementation should be impartial, fair, just, and equitable, but no mention was made of policy advice.[53]

During the 2019 protests, the government's failure to address the protesters' demands and to take action to control the Police Force heightened tensions within the civil service. In July 2019, 100 administrative grade officers submitted a petition to the Chief Executive calling on her to appoint an independent inquiry into the unrest.[54] The next month saw many thousands of civil servants take to the streets, demanding that the Extradition Bill be withdrawn.[55] A subsequent petition, signed

---

50. Chan, A. (2001, 19 April), op. cit.; see also Chan, A. (2002, 1 July). Beware of blurring the dividing line. *Financial Times*.
51. Cheung, J. (2003, 17 October). Civil service neutrality is a British thing: State leader. *SCMP*.
52. Civil Service Bureau (2009). *Civil Service Code* (para 3.7), op. cit.
53. Ibid., para 3.6.
54. Lum, A., Ting, V., & Cheung, E. (2019, 26 July). One in seven of Hong Kong's elite civil servants call on Carrie Lam to hold independent inquiry into extradition bill unrest but police remain firmly opposed. *SCMP*. https://www.scmp.com/news/hong-kong/politics/article/3020206/one-seven-hong-kongs-elite-civil-servants-call-carrie-lam
55. Chung, K., Su, X., & Lum, A. (2019, 3 August). Hong Kong civil servants embarrass the government with protest against extradition bill and determination to "stand together with citizens". *SCMP*.

by 350 civil servants, warned of a strike and said that the petitioners were "absolutely disgusted" at the use of force.[56] The government responded by warning demonstrators that they were violating the provisions of the *Civil Service Code* on political neutrality and that they could be disciplined for their actions.[57] In 2020, during the COVID-19 crisis, 5,000 public health workers staged a week-long strike against the government for its failure to close all the borders with mainland China.[58]

Evidence of dissent within the civil service alarmed the Hong Kong and Chinese governments. After the national security legislation was passed by the NPC, the Civil Service Bureau proposed that all new appointees to the civil service after 1 July 2020 should sign an oath of allegiance to the HKSAR and pledge to uphold the Basic Law, subsequently extending this to all civil servants, accompanied with the penalty that, if they did not sign, they would lose their jobs (see p. 28). It was not clear what this was intended to achieve that was not already in the *Civil Service Code*, but the bureau thought that it would give civil servants a "clearer awareness of [their] responsibilities and requirements".[59] What has been lost from the original concept of political neutrality is the notion that civil servants have a responsibility to act in the best public interest and that, in providing policy advice, they should speak truth to power. Political neutrality is now defined as loyalty to the political executive. While the value of impartiality has been retained, it does not override the heavy stress on obedience to political orders.

Problems with the Post-handover Structure of Government

A major structural problem that has faced the government is that the system is highly centralised, leading to the overloading of senior personnel, lines of command that are not always clear and bureaus and departments that often act in uncoordinated and autonomous ways. In any public administration system, it is difficult to find the appropriate balance between the degree of centralisation and control and the ability to deal effectively with the many issues that require decisions. One aim of the POAS was to centralise the government to an even greater extent than under colonialism. By reducing the number of directors of bureaus, Tung created a situation in which they were overloaded and where matters requiring decision might in practice either still revert to senior civil servants or would not be dealt with expeditiously. One of

---

56. Lum, A. (2019, 15 August). "Disgusted" Hong Kong civil servants warn of strike in second petition to government over handling of protests. *SCMP*.
57. Hong Kong Government (2019, 3 August). Civil service neutrality restated. https://www.news.gov.hk/eng/2019/08/20190803/20190803_205232_873.html
58. Wong, J., Chen, L. Y., & Kwan, S. (2020, 4 February). Hong Kong's striking health workers pose new threat to Beijing. *Bloomberg*. https://www.bloomberg.com/news/articles/2020-02-03/hong-kong-s-striking-hospital-workers-pose-new-threat-to-beijing
59. Legislative Council Panel on Public Service (2020, 10 July). *Progress of the study on oath-taking by civil servants and political neutrality of civil servants*. https://www.legco.gov.hk/yr19-20/english/panels/ps/papers/ps20200710cb4-797-1-e.pdf

the defences offered by the Secretary for Financial Services and the Treasury in the Penny Stocks incident, for example, was that the "papers and files in my office were piling up like a mountain and I could not possibly have read every document".[60] Overloading continues to be a problem despite the substantial increase in the establishment of the civil service over the past decade.

Under Tung, the reduction in civil service numbers and pay was compensated, to some extent, by outsourcing services and by the prospect that public bodies and other agencies might be used to deliver goods and services. The Home Affairs Department conducted an enquiry in 2002 to examine the role and functions of statutory bodies, recommending that they should be de-layered and restructured to avoid duplication and that principal officials should be "ultimately accountable for the statutory bodies under their purview".[61] In 2004, Tung outlined his vision of "partnership" between the government and the statutory bodies although, in practice, the government wanted to exert greater control over them.[62] Scandals and friction with statutory bodies, concerning cost overruns, salaries of employees, performance, and appointments, probably shaped that view.[63] Neither Tung nor his successors were convinced that more decentralisation was desirable, especially since the public bodies provoked much critical comment in the Legislative Council, from the Director of Audit, and the media.[64]

The government's lines of command and control over public bodies did not noticeably improve under the Tsang, Leung, and Lam administrations. Painter and Yee found that heads of agencies thought they had a good deal of policy autonomy and concluded that this was not because they were seeking to avoid government control but rather because they had to fill "gaps in the power structure where the political leaders have chosen to vacate the field and to surrender policy roles".[65] The most likely reason for this was that directors of bureaus were overloaded and had too many other pressing issues to take on the statutory bodies and agencies. Politically, the pan-democrats in the Legislative Council, as C. Y. Leung discovered when he tried to create a new bureau, created problems for the government when it attempted to make structural changes. Public bodies and agencies, but also government departments, were often left to follow their own long-established, but often outdated, procedures.

---

60. Quoted in Kotewall, R. G., & Kwong, G. C. K. (2002). *Report of the panel of inquiry on the penny stocks incident* (p. 109). Hong Kong: Printing Department.
61. Home Affairs Bureau (2003). *Review of the role and functions of public sector advisory and statutory bodies* (p. 6). Hong Kong: The Bureau.
62. Tung, C. H. (2004). *Seizing opportunities for development, promoting people-based governance* (para 67). Hong Kong: Government Logistics Department. https://www.policyaddress.gov.hk/pa04/eng/pdf/speech.pdf
63. Scott, I. (2006). The government and statutory bodies in Hong Kong: Centralization and autonomy. *Public Organization Review, 6*, 185–202.
64. Hansard, 12 December 2001, 2449–2525; Director of Audit (2004). *Report No. 42*, Chapter 4. Shamdasani, R., & Lee, S. (2003, 31 October). EOC chief faces "gifts" enquiry. *SCMP*.
65. Painter, M., & Yee, W. H. (2012). Agencies and policy in an administrative state: The case of Hong Kong. *Policy and Society, 31*(3), 223–235.

In strongly hierarchical administrative systems, such as Hong Kong, there are often problems with horizontal coordination between departments.[66] Hierarchies tend to maximise vertical coordination within the departments, but many policies cut across departmental lines, requiring collaboration and cooperation in implementing policies. Painter and Yee's finding that public bodies were not averse to following directions if the centre provided them probably applies equally to departments. If there is strong political direction, then departments will follow orders, but left to their own devices they give priority to departmental interests. Policy implementation may fall through the cracks, leaving services poorly delivered or entirely neglected. The Ombudsman, for example, found lack of horizontal coordination was a major cause of such problems as dealing with water seepage,[67] identifying and reporting child abuse cases,[68] and the attempt to set up a one-stop shop for handling all departmental complaints and enquiries.[69]

Why does the Hong Kong government not do more to resolve the problem of horizontal coordination? The fundamental reasons are structural, derived from the politics/administration dichotomy bequeathed to the government in the 1973 McKinsey reforms.[70] In the Hong Kong context, put simply, the politics/administration dichotomy means that formally, although not in practice, bureaus make policy and departments implement it. This separation of responsibilities works against horizontal coordination. The director of a bureau has many political and policy issues to consider. Unless the matter assumes political dimensions, there is no time or reason to intervene in the implementation of collaborative policies between departments.

If a department can deliver a policy itself without relying on input from other departments, implementation may proceed smoothly. But when more than one department is involved in implementation, a host of factors come into play. If the political direction is precise and clearly a priority of the centre, it may be implemented according to plan. If it is not—and very often on medium-range issues it is not—there is a policy vacuum. Department heads may not regard the matter as important as deploying personnel to implement departmental objectives. Other issues may also impede implementation. Departmental officers charged with implementing collaborative projects with other departments or private sector organisations may be very wary of cost overruns, especially if costs have not been clearly

---

66. Scott, I. (2020). Governing by silos. In B. G. Peters & I. Thynne (Eds.), *The Oxford research handbook of public administration*. Oxford: Oxford University Press. https://oxfordre.com/politics/view/10.1093/acrefore/9780190228637.001.0001/acrefore-9780190228637-e-1414
67. Office of the Ombudsman (2008, 10 April). *Direct investigation of handling of water seepage complaints by the Food and Environmental Hygiene Department, Buildings Department and Water Supplies Department*. https://ofomb.ombudsman.hk/abc/files/ombe_4_0708.pdf
68. Office of the Ombudsman (2019). Mechanism for identifying and reporting suspected child abuse cases. https://ofomb.ombudsman.hk/abc/en-us/direct_investigations
69. Office of the Ombudsman (2008b). *Direct investigation report: Effectiveness of the Integrated Call Centre in handling complaints*. https://ofomb.ombudsman.hk/abc/files/6-2008-1.pdf
70. McKinsey and Company (May 1973) op. cit.

determined initially. In other cases, they may feel that the collaborative policy is not a departmental priority.

Two other factors have caused the policy vacuum at the departmental level to grow. First, the decline in the political role of administrative officers has meant less coordination between departments on policy implementation. Political appointments were intended to take over the "political work" of administrative officers in the bureaus.[71] But the political appointees have no brief to work on departmental coordination or to deal with line management and so the problem of horizontal coordination between departments has increased. A second related factor is that, in the maelstrom of politics and widespread opposition to the government in post-handover Hong Kong, senior civil servants have been inclined, understandably, to keep their heads beneath the parapet. Their predisposition has been to recommend safe, incremental policy choices within the self-contained confines of departmental competence rather than potentially more contentious initiatives requiring horizontal coordination. The exceptions have come when external pressures, from the Chinese government or deteriorating economic conditions, have left little option but to pursue more controversial options (see Chapters 9 and 10).

The broader question is whether the Hong Kong government needs such a centralised system. Faced with political unrest, the government's reaction seems to have been to centralise decision-making even more, which has increased the overload on directors of bureaus and senior civil servants. Decentralisation was not seen as an option and divesting government functions by outsourcing provoked criticism from unions and Legislative Councillors. An alternative strategy would have been to create more bureaus and decrease the span of control of the directors of bureaus, but Legislative Councillors might well have opposed such changes on grounds of cost and there would have been opposition at that time from the democrats. The structural options available to the government are constrained by the Chinese government's preferences and by public reaction in Hong Kong; the government has been able to do little more than increase the size of the establishment. More centralisation has been a response to continuing political unrest and low trust in government, but it does not resolve problems of service delivery or the lack of community participation in decision-making.

The Functions of Government

Small government has been a basic principle of governance in Hong Kong and still serves as a point of reference although commitment to the idea has declined since 2013. It has at least three closely related meanings: limiting the functions of government and ensuring that the government is fiscally frugal and cost-effective; limiting

---

71. Constitutional Affairs Bureau (2006). *Consultation document on further development of the political appointments system* (pp. 5–7). https://www.legco.gov.hk/yr05-06/english/panels/ca/papers/ca0731cb2-consultation-e.pdf

the size and cost of the civil service; and enabling the private sector to deliver services that might otherwise have to be provided by government. While each of these elements was an article of faith under colonial administration, after the Leung administration took office small government was occasionally mentioned approvingly[72] but was subject to government intervention to correct market failures.[73]

Limiting the Functions of Government

The original functions of the colonial government—the maintenance of law and order, the administration of justice, public works, port administration, and the prevention and control of epidemics and relief from the effects of natural disasters—remained the main tasks undertaken by the civil service for well over a century. The prevailing belief was that government should only undertake those functions that were absolutely necessary and that its main role was to regulate the society in ways that would encourage the economy to prosper. So entrenched was this view that, even after it had begun to provide public housing and some social services and was no longer a small government, it was still regarded as a model for capitalist systems.

Limiting the functions of government was closely related to the belief in the need for fiscal frugality and a balanced budget. The colonial government did not want, and could not afford, to fund major social policies which were provided instead by the churches, Chinese traditional organisations, and voluntary agencies.[74] The government did not become actively involved in social service provision until after the Second World War.

"Value for money" became a central plank in the government's financial practices. As the colony prospered, the government began to accumulate large reserves and the Financial Secretary was usually able to budget for a surplus. In only five of the 50 years before 1997 did the government experience a budgetary deficit.[75] The Financial Secretary exercised tight control over expenditure and new proposals were vetted very carefully even for relatively minor items.[76] In February 1989, when it was clear that the system was too centralised, the branch produced its own proposals for reform, which included a redefinition of its role. It stated its difficulties very clearly:

---

72. Hong Kong Government (2014, 7 October). *Government welcomes Fraser Institute ranking HK first in economic freedom again* [Press release]. https://www.info.gov.hk/gia/general/201410/07/P201410070840.htm
73. Leung, C. Y. (2013) op. cit.
74. Lethbridge, H. J. (1978). *Hong Kong: Stability and change*. Hong Kong: Oxford University Press; Sinn, E. (1989). *Power and charity: The early history of the Tung Wah Hospital, Hong Kong*. Hong Kong: Oxford University Press.
75. Jao, Y. C. (2001). *The Asian financial crisis and the ordeal of Hong Kong*. Westport, CT: Quorum Books.
76. McKinsey and Company (May 1973) op. cit.

> Traditionally, financial control has been highly centralised . . . This incremental approach is fundamentally limiting. Attention is focused on new services, and seldom on a re-appraisal of the need for current activities.[77]

In the future, the Finance Branch was to be responsible for "global totals and controlling the overall allocation of resources to Policy Secretaries".[78] Some within the Finance Branch continued to favour centralised control.

The functions of the colonial government gradually began to expand in the 1950s when the influx of refugees from China caused the population to increase fourfold in the space of a few years, putting pressure on the housing supply and stretching other facilities. A Department of Labour and a Social Welfare Department were created although not with the aim of providing unemployment support as of right but with the intention of reintegrating the recipient into the workforce as quickly as possible.[79] The public housing programme was based on similar logic. It became policy not because the government was moved by the plight of homeless squatters but because it believed that freeing up land would be good for the economy.[80] Social policies were introduced either because they served economic ends or because there were fears that if nothing was done the Communist Party might exploit the situation.

By the 1960s, this approach was insufficient to deal with the social problems of a much larger population. The commission which investigated the 1966 riots found serious problems with the labour laws and a "gap" between government and the people.[81] The riots and further disturbances in 1967, which resulted from the Cultural Revolution, were not immediately reflected in new social policies, aside from reforms to the labour laws. By the 1970s, however, following the government's commitment to much greater provision of housing, education, health, and social welfare, the functions of government expanded and the size of the civil service increased rapidly. Between 1972 and 1982, the establishment grew from 94,816 to 168,298, an increase of over 56%.[82]

In the transitional period between 1984 and 1997, there were political and structural considerations that made it difficult to reduce the functions of government or the size of the civil service. The commitment to funding social policies created expectations that the new services would continue to be provided. There was no financial pressure to cut those services or the size of the civil service because the economy was strong and the budget was in surplus. Moreover, the British and

---

77. Finance Branch (1989). *Public sector reform* (p. 3). Hong Kong: The Branch.
78. Ibid.
79. Hong Kong Government (1949). *Report of the Hong Kong Salaries Commission 1947* (p. 33). Hong Kong: Government Printer.
80. Hong Kong Government (1955). *Annual report by the Commissioner for Resettlement for the financial year 1954–55* (pp. 44–45). Hong Kong: Government Printer.
81. Commission of Inquiry (1967). *Kowloon disturbances 1966: Report of the commission of inquiry* (p. 127). Hong Kong: Government Printer.
82. Civil Service Branch (1982). *Civil service personnel statistics* (p. 1). Hong Kong: The Branch.

Chinese governments were agreed on the need to keep the civil service stable in the potentially volatile years before the handover. Rather than devolving functions or reducing the size of the civil service, the government tried to avoid controversy and focused instead on maintaining the status quo. It created more statutory bodies, some of which were intended to alleviate fears about the handover. Public expenditure increased, notably welfare spending, although not all of its new programmes, such as small class teaching and civil service reform, were immediately implemented.

In 1995, the government issued a document, "Serving the Community", which formally remains the rationale for the system of government. "Living within its means" was identified as one of the key principles.[83] It was defined as how much government could afford to spend and how to set priorities to meet community needs within that limit. In the narrow sense, this meant that expenditure should not exceed revenue, a principle which was embodied in the Basic Law but was of little concern to a government that continued to enjoy large surpluses. Consequently, Hong Kong arrived at the handover with anything but a small government. In 1997, the civil service had a strength of 189,136.[84] Much of the substantial public sector outside the civil service was also largely funded by the government. Government pervaded the lives of the citizens. Yet the value and commitment to small government and to the belief that it was the appropriate form for a capitalist system remained unimpaired. By 1997, the government knew that it should slim down but was not ready to do so; recruitment to the civil service again began to rise. Increased public expenditure was implicitly justified by the need to maintain political stability and blur the consequences of change.

The Size and Cost of the Civil Service

The post-handover government was initially as expansionary as its colonial predecessor. Major initiatives were announced in Tung's first policy address, including new programmes in education, housing, and infrastructure.[85] There was no mention of cost-cutting in the civil service; the focus instead was to be target-based management and achieving results.[86] Thereafter, the effects of the Asian financial crisis, a further downturn, and the economic consequences of the SARS epidemic resulted in six consecutive years of budgetary deficits. As unemployment rose, there was political and business pressure on the civil service to reduce its costs and to return to the principle of small government.

The government took three measures to attempt to reduce costs: to downsize the civil service, to cut civil service salaries, and to introduce an Enhanced

---
83. Hong Kong Government (1995). *Serving the community* (p. 29). Hong Kong: Government Printer.
84. Civil Service Bureau (1997). *Civil service personnel statistics 1997* (p. 12). Hong Kong: The Bureau.
85. Tung, C. H. (1997) op. cit., pp. 16–23.
86. Ibid., p. 51.

Productivity Programme and an Efficiency Savings Exercise scheme to cut expenditure. The government's objective was to reduce the size of the civil service to 160,000 by 2006–2007 without compulsory redundancies.[87] The establishment of the civil service then stood at 174,116, which was already substantially down as a result of a freeze on recruitment and a voluntary retirement scheme that had targeted 59 grades with surplus staff. A second voluntary retirement scheme, with less generous conditions but covering 200 grades, was introduced in 2003. At that time, the government did not expect to balance its budget before 2008 and saw the task of cutting the size and salaries of the civil service as essential. The effect of the voluntary redundancy schemes, coupled with the deletion of posts through other cost-savings schemes, outsourcing, and privatisation, reduced the size of the civil service by about 19% from its peak in the 1990s.[88] By April 2007, the economy had recovered and the freeze on recruitment was lifted.

Although the government's efforts in reducing costs and the size of the civil service were applauded by business and some legislators, the decline in numbers was not quite as impressive as the raw figures suggested. In 1999, the government introduced a non-civil service contract (NCSC) scheme to enable departments to continue to provide services that would be affected by downsizing.[89] The contracts, mainly for lower-level positions, were usually for three years at salaries no greater than equivalent positions in the civil service and with inferior conditions of service.[90] By 2006, NCSC staff, who were not included in the government numbers for the civil service, amounted to more than 16,000 or over 10% of the civil service.[91] NCSC staff were not supposed to take on the work of civil servants, but a review discovered that over 4,000 of them were doing so. The government then acknowledged that the staff were being inappropriately employed and undertook to phase out the positions or to create new ones in the civil service.[92]

By 2018, the government had created 7,930 new civil service posts and NCSC staff numbers had dropped to 10,380 or about 5.5% of the civil service.[93] However, their employment has remained a politically sensitive issue with the unions and has been a regular item on the agenda of the Legislative Council's panel on public service. The concerns about NCSC employment relate principally to conditions of service, including comparability with staff employed on outsourced contracts, the

---

87. Ibid., p. 22.
88. Legislative Council Panel on Public Service (2008, 16 June). *General overview of the civil service strength, retirement and resignation*, LC Paper CB (1)1817/07-08(01). csb.gov.hk/english/info/files/20080610_panel_eng.pdf
89. Chan, A. K. W. (2008). *A review of the non-civil service contract scheme of the Hong Kong government* [Unpublished master's thesis]. The University of Hong Kong.
90. Legislative Council Panel on Public Service (2006). *Review of employment situation of non-civil service contract staff*, LC Paper No. CB (1)471/06-07(03) (pp. 3–4).
91. Ibid., p. 2.
92. Ibid., p. 7; Legislative Council Panel on Public Service (2007). *Employment of non-contract staff*, LC Paper No. CB (1)377/07-08(03) (p. 3).
93. Legislative Council Panel on Public Service (2018, 15 January). Non-civil service contract staff. https://www.legco.gov.hk/yr17-18/english/panels/ps/papers/ps20180115cb4-455-2-e.pdf

slow speed at which bureaus and departments have created new posts to absorb NCSC staff, and the long tenure of some NCSC staff on what were supposed to be short-term contracts.[94] The government has nonetheless remained committed to employing NCSC staff, arguing that it provides flexibility in the deployment of personnel.[95]

Apart from employing NCSC staff, which was one way for bureaus and departments to reduce the impact of the freeze on recruitment, there were some exemptions. The Police Force, for example, continued to recruit even at the height of the freeze.[96] In most departments, staff tended to be overworked and morale declined. The government's tendency to save costs by creating and extending acting appointments and by keeping the strength of the civil service at 2% to 3.5% below the establishment exacerbated the problem.[97] The freeze on recruitment also affected the demographic profile of the service with a dearth of new young recruits available to succeed to senior positions. In 2008, only 32% of the civil service was in the 20–39 age group.[98]

Despite the freeze, the cost of the civil service continued to rise. Annual increments enabled civil servants to proceed unimpeded to the top of their salary scales. For those on permanent terms, there were also generous housing, education, and pension benefits. The government tried to address the problem of growing operating costs by cutting civil service salaries. In 1999, changes to conditions of service lowered the salaries of new recruits (see pp. 150–153) but not the salaries or benefits of those already employed. Thus, although there was a fall in civil service numbers (see Table 4.5), despite the freeze on salaries and pay cuts from 2002 onwards, there was only a slight reduction in recurrent costs.[99]

As the economy worsened, the government came under strong pressure from the business lobby to bring salaries in line with those of the private sector. In February 2000, the Liberal Party chairman, James Tien Pei-chun, argued that there was a substantial gap between conditions of service in the private and public sectors and called on the government to take action. "Civil servants must choose", he said, "between high pay and job security—because taxpayers cannot afford to let them have both".[100] The government responded initially by freezing civil service salaries but later decided to take more drastic action by cutting salaries.

---

94. Legislative Council Panel on Public Service (2019, 16 December). Non-civil service contract staff. https://www.legco.gov.hk/yr19-20/english/panels/ps/papers/ps20191216cb4-177-6-e.pdf
95. Ibid.
96. Chang, L. Y. (2008). *An analysis of the impact of civil service reform on recruitment and retention in the Hong Kong Police Force* (p. 24) [Unpublished master's thesis]. The University of Hong Kong.
97. Public Service Commission (2008). *2007 Annual report* (pp. 42–45). www.psc.gov.hk; Civil Service Bureau (2008). *Civil service personnel statistics 2008* (Table 1.1). Hong Kong: Civil Service Bureau.
98. Civil Service Bureau (2008) op. cit., Figure 1.4a. https://www.psc.gov.hk/english/ann_rep/files/08rep.pdf
99. Civil Service Bureau (2003). *Civil service personnel statistics 2003* (Table 1.6). Hong Kong: Printing Department.
100. Tien, J. (2000, 29 February). Stop indulging the civil service. *SCMP*.

Table 4.5 *Establishment and Strength of the Civil Service 1997–2021*

Year	Establishment	Strength
1997	190,503	184,639
2002	179,740	173,029
2005	163,593	157,300
2007	159,401	153,805
2012	165,343	159,195
2017	175,156	167,671
2021	192,000	178,000

Sources: Civil Service Bureau (2008, 2013). Civil service personnel statistics 2008, 2013. Hong Kong: Civil Service Bureau, Table 1.1; Legislative Council Panel on Public Service (2018). *An overview of the civil service establishment, strength, retirement, resignation, age profile and gender profile* (p. 2). https://www.csb.gov.hk/english/info/files/common/Panel_paper_strength_e.pdf; Legislative Council Panel on Public Service (2021, 17 May). *An overview of the civil service: establishment, strength, retirement, age profile and gender profile* (p. 2). LC Paper No. CB(4) 986/20-21(03).

Note: With the exception of the Lam administration, the selected dates are establishment and strength figures at the beginning and end of each Chief Executive's administration. The figures for 2021 are approximate.

The government chose to legislate its proposed reductions by introducing a bill in the Legislative Council. Pay was reduced by 4.42% for the directorate and upper salary band, 1.64% for the middle salary band and 1.58% for the lower salary band. The bill was fiercely debated in the Legislative Council but was eventually narrowly approved in July 2002. The civil service associations immediately organised a demonstration; an estimated 25,000 civil servants and 113 staff associations took to the streets.[101]

Civil servants were not only annoyed that their pay had been cut but were also aggrieved that the civil service pay adjustment system was not followed and that there had been little consultation.[102] The Hong Kong Confederation of Trade Unions, whose membership included some civil service associations, argued that the "pay cuts exposes the failure of 'consultation' which can never replace collective bargaining rights".[103] Other civil servants argued that the pay cuts constituted a dispute under the 1968 agreement with civil service unions and that a commission of inquiry should have been appointed. Civil servants took four court actions over the decision, including a petition for judicial review.

When the government sought to reduce civil service pay even further in 2003, it tried a more conciliatory and consultative approach. In February 2003, the

---
101. Lee, K., & Bradford, S. (2003, 11 June). Case has not ended legal battle for redress. *SCMP*.
102. Legislative Council Panel on Public Service (2002). *Minutes of a meeting held on 23rd May*, LC Paper No. CB (1)2628/01-02. https://www.legco.gov.hk/yr01-02/english/panels/ps/minutes/ps020523.pdf
103. Hong Kong Confederation of Trade Unions (2002). No pay cuts. Collective bargaining rights now! www.hkctu.org.hk.

Secretary for the Civil Service announced that he had reached a consensus with the staff sides of the four Central Consultative Councils and representatives of the four major unions.[104] The government decided to reduce salaries for all civil servants below the third pay scale point on the directorate pay scale to dollar values at June 1997 levels. Civil service salaries cost approximately the same as they had in 2001 at $69.5 billion but, as a percentage of recurrent expenditure, they had dropped from about 36% to 27%.[105] The savings came at a high political cost. The unions were unable to exact any major concessions and morale in the civil service was already low when the pay cuts were introduced. They alienated a substantial proportion of the civil service still further and added to the growing list of the discontented.

The pay cuts and downsizing of the civil service can be seen as the last significant effort to maintain a small and cheap government. Once the economy began to improve, the civil service was again offered large pay increases based on factors that included "the state of civil service morale".[106] As Table 4.5 shows, the establishment numbers rose until, by 2021, they were back to 1997 levels. The rise was a reflection of the continuing trend to greater centralisation and less divestment of functions to the private sector. The increase may also be attributed to the changing attitudes of Chief Executives towards the functions of government. Leung Chun-ying maintained that expenditure should be kept within the limits of revenue but that government should play a more positive role in dealing with market failures.[107] Lam was even more committed to big government. In 2017, she promised that she would address large policy issues, such as public housing, welfare, and health care, that had festered under her predecessors. She proposed to expand the civil service by 3%, a figure, which the civil service associations argued, was insufficient to realise her objectives.[108]

Small government in Hong Kong has traditionally been related to the state of the economy: in good times, public expenditure would rise; in bad times, it would contract. By 2020, however, there was a disjunction between the two. The economy was in recession as a result of the impact of the 2019 protests, the COVID-19 pandemic, and the Chinese government's enactment of national security laws for Hong Kong. But the government was also spending beyond its means. In his 2020 budget speech, the Financial Secretary said the problem was that "government revenue cannot keep up with drastic increases in government expenditure, especially recurrent expenditure".[109] Between 1997 and 2020, recurrent expenditure had risen from

---

104. Secretary for the Civil Service (2003, 21 February). *SCS's transcript on the pay cut consensus reached with the staff sides* [Press release].
105. Hong Kong Government (2008, 31 March). Civil service establishment to rise 1%. news.gov.hk
106. Civil Service Bureau (2008, 3 June). 2008–09 civil service pay adjustment. *Information and News*. www.csb.gov.hk
107. Leung (2013) op. cit., para 19.
108. Ng, K. C. (2017, 29 October). Proposed headcount increase in Hong Kong's civil service is just drop in ocean, unions say. *SCMP*. https://www.scmp.com/news/hong-kong/politics/article/2115433/proposed-headcount-increase-hong-kongs-civil-service-just
109. Financial Secretary (2020b) op. cit., para 176.

$150 billion to $440 billion (see Chapter 7, Figure 7.2). Although at that time he did not expect to balance the budget for the next five years, he gave cash handouts of $70 billion to the public and increased the Police Force's recurrent expenditure by 25%. As the Financial Secretary remarked, this was not sustainable but in his 2022–2023 budget, he still reported a rise in recurrent expenditure from $361.8 billion in 2017–18 to a projected amount of over $510 billion in the coming year.[110] In June 2020, the government did decide to freeze civil servants' pay increases but had no plans to downsize.[111] By 2021, the government was already granting substantial pay increases, especially in the disciplined services.[112] The idea of small government that had driven colonial government and the Tung and Tsang administrations appeared to have been superseded by attempts to find financial panaceas for political unrest and the pandemic.

Divesting Functions to the Private Sector

In theory, a government that follows minimalist principles should be prepared to divest its non-core functions to the private sector or voluntary agencies. Throughout its history, the Hong Kong government has asked voluntary agencies to deliver services that it has subsidised. Under colonialism, control over those agencies was quite loose unless the government thought that their activities threatened political stability. After 1997, Tung's belief that there should be more private sector involvement in the provision of services led to even greater stress on the divestment of some government functions to the private sector or voluntary agencies. This divestment did not mean that the government relinquished control. While it was willing to encourage purchaser/provider relationships, its control over providers tightened to the point where some agencies complained that they had too little autonomy.[113] The government increased its supervision of service delivery through the lump sum grant scheme for voluntary agencies and was often more interventionist than was its colonial predecessor.

In education, there has been a long history of contention between the post-handover government and providers. School management reform, introduced in 2000 and legislated in 2004, resulted in changes to the school boards, which the

---

110. Financial Secretary (2022). *The 2022–23 budget* (para 178). https://www.budget.gov.hk/2022/eng/speech.html
111. Legislative Council Panel on Public Service (2020). Updated background brief on 2020–21 civil service pay adjustment. https://www.legco.gov.hk/yr19-20/english/panels/ps/papers/ps20200619cb4-699-3-e.pdf
112. Standing Committee on the Disciplined Services Salaries and Conditions of Service (2021, June). *Report on the grade review of the disciplined services grades*. https://www.jsscs.gov.hk/reports/en/scds_gsr_2021_eng.pdf
113. Leung, J. Y. H., & Chan, H. M. (2001). The school management reform in Hong Kong: Administrative control in a new cloak of managerialism. In A. B. L. Cheung & J. C. Y. Lee (Eds.), *Public sector reform in Hong Kong: Into the 21st Century*. Hong Kong: The Chinese University Press; Leung, J. C. B. (2002). The advent of managerialism in social welfare: The case of Hong Kong. *The Hong Kong Journal of Social Work, 36*(1/2), 61–81.

Catholic Church argued violated the partnership between the church and the state and was in conflict with the Basic Law.[114] The government won the legal challenge, but the Catholic primate, Bishop Zen, believing that the measures were prompted by the Chinese government's desire to reduce the influence of the church, refused to implement them.[115] The school management reform caused stress among teachers and 10,000 of them subsequently protested.[116]

In 2007, in the government's failed attempt to merge the Chinese University of Hong Kong and the Hong Kong Institute of Education, it argued that it had the right to ensure that its policies in higher education were implemented (see Chapter 3).[117] In 2012, the government unsuccessfully tried to impose a "moral and national" education curriculum on the schools, triggering large protests of students, parents, unions, and democrats.[118] Pro-establishment and pro-Beijing politicians increasingly blamed political unrest on the "liberal" curriculum. In 2020, Carrie Lam said that the curriculum was "politicised" and that anti-government forces had "infiltrated" the campuses.[119] Articles 9 and 10 of the national security law state that the Hong Kong government shall "take necessary measures to strengthen public communication, guidance, supervision and regulation over matters concerning national security, including those relating to schools, universities, social organisations, the media, and the internet" and that it "shall promote national security education in schools and universities."[120]

Divestment of social welfare and education provision to voluntary agencies and the private sector is a common feature of most administrative systems. But when it is accompanied, as in Hong Kong, by the intention to exert control over the way the service is provided, the government must necessarily employ more civil servants to monitor the providers, adding to its costs. A second, less tangible, cost is that repeated intervention often provokes political resistance. Government intervention in social welfare and education was not the primary cause of political unrest in Hong Kong, but it did sharpen differences between the government and providers and raised questions about civil liberties, such as academic autonomy.

---

114. Cheng, Y. C. (2009). Hong Kong educational reforms in the last decade: Reform syndrome and new developments. *International Journal of Educational Management*, 23(1), 65–86.
115. Wang, J. (2010, 2 April). Appeal Court rejects Catholic Church's argument on school freedom. *AsiaNews.it*, http://www.asianews.it/news-en/Appeal-court-rejects-Catholic-Church%E2%80%99s-argument-on-school-freedom-17540.html
116. Cheng (2009) op. cit.
117. Education Bureau (2007, 17 September). *Education Bureau launches judicial review* [Press release]. https://www.info.gov.hk/gia/general/200709/17/P200709170128.htm
118. Morris, P., & Vickers, E. (2015). Schooling, politics and the construction of identity in Hong Kong: The 2012 "moral and national education" crises in historical perspective. *Comparative Education*, 51(3), 305–326.
119. Ho, K. (2020, 13 July). Hong Kong's Carrie Lam says education is "politicised" and blames media for "negative, smearing" coverage. *HKFP*. https://hongkongfp.com/2020/07/13/hong-kongs-carrie-lam-says-education-is-politicised-blames-media-for-negative-smearing-coverage/
120. Government of the People's Republic of China (2020). *The Law of the People's Republic of China on safeguarding national security in the Hong Kong Special Administrative Region*. https://www.elegislation.gov.hk/doc/hk/a406/eng_translation_(a406)_en.pdf

Outsourcing has been another means of divestment employed by the government. Under Tung, it was regarded as an attractive option for three reasons. First, it helped to downsize the civil service and involve the private sector in the provision of services. Second, it reduced costs because some services, such as cleaning, could be provided at a lower cost if they were outsourced. Third, responsibility for providing the function remained with the government because the contract could be terminated if the service was not satisfactory.[121]

By 2006, the government had about 4,000 outsourcing contracts with a value of about $200 billion, over six times the value of contracts in 2002 although the number of contracts awarded had declined.[122] Many larger contracts were in public works, but most departments outsourced small short-term contracts for cleaning, horticultural, and guard-duty services. Over time, the number of public works contracts dropped and the value of the contracts declined. By 2012, of 6,456 outsourced contracts, 82% were non-works contracts.[123] Of these, 70% were under $1.43 million in value and did not require an open tender.[124] There have been major criticisms of the government's outsourcing policy. The Director of Audit has identified weaknesses in the government's tendering and monitoring procedures.[125] There have also been complaints about the government's lack of transparency on what outsourcing saves in costs.[126] Academics and unions have argued that outsourcing should be stopped because it means more work and less pay for the workers.[127] In 2019, the government did introduce an improved scheme for the employment of low-paid workers although it did not apply to existing contractors.[128]

Other forms of private sector involvement have not led to any divestment of functions. There have been successful "build, operate and transfer" projects for tunnels for many years, but public-private partnerships, such as Harbour Fest, Disneyland, and the West Kowloon Cultural Development District, have experienced cost overruns or were criticised because the government had not obtained value for money (see Chapter 6).[129] For a government under pressure from all sides

---

121. Efficiency Unit (2008b). *Serving the community by using the private sector: A general guide to outsourcing* (3rd ed., p. 11). https://www.effo.gov.hk/en/reference/publications/guide_to_outsourcing_200803.pdf
122. Ibid., p. 7.
123. Legislative Council Secretariat Research Office (2017). *Government outsourcing* (p. 1). https://www.legco.gov.hk/research-publications/english/1617in04-government-outsourcing-20170207-e.pdf
124. Ibid., p. 3.
125. Director of Audit (2014). *Report No. 63: Hiring of service contractors and professionals.* https://www.aud.gov.hk/eng/pubpr_arpt/rpt_63.htm
126. Yip, P. (2015, 3 June). Hong Kong government should stop outsourcing its low-paying jobs. *SCMP.* https://www.scmp.com/comment/insight-opinion/article/1815705/hong-kong-government-should-stop-outsourcing-its-low-paying
127. Ibid.; Goodstadt, L. F. (2013). *Poverty in the midst of affluence: How Hong Kong mismanaged its prosperity* (pp. 36–37). Hong Kong: Hong Kong University Press.
128. Hansard, 9 January 2019, 4679–4715.
129. Brewer, B., & Hayllar, M. (2005). Building public trust through public-private partnerships. *International Review of Administrative Sciences, 71*(3), 475–492; Director of Audit (2004). *Report No. 42 Harbour Fest.*

and with an inclination towards greater exerting greater control, public-private partnerships seem to have lost their appeal. In addition to public/private partnerships, some privatisation measures have helped to reduce the size of the civil service. The privatisation of the management of some public housing estates, for example, reduced numbers in the Housing Department significantly (see Table 4.3). From a broader perspective, however, the government's attempts to privatise housing provision has been a failure. The private sector does not have the capacity or the inclination to deliver a sufficient quantity of housing units at reasonable prices, resulting in long waiting lists for public housing.[130]

The structure and functions of the Hong Kong government have been greatly influenced by the core principles of centralisation and hierarchy, by the traditional, but now questioned, belief in the values of a generalist administrative elite and political neutrality, and by the notions, also now in doubt, of small government, efficiency, and fiscal frugality. Specific political and economic circumstances have persuaded the government to deviate from these principles. In the 1990s, for example, the colonial government could not afford to downsize its large civil service because its first priority was to maintain political stability. When economic circumstances did not permit such a large establishment, business groups were able to make a persuasive case that Hong Kong should return to its previously proclaimed belief in "big market, small government". When the concept of political neutrality came under threat, senior civil servants were quick to point out that the quality of policy advice would be affected. When lines of command, and consequently effective centralisation, were threatened after the introduction of the POAS, Tsang soon reverted to the time-tested structure of control through the Chief Secretary and the Financial Secretary. There has, in short, been something of a default model at work. If the government's structure and functions deviated too far from core principles, and there was no good reason for doing so, there was usually sufficient political and public pressure to require the government to revert to previous practice.

The post-2012 period has seen challenges of a different order, however. When C. Y. Leung became Chief Executive, his attempt to address market failures through government intervention meant more functions, more staff, and more expenditure. Carrie Lam continued this policy, expanding the size of the civil service and bringing about even greater centralisation. Both Chief Executives were faced with major political unrest and an increasingly intrusive Chinese government. For the Hong Kong government, centralisation and the cultivation of loyal political support seemed a better option than the time-honoured values of rule by an administrative elite and political neutrality. Divestment, such as devolving or outsourcing major services or privatising government functions to reduce the size and cost of

---

https://www.aud.gov.hk/pdf_e/e42ch04.pdf; Higgins, C. D., & Huque, A. S. (2015). Public money and Mickey Mouse: Evaluating performance and accountability in the Hong Kong Disneyland joint venture public-private partnership. *Public Management Review*, *17*(8), 1103–1123.

130. Goodstadt (2013) op. cit., pp. 87–110; Lam (2017) op. cit., paras 144–152.

the civil service, came to be regarded as potentially dangerous because it would loosen political control. Whether this system can be sustained remains to be seen. Without popular support and a predicted budget deficit for the foreseeable future, the government may have to return to the reality of its traditional principles of administration.

5
The Civil Service
Personnel Policies and Integrity Management

This chapter focuses on two key principles of public administration in Hong Kong:
- a permanent tenured civil service selected on merit and
- personnel whose integrity is above question and who are subject to the rule of law.

Both principles have been sustained in the post-handover era but not without challenge. Tung's attempts to introduce reforms raised prospects that the administration would evolve beyond a permanent tenured civil service into something resembling the new public management systems in some Western countries. But resistance to the reforms meant that, although there was downsizing and cuts to civil service salaries, contracts did not replace permanent terms for the working life of most civil servants. Similarly, although the practices of the ICAC have expanded well beyond its traditional concern with combating bribery to include more complex conflicts of interest, its commitment to a zero-tolerance corruption policy has remained unchanged. It has been cogently argued that attempts to reform the public sector have been more a reaction to political and economic problems, and in the ICAC's case to changing patterns of corruption, than an intention to converge with new public management concepts.[1]

By 2020, the civil service was demonstrating the characteristics that had prompted the original reform programme: it was too large, too expensive, and not as productive or as well managed as politicians wanted. We analyse the reform programme and subsequent developments in four major areas of human resource management: recruitment, selection, and terms of service; pay and fringe benefits; performance management and training; and integrity management and discipline.

---

1. Common, R. (2001). Are Hong Kong's public sector reforms converging with international trends? In A. B. L. Cheung & J. C. Y. Lee (Eds.), *Public sector reform in Hong Kong: Into the 21st century*. Hong Kong: The Chinese University of Hong Kong Press; Painter, M. (2004). Against the trend: Public management reforms in Hong Kong. In A. Nakamura (Ed.), *Public reform, policy change and new public management: From the Asia and Pacific perspective* (pp. 31–49). Tokyo: EROPA Local Government Center.

Human Resource Management Reform

In January 1999, Tung Chee Hwa announced a major review of the civil service, citing a need to increase efficiency and "to improve the system at the fundamentals".[2] The consultation document, which followed the Chief Executive's speech, spelt out the need for reform in slightly greater detail: the Asian financial crisis had increased the community's expectations of government, there had been incidents in which civil service performance had been below standard and criticisms of inefficiencies in some departments.[3] The civil service review aimed to make recommendations that would ensure that the government had "a clean, trustworthy, quality and efficient Civil Service".[4]

The proposed reforms had some history in the late colonial period, but they might equally be seen as a prelude to more radical changes than had ever been envisaged under colonialism. The Civil Service Branch (later the Civil Service Bureau (CSB)) had considered changes in personnel policies for the entire decade before the 1999 reform document. In 1993, for example, it argued for a more flexible appointment system and subsequently introduced some changes in human resource management within the service.[5] The localisation of senior levels of the civil service, the issue of expatriates in the Police Force, and questions of compensation for those who were to be displaced or to lose their promotion prospects after the change of sovereignty in 1997 were all central concerns. There was also a slate of reform measures, many of them initiated by the Efficiency Unit, which were designed to make the civil service more managerial, more entrepreneurial, and more customer-friendly. None of these measures threatened the permanent and pensionable conditions of service of civil servants. The assumption was that reform was desirable—for example, many civil servants strongly favoured the changes to their work culture in the 1990s—but that it could be accommodated without disruptions to their pay and conditions of service.[6]

The 1999 reform proposals could be interpreted to call that assumption into question. Radical reform of the civil service had wide and vocal support from Tung, the business community, and many others who saw the civil service as over-privileged in a time of economic hardship.[7] The Liberal Party argued strongly that civil service salaries and fringe benefits should be brought in line with the private sector

---

2. Hansard, 14 January 1999, 4652.
3. Civil Service Bureau (CSB) (1999). *Civil service reform: Consultation document: Civil service into the 21st Century* (p. 5). https://www.info.gov.hk/archive/consult/1999/reforme.pdf
4. Ibid., p. 5.
5. Civil Service Branch (1993). *Civil service consultation document on civil service terms of appointment and conditions of service* (p. 23). Hong Kong: Government Printer; Civil Service Branch (1995). *Human resource management* (p. 54). Hong Kong: Government Printer.
6. Scott, I. (2000). Public sector reform and middle managers in Hong Kong. *Asian Journal of Public Administration*, 22(2), 107–134.
7. Cheng, C. (2003, 8 January). Public service must change with the times. *SCMP*.

and that the service was overstaffed.[8] The aim of those who favoured radical reform was to create a less permanent, more managerial, more productive civil service that would remove civil servants from the protective cocoon of tenured employment and generous salaries and instead move them along the path towards greater accountability for their actions.

On the other side, civil servants and their staff associations saw the reform proposals as detrimental to their interests. The staff associations objected to the changes to recruitment, promotion, and disciplinary procedures and were incensed by the subsequent pay cuts (see pp. 150–153). Initially, the government handled the implementation of the reforms very cautiously. A central pledge, for example, was that no civil servant would be made redundant as a result of the reforms. The government was also constrained by Article 100 of the Basic Law, which provides that all public servants, "including the police department . . . may remain in employment and retain their seniority with pay, allowances, benefits and conditions of service no less favourable than before". This was designed to reassure civil servants during the transition but was not expected to be a concern after 1997 because salaries and conditions of service of civil servants had almost always improved rather than deteriorated. The Secretary for the Civil Service said Article 100 would be treated as a specific commitment and that pay would not be reduced to levels below those of July 1997.[9]

Senior civil servants played down some of the more radical statements in the consultation document, stressing the need to achieve what the document called a "balance between stability and flexibility".[10] In 2000, the Chief Secretary for Administration spoke of "maintaining stability while introducing reforms and protecting existing staff while introducing changes at entry levels",[11] which perhaps implied a slower pace of change than some of the proponents of reform wanted. She also spoke of the potential effects of reform on morale in the civil service and of the concerns of the community. If the reforms had been fully implemented, they would have undermined the Weberian character of the civil service and, in combination with the POAS, would have significantly affected its mode of operation.

The proposals anticipated major changes even if the civil service was intent on mitigating what it saw as their potentially adverse effects.[12] They envisaged a performance-oriented system that would more closely mirror private sector practice and would allow a much greater interchange between the public and private sectors. The public sector outside the civil service was expected to expand, encouraging the greater mobility of all civil servants who would be able to transfer their pensions and benefits. Decentralisation of many personnel functions to the departmental

---

8. Hansard, 29 March 2000, 5383–5384.
9. CSB (1999) op. cit., p. 12.
10. Ibid., p. 9.
11. Hansard, 5 April 2000, 5660.
12. CSB (1999) op. cit., p. 9.

level would mean an erosion of service-wide relativities in salaries and conditions of service and would increase the powers of principal officials. In the following sections, we look at the specific issues that were raised in the reform proposals and how they have been implemented and/or modified.

Recruitment, Selection, and Terms of Service

Recruitment to the Hong Kong civil service is on grounds of merit defined according to "the best person for the job".[13] Ensuring that the correct choice has been made for senior positions is the task of the Public Service Commission (PSC), an independent statutory body established in 1950. Recruitment is undertaken by the bureaus and departments, but the commission has a monitoring role to determine if open and fair procedures have been correctly followed. In 2020, it advised the Chief Executive on appointments and promotions to posts with a monthly salary of $53,500 or above with 49,133 posts falling under its purview including the positions of Permanent Secretary and head of department. The commission also advises the Chief Executive on termination of probationary and agreement appointees, retirement in the public interest, and on disciplinary issues.[14] Some senior appointments in the civil service are bound by the provisions of Article 101 of the Basic Law. The positions of Secretaries and Deputy Secretaries of Departments, Directors of Bureaus, the Commissioner against Corruption, the Commissioner of Police, the Commissioner of Customs and Excise, and the Directors of Audit, Immigration, and Customs and Excise may only be held by Chinese citizens with no right of abode in a foreign country.

Recruitment boards are set up in the bureaus and departments to exclude candidates who do not meet basic entry requirements and to ensure competitive selection. Entry requirements involve relevant academic or professional qualifications, working experience, language proficiency, and any other qualities or attributes that the grade requires.[15] Applicants may also have to pass written examinations and to perform well at a selection interview. They must also pass medical examinations and integrity checking and must meet certain physical and fitness standards in the disciplined services. All successful applicants are required to be permanent residents of Hong Kong except for foreign nationals who may be employed as advisers at the discretion of the government.[16] Since 2008, applicants have also been required

---

13. Public Service Commission (PSC) (2021). *Annual report 2020* (p. 11). https://www.psc.gov.hk/eng/ann_rep/files/20rep.pdf
14. Ibid., pp. 5–6.
15. Civil Service Bureau (2021). Recruitment. https://www.csb.gov.hk/english/recruit/7.html; Legislative Council Panel on Public Service (2008). *Background brief on civil service recruitment policy* (p. 1), LC Paper No. CB (1)974/07-08. Hong Kong: mimeo.
16. Ibid., p. 2.

to sit a written test on the Basic Law, the results of which are given "appropriate weighting" in the selection decision.[17]

New appointees usually enter the service at a relatively young age and, before June 2000, would normally expect to be permanently employed until retirement. The 1999 consultation document, argued instead that permanent appointment discouraged able applicants who wanted flexibility, stifled the exchange of talents with the private sector, and led to some civil servants "being less than fully motivated".[18] These are debatable assumptions, but they were at the heart of the 1999 proposals to change recruitment policy. A permanent career was redefined to mean "the promise of a structured career and long-term employment for those who continue to contribute their best".[19]

Before 2000, depending on their place of origin and the requirements of the position, successful applicants were usually offered one of four terms of appointment: permanent and pensionable terms (either local or overseas) or agreement (contract) terms (either local or overseas). After the signing of the Sino-British agreement, the government's main human resource concern was how to localise the civil service, especially at the most senior levels and in the Police Force. The localisation policy was introduced in 1946, but progress was very slow. In 1982, for example, at the start of the Sino-British negotiations, expatriates held 54.3% of directorate-level positions (343 of 632 positions), 49.3% of administrative grade positions (159 of 329 positions) and 40.6% in the ranks of inspector and above in the Police Force (877 of 2,160 positions).[20]

After 1984, expatriate administrative officers were required to retire at 57 and a "golden handshake" scheme was introduced to retire some 70 administrators and 30 police officers.[21] Some professional grades, such as engineers, were soon entirely localised and newly appointed expatriates were only employed on agreement terms.[22] Expatriate officers became concerned about their futures and challenged the plans to localise rapidly, using the Bill of Rights, which prohibits discrimination, as the basis of their case. Local civil service associations and Legislative Councillors argued to the contrary for faster implementation of localisation policies.[23] The government sought to avoid further court cases and released a consultation document in 1993 which, it was hoped, would keep both sides happy.

The government proposed that all serving local and overseas officers on agreement terms would be offered permanent and pensionable terms, provided they

---

17. Civil Service Bureau (2021). Basic Law test in civil service recruitment. https://www.csb.gov.hk/english/recruit/basiclaw/1372.html
18. CSB (1999) op. cit., pp. 9–10.
19. Ibid., p. 11.
20. Civil Service Branch (1982). *Civil service personnel statistics* (pp. 19–20). Hong Kong: The Branch.
21. Harte, S. N. (1987, 30 August). Redundancy boost for expatriates. *Sunday Morning Post*.
22. Civil Service Branch (1993) op. cit., p. 3.
23. Hansard, 13 October 1993, 136–139; 24 November 1993, 1093–1138; 15 December 1993, 1635–1657; Cheung, T. M. (1993, 23 September). Patriots, expatriates. *Far Eastern Economic Review*.

qualified as a local under the Basic Law, were proficient in the Chinese language, met a service need, had a satisfactory conduct and performance record, and were physically fit.[24] The provisions were aimed largely at expatriate officers and had little effect on locals. Most civil servants continued to be employed on local permanent and pensionable terms. In 1997, for example, of a civil service strength of 184,639, 155,012 were on local permanent and pensionable terms. A further 2,902 were on agreement terms. Of those on overseas terms of service, 530 were on permanent and pensionable terms while 715 were on agreement terms.[25] The 1993 consultation document assumed that all recruits would enter the service on what was called "new permanent and pensionable terms"[26] (see Table 5.1). The trend was clearly towards an almost exclusively local civil service, fluent in Cantonese and, increasingly, in Putonghua.[27] Most expatriates were not disadvantaged by the new conditions because the majority of contracts were renewed. After 1997, however, there was a gradual decline in overseas officers. By 2020, there were only 48 civil servants on overseas terms (see Table 5.1).

The 1993 document did not challenge the fundamental premise on which the civil service had been based. If the employee was on permanent and pensionable terms, apart from unsatisfactory performance during the probation period or serious misconduct, the job was held until retirement. An internal document, *The consultation document on human resource management review*, circulated to senior management in the branches and departments in 1993, did foreshadow some important future issues. The central argument was that the terms of appointment had "reduced responsiveness to service needs"[28] and that there was a need to introduce more flexible contract terms. No changes were made in appointment policy, however, until January 1999 when "common terms" of appointment and conditions of service, that is, those that did not distinguish between overseas and local terms, were finally introduced. After June 2000, the "new" terms for fresh recruits came into effect.

The 1999 proposals recommended that recruits be appointed on agreement (contract) terms rather than on permanent and pensionable terms as in the past. The first step in the implementation process occurred in June 1999, when starting salaries were significantly reduced.[29] The overall decrease was between 6% and 31% for new civil servants on the Master Pay Scale (MPS) and between 3% and 17% for disciplined services staff. The entry point for professional and related grades was lowered from MPS point 27 ($35,285) to MPS point 22 ($28,075) and for degree

---

24. Civil Service Branch (1993) op. cit., p. 19.
25. CSB (1997). *Civil service personnel statistics* (pp. 14–15). Hong Kong: Government Printer.
26. Civil Service Branch (1993) op. cit., Annex E.
27. Ibid.
28. Kue, K. M. W. (2001). *Civil service reform in Hong Kong: New appointment policy* (p. 74) [Unpublished master's thesis]. The University of Hong Kong.
29. Standing Committee on Civil Service Salaries and Conditions of Service (SCCSS) (1999). *Civil service salaries: Starting salaries 1999 (Report No. 36)* (pp. 18–19). Hong Kong: Printing Department.

Table 5.1 *The Civil Service by Gender and Terms of Appointment 2020*

Gender	Local	Overseas	Common	New	Total	Percentage
Male	43,325	48	1,066	64,788	109,217	61.5
Female	28,278	0	218	39,943	68,439	38.5
Total	71,603	48	1,284	104,721	177,656	100
Percentage	40.3	(*)	0.7	58.9		

Source: Civil Service Bureau (2020). *Quarterly updated civil service personnel statistics*. https://www.csb.gov.hk/english/stat/quarterly/541.html

holders from MPS point 16 ($21,010) to MPS point 11 ($16,095).[30] All entry points on the MPS were reduced from their previous levels.

New appointees were further disadvantaged by the extension of their probationary period. Before the reforms, the normal probationary period had been two years when, subject to satisfactory performance, the appointee would be offered permanent and pensionable terms. Under the new system, an appointee would serve an initial probationary contract of three years. Subject to satisfactory performance, the civil servant would be offered a further contract of three years and, after further satisfactory performance, could only then accede to permanent and pensionable terms. The CSB was careful to assure the civil service staff associations that the conditions of service would only apply at entry level and that civil servants already in post would not be affected by the new provisions.[31] The PSC also recommended that the offer of permanent terms after three years be retained for the disciplinary services.[32] Because there was a freeze on civil service recruitment in most grades, except the Police Force, the initial impact of the recommendations was limited.[33]

In the early 2000s, the Hong Kong government tried various means to reduce the size and cost of the civil service: by encouraging civil servants to retire early through voluntary retirement schemes, by introducing a provident fund in place of pensions and mandating it for new recruits, by employing non-civil service contract staff, and by outsourcing some government activities (see Chapter 4). New recruitment policies provided an additional and long-term solution to the problem of the cost of the civil service. But there were also adverse consequences and little impact on flexibility and interchange with the private sector.

The new system made it less attractive to join the service. The length of the probation period was increased threefold, there was greater uncertainty over whether tenure would be granted, and starting salaries were reduced. Soon after the new terms were introduced, there was a freeze on civil service recruitment so that the

---

30. Ibid.
31. Hong Kong Government (2000, 7 April). *New civil service entry system and fringe benefits package* [Press release].
32. PSC (2001). *Annual report 2000* (p. 14). Hong Kong: Printing Department.
33. Kue (2001) op. cit., p. 76.

impact was not entirely felt until 2007 when recruitment resumed. For all those who were recruited after April 2000, however, there was a yawning gap between their salaries and conditions of service and those on local conditions. In many cases, the new appointees were doing the same job as those on local terms, violating the principle of equal pay for equal work. Morale declined. Probationers were rumoured to spend a good proportion of the latter periods of their contracts looking for alternative employment.

Those who were able to join the civil service may have done so because there was nothing better available during the economic downturn. In the Police Force, which was allowed to recruit despite the freeze, 43% of the new constables in 2003–2004 held degrees.[34] By 2006–2007, this had declined to 17%. With better opportunities in the private sector and at the officer level in other disciplined services, the force had difficulty retaining its degree holders.[35] After recruitment recommenced in 2007, starting salaries across grades had to be increased to attract better-quality applicants and some of the cost-saving benefits of the reforms were lost.

Stop-start recruitment policies had negative consequences for succession planning and the demographic profile of the civil service. If large numbers of civil servants in a permanent civil service are recruited at the same time, they will retire at approximately the same time. If a large recruitment exercise is followed by a lengthy freeze, there will a gap in succession planning and a shortage of experienced personnel to fill senior positions. Once economic conditions improved, the new appointment system, together with the reduction in starting salaries and the replacement of pensions with a provident fund, resulted in greater turnover, increasing the difficulty of retaining sufficient able people. By 2008, with only 26% of civil servants under the age of 40, and many of those in the junior ranks of the disciplined services, the civil service knew that it had a major problem of succession planning.[36] There were some attempts to improve recruitment procedures, reducing the time required to appoint new employees and conducting research on the employment market.[37] But the problem did not go away.

The effect of a recruitment freeze can be seen in the age profile of the directorate in 2019–2020 when 77% of officers were 50 years of age or older.[38] The percentage of officers in the age group between 40 and 49 years of age, who would expect to succeed to these positions, has been in almost continuous decline since the recruitment freeze of the 2000s.[39] Although, as the government argues, this percentage is consistent with the overall age profile of Hong Kong's labour force, it also seems

---

34. CSB (2007, June). *Civil service newsletter*. No. 69, p. 13.
35. Ibid. See also Chang, L. Y. (2008). *An analysis of the impact of civil service reform on recruitment and retention in the Hong Kong Police Force* [Unpublished master's thesis]. The University of Hong Kong.
36. Legislative Council Panel on Public Service (2008). *General overview of the civil service strength, retirement and resignation* (p. 2). LC Paper CB (1)1817/07-08(01). Hong Kong: mimeo.
37. PSC (2008). *2007 annual report* (pp. 13–14). https://www.psc.gov.hk/english/ann_rep/files/08rep.pdf
38. Legislative Council Panel on Public Service (2021, 17 May). *An overview of the civil service: establishment, strength, retirement, age profile and gender profile* (p. 4). LC Paper No. CB(4) 986/20-21(03).
39. Ibid., Annex G.

likely that able young potential civil servants in the 2000s could not find positions in the civil service and either delayed their entry to the service or found employment elsewhere. In 2020, when government directed that civil service staffing should be kept at the same level and that expenditure should be cut by 1%, an already difficult succession planning problem was exacerbated. With retirements at nearly 10% per annum at the directorate level, a widening gap between establishment and strength, a prohibition on recruitment, and an insufficient pool from which to draw potential successors, the workload of officers in post inevitably increased considerably.[40] The wastage rate across the civil service at 4.8% of strength in 2021 was much lower than that of the directorate, but there were similar problems with consequential effects for morale.

The government's solution to the problem was to create more time-limited supernumerary positions and to extend the retirement age in the civil service as a whole. In 2015, the government raised the retirement age to 65 for anyone joining the service after June 2015.[41] In 2018, the same offer was made to civil servants who had joined civilian grades between June 2000 (that is, on the new appointment terms) and May 2015 and allowed disciplined services officers to continue working to the age of 60.[42] About 83% of those eligible accepted the option.[43] In the Police Force, which had the highest civil service vacancy rate of 8% in 2021, the government extended the retirement age of non-directorate officers to 60 for officers who had joined before 2000 and was considering making similar arrangements in the other disciplined services.[44] The extension may help provide greater continuity in the service—at an estimated cost of $5.8 billion[45]—and make succession planning easier, but it has not addressed the problem of recruiting able young people, who seem much less attracted to civil service careers than previous generations, or of resolving the fundamental issue of how to ensure that the age profile of the civil service is congruent with its needs.

The numbers on new terms of service have grown and those on local terms have become a declining minority (see Table 5.1), but the system has never delivered the benefits that were promised. By 2019, most civil servants were on permanent terms, recurrent costs had spiralled, seniority was still the determining factor in most promotions, and there were few signs of the flexibility that the reformers had sought to

---

40. Ibid., p. 2, 3.
41. CSB (2015, 14 January). Extension of the service of civil servants. https://www.csb.gov.hk/english/letter/2612.html
42. CSB (2018, 19 June). Extension of service of civil servants who joined the government between 1 June 2000 and 31 May 2015. https://www.csb.gov.hk/english/info/files/common/LegCoBrief_ExtofSer_20180619_e.pdf
43. Legislative Council Panel on Public Service (2022, 9 February). *Policy measures of the Civil Service Bureau in 2021 policy address* (p. 9). LC Paper No. CB(4) 57/2022(01).
44. Legislative Council Panel on Public Service (2021, 17 May). Minutes of meeting (p. 8). LC Paper No. CB(4)1340/20-21.
45. CSB (2018, February). *Consultation paper: Extension of service of civil servants who joined the government between 1 June 2000 and 31 May 2015* (p. 5). https://www.csb.gov.hk/english/publication/files/Consultation_Paper_2018_Eng.pdf

achieve. Civil servants appeared to be less motivated than they had been before the reforms and less willing to undertake new initiatives. Much of this, of course, may relate to an increasingly fractious political environment, but the changes in terms of service did not help.

Pay and Fringe Benefits

Civil service salaries are based on two principles, which are often quoted, sometimes criticised, and much debated. The first is that remuneration should be sufficient to attract, retain, and motivate staff and that it "should be regarded as fair both by themselves and the public they serve".[46] The second, much more contentious, principle is that civil service pay should be broadly comparable with pay in the private sector.[47] Both principles date from the 1960s. The "comparability" with the private sector principle was introduced by the 1965 Salaries Commission and the "fairness" principle can be traced to the government's agreement with the staff associations in 1968.[48] This has meant that when times are prosperous the civil service thinks that it is underpaid and when times are bad the private sector thinks that the civil service is overpaid. But both principles raise a host of questions about whether pay levels are or are not attracting the best people and how comparisons can be drawn between very different positions in the public and private sectors.

Before 1979, civil service salaries were determined by periodic salaries commissions. When inflation was relatively low, these commissions were appointed every five or six years. After 1971, it became clear that continuous management of the pay determination process was necessary. The initial attempt to ensure comparability with the private sector was through the use of an occupational class system whereby the government's Pay Investigation Unit tried to identify similar occupational classes in the public and private sectors and then made appropriate changes to salaries. This resulted in unrest and strikes because the salaries of grades could change quickly, depending on the often volatile situation in the private sector. This approach was abandoned in 1974 when the government moved to annual pay trend surveys.

The government responded to its worsening staff relations situation by creating a Standing Commission on Civil Service Salaries and Conditions of Service (SCCSS) in 1979. The commission, with a later improved pay determination mechanism, has decided civil service pay levels ever since. Subsequently, three further standing committees were created, one for the six disciplined services and the ICAC, one for the directorate, and one for the Judiciary. They have similar terms of reference to the SCCSS although their procedures have evolved in different ways. The principal

---

46. CSB (2020). Pay policy. https://www.csb.gov.hk/english/admin/pay/38.html
47. Ibid.
48. CSB (2003). *Development of an improved pay adjustment mechanism for the civil service* (Annex A). https://www.csb.gov.hk/english/admin/pay/1570.html

roles of the SCCSS are to review the principles and practices governing the grade, rank, and salary structure of the civil service, the salaries of individual grades and the methodology used to determine comparability with the private sector, and to recommend any changes to the Chief Executive.

The commission replaced the occupational class method with a qualification group approach, establishing educational qualification entry benchmarks for new recruits and delinking the pay scale from direct comparison with groups in the private sector. Civil service associations might still claim that particular grades were underpaid or that they should be paid more to attract necessary new staff, but they could no longer claim that they should be paid the same as their private sector counterparts. The educational qualification method enabled the commission to "broad-band" grades with similar requirements for appointment, which are then collapsed into 11 qualification groups, in each of which a common pay structure prevails.[49] Broad-banding has been defended on the grounds that it promotes equity, but it is also a useful management tool because it forestalls the argument for special treatment for particular grades. The staff associations have frequently made cases for "other factors", such as obnoxious duties, excessive workloads, or unreasonable hours, to be taken into consideration in pay determination. The commission has responded by making rules about the remuneration these "other factors" should attract. It has never ruled out using pay as an incentive and some grades have seen their pay increased because of a shortage of new applicants. The overall effect has been to enhance stability, possibly at the expense of efficiency.[50]

The SCCSS also took on board the wider issue of staff relations. Staff relations was a concern after the government's 1968 agreement with three service-wide staff associations that led to the formation of the Senior Civil Service Council, a body on which the staff associations were represented and which the government agreed to consult on any proposed changes in conditions of service.[51] Other central consultative bodies were established later: a Model Scale 1 Staff Consultative Council in 1982 constituted by representatives of staff associations mainly representing labourers and artisans; a Police Force Council formed in the same year with representation from four police staff associations; and a Disciplined Services Consultative Council created in 1990 with representation from staff associations in other disciplined services.[52] The councils have remained in force as peak organisations in staff consultative relations in the post-handover period.[53]

---

49. CSB (2016). Qualification groups. https://www.csb.gov.hk/mobile/english/admin/csr/407.html
50. Cheung, A. B. L. (2005). Civil service pay reform in Hong Kong: Principles, politics and paradoxes. In A. B. L. Cheung (Ed.), *Public service reform in East Asia: Reform issues and challenges in Japan, Korea, Singapore and Hong Kong* (pp. 157–192). Hong Kong: The Chinese University of Hong Kong Press.
51. For the text of the 1968 agreement, see Burns, J. P. (2004). *Government capacity and the Hong Kong civil service* (Appendix D). Hong Kong: Oxford University Press.
52. Legislative Council Panel on Public Service (2005). *Staff consultation mechanism in the civil service* (pp. 1–3). LC Paper No. CB (1) 1769/04-05. Hong Kong: mimeo.
53. CSB (2020). Channels of consultation. https://www.csb.gov.hk/english/admin/relations/151.html

Staff consultative mechanisms at the departmental level were not well developed until 1980. In a wide-ranging report in that year, the SCCSS laid down uniform rules covering such matters as membership, frequency of meetings, the use of Cantonese, and attendance by CSB representatives.[54] These measures, coupled with the new method of determining pay, probably helped to prevent issues from escalating into the territory-wide disputes of the late 1970s. Departmental consultative committees are now the major institutional mechanism for resolving differences between staff and management in all departments with staff of over 100. Their meetings are attended by representatives of the staff associations and by a member of the CSB who explains government policies. Pay and conditions of service are important topics for discussion although the committees also deal with appointment and promotion criteria, welfare and recreational activities, and improvements in productivity.[55]

Civil servants are paid on one of 11 pay scales, but most fall within the five major pay scales (see Table 5.2) with over 60% coming under the MPS. The other scales are for the directorate-level staff; the directorate (legal) officers; the police; other disciplined services which have three pay scales for commanders, officers, and rank and file; the Model Scale 1 for labourers and artisans; and the training, technician, and craft apprentice pay scales.[56] Since pay increases (or reductions) are normally issued in three bands for upper-, middle-, and lower-ranking civil servants, and relativities between the bands are approximately maintained, the pay scales tend to re-enforce the hierarchy within the civil service. The ratio between the lowest-paid and highest-paid civil servant tends to be considerably greater than it would be in most developed countries. However, because the government considers itself to be a good employer, the lowest-paid civil servants have historically been better paid than their private sector counterparts.

Comparability with the private sector is determined by an annual pay trend survey of salaries in private sector companies. The Joint Secretariat, which is attached to the SCCSS, houses the Pay Survey and Research Unit, which carries out the surveys based on a methodology established by an independent Pay Trend Survey Committee.[57] The methodology is based on improvements to the survey introduced in 2007 and now includes not only large typical companies in the major economic sectors but also gives a 25% weighting to smaller companies with between 25 and 99 employees.[58] Companies are chosen because they have stable, rational, and systematic salary administration. In 2020, the survey covered 107 companies (80 large companies, 27 smaller ones) with 146,000 employees over a 12-month period.[59]

---

54. SCCSS (1980). *Report No. 4*. Hong Kong: Government Printer.
55. Legislative Council Panel on Public Service (2005) op. cit., pp. 3–4.
56. CSB (2020). Pay scales. https://www.csb.gov.hk/english/admin/pay/952.html
57. SCCSS (2008). *Report No. 42* (p. 5). https://www.jsscs.gov.hk/reports/en/42/42.pdf
58. Ibid., pp. 4–5.
59. Hong Kong Government (2020, 19 May). *Pay trend survey committee meeting on May 19, 2020* [Press release]. https://www.info.gov.hk/gia/general/202005/19/P2020051900528.htm

Table 5.2 *Civil Service Pay Scales*

Type	Scale	Salary Range ($ per month)	Strength
Directorate	D1–D8	$150,950–$303,950	1,378
Master Pay Scale	MPS 0–49	$12,915–$135,470	110,613
General Disciplined Services (Officer) Scale	GDS 1d–39	$25,125–$147,235	29,280[1]
General Disciplined Services (Rank and File) Scale	GDS 1a–29	$20,000–$48,395	
Police Pay Scale	PPS 1a–59	$23,250–$303,950	28,875[2]
Model Scale 1	MOD 0–13	$13,730–$17,870	7,263

Source: Civil Service Bureau (2020). *Quarterly updated civil service personnel statistics*. https://www.csb.gov.hk/english/stat/quarterly/541.html
Notes:
1. The personnel statistics do not differentiate between officers and rank and file in the General Disciplined Services.
2. The establishment of the Police Force on 30 June 2020 was 31,190 supported by 4,611 additional civilian staff, mainly on the Master Pay Scale.

The survey includes all full-time employees of the company, whose basic salaries are the equivalent of three broad salary bands in the non-directorate staff of the civil service and takes into account salary adjustments and any additional payments, merit increases, and increments. When these have been calculated, they are translated into indicators that represent the weighted average pay adjustment for all surveyed employees within each salary band. The findings are then sent to the Secretary for the Civil Service. Once the findings have been confirmed, the major staff associations make a claim for an adjustment. The government considers the submission and then makes a pay offer. The staff side comments on the offer and a proposal is then submitted to the Executive Council, which decides on the annual adjustment subject to the provision of funds by the Finance Committee of the Legislative Council. Although pay increases are normally granted based on the pay trend findings, in 2020, despite findings suggesting that there should be an increase, the government instead decided to freeze salaries.[60]

The pay trend surveys assess changes in remuneration within the service, but they do not address the more difficult question of establishing whether the annual determination of the trend accurately reflects pay levels in the private sector. Until December 2001, the difficulty of making the comparison, and the opposition of the staff associations to it, persuaded the government that it should be left unresolved. A pay level survey conducted in 1986 found that most civil servants' salaries and fringe benefits outstripped private sector compensation by as much as 23% on the

---
60. Hong Kong Government (2020, 2 June). *Decision of 2020-21 pay adjustment*. https://www.info.gov.hk/gia/general/202006/02/P2020060200599.htm

lower pay band and by up to 52% on the upper pay band.[61] The civil service staff associations raised strident objections to the consultants' methodology.[62] Under the 1968 agreement, the government was obliged to appoint a committee to investigate the issue. The committee duly reported that the "pay level survey does not provide a sufficient basis for making adjustments to civil service pay either now or in the future".[63] There the matter rested. Faced with the political problems of the transitional period, the government had no desire to create more friction by raising the matter of the civil service pay level and the staff associations saw no advantage in doing so.

The 1999 civil service reform document, however, foreshadowed potentially major changes to the civil service pay system. It noted, for example, that pay was not linked to performance, that pay and fringe benefits should be more closely linked to private sector practices and performance appraisal, and that the pay trend system might have to be improved.[64] A less costly civil service was critically important to the government's reform agenda and the issue of the comparability of pay with the private sector had to be confronted if it wished to maintain credibility. In December 2001, the Secretary for the Civil Service invited the SCCSS to review the pay policy and system of the civil service. The review included comparability with private sector pay and the methodology for determining pay levels, the rationalisation of the grading structure of the 400 grades and over 1,000 ranks in the service, the possibility of increasing motivation through an improved and more flexible salary system, the annual pay adjustment mechanism, and the preservation of the integrity and stability of the civil service. The Task Force's terms of reference suggested that it should make recommendations for radical changes to the pay policy system and to the civil service itself. The civil service staff associations, predictably, were opposed to the review because, they argued, economic conditions were too volatile to arrive at conclusions that would stand the test of time.

The Task Force produced an interim report in April 2002. The issue of reducing the cost of the civil service was clearly on its collective mind, particularly because its members believed that it was "obvious that the community would like to see a thorough re-thinking of the basic principles of the existing pay system".[65] A second report released in September 2002 outlined its long-term vision for the pay system. It reiterated many basic principles that had previously governed the system, including that it should be able to attract and retain staff of suitable calibre; that it should be fair; and that it should be flexible but stable enough to assure civil servants of

---

61. Committee of Inquiry into the 1988 Civil Service Pay Adjustment and Related Matters (1989). *Report* (p. 21). Hong Kong: Government Printer.
62. Ibid.
63. Ibid., p. 105.
64. CSB (1999) op. cit., pp. 15–17.
65. Task Force on the Review of Civil Service Pay Policy and System (April 2002). *Interim report: Phase 1 study* (Appendix IX). Hong Kong: Printing Department.

their reasonable expectations.[66] But it left the door open for the introduction of performance pay, enhanced performance management systems, measures to allow managers to use resources more effectively, and regular reviews of the system.[67] The Task Force favoured regular and comprehensive pay level surveys but recognised the methodological difficulties involved and deferred the issue of comparability with the private sector for a further study. The Task Force also recommended studies on how pay ranges could replace fixed pay scales, how the staff appraisal system could be improved in support of performance pay and flexible pay ranges, and how practical problems associated with a simplified and decentralised pay administration could be overcome.[68]

The CSB proceeded very cautiously with the work of reforming the pay system, and with good reason. The government had introduced the first round of civil service pay reductions in 2002 when the Task Force's reports were being considered, a move that aroused strong opposition from the staff associations.[69] The associations took unsuccessful legal action and demonstrated against the salary cuts and violations of the pay system process, but the government remained determined to bring civil service salaries more in line with equivalent levels in the private sector (see p. 129).[70] By April 2003, the government had decided to introduce a second round of cuts to reduce "the value of all pay points on all civil service pay scales to the levels as at 30 June 1997".[71] Reductions to salaries were introduced in two phases in January 2004 and January 2005. To make additional radical changes to the pay system when staff associations were incensed by the government's decision and when the government was already under pressure over its decision to legislate under Article 23 of the Basic Law would have been very difficult. The Task Force's strong advocacy of a pay level survey could have caused unrest in the service and its acceptance in principle of performance pay, pay ranges, and the decentralisation of the system had potentially far-reaching effects on the structure of the civil service and of performance appraisal, if it were related to pay.

Nonetheless, in April 2003, when the government decided to legislate the second round of pay cuts, the CSB began to consider how change might be implemented.[72] In a report produced in November 2003, it retreated from some of the more radical possibilities raised by the Task Force. The principle of comparability, for example, was to be expressed as broad comparability rather than any attempt to identify appropriate private sector analogues for every position in the public sector.[73] In setting pay levels, the government should continue to observe "the established

---

66. Task Force (final report) (September 2002) op. cit., pp. 12–13.
67. Ibid.
68. Ibid.
69. Hansard, 5 June 2002, 7010–7015.
70. Lee, K., & Bradford, S. (2003, 11 June). Case has not ended legal battle for redress. *SCMP*.
71. CSB (2003). *Brief for the Legislative Council: Public officers pay adjustments (2004/2005) Bill* (p. 6). CSB CR PG 4-085-001/33.
72. CSB (2003). Improved pay adjustment mechanism, op. cit.
73. Ibid., pp. 7–8.

principle that the government should follow, but not lead the private sector".[74] The bureau was also cautious about internal pay relativities and did not comment on the introduction of performance pay or linkages between performance appraisal and pay. It proposed to employ consultants to advise on developing a feasible pay level survey methodology, to review pay trend survey methodology, and to introduce enabling legislation to allow it to make downward adjustments in salary.[75]

The CSB's mood remained conciliatory. There was wide consultation with the staff associations, the SCCSS, and the public[76] and an evident attempt to achieve a consensus. The proposed pay level survey system had important features that won support both from the SCCSS and the staff associations. It was to use the job-family and job-level method, drawing on broad categories of positions to make comparisons; select and match civil service benchmark jobs with those in the private sector; select "steady and good employers" in the private sector for the surveys; and collect cash-based pay data.[77] The civil service stood to benefit on several counts from the application of the collected information from the survey. First, the upper quartile of private sector pay was to be used to arrive at the market pay indicator. Second, the market pay indicator of a defined job level would be compared with the notional mid-point salary of the civil service plus average expenditure on fringe benefits. Finally, the range of difference between civil service and private sector pay was set at plus or minus 5% with no adjustment made to pay levels if the findings fell within this range.[78]

When the pay level survey was carried out in 2006, the consultants collected data from 97 companies and matched them against 166 civil service ranks. They then divided the civil service into five job levels, ranging from the lowest to the highest levels. Since each level was within the plus or minus 5% range, the Secretary for the Civil Service was able to announce that there would be no changes to civil service pay scales because of the evidence of broad comparability with the private sector.[79] There was no mention of linking the performance pay system to appraisal or bringing in pay ranges or decentralising the pay system, all of which had been mooted in the Task Force document.[80]

Thereafter, pay level surveys were held at six-year intervals[81] and starting salary surveys every three years. Pay trend surveys were reintroduced on an annual basis

---

74. Ibid., p. 9.
75. Legislative Council Panel on Public Service (2006). *Progress update on the pay level survey and the development of an improved pay adjustment mechanism for the civil service*. LC Paper No. CB (1)248/06-07(04).
76. Hong Kong Government (2007, 24 April). *Improved civil service pay adjustment mechanism announced* [Press release].
77. Ibid.
78. Ibid.
79. Ibid.
80. CSB (1999) op. cit, pp. 15–17.
81. SCCSS (2013). *Report No. 52: Civil service pay level survey 2013*. https://www.jsscs.gov.hk/reports/en/52/R52e.pdf; SCCSS (2018). *Report No. 59: Review on civil service pay level survey and starting salaries survey*. https://www.jsscs.gov.hk/reports/en/59/R59_e.pdf

with an improved methodology. None of these surveys was controversial. They found in favour of increasing civil service salaries and did not try to reintroduce any of the radical ideas in the 1999 reform proposals. The 2013 pay level survey led to a 3% increase in salaries[82] and, in 2018, the pay-level and starting salaries survey recommended that graduate starting salaries should continue to be above those in the private sector because graduates joining the private sector had potentially faster salary increases.[83] The consequences of such decisions were that the cost of the civil service rose rapidly. By 2020, the government's recurrent expenditure was over threefold what it had been in 1997.[84]

Why did the government not rein in the cost of civil service salaries and fringe benefits? Economic and political conditions probably underlie its retreat from the managerial recommendations of the reform document and the Task Force. First, Hong Kong governments have always believed that a stable civil service is necessary for prosperity and maintaining law and order. The stability of the civil service would have been greatly affected by radical changes to the pay system. Politically, the government did not want to create more opponents within its own camp. Second, both Leung and Lam required more civil servants to implement their expansionist agendas, increasing the size and cost of the civil service. Third, as economic conditions improved, the heat was taken out of the pay issue. Part of the public support for pay reductions had been based on a feeling of relative deprivation, that the civil service should experience the same economic hardship as the rest of the community was facing. When wages in the private sector began to rise, less attention was paid to civil service pay. After the 2019–2020 protests, COVID-19, and the Chinese government's enactment of national security legislation, the subsequent economic downturn left Hong Kong with a bloated civil service funded by a government living beyond its means.

Performance Management and Training

Performance Appraisal

Performance appraisal has been a perennial concern for the Hong Kong civil service and its deficiencies have long been recognised. There has been a persistent "central tendency" for civil servants, who are assessed annually on their performance, to be marked in the middle or at the top end of the scale. Attempts to move away from the annual reporting system to more continuous and qualitative "coaching" have largely failed. Performance appraisal has been grounded in a competency-based approach

---

82. CSB (2015). *Legislative Council brief: 2013 pay level survey: Application to the civil service* (p. 1). https://www.csb.gov.hk/english/info/files/2013_PLS_eng.pdf
83. SCCSS (2018) op. cit., pp. 43–46.
84. Financial Secretary (2020). *The 2020/2021 budget* (para 176). https://www.budget.gov.hk/2020/eng/speech.html

supplemented by departmental assessment panels that are expected to moderate and level out the results of the exercise.[85] The intention remains to evaluate performance to enable management to distinguish the diligent and the able from the lazy and the incompetent. However, experience elsewhere and in Hong Kong itself suggests that this objective is not easily achieved.

The 1999 reform proposals on performance appraisal were based on the assumption that reporting officers were too generous in their assessments. The PSC supported this view, favouring strong action against civil servants who performed poorly and condemning departmental failures to conduct annual exercises.[86] After 2007, however, it took a more benign attitude, laying down correct procedures and providing examples of good and bad practice. It noted that departments should not use quota systems in rating civil servants and that assessment panels should avoid downgrading "very effective" ratings to "effective" which, it felt, created "a lot of grievances and complaints from staff".[87] It also supported the CSB's efforts to introduce a competency-based approach, defined according to the "knowledge, attributes, attitudes and skills"[88] required to do a job effectively.

In 2009, and again in 2013, the CSB revised the performance appraisal form, both for the annual exercise and for promotion, and gave some indication of what was expected from the process.[89] Civil servants are graded annually on a six-point scale, ranging from "outstanding" to "poor", the bottom three categories giving cause for concern and potential action.[90] A persistently substandard performance can lead to the civil servant's retirement in the public interest. The procedures require face-to-face interviews between the supervisor and the civil servant, who discuss the appraisal with a view to improving performance. Civil servants have the right to appeal the results of the appraisal. Performance appraisals are also used by promotion boards to determine whether the candidate has the potential to serve at a higher level. The bureaus and department conduct the appraisals and, inevitably, take specific work conditions into account in arriving at decisions. The government has attempted to respond to these differences by providing more training courses in performance appraisal writing and customised training courses for individual bureaus and departments.[91]

The performance appraisal system is expected to play a role in three respects. It is supposed to be an important means of linking pay to performance and improving productivity. Withholding the annual incremental pay increase was initially thought to be one way to signal that performance was not up to standard. The

---

85. Civil Service Bureau (2013). Circular 6/2013: Performance management in the civil service. http://www.agtso.org/update/download/c201306e.pdf
86. PSC (2002). *Annual report 2001* (pp. 18–19). https://www.psc.gov.hk/english/ann_rep/files/01rep.pdf
87. PSC (2008). *Annual report 2007* (p. 50). https://www.psc.gov.hk/english/ann_rep/files/07rep.pdf
88. CSB (1999). *Performance management guide* (p. 6). https://www.csb.gov.hk/english/publication/files/PM_Guide_e.pdf
89. CSB (2013) op. cit.
90. Ibid., p. 3.
91. PSC (2019). *Annual report 2018* (p. 34). https://www.psc.gov.hk/english/ann_rep/files/18rep.pdf

CSB mandated that increments would only be granted if performance, including conduct, diligence, and efficiency, was satisfactory.[92] The Task Force further suggested that successful performance appraisal might be applied more rigorously to determine whether increments should be awarded. However, by 2008, 77% of civil servants were already on the highest point of their salary scale[93] so that withholding increments would have had no impact on most officers. Increments have occasionally been withheld as a disciplinary measure but have not often been used as a punishment for poor performance.

Performance appraisal was also expected to be useful in identifying underperformers and, if necessary, dismissing them. In March 2003, the CSB stipulated that an "unsatisfactory" rating over a 12-month period could mean that the offender would be retired in the public interest under Section 12 of the *Public Service (Administration) Order*.[94] In October 2005, the period allowed for unsatisfactory performance was reduced to six months.[95] The subsequent revision of the rules in 2009 and 2013 did not put a time limit on dismissal but suggested a process of counselling followed, if performance did not improve, by withdrawing the increment and then retirement in the public interest. The number of civil servants compulsorily retired under Section 12 declined from 24 in 2005 to six in 2019 and eight in 2020.[96] In 2005, 21 civil servants were dismissed; in both 2019 and 2020, only four.[97] Unsatisfactory performance was not the main reason for either dismissal or compulsory retirement; the most common reason for dismissal was absenteeism.

Performance appraisal is also relevant in supporting or hindering candidates' chances of promotion. Promotion boards have applicants' performance records on hand. A negative or lukewarm appraisal or any concern about integrity may adversely affect a candidate's case although seniority is usually the most important factor determining promotion. The staff associations regard reliance on the performance appraisal report as unfair although the promotion boards also interview all the candidates. The assessment panels' moderation of appraisal results has added to the perception of unfairness in some instances.[98]

The difficulty with attempts to link performance appraisal reports to pay, dismissals, and promotions has been that insufficient attention has been paid to the informal culture within the organisation. Performance appraisal runs into resistance from supervisors who often value a harmonious and productive working culture above a more friction-laden, performance-based assessment process. Supervisors

---

92. Legislative Council Panel on Public Service (2003). *Performance management in the public service* (p. 1). LC Paper No. CB (1) 1459/02-03(04). Hong Kong: mimeo.
93. Personal communication, CSB, 29 July 2008.
94. Legislative Council Panel on Public Service (2003) op. cit., p. 3.
95. Legislative Council Panel on Public Service (2007). *Updated overview of civil service conduct and discipline* (p. 5). LC Paper No. CB (1) 1915/06-07(02) Hong Kong: mimeo.
96. PSC (2006). *Annual report 2005* (Appendix VI). https://www.psc.gov.hk/english/ann_rep/files/05rep.pdf; PSC (2020) op. cit., Appendix IX. PSC (2021) op. cit., Appendix X.
97. Ibid. Dismissal means a loss of pension rights; compulsory retirement does not.
98. PSC (2008) op. cit.

seem to dislike the entire performance appraisal process, complaining that it causes resentment, is a waste of time, and that they are asked to report on too many officers. Their behaviour is sometimes antithetical to the performance management goals of the CSB and the PSC. In 2018, for example, the PSC noted instances of failure to complete the annual reporting exercise and of the "central tendency".[99] In one case, a large cohort of officers had all been marked as "very effective".[100] Some departments have tried to improve their procedures, and the CSB and the PSC keep the issue under review, but the problem of producing assessments that are perceived to be fair and adequately reflect performance remains unresolved.

Training

From a public management perspective, a key assumption underlying the need for training is that it will increase productivity and efficiency.[101] Training is about acquiring a competency that is expected to benefit the organisation by cutting its operating costs. But training may also be used as a means of imparting values to civil servants. The balance between competency training and imparting values is indicative of the kind of approach that a government takes to public management. In the 1999 consultation document, for example, there is little mention of values; the stress is on "tailor-made plans" which will enhance "organizational and grade competence".[102] After 2006, however, training programmes reflected an increased concern with value-based integrity management and much more emphasis on the Basic Law and China studies programmes.[103]

Until 2004, training was provided through a relatively independent Civil Service Training and Development Institute (CSTDI), which ran courses in Chinese and English writing, management development, general grades training, information technology, China studies, training in support of the civil service reforms, a Leadership Enhancement and Development programme, and overseas visits for senior staff.[104] In December 2003, the CSB announced plans for a radical restructuring of the institute.[105] It was to concentrate on four areas: senior executive training and development; national studies programmes; consultancy services on human resource management initiatives; and promotion of a continuous learning culture within the civil service. The institute was incorporated into the CSB and lost 47

---

99. PSC (2019). *Annual Report 2018* (pp. 34–36).
100. Ibid.
101. CSB (1999) op. cit., pp. 23–24.
102. Ibid.
103. Legislative Council Panel on Public Service (2008, 18 February). *Integrity enhancement initiatives for civil servants*. LC Paper No. CB (1)764/07-08(05). Legislative Council Panel on Public Service (2008, 25 April). *Update on national studies and Basic Law training for civil servants*, LC Paper No. CB (1) 764/07-08(04).
104. Hong Kong Government (2002). *Hong Kong 2001* (p. 23). Hong Kong: Printing Department.
105. Legislative Council Panel on Public Service (2003). *Reorganization of the Civil Service Training and Development Institute*. LC Paper No. CB (1) 551/03-04 (03). Hong Kong: mimeo.

posts. This was consistent with cost-cutting initiatives and with the stress on decentralising training to the departments, particularly the disciplined services.

Until 2020, when COVID-19 cut numbers, about 56,000 civil servants per year attended a variety of management and communications courses at the CSTDI.[106] They included induction programmes for new recruits, programmes for enhancing managerial competencies such as financial management and decision-making, courses for front-line staff in improving customer service, handling complaints and managing conflicts, performance management courses, language courses in written Chinese and English and effective Putonghua telephone skills, and other more specialised courses.[107] In 2017, after visiting Singapore, Carrie Lam announced that Hong Kong would have a new Civil Service College which would further expand the scope of the CSTDI. She thought that it would help civil servants to "think outside of the box" and handle new technology.[108] The college, which will be located on a new site, is not expected to be operational until 2026.

In 2007, Tsang, under some pressure from leading Chinese officials and some Hong Kong politicians, announced that national education was a community undertaking and that civil servants would have enhanced Basic Law training.[109] Teaching Hong Kong civil servants about China through visits, exchanges, and studies programmes soon developed into a small industry. Aside from the innumerable courses on China available through the CSTDI and local universities, there are now short courses to suit all levels of the civil service on the Mainland.[110] About 700 senior and middle-level civil servants take courses and visit Mainland departments annually.[111] Directorate-level officials and administrative officers may study Chinese government policies and practices at the Chinese Academy of Governance. For those above point 45 on the MPS and the senior ranks of the disciplined services, there are courses available at Tsinghua and Peking Universities.[112] At levels between points 34 and 44 on the MPS, civil servants are required to undertake Chinese studies and training in the Basic Law within six years of reaching point 34 and may study for a week at Zhejiang, Nanjing, or Wuhan universities.[113] There are also a variety of exchange programmes on thematic topics, particularly with Guangdong province. The immediate aim is to enhance civil servants' understanding of the Chinese

---

106. Legislative Council Panel on Public Service (2020, 4 May). An overview of training and development for civil servants (p. 5). https://www.legco.gov.hk/yr19-20/english/panels/ps/papers/ps20200504cb4-506-5-e.pdf
107. Ibid.
108. Lam, J. (2017, 3 August). Hong Kong leader Carrie Lam pledges to set up civil service training academy after visiting facility in Singapore. *SCMP*. https://www.scmp.com/news/hong-kong/politics/article/2105298/hong-kong-leader-carrie-lam-pledges-set-civil-service
109. Tsang, D. Y. K. (2007). *A new direction for Hong Kong* (para 115, 119). https://www.policyaddress.gov.hk/07-08/eng/policy.html
110. Legislative Council Panel on Public Service (2020, 4 May) op. cit.
111. Legislative Council Panel on Public Service (2020, 25 April). *Updated background brief on training and development for civil servants* (p. 3). https://www.legco.gov.hk/yr19-20/english/panels/ps/papers/ps20200504cb4-506-6-e.pdf
112. Legislative Council Panel on Public Service (2020, 4 May) op. cit., p. 6.
113. Ibid.

environment, but the wider goal is to ensure that they follow national policies rather than acting solely in Hong Kong interests.

There are three main lines of criticism of training policy. First, legislators have claimed that the goal of Mainland national studies programmes is to brainwash Hong Kong civil servants into a "one country, one system" frame of mind and that such programmes should only be arranged for those with close working relationships with Mainland authorities.[114] Second, there is a view that training in the Basic Law is superfluous, more symbolic than of any practical value. The Basic Law is taught in schools and, since 2008, civil service applicants are required to demonstrate some knowledge of it; most civil servants are well aware of its provisions.[115] Third, there is some feeling, perhaps implicit in Carrie Lam's rationale for the creation of a Civil Service College, that the strong competency-based element of many CSTDI programmes does not allow many opportunities to think innovatively. The courses available in overseas universities and exchange visits with mainland Chinese government departments provide skills and information but do not usually allow sufficient time for reflection. Even if new ideas do emerge from CSTDI competency-based courses or from overseas visits, the structure and long-established practices of the Hong Kong government do not provide a receptive setting for innovation. Training does not, and cannot be expected to, make up for system-wide deficiencies in the bureaucratic environment.

Integrity Management and Discipline

A second principle that has been sustained since the handover, but has not gone entirely unchallenged, is that Hong Kong should have a corruption-free civil service subject to the rule of law. Public sector corruption, defined as bribery, has long ceased to be a major problem in the civil service, but there have been serious conflicts of interest and a need for the ICAC to adapt to combat the problem. Until 1998, it relied mainly on the stringent provisions and rigorous enforcement of the *Prevention of Bribery Ordinance* (POBO). The emergence of serious conflicts of interest after 1997 led to supplementing the POBO with the common law offence of misconduct in public office and to introducing a value-based integrity management programme for the civil service with the CSB. The POBO remains the cornerstone of the ICAC's corruption prevention efforts, but private sector cases now far outstrip those from the civil service. In 2020, only five civil servants and seven from public bodies were prosecuted compared with 136 from the private sector.[116] The ICAC has always taken a zero-tolerance policy towards corruption. In addition to its Operations Department, its Community Relations Department conducts major campaigns and uses comprehensive publicity to spread its message throughout the

---

114. Legislative Council Panel on Public Service (2020, 25 April) op. cit. pp. 2–3.
115. Legislative Council Panel on Constitutional Affairs (2018, 15 January). LC Paper No. CB(2)661/17-18(03).
116. ICAC (2021). *Annual report 2020* (Appendix 7). https://www.icac.org.hk/icac/annual-report/2020/

society and its Corruption Prevention Department has enabled both public and private organisations to establish effective anti-corruption systems.

In the immediate post-handover period, there was widespread public concern that corruption, imported from China, would increase. Corruption reports to the ICAC, which are used as an indicator of the incidence of corruption, rose to the highest levels ever recorded although the major cause may have been an economic downturn rather than cross-border corruption. Ethical conduct in the civil service was also a concern. In 1996, the Director of Immigration, Leung Ming-yin, was compulsorily retired from the civil service. Leung had been investigated by the ICAC but had been cleared of corruption. The Secretary for the Civil Service said that he had violated civil service regulations by breaching the Housing Loan Scheme, had not fully declared his investments, and had a possible conflict of interest because of a business relationship with a Legislative Councillor. As a consequence, the government had lost confidence in his integrity.[117] It was later revealed that Leung had links with organised crime.[118]

In 1998, the Chief Secretary for Administration, Anson Chan, addressed some of these ethical issues by laying down six core values which, with slight modifications, have remained in place. The values are: commitment to the rule of law; honesty and integrity above private interests; accountability and openness in decision-making; political neutrality; impartiality in the execution of public functions; and dedication and diligence in serving the community. The values may be seen as a precursor of government action to enhance civil service integrity, to introduce an integrity management programme, and to promulgate the *Civil Service Code* in 2009.[119]

The announcement of the core values resulted in a flurry of activity within the government. In 1998, the Ombudsman published an administrative ethics checklist.[120] In the following year, the CSB circulated within the civil service *The civil servants' guide to good practice*, which covered the major corruption offences and ethical issues, such as conflicts of interest, post-public employment, and misconduct in public office.[121] In 2000, the CSB and the ICAC jointly published *Ethical leadership in action*, which created a framework for the integrity management programme.[122] Departments were advised to set up integrity promotion committees headed by a directorate officer and comprising senior officers from functional

---

117. Legislative Council (1997). *Report of the select committee to inquire into the circumstances surrounding the departure of Mr Leung Ming-yin from the government and related issues* (Vol. 1, pp. 31–32). Hong Kong: Government Printer.
118. Cheung, G. (2019, 31 March). Real reason for mysterious departure of Hong Kong's immigration chief in 1996 finally revealed—His links with organised crime. *SCMP*. https://www.scmp.com/news/hong-kong/politics/article/3003984/real-reason-mysterious-departure-hong-kongs-immigration
119. Scott, I., & Gong, T. (2019). *Corruption prevention and good governance in Hong Kong* (pp. 100–103). Abingdon: Routledge.
120. Office of the Ombudsman (1998). *Administrative ethics checklist* (pp. 1–4). Hong Kong: Printing Department.
121. CSB (2005). *Civil servants' guide to good practices*. Hong Kong: Civil Service Bureau.
122. ICAC and CSB (2000). *Ethical leadership in action: Handbook for senior managers in the civil service*. Hong Kong: ICAC and CSB.

areas.[123] Managers were asked to warn their staff about the dangers of "sweeteners", becoming indebted, accepting excessive entertainment and gifts, and taking out loans from dubious sources.

In 2002, the ICAC and the CSB set up an integrity enhancement programme that was intended to incorporate more value-based training into departmental programmes. The Public Works Department, which had many potential opportunities for corruption, was chosen for a pilot study. In 2006, after a successful trial, the ethical leadership programme was extended to the whole civil service except for the Police Force, which already had a value-based integrity programme. The ethical leadership programme requires that an ethics officer, appointed from among directorate staff, develop an annual plan for the department. The plan is considered by a departmental committee which includes a representative of the ICAC's Corruption Prevention Department. If the committee decides that particular areas need investigation, the Corruption Prevention Department may carry out an assignment study and make recommendations to deal with the problem. The plan also includes a training programme, devised with departmental needs in mind. The larger departments develop their own training programmes; smaller ones are reliant on material provided by the ICAC and the CSB.[124] Ethics officers are also supposed to play a role in following up any disciplinary cases referred to them by the ICAC and to deal with any potential departmental conflict of interest cases.

Surveys and interviews with ethics officers suggest that the programme bedded down comparatively quickly within the civil service system.[125] One difficulty was integrating value-based objectives, focusing on ethical conduct, with the rule-based sanctions that applied to violations of the civil service regulations and the POBO.[126] Until the 2000s, training was rule-based and civil servants were constantly reminded of the penalties for corrupt behaviour. With the announcement of core values and the ethical leadership programme, more value-based considerations were introduced and found further expression in the *Civil Service Code*. The code explains what the values are but also alludes to the penalties that may apply if they are violated.[127] Value-based integrity issues raised concern among civil servants because the misconduct in public office offence was originally vaguely defined and applied not only to serious conflicts of interest but also to cases where there was no evident corruption.[128]

---

123. Ibid., p. 38.
124. Brewer, B., Leung, J. Y. H., & Scott, I. (2011). *Report on interviews with ethics officers and assistant ethics officers* (pp. 19–20). Hong Kong: City University of Hong Kong.
125. Ibid.
126. Brewer, B., Leung, J. Y. H., & Scott, I. (2015). Value-based integrity management and bureaucratic organizations: Changing the mix. *International Public Management Journal, 18*(3), 390–410; Scott, I., & Leung, J. Y. H. (2012). Integrity management in post-1997 Hong Kong: Challenges for a rule-based system. *Crime, Law and Social Change, 58*(1), 39–52.
127. CSB (2020). *The Civil Service Code*, op. cit.
128. Leung, J. Y. H., & Scott, I. (2012). *Misconduct in public office: An analysis of Hong Kong cases*. Hong Kong: City University of Hong Kong.

The misconduct in public office offence can be applied when a public official "seriously misconducts himself" and where power has been abused[129] and has been used in cases where it was uncertain that a conviction would be secured under the POBO. The POBO provides that, if an accused can be shown to have accepted an advantage without permission of the Chief Executive or the principal in the private sector, then an offence has been committed.[130] In conflict of interest cases, however, there is not always an immediate advantage to the accused: benefits may be deferred, such as offers of post-service employment, or provided to relatives or friends. In the first major misconduct in public office case in 1998, Shum Kwok-sher, who was the government's Chief Property Manager, was found guilty of awarding contracts worth $150 million to companies controlled by his relatives.[131] Initially, prosecutors also sometimes used the offence to charge civil servants who violated civil service regulations but who were not necessarily guilty of corruption. In 2012, the CFA restricted the meaning of misconduct in public office to focus on the abuse of power which excluded matters more properly treated under the civil service regulations.[132]

The misconduct in public office offence has been used to charge and convict officials at the highest level. In March 2012, a former Chief Secretary of Administration, Rafael Hui Si-yan, was prosecuted for accepting loans, a rent-free apartment, and bribes of $8.5 million from Sun Hung Kai Properties. The prosecution successfully contended that the bribes had been paid to persuade Hui to act favourably towards the company and its interests. He was sentenced to seven and a half years in prison. In 2014, the former Chief Executive, Donald Tsang Yam-kuen, was charged on two counts of misconduct in public office.[133] The first related to an honour given to his interior decoration, the second to a digital broadcasting licence granted to a company, partly owned by a tycoon with whom he was negotiating to rent a residence at a below-market price. Tsang was convicted on the second charge and served a custodial term. His conviction was eventually quashed.

These high-profile convictions did nothing to increase the public's belief that those who transgressed would be punished. As the judge in the Hui case remarked, they confirmed the long-held perception that government and business leaders were cosying up to one another.[134] Tsang's successor, C. Y. Leung, was dogged with allegations of misconduct throughout his term in office and high-ranking officials, including a former Commissioner of the ICAC, have been asked to explain their behaviour by the CSB or the Legislative Council.[135] Surveys suggest that trust in

---

129. *Shum Kwok-sher v HKSAR* (2002) 5 HKCFAR 381.
130. *Prevention of Bribery Ordinance*, Cap 201, S.4 & S.9.
131. *Shum Kwok-sher v HKSAR* op. cit.
132. *HKSAR v Wong Linkay* FACC No. 3 of 2011.
133. Scott, I. (2014). Political scandals and the accountability of the Chief Executive in Hong Kong. *Asian Survey*, 54(5), 966–986.
134. *HKSAR v Rafael Hui Si-yan and Others* (2014) HCCC 98/2013.
135. Gong, T., & Scott, I. (2016). Conflicts of interest and ethical decision-making: Mainland China and Hong Kong comparisons. In A. Lawton, Z. van der Wal, & L. Huberts (Eds.), *Ethics in public policy and management: A global research companion* (pp. 257–276). Abingdon: Routledge.

government and, by implication, in the integrity of politicians and senior civil servants has steadily declined.[136]

The CSB has faced many difficult decisions on conflict of interest matters and what constitutes ethical conduct. In the 2000s, the post-retirement employment of former senior civil servants aroused particular public concern. In 2005, Elaine Chung, who had been Director of Urban Services, was accused of lobbying for government contracts for her new employers.[137] Chung noted that it was five years since she had been involved in the cultural activities to which the contracts related.[138] The CSB subsequently agreed that there was no conflict of interest but warned her not to participate in bids for the contracts. In 2008, a former Director of Housing, Leung Chin-man, was implicated in a conflict of interest over his role in the government's sale, at a below-market price, of an unoccupied home ownership housing project. After retirement, Leung joined the company that had bought the project. In the face of public outrage, Leung resigned and the Chief Executive set up a committee to examine the rules on post-service retirement.[139] Many favoured stricter rules and the government initially took that approach. Civil service staff associations then argued that tighter regulations were a restriction on their future right to work and the application of the rules appears to have been moderated as a consequence.

Directorate-level civil servants must apply for permission to an advisory committee to take up post-public employment.[140] In 2019, all 43 applications at the directorate level were approved although additional restrictions were added in most cases.[141] Applications below the directorate level are considered at the bureau and departmental levels and then forwarded to the advisory committee. In 2019, 647 of 654 applications were approved.[142] The Secretary for the Civil Service considers, and invariably approves, the advisory committee's recommendations. The committee draws a distinction between the sanitisation period of six to 12 months when the applicant may not work, and the control period of two to three years where the work is monitored. These are generous provisions compared with those of civil services elsewhere.[143]

The CSB is also responsible for maintaining discipline and enforcing civil service regulations. The measures employed range from positive attempts to

---

136. PORI (2021). On the whole, do you trust the HKSAR government? https://www.pori.hk/pop-poll/government-en/k001.html?lang=en:
137. Legislative Council Panel on Public Service (2005). *Post-retirement employment of Ms Elaine Chung* (p. 5). LC Paper No. CB (1)1095/04-05(01). Hong Kong: mimeo.
138. Legislative Council Panel on Public Service (2004). First letter dated 16 December from Ms Elaine Chung Lai-kwok. https://www.legco.gov.hk/yr04-05/english/panels/ps/papers/ps1221cb1-532-3e.pdf
139. Committee on Review of Post-Service Outside Work for Directorate Civil Servants (July 2009). *Report on review of post-service review of outside work for civil servants*. https://www.dcspostservice-review.org.hk/english/review.html
140. Advisory Committee on Post-Service Employment of Civil Servants (2020). *31st report*. https://www.jsscs.gov.hk/reports/en/31st_AC_Report_eng.pdf
141. Ibid., 8, Annex B.
142. Ibid., Annex D.
143. OECD (2010). *Post-public employment: Good practices for preventing conflicts of interest*. Paris: OECD.

motivate personnel and encourage greater productivity, to the penalties applied for breach of the regulations and gross misconduct. Under the colonial government, the *Letters Patent* and the *Colonial Regulations*, which covered discipline, lapsed at the handover. After 1997, the Basic Law (Article 48(7)) empowered the Chief Executive to take disciplinary action against civil servants. The *Public Service (Administration) Order* further expanded those powers, specifying procedures if a civil servant is charged with an offence warranting dismissal, suspension, or compulsory retirement.[144] Section 10, for example, permits the Chief Executive summarily to dismiss an officer who is absent from duty without leave for more than 14 days. Further provisions on discipline are contained in the *Public Service (Disciplinary) Regulation*, a regulation made under the authority of the order.

Between July 2018 and the end of March 2020, the CSB reported that there were 1,228 disciplinary cases, of which 29 resulted in dismissal.[145] While it is not possible to disaggregate these figures precisely, a large majority of the cases involved civil servants at lower levels in the service. The PSC statistics, for example, show that the commission advised on 76 disciplinary cases in 2018 and 2019 but only six of those involved civil servants above point 34 on the MPS.[146] Since 2002, departments have resolved minor infractions of the rules involving most civil servants on salaries up to the middle ranges of the MPS. The ICAC is also engaged in the disciplinary process, forwarding cases of alleged misconduct to heads of bureaus and departments. Of 63 completed cases received from the ICAC in 2019, disciplinary action was taken against 42 officers.[147]

Until the political unrest of 2014 and 2019/2020, discipline within the civil service was only a matter of public concern when scandalous behaviour was revealed. With the Umbrella Movement in 2014, police action was more closely scrutinised and questions were asked about whether they were being disciplined if they broke the rules. In 2019/2020, many civil servants demonstrated against the government. By January 2020, 41 had been arrested and 31 had been suspended from duty. The Secretary of the Civil Service said that, if civil servants were convicted, the government would take disciplinary action, resulting in possible dismissal or a warning. A civil service association claimed that suspension violated the presumption of innocence.[148]

As the unrest continued, there was growing public outrage that the behaviour of the riot police, who were widely perceived to be out of control, did not result in more disciplinary action. By November 2019, there had been over 1,200 complaints

---

144. Hong Kong Government (1997). *The Public Service (Administration) Order*. https://www.csb.gov.hk/english/admin/conduct/files/psao103e.pdf
145. CSB (2020). Conduct and discipline. https://www.csb.gov.hk/english/admin/conduct/134.html
146. PSC (2019) op. cit., Appendix IX; PSC (2020) op. cit., Appendix IX.
147. ICAC (2020) op. cit., p. 45, Appendix 10.
148. Cheung, G. (2020, 10 January). Hong Kong protests: 31 arrested civil servants suspended from posts. *SCMP*. https://www.scmp.com/news/hong-kong/politics/article/3045494/hong-kong-protests-31-arrested-civil-servants-suspended

about police behaviour.[149] A *Washington Post* report, based on a leaked police document, revealed that no officer had been suspended, charged, or prosecuted for any incident relating to the riots.[150] By May 2020, 21 officers had been "rebuked", the mildest punishment in the police disciplinary chain.[151] One officer who repeatedly ran his motorbike directly at crowds was temporarily suspended but then reinstated. Many NGOs and concerned groups presented evidence of alleged police brutality, but senior police officers continued to argue against a commission of inquiry and contended that the protesters were to blame for the violence.[152] The contrast between how protesting civil servants were treated and the free rein given to the riot police was very marked.

The Hong Kong public service devotes much time and many resources to issues of corruption, integrity management, and discipline. Aside from the CSB, the ICAC, and the PSC, all of which play major roles, the amount of departmental time spent on those issues is considerable. Why is the government so concerned about such matters? Three reasons are particularly important. First, the civil service is still a traditional bureaucracy. The enforcement of rules is required for the maintenance of the system and the hierarchy. Second, the government has been committed to ensuring that the civil service remains bribery-free and does not return to past corrupt practices. Third, there has been some pressure on the government to improve its monitoring and disciplinary mechanisms. The reform proposals, for example, came under consideration at a time when some cases of shirking and poor performance were widely publicised.[153] Latterly, political unrest has resulted in intense interest in the accountability of civil servants and, particularly, the Police Force.

Assessing whether the measures taken to ensure integrity and enforce discipline have worked is problematic. The best means of avoiding potential conflicts of interest is to ensure that civil servants have an appropriate set of values that will enable them to steer clear of situations where their integrity is compromised. From the 1970s until the last decade, most civil servants have shown a high level of commitment to core values. Since then, there have been doubts about the integrity of the government at the most senior levels after the convictions of Rafael Hui and Donald Tsang and the issue of Leung Chun-ying's business affairs.[154] A cynic might

---

149. Sum, L. K. (2019, 27 November). Hong Kong police receive 1200 complaints over handing of anti-government protests. https://www.scmp.com/news/hong-kong/law-and-crime/article/3039603/hong-kong-police-receive-1200-complaints-over-handling
150. Mahtani, S., McLoughlin, T., Liang, T., & Kilpatrick, R. H. (2019, 24 December). In Hong Kong crackdown, police repeatedly broke their own rules and faced no consequences. *The Washington Post*.
151. Hansard, 20 May 2020, 6792–6802.
152. All-Party Parliamentary Group on Hong Kong (2020). *The shrinking safe space for humanitarian aid workers in Hong Kong: Inquiries into violations of human rights and humanitarian principles by the Hong Kong Police Force*. https://hongkongfp.com/wp-content/uploads/2020/08/APPG.pdf; Amnesty International (2020). *Hong Kong: Missing truth, missing justice; the case and international legal framework for the establishment of a commission of inquiry into the 2019 protests*. London: Amnesty International.
153. Brewer, B. (2001). Human resource management reforms in the Hong Kong government. In A. B. L. Cheung & J. C. Y. Lee (2001) op. cit., p. 274; Burns (2004a) op. cit., pp. 254–257.
154. See Gong & Scott (2016) op. cit.

observe that enforcement of the rules is selective. Disciplinary measures have been applied largely to civil servants in lower-level positions except for the Police Force. At senior levels, the civil service has become increasingly politicised with adverse consequences for the ethos that drove civil servants in Anson Chan's era.

Conclusions

Attempts to reform the personnel system have had mixed success. The vision of a civil service whose size and cost would be reduced, where many more appointments would be on contract, where pay would be linked to performance, and where appraisals would be conducted rigorously and would enable management to identify and promote the competent and coach or punish underperformers, has not been realised. The civil service has reverted to the way it looked in 1997: somewhat bloated in size and expensive to run; a largely permanent establishment; a pay-determination system not linked to performance; an ineffective performance management system; and a disciplinary system which, some high-profile cases notwithstanding, seems mainly to affect lower-level staff.

Why has this happened? The contextual factor is that constant political turmoil and economic downturns have reinforced the long-standing belief that Hong Kong needs a stable civil service. Challenging the traditional expectations of civil servants by introducing reform measures risks increasing dissatisfaction, loss of morale, and problems with recruiting and retaining staff. Since 2007, in each of the personnel policy areas that we have considered, a more benign interpretation of practice in favour of civil servants seems to have been employed. In summary:

Tung's reforms effectively downsized the civil service but, subsequently, there has been a gradual increase in establishment, spurred by the expansionist agendas of Leung and Lam, to the point where, by 2021, the civil service establishment was as large as it had been at the start of the reform process.

Tung's salary cuts and pension changes temporarily reduced the cost of the civil service. Between 2007 and 2020, however, the recurrent costs of the civil service increased over threefold. Despite concerns over the methodologies used in pay determination, the changes have been relatively minor and have not disadvantaged civil servants. The system remains largely as it was in 1979.

There has been continuing concern over performance appraisal. Since the promotion system is primarily based on seniority and most civil servants receive a "very effective" or "effective" rating, it may be that effort could be better expended elsewhere. Training programmes do not appear to deliver the innovative civil servants that the government says it wants. But this is as much a problem of a highly bureaucratic system as of the training programmes as such.

Integrity management, based on the inculcation of values, was a new posthandover initiative. Coupled with the ICAC's use of the misconduct in public office offence, it promised much as an antidote for the increasing number of conflicts of interest. Integrity management has had some effect in requiring civil servants to think about their conduct but, in some cases, the interpretation continued to be that, if it was legal, it was permissible.

With the government facing a large budgetary deficit for the foreseeable future, the government is not meeting one of its most important principles: living within its means. Resources have been spent on bolstering the civil service in ways that do little to meet other pressing concerns (see Chapters 8 to 10). The system requires urgent reform, but the continuing belief that a stable civil service is a necessity in times of political volatility may act as a brake on change.

6
Government and Public Bodies

Over the years, the Hong Kong government has created and funded many different types of organisation to provide advice or deliver services. These quasi-government public bodies have varying degrees of formal autonomy to run their affairs. Their complex relationship with core government raises important questions about whether the extent of their autonomy, their organisational structures, their funding, and their methods of coordination are appropriate for the functions they are expected to perform and for their accountability.[1] Although public bodies are not part of the civil service, they have become an established part of the governance framework and of public expectations about service delivery. Their relationship with core government has gradually changed. Until the 1950s, the government relied mainly on churches and charitable organisations to supply social services. When the government itself became more involved in social policy provision, it decided to establish more public bodies, such as the Hospital Authority, to deliver some services. The Tung administration took this a step further by supporting privatisation, public-private partnerships, outsourcing, and greater devolution of government functions. With the failure of many of these initiatives, several scandals, and more concern with centralisation and political unrest, the enthusiasm for creating new public bodies or expanding the functions of existing organisations declined. In 2008, a government survey found that there were 509 advisory and statutory bodies.[2] By 2018, the Home Affairs Bureau estimated that there were about 490.[3]

What explains these shifts in the government's attitudes towards public bodies? Underlying the fluctuations have been different conceptions of the functions that government should perform. Changing beliefs about what core government should do and how much should be left to public bodies or the private sector have affected

---

1. Thynne, I. (2018). Fundamentals of government structure: Alignments of organizations at and beyond the center of power. In W. R. Thompson (Ed.), *Oxford research encyclopedia of politics*. New York: Oxford University Press. https://oxfordre.com/politics/view/10.1093/acrefore/9780190228637.001.0001/acrefore-9780190228637-e-128
2. Home Affairs Bureau (2005). *Legislative Council Panel on Home Affairs: Review of advisory and statutory bodies: Interim Report No. 14. Review of the classification system of advisory and statutory bodies in the public sector* (Annex 1). Hong Kong: The Bureau.
3. Hansard, 31 October 2018, 869–872.

the size, autonomy, legal status, and funding of the public bodies. Shifting concepts of the appropriate relationship between government and non-government providers of public services have also raised important questions about the accountability, transparency, and representativeness of quasi-government organisations. In this chapter, we consider, first, how the public bodies have evolved; second, their legal status and funding; third, their representativeness, autonomy, and accountability; and, finally, contentious issues arising from the composition of their boards and the remuneration of their senior executives.

The Evolution of Government's Relationship with Service Providers

Under colonial rule, the Hong Kong government's involvement in social policy was initially restricted to regulating education and health care, making occasional benevolent donations and grants of land to schools and hospitals, and providing limited support for the destitute and for refugees. The colonial government was strongly disinclined to develop social policy programmes for two reasons. First, the prevailing philosophy was that government should be kept small and its functions should be limited. Business leaders believed that any social policy programmes could only be funded by increased taxes, to which they were fiercely opposed. Second, the British government put pressure on the Hong Kong authorities to balance the budget and there was little slack for expenditure on social policy. Instead, the government monitored providers to prevent schools from becoming hotbeds of political dissent or condoning unhygienic health practices causing epidemics.

After the Second World War, regulation of the social policy system alone could no longer adequately address the colony's problems. The influx of refugees from China created major housing problems, led to communist activities in the schools and labour unions, and aggravated economic difficulties. The government began to reconsider its relationship with service providers. In 1947, it set up a Social Welfare Office and supported the creation of the Hong Kong Council of Social Service, which was incorporated in 1951 and has since served as the peak organisation and mediator between the government and the welfare providers. There was little funding support for welfare; the government's view was that any aid that recipients received should be used to encourage them to return to the workforce as quickly as possible.

In two other areas, the government was more interventionist. The housing problem was acute; there were thousands of squatters and the constant danger of fire. Despite some pressure from Britain, the government was reluctant to intervene, believing that it did not have sufficient capacity to resolve the problem.[4] In December

---

4. Ure, G. (2012). *Governors, politics and the Colonial Office: Public policy in Hong Kong, 1918–58* (pp. 135–161). Hong Kong: Hong Kong University Press.

1953, the Shek Kip Mei fire finally led to government action. The land occupied by the squatters was resumed and a public housing programme was started that eventually provided accommodation for nearly half the population.[5] In education, fear of communist activities in the schools led to a greatly expanded public primary education programme.[6] By the 1960s, the government was providing important housing and education benefits, but it did so grudgingly under pressure from social and political forces that it could not entirely control.

After the riots of 1966 and 1967, there was a sea change in attitudes. Policy outputs—more housing, better education, better health facilities, more social welfare—provided the underpinning for the administration's attempt to bolster its legitimacy. Ancillary changes to devolve responsibilities to government-owned public corporations occurred at the same time. In 1973, the government introduced a new *Housing Authority Ordinance* which established the Housing Authority as a public corporation responsible for the construction and management of public housing estates. The housing powers and functions of the existing Housing Authority, the Housing Board, the Urban Council, and the Commissioner for Resettlement were consolidated in a single body, but the government did not see the Housing Authority as a new form of organisation.[7] The Housing Department, which was the executive arm of the authority, remained part of the civil service.

In 1975, the government did believe that it was breaking new ground when it established the MTRC as a wholly owned public corporation to build and then run Hong Kong's underground railway system.[8] The principal reason for setting up the MTRC lay in its commercial possibilities. It followed that Hong Kong's other railway, the KCRC, which had been a government department since 1910, should also be set up as a public corporation and an ordinance was passed in 1982. Measures were also introduced to provide for government regulation of the electricity companies and the bus companies, which operated under schemes of control that capped their charges and required that certain performance standards be met.[9]

Increasing social policy outputs had considerable political advantages.[10] It enabled the government to claim that it deserved to rule because it was an efficient government and provided the kind of services that people wanted. The government began to look more favourably at other means of providing these services. In 1985, consultants were appointed to investigate more cost-effective ways of delivering health services. Their recommendation was to establish a single authority because

---

5. Smart, A. (2006). *The Shek Kip Mei myth: Squatters, fires and colonial rule in Hong Kong, 1950–1963* (Ch. 6). Hong Kong: Hong Kong University Press.
6. Sweeting, A. (1993). *A phoenix transformed: The reconstruction of education in post-war Hong Kong* (pp. 218–219). Hong Kong: Oxford University Press.
7. Hansard, 14 February 1973, 440.
8. Hansard, 2 April 1975, 658.
9. Lam, P. L. (1996). *The scheme of control on electricity companies* (pp. 17–29). Hong Kong: City University of Hong Kong Press.
10. Scott, I. (1989). *Political change and the crisis of legitimacy in Hong Kong* (pp. 152–165). London: Hurst; Lee, J. (1999). *Housing, home ownership and social change in Hong Kong* (p. 13). Aldershot: Ashgate.

"the current system of medical services delivery will become increasingly ... costly to maintain and less able to cope with the demands placed upon it".[11] When the Hospital Authority was created in 1990, the model adopted, after some years of contentious debate, was similar in form to the Housing Authority.[12] The Hospital Authority was given overall responsibility for the management of public hospitals although public health remained under departmental control. In 1988, the government also made further changes to the Housing Authority, permitting greater financial flexibility for the implementation of its long-term housing strategy.[13]

There were good political reasons for strengthening the powers of the authorities. Complaints about the quality of social policy outputs were rising and added to the pressures on government. Demands for more representative political institutions, fears about the Chinese resumption of sovereignty, and the Tiananmen Square incident all meant declining legitimacy for the government. To deflect complaints to public bodies outside government was politically desirable because criticism was directed away from what was becoming an overloaded government. The Broadcasting Authority was set up as a statutory body in 1987 and was made responsible for answering complaints about radio and television. To deal with complaints more broadly, a Commissioner of Administrative Complaints was established in 1989, predictably receiving the largest number of complaints about housing.

In the 1990s, the government began to devolve even more responsibilities to statutory bodies and to allow them to charge more for their services. These measures were driven by both commercial considerations and wider political concerns. A strongly expressed fear during the transitional period was that a centralised bureaucracy with the autocratic powers held by the colonial regime could be used to suppress civil liberties after 1997. Consequently, there was support in government for spreading more of the public sector beyond the traditional civil service. The powers of the Commissioner of Administrative Complaints were strengthened and an Equal Opportunities Commission was established. An attempt was also made to corporatise Radio Television Hong Kong although this was abandoned after opposition from the Chinese government.[14] In similar vein, the government passed legislation to protect the privacy of individual data and to provide access to information.

On the commercial side, the government began to experiment with changing the ways departments conducted their business. A *Trading Funds Ordinance* was passed in 1993, which enabled government departments to operate in a commercial manner, provided that they were efficient and effective and had "the capacity

---

11. W. D. Scott & Company (1985). *Report on the delivery of medical services* (pp. 2–3). Hong Kong: The Company.
12. Gauld, R., & Gould, D. (2002). *The Hong Kong health sector: Development and change* (pp. 51–73). Hong Kong: The Chinese University of Hong Kong Press.
13. Hansard, 9 March 1988, 899.
14. Cheung, A. B. L. (1997). Reform in search of politics: The case of Hong Kong's aborted attempt to corporatise public broadcasting. *The Asian Journal of Public Administration 19*(2), 276–302.

to meet the expenses incurred in the provision of the government service".[15] Six trading funds were eventually established: the Lands Registry, the Companies Registry, the Office of the Telecommunication Authority, the Post Office, Electrical and Mechanical Services, and Sewage Services. In 1998, the Sewage Services Fund was terminated after members of the Legislative Council criticised it for raising charges.[16] The funds were not usually given the liberty to set their prices, continued to operate as monopolies, and they did not live up to the expectations of those who wanted to see more commercial activity in government.[17] Another major commercial venture was the building of an international airport at Chek Lap Kok. The government established an Airport Authority, drafting the legislation along similar lines to that of the MTRC.[18] This raised concerns that there was insufficient government control over the new public corporation, a fear that seemed justified after the disastrous opening of the airport when the Legislative Council's investigation laid some of the blame for inadequate monitoring of the authority at the door of senior officials.[19]

After the handover, the Tung administration based its commitment to small government on the belief that the private sector could undertake many public functions in more efficient ways than the civil service. The measures that were taken mostly involved public-private partnerships, establishing government-owned public corporations and subvented bodies. Outsourcing also occurred, but it was mainly for public works or government services such as cleaning or parking. There were cross-cutting values at work. Although the government wanted to devolve some of its responsibilities, it also wanted to strengthen its grip on subvented organisations to make them financially accountable for taxpayers' money and to retain control of service delivery. Many senior civil servants believed that statutory bodies and subvented organisations were inefficient.

An important obstacle to greater privatisation has been actual or prospective political opposition. There were many fronts on which the government has had to battle to win or retain support. To introduce further controversial measures would have aroused the ire of the unions, members of the Legislative Council, and perhaps civil servants. The Chinese government, too, has favoured the centralisation of functions and opposed both the corporatisation of government broadcasting and the

---

15. *Trading Funds Ordinance*, Cap 430, S.3(2).
16. Cheung, A. B. L. (2001). The "trading fund" reform in Hong Kong. In A. B. L. Cheung & J. C. Y. Lee (Eds.), *Public sector reform in Hong Kong: Into the 21st century* (p. 204). Hong Kong: The Chinese University of Hong Kong Press; Lam, P. L., & Chan, Y. C. (1997). *Privatising water and sewage services* (p. 3). Hong Kong: City University of Hong Kong Press.
17. Cheung (2001) op. cit., pp. 218–220; Huque, A. S., Hayllar, M. R., Cheung, A. B. L., Flynn, N., & Wong, H. K. (1999). *Public sector reform in Hong Kong: The performance of trading funds* (p. 1). Occasional Papers Series. Hong Kong: Department of Public and Social Administration, City University of Hong Kong.
18. Cheung, A. B. L. (2006). How autonomous are public corporations in Hong Kong? The case of the Airport Authority. *Public Organization Review* 6(3), 221–236.
19. Legislative Council (1999). *Select committee inquiry report on the new airport* (Vol. 1, pp. 187–191). https://www.legco.gov.hk/yr98-99/english/sc/sc01/papers/chapter7.pdf

partial privatisation of the Airport Authority.[20] Politicians and academics also questioned whether privatisation and devolution were more efficient and cost-effective than the services provided by the government. Legislative Councillors were critical of the lack of accountability of public bodies, outraged over the large salaries paid to their senior executives, scandalised over the misuse of public money, fearful of possible job losses in the civil service, and concerned about the seemingly inevitable increase in fees for public services that were once free or relatively inexpensive.

Many of these concerns were raised in a debate in the Legislative Council in 1999 on the privatisation of government departments. Lee Cheuk-yan, the head of the Hong Kong Confederation of Trade Unions, introduced a motion urging the government to oppose privatisation.[21] He said that the government was ignoring

> the five big evils accompanying the privatisation of government services, namely a drop in service quality; heavier burden for the people as a result of loss of control on the monitoring of charges; retrogression in democracy due to dwindling accountability; adverse effects . . . from piecemeal implementation of government policies; and the smashing of the "rice bowls" of staff that might lead to unemployment, social unrest and suppressed wages.[22]

Against the "five big evils", the then Financial Secretary, Donald Tsang, posited what he saw as the four virtues. Corporatisation, he said, had distinct commercial advantages. The service providers could develop a customer-oriented culture. The cost-effectiveness of services could be more accurately assessed. Corporations would no longer be subject to government rules and could adjust to changing market conditions. Private sector organisations could take part in offering services previously provided by government.[23] Tsang noted that staff would be consulted on changes, redundancies would be avoided as far as possible, service quality would be enhanced, and the level of charges would be monitored or included in the operating agreement with the new public body.[24]

The Asian financial crisis increased the pressure on the government to do more for business and to decrease the cost of running the civil service. In the heyday of its support for privatisation, the government had an extensive agenda of assets that it intended to sell off to the private sector. In the 2003 budget, the Financial Secretary announced that the government would sell $112 billion in assets over the following five years.[25] In 2004, his successor noted that about $21 billion had been realised through selling housing loans to the Hong Kong Mortgage Corporation and the securitisation of revenues from government toll tunnels and bridges.[26] There were

---

20. Cheung (1997) op. cit.; Cheung (2006) op. cit.
21. Hansard, 16 June 1999, 8791.
22. Ibid., 8787–8788.
23. Ibid., pp. 8855–8856.
24. Ibid., p. 8858.
25. Financial Secretary (2003). *The budget 2003–04* (p. 25). Hong Kong: Printing Department.
26. Financial Secretary (2004). *The 2004–05 budget* (p. 25). Hong Kong: Government Logistics Department.

proposals to contract out welfare services and water supplies and to privatise public corporations of which the MTRC was to be the first example. Future candidates for privatisation were thought to include 25%–49% of the Airport Authority, car parking spaces and shopping centres owned by the Housing Authority, the remaining shares in the MTRC, the Post Office, the KCRC, the Water Services Department, the Environmental Protection Department, and the government's holding in Disneyland.[27]

By 2008, the only project that had been fully implemented was the sale of the Housing Authority's car parking and shopping centres and even that was delayed by a court case brought by activists.[28] The KCRC's rolling stock was all leased to the MTRC for 50 years in December 2007 but not without opposition from the democratic parties, who voted against the bill, and from some MTRC shareholders who were opposed to the corporation's reduced autonomy in deciding on fares.[29] Other reasons for the inability to divest government assets were the Chinese government's opposition to privatisation of the Airport Authority and the political fallout from attempting to privatise a government department.

The government's attitude to privatisation also changed. It had less need to sell assets once the economic situation began to improve. Tsang was also less willing to court controversy by doing so. Rather than divesting assets, the government became more interested in regulating the commercial sector through the introduction of competition law and by rewriting the *Companies Ordinance*.[30] After conducting a major review of advisory and statutory boards between 2003 and 2005,[31] the government may have concluded that its relationships with public bodies had been clarified and that further initiatives were neither necessary nor desirable. The Tung administration also left a legacy of public-private partnerships failures and financial losses and other problems associated with government companies and statutory boards. The Harbour Fest project with the American Chamber of Commerce lost the government $100 million and generated much adverse publicity.[32] The joint venture Disneyland project was widely seen to be a bad deal for the government.[33] In the technology field, the performance and financial losses of government-owned companies and statutory boards, such as Cyberport, the Science and Technology Parks Corporation, and the Applied Science and Technology Research Institute

---

27. Baglole, J. (2003, 23 October). Hong Kong's big sell-off. *Far Eastern Economic Review*; Chong, F. (2004, 5 February). Bonkers over property float. *The Australian*.
28. *Lo Siu Lan v Hong Kong Housing Authority*, FACV 10/2005.
29. Yeung, R. (2008). *Moving millions: The commercial success and political controversies of Hong Kong's railways* (pp. 264–265). Hong Kong: Hong Kong University Press.
30. Financial Secretary (2008). *The 2008–09 budget* (p. 30). Hong Kong: Government Logistics Department.
31. Legislative Council Panel on Home Affairs (2005). *Progress report on the review of advisory and statutory bodies*. https://www.legco.gov.hk/yr04-05/english/panels/ha/papers/ha0513cb2-1488-1e.pdf
32. Director of Audit (2004). *Report No. 42: Harbour Fest*. https://www.aud.gov.hk/pdf_e/e42ch04.pdf; Rowse, M. (2009). *No minister and no, minister: The true story of HarbourFest*. Hong Kong: Blacksmith Books.
33. Higgins, C. D., & Huque, A. S. (2015). Public money and Mickey Mouse: Evaluating performance and accountability in the Hong Kong Disneyland joint venture public-private partnership. *Public Management Review*, *17*(8), 1103–1123.

(ASTRI), resulted in more bad press. To cap this litany of failures, the Director of Audit found that the Tourism Board (HKTB) had been badly mismanaged, leading to the resignation of the chair and its executive director.[34]

It is not surprising that Tung's successors did not share his zeal for public-private partnerships and the creation of new public bodies. But the government could scarcely reduce funding or abolish those organisations because they delivered many public goods and services, furnished policy advice, and managed some regulatory functions. After the 2005 review, the government wanted to make public bodies more cost-effective. Its strong regulatory and financial controls over statutory bodies, subvented organisations, and government corporations were mainly exercised in cases of poor implementation or where it thought that the agency was acting contrary to policy. Managerial procedures and financial controls had often been tightened on the recommendations of the Audit Commission. After the HKTB audit, the commission devoted more attention to public bodies and any schemes devolved to them. Overall, however, the government has tended to keep public bodies at arm's length.[35]

Aside from the important functions that statutory bodies, subvented organisations, and government corporations perform in delivering goods and services, public bodies have also proved useful as a means to implement policies that the Chinese government wants Hong Kong to pursue. In 2012, it was announced that the MTRC would be responsible for the construction of the high-speed rail link to connect with the Mainland network. Although the devolution of responsibilities did not allow the government to avoid organised opposition and strong criticism of the cost and utility of the project, it did deflect problems of implementation to the corporation.[36] In 2019, further large sums were diverted to Hong Kong government corporations to pursue a Chinese government initiative when the Financial Secretary announced that the Science and Parks Technology Corporation and Cyberport would receive most of a $50 billion allocation to support Hong Kong's part in the further development of a technology hub in southern China.[37]

Despite these substantial projects, the more common pattern of recent interaction between government and the public bodies has been that of a steady-state relationship rather than one of radical changes. The enthusiasm for new public bodies in the 1990s and 2000s has waned. The failure of many devolved initiatives under the Tung administration, declining belief that the private sector can perform more

---

34. Director of Audit (2007). *Report No. 49: Hong Kong Tourism Board: Corporate governance and administrative issues*. https://www.aud.gov.hk/pdf_e/e49ch05.pdf
35. Painter, M., & Yee, W. H. (2012). Agencies and policies in an administrative state: The case of Hong Kong. *Policy and Society*, *31*(3), 223–235.
36. SCMP (2015, 25 September). Over-budget and behind schedule: Hong Kong must now make haste on high-speed rail link to Guangzhou. Editorial.
37. Financial Secretary (2019). *Budget speech by the Financial Secretary* (paras 64–75). www.budget.gov.hk/2019/eng/speech.html; Government of the People's Republic of China (2019). *Outline development plan for the Guangdong-Hong Kong-Macao Greater Bay Area*. https://www.bayarea.gov.hk/filemanager/en/share/pdf/Outline_Development_Plan.pdf

efficiently than the public sector, the increasing tendency of the Hong Kong government supported by the PRC to centralise rather than decentralise its functions, and the absence of major new social policies have all contributed to the view that the role of government should be expanded and that public bodies should simply do what they have traditionally done.

The Legal Status and Funding of Service Providers

The bewildering range of relationships that exist between the Hong Kong government and public bodies is a consequence of their piecemeal development. To understand how this affects their accountability, it is necessary to classify these relationships. By public bodies, we mean organisations that perform public functions but which, because of their legal status or primary roles as private sector organisations, enjoy varying degrees of autonomy from core government. In June 2005, the government attempted to classify the 509 advisory and statutory bodies.[38] At that time, 229 of those organisations were statutory bodies established under ordinance. By 2020, the number of advisory and statutory bodies was similar, but the number of statutory bodies had risen to 270.[39] The advisory and statutory bodies range in type from executive agencies to statutory corporations to some private companies. They also include funded voluntary welfare organisations but not other civil society organisations unless they are funded by government.

The government's 2005 classification of advisory and statutory bodies comprised seven categories: advisory boards and committees (287); non-departmental public bodies (15); regulatory bodies (48); appeal boards (59); advisory and management boards of trusts and funds (74); public corporations (5); and miscellaneous boards and committees (21).[40] This classification is not entirely satisfactory because the category "non-departmental public bodies" is a catchall for public bodies which had financial or organisational problems or were in conflict with the government at the time. The classification used here is based on three variables:

- the extent to which the public sector organisation is funded by government,
- the legal framework under which the public sector organisation has been established, and
- the extent to which specific circumstances influence attempts to ensure accountability.

In this section, public bodies are classified according to their legal status and their funding relationships with government.

Public bodies range from quite closely supervised bodies, such as executive agencies established by government under executive orders or delegated legislation,

---
38. Legislative Council Panel on Home Affairs (2005) op. cit.
39. Hansard, 3 June 2020, 7538–7547.
40. Legislative Council Panel on Home Affairs (2005) op. cit.

to bodies such as the Hospital Authority, which have close relations with government departments and policymaking bureaus, to public corporations such as the MTRC, which once enjoyed a much greater degree of independence. Between these extremes, many organisations—for example, voluntary welfare organisations, tertiary-level educational institutions, the Trade Development Council, the Productivity Commission and the ICAC—receive most, or all, of their funding from government and are accountable for how that money is spent. Some companies, such as the bus companies and the electricity companies, operate monopolies or duopolies and are subject to regulation under schemes of control. Other arrangements apply to property that the government may own but does not always choose to operate. The government owns some tunnels and bridges, but others are run by private companies on long-term contracts. The HZMB is jointly owned and operated in partnership with the Chinese government.

Although there has been no coherent pattern to the Hong Kong government's efforts to oversee these many different kinds of organisation, they do fall into certain categories according to their funding arrangements and legal status. Table 6.1 presents a classification based on these variables. The relationship between the government and public bodies can, however, sometimes change quite quickly. The government can alter the legal status of public bodies, as it tried to do with its unsuccessful attempt to amend the *Airport Authority Ordinance* to allow for partial privatisation.[41] There may also be functional changes that might result in more or less autonomy from government. In 2002, the Housing Authority, for example, was given a role as a housing facilitator, rather than a provider, and came under more direct government control.[42] Public bodies themselves sometimes lobby for a change in their status, as the Examination and Assessment Authority did when it argued for government funding rather than relying wholly on student fees.[43] A difficulty in classifying public bodies is that their legal status is not wholly exclusive. Thus, a statutory body established under an ordinance can also be a charitable trust for income tax purposes and a public corporation. Consequently, the classification is based on both the organisation's legal status and its funding relationship with government.

With these caveats in mind, we can examine specific types of public body and the reasons why government has established a particular kind of relationship with them.

---

41. Cheung (2006) op. cit.; Legislative Council Panel on Economic Services (2004). *Privatization of Airport Authority*. https://www.legco.gov.hk/yr03-04/english/panels/es/papers/es0223cb1-1017-5e.pdf; Legislative Council (2004). *Background brief on Airport Authority (Amendment) Bill 2004*. LC Paper No. CB (1) 1693/03.
42. Hong Kong Government (2002, 20 June). *Statement by CS on the review of the institutional framework for housing* [Press release].
43. *SCMP* (2017, 10 August). Hong Kong exam authority seeks government cash as fewer students take tests. https://www.scmp.com/yp/learn/learning-resources/article/3065692/hong-kong-exam-authority-seeks-more-government-cash

Table 6.1 *The Organisation of the Public Sector*

Type	Legal Foundation	Funding	Examples
A. *Core Government Organisations*			
1. Policy bureau	Recognised under the Basic Law but established by an executive order or decision.	Fully funded by government.	Development Bureau; Education Bureau; Transport and Housing Bureau.
2. Government department	Recognised under the Basic Law but established by an executive order or decision.	Mostly fully funded by government. Some departments may operate as trading funds.	Home Affairs Department; Social Welfare Department. The Post Office operates as a trading fund.
B. *Quasi-government Organisations*			
3. Executive body	Established by executive order or directive.	Usually fully funded by government.	Hong Kong Monetary Authority; University Grants Committee; Women's Commission.
4. Trusts/Funds	Established as trust with the Permanent Secretary of the relevant department as trustee.	Funded by government but may also receive financial support from charities.	Child Development Fund; Quality Education Fund.
5. "Not-for-profit" subvented statutory body	Established by ordinance.	Fully or nearly fully subvented by government.	Independent Commission Against Corruption.
6. "Not-for-profit" non-subvented body	May or may not be established by ordinance.	Organisation charges fees and is self-financing.	Hong Kong Examination and Assessment Authority.
7. Partially commercial entity underwritten by government	Established by an ordinance as an incorporated statutory body.	May charge fees or rents or sell property but may be dependent on government backing for capital expenditure.	Hospital Authority; Airport Authority.
8. Commercially viable entity	Established by an ordinance as an incorporated statutory body.	Wholly self-financing but government may forego dividends to support further capital expenditure.	Kowloon-Canton Railway Corporation. After 2007, the KCRC remained a statutory corporation managing the service concession to the MTRC.

Table 6.1 (continued)

Type	Legal Foundation	Funding	Examples
9. Company in which government holds all or a majority of shares	Established by its own constitution, pursuant to the *Companies Ordinance* and sometimes also subject to a special ordinance.	Wholly self-financing but government may waive or defer dividends in the interest of further capital expenditure.	Mass Transit Railway Corporation Limited.
C. Private Organisations with Public Functions			
10. "Not-for-profit" private (voluntary) welfare organisations	Established by its own constitution or deed of trust under such ordinances as the *Societies Ordinance* and sometimes incorporated under an ordinance.	Regularly or partially subvented by government grants with supplementation from charities.	Hong Kong Aids Foundation; Hong Kong Council on Smoking and Health; Community Drug Advisory Council; Po Leung Kuk.
11. Publicly listed company or private company with public functions	Established by its own constitution pursuant to the *Companies Ordinance*, operating under a contract, franchise, build-own-operate agreement with government.	Company contracts with government to manage a public function at a profit but with controls over prices and standards and sometimes with build-own-operate arrangements.	Bus companies; tunnel companies.

Sources: This table is based on the legislation and annual reports of the government departments and organisations mentioned in this chapter. I am grateful to Ian Thynne for his help in clarifying many of these relationships and for his suggestions on the wording of the categories.

Core Government Functions

The Hong Kong government has delegated power under Article 16 of the Basic Law to conduct, on its own, the administrative affairs of the HKSAR. Core government functions are provided by the bureaus and departments which are staffed by civil servants. Article 60 of the Basic Law provides that a "Department of Administration, a Department of Finance, a Department of Justice and various bureaus, divisions and commissions shall be established" in the government. Structural changes in government, such as the creation of a new bureau, may involve seeking the approval of the Legislative Council if new positions are required. But the authority to change the structure of government rests with the executive.

The funding of bureaus and departments comes from revenue raised by the government. Some departments may have income from their activities, but most are reliant on funding granted by the Legislative Council when it approves the budget estimates. This enables the council, through its Finance Committee, the Panel on Public Service, and other specialised panels, to monitor how the government spends its money and whether requests for new positions are justified.

Quasi-Government Organisations

Public bodies may be created in different ways: by executive decree; by the creation of a trust; under an ordinance passed by the Legislative Council; or by their constitutions which may provide for functions that are in the public interest and for which they may receive government funding. We consider examples of each of these types of public body.

Executive Body

In purely legal terms, the simplest way to create a relatively autonomous organisation to perform specific functions is by government decree. This may be done either through an executive order or under delegated legislation. The Hong Kong Monetary Authority, for example, serves as the equivalent of a Central Bank and administers the *Banking Ordinance*, the Exchange Fund and the fiscal reserves, and the government's investments in the stock market. It was formed in 1993 from the Monetary Affairs Branch and the Banking Commissioner's Office of the Hong Kong government. It was not established under its own ordinance, but its functions are clearly laid out in the *Banking Ordinance*, the *Exchange Fund Ordinance*, and various other ordinances.[44] The relationship between the authority and the government is very close. The government funds the authority directly from the fiscal reserves without the oversight of the Legislative Council; the Financial Secretary retains the chair of its major committees, and many of its senior officials are former civil servants.

Fully funding an executive agency is quite common in Hong Kong, but there is no reason why these agencies should not be set up as self-financing bodies if they can generate revenue. Despite the financial dependency of most agencies on government, there is no guarantee that friction will be avoided. Specific funding and political issues may arise and can be a source of conflict if powers and duties are not carefully defined. There are also accountability issues. In setting up such agencies, the government does not always make provision for legislative oversight of their work. The Hong Kong Monetary Authority, for example, has been required to work hard to develop its relationship with legislative committees to keep them apprised of what it is doing; its chief executive meets with the Legislative Council

---

44. Hong Kong Monetary Authority (2020). Governance structure. https://www.hkma.gov.hk/eng/about-us/the-hkma/governance-structure/

Panel on Financial Affairs three times a year and other members of the authority appear before the Bills Committee if required.[45]

Trusts/Funds

The government often sets up trusts to manage funds aimed at providing specific services. The trust is created by a Declaration of Trust and the permanent secretary of the supervising department is appointed as the trustee. A steering committee composed of civil servants and specialists in the field makes decisions on the development of schemes and the allocation of grants. The Quality Education Fund, for example, which was established in 1998 with an allocation of $5 billion from the government, supports educational initiatives that would not otherwise be funded by government or other sources.[46] The Permanent Secretary of the Education Bureau is the trustee and the Bureau provides 25 civil servants to run the fund's secretariat and to assist its steering committee. Similarly, the Child Development Fund allocates grants for projects assisting disadvantaged children and receives its funding principally from the government although it is also supported by many businesses and charities. Its steering committee, which is largely composed of *ex officio* members, is chaired by the permanent secretary of the Labour and Welfare Bureau.[47]

"Not-for-Profit" Subvented Statutory Body

Unlike the executive agencies and the trusts, subvented statutory bodies are established under ordinance. The powers and duties of the subvented body are subject to scrutiny by the Legislative Council, which approves their funding. For the government to propose such an arrangement there must be some function that it believes can be performed better by an independent or autonomous agency. The ICAC is a classic example of this type of organisation. Its principal purpose—to prevent corruption and to pursue and prosecute those who engage in corrupt activities—cannot easily be undertaken by the government. If the government did bring corruption prevention directly under its control, its impartiality would be called into question. Given the nature of its functions, the ICAC could scarcely be expected to raise money to fund its own activities. It is necessarily a fully subvented statutory body whose officers are employed on contract.

---

45. Hong Kong Monetary Authority (2020). Legislative Council issues. https://www.hkma.gov.hk/eng/data-publications-and-research/legislative-council-issues/
46. Quality Education Fund (2019). *Collaborate for pedagogical innovation: Cultivate for quality education.* https://www.qef.org.hk/
47. Labour and Welfare Bureau (2020). Child Development Fund. https://www.cdf.gov.hk/en/

"Not-for-Profit" Non-subvented Body

Some organisations, which may or may not be established under ordinance, perform public functions but are permitted to charge for their services. Since the function is in the public interest, the organisation is not allowed to charge fees to make a profit although it will seek to cover its costs. The Examinations and Assessment Authority is an example of this type of public body although it has argued that fees paid by students are insufficient to cover its costs.[48]

Partially Commercial Entity Underwritten by Government

Some organisations have been set up outside the government to implement policy without the constraints of normal bureaucratic practice. The Housing Authority, the Hospital Authority, and the Airport Authority have several significant features in common.

First, they are public corporations established under ordinances passed by the Legislative Council. In some respects, they may act in ways similar to private companies: they may sue and be sued, for example. But they also have legal entitlements that private companies may not have; they may be charitable trusts, for example, which would give them favourable income tax benefits.

Second, they have large capital expenditures that may be provided or underwritten by government or financed from their activities. The government is necessarily concerned about expenditure in these areas. The Housing Authority, for example, changed its role from the "bricks and mortar" provision of public housing to advising government on a housing strategy to encourage more private sector involvement. Although a majority of the board are from the private sector, its chair and three other public officials represent the government.[49] The Airport Authority and the Hospital Authority, by contrast, are chaired by members from the private sector although there are public officials on their boards.[50]

Third, the authorities can make money themselves. The Housing Authority charges rent and sells flats; the Hospital and Airport Authorities charge fees. The Housing Authority and the Airport Authority realised financial surpluses in 2018/2019 and 2019/2020 respectively, but the Hospital Authority operated at a loss despite a government subvention of $64.3 billion for recurrent expenditure.[51]

---

48. *SCMP* (2017) op. cit.
49. Housing Authority (2019). *Annual report 2018/2019* (p. 97). https://www.housingauthority.gov.hk/mini-site/haar1819/en/view.html
50. Airport Authority (2020). *Annual report 2019/2020*. https://www.hongkongairport.com/en/airport-authority/board-management/the-board.page; Hospital Authority (2020). *Annual report 2019/2020*. https://www.ha.org.hk/ho/corpcomm/AR201920/PDF/HA_Annual_Report_2019-2020.pdf
51. Hospital Authority (2020) op. cit., pp. 48, 56; Airport Authority (2020) op. cit., p. 16; Housing Authority (2019) op. cit., pp. 94–95.

Fourth, each of these public bodies is involved in the difficult task of establishing a proper balance between the public need for the service and the economic cost of providing it. For the Housing Authority, this is complicated by its changed role and the problem that the inadequate supply of housing is not met by private providers at an acceptable price. The difficulty for the Housing and Hospital Authorities is that they are not purely commercial operations; they provide services subsidised by government. While they can charge economic prices, if they were to do so, the political cost to the government would be unacceptable.

Commercially Viable Public Entity

Until 2007, the government did wholly own at least one public enterprise that could charge the full economic price for its service and make a profit. The KCRC, which was then a public corporation, made consistent profits although in some years the corporation claimed a loss for tax purposes.[52] The government, as its only shareholder, was entitled to dividends from these profits but usually waived the dividend to assist further capital expenditure. Since 2007, although it no longer has an operational role following the decision to lease its rolling stock to the MTRC, a rump KCRC company has continued to manage the company's service concessions.

Company in Which Government Holds All or a Majority of Shares

Before 1999, the MTRC was a wholly government-owned public corporation and had the same legal status as other public corporations such as the Housing, Hospital, and Airport Authorities, and the KCRC. Since 1999, the MTRC has been a public company in which the government has a majority (75.6 %) stake. The changed status of the MTRC raised issues about the relationship between commercial practice and the public interest, which had previously been treated as an internal negotiating matter between the government and the corporation. When the MTRC was created in 1975, the government stressed that the corporation could only operate "having regard to the reasonable requirements of the public transport system of Hong Kong" and that it was "highly important" that it took into account the government's transport policies.[53]

Nonetheless, the government has been supportive of the independence of the corporation. Critically, the MTRC has been allowed to build and manage 47 residential and commercial projects constructed above its subway stations, which have

---

52. Kowloon Canton Railway Corporation (2021). *Annual report 2020*. https://www.kcrc.com/download/en/corporate-and-financial-information/annual-reports/annual-report-2020.pdf
53. Hansard, 2 April 1975, 659–660.

made substantial profits.[54] Setting fares has been a perennially politically sensitive issue.[55] After the agreement with the KCRC, the government wanted an "objective and transparent" fare adjustment mechanism and an assurance that the company would not engage in cut-throat competition with other transport providers.[56] The MTRC sets fares based on government data, but there have been complaints that, given its profits, fares are too high. Cost overruns, controversies, and delays over the high-speed rail link with the Chinese network and the Shatin-Central link have caused greater friction with government. The corporation remains, however, one of the most profitable railways in the world, realising a net profit of $11.9 billion in 2019, a fall of 25% from the previous year.[57]

Private Organisations with Public Functions

The government has permitted voluntary welfare organisations and the private sector to provide necessary public functions, such as community care, electricity supplies, and bus services, while retaining some control over pricing and standards through funding and licensing arrangements. For welfare, the government has historically tended to prefer public bodies to provide services. When private companies have taken on public functions, the government has usually been sympathetic if it believes that the service can be provided more efficiently. Occasionally, political considerations have meant that the government has had to provide a service that it would probably have preferred private companies to deliver. Water, for example, is a political issue because 70% to 80% of supply comes from the Mainland and is subject to negotiations over availability, price, quality, and quantity.[58] With sewage, a political consideration—increased charges—led the government to close down its trading fund and return responsibility to departmental control.[59] In other areas, such as the supply of electricity, gas, and buses, the government has been less interested in playing a direct role.

Where there are multiple providers of social services, the appropriate mix between government, subvented bodies, and the private sector is often an issue because of potential duplication of services, varying quality for the same service, and pricing differentials. The government has tried to introduce more uniformity in standards through such management methods as schemes of control over the power and bus companies, the school management system, and the lump sum grant

---

54. Leong, L. (2016). The "rail plus property" model: Hong Kong's successful self-financing formula. McKinsey and Co. https://www.mckinsey.com/industries/capital-projects-and-infrastructure/our-insights/the-rail-plus-property-model
55. Yau, C. (2018). Hong Kong MTR's fares set to rise 3.4 percent. *SCMP*. https://www.scmp.com/news/hong-kong/economy/article/2139131/hong-kong-mtr-fares-set-rise-314-cent
56. Yeung (2007) op. cit., Annex B.
57. MTRC (2020) *Annual report 2019*. https://www.mtr.com.hk/en/corporate/investor/2019frpt.html
58. Lin, J. (2019). *Modernising Hong Kong's water management policy Part 1* (p. 17). Hong Kong: Civic Exchange. https://civic-exchange.org/wp-content/uploads/2019/06/Conservation-and-Consumption.pdf
59. Cheung (2001) op. cit., pp. 215–217; Lam & Chan (1997) op. cit.

scheme for welfare agencies. In some areas, such as the school management system and the lump sum grant scheme, its attempts to establish uniformity have caused continuing friction with providers. Achieving the balance between different providers and cost-effectiveness and the equitable provision of services requires constant adjustment and review to ensure that the system works well.

Voluntary Welfare Organisations

Legally, voluntary welfare organisations are private bodies although most receive a high percentage of their revenue from the government, the Community Chest or the Jockey Club, or from more than one of these sources. In 2021/2022, the Social Welfare Department expected to pay out $23.1 billion to 169 subvented agencies;[60] over 70% of funding was provided for services for the elderly and for rehabilitation and medical social services.[61] The Community Chest disbursed a further $302 million to 165 welfare agencies and, in 2020/2021, the Jockey Club donated $4.5 billion to 528 charities and community groups.[62] Most voluntary welfare agencies are members of the Hong Kong Council of Social Service, which negotiates with government on their behalf, conducts research and serves as a planning body for the provision of services.[63]

The subvention system means that welfare agencies are highly dependent on the government. In 2001, the government introduced the lump sum grant scheme, which gave the agencies more autonomy over their budgets but also meant that they were required to meet overall government expenditure caps. By 2008, 162 of 173 NGOs had joined the scheme.[64] The scheme was popular with the Hong Kong Council of Social Service and with heads of agencies but much less so with members of staff whose salaries and ability to move to equivalent organisations were affected.[65] The government has also imposed further extensive controls on the agencies. The Director of Social Welfare is empowered to undertake audits, to have access to the agency's records and accounts, to have representation on its executive and management committees, and to withhold or impose conditions on any grant.[66]

---

60. Social Welfare Department (2021). Subvention allocation information. https://www.swd.gov.hk/en/index/site_ngo/page_subventions/sub_modesofsub/id_subvention/
61. Ibid.
62. Community Chest (2021). Services and projects. https://www.commchest.org/event/allocation/currentyear/en/index.html. The Jockey Club (2021). Community and charities. https://charities.hkjc.com/charities/english/index.aspx
63. Hong Kong Council of Social Service (2019). About us. https://www.hkcss.org.hk/about-us/?lang=en
64. Social Welfare Department (2008). *Review report on the Lump Sum Grant subvention system* (p. 4). https://www.swd.gov.hk/en/index/site_ngo/page_subventions/sub_rrlsgss/
65. Yan, M. C., Cheung, J. C. S., Tsui, M. S., & Chu, C. K. (2017). Examining the neoliberal discourse of accountability: The case of Hong Kong's social services sector. *International Social Work*, 60(4), 976–989.
66. Social Welfare Department (2016). *Lump Sum Grant manual* (pp. 29–30). https://governance.hkcss.org.hk/node/79

Some subvented organisations are incorporated under an ordinance that governs their operations. The reasons for incorporation vary. The charitable organisations, the Tung Wah and the Po Leung Kuk, were incorporated under ordinance because the government wanted greater control over their activities. Generally, incorporation does imply a stronger relationship between the private organisation and the government, but other than a purely commercial relationship between government and a private company, it still represents the loosest form of contact; the incorporated body is responsible for its own funding although it may also hope to receive some government largesse.

Publicly Listed Company or Private Company with Public Functions

The government also controls the bus companies, the tunnel companies, and certain utilities to some extent. In their day-to-day operations, the companies function as any other private company would. However, under their schemes of control, they are required to submit increases in charges and fares to government and to meet performance standards laid down by the government.[67] Since the companies cannot operate without government approval, they are dependent upon it. Until 1993, there were only two franchised bus companies. In 1998, the government put out tenders for a new bus franchise with the result that the New World First Bus Company was awarded much of the China Motor Bus Company's network, which then ceased to be a franchised operator.[68] There are now five franchised bus companies.

The construction and operation of Hong Kong's tunnels involve equally complex relationships between government and private companies. In 2020, there were 22 tunnels in Hong Kong, either constructed under "build, operate and transfer" provisions or managed and operated under contract by private companies.[69] There have been problems with congestion in some cases and underutilisation in others. Other difficulties have arisen from the tolls charged. If tolls are too high, as some consumers believe, the government may be called upon to put pressure on the company to reduce them. The relationship of the government to the bus companies and the tunnel operators may be appropriately described as a public-private partnership in which government regulates and coordinates and the private company provides the service.

Under the Tung administration, the government's relationship with the private sector was influenced by the emphasis on outsourcing services and the requirement that departments should consider the private sector as an alternative to providing the services themselves (see pp. 132, 134). Many large capital expenditure projects

---

67. See CLP Power (2021). Scheme of control. https://www.clp.com.hk/en/about-clp/scheme-of-control.html
68. Transport Department (2021). Franchised buses. https://www.td.gov.hk/en/transport_in_hong_kong/public_transport/buses/index.html
69. Transport Department (2021) Tunnels and bridges. https://www.td.gov.hk/en/transport_in_hong_kong/tunnels_and_bridges_n/index.html

were based on the assumption that the private sector would be actively involved in design, construction, and operations. However, projects such as Cyberport,[70] Disneyland,[71] the West Kowloon Cultural District,[72] and the creation of parastatals to encourage innovation in technology were either failures or took many years to perform effectively. In the process, they generated political controversies over performance and costs. Under the Tsang, Leung, and Lam administrations, the government has been rather more wary of underwriting grandiose projects. In principle, the government supports public-private partnerships and outsourcing; in practice, the trend has been towards centralisation and keeping public functions in-house, especially as the political environment has become more volatile.

In its dealings with public bodies, the government possesses very considerable powers over the funding and legal status of public bodies. It may decide, for example, to increase or reduce subventions or capital expenditure. It may slow or speed up the pace with which housing estates or railway lines come into operation. It may even affect the fortunes of private companies by awarding or failing to award franchises and contracts. In addition to controlling the purse strings, the government can change the legal status of public bodies through its executive powers or the introduction of new ordinances or amendments to existing ordinances. A public body could have its powers shorn, or its autonomy expanded, depending on whether the government believes that its aims would be better achieved by a change in legal status.

Yet, despite these formidable powers, it would be wrong to assume that the government always gets its way and that public bodies do not exercise some control and direction over their affairs. Points of friction do emerge between the Hong Kong government and the NGOs over funding and legal authority. Many fractious issues also arise from commercial operations, project implementation, or service provision of the public bodies. Since public money is likely to be involved, this becomes an accountability issue: how are these organisations to be held accountable when they were intended to be somewhat autonomous? In the following section, we examine this issue in greater detail.

Accountability and Public Bodies

When there is little political friction over the performance of public bodies, the government leaves them largely to their own devices. Once major issues or scandals emerge, the government sometimes serves as a proxy for the wrath of the public or

---

70. Hammond, G., & Ruehl, M. (2020, 6 February). Why Hong Kong is failing to produce more tech start-ups. *Financial Times*. https://www.ft.com/content/458bc9d0-3e79-11ea-a01a-bae547046735
71. Higgins & Huque (2015) op. cit.
72. Tsui, E., & Kwong, K. (2017). Is the West Kowloon Cultural District finally taking shape? *Post Magazine*. https://www.scmp.com/magazines/post-magazine/arts-music/article/2071461/west-kowloon-cultural-district-finally-taking

their representatives. It may be accused of failing to ensure that there was sufficient oversight over the organisation, or it may be held to be negligent in the fulfilment of its duties on the boards of public corporations, or it may even be judged to have made a mistake in removing the agency from the government. Whatever the charge, accountability relationships between the government and public bodies have generally been weak.

Major scandals have raised serious questions because public bodies have not been seen to be accountable either to government or the legislature. A few examples illustrate the kinds of problem that have occurred. The opening of the Chek Lap Kok airport was marked by failures in the computer, cargo-handling, and baggage systems, causing considerable inconvenience to passengers and a detrimental effect on the economy as many perishable goods rotted.[73] Between 2014 and 2020, the MTRC, long held to be a model of railway management, came under scathing criticisms for repeated delays and cost overruns on two major projects, the high-speed rail link and the Shatin-Central link.[74] The Director of Audit's increased number of investigations into public bodies has also uncovered many organisational and financial irregularities.[75]

Would these problems have arisen if tighter accountability systems had been in place? To try to answer that question, we examine the four major institutional checks on public bodies. First, the powers of direction vested in the Chief Executive or principal officials. Second, the power of the Chief Executive to appoint representatives to sit on the boards of advisory and statutory bodies. Third, Legislative Council scrutiny, mostly conducted by committees, through the evaluation of tabled reports or meetings with the executives of public bodies. Fourth, the audit process, identifying shortcomings in the financial management or organisation of the public bodies.

Powers of Direction

The Chief Executive has the power to direct the work of statutory bodies both generally through the *Interpretation and General Clauses Ordinance* and, more specifically, through the ordinances governing the statutory bodies and the appointment of commissions of inquiry. The Chief Executive may appoint members of the statutory bodies and may dismiss the board and reconstitute it.[76] There are also specific

---

73. Lee, E. W. Y. (2000). The new Hong Kong international airport fiasco. *International Review of Administrative Sciences*, 66(1), 57–72.
74. Cheng, K. (2018). Cost overruns and constitutional debate: Hong Kong's controversial express rail link explained. *HKFP*. https://hongkongfp.com/2018/09/23/cost-overruns-constitutional-debate-hong-kongs-controversial-express-rail-link-explained/; Hartmann, M., & Hansford, P. (2020). *Final report of Commission of Inquiry into the construction works at and near Hung Hom station extension under the Shatin to Central link project*. https://www.coi-hh.gov.hk/pdf/COI_Final_Report_Eng.pdf
75. See, for example, Director of Audit (various dates). *Reports Nos. 49, 67, 69, 74, 75*. https://www.aud.gov.hk/eng/pubpr_arpt/rpt.htm
76. *Interpretation and General Clauses Ordinance*, Cap 1, S.42.

powers that may be exercised under the ordinances that govern the boards of statutory bodies. The *Urban Renewal Authority Ordinance*, for example, provides that:

> The Chief Executive may, if he considers the public interest so requires, give directions in writing to the Authority in relation to the exercise of its powers or the performance of its duties and the authority shall comply with those directions.[77]

These are very broad powers, sufficient to ensure that the government could, if it so wished, shape some public bodies in any way it saw fit. The government has always maintained that, because it is responsible for policy and often funding, it has the right to tell public bodies what to do.[78] Generally, however, it has used its powers to reorganise public bodies quite sparingly. Only when major issues of competence, delays to projects, or unacceptable financial irregularities have been involved has the government unequivocally asserted its authority.

Two MTRC cases provide examples where the government was late in taking remedial action. The MTRC was responsible for the construction of the high-speed rail link to Guangdong but was beset by problems, from technical difficulties, to cost overruns, to major political opposition on the streets and in the Legislative Council. In 2014, the MTRC's chief executive and its projects manager resigned and were awarded "golden handshakes" of $15.5 million and $400,000 respectively.[79] The government was not kept fully informed of project delays and had to seek a hostile Legislative Council's approval for substantial additional funding. When the project was finally completed, it was over double its initial projected cost and three years overdue.[80]

The Shatin-Central subway line was a reprise of problems faced by the high-speed rail link. There were two delays in starting the project. Then, in May 2018, with construction in progress, a whistle-blower claimed that the work on the Hung Hom station was substandard. In June, the government appointed a commission of inquiry to examine the construction works on the line. In August, the Secretary for Transport and Housing, himself a member of the MTRC board, called on the board to "remove" those in charge of the rail link.[81] Shortly thereafter, the MTRC's Chief Executive and four senior members of the company resigned and were told

---

77. *Urban Renewal Authority Ordinance*, Cap 563, S.33.
78. Hansard, 12 December 2001, 2519; Education Bureau (2007, 17 September). *Education Bureau launches judicial review* [Press release].
79. Sung, T. (2015, 16 April). Hong Kong MTR chief pocketed $15.5 million when he quit. *SCMP*. https://www.scmp.com/news/hong-kong/politics/article/1767266/hong-kong-mtr-chief-jay-walder-pocketed-hk157m-golden
80. Cheng (2018) op. cit.; Legislative Council Public Works Committee (2009). Hong Kong section of the Guangzhou-Shenzhen-Hong Kong express rail link—Construction of railway works (p. 7). https://www.legco.gov.hk/yr09-10/english/fc/pwsc/papers/p09-68e.pdf
81. Tsang, D., Leung, K., Ng, K. C., & Sum, L. K. (2018, 7 August). Hong Kong MTR to revamp top management as chief executive Lincoln Leong to leave over Sha Tin-Central rail link scandals. https://www.scmp.com/news/hong-kong/hong-kong-economy/article/2158639/mtr-fires-projects-director-philco-wong-over

by the government not to expect "golden handshakes".[82] In the meantime, costs had blown out from an approved estimate of $79.8 billion to $97.1 billion. The commission of inquiry's report criticised the government's failure to monitor the project adequately and recommended that it should carry out a comprehensive review of how it monitored and controlled major projects.[83]

The government's response to the MTRC's failures was to tighten control. It proposed creating a new department to supervise rail development and promised closer government monitoring of MTRC projects.[84] While this may increase the level of monitoring of rail projects, it also diminishes the relative autonomy of the MTRC, overriding the rationale for its organisational form and adding another bureaucratic level to decision-making.

Boards and Government Representation

Potentially, the most important means by which the government ensures that the public body is accountable is through the power exercised by the Chief Executive to appoint members of the board. These often include the relevant senior government official. The actual role that these representatives may play is dependent on the type of organisation. In simple voluntary organisations, for example, the board may only play an advisory role. In more commercial organisations, by contrast, the board, as a body corporate, may have the power to sue and be sued and assumes collective responsibility for the actions, direction, and profitability of the organisation.

The different types of board reflect what government perceives to be the function of the public body. A representational board attempts to replicate community concerns. In 2020/2021, for example, the Housing Authority and the Hospital Authority had memberships of 32 and 27 respectively drawn from government officials, politicians, academics, and professionals.[85] The HKTB had 20 chosen from a more restricted pool of business people with travel and trade interests.[86] The representational model, if it draws solely on functional interests, may not be the best way to ensure unity of action because board members may have very different views on the way forward. Larger boards more often resemble class reunions than groups focused on clear policy objectives and it is difficult to see how they can hold executives accountable for administrative or policy failures.

---

82. Lum, A., Leung, C., & Sum, L. K. (2018, 8 August). No rewards for outgoing MTR bosses, Hong Kong leader Carrie Lam says. *SCMP*. https://www.scmp.com/news/hong-kong/politics/article/2158878/no-rewards-outgoing-mtr-bosses-hong-kong-leader-carrie-lam
83. Hartmann & Hansford (2020) op. cit., pp. 200–202.
84. Hong Kong Government (2020, 12 May). *Government releases and responds to the final report of commission of inquiry into construction works at and near Hung Hom station extension under the Shatin to Central project* [Press release]. https://www.info.gov.hk/gia/general/202005/12/P2020051200455.htm#:~:text=The%20Government%20released%20today%20(May,Carrie%20Lam%2C%20on%20March%2027.
85. Hospital Authority (2020) op. cit.; Housing Authority (2021) op. cit.
86. Hong Kong Tourism Board (2021). *Annual report 2020/2021*. https://www.discoverhongkong.com/eng/about-hktb/annual-report/annual-report-20202021/board-members.html

A technical board is usually much smaller and draws on the specific expertise of its members. Until 2013, the MTRC had a technical board of 13 members, including three senior civil servants, and drew on governmental, financial, and engineering expertise. The board then gradually expanded to become more representational. By 2019, it had a membership of 20 and a commitment to gender equality. Technical boards are usually more focused on operating efficiently rather than on providing a forum for the articulation of their customers' demands, which is more of a concern for the representational boards. Companies functioning under schemes of control or build-own-operate arrangements with the government generally have technical boards and no government representation on the board.

How exactly does the *ex officio* board member express government's interests? The senior civil servants who sit on the boards are in a delicate position. In commercial organisations, they must always be conscious of conflicts of interest and may have to recuse themselves on some issues. If they assert the government's position to the exclusion of commercial considerations, they fall into the danger of rescinding the powers they gave to the public body in the first place. The government believes that it can use membership on the boards to liaise with key players in service provision and as a means of exercising some control. In introducing the lump grant scheme for subvented welfare organisations, for example, the Social Welfare Department stipulated that a government official should sit on the boards of subvented bodies, which had not previously been the case, and which, coupled with new monitoring and control mechanisms over social welfare spending, could be taken to mean that the government wanted stronger controls over expenditure.[87]

The role that government officials play on boards appears to vary from passive receipt of information to active participation, depending on the personalities involved, circumstances, and the degree of government funding. The presence of senior public servants on the boards does not prevent public bodies from making mistakes or ensuring that executives are held accountable for those mistakes. In the case of a construction scandal which eventually required the destruction of defective housing blocks, it is unlikely that the members of the Housing Authority, without appropriate technical advice, would have been able to detect what was corrupt practice. The Chairman of the Housing Authority, who was not a civil servant, did resign following the incident, but the extent to which she could be held accountable given the complex lines of decision-making within the authority is questionable. The Director of Housing, who was the subject of a no confidence vote in the legislature, did not resign.

In the case of the opening of the airport, Legislative Councillors argued that the Chief Secretary, Anson Chan On-sang, who chaired a key committee, should have delayed the opening of the airport and was therefore accountable for the mistake. The difficulty in ensuring accountability in cases such as this is establishing the

---

87. Social Welfare Department (2015). *Guide to corporate governance for subvented organizations* (2nd ed., pp.31–32). https://www.effo.gov.hk/en/reference/publications/guide_to_cg_for_so_2015.pdf

difference between decisions taken in good faith with as much relevant information as possible, repeated poor judgements where the calibre of the official may be in question, and reckless, irresponsible decisions made without due process. Disentangling the many hands often involved in these decisions and ensuring that responsibility is located in the right place is a difficult process. Boards are given the authority to act and must certainly bear responsibility for the way public bodies function. But until the government spells out in more precise detail what it expects of senior civil servants on these boards, it is not likely that their presence alone will ensure more accountable public organisations.

Legislative Scrutiny

Legislative Councillors have repeatedly asserted their wish to monitor public corporations rather better and have graphically described their difficulties in doing so. One Councillor described his role as a "man dressed in black trying to catch a crow on a dark night".[88] The council has weak powers and faces the difficulty that most problems that come before it occurred in the relatively distant past and have already been remedied or justified.

Through its Public Accounts Committee, the council has a role in determining responsibility for poor practice and misspent public funds and powers under some ordinances to call the chairs and executive directors of statutory bodies to account. Under the *Urban Renewal Authority Ordinance*, for example,

> The committees and subcommittees of the Legislative Council may request the Chairman and the executive directors to attend its meetings and they shall comply.[89]

The Legislative Council's main powers are reviewing the annual reports of the public bodies, discussing the Director of Audit's findings on their performance, asking questions of the responsible policy secretary and, rarely, in investigating their activities and censuring their executives for inappropriate behaviour. Although these functions bring greater transparency and publicity to the work of the public bodies, they have suffered from the limitation that the Legislative Council is understaffed and has no effective sanctions. Questions in the chamber raise issues temporarily, debates in the Public Accounts Committee dissect past events, annual reports often gather dust, and high-level investigations and votes of no confidence make transitory headlines. Public bodies do not always see themselves as accountable to the legislature and they seldom appear to concern themselves with its powers of review and sanctions.

To illustrate the process by which potential malpractice in public bodies reaches the attention of the Legislative Council, we can consider two cases in which the

---
88. Hansard, 12 December 2001, 2496.
89. *Urban Renewal Authority Ordinance*, Cap 563, S. 9.

Audit Commission conducted investigations of statutory bodies. In 2007, the Audit Commission investigated the affairs of the HKTB, 94% of whose income of $725 million was subvented by the government.[90] The commission found irregularities in corporate governance and questioned the absence of long-term planning, spending priorities, marketing strategies, and some financial irregularities.[91] In this case, the Public Accounts Committee was able to respond almost immediately. It found that:

> The top management of the HKTB should be held directly responsible for the deficiencies in corporate governance. It had failed to ensure that the HKTB adopted high standards of corporate governance, effective operations, compliance and administration systems . . . In particular, the Committee condemns the former E(xecutive) D(irector) who has failed in her duties.[92]

Although the committee responded promptly, the resignation of the chair and the executive director effectively took the steam out of its recommendations. As the former chair explained, many of the recommendations had already been implemented and the rest were in train.[93] It was the Audit Commission—not the Legislative Council—that held the HKTB accountable. In 2020, it returned to the task, finding more corporate governance and administrative problems.[94]

In March 2013, the Audit Commission uncovered irregularities in the funding of two official ICAC dinners and there were subsequent press revelations of excessive expenditure on duty trips, gifts, and 20 receptions for Chinese liaison officials.[95] The Legislative Council sought to hold the ex-ICAC Commissioner, Timothy Tong Hin-ming, accountable through its Public Accounts Committee and by establishing a Select Committee to investigate what had happened. The Public Accounts Committee called on Tong to respond to the charges and although he refused to do so, the committee then used its powers to require him to testify. The committee found that there had been overspending for many ICAC lunches and dinners on hard liquor and gifts and that Tong had spent 146 days of his time in office on duty trips to China and elsewhere.[96] The Select Committee covered the same matters discussed in the Public Accounts Committee and reached the same conclusions.[97]

---

90. Audit Commission (2007). *Report No. 49* (Ch. 5). https://www.aud.gov.hk/pdf_e/e49ch05.pdf
91. Ibid., pp. 14, 26, 37–38.
92. Public Accounts Committee (2008). *Report No. 49A* (Part 4, p. 92). https://www.legco.gov.hk/yr07-08/english/pac/reports/49a/49a_rpt.pdf
93. Ibid., p. 10.
94. Director of Audit (2020). *Report No. 75: Hong Kong Tourism Board: Corporate governance and administrative issues* (pp. x–xii). https://www.aud.gov.hk/pdf_e/e75ch07.pdf
95. Director of Audit (2013). *Report No. 60–Chapter 7*. https://www.aud.gov.hk/pdf_e/e60ch07.pdf; Cheung, S., Tam, J., & Lee, C. (2013, 26 April). Ex-ICAC boss faces graft probe for allegedly dining out on public money. *SCMP*. https://www.scmp.com/news/hong-kong/article/1223227/ex-icac-boss-faces-graft-probe-allegedly-dining-out-public-money
96. Public Accounts Committee (2013). *Report 60A—Part 4: Preventative education and enlisting public support against corruption*. https://www.legco.gov.hk/yr12-13/english/pac/reports/60a/m_4.pdf
97. Legislative Council (2014). *Report on matters relating to Mr. Timothy Tong's duty visits, entertainment, and bestowing and receipt of gifts during his tenure as Commissioner of the Independent Commission Against Corruption*. https://www.legco.gov.hk/yr12-13/english/sc/sc_ttong/report/ttong_rpt.htm

Both committees were concerned about the effects of the scandal on the credibility of the ICAC. The Select Committee found that Tong's contacts with Mainland officials had been unduly close, "shaking confidence in [its] impartiality".[98] Public complaints about corruption, an indicator of trust in the ICAC, dropped sharply after the scandal was revealed.

The value of the Legislative Council's investigations is that they increase transparency and provide information about performance and conduct in public bodies. But the council has no sanctions that it can bring to bear on offenders. In the Tong case, the Select Committee did raise the question of whether he might be charged under the misconduct in public office offence, but the Secretary for Justice, on advice from the Director of Public Prosecutions, said that there was no evidence of a corrupt motive and no charges were laid.[99] There have been some attempts to strengthen the role of the legislature by asking heads of public bodies to appear regularly before legislative committees and the increasing number of Audit Commission reports on public bodies has also enabled legislators to expand their investigative role.[100]

Auditing Public Bodies

Under the *Audit Ordinance*, the Director of Audit has the power to investigate more than 60 statutory and non-statutory funds.[101] Until the 2000s, for the Audit Commission to audit organisations other than a government department was a relatively rare event. Its focus had been primarily on the government accounts, "value-for-money" studies, and improving programme implementation. These are critical functions that legislators now expect to be applied to public bodies, especially those funded by the taxpayer. Its reviews of public finances and practices and its reports to the Public Accounts Committee are an important element in the accountability process. Legislators have been steadfast in their support for the independence of the commission.

The independent auditors of public bodies' accounts also have important responsibilities. Instead of reporting to shareholders and the market as they would in the case of private companies, their responsibilities extend to a much larger audience: taxpayers, government, and the Legislative Council. Independent auditors play an important role in uncovering malpractice and in holding the public bodies

---

98. Ibid., p. 97.
99. Lee, E., Lau, S., & Lau, C. (2016, 27 January). Former Hong Kong anti-corruption commissioner Timothy Tong Hin-Ming to face no further criminal probe. *SCMP*. https://www.scmp.com/news/hong-kong/law-crime/article/1905876/former-hong-kong-anti-corruption-commissioner-timothy-tong
100. See Public Accounts Committee (2020). *Report of the Public Accounts Committee on Report No. 74 of the Director of Audit* (Part 4). https://www.legco.gov.hk/yr19-20/english/pac/reports/74/74_rpt.pdf; Public Accounts Committee (2018). *Supplemental report of the Public Accounts Committee on Report No. 69*. https://www.legco.gov.hk/yr17-18/english/pac/reports/69a/69a_rpt.pdf
101. *Audit Ordinance*, Cap 122, S.14.

accountable by communicating their findings to executive and legislative authorities. Transparency on the accounts of public bodies has improved although more could be done. The Social Welfare Department, for example, does release information on the financial reports and salaries of senior personnel funded under the lump sum grant scheme, but many agencies are exempt from reporting.[102]

Holding public bodies accountable involves many different actors: a free press, representatives of the government and independent directors on the boards, the responsible government department, the Legislative Council, especially its Public Accounts Committee, independent auditors, and the Audit Commission. Obtaining and acting on information requires a process that does not seem to be fully developed. There are too many instances of important information that has not been made publicly available as soon as it was known, such as the time taken to reveal the delays in the high-speed rail link. Even when such information is available, the process of taking action and resolving the situation is often very slow. Some of this is unavoidable. An audit usually takes place after relevant events have occurred and sometimes when information has been concealed. But action within the civil service, the government, and the legislature could be speeded up to ensure that problems with public bodies do not become long-running sagas.

Public Sector Appointments and Salaries

The appointments and salaries of those in senior positions in public bodies are accountability issues. If opaque committees determine these matters, public confidence in the recruitment and wage determination process is likely to be affected. For legislators, in particular, the membership of boards and the remuneration of their senior executives have been perennial issues. In 2001, for example, government data showed that 91 senior executives of five major public corporations were being paid three to five times as much as senior civil servants with comparable levels of responsibility.[103] The government came under attack in the Legislative Council and eventually agreed to appoint Hay Management Consultants to investigate the comparability of the salaries of the top 100 executives in nine statutory bodies with equivalents in the private sector.

Perhaps predictably, the consultants found that 70% of the chief executive positions had current remunerations within a range of 15% of the market medians. They did recommend that committees be established that would disclose the full remuneration packages for chief executives and the aggregate or average remuneration for second- and third-tier executives.[104] The consultants' terms of reference

---

102. Social Welfare Department (2019). NGOs' annual financial reports and review reports on remuneration packages in the top three tiers. https://www.swd.gov.hk/en/index/site_ngo/page_AFRandRR/
103. Hansard, 12 December 2001, 2448–2475.
104. Hong Kong Government (2002, 26 June). *CS' statement on remuneration of senior executives of statutory and other bodies* [Press release].

meant that the report did not address the fundamental issues raised by Legislative Councillors, some of whom argued that executives in statutory bodies were public employees and that they should be paid accordingly. The government did introduce a rule that no senior executive of a subvented body should be paid more than the top of the civil service directorate pay scale.[105] Public corporations and some other statutory bodies are not subject to this rule although the government reviews senior executives' salaries periodically. Legislative Councillors and the media have continued to raise the issue,[106] but there has remained a substantial salary differential between the principal officials overseeing public corporations and some statutory bodies and the senior executives of those organisations.[107]

The government's benign view on the salaries of senior executives is sometimes linked to criticism of the recruitment system and the seemingly disproportionate number of former senior civil servants appointed to high office in the public bodies. Where those bodies take on functions previously performed by government, such as, for example, the Monetary Authority and the Urban Renewal Authority, it is perhaps not surprising that former senior civil servants with knowledge of the field have been employed. In the case of the Urban Renewal Authority, the appointment of the managing director, who happened to be a former senior public servant, was undertaken by a selection panel composed of the Chief Secretary, the Financial Secretary, the Secretary for Planning and Lands, the Chairman of the Urban Renewal Authority Board, and an Executive Council member.[108] Although candidates from both the public and private sectors were considered for the position, the heavy representation of senior civil servants on the selection panel gives pause for thought. The absence of Legislative Councillors from the panel is striking.

In public corporations with largely commercial operations, it is more difficult to see why so many senior civil servants have been appointed to executive positions. There is a danger that those approaching retirement or anticipating resignation could begin to make decisions with one eye to lucrative future positions in either the public bodies or the private sector. There has been considerable concern about conflicts of interest when senior civil servants join the private sector and where there is the prospect of using sensitive information and contacts in government to obtain an unfair advantage (see p. 162). However, the same concern does not seem to apply to public bodies which the government seems to regard as an extended version of its own operations, even though some corporations and agencies have

---

105. Legislative Council (2003). *Internal review of remuneration of senior executives of government-funded bodies.* https://www.legco.gov.hk/yr02-03/english/panels/ps/papers/cso_admcr2_1136_01-e.pdf
106. Hansard, 9 May 2007, 6766–6775; Hansard, 26 February 2014, 8112–8121; Hansard, 17 December 2014; *SCMP* (2019, 15 April). Keep better track of MTR bosses' pay. Editorial. *SCMP.* https://www.scmp.com/comment/insight-opinion/article/3006279/keep-better-track-mtr-bosses-pay
107. Hansard, 8 May 2019, 9288–9290.
108. Hong Kong Government (2001, October 12). *Managing director of the Urban Renewal Authority appointed* [Press release].

been created on the assumption that they will benefit from private sector rather than public sector skills.

From 1996 onwards, Legislative Councillors repeatedly sought a review of the role and functions of the advisory and statutory bodies to improve their transparency and appointment procedures. In April 2002, the Secretary for Constitutional Affairs finally announced that a review would take place.[109] The Home Affairs Bureau, which took charge of the process, decided on a two-stage approach. During the first stage, the aim was to determine the guiding principles; the second stage was to conduct in-depth reviews of particular problems. A consultation paper, released in April 2003, laid out the government's view of what the guiding principles should be. Principal officials should be "ultimately accountable for the advisory and statutory bodies under their purview".[110] Public bodies should be structured to ensure that there was no duplication in their work; appointment criteria should be set out; appointments should be on merit; the service of non-official members should be unpaid; there should be equal opportunities for individuals from all sectors of the community to participate; steps should be taken to promote the participation of women; members should declare their interests; their work should be open and transparent; and members should not serve for more than six years or on more than six boards (the "6 plus 6" rule).[111] These rules formally remain in place although they have often been honoured more in the breach.

Even by the time the Home Affairs Bureau released its first individual reports, it was clear that the government had no intention of enforcing its own rules. Its 2005 report on the "6 plus 6" rule showed that the numbers of those who had been on boards for more than 10 years had increased.[112] In his first election manifesto, Donald Tsang claimed that he would strictly enforce the "6 plus 6" rule. Yet, by January 2008, there were still 137 statutory board members who had served for more than six years.[113] By 2020, the number who had been on boards for more than six years had increased to 298 members; four were serving on more than six boards.[114] The consequence is that some boards are composed mainly of ageing veterans.

There appears to be little monitoring of the performance of board members. The Audit Commission's investigation of the HKTB in 2007 revealed that one

---

109. Constitutional Affairs Bureau (2002). *Legislative Council paper: Accountability system for principal officials* (p. 18). https://www.legco.gov.hk/yr01-02/english/panels/ca/papers/ca0418cb2-paper-e.pdf
110. Home Affairs Bureau (2003). *Review of the role and functions of public sector advisory and statutory bodies: Consultation paper* (p. 6). Hong Kong: The Bureau.
111. Ibid., pp. 6–8; Scott, I. (2006). The government and statutory boards in Hong Kong: Centralization and autonomy. *Public Organization Review* 6(3), 185–202; Thynne, I. (2006). Statutory bodies as instruments of government in Hong Kong: Review beginnings and analytical challenges ahead. *Public Administration and Development* 26(1), 45–53.
112. Home Affairs Bureau (2005). *Progress report on the review of advisory and statutory bodies.* Hong Kong: The Bureau.
113. Hansard, 30 January 2008, 75–76.
114. Home Affairs Bureau (2020). Advisory and statutory bodies. https://www.hab.gov.hk/en/policy_responsibilities/District_Community_and_Public_Relations/advisory.htm

member had missed 15 consecutive meetings and had still been reappointed twice to the board.[115] Others had failed to sign declaration of interest forms and there has been little progress on the transparency of board meetings. The number of women has increased. In 2010, the government set a target of 30% female membership on boards but, by 2013, 142 boards had failed to meet that target and the overall representation of women fell below 30%.[116] In 2017, 32% of board members, compared with 16% in 1998, were female.[117]

There has also been lasting concern that the government is using its power to appoint approximately 4,600 members to reward its political supporters and to exclude opponents.[118] Formally, the government makes appointments to boards on grounds of merit, taking into account the candidate's ability, expertise, experience, integrity, and commitment to public service.[119] Democrats argue that few of their numbers are ever appointed to boards and that one was allegedly removed on grounds of political affiliation.[120] After the November 2019 District Council elections, the Chief Executive, Carrie Lam, apologised to the defeated pro-Beijing/pro-government candidates for their losses and reportedly said that they might be appointed to boards.[121] Later, when asked about the alleged remark, she simply said that the government would continue to have a strong relationship with the defeated candidates.[122]

What the government has been particularly intent on ensuring is that advisory and statutory bodies with which it has problems over policy, management, or performance are brought under control. In June 2005, the Home Affairs Bureau lumped all these problematic boards into the category "non-departmental public bodies".[123] They included the Applied Science and Technology Institute, the Examinations and Assessment Authority, the Prince Philip Dental Hospital, the Sports Development Board, which was restructured and later removed from the list, the Vocational Council, the Hospital Authority, and the Equal Opportunities Commission, which had won a ruling from the courts that the government's secondary school allocation

---

115. Audit Commission, *Report No. 49*, op. cit., Ch. 5.
116. Hansard, 20 June 2013, 13507–13531.
117. Legislative Council Secretariat Research Office (2018). *Women's participation in public affairs in Hong Kong* (p. 15). https://www.legco.gov.hk/research-publications/english/1819issf02-womens-participation-in-public-affairs-in-hong-kong-20181016-e.pdf
118. Cheung, A. B. L., & Wong, P. C. W. (2004). Who advised the Hong Kong government? The politics of absorption before and after 1997. *Asian Survey*, 44(6), 874–894; Hansard, 22 January 2014, 5851–5855; Hansard, 29 June 2016, 12848–12850; Kwong, B. K. K. (2009). *Patron-client politics and elections in Hong Kong* (pp. 41–43). London and New York: Routledge.
119. Hansard, 29 June 2016, op. cit.
120. Ibid.
121. Cheng, K. (2019, 10 December) "Natural" to apologise to defeated pro-Beijing election candidates says Hong Kong chief Carrie Lam. *HKFP*. https://hongkongfp.com/2019/12/10/natural-apologise-defeated-pro-beijing-camp-election-candidates-says-hong-kong-chief-carrie-lam/
122. Chung, K., & Wong, N. (2019, 10 December). Hong Kong leader Carrie Lam reveals apology to defeated pro-Beijing candidates after district council elections. *SCMP*. https://www.scmp.com/news/hong-kong/politics/article/3041386/hong-kong-leader-carrie-lam-reveals-apology-defeated-pro
123. Scott (2006) op. cit.

system was discriminatory (see pp. 365–367).[124] The Tourism Board and the MTRC also subsequently came under scrutiny, resulting in changes. In each case, the government asserted greater control over the operations and organisation of the public body. It has also shown intent in keeping mid-range salaries in subvented organisations in check, benchmarked against their civil service counterparts.

The recruitment and appointment of executives and board members, salary structures, and the accountability of public bodies have all been, and remain, highly contentious matters. There is a deep suspicion that the government is either deliberately or inadvertently running a patronage network, a perception that tends to be reinforced when scandal or poor performance comes to light. The principles and rules that should guide the advisory and statutory bodies are not in question; rather, it is the government's commitment to ensuring compliance that is the issue.

Conclusion

The government is caught between two values, centralisation and autonomy, that it seeks to maximise in its relationship with the public bodies. Since the values are polar opposites, it is difficult, if not impossible, to have the best of both worlds. Under the Tung administration, the pendulum swung towards autonomy. The government wanted to devolve more government business to the private sector or to statutory bodies, based on the belief in the importance of small government and the notion that the private sector was more efficient than the civil service. Under Tung's successors, the pendulum has swung the other way, towards greater centralisation. Initially, the major reason for the change of direction, and the partial freeze on new public-private partnerships and government-owned companies, was the failure of many of Tung's projects. Subsequently, however, the expansionist agendas of Leung and Lam and their desire to keep major new initiatives within government, Chinese government support for centralisation, and problems with some statutory bodies have all led to moves towards more central control.

The government has certainly ensured that it has the power to control the advisory and statutory bodies. But possessing the power and exercising it are different matters. The Home Affairs Department and the Social Welfare Department are too busy to pay attention to the many public bodies under their purview unless there is a major political problem in the offing. Control tends to be exercised reactively: if the public body is performing within the broad parameters set by the government, it is mostly left to follow its own path.

The wider issue of accountability remains. A saving grace is that the Audit Commission has identified financial and organisational problems very efficiently and made recommendations for improvements. That aside, however, the

---

124. Home Affairs Bureau (2006). *Interim Report No. 15—Review of the corporate governance of the Equal Opportunities Commission.* LC Paper No. CB (2) 786/05-06.

appointment of government officials, unofficial council members and independent directors to boards, the important, but necessarily belated, efforts of the Public Accounts Committee, questions in the legislature, and the rules governing inflated executive salaries, have all failed to hold public bodies accountable. Good governance and the taxpayer have paid the price.

Part III

Policy Formulation and Implementation

7
Policy and the Budgetary Cycle

One criterion used to evaluate the performance of governments is their ability to formulate and implement sound policies that will deliver collective benefits as efficiently, effectively, and economically as possible. Public policy may be defined as:

> A set of inter-related decisions taken by a political actor or group of actors concerning the selection of goals and the means of achieving them within a specified situation when these should, in principle, be within the power of these actors to achieve.[1]

If this aim is subsequently attained, decision-makers may formulate and implement sound policies. But it is also quite possible, indeed perhaps likely, that the decision-makers will fall far short of their goals or that those elusive objectives—efficiency, effectiveness, and economy—will prove to be contradictory, or that one may be maximised at the expense of the others. This definition of policy is perhaps a little optimistic. It assumes a logical and rational sequence of events from the formulation of goals, through consideration of the most beneficial means of achieving those ends, to actual strategies of implementation. It is considerably easier for policy-makers when this does occur or when they can structure their decisions so that they follow logically, one from another. However, events do not always allow such a careful assessment of the problem and its optimal solution. The need for action may be so immediate that policymakers do not have time to reflect on the most rational strategy or the political environment may influence outcomes so that the resulting policy is not efficient, effective, or economic.

In the following four chapters, the overarching argument is that two policy-making systems coexist uneasily in Hong Kong. Under colonial rule, the policy-making system was closed and well insulated from political pressures. It was based on a budgetary system that so effectively controlled resources that the government was able to build up large fiscal reserves. On the back of a buoyant economy, it had ample means to fund its policies. Under such circumstances, it is relatively easy to fend off political pressures and to co-opt potentially dissident elites by the

---

1. Jenkins, W. I. (1978). *Policy analysis* (p. 15). London: Martin Robertson.

"administrative absorption of politics".[2] Civil servants, not politicians, decided what the policy problems were and how they should be addressed. Once the problem was identified and under active consideration, advice could be sought from advisory committees or from the community and could be accepted or rejected as senior civil servants saw fit. Policy could be formulated in what appeared to be a rational and logical way. Options could be considered, the relative benefits of different public investments discussed, and final policies put before a public, often prepared well in advance for the measures that the government intended to introduce. There were, of course, events that did not always allow slow and considered progress towards a measured conclusion. Although mistakes were often made, problems misidentified, and policies poorly implemented, a formal rational system remained in place. It was gradually modified after the handover as pressure groups and political parties emerged and as the influence of the Chinese government on policymaking grew, leading to more ad hoc decisions, less rationality and, in some areas, the inability to implement policy.

After 1997, the system that evolved was very different from the traditional way in which policy had been made. Policymaking processes did not always proceed chronologically but often unfolded independently and simultaneously rather than in neat, logical stages.[3] Three important changes affected how policy was formulated and implemented and created the conditions which encouraged the development of a different policymaking style. First, the political executive wanted to put its imprint on policy. Colonial government policymaking, with the partial exception of the 1970s, had tended to be reactive rather than proactive. The Chief Executive and the principal officials sought to introduce initiatives that would reduce the backlog of policy problems left over from the transitional period and establish the government's credentials, as its predecessor had done, based on performance legitimacy. The political executive expected its ideas to be translated into action quickly through the civil service. The consequence was that some of the new initiatives were not always as carefully costed and assessed as they had been in the past and were less subject to the moderating influence of the budgetary system. Many were failures (see Chapters 5 and 6). The policy agenda, within a system that had become more disarticulated and characterised by friction between the legislature, executive, judiciary, and bureaucracy, was increasingly less under the control of senior civil servants.[4]

A second factor was that changes in the political environment meant that policymaking could no longer be insulated from actors outside the system The Chinese government became an increasingly important influence on what should be on

---

2. King, A. Y. C. (1981). Administrative absorption of politics in Hong Kong: Emphasis on the grassroots level. In A. Y. C. King & R. P. L. Lee (Eds.), *Social life and development in Hong Kong* (p. 130). Hong Kong: The Chinese University Press.
3. Kingdon, J. W. (1995). *Agendas, alternatives and public policies* (2nd ed., p. 78). New York: Harper Collins.
4. Scott, I. (2007). Legitimacy, governance and public policy in post-handover Hong Kong. *Asia Pacific Journal of Public Administration*, 29(1), 29–49.

the agenda and on expenditure. On the domestic front, political parties, pressure groups, and civil society organisations gradually became more able to obstruct policy implementation. Although these organisations still had relatively little influence on policy formulation, they had enough support in the community to delay new measures and demonstrate against their implementation. In several cases, the government was forced to retreat, to revise its proposals, or not to make major policy reforms. Problems in major social policy areas, such as health and housing, were left unattended with consequential incremental drift leading to complaints about service delivery.

The third factor that changed the nature of policymaking after 1997 was a persistent structural budgetary deficit. Budgeting was a relatively relaxed exercise when the government had sufficient revenue to obviate the need to make hard choices. After the Asian financial crisis, however, when tensions arose over which services would be funded and which would not, there was less time, and perhaps even less inclination, for economic rationality. More explicitly, political agendas had to be met. After 2007, the economy improved, but it became more difficult to introduce new policies. Civil society organisations increasingly acted as a brake on what could be successfully implemented, the pan-democrats in the legislature blocked constitutional changes, and the memory of the 2003 demonstration was sufficient to persuade the government that it should proceed cautiously on domestic issues. Large expenditure was made on projects favoured by the Chinese government, such as the high-speed rail link to Guangdong and the HZMB, but major problems of insufficient public housing supply, health financing, inadequate welfare services, and poverty remained unresolved. Under the Leung and Lam administrations, expenditure continued unabated but did not address or make much progress on social policy problems (see Chapter 8). By 2020, the government was once more budgeting for a deficit after the 2019 protests, COVID-19, and the Chinese government's decision to enact national security laws for Hong Kong had badly affected the economy. An unexpected recovery in 2021 was met with pent-up demands for salary increases from civil service and the need to provide substantial funding to combat a new wave of the pandemic.

The post-1997 system is more porous than its colonial predecessor with the consequence that policy formulation and implementation are less easily controlled and outcomes are more difficult to predict. That said, policy in some areas, particularly well-established policies which require fine-tuning rather than radical change and those which are of little immediate political interest, remain rationally driven from within the civil service rather than by the political executive. The attempt to exert political control over the civil service is uneven; old ways of doing things persist and the imperative to ensure that the costs and benefits of public policies are properly assessed continues to be important.

We will explore this argument over the next three chapters. In this chapter, we describe and analyse the budgeting system which has been the bedrock of the traditional policymaking system. We look at the principles underlying the budget, constraints on budget-making, the budgetary cycle, and what we can learn from it about patterns of expenditure and policy priorities. Although the budgetary system has largely remained procedurally the same as it was before 1997, the principal actors are now politicians rather than civil servants and have had to respond to different demands and pressures. In Chapter 8, we consider the political factors influencing policy more directly, how issues reach the agenda, the extent to which the system is open or closed to demands from the community, and the results of the two different policymaking styles. In Chapter 9, we will analyse the means of achieving policy objectives, the way these have changed over time, the role played by pressure groups and parties in the implementation process, and the contrasting features of policy driven by the civil service from that of policy driven by the political executive. Chapter 10 analyses the increasing influence of the Chinese government on Hong Kong policymaking and the areas in which policy has been shaped by its objectives.

Budgetary Principles

The budgetary process has been described as "a mechanism for making choices among competing claims for resources under conditions of scarcity".[5] The scarcity arises because there are never enough resources to meet demands; an authoritative decision, which the budget represents, is needed to determine which policy areas will be funded and how revenue will be raised to meet that expenditure. What principles guide the government in deciding how much money it will make available to meet demands? Is the government willing to go into deficit to fund critical policy areas? How does the budgetary process assist in establishing what should be funded and what should not? Answering these questions requires an examination of the evolution of budgetary principles.

The budget is based on propositions that date to the origins of Hong Kong as a colony. The British government wanted to keep the cost of running its empire as low as possible and regarded a balanced budget as a highly desirable feature of colonial administration. Since the Hong Kong government benefited from greater autonomy from London when the budget was balanced, and because it was constantly being criticised by local entrepreneurs for spending too much, and perhaps also because senior officials were themselves believers in fiscal frugality, Financial Secretaries put a great deal of effort into ensuring that the government remained small and that it did not spend beyond its means. This was particularly true after the Second World War when the colony was devastated and had to rely on financial support from the British government to re-establish itself. A condition of its subsequent financial

---

5. McCaffery, J. (1999). Features of the budgetary process. In R. T. Myers (Ed.), *Handbook of government budgeting* (p. 27). San Francisco: Jossey-Bass.

autonomy, or so it was perceived, was that the colonial government should operate with a budgetary surplus. A series of long-serving Financial Secretaries made "value for money" and a balanced budget the central tenets of their fiscal credo.[6] This was based on assumptions about revenue and expenditure: that revenue would be sufficient for the needs of a small government if the colony continued to prosper economically and that expenditure would be kept to a minimum by stringent financial controls. The result was that the government accumulated large fiscal reserves and had virtually no debt.

These principles came under pressure in the 1970s when MacLehose vastly expanded social policy outputs, putting the budget under strain even though the economy was prospering. In the end, however, fiscal discipline was maintained. MacLehose's ambitious public housing targets could not be entirely met because the Finance Branch was adamant that there were no funds available. By the end of the 1970s, Financial Secretaries had refined their budgetary principles to the point where there were prescribed rules to guide best practice.[7] In 1982, the Financial Secretary laid down four principles which were to serve as the basis of the budgetary system:

- the growth rate of public expenditure should have regard for the growth rate of the economy;
- the pattern of public sector expenditure should reflect the government's conscious view of its priorities;
- there should be a balance between direct and indirect taxation, and between taxation and other recurrent revenue, and the taxation system should be simple to administer, equitable, and generate enough revenue for policy priorities to be met;
- guidelines should be borne in mind in preparing the annual estimates of revenue and expenditure so that recurrent revenue did not consume such a proportion of the budget that capital expenditure suffered.[8]

In 1995, a Finance Branch publication put these principles in the context of the continuing importance of the historical constraints of business interests and small government:

> in Hong Kong, it is the private sector, not the public sector which largely generates the wealth on which all else depends. Disproportionately large public sectors not

---

6. Brown, S., Fung, E. W. K., Loh, C., Uebergang, K., & Xu, C. (2003). *The budget and public finance in Hong Kong*. Hong Kong: Civic Exchange; Fong, B. C. H. (2022). *Hong Kong public budgeting*. Singapore: Palgrave Macmillan; Rabushka, A. (1976). *Value for money: The Hong Kong budgetary process*. Stanford: Hoover Institution Press.
7. Rabushka, A. (1979). *Hong Kong: A study in economic freedom* (pp. 31–32). Chicago: University of Chicago Press.
8. Financial Secretary (1982). *The 1982–83 budget* (Appendix A). Hong Kong: Government Printer.

only reduce the real resources available to the private sector but may also impose a burden on the community through higher taxation.[9]

The Basic Law endorsed the stringent fiscal practices that the colonial administration had adopted. During the drafting process, some wanted to include the mandatory requirement of a balanced budget into the constitutional arrangements on the assumption that revenue would usually be sufficient to meet expenditure. A slightly milder form of the importance of a balanced budget was eventually adopted. Article 107 provides that:

> The Hong Kong Special Administrative Region shall follow the principle of keeping expenditure within the limits of revenue in drawing up its budget, and strive to achieve a fiscal balance, avoid deficits and keep the budget commensurate with the growth rate of its gross domestic product.

If these conditions cannot be met, how long can the government be in breach of the Basic Law and what happens to its existing programmes if "keeping expenditure within the limits of revenue in drawing up its budget" cannot be maintained? The phrase "strive to achieve a fiscal balance" has been interpreted to mean that a short-term deficit might be acceptable but that a balanced budget should be restored as soon as possible.

There are frequent fluctuations in GDP in Hong Kong, reflecting the situation of a small open economy exposed to external forces over which it has little or no control.[10] Trying to maintain a balanced budget and to relate public expenditure to economic growth under such circumstances is not always possible. Financial Secretaries have fixed obligations to provide public services and the government has sometimes been forced to operate in deficit, notably between 1998 and 2004 and after 2019. Figure 7.1 shows public expenditure as a percentage of GDP. The aim is to keep expenditure below 20% of GDP, but that has often been breached and reached 32% in 2021. In prosperous times, it has proved possible to bring in the budget at under 20% of GDP, principally because Hong Kong does not have an army and its spending on health and welfare is much lower than that of most developed countries. When times are hard, the government has to rely on its reserves and/or the sale of land to meet the difference between revenue and expenditure.

Between 1998 and 2004, there were six consecutive years of budgetary deficits on the operating account, which comprises only recurrent revenue and expenditure, and deficits on five out of six years on the consolidated account, which includes both recurrent and capital revenue and expenditure.[11] In 2003, the Financial Secretary, Antony Leung, noted that the causes lay in the "consolidation" of the

---

9. Finance Branch (1995). *Practitioner's guide: Management of public finances* (p. 33). Hong Kong: Government Printer.
10. Luk, P., Cheng, M., Ng, P. & Wong, K. (2020). Economic policy spillovers in small open economies: The case of Hong Kong. *Pacific Economic Review*, 25(1), pp. 21–46.
11. Financial Secretary (2004). *The 2004–05 budget* (p. 17). Hong Kong: Government Logistics Department; Financial Secretary (2003). *The 2003–04 budget* (p. 3). Hong Kong: Printing Department.

Figure 7.1 *Public Expenditure as a Percentage of GDP*

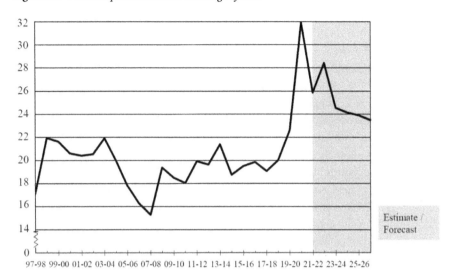

Source: Adapted from Financial Secretary (2022). *The 2022–23 budget* (Appendix B, p. 19). https://www.budget.gov.hk/2022/eng/pdf/e_appendices_b.pdf

Note: The government distinguishes between public and government expenditure. Public expenditure includes both government expenditure and expenditure on public bodies outside government. Government expenditure is expenditure directly attributable to government bureaus and departments.

property market and the bursting of the "bubble economy", economic restructuring with most of Hong Kong's industrial production processes moving to China, an ageing population, and increases in recurrent expenditure resulting from a rigid pay adjustment mechanism for civil servants and subvented organisations.[12] By 2005–2006, the government was once more in surplus and returning to the discipline applied to traditional Hong Kong budgets. Budgetary surpluses, however, created their own politics and did not necessarily appease the public.[13]

John Tsang Chun-wah, who was Financial Secretary between 2007 and 2017, was a fiscal conservative who reaffirmed the original principles of budgeting, "to keep expenditure within the limits of revenue, avoid deficits, and keep the budget commensurate with economic growth".[14] The problem was that neither the domestic nor the external political environment was conducive to the kind of budgeting process that had been successful under colonial rule. The post-handover system was far less insulated and far more open to pressure for greater expenditure from Chief Executives, local business, the Chinese government, and civil society organisations. Thus, although Tsang built Hong Kong's reserves from $369 billion in 2007 to $868

---

12. Financial Secretary (2003). *The 2003–04 budget* (p. 5).
13. Fong (2022) op. cit., pp. 48–54.
14. Financial Secretary (2016). *The 2016–17 budget* (p. 45). Hong Kong: Government Logistics Department.

billion in his last budget in 2016, the rate of increase in expenditure was so high that both figures were equivalent to about 25 months of government spending.[15]

Carrie Lam and her Finance Secretary, Paul Chan Mo-po, introduced "a new fiscal philosophy" in 2018. The 1982 principles were still reiterated in the budget and, at first sight, the new policy seemed little more than platitudes. Fiscal policy would "promote economic development", "invest for our future", "relaunch Hong Kong", "continue to support enterprises, safeguard jobs", "improve people's livelihood", and "enhance public services".[16] All this was to be wrapped in a blanket of "fiscal prudence" and using the reserves "wisely for the community".[17] The new fiscal philosophy did allow the government to try to spend its way out of its accumulated political and social problems and to allow the Future Fund, in which a portion of the reserves was held, to make "direct investments in projects with a 'Hong Kong nexus'".[18] But it came at the expense of a balanced budget. Figure 7.2 shows that a major reason for the deficit was the rapid rise in recurrent expenditure (the operating account) which far outstripped economic growth. Successive Chief Executives introduced new projects that required a larger civil service. An increasingly volatile political situation meant that the government found it more difficult to resist claims

Figure 7.2 *Growth of Government Recurrent Expenditure 1997–2020*

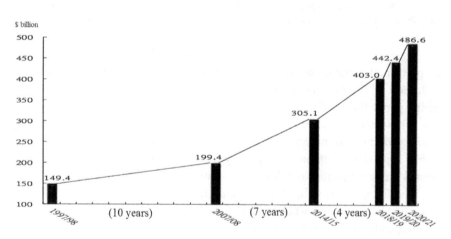

Source: Adapted from Financial Secretary (2020). *The 2020–21 budget* (para 176). https://www.budget.gov.hk/2020/eng/budget33.html

---

15. Ibid., p. 47; Financial Secretary (2008). *The 2008–09 budget* (Appendix A, p. 7). Hong Kong: Government Logistics Department.
16. Legislative Council (2019). *Budget consultation*. LC Paper No. CB (1)175/19-20 (04) (p. 25). https://www.legco.gov.hk/yr19-20/chinese/panels/fa/papers/fa20191202cb1-175-4-ec.pdf
17. Hong Kong Government (2019). *The Chief Executive's 2019 policy address supplement* (Ch. 2, p. 3). https://www.policyaddress.gov.hk/2019/eng/supplement.html
18. Financial Secretary (2020). *The 2020–21 budget* (para 184). https://www.budget.gov.hk/2020/eng/index.html

for substantial salary increases. By 2021, the operating deficit had reached $280 billion. Although the Financial Secretary expected that the deficit would be nearly halved in the following financial year, the Medium Range Forecast still showed that the government would remain in deficit for the next five years.[19] Fortuitously, the economic recovery in 2021 reduced the forecast deficit to $125 billion in 2002–2023 and even led the government to predict a small budgetary surplus for 2023–2024 (see Table 7.2).

On the capital expenditure account, there were considerable fluctuations, depending largely on whether the government sold land. Mega-infrastructural projects, such as the high-speed and subway rail links and the HZMB, resulted in billions of dollars in cost overruns, put pressure on efforts to balance the consolidated account. The deficit between capital revenue and capital expenditure gradually grew. However, in 2019, the government sold land for $118 billion, which returned the capital account to a surplus.[20]

Budget allocations on both the operating and the capital account faced increasing criticism and obstruction from democratic legislators.[21] On the operating account, they argued that the growing number of elderly people, those living in poverty, the income inequality gap, long public housing waiting lists, and poor access to public health care justified vastly increased social policy spending. By the end of John Tsang's term in office in 2017, these issues had become pressing concerns. The number of people over the age of 65 rose from 0.46 million, or 8.2 % of the population in 1988, to 1.27 million, or 27% of the population in 2018, and was expected to almost double in the 20 years to 2038.[22] Many of the 1.35 million (20% of the population) who were living in poverty were elderly. By 2016, the Gini coefficient, which measures income inequality, increased to 0.539, its highest level in 40 years and the eighth highest in the world.[23] In 2018, the average waiting time for the 268,500 applicants for public housing was over five years, the highest number in 18 years.[24] The problem was compounded by low levels of government expenditure on public housing.[25] As the Legislative Council's Research Office pointed out:

---

19. Financial Secretary (2021). *The 2021–22 budget* (Appendix A). https://www.budget.gov.hk/2021/eng/pdf/e_appendices_a.pdf
20. Ibid., Appendix A, 10.
21. For the effects of disputes on budgetary outputs, see Xiao, H., Wang, X., & Liu, C. (2019). Budgetary punctuations: A fiscal management perspective. *Policy Studies Journal*, 48(4), 896–925.
22. Wong, K., & Yeung, M. (2019). *Population ageing trend of Hong Kong* (pp. 2–3). Hong Kong: Office of the Government Economist. https://www.hkeconomy.gov.hk/en/pdf/el/el-2019-02.pdf
23. Social Indicators of Hong Kong (2020). *Gini coefficient*. https://www.socialindicators.org.hk/en/indicators/economy/11.6
24. Ng, N., & Su, X. (2018, 10 August). Waiting time for a Hong Kong public housing flat longest in 18 years: Five years, three months. *SCMP*. https://www.scmp.com/news/hong-kong/community/article/2159237/waiting-time-hong-kong-public-housing-flat-longest-18-years
25. Legislative Council Secretariat Research Office (2020). *Research brief: The 2020–21 budget* (pp. 5–6). https://www.legco.gov.hk/research-publications/english/1920rb01-the-2020-2021-budget-20200403-e.pdf. See also Goodstadt, L. F. (2013). *Poverty in the midst of affluence: How Hong Kong mismanaged its prosperity* (pp. 96–98). Hong Kong: Hong Kong University Press.

Public housing plays a key role in local social mobility, with greater poverty alleviation effect than Comprehensive Social Security Assistance. Yet its share in public expenditure halved to 5% in 22 years, with continued impact on income disparity.[26]

The health care system, among its many other problems, was understaffed and access to medical attention in public facilities was poor.[27]

On the capital account, expenditure on the mega-projects angered many democrats because they saw them as expensive, not justified on a cost-benefit analysis, and an unnecessary diversion of resources from required social policy spending. They also believed that the infrastructural projects were an attempt to speed up the integration of Hong Kong and China. The projects resulted in demonstrations, filibusters in the Legislative Council, and opposition to the government's request for additional funding when the mega-projects exceeded their original estimated cost.

It is a moot point whether budget allocations were an underlying cause of the 2019 protests. The government's position was that the protests were a "social incident" that stemmed—implicitly—from its failures in social policy provision. The Chief Secretary for Administration, Matthew Cheung Kin-chung, who was also chair of the Commission on Poverty, added $100 million to the public housing budget in July 2019 and there were further plans to ameliorate housing problems in the Chief Executive's 2019 policy address. In her speech, Carrie Lam conceded that, despite its efforts to provide public housing, the government may not have "eased the minds of the general public".[28] There were nonetheless no promises of significant injections of capital into public housing. Cheung's $100 million was but a drop in the ocean compared to the problems that poor families and the elderly were suffering from lack of affordable housing supply.[29] Whether public housing and income inequality were underlying causes of the protests, however, is by no means certain. The protesters' demands did not mention inadequate social policy provision but were overtly political calls for universal suffrage and an inquiry into the actions of the Police Force. When Cheung took to the radio to explain government policies, several young people phoned in to tell him that housing was not the primary cause of their despair.[30]

The economy performed reasonably well until the onset of the 2019 protests, COVID-19, and the enactment of the national security laws led to a severe economic downturn and brought the problems of the budget into high relief. Despite providing a $71 billion cash handout to the public and slashing income tax, the

---

26. Legislative Council Secretariat Research Office (2020), op. cit., p. 1.
27. Schoeb, V. (2016). Healthcare service in Hong Kong and its challenges. *China Perspectives*, 4, 51–58.
28. Chief Executive (2019). *2019 policy address* (para 12). https://www.policyaddress.gov.hk/2019/eng/index.html
29. See Oxfam (2018). *Hong Kong inequality report* (pp. 19–22). https://www.oxfam.org.hk/tc/f/news_and_publication/16372/Oxfam_inequality%20report_Eng_FINAL.pdf
30. *The Standard* (2019, 17 October). Youngsters tell Cheung despair isn't due to housing. https://www.thestandard.com.hk/breaking-news-print/135654/Youngsters-tell-Cheung-despair-isn't-due-to-housing

Financial Secretary, Paul Chan Mo-po, declared that current practices could not be sustained.[31] The budget was increasingly hostage to political and economic headwinds. The evident disjunction between policy problems and patterns of expenditure in budget allocations continued. Yet the traditional budgetary principles remain in place. The government still formally believes that it is desirable to balance the consolidated account, that the growth of expenditure should not exceed the growth rate of the economy, and that public expenditure should be below 20% of GDP.[32] The principles underlying the budget are important because they embody the government's fiscal strategy and constitute the macro-economic background against which policy is constructed. However, budget allocations under the Lam administration suggest that in practice the 1982 principles are now less relevant, superseded by the new fiscal philosophy or driven by political and economic forces beyond the control of the government.

Constraints on Fiscal Policy

Aside from political and economic forces, there are other significant constraints on the implementation of the budgetary principles. These relate to problems of forecasting revenue, to built-in assumptions about the importance of maintaining a low tax regime, and the necessity to continue funding essential services.

Financial Forecasting

Financial Secretaries face the imprecision of economic growth figures from which they must derive estimated revenue and expenditure figures for the next financial year. GDP has fluctuated wildly since 1997, initially affected by the Asian financial crisis, the subsequent economic malaise, and the SARS epidemic, recovering strongly after 2004 but again experiencing a major downturn from 2019 onwards. GDP is the starting point for the calculation of the Medium Range Forecast (MRF), which determines expenditure for the following year. There is a bias towards an optimistic forecast because the Financial Secretary has to cover existing services and commitments. The projections of future growth have tended to exceed actual growth; consequently, expenditure outstrips growth.

The inability to predict economic growth figures accurately has a direct impact on the determination of revenue and expenditure levels. The government is never entirely sure how much revenue it will collect and therefore how much it will have to spend. In prosperous times, the government will usually receive more than it expects; in difficult economic conditions, it will need to rely on its fiscal reserves or the sale of land to meet its commitments. The introduction of accrual-based

---

31. Financial Secretary (2020a) op. cit., p. 56.
32. Ibid., Appendix A, p.6.

accounting in 2004 helped to improve economic forecasting, but other factors continue to result in volatile, short-term changes to the government's revenue base. The land premium, stamp duties, and profit tax all vary considerably depending on the state of the economy. As Figure 7.3 shows, approximately 23% of revenue in 2022/2023 was expected to be derived from profits and salaries tax. The companies are dependent on economic circumstances for their profits, which determine the amount of tax that they pay. Company tax on profits is low at 8.2% for the first $2 million and 16.5% thereafter. For individuals, the maximum standard rate of salaries tax is 15% of assessable income. There are substantial deductions for children, education allowances, and home loans. In 2020, in light of the economic situation, tax concessions were granted both to companies and individuals. The tax base for both companies and individuals is consequently very narrow. In 2019, the top 5% of tax-paying companies (about 5,700 corporations) contributed 87% of profits tax and 91% of registered corporations paid no tax at all.[33] Of an estimated working population of 3.83 million, some 1.96 million did not pay any salaries tax; of those

Figure 7.3 *Estimated Government Revenue 2022–2023*

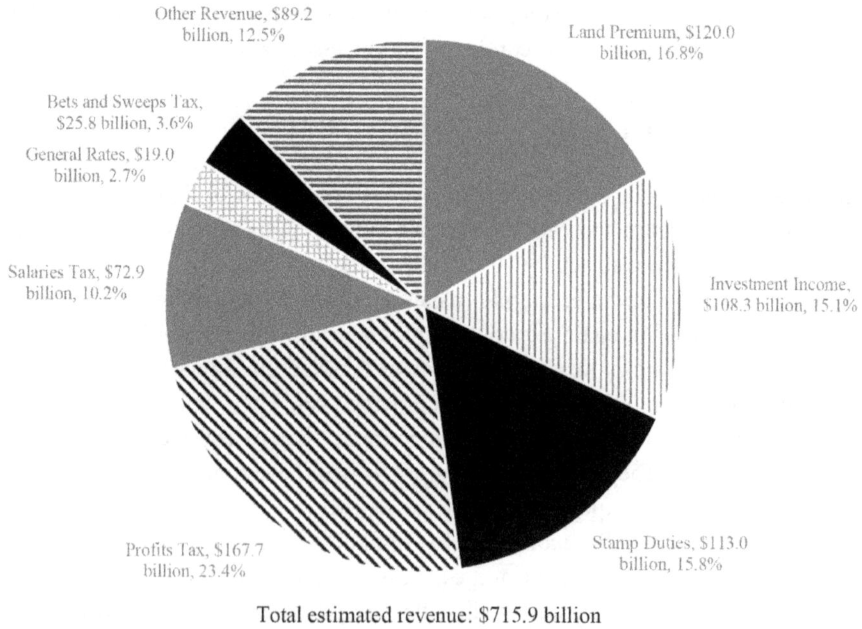

Other Revenue, $89.2 billion, 12.5%
Land Premium, $120.0 billion, 16.8%
Bets and Sweeps Tax, $25.8 billion, 3.6%
General Rates, $19.0 billion, 2.7%
Salaries Tax, $72.9 billion, 10.2%
Investment Income, $108.3 billion, 15.1%
Profits Tax, $167.7 billion, 23.4%
Stamp Duties, $113.0 billion, 15.8%

Total estimated revenue: $715.9 billion

Source: Adapted from Financial Secretary (2022). *The 2022–2023 budget* (Appendix B, p. 31). https://www.budget.gov.hk/2022/eng/pdf/e_appendices_b.pdf

---

33. Legislative Council (2019) op. cit., p. 22.

who did, the top 5% of taxpayers (93,000 people) paid 66% of the personal tax revenue.[34] In 2020, even for those who did pay tax, the Financial Secretary reduced income tax by 100% except for a cap of $20,000.[35] The figures reflect both the problems with the budget and the inequalities in society.

A Low Tax Regime

Historically, a low tax regime has been an important factor in Hong Kong's economic growth and has long been defended by business groups.[36] Government attempts to broaden the tax base have been obstructed and eventually abandoned. The most serious attempt began in March 2000, when the Financial Secretary appointed a Task Force to review public finances and an Advisory Committee to make recommendations on new broad-based taxes. When their reports were delivered in early 2002, it was clear that their members believed that there was an urgent need for financial reforms. The Task Force concluded that there were:

> unequivocal signs that even when the economy returns to "normal" growth, the budget deficits will remain and indeed worsen. To continue the current fiscal "lifestyle" is therefore not an option.[37]

It recommended that the government give priority to controlling the growth of public expenditure and that it should try to make the tax base more broad-based.[38] After a wide review of the available options, the Advisory Committee recommended that, rather than raising salaries taxes, a consumption tax should be considered.[39]

The government was supportive and believed, in principle, that a goods and services tax (GST) was the best way to broaden the tax base. However, in 1998, the government had frozen most charges to ease the financial burden and then had difficulty in reimposing them, let alone introducing a GST. Unemployment was running at 7% and, in 2001, only about 60% of the proposed measures to increase taxes were approved by the Legislative Council.[40] In 2003, legislators persuaded the government to withdraw a proposal to levy a Boundaries Facilities Improvement tax on departing passengers that was estimated to raise HK$1 billion.[41] The GST was a much more significant proposal and attracted widespread opposition from

---

34. Ibid., p. 21.
35. Financial Secretary (2020) op. cit., para 33(a).
36. See Littlewood, M. (2010). *Taxation without representation: The history of Hong Kong's troublingly successful tax system*. Hong Kong: Hong Kong University Press.
37. Task Force on Review of Public Finances (2002). *Final Report to the Financial Secretary* (p. 43). Hong Kong: Printing Department.
38. Ibid.
39. Advisory Committee on New Broad-Based Taxes (2002). *Final report to the Financial Secretary* (p. 27). Hong Kong: Printing Department.
40. Financial Secretary (2004). *The 2004–05 budget: Information pack for the Financial Secretary's consultations* (p. 23). https://www.budget.gov.hk/2004/eng/20031028-eng.pdf
41. Ibid.

within the legislature and from the business lobby, which agreed on the need to broaden the tax base but thought that it was not an appropriate time to introduce the new tax.[42]

The government introduced its proposals as a consultation document in July 2006. By that stage, the budget was in surplus and unemployment had dropped. The government's rationale for the tax was simply to increase the revenue base to provide additional funding to support an ageing population.[43] The Financial Secretary gave assurances that there would be no threat to Hong Kong's low tax regime, that the GST would be low at about 5% and would be expected to generate $30 billion annually, and that registration would exclude many small and medium-size businesses.[44] Opposition to the GST continued to mount. In October 2006, the Democratic Party lodged a motion in the Legislative Council opposing its introduction, claiming that 70% of the public was against it.[45] There was cross-party support for the motion. Many legislators questioned the assumption that the tax base was too narrow and raised concerns about its impact on the poor and on Hong Kong's economic competitiveness. The motion passed with 40 legislators voting for it, four voting against, and five abstaining.[46] In December 2006, the Financial Services and the Treasury Bureau conceded that "it is clear that the public is strongly against GST . . . there is insufficient public support nor are the conditions right for the introduction of GST".[47]

The government has continued to study options for creating a more stable revenue base. One way in which it might raise revenue and reduce costs is to charge for services that it now offers at highly subsidised rates. It has remained government policy to try to introduce more realistic fees and "user-pays", but opposition from legislators and the public have prevented much progress. A critical area is health care financing. Hong Kong people enjoy a health care system that is heavily subsidised by the government and which, with an ageing population, is likely to become increasingly expensive. The government's proposals for reforming the system have always entailed larger personal contributions to health care financing[48] and are always likely to be challenged by the public, political parties, and civil society groups.

---

42. Hong Kong General Chamber of Commerce (2007, 22 August). Policy statement and submission. https://www.chamber.org.hk/en/advocacy/policy_comments.aspx?ID=37
43. Financial Secretary (2006, July). *Broadening the tax base: Ensuring our future prosperity: What's the best option for Hong Kong*. www.taxreform.gov.hk
44. Ibid.
45. Hansard, 19 October 2006, 479–480.
46. Ibid, 580.
47. Financial Services and Treasury Bureau (2006). *Public consultation on tax reform: Interim report* (p. iii). Fin(CR)/11/2306/06, https://www.legco.gov.hk/yr06-07/english/panels/fa/papers/fa-fincr11230606-e.pdf
48. Benitez, M. A. (2018, 4 July). Hong Kong's plan to steer 1.5 million people towards private health care through Voluntary Health Insurance Scheme will be "challenging". *SCMP*. https://www.scmp.com/news/hong-kong/health-environment/article/2153647/hong-kongs-plan-steer-15-million-towards-private; Food and Health Bureau (2006). *Your health, your life: Health care reform consultation document*. https://www.fhb.gov.hk/beStrong/files/consultation/reportcover_eng.pdf

Other than raising charges for government services, the government's options for raising revenue appear to be limited. It does not want to raise salaries or companies' tax because it fears that this might affect foreign investment and Hong Kong's competitiveness. It could sell government-owned assets, but there has been political opposition in the past and this does not resolve the problem in the longer term. It has tentatively moved towards issuing some government bonds. The retail government bond programme began in 2009 with a maximum outstanding amount at any time raised to $200 billion in 2013. In 2018, the government also introduced "green" bonds, aimed at financing public works projects with environmental benefits, with a maximum outstanding amount of $100 billion.[49] In his 2022–2023 budget, the Financial Secretary committed to issuing at least $15 billion inflation-linked retail bonds, $35 billion inflation-linked silver bonds aimed at the elderly, and $15 billion green bonds.[50] The amounts remain small in the context of the overall budget, and the government has stressed that it "maintains a strong fiscal position and does not need to finance its expenditure by issuing government bonds".[51] When the recession caused by the protests, COVID-19, and the introduction of the national security measures struck in 2020, the government looked to its old allies, fiscal reserves and the sale of land, to prevent a deficit from becoming a disaster.

Funding Essential Services

Expenditure patterns are usually less liable to rapid fluctuation than revenue. As in many governments, a large proportion of services continue to be funded with slightly increased amounts from year to year. A large percentage of the budget is spent on education, health, housing, and social welfare (see Figure 7.4). When revenue is higher than expected, this does not create any problems; the surplus simply goes into the fiscal reserves and legislators complain that more services should have been funded. When revenue is below expectation and the government still needs to fund existing services, then it may need to tap the fiscal reserves or sell some land to meet its commitments.

The Financial Secretary has few options other than to continue to budget for most of the vast range of services that the government funds and this means that room for manoeuvre in any particular budget may be quite limited. Unless programmes have a "sunset" provision requiring their completion within a specified period, it is difficult to terminate them because tenured civil servants have to be redeployed. The best chance of changing the direction of fiscal policy is usually to

---

49. Hong Kong Monetary Authority (2020). *Government green bond programme*. https://www.hkma.gov.hk/eng/key-functions/international-financial-centre/bond-market-development/government-green-bond-programme/
50. Financial Secretary (2022). *The 2022–23 budget* (para 77). https://www.budget.gov.hk/2022/eng/pdf/e_appendices_b.pdf
51. Hong Kong Government (2020). Government bonds. https://www.hkgb.gov.hk/en/overview/introduction.html

Figure 7.4 *Estimated Government Expenditure 2022–2023*

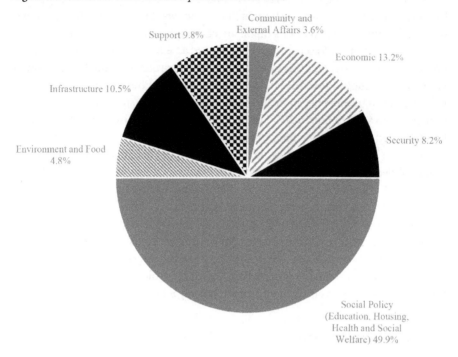

Source: Adapted from Financial Secretary (2022). *The 2022–2023 Budget*, Appendix B, pp. 26–27.
Notes:
1. For an explanation of the categories, "support" and "economic", see Table 7.5n.
2. For estimated total public expenditure in 2022–2023, see Table 7.5.

make gradual reductions and to look for savings in delivering services. In 2008, the Financial Secretary estimated that if expenditure on health and social welfare programmes were to remain unchanged, this would lead to increases of 400% and 140% respectively in real terms by 2033.[52] He argued that a central principle of public financial management should be sustainability and that the government should avoid measures either to raise revenue or increase expenditure that "the community will find hard to bear in the long run".[53] An alternative view might be that, if the demand is there, the government should try to meet it. Incremental drift and declines in public expenditure in real terms can lead to situations where inadequate social provision becomes permanently institutionalised in the budgetary system.

The budget allocations for 2022–2023 in Figure 7.4 represent a fairly normal distribution of resources in a post-handover state of equilibrium. They do not reveal,

---

52. Financial Secretary (2008). *The 2008–09 budget* (paras 39, 41). https://www.budget.gov.hk/2008/eng/budget11.html
53. Ibid., para 52.

Policy and the Budgetary Cycle 219

however, the considerable pressure to expand expenditure arising from the erosion of traditional budgeting principles, the long-standing constraints on fiscal policy, a weak government, and external crises caused by the protests, the pandemic, and Chinese government policies.

Public expenditure has shown a strong upward trajectory. In the 2018/2019 budget, the government forecast a surplus and put total public expenditure at $598.6 billion and made some effort to address its previous shortfalls in health and social welfare spending. In the 2019/2020 budget, total public expenditure increased to $611.4 billion, partly driven by "helping measures" of about $40 billion to alleviate financial distress and $50 billion to support the development of a technology hub in southern China.[54] Shortly before the 2020/21 budget was announced, the government set up a $30 billion anti-epidemic fund, adding another $137.5 billion to the fund in April 2020.[55] In the 2020/2021 budget itself, estimated public expenditure rose sharply to $773.1 billion, an increase of 26.6% over the previous year, and in actual practice came in at $860.1 billion.[56] The growth in expenditure reflected rising recurrent expenditure, a cash handout of $71 billion to the public, and a Police Force budget that soared by 25% to $25.8 billion.[57]

In the 2021/2022 budget, the Financial Secretary was faced with major economic and social problems. The economy had contracted by 6.1%. Although reducing public expenditure was still a major objective, he felt that its three largest components, education, welfare and healthcare, and contributions to the anti-epidemic fund could not be cut.[58] In order to lower public expenditure, particularly recurrent expenditure, he imposed a freeze on the civil service establishment.[59] Public expenditure was projected to decline by 11.8% in real terms to $771.3 billion.[60] By 2022–2023, although total public expenditure was still expected to rise to $851,824 billion[61] and the budget was in deficit, the government was still trying to rein in expenditure.[62] But it was uphill task. The improvement in public finances led to pressure for pay rises and an increased establishment. In March 2022, the Secretary for the Civil Service reported that the civil service establishment was projected to reach an all-time high of 197,646.[63]

---

54. Financial Secretary (2019). *The 2019–20 budget* (paras 64–70, 108). https://www.budget.gov.hk/2019/eng/index.html
55. Hong Kong Government (2020). Anti-epidemic fund. https://www.coronavirus.gov.hk/eng/anti-epidemic-fund.html
56. Financial Secretary (2021) op. cit., Appendix B:25.
57. Financial Secretary (2020). *The 2020–21 budget estimates* (p. 593). https://www.budget.gov.hk/2020/eng/pdf/head122.pdf
58. Financial Secretary (2021) op. cit., Paras 10, 172.
59. Ibid., Para 173.
60. Ibid., Appendix B, p. 25.
61. Financial Secretary (2022). *The 2022–2023 budget*, op. cit., Appendix B, p. 25.
62. Ibid., paras, 176, 178.
63. Legislative Council Panel on Public Service (2022, 9 February). Policy measures of the Civil Service Bureau in 2021 policy address (p. 8). LC Paper No. CB(4)57/2022(01).

Escalating public spending is partly an outcome of the government's failure to control the expansion of the civil service, salaries, and other costs associated with employing its personnel. On capital expenditure, the increases relate to infrastructural cost overruns and other projects under construction. To that extent, success or failure is within the grasp of a government still formally committed to traditional budgetary principles. What has not been under its control is the turbulent political and economic environment within which it has had to work. On the domestic front, its political, economic, and social problems continue to multiply. Its relations with the Chinese government and the pandemic influence its policy expenditure and leave its economic expectations as a matter of guesswork rather than rational economic calculation.

The budget is an overtly political exercise and one in which the Legislative Council, political parties, civil society organisations, and the public have all, up to this point, played an active role. There have been cleavages between business groups and the more populist parties which have fuelled the debate on how money will be raised and spent. The democrats and the unions have often challenged the basic principle that the budget should be balanced, maintaining that expenditure on welfare, education, housing, and health care is indispensable and should be accorded higher priority than mechanical efforts to balance the books.[64] Business groups have different agendas. The Chamber of Commerce regularly lobbies the government on matters such as maintaining an unchanged statutory minimum wage, tax concessions, and help for the small and medium-size enterprises affected by COVID-19.[65] In the Legislative Council, business representatives have consistently argued that the cost of the civil service is too high, that taxes should be lowered, and that the government is not showing sufficient concern about Hong Kong's regional economic competitiveness. The government has tried to reconcile some of these conflicting interests by increasing expenditure during the recession, in the process "punctuating" the equilibrium[66] of incremental budgets and depleting its reserves and land supply.

Despite their reservations about policy on particular issues, business groups and the DAB generally support the government, which has remained committed to their aims. This is important because the Legislative Council's most potent powers over the executive lie in the approval, modification, or rejection of the government's budgetary plans. It is a traditional function of legislatures to hold governments accountable by voting for supply and Article 52 of the Basic Law permits the Legislative Council to do so. It is highly unlikely, especially since the national security legislation was introduced, that the government's budget proposals could

---

64. Sum, L. K., & Leung, R. (2019, 7 February). Parties call for bigger spending on health care and welfare but avoid asking for direct cash after handout debacle. *SCMP*. https://www.scmp.com/news/hong-kong/politics/article/2185268/parties-call-bigger-spending-health-care-and-welfare-hong
65. Chamber of Commerce (2021). Submissions and reports. https://www.chamber.org.hk/en/advocacy/Policy.aspx
66. Xiao, Wang, & Liu (2020) op. cit.

be defeated. Nonetheless, a Financial Secretary has to tread carefully on social policy expenditure even in a legislature without democrats, but with many business supporters of a low tax regime and small government.

The Budgetary Cycle

The Financial Secretary has greater room for manoeuvre in the committees that determine whether proposals will be funded and whether existing programmes continue to be funded at the same level. Senior policymakers take these decisions formally in such bodies as the Executive Council and the Star Chamber and less formally in discussions with department heads and legislators. Many different values are involved: pressure groups, political parties, legislators, and individual departments all have an interest in getting their proposals funded and preventing existing programmes from having their budgets cut. Since resources are scarce, some will inevitably be disappointed and others will have to make do with less than they wanted. The Financial Secretary and the Secretary for Financial Services and the Treasury are central to the process of deciding who gets what. If the decisions are not to be contradictory or wasteful, there must be a clear understanding of how they relate to broader questions of policy: what those policies are, the directions in which revenue and expenditure plans will take the economy and the society, and how fiscal policy is coordinated with the policy objectives of the government.

The process of deciding on the new budget begins soon after the last one has been agreed (see Table 7.1). In June, the Financial Services and Treasury Bureau update the MRF, which is intended to provide a perspective on the direction of government revenue and expenditure beyond that of the annual resource allocation exercise. The MRF is based on assumptions about the future macro-economic picture—particularly the GDP and the rate of inflation—and of the government's fiscal intentions over the period. Table 7.2 shows the MRF over the period 2018/2019 to 2025/2026. Economic forecasting is difficult at the best of times and no forecasting could have predicted the impact of the kinds of political and social problems that the economy faced since 2019. The MRF is now strikingly different in its predictions from that of the previous years. Instead of the benign forecast of a budget in surplus, the 2021 MRF shows successive large budget deficits that are expected to be met from fiscal reserves. However, it failed to predict the economic rebound with the consequence that in 2022 the MRF presented a very different forecast for the future (see Table 7.2). Despite its forecasting inadequacies, the MRF is important because it sets the targets that the government aspires to meet and the amounts that bureaus and departments will be able to spend in the coming financial year.

After the MRF is determined, the next step in the budgetary process is for the Financial Services and Treasury Bureau to examine the expenditure proposals of the bureaus and departments. Policy programmes are costed at the departmental level and brought together by the bureau. Public expenditure has to be defensible,

Table 7.1 *The Budgetary Cycle*

Date	Activity
1 April	*Financial year begins.*
June/July	The Financial Services and the Treasury Bureau updates the medium-range forecast (MRF) and advises the Financial Secretary on the amount of "new money" for which bureaus/departments may bid. The Financial Secretary issues "envelopes" to Directors of Bureaus advising them of funding available for the coming year. Allocations for the next four years are also given for indicative planning purposes. Each Director of Bureau is required to confirm acceptance of the figures and to advise FSTB of the allocation of resources to each department under the bureau.
July–September	The Resource Allocation Exercise (RAE) begins. All Controlling Officers are invited to bid for resources for new initiatives in the coming year. All bids are submitted through the Director of Bureau who ranks the bids in order of priority. In a parallel exercise, Directors of Bureaus submit new initiatives for inclusion in the policy address. If they secure RAE funding, they are included in the policy address. The Star Chamber considers all bids and advises Directors of Bureaus of the results. Controlling Officers proceed to finalise their heads of expenditure for inclusion in the estimates.
October–December	The Chief Executive delivers the policy address in October. The Financial Secretary discusses budget proposals with Legislative Councillors and invites public submissions on the shape of the future budget and the constraints which the government faces. The bureau produces a budget consultation document which is intended to set the parameters for these discussions.
February–March	The draft estimates of expenditure and the Appropriation Bill to raise revenue to meet expenditure are introduced in the Legislative Council. The Financial Secretary moves that the Appropriations Bill (the budget speech) be read a second time. The debate is then adjourned to allow the Finance Committee, which is a committee of the whole Legislative Council, to examine the draft estimates of expenditure. The Chair of the Finance Committee reports to the Legislative Council.
March	Debate in the Legislative Council on the budget. Financial Secretary sums up the budget debate. The Appropriations Bill is amended, if required, and passed by the Legislative Council.
31 March	*Financial year ends.*

Source: I am grateful to Alan N. Lai, former Permanent Secretary of the FSTB, for his comments on this table. See also Financial Secretary (2020). *The 2020/2021 budget*. https://www.budget.gov.hk/2020/eng/speech.html; Legislative Council (2019). *Budget consultation*. LC Paper No. CB (1)175/19-20 (04). https://www.legco.gov.hk/research-publications/english/1920rb01-the-2020-2021-budget-20200403-e.pdf; Legislative Council (2016). *A companion to the history, rules and practices of the Legislative Council of the Hong Kong Special Administrative Region* (Ch. 12). https://www.legco.gov.hk/general/english/procedur/companion/main_toc.html

Policy and the Budgetary Cycle

Table 7.2 *The Medium Range Forecast*

($ million)	2020–21 Revised Estimate	2021–22 Revised Estimate	2022–23 Estimate	2023–24 Forecast	2024–25 Forecast	2025–26 Forecast
Operating revenue	440,351	519,478	556,911	584,878	613,605	658,905
Operating expenditure	721,192	593,057	682,500	584,400	601,500	627,600
Operating deficit	(280,841)	(73,579)	(125,589)	478	12,105	31,305
Capital revenue	103,144	163,255	158,947	148,629	153,872	170,009
Capital expenditure	99,193	105,898	124,879	141,266	148,316	148,319
Capital surplus/deficit	3,951	57,357	34,158	7,363	5,556	21,690
Fiscal reserves	902,721	946,669	890,338	933,279	968,976	1,034,221
Fiscal reserves as number of months of government expenditure	13	16	13	15	16	16

Sources: Figures for the 2020–21 revised estimate are from Financial Secretary (2021). *The 2021–22 budget* (Appendix A). https://www.budget.gov.hk/2021/eng/pdf/e_appendices_a.pdf. The remaining figures are from Financial Secretary (2022). The 2022–23 budget (Appendix A). https://www.budget.gov.hk/2022/eng/speech.html

initially against the scrutiny of senior officials and eventually before the Legislative Council. In considering their proposals, departments are expected to have regard for longer-term as well as short-run considerations. Policies do not usually fit neatly into the annual budgetary time frame and the department may be required to devise programmes that run over several years or indefinitely. Departments will also be asked by their bureaus to account for their progress on existing programmes and to explain any shortcomings. If they are proposing new policy initiatives, they will be subject to particular scrutiny on the recurrent expenditure side. Additional recurrent expenditure means new posts which need to be justified to the Legislative Council's Finance Committee.

Departmental bids for new resources are forwarded through the bureau for consideration by the Financial Services and Treasury Bureau and by the Star Chamber. The Star Chamber is a body composed of high-ranking principal officials: the Chief Secretary for Administration, the Financial Secretary, the Secretary for Financial Services and the Treasury, and the Secretary for the Civil Service. It is the gatekeeper for what will proceed as a funded proposal and what will be rejected or deferred for future consideration. The Star Chamber interviews principal officials on the spending plans of their bureaus and departments. It may also interview the heads of departments although it does not normally do so. The Star Chamber begins its work in July after the MRF has been decided. This is an essential prerequisite because the determination of expenditure can only be made after the amount of available money is known.

The Star Chamber normally begins by conducting a baseline review, assessing how well the bureau or department has performed in cutting costs and improving services, indicating where there might be improvements, and determining the "baseline" of future expenditure. Since much of this expenditure is already committed in the form of civil service salaries, there is relatively little leeway, especially when the budget is under pressure. If the current MRF forecasts are correct, there will be little "new money" until 2025 at the earliest. Despite its limited role in deficit years, the Star Chamber does have the power to make significant changes in resource allocation by requiring bureaus and departments to re-deploy personnel or eliminate positions. In surplus years, it plays a very important role in deciding on policy priorities and how government funds should be spent. The resource allocation process is to some extent decentralised to the bureau level. The principal official is given an "envelope" of funding which is then divided between the departments coming under his or her bureau. This moves the politics of the process to debates between the principal official and heads of departments although the amount that is in the "envelope" is determined by the Star Chamber, the Financial Secretary, and the Financial Services and Treasury Bureau.

We do not know what proposals the department may have put up which were rejected by its bureau, by the Financial Services and Treasury Bureau or by the Star Chamber, but from the funded programmes it is possible to determine how the allocation between programme areas was decided and where the department was looking to put more resources in the future. Each policy programme has a general objective that may never be fully achieved, let alone within a budgetary year. For the Police Force, for example, the aim of the law and order programme is "to maintain law and order through the deployment of efficient and well-equipped uniformed police force throughout the land and waters of Hong Kong".[67] Similarly, the aim of the Social Welfare Department's social security policy is "to provide a non-contributory social security system to meet the basic and essential needs of the financially vulnerable and the special needs of the severely disabled and elders".[68] In determining their personnel needs for particular programmes, departments take into account public demand for existing services and the need for more rapid delivery. To assess these factors, the departments look at indicators (to determine demand) and targets (to attempt to improve the speed with which the service is delivered). Expenditure in many cases cannot easily be substantially decreased without damaging effects, but areas within programmes may see a shift in expenditure as demand changes.

---

67. Financial Secretary (2020b) op. cit., p. 581.
68. Ibid., p. 857.

In the Social Welfare Department, for example, indicators for its largest programme, social security, relate particularly to the numbers who request support and are eligible for benefits under the Comprehensive Social Security Assistance (CSSA) Scheme and the Social Security Allowance (SSA). The CSSA is paid to residents who have lived in Hong Kong for more than one year and are unable to support themselves.[69] Eligibility is determined after an assessment of income and assets. Until 2007, the CCSA Scheme was a continual source of concern because of the spiralling number of cases and increasing expenditure. Between 2007 and 2017, cases dropped from 288,000 to 232,000 but expenditure rose from $17 billion to $20 billion.[70] Although there was a spike in unemployment cases during COVID-19, the caseload was 224,000 in December 2020, possibly because of the stringent eligibility criteria.[71] The SSA, which is comprised of the old age pension and various disability allowances, has become a major problem with the estimated number of cases expected to rise from 1.07 million in 2018 to 1.137 million in 2021.[72] It might be expected that with an ageing population the relative proportion of budgetary expenditure on the SSA might rise, provided that unemployment does not result in a flood of new applicants on the CSSA Scheme. These delicate issues of government responses to demand are difficult to predict and the budgetary process often lags behind community need.

In comparison with established programmes, such as social security, the development of new initiatives may be limited in times of budgetary austerity. New programme areas nonetheless provide important recognition that the government is responding to community needs. There is keen competition for "new money" among bureaus and departments and from many groups outside government who would like to see expenditure on their favoured projects. The Star Chamber, in consultation with the Chief Executive, vets new proposals, deciding on those that will go forward for inclusion in the policy address and which will subsequently be funded in the budget. The fate of new proposals has much to do with the politics surrounding the issue. Whether it is accepted will also depend on the contribution that it makes to the government's general policy direction, the perception that it addresses an important problem, pressure in the community for its adoption, and the vigour with which the policy secretary makes the case for funding. If the proposal is accepted as part of the policy address and further financial provision is contained in the budget, it becomes part of the institutional agenda that the government is actively implementing.

---

69. Social Welfare Department (2020). Comprehensive Social Security Assistance (CSSA) scheme. https://www.swd.gov.hk/en/index/site_pubsvc/page_socsecu/sub_comprehens/
70. Census and Statistics Department (2018). *Statistics on Comprehensive Social Security Scheme* (para 2.8). https://www.statistics.gov.hk/pub/B71809FB2018XXXXB0100.pdf
71. Hong Kong Government (2020, 17 December). *CSSA caseload for November 2020*. [Press release]. However, the figures are debatable. In the 2020 budget estimates, the Social Welfare Department claimed to have handled 268,000 cases in 2018 and estimated that it would have 260,000 cases in 2020/2021 but Census and Statistics figures are much lower. Financial Secretary (2020b) op. cit., p. 858.
72. Ibid., p. 858.

Until 2017, the Chief Executive's policy address was produced by the Central Policy Unit (CPU) which collated approved new proposals. Despite its name, the CPU did not have any say in deciding which policies would proceed. Before 1997, it produced papers on policy problems for the attention of senior policymakers, some of which were acted upon. After 1997, apart from its role in preparing the policy address, it focused mainly on research into policy issues but appears to have had only a marginal influence on agenda-setting. In 2017, Carrie Lam decided to change the name of the unit to the Policy Innovation and Coordination Unit. The unit is staffed by non-civil service staff and has been given responsibility for policy research and innovation, coordination across bureaus and departments, and enhancing public participation.[73]

The policy address is delivered in October and includes an indication of future directions and areas that will receive special emphasis. Accompanying the policy address is a booklet entitled the *Policy Address Supplement*, previously called the *Policy Agenda*, which reports on progress on previous and future initiatives.[74] While the agenda/supplement includes an overview of factors shaping policy outcomes, its main aim is to present in a favourable light what the government thinks that it is doing.

The debate in the Legislative Council following the policy address gives members the chance to praise the government for its foresight or, more usually, to castigate it for its shortcomings. Since members may not propose additional expenditure in the budget debate, the debate on the policy address is a convenient opportunity to bring alternative spending suggestions to the government's attention. The government cannot entirely ignore legislators' views although, since the Legislative Council is now entirely composed of pro-establishment/pro-Beijing members, it is highly unlikely that the budget would ever be rejected.

Following the debate on the policy address, the Financial Secretary is bound by convention to consult with legislators in advance of the budget. The process has become institutionalised. The Financial Secretary puts out a budget consultation document that contains information on the state of the economy, presents expenditure and revenue patterns and outlines the direction that the government thinks that policy should take.[75] He then invites comments from legislators as well as the public. There is a good deal of scepticism about whether the government's apparent receptivity to new ideas is any more than good public relations. As one commentator remarked, "it is mostly a cosmetic exercise, with the government seeking and listening to the views of the community and then going off and doing exactly what it wanted to do before the start of the so-called "consultation".[76] In times of equilib-

---

73. Legislative Council Panel on Public Service (2017). Review and revamp of the Central Policy Unit (pp. 3–4). https://www.legco.gov.hk/yr17-18/english/panels/ps/papers/ps20171120cb4-212-4-e.pdf
74. Hong Kong Government (2019) op. cit.
75. Legislative Council (2019) op. cit.
76. Perkin, I. K. (2003, December). Tang: Is he going to have it both ways? *Hong Kong Business*, 18–20.

rium, the main features of the following year's budget are usually in place when the Financial Secretary meets with legislators.

The Financial Secretary presents the budget to the Legislative Council at the end of February or in the first or second week of March. The first reading of the Appropriations Bill, which is the budget, is a purely formal exercise to table the bill. On the same day that it is read, the estimates of expenditure are tabled. The budget itself is the Financial Secretary's speech in support of a motion to read the Appropriations Bill for a second time. In his speech, the Financial Secretary will normally range widely over the state of the economy and the government's financial position, explaining how the budget takes account of these factors. Until 2019, major economic changes were rarely announced in the budget. Taxes might be adjusted slightly upwards or downwards, special provisions might be announced for particular groups, such as the elderly or charities, and mention may be made of the projects which will be funded by new money. But most changes are likely to be incremental and relatively innocuous, reflecting a state of economic equilibrium or growth and the kinds of constraint under which the budget has been formulated.

The February 2020 budget deviated from usual practice. The economic impact of the protests and COVID-19 were not entirely clear before the budget speech although it was evident that the government was going to be operating at a sizeable deficit. What was unexpected was the size of a cash handout to the public of $71 billion, the 25% increase in the Police Force budget, and increased expenditure in eight of the 10 policy areas. To compound matters, the government included all police expenditure in the Vote on Account, a measure introduced before the budget debate to allow essential spending after the end of the financial year without formal Legislative Council approval. The move riled the democrats, who introduced an amendment to cut expenditure in the Chief Executive's Office and the Police Force to zero, arguing that their performance had been unacceptable.[77] The democrats were also concerned that the Legislative Council had not been able to exercise sufficient scrutiny over the $2.5 billion spent on police overtime and other allowances during the protests and the spread of some Police Force costs over 22 other departments.[78] The Vote on Account was nonetheless passed by the council. In 2021, with the democrats absent from the chamber through disqualification or resignation, the Finance Committee's examination of police expenditure was a much more muted affair. Only 97, often congratulatory, questions were asked compared with the many hundreds of questions and often prolonged and heated debate that had accompanied the 2020 examination of police expenditure.[79]

---

77. Hansard, 18 March 2020, 4944ff.
78. Ho, K. (2020, 27 February). Hong Kong budget 2020: Democrats angered as police receive $2.5 billion boost in manpower and gear. *HKFP*. https://hongkongfp.com/2020/02/27/hong-kong-budget-2020-democrats-angered-police-receive-hk25-8-billion-boost-manpower-gear/
79. Finance Committee (2020). *Report on the examination of estimates of expenditure.* https://www.legco.gov.hk/yr19-20/english/fc/fc/minutes/sfc_rpt.pdf

After the Vote on Account, the President of the Council refers the estimates to the Finance Committee. The Finance Committee is composed of all members of the Legislative Council except the President. The committee has a continuous role in the budgetary process. It is required to approve any supplementary expenditure and its two subcommittees, on establishment and public works, meet frequently to consider new posts and capital expenditure respectively. The committee's most important task, however, is to ensure that the estimates of expenditure requested in the budget are "no more than necessary for the execution of the approved policies".[80]

The Legislative Council becomes the Finance Committee to consider the specific heads of expenditure, proposed by bureaus and departments. Members may move amendments provided that they reduce rather than increase expenditure and may raise questions about the plans of the bureau or any of its departments. Tables 7.3 and 7.4 show the proposed expenditure of the Police Force and the Social Welfare Departments respectively in the 2022/2023 budget estimates.

Departments divide their expenditure into policy programme areas. Expenditure reflects the relative importance of the programme area and may change quickly depending on circumstances. In the case of the Police Force, however, the maintenance of law and order has always been its primary goal. Justifying the maintenance of law and order was not difficult during the 2019 disturbances when the force duly received an increase of 25% in expenditure in the 2019/2020 budget. In the 2022/2023 budget, the request for an increase was based partly on a review of grade structure of the disciplinary services in 2021 which concluded that responsibilities of the force under the national security law had increased, that pay points throughout the force should be raised by one or two points, and that additional points should be added to the scale.[81] There was little discussion of the cost of these proposals in the Standing Committee's report or in the government and Finance Committee's acceptance of its findings, but they were important in the force's justification of its proposed expenditure in the 2022/2023 budgetary estimates.[82]

Social welfare expenditure has long been a concern of members of the legislature. Some have been concerned about cost, others about inadequate provision. In 2020, of the 6,722 questions asked of controlling officers during the Finance Committee meetings, 798 were on welfare, the second highest number after police expenditure.[83] In 2021, with only two democrats left in the Legislative Council, there were still 244 questions on social welfare expenditure for the controlling

---

80. Legislative Council (2016). *A companion to the history, rules and practices of the Legislative Council of the Hong Kong Special Administrative Region* (12.47). https://www.legco.gov.hk/general/english/procedur/companion/main_toc.html
81. Standing Committee on the Disciplined Services Salaries and Conditions of Service (2021, June). *Report on the grade review of the disciplined services grades* (pp. ix–xi, 14–15, 23–24). https://www.jsscs.gov.hk/reports/en/scds_gsr_2021_eng.pdf
82. Finance Secretary (2022). *The 2022–23 budget – estimates* (p. 597). https://www.budget.gov.hk/2022/eng/pdf/head122.pdf
83. Ibid., Appendix 2.

Policy and the Budgetary Cycle

Table 7.3 *Police Force: Analysis of Financial Provision 2021–2022 and 2022–2023*

Programme Area	2021–2022 (Revised) $ million	2022–2023 (Estimate) $ million
Maintenance of law and order in the community	11,379.8	12,759.2
Prevention and detection of crime	4,791.7	5,398.9
Road safety	2,349.3	2,650.7
Operations	4,721.9	5,859.4
Total	$23,260.7 (−7.2% on the original estimate)	$26,668.2 (+14.7% or +6.4% on the original estimate)

Source: Adapted from Financial Secretary (2022). *The 2022-23 budget-estimates.* https://www.budget.gov.hk/2022/eng/pdf/head122.pdf

Note:
1. Operations involves action to prevent illegal immigration and terrorism and measure to maintain internal security.

Table 7.4 *Social Welfare Department: Analysis of Financial Provision 2021–2022 and 2022–2023*

Programme Area	2021–22 (Revised) $ million	2022–23 (Estimate) $ million
Family and Child Welfare	4,560.4	4,781.2
Social Security	64,892.9	71,498.8
Services for Elders	13,059.8	14,022.6
Rehabilitation and Medical Social Services	9,945.1	10,414.8
Services for Offenders	423.0	426.1
Community Development	214.4	212.2
Young People	2,659.5	2,706.3
Total	95,755.1 (−8.2% on the original estimate)	102,270.0 (−0.2% on the original estimate)

Source: Adapted from Financial Secretary (2022). *The 2022-23 budget – estimates.* https://www.budget.gov.hk/2022/eng/pdf/head170.pdf

officer.[84] Questions usually cover all seven welfare programmes, but most focus on services for the elderly, family and child welfare, social security, and rehabilitation and medical social services.[85] Relatively less attention has been paid to the services offered for offenders, community development, and young people. Such differences in scrutiny often reflect the size of the programme's budget and the extent to which it is a matter of public concern.

After the Finance Committee has concluded its review of the expenditure of all bureaus and departments, the chair presents a report on the proceedings of the meeting to the full council. The resumption of the debate on the second reading of the Appropriations Bill follows the Finance Committee meetings. Members of the council are free to express their views on the general direction of the budget, on what it will achieve, and the areas in which it has failed to bring about improvements. This is an opportunity for Legislative Council members to voice their particular concerns. Members are given 15 minutes each to elaborate on what they feel are the pressing issues facing Hong Kong. The debate always ranges widely. On the 2020 budget, for example, members raised such issues as the protests and police expenditure, COVID-19 and health policy, fiscal policy and tax concessions, the speed at which the cash handouts would be paid, the economy, welfare and the elderly, and many other issues, both those which were funded and those which were not.[86] Once members have spoken, the policy secretaries then ask for the council's support for bureau proposals and the Financial Secretary closes the discussion on the second reading, usually dwelling on the general direction of the budget and noting points raised by members. Members may then call for a vote.

The final stage is the consent of the Chief Executive, which is a formality, provided that the budget has not been so substantially amended that it no longer reflects the government's original intentions. If the Legislative Council refuses to pass the budget, the Chief Executive may dissolve the council (Article 50 of the Basic Law). If the newly elected council still refuses to pass the budget, the Chief Executive must resign (Article 52(3)).

The budgetary process raises important questions about accountability, how government departments spend their money, how they allocate it within programmes, and whether it meets community needs. Most Legislative Councillors are diligent in their efforts to hold the government to account over its revenue collection and spending intentions. But it is the government that has the definitive say on the final allocation of resources. It would be too time-consuming for members to scrutinise every item in detail and, even if they could, the government could still push through its proposals as long as it maintained a majority in the council. The

---

84. Finance Committee (2021). *Replies to questions raised by Finance Committee members in examining the estimates of expenditure 2021–22* (Social Welfare). https://www.swd.gov.hk/storage/asset/section/2252/en/2021_22_Questions_and_Replies_(Sorted_by_Reply_No.).pdf
85. Ibid.
86. Hansard, 22, 23, April, passim.

best that members can achieve is to be alert to any unnecessary or extravagant proposals and, in conjunction with the Public Accounts Committee, to keep a watchful eye on how money is spent in the following financial year.

Policy and the Budget

Our definition of public policy starts with the notion that it is comprised of "a set of inter-related decisions". Ideally, the budget should reflect a series of coherent decisions that eventually come together as an integrated policy. Decisions are expected to be coherent in at least two different senses. First, they should not be contradictory. With the thousands of individual decisions that make up a budget, it is quite conceivable that individual departments or policy bureaus will formulate or implement policies that either cancel each other out or not achieve the desired outcome. In some cases, the swift intervention of senior officials can resolve the problem quite quickly. In other cases, the values on which the policies are based may be in total or partial conflict. The policy to provide public housing for those below a certain income level, for example, is more difficult to achieve since the government has reduced funding for new public housing projects.[87] Values, such as equity, often break down in the face of the political reality that policies sometimes benefit some groups at the expense of others. Traditionally, the structure of the Hong Kong government has not been designed to minimise problems that require both extensive horizontal coordination between departments and strong leadership to resolve the value differences reflected in policy. Ideally, the government should concern itself with the possibility of such conflicts and attempt to resolve them before policies are introduced and implemented. But some slip through the net.

The second sense in which government policy should be coherent is that it should represent conscious policy choices. The match between stated policy objectives and how the government spends its money provides one indication of how well the budget comes together in broad policy streams. In this respect, it is necessary to consider total public expenditure because, in the social policy field, in particular, implementation is often undertaken by subvented bodies. The relationship between aggregated expenditure decisions and intended policy objectives may be considered from both a short-term perspective, examining year-on-year changes in budget allocation, and a longer-term perspective to determine how allocation has been made to different sectors over the last decade (see Tables 7.5 and 7.6). If the budget is consciously goal-oriented, it should provide an important indication of the issues that have priority on the policy agenda.

Table 7.5 shows the budget allocation by sector in 2021 and 2022. In such a short period, the budget would usually reflect incremental policies because a large proportion of expenditure is already committed to existing programmes which are

---
87. Legislative Council Secretariat Research Office (2020) op. cit., pp. 5–6.

Table 7.5 *Total Public Expenditure: Year-on-Year Change 2021–2022 and 2022–2023*

Sector	2021–2022 Revised Estimate ($ million)	2022–2023 Estimate ($ million)	Increase/decrease in real terms (%)
Community and External Affairs	23,749	28,819	18.4
Economic[1]	75,071	113,789	48.7
Education	106,785	111,887	3.9
Environment and Food	33,651	39,060	13.7
Health	114,389	162,760	40.5
Housing	38,257	44,914	13.7
Infrastructure	80,448	85,429	3.0
Security	56,232	65,851	15.9
Social Welfare	103,910	120,031	13.4
Support[2]	107,412	79,284	–27.6
Total	739,904	851,824	13.1

Source: Adapted from Financial Secretary (2022). *The 2022-23 budget*. https://www.budget.gov.hk/2022/eng/pdf/e_appendices_b.pdf

Notes:
1. Economic covers air and sea communication, commerce and industry, employment, financial services, information technology and broadcasting, posts, power, competition policy and consumer protection, public safety and travel and tourism.
2. Support covers the central management of the civil service, complaints against maladministration, constitutional affairs, intra-governmental services, revenue collection and financial control and support for members of the Legislative Council.

regarded as essential. But the years between 2019 and 2022 were not normal years and the budgets show some of the strains that the economy, polity, and society were experiencing.[88] Some policy areas saw percentage gains that were outside the normal range. In 2020, for example, the 223.9% increase in the "economic" sector reflects the decision in the 2020 budget to provide a cash handout of $10,000 for each Hong Kong resident at a cost of $71 billion. The Financial Secretary said that this was designed to boost local consumption and to relieve the people's burden.[89] Although there was support in the legislature for the decision, there were also criticisms of this means of alleviating financial distress. It was argued that there was an opportunity cost involved because the money could have been spent on social policy improvements with potentially longer-term benefits than a one-off payment.[90] Studies on

---

88. Tobin, D. (2019). *Hong Kong's balancing act: Fiscal conservatism, northbound financial flows and poverty*. Nottingham: University of Nottingham Asia Research Institute. https://theasiadialogue.com/2019/06/05/hong-kongs-balancing-act-fiscal-conservatism-northbound-financial-flows-and-poverty/
89. Financial Secretary (2020) op. cit., para 36.
90. Wong, R. (2020, 26 February). Hong Kong budget 2020: HK$10,000 cash handout does nothing to tackle systemic justice, says democrat. *HKFP*. https://hongkongfp.com/2020/02/26/hong-kong-budget-2020-hk10000-cash-handout-nothing-tackle-systemic-injustice-says-democrat/

such payments in Australia and the United States have concluded that cash handouts stimulated savings rather than boosting consumption.[91] Economists have suggested that there is no compelling reason why Hong Kong should be any different, noting that a previous cash handout in 2011 had not demonstrated any significant economic benefits.[92] Finally, there were suspicions that the handout was an attempt to buy political support ahead of a scheduled (but later postponed) Legislative Council election.[93] Although most areas benefited from greatly increased expenditure in the budget, there were also evident spikes in spending in the security budget on police expenditure and in most social policy areas.

Table 7.6 *Total Public Expenditure by Percentage by Policy Area Group*

Policy Area Groups	1992–93 Actual	2005–06 Actual	2013–14 Actual	2018–19 Actual	2021–22 Revised estimate	2022–23 Estimate
Community and External Affairs	3.4	3.2	6.1	4.4	3.2	3.4
Economic	4.6	5.3	8.2	4.6	10.1	13.4
Education	18.7	22.0	16.7	19.0	14.4	13.1
Environment and Food	4.6	3.9	5.2	4.3	4.5	4.6
Health	11.8	12.9	14.8	13.8	15.5	19.1
Housing	17.0	6.3	4.6	5.5	5.2	5.3
Infrastructure	8.5	10.4	16.1	13.3	10.9	10.0
Security	9.6	10.1	7.7	8.9	7.6	7.7
Social Welfare	10.2	13.6	12.1	15.9	14.0	14.1
Support	11.6	12.3	8.5	10.4	14.5	9.3
Total Public Expenditure ($ million)	123,490	244,982	457,346	567,578	739,904	851,824

Sources: Calculated from Financial Secretary (1997). *The 1997-1998 budget.* Hong Kong: Government Printer, 1997, Appendix B; Financial Secretary (2007). *The 2007–08 budget.* Hong Kong: Government Logistics Department, Appendix B; Financial Secretary (2022). *The 2022-23 budget* (Appendix B). https://www.budget.gov.hk/2022/eng/pdf/e_appendices_b.pdf

Notes:
1 and 2. For an explanation of the categories of "Economic" and "Support", see Table 7.5, notes 1 and 2.
3. Figures have been rounded.

---

91. Davidson, S., & de Silva, A. (2013). Stimulating savings: An analysis of cash handouts in Australia and the United States. *Agenda: A Journal of Policy Analysis and Reform, 20*(2), 39–57.
92. Kwong, B. K. K. (2013). A comparative analysis of the cash handout policy of Hong Kong and Macau. *Journal of Current Chinese Affairs, 42*(3), 87–100; Lam, E., Curran, E., & Bloomberg (2020, 26 February). Hong Kong is giving every adult resident $1200—no strings attached. *Fortune.* https://fortune.com/2020/02/26/hong-kong-economy-stimulus-cash-handout/
93. Chow, N. (2020, 6 March).「派錢」710億——背後的政治考量 [Political considerations behind the $71 billion handout]. *Ming Pao.*

The 2022–2023 budget saw a significant jump in health expenditure, resulting from the pandemic. Expenditure on health increased by over 40% and constituted over 19% of the entire budget (see Tables 7.5 and 7.6). Financial Secretaries have no control over such unexpected developments which must be funded but which disrupt other policy-making plans. Despite the cost of the pandemic and a deficit that was still expected to amount to $125 billion, the Financial Secretary remained in expansionary mood with government expenditure projected to rise by over 15% and the intention to raise funds for other projects by issuing bonds. Where this fiscal strategy differs that of previous Financial Secretaries is that spending seems set to continue, relying if necessary on reserves and the sale of land, even under economic circumstances that, in the past, would have led to austerity programmes.

Table 7.6 shows the allocation of resources within policy sectors over a lengthier period. The major decline in spending has been in housing where a change of policy has meant that the private sector is supposed to meet demand with increased supply, a requirement that it has singularly failed to achieve. In comparison with the colonial period, spending on education increased until 2019 but has declined somewhat since then. More social welfare spending is a function of an ageing population and uncertain economic conditions: the post-1997 government is no more sympathetic to the idea of comprehensive social security than was its colonial predecessor. However, social policies continue to consume the bulk of expenditure and present the major challenge for any Financial Secretary seeking to balance many competing demands. As Table 7.6 shows, the Hong Kong government's allocation of funding to the various policy areas was relatively consistent in percentage terms from late colonial times until 2019. More dramatic shifts in funding allocation over the period 2019–2022 may reflect both a new fiscal philosophy and an attempt to find political answers to the unprecedented range of pressing issues facing the government.

Conclusion

The policymaking system in Hong Kong has undergone significant change, from a decision-making process that was largely closed and controlled by the bureaucracy to one that became more fractious and lately to one more subject to political direction from the executive and the Chinese government. The budgetary process provides some illustration of how this change is occurring. The allocation of resources has gradually evolved into a more public exercise than was previously the case. Financial Secretaries now consult with legislators, political parties, and pressure groups on the shape of the budget although the extent to which that consultation influences their decision is debatable. That does not mean that decisions are taken more rationally or logically. Conflicting pressures may result in decisions that are less than optimal, particularly in an environment where resources have become scarcer. The constraints on decision-makers have increased and their room for manoeuvre has declined because the political environment has changed. Where large new expenditure has occurred, it has tended to be one-off charges, such as cash handouts, or taken in line with Chinese government policies on infrastructure and innovation. Financial Secretaries now seem to generate more surprises with their budgets and arrive at some decisions that might cause their more miserly colonial predecessors to turn in their graves. In the next chapter, we examine the wider ramifications for the policy process of superimposing one policymaking system on another.

8
The Policy Process

Definitions of policy are often recognised to be inadequate to cover the many practical and analytical difficulties that the term encompasses.[1] Policy may involve debates over values, establishing an agenda to determine priorities, consultation with the public, negotiations between politicians and stakeholders, and deciding authoritatively on which course of action should be followed. It will also involve the use of state power, interactions between institutions and organisations outside the governmental structure, strategies to ensure successful implementation, assessments of the impact of the policy on citizens, and much more besides. Importantly, it also includes what a government chooses not to do, which may itself reflect many different considerations. It may be that the government does not have sufficient resources to achieve a particular goal because of other policy priorities, or because there is actual or anticipated political opposition, or because the timing is perceived to be unfavourable. It is difficult to find a definition that will cover this complex interaction between values, agendas, institutions, groups, and the impact of policy on people. Some analysts seek to avoid this complexity by defining policy simply as the output, in terms of decisions, of any public sector organisation. The difficulty with this approach is that it may miss the substantively important political issues in the process of arriving at decisions. It also fails to distinguish between different types of policy: a decision to raise the fines for illegal parking, for example, would fall into the same category as government policy on education.

Our definition of public policy takes it to be a broad course of action, a set of related decisions rather than random choices, involving "the selection of goals and the means of achieving them within a specified situation when these should, in principle, be within the power of these actors to achieve".[2] Even with this definition, we have some conceptual problems. Not all elements of the process can easily be incorporated within the dynamics of policymaking and there are, moreover, important debates among scholars about the degree of rationality in policy formulation and the extent to which goals can be realised by employing rational means.

---

1. Howlett, M., & Cashore, B. (2014). Conceptualizing public policy. In I. Engeli & C. R. Allison (Eds.), *Comparative policy studies* (pp. 17–30). New York: Palgrave Macmillan.
2. Quoted in Jenkins, W. I. (1978). *Policy analysis* (p. 15). London: Martin Robertson.

It would be helpful if we could escape from some of these conceptual difficulties by analysing policymaking as a sequence. We might begin with the observation that policy is, first, a debate about values. There is a constant debate in policymaking over the values that will be promoted or adversely affected by particular measures. Government officials, pressure groups, political parties, and anyone else who chooses to join the public debate are all policy actors in this process although not everyone has the same influence on the final decision.[3] The debate may be about whether the value is of such importance that it should reach the policy agenda or about the means to achieve it. The government will also have goals that may require some discussion to ascertain whether they have sufficient public support. The institutional agenda will consist of those items up for "active and serious" consideration by the policymakers within the political and administrative system.[4]

In Hong Kong, key policymakers comprise the Chief Executive and the principal officials, Chinese government officials, Executive Councillors, senior civil servants, Legislative Councillors, and advisory committees. Not all of these actors are involved in considering every policy. Assuming that the relevant actors agree on the need for action and formulate their proposals, the policy then becomes part of the institutional agenda. The next stage is implementation, a process fraught with problems and unrealised expectations. In seeking to realise their values—to translate words into action—policymakers have to identify the most appropriate instruments for implementation. This could involve not only institutions, such as government departments and quasi-governmental agencies, but also the private sector and civil society organisations. If these stages are completed, some judgement can then be reached on the type of output, the policy content. Finally, the success or failure of the policy is evaluated to see whether its objectives have been achieved and public funds have been properly spent.

The idea that policy might begin as a debate over values, proceed through agenda-setting to formulation, and emerge as a tangible policy, which is then implemented and evaluated, provides a convenient analytical map from which we can follow the stream of policy from its formative stages to its conclusion. Unfortunately, it may also be an idealised, unrealistic, and misleading view of the policymaking process.[5] This is a matter of degree, however. Under some circumstances, policy might move forward in steps or stages, provided that the decision-making system is insulated from politics and that policymakers enjoy relative autonomy from business and other influential elites. Such conditions applied in Hong Kong in a colonial system where the government controlled the policy process, where there were no

---

3. Wu, X., Ramesh, M., Howlett, M., & Fritzen, S. A. (2017). *The public policy primer: Managing the policy process* (pp. 11–17). London: Routledge.
4. Zahariadis, N. (2016). Setting the agenda on agenda setting: Definitions, concepts and controversies. In N. Zahariadis (Ed.), *Handbook of public policy agenda setting* (pp. 1–22; 4). Cheltenham: Edward Elgar.
5. Kingdon, J. W. (2011). *Agendas, alternatives and public policies* (updated 2nd ed.). Boston: Longmans; Béland, D. (2016). Kingdon reconsidered: Interests and institutions in comparative policy analysis. *Journal of Comparative Policy Analysis, 18*(3), 228–242.

political parties or pressure groups (other than business) and where the process, for the most part, took place behind closed doors. The political system is a key variable determining the dominant mode of policymaking, but not all policy will be made in exactly the same way. Some issues are more controversial than others, some have a more direct impact on the public, and some "wicked" problems persist over time without any durable solutions.

Kingdon's model of three streams of action—problems, politics, and policy—is perhaps better suited to an explanation of the type of system that emerged during the later transitional period and in post-colonial Hong Kong where a more turbulent environment made policymaking less predictable.[6] In Kingdon's model, values are debated up to, and sometimes after, implementation. Policies may be reformulated at the point of delivery and may have to be revisited to take account of spectacular failures or unexpected problems. Resources may dry up; governments may change their minds; success may owe more to accidental good fortune than to planned, rational calculation. Policymaking, in this conception, is a messy, political business whose outcomes may be fortuitous or disastrous and often unintended. For Kingdon, the chances of achieving policy goals are greater when there is a window of opportunity in which the three streams of action come together to enable decisions to be made authoritatively.

In Hong Kong, bearing in mind the caveat that policymaking might not always occur as a logical sequence of events, it may still be helpful to distinguish the different processes involved in policymaking—the role of values and policy actors, the role of public institutions, and the location of power within the system, and so on. The policymaking framework of the colonial period has formally persisted beyond 1997, but the government is now operating in a new political environment and is seeking to deal with policy issues in very different ways from those of its predecessor. Consequently, there is a striking contrast between two different types of policymaking. One mode of policymaking, which we characterise as rational, has its origins in modes of policy formulation in colonial times. The other, which is much closer to the situation which Kingdon describes, reflects to a greater extent the politics of policymaking in the post-1997 period.

The stages outlined below cannot be assumed to follow each other sequentially but, in whatever order they occur, they are central to the policy process and are used to structure this chapter:

- the predominant values represented in policy formulation (values and the policy agenda);
- the location of power and the role of institutions in formulating specific policies (power and the institutional framework);
- consultation and participation, that is, whether the policymaking system is open or closed (consultation and participation); and

---

6. Kingdon (2011) op. cit., Ch. 7, 8.

- the types of policy that are produced (content and outputs).

For much of the colonial period, policymaking gives the impression of a rational sequence in the order listed above. The administration was insulated from popular pressures and debates over values and the policy agenda were decided with minimal public consultation. Policy decisions were reached after careful consideration within the government and were usually incremental adjustments to long-established practices. This eventually proved insufficient to meet community demands. In the 1970s, the MacLehose administration introduced more distributive policies and more attention was given to government provision of collective goods, such as education and housing.

After the Sino-British Agreement in 1984, the character of policymaking changed. Values were often agreed, but implementation sometimes faltered when faced with opposition from political and social groups; policy initiatives were often symbolic, an expression of ideals rather than an immediate intent to implement. In the post-1997 era, lack of institutional coordination in a disarticulated system contributed to the emergence of disjointed policies which were sometimes poorly implemented (see Chapter 9). Policy became much more contentious and seemingly less rational and ordered and the policymaking process became more fragmented and less authoritative. It was more difficult to reach decisions, prompting the former Chinese premier, Zhu Rongji, to characterise the Hong Kong policymaking process as "discussing without deciding, deciding without acting".[7] There is still some historical continuity in the policymaking process so that long-standing values and processes may be incorporated in the new mix. Uncontroversial policies may continue to be made in largely the same way as before the retrocession.

The most significant new factors affecting policymaking in post-1997 Hong Kong have been the rise of civil society and the growing influence of the Chinese government. The Tung administration's initial inclination was to implement policy even if this brought the government into conflict with civil society organisations. After the 2003 mass demonstrations, the ability to introduce new policies gradually became more constrained in anticipation that they could result in similar public reactions to the attempt to legislate the national security law.[8] Civil society groups grew in strength[9] and policies, such as the goods and services tax (see pp. 215–216), were abandoned when it became clear that there would be substantial organised

---

7. Quoted in Wong, M. Y. H. (2017). Discussing without deciding, deciding without acting: Veto players in Hong Kong, and Beijing's response. *Asian Journal of Comparative Politics, 2*(4), 347–361.
8. Cheung, A. B. L. (2007). Policy capacity in Hong Kong: Constrained institutions facing a crowding and differentiated polity. *Asia Pacific Journal of Public Administration, 29*(1), 51–75; Lowe, C. J. G. (1980). How the government in Hong Kong makes policy. *Hong Kong Journal of Public Administration, 2*(2), 63–70; Scott, I. (2007). Legitimacy, governance and public policy in post-handover Hong Kong. *Asia Pacific Journal of Public Administration, 29*(1), 29–49.
9. See Ma, N. (2007). *Political development in Hong Kong: State, political society, and civil society* (Part C). Hong Kong: Hong Kong University Press; Chan, E., & Chan, J. (2007). The first ten years of the HKSAR: Civil society comes of age. *Asia Pacific Journal of Public Administration, 29*(1), 77–99.

opposition to their implementation. At the same time, the Chinese government's influence, particularly on economic policies aimed at the greater integration of Hong Kong with the Mainland, was increasing (see pp. 310–318). After 2014, when the Chinese government redefined its relationship with the Hong Kong government[10] and curtailed democratic aspirations,[11] civil society organisations became increasingly active and policy implementation became even more difficult.[12] The Hong Kong government was sandwiched between Chinese government demands and the obstructionist tactics of civil society organisations.

In this chapter, we analyse why these changes have taken place, why some features of the system remain and others do not, why policy capacity and the ability to introduce major new policies is low, and the implications these problems have for policy formulation and implementation.

Policymaking under Colonial Rule

Values and the Policy Agenda

Values impinge on the policy process in many different ways. At a general level, they are implicit in what has been called regime values, values that are part of the constituent make-up of the political system and which may have a determining influence on how concrete policies are devised.[13] Regime values help to provide a polity with its legitimacy. They provide the justification for the use of coercive action and the persuasive reference point when a government needs popular support. Ideally, regime values should relate closely to specific policy values, ensuring that there is congruence between what a regime stands for and its specific policies. In practice, there is often some distance between regime values and the government's actual policies. What were the regime values in colonial Hong Kong? How did they translate into specific policies?

The dominant form of policymaking is determined largely by political factors. Until the 1970s, the colonial government was principally concerned with maintaining its rule and with the associated problems of political stability and legitimacy. It wanted to encourage economic growth by keeping government small and by allowing business to have free rein, largely unrestricted by regulation. The concern with political stability placed some constraints on what the government could do. Its functions were limited. Its funds were used to support a basic administrative

---

10. State Council of the People's Republic of China (2014). *The practice of the one country, two systems policy in the Hong Kong Special Administrative Region*. http://english.www.gov.cn/archive/white_paper/2014/08/23/content_281474982986578.htm
11. NPCSC (2014, 1 September). Full text of NPC decision on Hong Kong's constitutional framework. https://www.mfa.gov.cn/ce/cohk/eng/syzx/tyflsw/t944943.htm
12. Chan, E., & Chan, J. (2017). Hong Kong 2007–2017: A backlash in civil society. *Asia Pacific Journal of Public Administration*, 39(2), 135–152.
13. Rohr, J. A. (1989). *Ethics for bureaucrats: An essay in law and values* (2nd ed., p. 68). New York: Marcel Dekker.

structure, the police, and rudimentary social policies. Policymaking tended to be incremental. To get new policies on the agenda was difficult because taxes were low and the government wanted to budget for a surplus. It could not raise tax revenue without encountering opposition from business.

Regime values also meant that the government did not make policy in what it regarded as inappropriate areas, including intervention in the market. Although business often accused it of doing little to help enterprise, benign neglect served the interests of commerce well. Most services were in the hands of private providers; the best that the government offered was an inadequate safety net. There were no representative institutions, political parties had yet to emerge, civil society organisations were embryonic, and there were few critics of the regime. The government legitimised its rule by arguing that the administration provided good government, order, and security which, implicitly, were missing across the border in China.

After the 1966 and 1967 riots, the government tried to address mounting social problems and to establish a better relationship with society. As the government attempted to bridge the gap between itself and the people, the values underlying policy began to change. In a keynote policy address in October 1972, the Governor, MacLehose, spoke of the need to improve housing conditions. He said:

> the inadequacy and scarcity of housing and all this implies . . . is one of the major and most constant sources of friction and unhappiness between the Government and the population. It offends alike our humanity, our civic pride and our political good sense.[14]

Before MacLehose, governors would have been reluctant to make speeches that so clearly acknowledged government's moral responsibility to improve the social conditions of the population.

MacLehose's initiatives resulted in vastly expanded publicly funded social policy outputs. More housing units were built, new towns were constructed, social welfare and health care provision was increased and education was eventually extended to three years of compulsory secondary school. The government quickly learned that distributing social policy outputs in greater quantity could positively increase its political support although this required a much more interventionist role in society than it had previously pursued. Of necessity, the civil service began to grow rapidly and the government became a major service provider. At the outset of MacLehose's decade-long tenure, the administration probably believed that creating a more prosperous, better-housed, healthier, and better-educated population could be accomplished without substantially changing its regime values.

But social policy outputs have their own dynamics. The kind of society that had emerged by the end of MacLehose's tenure in 1982 was markedly different from that of the immediate post-1967 period. It was a society that played a more active part in the affairs of the colony (now known as a territory). The number of pressure groups

---

14. Hansard, 18 October 1972, 4.

had increased and labour had become more belligerent, particularly within the civil service. The new public sector services required more professionals who had their own views about what should be provided and what they should be paid. New values began to infiltrate the policy process. Consultation with the people became the *leitmotif* of the administration although government still claimed the right to make the final decision.

While the economy prospered and government could deliver desired collective goods, the values on which policy was based continued to receive widespread public support. But after 1984 and the agreement to return Hong Kong to Chinese sovereignty, the government's control over the policy process gradually declined. The population was more politicised, not confident about the government's assurances on their future. Some wanted to see a more democratic system in place before 1997; civil liberties became a major issue; and civil service unions and professional organisations wanted guarantees that their positions would be safeguarded. The Chinese government asserted its stance on policies that had implications after 1997, sometimes contradicting the Hong Kong government's stated goals. The government was able to maintain its distributive social policies, but it was unable to implement those policies quite as forcefully as before, avoiding decisions adversely affecting political confidence. Policymaking was sometimes more symbolic than effective, the articulation of the value seemingly more important than the policy.

By 1997, a more dynamic mix of values was influencing policymaking. There was local pressure for a more active government that would address enduring social problems and entrench civil liberties. The Chinese government seemed to want to inherit a system unchanged from unreformed colonial days, excluding democratic parties from power. The British government's principal aim was to leave the territory with minimal possible disruption and with its dignity intact. It tried to do as little as possible to offend the Chinese government. Policy became a hostage to these conflicting forces. When Patten became governor in 1992, the government did begin to take measures to address some concerns more actively by improving social conditions and trying to protect civil liberties. In other areas, policy remained largely symbolic because the government preferred not to risk potentially more confrontational politics.[15]

Power and the Institutional Framework

Where does power reside in a system? Who has the authority to decide which policies should be pursued and implemented and which should not? The location of power is important because it is a critical factor influencing how policy is made. If, as in Hong Kong's colonial system, power is centralised, civil society relatively

---

15. Morris, P., & Scott, I. (2003). Educational reform and policy implementation in Hong Kong. *Journal of Education Policy, 18*(1), 71–84.

weak, and decisions can be effectively implemented, then the chances of following a sequential, rational policy process from formulation to implementation are greater. If power is diffuse, scattered among various institutions, groups, and political forces, then the policymaking process is likely to be more fragmented as different power centres seek to influence both policy formulation and implementation.

Power in the classical Hong Kong colonial system was invariably centralised and exercised through a hierarchically organised civil service. No institution challenged the authority of the Governor and the Civil Service Secretariat. The government spoke with one voice and whatever disagreements existed between civil servants over policy were kept behind closed doors. The only occasional constraint on the local administration's ability to make policy autonomously was pressure from the British government to ensure that social and labour conditions met basic standards.[16] Apart from these sporadic interventions, the colonial administration was largely left to its own devices. The Colonial Secretariat was the principal source of policy advice for the Governor and policy ideas were either generated within the Secretariat or from departmental proposals. Once policies were established, subsequent changes were usually incremental, mainly changing or tightening a regulation here or there. The Secretariat was not particularly responsive to attempts by government departments to change policies and vetted new proposals carefully. It held a monopoly over decision-making and to change policy required the approval of the senior officials, the Governor, the Chief Secretary, and the Financial Secretary. Without their support, nothing could be achieved; even with their support, a period of bargaining over resources followed.[17] When policy papers were finally agreed internally, they went to the Executive Council and the Finance Committee of the Legislative Council for further discussion and approval.

The changes introduced in the 1970s from an incremental to a more distributive system had important repercussions for how policy was made. In 1973, the McKinsey consultants recommended the establishment of policy branches, staffed almost entirely by administrative officers, and departments that would implement policy.[18] The division was never quite so clear-cut because the separation between politics and administration implicit in the concept is not how policymaking normally works. The departments had long experience of implementing policies and often firm ideas on what, if anything, was needed. Administrative officers making policy in the branches were liable to transfer every few years and usually had no specialist knowledge of the field. There were other important shortcomings in the reforms. The consultants called for more programme and resource plans.[19] But there

---

16. Miners, N. J. (1987). *Hong Kong under imperial rule 1912–1941* (pp. 153–169, 280–282). Hong Kong: Oxford University Press; Ure, G. (2012). *Governors, politics and the Colonial Office: Public policy in Hong Kong, 1918–58*. Hong Kong: Hong Kong University Press.
17. Lowe (1980) op. cit.
18. McKinsey and Company (May 1973). *The machinery of government: A new framework for expanding services in Hong Kong* (p. 16). Hong Kong: mimeo.
19. Ibid., pp. 9–11.

was some opposition within the civil service, especially from the Finance Branch, which was concerned that it might lose some control over resources and from the Financial Secretary himself, who thought that his position was being downgraded.

Power was more diffused after the McKinsey reforms than under the old colonial system. The Secretariat remained the central policymaking body and the administrative grade was still the dominant force in policy formulation. After 1984, the British and Chinese governments were able to exercise vetoes on policy proposals, which they had not previously been able to do. As the civil service grew, the Secretariat's control over departments was diminished because the thin layer of senior administrators was no longer able to supervise every aspect of government. Power remained centralised, but there were many more actors in the policymaking process, both within the civil service and outside it.

Hong Kong's colonial political system could not easily incorporate emerging civil society groups. Business people and professionals continued to be over-represented on the Legislative and Executive Councils and the advisory committees. New pressure groups were under-represented and could not be co-opted because political arrangements for the future were beyond the control of the Hong Kong government. Policymaking, by default, remained in the hands of the civil servants although, as 1997 approached, they had difficulty in persuading the Legislative Council that their policies were the best solutions to the territory's problems.

Consultation and Participation

During the colonial era, consultation and participation in policymaking were restricted and controlled. Until the 1970s, the administrative system was strongly supported by the most powerful figures in the business world and in Chinese society, which meant that other elements of society were starved of access to the policymaking process. There were no political parties and pressure groups were slow to develop. When pressure groups did develop, they tended to lobby branches and departments, which did not have final decision-making power. The Legislative Council was also largely excluded from the policymaking process. Its members were sometimes influential behind the scenes in advisory committees, but their role was essentially to validate policy rather than to formulate it or criticise it. The council was entirely appointed by the Governor and was composed of supporters of the government rather than its critics.

Because expectations were limited, popular protests were not concentrated on the government's policy shortcomings. Occasional riots and demonstrations were seen as aberrations from normal social stability and were usually dealt with by introducing tighter regulations. After MacLehose introduced social policy reforms, political participation increased considerably. This was encouraged by the government and it tried to build its policies on "consultation and consent". New policy initiatives were often presented as green papers that were put to the public for comment. The government would then issue a white paper which, it said, reflected the views of the community. The system fell into disrepute when it became clear that the government tended to ignore those views that did not correspond with its own. This happened, most importantly, over the question of introducing directly elected representatives to the Legislative Council, but it was also characteristic of other policymaking areas, notably education and the redress system.[20] The government made some effort to consult groups affected by policy, especially business, but it had little contact with, or control over, the new pressure groups that began to emerge in the 1970s.

The government's policy towards groups was based on long-standing measures under the *Societies Ordinance* and on its efforts to fragment the labour movement. One consequence was the emergence of many small and fragmented groups and unions. There were exceptions, such as the Professional Teachers Union, which was able to build a more comprehensive organisation on the back of confrontations with the government over the status of certified teachers and the closure of the Precious Blood Jubilee School.[21] Although the government might have wished to include new pressure groups in the policy process, it was increasingly constrained by the politics of the transition. Neither the British nor the Chinese governments favoured more democracy for Hong Kong in the 1980s. The Governors of the period, Youde and Wilson, tended to rely on traditional elites and the new democratic groups were excluded from the process.

During the Patten years, consultation took rather different forms. Patten came to office with a commitment to more open government and spent much more time in discussions with legislators. With the introduction of direct elections for some seats in 1991, there was also much more bargaining between government and Legislative Councillors. Yet political constraints on greater consultation and participation remained. The government could not afford protracted conflict with pressure groups at a time when relations with the Chinese government were tense and when public confidence in the future of the system was low. Its strategy was to try to establish a value consensus—for example, that the education system needed to be reformed or that the quality of public housing needed to be improved—and formulated policies to meet those ends. Where it might be involved in conflict with pressure groups, it tended not to force the issue. Policymaking was symbolic; it would only be implemented if there were no groups likely to engage in political or industrial action.

---

20. Hong Kong Government (1986). *Consultation document: Redress of grievances*. Hong Kong: Government Printer; Hong Kong Government (1987). *Green paper: The 1987 review of developments in representative government*. Hong Kong: Government Printer.
21. Leung, J. Y. H. (1999). *State and society: The emergence and marginalization of political parties in Hong Kong* (pp. 149–154) [Unpublished doctoral dissertation]. The University of Hong Kong.

Policy Content

By content, we mean the kinds of policy output that the system produces and permits. Thus, following Lowi, we might describe the policies of the old colonial period as mainly regulatory, those of the later colonial period as largely distributive and symbolic, and those of the post-colonial period as stuck in gridlock on many major policies but with elements of some of the policymaking styles of the preceding systems.[22] These general descriptions of policymaking do not encompass all policies made within a particular historical period. In each period, there was nevertheless a dominant form of policymaking determined by prevailing values, the location of power and the institutional framework, and the nature of consultation and participation.

Under colonialism, regulatory policy was seen to be the appropriate way to maintain the stability of the regime. The *Societies Ordinance*, the *Education Ordinance*, and various labour regulations were used to control organisations, intervene in the school system, and fragment trade unions.[23] After the Second World War, regulatory policy was no longer sufficient and the administration began to make grudging accommodations in health, welfare, housing, and education.[24] The MacLehose reforms brought collective goods in much larger quantities: more school places, more hospital beds, increased social welfare, and a greater likelihood of securing a public housing flat. This expansion of social policy was a means of re-legitimating a regime that had singularly failed to provide adequately in these respects in the 1950s and 1960s. It increased political support and heightened levels of expectation for even more, qualitatively better, collective goods.

After the 1984 agreement, policy remained largely distributive but also took on more symbolic aspects. The economy required different types of regulation and important reforms were made in the banking sector. Regulation changed from a concern with control in the interests of maintaining stability to an attempt to ensure that standards were met in the provision of services. The government also sought to build confidence by other means: by providing for a Bill of Rights and various forms of safeguards for civil liberties, by creating new universities, and by constructing a new airport. Policy was used to try to persuade the population that the future would be at least as prosperous and pleasant as the past. Where possible, the government avoided becoming embroiled in contentious policy issues. In areas where it had no option but to make policy, the process of implementation was designed to minimise

---

22. Lowi, T. A. (1972). Four systems of policy, politics and choice. *Public Administration Review, 32*(4), 298–310.
23. Sweeting, A. (1992). Hong Kong education within historical processes. In G. A. Postiglione (Ed.), *Education and society in Hong Kong: Toward one country and two systems* (pp. 39–81). Hong Kong: Hong Kong University Press.
24. Hong Kong Government (1955). *Annual report by the Commissioner for Resettlement for the financial year 1954–55*. Hong Kong: Government Printer; Sweeting, A. (1993). *A phoenix transformed: The reconstruction of education in post-war Hong Kong*. Hong Kong: Oxford University Press; Wong, V. C. W. (1999). *The political economy of health care development and reforms in Hong Kong* (Ch. 4). Aldershot: Ashgate.

conflict and to allow the government to retreat if its proposed measures proved to be too controversial.[25]

The Rational Policymaker

The political preconditions which aid rational policymaking include: government monopoly of the policy agenda; restrictions on public influence on the decision-making system and the insulation of decision-makers from the political process; centralising the decision-making system to attempt to obtain value for money and avoid potentially conflicting policies; acting authoritatively to reinforce the image of a government in command; using cost-benefit analysis to determine best possible public investments; and trying to match policy outputs to the prevailing political circumstances. How did these political preconditions translate into rational policymaking? Did the policymakers hold a set of beliefs about the best way to make policy? If so, what were those beliefs?

Between 1998 and 2002 and again in 2006 and 2007, I conducted interviews with 32 senior officials from seven different policy bureaus and 16 different departments and statutory bodies. All held high office in the final years of the colonial administration and continued in senior positions after 1997. Seventeen of the 32 were administrative officers and had been transferred between bureaus, departments, and statutory bodies during their careers. What follows is a distillation of their views on how policy should or should not be made, tempered by the change of regime.

A central element in policymaking, although few of the interviewees used the word, was that policymaking should be rational, that is, that the government's response to a problem should be appropriate to provide a solution to present or future difficulties. The respondents drew attention to the need to ensure that there were adequate financial resources, that alternatives had been considered, that the problem had been properly discussed with all the relevant stakeholders, and that proper "homework" had been undertaken to stave off criticism and to defend the policy proposal against charges that there were better ways to proceed. The means of achieving these conditions for successful policymaking varied according to the nature of the problem. In some cases, the policymakers sought expert advice; in others, they surveyed public opinion; in still others, they undertook pilot schemes or conducted experiments. In each case, the aim was to construct a case for change as watertight as possible or to put the issue to the public so that the problem was canvassed and the options presented, usually with the government making its preferred position clear.

A second element that was heavily stressed was the need for flexibility. One respondent quoted with approval the words of a long-standing Executive Councillor

---
25. Morris & Scott (2003) op. cit.

who advised policy secretaries that they should always give themselves room to "wriggle". By the end of the colonial administration and after the handover, policy secretaries found it increasingly difficult to take unequivocal positions because criticism of their role had become more intense and more informed. Most respondents felt that, ideally, there should be a preferred and publicly articulated government stance but that fall-back positions and contingency plans were a necessary part of the process.

A third element was that policymakers should keep their distance from the politics of the process. "Don't eat with your chin" said one highly experienced official, meaning that the policymaker should avoid becoming part of the public debate until an authoritative decision was required. This was, of course, part of the colonial culture of maintaining distance from the population. No government likes to back down on policy, but there was always the feeling that, if the colonial government did so, the legitimacy of its rule might be called into question. Decisions were generally not negotiable once the government had put its prestige on the line. Distance from politics was also related to decision-making within government. Most respondents believed that they should be politically neutral and that they should give the "best" impartial advice that they could. Many noted, though, that "politics" was now determining decision-making and that the "best" decision could not always be reached because of the need for political expediency. The ideal administrator remained distant from the process and arrived at rational decisions after appropriate consultation with other policy actors.

In the following case study, we consider the application of rational decision-making to a volatile political issue, the reduction of social security assistance. The key policy actor in the process was Carrie Lam, then Director of Social Welfare. She later served as Chief Secretary for Administration under Leung Chun-ying before becoming Chief Executive in 2017. Later in this chapter, her approach to handling reductions in social security assistance in 2003 is compared with her attempts to introduce the Extradition Bill in 2019.

Rational Policymaking: Reducing Social Security

The CSSA Scheme was introduced in 1993, replacing a public assistance scheme that had provided only the most basic social security benefits. The new scheme was more generous although its philosophy was very similar to the one that had preceded it. Social security assistance was given to those in need to raise their incomes to meet essential requirements. The benefits were means-tested and all able unemployed people between 15 and 59 years of age were required to register with the Labour Department for job placement. The scheme provided a range of standard rates for different categories of applicants, for rent, and to meet special needs. In 1993, there were 92,000 CSSA cases compared with 79,700 public assistance cases in the previous year. Expenditure rose to $2,073.8 million, an increase of 54.9 % from the previous year.[26] By 1997, CSSA cases had more than doubled to 195,645.[27] The unemployment numbers rose from 3,876 in 1993–1994 to 14,964 in 1996–1997.[28] Since there was almost full employment, it was suggested that those claiming unemployment benefits might be doing so because the payments were more attractive than working.[29]

In 1997, Tung announced that the CSSA system would be reviewed and stressed that "we should not remove the incentive to work".[30] From the outset, the agenda was controlled by the civil service. The Steering Group that conducted the review was chaired by the Director of Social Welfare and its membership, except for a member of the Employees Retraining Board, a statutory body, was composed entirely of civil servants.[31] There was no outside representation from those who might be affected by its decisions or from organisations, such as the Hong Kong Council of Social Service, which might have spoken for the disadvantaged. Controlling the agenda meant that the Steering Group could define the problem. There was, it said,

> growing public concern about the rapid growth in the CSSA caseload and its expenditure, the high level of CSSA benefit for larger families as compared with market wages, and sharp increases in the number of people of working age turning to CSSA. There is also an increasing perception that some people are abusing the system and . . . increasing calls . . . for the Government to take more measures to prevent such abuses.[32]

The identification of the problem was accompanied by supporting statistics: the number of CSSA cases had increased by 146% between September 1993 and September 1998; expenditure had grown threefold and was certain to rise further; benefits were becoming more attractive because of the slow growth in wages; and CSSA payments for a family of four or more were much higher than low-end wages.[33]

The definition of the problem rested on assumptions about the motives of the recipients and pointed to possible solutions. The group felt that there was "a tendency for some employable adults to consider reliance on welfare assistance a preferred option even when there is employment available".[34] This conflicted with the long-standing value that welfare should only be provided for as long as it took to return the employable to the workforce. The solutions offered, therefore, aimed

---

26. Hong Kong Government (1995). *Hong Kong 1994* (pp. 175–176). Hong Kong: Government Printer.
27. Census and Statistics Department (2003). *Hong Kong annual digest of statistics* (p. 315). Hong Kong: Printing Department
28. Tsoi, K. W. (2002). Poverty eradication and social security in Hong Kong. In D. T. L. Shek, M. C. Lam, C. F. Au, & J. J. Lee (Eds.), *Advances in social welfare in Hong Kong* (p. 124). Hong Kong: The Chinese University of Hong Kong Press.
29. Liu, P. W. (2000). Financing the CSSA Scheme. https://hkcer.hku.hk/Letters/v58/cssa.htm
30. Tung, C. H. (1997). *Building Hong Kong for a new era* (p. 40). Hong Kong: Printing Department.
31. Social Welfare Department (1998). *Review of the Comprehensive Social Security Assistance (CSSA) Scheme.* (Annex 1). https://www.lwb.gov.hk/en/consult_paper/cssa.html
32. Ibid., p. 3.
33. Ibid., pp. 3–5.
34. Ibid., p. 5.

at the unemployed and at benefits enjoyed by large families. The proposals included slashing benefits, unpaid community work programmes for unemployed CSSA beneficiaries, reassessing the asset limits for the unemployed, provisions to terminate payments if the recipient refused reasonable employment opportunities, and strengthening arrangements to prevent fraud.[35] Even these measures, the Steering Group warned, would not prevent the growth in CSSA expenditure from increasing to an unsustainable level.[36]

Their predictions proved to be correct. With the subsequent economic downturn, more poor migrants from China, and the growing number of elderly recipients of CSSA, the number of applicants and government expenditure both rose dramatically. Cases increased from 195,645 in 1997 to 288,648 in October 2003.[37] The budget increased from $2.4 billion in 1993 to $9.4 billion in 1998 to $16 billion in 2002.[38] The implementation of the Steering Group's recommendations appears to have had some effect in discouraging new applicants for unemployment benefits. New cases rose to 31,942 in 1998–1999, but stabilised thereafter and even dropped in 2000.[39] Low earnings cases, which were supplemented by benefits, continued to rise, suggesting that the slowing growth in wages and CSSA payments were coming closer together than the government would have wished. As economic conditions worsened, unemployed CSSA cases rose sharply. By September 2003, there were 51,372 unemployed cases, nearly double the number in March 2000.[40]

The government faced a potentially explosive situation. Any move to cut benefits could have resulted in an even greater loss of political support and more protest movements, but CSSA expenditure was spiralling out of control. In October 2002, the Director of Social Welfare, Carrie Lam, put the government's case in an article in the *South China Morning Post*.[41] The tone was coolly rational. The problem, she said, was not simply a matter for the government but how welfare provision should best reflect community values. "The community" wrote Lam "is compassionate towards the vulnerable when the economy is good and public finances permit . . . [but] expects vigilance by the administration in guarding CSSA from becoming a preferred alternative to work."[42] She presented figures which showed that, as a result of negative growth in the economy, the purchasing power of the CSSA was 12.4% higher than when it was set in 1996. She concluded:

---

35. Ibid., passim; Chau, K. L., & Wong, C. K. (2002). The social welfare reform: A way to reduce public burden? In S. K. Lau (Ed.), *The first Tung Chee-hwa administration* (pp. 209–213). Hong Kong: The Chinese University of Hong Kong Press.
36. Social Welfare Department (1998) op. cit., p. 4.
37. Census and Statistics Department (2003, 9 October) op. cit.; Social Welfare Department (2003). *CSSA recipients encouraged to move towards greater self-reliance* [Press release].
38. Social Welfare Department (1998) op. cit.; Tsoi (2002) op. cit., p. 125; *Hong Kong Standard* (2002, 12 November). Lam warns of "drastic steps" if benefits not cut. *Hong Kong Standard*.
39. Census and Statistics Department (2003) op. cit.
40. Ibid.; Social Welfare Department (2003) op. cit.
41. Lam, C. (2002, 24 October). Will we have to cope with less? *SCMP*.
42. Ibid.

The issue now is whether CSSA rates should be reduced to restore purchasing power to the intended level, freeing up existing resources to help an anticipated increase in applicants . . . with the growing number of elderly, and an increasing number of low-income families, what should be done to ensure CSSA will continue to provide a strong financial safety net for the most vulnerable? These are questions on which we welcome public views.[43]

The government, of course, had firm views on what should be done. It had framed the agenda and articulated what it thought was the principal problem. It wanted to reduce CSSA benefits by 11.1%. The invitation for public comments was not because the government was uncertain of its policy direction but because it had to gauge whether a CSSA reduction might spill over into a wholesale indictment of an unpopular regime.

Over the next few weeks, the debate intensified. Carrie Lam met with the Legislative Council Panel on Welfare Services, some invited individuals and representatives of 10 pressure groups, and the Hong Kong Council of Social Service to discuss the CSSA issue.[44] She stressed that the administration had not yet come to a view on whether the CSSA should be adjusted downwards by 11.1% although she explained how the figure had been calculated. Predictably, the pressure groups and many legislators were opposed to any reduction. In her concluding remarks, Carrie Lam sought to address some of their concerns. She emphasised that the effects of deflation on wages and the CSSA benefits had been calculated methodically, that the government had always drawn a distinction between the able-bodied who could work and those who could not, and that the reduction was not about saving money but about distributing benefits more equitably.[45]

A few days later, Christine Fang, the Director of the Hong Kong Council of Social Service, challenged many of the government's central assumptions.[46] She noted that almost 80% of CSSA recipients were elderly, disabled, or infirm, or single-parent families and had little chance of finding work and that the unemployed had been unfairly maligned. People who lost their jobs did not immediately turn to the Social Welfare Department; only 14.3% of the unemployed received CSSA benefits.[47] She also cast doubt on the government's argument that CSSA benefits were too high, claiming instead that wages were too low and would be pushed lower if the CSSA was cut. In place of reduced benefits, Fang suggested that there was a need for a comprehensive review of the CSSA Scheme and that reductions in benefits should not be treated simply as a budget deficit issue.

Some political parties and the major unions were also highly critical of the government's planned course of action. The government remained steadfast. The

---

43. Ibid.
44. Legislative Council Panel on Welfare Services (2002). *Minutes of the meeting held on Monday 11th November 2002*. https://www.legco.gov.hk/yr02-03/english/panels/ws/minutes/ws021111.pdf
45. Ibid., pp. 13–14.
46. Fang, C. (2002, 15 November). Why we should not cut social welfare. *SCMP*.
47. Ibid.

following day a motion was introduced in the Legislative Council opposing the "cutbacks in welfare benefits for the elderly, the vulnerable and the disabled".[48] The motion condemning the cutbacks was passed without dissent and 90 pressure groups later demonstrated against the government's action.[49] But the planned reductions went ahead. The measures were approved by the Executive Council in February 2003[50] and were given legislative effect in the budget in April 2003. With two minor concessions, the changes reduced the standard rate allowances for the able-bodied by 11.1% from June 2003 and the benefits for the elderly, disabled, and infirm by the same amount in two phases, starting in October 2003.

From the government's standpoint, the reduction in the CSSA was an example of successful policy formulation and implementation. Why did the government succeed in this instance when it failed in so many others? Each of the characteristics of rational policymaking, identified earlier in interviews with senior officials, was present in the process. First, the government controlled the agenda, defined the problem, and focused its energies on a specific change. Carrie Lam did not allow herself to be drawn into a political debate on other possible conceptions of the problem. She defended the proposal with an array of statistics and became known, to her annoyance, as the "figures lady". "Figures," she said, "have helped me to convince others when implementing some policies. We could not solve problems with emotions alone."[51] The proposal was carefully explained in the context of welfare policy goals and the greater equity that would result from a redistribution of benefits to new, deserving applicants. It was presented as the only logical and rational course of action.

A second characteristic of rational policymaking identified in the interviews with senior officials was flexibility. The government made its views known on its preferred proposal from a very early stage. It did not, however, finally commit itself until the inclusion of the reductions in the budget. Even in the motion debate in February 2003, the Secretary for Health, Welfare and Food spoke of the reductions as a proposal. Flexibility also meant listening to the proposals from interested individuals and pressure groups even if the government made few concessions. It delayed the cuts to non-able-bodied recipients to October 2003 and October 2004, a similar strategy to that employed over civil service pay reductions. But there were no other substantive concessions.

Finally, Carrie Lam was careful to keep her distance from the political process. She met with pressure groups and representatives of the political parties, but she did not bargain with them. Rather, she listened to their arguments, maintaining the flexibility of the government's position to develop contingency plans should they

---

48. Hansard, 26 February 2003, 4148.
49. Yeung, C. (2003, 26 February). Rising heat. *SCMP*.
50. Hong Kong Government (2003, 25 February). ExCo endorses rate adjustment of CSSA and SSA [Press release].
51. Lee, E. (2003, 30 October). I hate being known as the figures lady. *SCMP*.

prove necessary. In the event, the CSSA reductions came when the government was considering implementing Article 23 and when SARS was becoming a serious problem and these developments soon took centre stage. The government's successful outcome was also helped by the different proposals canvassed by parties and pressure groups. In comparison with these other options, the government's proposal had the advantage of clarity, political appeal to the values of hard work, programmes to return recipients to gainful employment, sensitivity to equity and the future requirements of the welfare system, and a continuing emphasis on the traditional governance virtue of fiscal frugality.

Policymaking in a Time of Turbulence

Although rational policymaking has persisted in the post-handover system, particularly in areas less controversial than reductions to welfare benefits, it is better suited to systems where policymakers can remain aloof from the politics of the process and retain control of the agenda. In the post-handover system, with the difficulties inherent in the system and the increasing politicisation of the policy process, a new mode of making policy, rather closer to the conditions underlying Kingdon's "three streams" approach, began to emerge. One characteristic of that situation was that policy formulation and implementation were often driven or prevented by forces beyond the control of the Hong Kong government. In the following sections, we analyse the post-handover political circumstances and their impact on policymaking.

The Post-1997 Policy Agenda

What values does the post-1997 government seek to realise through policy? And how do these differ from those that it inherited? In his first policy address, Tung stressed many traditional values: government was to be more proactive in meeting the needs of business; the new political system would promote stability; government would look after the interests of the population; law and order would be maintained; and the administration would continue to deliver policy outputs efficiently, effectively, and economically.[52] Aside from stressing that Hong Kong was now part of China, the 1997 policy address might have been delivered by a British Governor.

Within a few years, the tone had changed. In his re-election speech, Tung claimed that the government had successfully taken a different direction since the handover although he conceded that some policy initiatives might have been handled differently.[53] There was more stress on economic restructuring, on

---

52. Tung (1997) op. cit., passim.
53. Tung, C. H. (2001, 14 December). I will bring solutions to our problems. *SCMP*.

enhancing relations with China, and on revamping the structure of government.[54] The administration faced an economic crisis almost immediately after it assumed office and this placed many traditional regime values under threat. The Chief Executive, Executive Councillors, and many Legislative Councillors favoured more deregulation and small government, for example, but the economic crises led to calls for more government intervention and help in times of hardship. The government was not averse to intervention in some circumstances.[55] However, this meant that policymaking was somewhat ad hoc and without the more consistent regime value parameters that had characterised the colonial government.

Similar problems arose with establishing policy values authoritatively on the agenda. The government came under challenge from many different groups, lacked support from the public, and found that introducing policy changes was much more difficult than it had anticipated. The Mainland government also became much more influential in the policymaking process. Initially, senior policymakers were inclined to treat advice from the local Chinese Liaison Office as a suggestion unless it received authoritative support from Beijing. Increasingly, however, and especially during and after the 2019 protests, the Liaison Office, backed by many united front groups and pro-Beijing legislators, became something of an alternative government.[56] Pan-democrats, searching for leverage to bring about a more democratic system, often obstructed government policy proposals in the Legislative Council. Although many street protests were about democratic issues and civil liberties, many others were concerned with the poor performance of successive Chief Executives. The disarticulated political system enabled diverse values to be expressed, to gain support, and to act as a brake on the realisation of the government's policy goals.[57] The government had lost its relative autonomy in policymaking and control over its agenda and capacity to implement new policies.[58]

The Institutional Framework

The institutional framework inherited by the political executive after 1997 was deficient in some important respects. The Basic Law assumed that institutions would cooperate and coordinate policy. In practice, there was considerable friction. Under Tung, the executive was not unified and there were major differences in approach and values between the business and professional appointees on the Executive

---

54. Tung C. H. (2004) *Seizing opportunities for development, promoting people-based governance* (pp. 2–15). Hong Kong: Government Logistics Department.
55. Cheung, A. B. L. (2000). New interventionism in the making: Interpreting state interventions in Hong Kong after the change of sovereignty. *Journal of Contemporary China*, 9(24), 291–308.
56. Cheng, E. W. (2020). United front work and mechanisms of countermobilization in Hong Kong. *The China Journal*, 83(1), 1–33.
57. Scott, I. (2000). The disarticulation of the Hong Kong's post-handover political system. *The China Journal*, 43, 29–53.
58. Wong (2017) op. cit.

Council and senior civil servants. The business people advocated change within the civil service to improve efficiencies, reduce costs, and remove what they saw as obstructions to rapid change. They favoured policies that would aid business, including government initiatives with the private sector. Senior civil servants were not directly opposed to those aims, but they wanted to continue to make policy within the civil service with careful attention to rationality, costs, and strategies for implementation. This resulted in a struggle on some issues between Executive Councillors and senior civil servants over policymaking style, the councillors favouring new, sometimes uncosted, initiatives and the civil servants preferring to rely on well-established procedures. Eventually, the introduction of the POAS in 2002 (see pp. 78–91) significantly reduced the policymaking powers of senior civil servants.

One of the consequences of the disarticulated system was that power was diffused rather than centralised. Kingdon remarks that, under such circumstances, policy ideas may come from anywhere and still have some prospect of reaching the agenda.[59] Whereas under colonialism, the senior civil service held a monopoly over which ideas would succeed and which would fail, in post-1997 Hong Kong, policy ideas and advice could potentially come from sources outside government. The dominant influences seem to have been the Chinese government and its supporters in Hong Kong and, on financial and housing policy, the business pressure groups.

Think tanks occasionally seemed to have some influence in shaping policy, but it is often difficult to establish a relationship between the ideas such organisations present and actual policies. The extent to which government listens to them also varies according to their political complexion and connections. Two chairs of the pro-Beijing think tank, the One Country, Two Systems Research Institute,[60] went on, respectively, to head the government's Central Policy Unit and to serve on the Executive Council under Leung Chun-ying. Other think tanks, such as the Our Hong Kong Foundation[61] founded by Tung Chee Hwa in 2014, and the Bauhinia Foundation, which had some former senior civil servants and business people among its members, may also have had sporadic influence. The Central Policy Unit itself generated many ideas but does not appear to have had much direct influence on policies.[62] It was eventually revamped in 2017 as the Policy Innovation and Coordination Office. Democratic influence as a source of policy advice and ideas appears to have been limited. Civic Exchange[63] made important contributions to environmental policies and on political reform, but the government did not fully

---

59. Kingdon (2011) op. cit., p. 71.
60. One Country, Two Systems Research Institute (2020). On think tanks. https://onthinktanks.org/think-tank/one-country-two-systems-research-institute/
61. Our Hong Kong Foundation (2020). https://ourhkfoundation.org.hk/en/ppi
62. See Chu, J. H. K., Lai, C. W., Ng, M. K. W., So, B. Y. B., & Yeung, K. L. K. (2014). *The Central Policy Unit in the governance of Hong Kong: A study of institutional dynamics* (p. 70) [Unpublished master's capstone project]. Hong Kong: University of Hong Kong.
63. Civic Exchange (2020). https://civic-exchange.org/

endorse its ideas. SynergyNet, which closed down in 2019, produced insightful academic studies on public policy and public sector reform but lacked financial support.

The prospects of formulating ideas into tangible policies can be increased with support from either the civil service or the political executive and might then follow either one of two routes. The first would see the policy move through the civil service to be eventually presented for public discussion with the agreement of the political executive. Alternatively, policy might be generated from the top down by the political executive. The latter route became more prevalent after the introduction of the POAS. The problem has been that top-down policy announcements sometimes unravel in the process of turning them into a concrete set of proposals for implementation. Gaining public acceptance for new policies has remained difficult and became worse under the Leung and Lam administrations. Major policy changes could not be introduced because the level of political conflict that they were likely to generate threatened the stability of a weak government. The government was caught between an often hostile domestic environment and a Chinese government that regarded political stability, at whatever cost, as a paramount objective.

Consultation and Participation after 1997

Initially, the post-1997 government did not face the same policy constraints as the transitional colonial administration and soon showed that it wanted to address some issues that had been swept under the carpet. The problem was that it did not have a mandate and that its claim to be able to act authoritatively was widely challenged. On education policy, for example, the government was faced with a shifting coalition of opposition from pressure groups. On the school-based management system, mother tongue teaching and the introduction of "moral and national education", the Professional Teachers Union, individual teachers, churches, parents, and students were in conflict with some aspects of government policy.[64] Moreover, because the government's policy intentions were often less ambivalently stated than during the transitional period, pressure groups could make their case to the public rather than accept a government-engineered consensus. The situation was further exacerbated by the tension between the government and the Legislative Council. Pan-democrats used filibusters in the council to delay government attempts to introduce new legislation.[65] Pressure groups frequently took to the streets in support of their demands.

---

64. Chan, E. (2002). Beyond pedagogy: Language and identity in post-colonial Hong Kong. *British Journal of Sociology of Education, 23*(2), 271–285; Morris & Scott (2003) op. cit.; Morris, P., & Vickers, E. (2015). Schooling, politics and the construction of identity in Hong Kong: The 2012 "national and moral education" crisis in historical perspective. *Comparative Education, 51*(3), 305–326.
65. Hansard, 18 May 2016, 9608–9615; Lam, J., & Su, X. (2017, 18 October). Hong Kong opposition filibuster blocks Lam's plan to prioritise joint checkpoint debate. *SCMP*. https://www.scmp.com/news/hong-kong/politics/article/2115921/hong-kong-opposition-filibuster-blocks-lams-plan-legco

The formal aspects of the consultation process remained in place. Green papers were replaced by consultation documents, but there was widespread scepticism about whether this meant very much. Consultation became largely window dressing. The Tung administration, in particular, was prone to make top-down announcements without adequately preparing for their public reception. In its decision to provide 85,000 flats a year, which was later abandoned, in its educational policies, in the decision to create a Cyberport, and to provide government funding for the construction of a Disneyland, in the bid for the Asian games, and in the announcement of proposals to merge the Chinese University, the Hong Kong University of Science and Technology, and the Hong Kong Institute of Education, the government simply laid out its proposals and bore the wrath of a highly critical polity.[66] In a remarkable *mea culpa* in 2005, Tung admitted the shortcomings of this approach and unwittingly forecast the weaknesses of policymaking under future administrations. He said:

> In formulating policies, we fell short of "thinking what the people think" and "addressing people's needs" ... we were not sufficiently mindful of ... the potentially controversial nature of those policies. We introduced too many reform measures too hastily ... We also lacked a sense of crisis, political sensitivity as well the necessary experience and capability to cope with political and economic changes. We were indecisive when dealing with emergencies. These shortcomings and inadequacies have undermined the credibility of our policy-making capability and our ability to govern.[67]

During Tsang's tenure in office, there were efforts to establish more consultative institutions. The Commission on Strategic Development, first established in 1998, was expanded and given the task of providing a "wide range of community views at the early stage of policy formulation".[68] Members were increasingly drawn from a narrow base of business people, professionals, academics and pro-establishment figures. No democrats or social activists were appointed as members and the commission's recommendations tended to follow what the government was already trying to do. In 2018, Carrie Lam replaced the commission with a Chief Executive's Council of Advisers composed of a largely similar membership.[69] A Commission on Poverty was established in 2005 but proved largely ineffective and was revamped in 2012. It has not had any more success than its predecessor in reducing the numbers

---

66. Tung (1997) op. cit., 19; Goodstadt, L. F. (2005). *Uneasy partners: The conflict between public interest and private profit in Hong Kong* (pp. 134–135). Hong Kong: Hong Kong University Press; Leung, J. Y. H., & Chan, H. M. (2001). The school management reform in Hong Kong: Administrative control in a new cloak of managerialism. In A. B. L. Cheung & J. C. Y. Lee (Eds.), *Public sector reform in Hong Kong: Into the 21st century* (pp. 229–259). Hong Kong: The Chinese University of Hong Kong Press.
67. Tung, C. H. (2005). *Working together for economic development and social harmony* (para 18). https://www.policyaddress.gov.hk/2005/eng/pdf/speech.pdf
68. Policy Innovation and Coordination Office (2020). Commission on strategic development. https://www.pico.gov.hk/en/archives/commission_on_SD.html
69. Ibid.

living below the poverty line. The Legislative Council's Research Office has observed that the provision of public housing is a critical means of alleviating poverty[70] and the Census and Statistics Department's figures show that the CSSA Scheme is the best way to reduce poverty quickly.[71] For ideological reasons, the government cannot easily pursue either option.[72] Housing has been devolved to developers who are unable or unwilling to produce an affordable supply. Social security has been seen as something that should be provided only as a last resort.

Civic engagement was also an option canvassed by the government to include greater participation and consultation with those directly affected by new proposals. On some issues, such as harbour reclamation, the government did seem to consult widely and with some effect on future decisions. On others, there appeared to be some consultation but little impact on decision-making.[73] The initiative soon died as the gap between the government and civil society organisations grew and the polity became more polarised.

The post-handover policy process has been significantly affected by the changing political environment. After the Tung administration's many failures, the easiest course of action for the government was to retreat from active policymaking and instead concentrate on marginal changes to existing policies. Initially, under Tsang, this was relatively successful in improving the provision of goods and services and increased the government's popularity (see Chapter 11, Figure 11.1). The problem was that fundamental social policy issues were not being addressed. The effects of incremental drift resulted in serious poverty, deteriorating health care services, and inadequate welfare support. More broadly, inequalities increased, wages remained static and opportunities for social mobility declined. When the government tried to play a more active role, as, for example, in education, organised opposition resulted in the withdrawal or modification of its proposals.

After 2014, following its redefinition of the "one country, two systems" concept and the insistence that candidates for the Chief Executive election be endorsed by a committee, the Chinese government began to play a more direct role in the policy-making process (see Chapter 10). The Hong Kong government's measures to implement the Beijing-backed high-speed rail link and the construction of the HZMB led to demonstrations and legal challenges that caused disruption and delays. Increasingly, the government found itself caught between its attempts to implement policy proposals from Beijing and opposition on the streets of Hong Kong. Where the Chinese government was not directly involved and where public suspicions were

---

70. Legislative Council Secretariat Research Office (2020). *Research brief: The 2020–21 budget* (p. 1). https://www.legco.gov.hk/research-publications/english/1920rb01-the-2020-2021-budget-20200403-e.pdf
71. Census and Statistics Department (2020). *Hong Kong poverty situation report* (pp. 25–27). https://www.censtatd.gov.hk/en/EIndexbySubject.html?pcode=B9XX0005&scode=461
72. Ngan, R., & Li, M. K. Y. (2007). Responding to poverty, income inequality and social welfare: The neo-liberalist government versus a social investment state. In J. Y. S. Cheng (Ed.), *The Hong Kong Special Administrative Region in its first decade* (pp. 535–563, 554–559). Hong Kong: City University Press.
73. Cheung, P. T. Y. (2011). Civic engagement in the policy process in Hong Kong. *Public Administration and Development*, 31(2), 113–121.

not aroused, it was still possible to make policies in a more orderly, rational fashion through the stages that we have previously identified. But in times of turbulence potentially any policymaking decision could be undermined by political opposition and expedient solutions.

In the following case study of the 2019 Extradition Bill, which triggered large-scale protests and led in 2020 to the Chinese government's enactment of national security laws for Hong Kong, we examine the difficulties of policymaking under conditions where the government found itself on the horns of a very serious dilemma. It could not ignore the Chinese government's strong support for its proposals, but it suspected that, if they were introduced, public opinion would be equally strongly opposed to the measures. The case study illustrates how policy was made when directives were issued from the top, when there was little substantive consultation, and when the characteristics of rational policymaking—precise identification of the problem, flexibility in seeking a solution, and distance from the political process—were either not observed or not possible.

Policymaking and the Extradition Bill

The Extradition Bill was formally an attempt to resolve problems resulting from the absence of legal provisions for the extradition of criminal suspects from mainland China, Taiwan, and Macau. When the *Fugitive Offenders Ordinance* was enacted in 1997, it was felt that the differences between criminal justice systems were such that there should be no formal agreement on extradition. Discussions with the Chinese government took place after the retrocession, but little progress was made. By 2019, Hong Kong had 20 extradition agreements with countries around the world but none with other parts of greater China. The major sticking points were that offences in Hong Kong that might result in a custodial sentence could meet with capital punishment in mainland China; offences were often defined differently on the mainland, and trials were not perceived to be fair. The absence of an agreement created problems. Mainland corruption suspects in Hong Kong often fled over the border and could not be extradited. After Xi Jinping's anti-corruption drive began in 2012, Mainland corruption suspects often sought refuge in Hong Kong and Mainland security forces sometimes entered Hong Kong without authority and took the suspects back to China. In 2016, the abduction of booksellers from Hong Kong who had published books about the alleged scandals of top Chinese leaders caused widespread concern.[74]

In February 2018, Chan Tong-kai, a Hong Kong resident, murdered his girlfriend, also a Hong Kong resident, in Taiwan. He then flew back to Hong Kong. Since the offence was committed elsewhere, Chan could not be charged with murder

---

74. Kuo, L. (2020, 25 February). Hong Kong bookseller jailed for 10 years in China. *The Guardian*. https://www.theguardian.com/world/2020/feb/25/gui-minhai-detained-hong-kong-bookseller-jailed-for-10-years-in-china

in Hong Kong but, because there was no extradition agreement with Taiwan, he could not be returned there to face trial. The Hong Kong government charged Chan with money laundering and he was sentenced to 29 months in prison. In October 2018, he voluntarily agreed to go back to Taiwan to face murder charges and the Taiwanese government offered to send police officers to escort him back to Taipei. However, the Hong Kong government rejected the offer, stating that the Taiwanese government had no jurisdiction in Hong Kong. The Taiwanese government then announced that it would bar Chan from entry. Chan was released from prison on 23 October and was still under police protection in Hong Kong until the following October.

A year later, in February 2019, the government announced that it had decided to amend the *Fugitive Offenders Ordinance* to allow for extradition arrangements with Taiwan, mainland China, and Macau. The proposal was sold principally as an attempt to plug "a loophole" to deal with the Chan Tong-kai case although the Secretary for Security noted that murder cases and economic crimes from other parts of greater China had created similar problems. The proposed amendment did not specify the places involved, stating that the amendment would apply to arrangements between the Hong Kong government and "the government of a place outside Hong Kong".[75] The democrats were quick to realise its implications. When the matter came before the Legislative Council's Panel on Security, they introduced a motion to restrict the application of the amendment to Taiwan. It was defeated by 17 votes to 12 votes.[76] The proposal then went forward for 20 days of public discussion.

The government argued that it had to enact the legislation before October 2019 to enable it to send Chan back to Taiwan. The public consultation was consequently much shorter than usual for a bill of this importance. By 4 March, the end of the consultation period, the government had received 4,500 submissions of which 3,000 were in support and 1,400 were opposed.[77] United front groups are often mobilised to launch signature campaigns on public consultation issues when the government needs support.[78] If that happened in this case, the effect may have been to mislead the government into thinking that it had more support than was subsequently proven to be the case. The opposition was widespread even at the consultation stage.

Business groups were concerned about the possibility that "economic crimes" could be broadly interpreted and could affect Hong Kong's future as an investment centre. The American Chamber of Commerce said that Hong Kong's reputation would be adversely affected and questioned the wisdom of introducing extradition

---

75. *Fugitive Offenders and Mutual Legal Assistance in Criminal Matters Legislation (Amendment) Bill*, S.3 (3).
76. Legislative Council Panel on Security (2019). *Minutes of meeting held on 15 February* (pp. 19–20). https://www.legco.gov.hk/yr18-19/english/panels/se/minutes/se20190215.pdf
77. Legislative Council Brief (2019). *Fugitive Offenders and Mutual Legal Assistance in Criminal Matters Legislation (Amendment) Bill* (pp. 11–12). https://www.legco.gov.hk/yr18-19/english/bills/brief/b201903291_brf.pdf
78. Cheng, E.W (2020). United front work and mechanisms of countermobilization in Hong Kong. *The China Journal*, 83, 1–33.

arrangements while there was "a lack of an independent judiciary, arbitrary detention, lack of fair public trial, lack of access to legal representation and poor prison conditions" on the Mainland.[79] A former Chief Secretary of Administration, an Executive Councillor, the Liberal Party, and the Business and Professional Alliance all called for the removal of some crimes that might result in extradition.[80] The Bar Association repeatedly expressed its opposition to the legislation. It noted that the original intention of the *Fugitive Offenders Ordinance* was to distinguish between the legal systems in place in Hong Kong and on the Mainland and that the government had to explain what had changed; that the means of transferring suspects from one jurisdiction to another could be achieved by other methods; and that the Hong Kong public had grave concerns about "the Mainland legal and judicial systems".[81] The Taiwan government said that it would not sign any extradition agreement with Hong Kong if it implied that Taiwan was part of China.[82]

Before the amendment reached the Legislative Council, the government revised the schedule of offences to make the Extradition Bill more palatable to business. The number of offences was reduced from 46 to 37, most of which involved removing economic crimes, such as bankruptcy, tax evasion, trade, and intellectual property offences, from the schedule.[83] The concessions allowed the government to retain the support of the business lobby. But it did nothing to assuage fears that extradition would become a political weapon and would seriously affect civil liberties. There were street demonstrations in March calling on the government to withdraw the legislation.[84] On 3 April, when Carrie Lam took questions from Legislative Councillors about the bill, she assured them that Hong Kong's autonomy and independent legal system would be maintained but made no further concessions.[85] When the first reading of the bill—normally a formality—was presented to the Legislative Council, democrats repeatedly interrupted on points of order.[86]

---

79. Lam, J. (2019, 6 March). Extradition agreement with mainland China would damage Hong Kong's "safe reputation", AmCham says. https://www.scmp.com/news/hong-kong/politics/article/2188915/extradition-agreement-mainland-china-would-damage-hong-kongs
80. Chung, K., Lam, J., & Lum, J. (2019, 7 March). Ex-Hong Kong chief secretary Henry Tang and Exco member Jeffrey Lam join business sector in criticising deal with mainland China. *SCMP*. https://www.scmp.com/news/hong-kong/law-and-crime/article/2189080/security-minister-wont-back-down-extradition-agreement
81. Hong Kong Bar Association (2019, 4 March). *Observations of the Hong Kong Bar Association on the proposal on the Security Bureau's proposal to amend the Mutual Legal Assistance in Criminal Matters Ordinance, Cap. 525 and the Fugitive Offenders Ordinance, Cap. 503*. https://www.hkba.org/sites/default/files/Security%20Bureau%27s%20%20Proposal%20to%20Amend%20the%20Mutual%20Legal%20Assistance%20in%20Criminal%20Matters...Fugitive.FOO%20and%20MLA%20%28Final%29%28website%29.pdf
82. Ng, K. C. (2019, 22 February). Taiwan won't sign any extradition deal with Hong Kong if it implies Taiwan is part of China, official says. *SCMP*. https://www.scmp.com/news/hong-kong/politics/article/2187224/taipei-wont-sign-any-extradition-deal-hong-kong-if-it
83. Legislative Council Brief (2019) op. cit., pp. 6–7.
84. Chan, H. (2019, 31 March). In pictures: 12,000 Hongkongers march in protest against "evil" China extradition law, organisers say. *HKFP*. https://hongkongfp.com/2019/03/31/pictures-12000-hongkongers-march-protest-evil-china-extradition-law-organisers-say/
85. Hansard, 3 August 2019, 8279–8281, 8288–8290.
86. Ibid., 8430–8446.

After the first reading, the bill was referred to the Legislative Council's Bills Committee for detailed examination, but no chair was elected because the democrats on the committee were intent on disrupting its business. On 20 May, the Secretary for Security asked instead that the House Committee prepare the Extradition Bill for the second reading.[87] On 29 May, the democrats tabled a motion of no confidence in the Chief Executive.[88] Many of their speeches in support of the motion focused on her decision to introduce the bill. The business lobby and pro-Beijing legislators again became concerned about the effects of the bill on commercial activities and on their political support. They called on the Secretary for Security to modify further provisions in the bill, which he duly did on 30 May, limiting extradition to offences warranting seven years' imprisonment and providing that requests for rendition would only be received from top-ranking judicial officials.[89] The concessions won the support of the pro-establishment legislators and most of the chambers of commerce but not the democrats or the protesters.

As the second reading of the bill on 12 June approached, the protests grew larger. By 28 April, tens of thousands of protesters were demonstrating peacefully against the bill.[90] On 6 June, 3,000 lawyers marched to government headquarters to stage a silent protest.[91] On 9 June, an estimated 500,000 people participated in a demonstration that was marked by violence. The Legislative Council meeting on the second reading was postponed, but on 12 June more than a million still protested, calling for the withdrawal of the bill. On 15 June, Lam suspended the bill. She spoke about the concessions that the government had made on the original bill and expressed her appreciation for the support of pro-establishment legislators and community groups. But, she said,

> our explanation and communication work has not been sufficient or effective . . . there are still supporting views and opposing ones on the bill, and their stances are often polarised . . . many members of the public still have concerns and doubts about the bill.[92]

She concluded by noting that work on the bill would continue but would not be resubmitted to the legislature until "our work in communication, explanation and listening to opinions is completed".[93]

---

87. Secretary for Security to Chair, Legislative Council House Committee, 20 May 2019.
88. Hansard, 29 May 2019, 10777ff.
89. Lum, A., Sum, L. K., & Lam, J. (2019, 30 May). Hong Kong extradition bill: Security chief announces safeguards to win support of business groups and political allies. *SCMP*. https://www.scmp.com/news/hong-kong/politics/article/3012498/hong-kong-security-chief-john-lee-rolls-out-new-measures
90. Pang, J., & Torode, G. (2019, 28 April). Thousands take to Hong Kong streets to protest new extradition laws. Reuters. https://www.reuters.com/article/us-hongkong-politics-extradition-idUSKCN1S405E
91. *SCMP* (2019, 7 June). Hong Kong lawyers hold silent march against controversial extradition bill. *SCMP*. https://www.scmp.com/video/hong-kong/3013537/hong-kong-lawyers-hold-silent-march-against-controversial-extradition-bill
92. Chief Executive (2019, 15 June). *Opening remarks by CE at media session* [Press release]. https://www.info.gov.hk/gia/general/201906/15/P2019061500707.htm
93. Ibid.

This was insufficient to mollify the protesters, who thought that a new variant of the bill would be reintroduced. On 16 June, almost two million protesters marched through the streets demanding the withdrawal of the bill.[94] On the same day, a government spokesperson said that "there is no timetable for restarting the process" and that the Chief Executive apologised to the people of Hong Kong and "admitted that the deficiencies in the Government's work had led to substantial controversies and deficiencies".[95] The demonstrations continued and became increasingly violent. On 4 September, Carrie Lam finally withdrew the bill.[96] By that time, the protesters had a wider agenda, which included demands for universal suffrage, the resignation of Carrie Lam, and an inquiry into the Police Force.[97]

The Extradition Bill is illustrative of the problems of a weak government trying to make policy in turbulent conditions. Kingdon's concept of coupling the three streams of problem identification, policy, and politics to enable successful policy implementation provides a helpful means of analysing the Extradition Bill and comparing it with the government's efforts to reduce social welfare expenditure. Problem identification in systems with a diffuse and, in Hong Kong's case, disarticulated distribution of power often results in contests over the definition of the problem. The government's definition of the problem as a need to address the murder in Taiwan and as a resolution of anomalies dating from the original enactment of the *Fugitive Offenders Ordinance* was highly contested. Many believed that there was a hidden agenda and that their civil liberties were in danger from Mainland intervention in Hong Kong affairs.[98]

In reducing social welfare expenditure, problem identification had been much less of a problem. There was broad agreement that social welfare expenditure should be reduced. The government controlled the political agenda. There was some opposition but it was *ex post facto* and easily sidelined. In the case of the Extradition Bill, there was no consensus on the problem and the government paid the consequences.

On the issue of the policy stream, it was not entirely clear who was formulating policy. The Hong Kong government claimed that it alone had come up with amendments to the bill to resolve the problem of returning the Hong Kong murderer to Taiwan. Even if this is so, there must have been close consultation with the

---

94. SCMP Reporters (2019, 17 June). "Nearly 2 million" people take to streets, forcing public apology from Hong Kong leader Carrie Lam as suspension of controversial extradition bill fails to appease protesters. *SCMP*. https://www.scmp.com/news/hong-kong/politics/article/3014737/nearly-2-million-people-take-streets-forcing-public-apology
95. Hong Kong Government (2019, 16 June). *Government response to public procession* [Press release]. https://www.info.gov.hk/gia/general/201906/16/P2019061600803.htm
96. SCMP Reporters (2019, 4 September). Hong Kong leader Carrie Lam announces formal withdrawal of the extradition bill and sets up a platform to look into the key causes of protest crisis. *SCMP*. https://www.scmp.com/news/hong-kong/politics/article/3025641/hong-kong-leader-carrie-lam-announce-formal-withdrawal
97. Amnesty International (2020). *Hong Kong: Missing truth, missing justice. The case and international legal framework for the establishment of a commission of inquiry into the 2019 protests* (p. 2). London: Amnesty International.
98. PORI (2019). Public sentiment report. https://www.pori.hk/research-reports-en/anti-extradition-bill-movement-2019.html?lang=en

Mainland government on its provisions because the legislation had a direct impact on relations between the PRC and Hong Kong. The Chinese government did not say much about the legislation, but what it did say was strongly supportive of, and consistent with, the Hong Kong government's approach.[99] It is possible, as many in Hong Kong suspected, that the genesis of the Extradition Bill came from the Mainland government although the Hong Kong government appeared to deny that this was the case.[100]

What is clear is that significant groups in Hong Kong were excluded from the policy formulation process. The short consultation period and the publication of the schedule of offences soon afterwards meant that there was inadequate dialogue with business. Yet the Hong Kong government must have known that it needed the business lobby on its side if it was going to stand any chance of enacting the legislation. Its failure to do so resulted in subsequent embarrassing concessions that weakened its credibility. It is perhaps not surprising that the government did not consult directly with the democrats because the proposed legislation was a zero-sum game—either it was enacted or it was not. Policy formulation could not be entirely rational because the government was not entirely in control of its agenda or of what was happening on the streets. By comparison, in reducing social welfare expenditure, the government held back on releasing its final proposals until it was certain that it could implement them. On the extradition bill, there was little flexibility. The government was committed to enacting the proposals as soon as they were released, leaving little room to "wriggle" apart from the concessions to business.

On Kingdon's politics stream, the difficulty was that the Hong Kong government maintained its distance from the public to such an extent that, in the early stages of selling the legislation, it was not aware of shifting public opinion. In both the unsuccessful attempt to legislate a national security law in 2003 and on the Extradition Bill, the government thought that it had sufficient support to get the legislation passed. The events on the streets proved otherwise. Even so, in both cases, the government continued to push on even in the face of the massive numbers opposed to the legislation. When asked repeatedly on 13 August whether the Hong Kong government had the autonomy to withdraw the Extradition Bill, Carrie Lam evaded the question.[101] On 30 August, a Reuters report claimed that the Chinese government had told her not to withdraw the bill or to meet any of the protesters' other demands.[102] Later, she explained that the length of time before withdrawing the bill—a period during which the protests grew into an attack on the

---

99. Wong, C. H. (2019, 10 June). Beijing digs in on Hong Kong extradition bill. *Wall Street Journal*. https://www.wsj.com/articles/beijing-digs-in-on-hong-kong-extradition-bill-11560167126
100. Legislative Council Panel on Security (2019) op. cit., pp. 11–12, 16.
101. BBC (2019, 13 August). Hong Kong's Carrie Lam pressed on her power to withdraw extradition bill. BBC News. https://www.youtube.com/watch?v=IOft2Y6mH_g
102. Pomfret, J., & Torode, G. (2019, 30 August). Exclusive: Amid crisis, China rejected Hong Kong plan to appease protesters—Sources. Reuters. https://uk.reuters.com/article/uk-hongkong-protests-china-exclusive/exclusive-amid-crisis-china-rejected-hong-kong-plan-to-appease-protesters-sources-idUKKCN1VK0HG

whole system of governance—was necessary because the Chinese government had to be consulted.

Managing the politics of the policy process had become much more difficult because multiple players have exercised vetoes that prevented implementation or required concessions on the government's part. The idea of a distant government absorbing, overruling, or ignoring opposition before announcing an authoritative decision, typical of Carrie Lam's rational policymaking in the reduction of social welfare expenditure, had long since disappeared. The government had to become more involved in politics and "eat with its chin" if it wanted to couple problem identification with its proposed policies. Otherwise, it was likely to suffer the loss of credibility that resulted from its attempt to pass the Extradition Bill.

Conclusion

It is perhaps helpful to think of the policy process in Hong Kong as a historical continuum. In its initial form, the government dominated policy formulation and implementation with little reference to society or those affected by its actions; policy was largely action taken in support of maintaining stability and colonial rule and was made rationally with those interests in mind. In the reformed colonial system, the government continued to control the policy agenda although some attempt was made to incorporate community interests. Policy continued to be made rationally, but the focus shifted from regulatory policies to distributive policies. In the transitional period, policy was sometimes more symbolic than substantive, but "stability and prosperity" remained the government's mantra. In the mixed policymaking system of post-1997 Hong Kong, rational policymaking has to some extent been superseded by *ex cathedra* pronouncements from the political executive, a government with low policy capacity, a volatile political environment, and a disarticulated system. This has the effect of compressing issues of values, formulation, and implementation into a single event rather than a series of distinct stages. The rational style of policymaking is based on the assumption that the political process can be controlled and that appropriate, cost-effective solutions can be developed to resolve problems. It is predicated on the insulation of the policymakers from partisan values which may deflect them from arriving at rational decisions. The post-1997 political environment does not insulate its policymakers from political pressures. It is much more diverse and pluralistic. While power is formally centralised, in reality, it has been diffuse. Successful policymaking consequently depends on a window of opportunity, a fortunate political conjunction of perceived problems with appropriate solutions. The prospect for failure is much greater than in a controlled political system not only at the formulation stage but also when policies have to be implemented in what is frequently a hostile environment.

9
Policy Implementation

The previous two chapters have focused on the formal rational procedures associated with budgeting and the policy process. Rational policymaking models tend to assume that, if financial resources are available, if policy is properly formulated, and if appropriate organisations are in place to achieve the intended objectives, the implementation process should be unproblematic. In practice, this assumption is not tenable. Many problems may prevent the realisation of policy objectives: communication with implementers may be inadequate, objectives may be imprecisely stated or subsequently distorted, the means chosen to implement the policy may be inappropriate or those affected by the policy may respond in ways that had not been anticipated. Policymakers cannot assume that their work is finished after their proposals have received official endorsement or legislative approval. If they wish to see their objectives achieved, they have to manage the process to its desired conclusion. In this chapter, we consider how policy implementation relates to the policy process and the political context, what policy instruments are used to attain goals, how and when the government consults or coerces to realise its objectives, and how results are evaluated by the government and the public.

A critical variable influencing policy implementation has been the turbulent political environment. Domestic and external political pressures have affected implementation strategies and success in achieving goals although there have been important continuities over time. Before 1984, the government based most of its policymaking on the assumptions underlying a rational policy model and implementation did not usually face serious obstacles. During the transitional period between 1984 and 1997, policy was implemented more cautiously because the regime was embroiled in political and constitutional controversies over the future of the territory and the British and Chinese governments had more influence on what should or should not be done. In the post-1997 period, the political impact on implementation has become much stronger and difficulties cannot be easily anticipated. Government has become weaker and less authoritative.

In this chapter, we consider three aspects of the process of policy implementation:

- **policy instruments**, defined as the means that the government uses, or tries to use, to achieve its policy objectives;

- **implementation strategies**, the major approaches and assumptions about how policy should be implemented; and
- **evaluation**, how the government and the public assess policy performance.

Policy Instruments

Policy instruments may be classified in many different and complex ways which reflect the wide range of methods that governments may use to achieve their objectives.[1] The macro-level typology adopted here is based on Etzioni's division of power into coercive, remunerative, and normative types. Coercive power involves the use or threat of force. Remunerative power implies the ability to control and distribute material resources and rewards. Normative power, also called persuasive power, "rests on the allocation and manipulation of symbolic rewards".[2] These three types of power may be further developed into a classification of policy instruments as regulations, economic means, and information. Vedung notes that:

> The popular expressions used in this context are the stick, the carrot and the sermon. The government may either force us, pay us or have us pay, or persuade us.[3]

To illustrate these categories, we can consider some examples, each of which has a prescriptive (positive) element and a proscriptive (negative) element. Regulations (or the stick) may be used both to prohibit and encourage desired behaviour. Certain kinds of behaviour can result in penalties, such as fines or jail sentences, for offenders; in this sense, regulations are proscriptive. In Hong Kong, for example, under the *Prevention of Bribery Ordinance*, it is an offence to attempt to bribe a public official. Yet even when regulations are used in a punitive way, there is very often a moral or prescriptive component in the intended outcome. The implicit message is that corruption is unacceptable. Littering is an offence punishable by a fine, but it also has the prescriptive objective to change public behaviour to create a cleaner Hong Kong. Codes of conduct for civil servants, similarly, are regulations designed to encourage appropriate behaviour but they may not have explicit sanctions punishing violations of all provisions of the code.

Economic policy instruments likewise may have positive and negative aspects. The positive aspects (the carrot) often relate to programmes that the government wants to introduce or expand but which it cannot itself provide. An example is the

---

1. Capano, G., & Howlett, M. (2020). The knowns and unknowns of policy instrument analysis: Policy tools and the current research agenda on policy mixes. *Sage Open*, 1–13; Peters, B. G. (2005). Policy instruments and policy capacities. In M. Painter & J. Pierre (Eds.), *Challenges to state policy capacity: Global trends and comparative perspectives* (pp. 73–91). Basingstoke: Palgrave Macmillan.
2. Etzioni, A. (1961). *A comparative analysis of complex organizations* (p. 5). New York: Free Press.
3. Vedung, E. (1998). Policy instruments: Typologies and theories. In M. L. Bemelmans-Videc, R. C. Rist, & E. Vedung (Eds.), *Carrots, sticks and sermons: Policy instruments and their evaluation* (pp. 29–30). New Brunswick, NJ: Transaction.

government's subsidy of higher education places when there is a shortage of trained personnel in particular fields. The negative aspect of economic policy instruments is that the government has to collect taxes to fund its programmes. This involves an element of coercion because it is a crime not to pay taxes. It may also sanction certain behaviour. For example, taxes on cigarettes and on companies that pollute the environment are designed to send a message that both are hazardous to health.

The final type of policy instrument, the sermon, is the effort that all governments make to persuade their people to act in certain ways, efforts that may be equally attempted through the use of regulation or economic policy instruments. With the sermon, governments usually employ public information campaigns as the principal means of achieving their objectives. Daily government press releases often contain sermons that include both positive (encouraging) elements and negative (warning) aspects. For example, on a single day, 30 June 2020, the Hong Kong government issued alerts about the importance of workplace safety, the dangers of hazardous waste, the requirement that food for sale should be fit for human consumption, and the need to comply with the national security laws. There are three messages that the government is often trying to convey: there is a problem about which we are concerned; there are benefits if you take heed of our warning; and, if you do not heed of our warning, we may prosecute you.

Macro-level policy instruments are often used in combination to address a particular problem. In its attempts to control the COVID-19 pandemic, for example, the government used all three policy instruments. It introduced regulations imposing restrictions on mobility and freedom to meet,[4] reduced taxation and provided relief to help those who were adversely affected by the disease,[5] and lectured the public on the need to avoid complacency.[6] The three types of policy instrument often come together because governments try to reach a consensus to enable them to implement policy smoothly. They may need to regulate undesirable or illegal activities and to provide guidance on future behaviour. There are also likely to be fiscal implications and the need to promote what the government believes to be desirable outcomes. There is no guarantee that, whatever policy instruments are adopted, the objective, or the means to achieve it, will succeed or meet with public approval. The government's efforts to control COVID-19 were widely criticised despite public acceptance of the need to take measures to prevent the spread of the disease.[7]

---

4. Hong Kong Government (2020). *Together we fight the virus.* https://www.coronavirus.gov.hk/eng/index.html
5. Hong Kong Government (2020, 29 September). Anti-epidemic fund steering committee convenes sixth meeting. https://www.info.gov.hk/gia/general/202009/29/P2020092900737.htm
6. Davidson, H. (2020, 27 March). "We can't let up": Hong Kong battles new wave of COVID 19. *The Guardian.* https://www.theguardian.com/world/2020/mar/27/we-cant-let-up-hong-kong-battles-complacency-amid-new-wave-of-covid-19
7. Hartley, K., & Jarvis, D. S. L. (2020). Policymaking in a low-trust state: Legitimacy, state capacity and responses to COVID-19 in Hong Kong. *Policy and Society, 39*(3), 403–423; Tufecki, Z. (2020, 12 May). How Hong Kong did it. *Atlantic Monthly.*

The choice of policy instruments, or combinations of those instruments, is based on how governments use power to achieve their policy objectives. But we may wish to go beyond this to ask questions about the specific instruments employed to implement policy or to deliver public goods and services. When does the government rely on its own resources and personnel to achieve its goals? When does it rely on partnerships with subvented bodies or the private sector to deliver goods and services? When would it rely on the private sector alone to do the work for it? The answers to these questions are important. If governments make mistakes and choose the wrong instrument, the results can be costly failures.

How policy instruments are chosen is determined by a complex mix of historical factors, the immediate consequences of present problems, and perceptions of whether the government has the capacity to achieve its objectives, possibly in cooperation with, or by devolution to, other organisations. In colonial times, the Hong Kong government relied on its own resources to provide limited functions: management of the economy, law and order, constitutional affairs, justice, water supplies, and domestic regulation (maintenance of standards of hygiene, hawker control, and the issue of licences and registration of births, deaths, marriages, and companies). By the 1970s, however, the government had been drawn into the provision of social services and was not simply a purchaser of services, as it would probably have preferred. Health, education, and social welfare were all public-private partnerships with varying degrees of government involvement.[8] The government provided nearly half of the housing supply.[9] In social welfare, until 1993 when the CSSA Scheme was introduced, it relied mainly on subvented bodies to deliver welfare services (see pp. 184–185).[10] In education, the government funded public schools and subsidised private schools and the tertiary sector.[11] In health, the government provided minimal services for those who needed care because private health care was too expensive for many.[12] The private sector provided some transport services and utilities, such as gas and electricity, under schemes of control.

In post-handover Hong Kong, these goods and services were initially delivered in the same way. But there was increasing demand and growing awareness within government that many services were becoming unaffordable. Increases in public housing were soon capped, resulting in a waiting list that eventually rose to over five

---

8. Scott, I. (1987). Policy implementation in Hong Kong. *Southeast Asian Journal of Social Science*, 15(2), 1–19.
9. Legislative Council Secretariat Research Office (2016). Housing. https://www.legco.gov.hk/research-publications/english/1617issh09-public-housing-20161122-e.pdf
10. Hong Kong Government (2021). Hong Kong: The facts: Social welfare. https://www.gov.hk/en/about/abouthk/factsheets/docs/social_welfare.pdf
11. Legislative Council Secretariat Research Office (2016). Education expenditure in Hong Kong. https://www.legco.gov.hk/research-publications/english/1617issh11-education-expenditure-in-hong-kong-20161125-e.pdf
12. Luk, S. C. Y. (2014). The politics of health care financing reforms in Hong Kong. *Public Administration and Policy*, 17(1), 15–31.

years.[13] Social welfare expenditure was cut but soon rose again to much higher levels (see pp. 248–253). Health services became increasingly expensive as the population aged and more people needed public services. Repeated attempts to find solutions for burgeoning costs failed.[14] There was increased expenditure on education, but it was a battleground between government attempts to impose its policies on the sector and resistance from providers.[15]

In the best of times, it would have been difficult to find solutions for the kinds of policy problem faced by the post-handover government. But the fractious political environment and the growing importance of the Chinese government, pro-establishment/pro-Beijing groups, the business lobby, and domestic pressure groups worsened those difficulties. Implementation was often blocked or delayed.[16] Increasing expenditure on social policy provided temporary solutions, but devising entirely new strategies to deliver goods and services met with opposition at every turn. The quality of provision began to suffer from incremental drift. Some makeshift solutions worked, some led to the gradual deterioration of the service, and some were abandoned in the face of opposition. In 2019, a Legislative Councillor asked the government to explain why there was so much dissatisfaction with its attempts to implement policies.[17] He cited the raising of the eligible age for elderly social assistance to 65, arrangements for a cash handout, a toll road adjustment proposal, and the health care workers' demonstrations against overloaded hospitals and the shortage of qualified personnel. But he could have added many more examples. In response, the Chief Secretary for Administration could only say that public consultation would be increased. However much public consultation was undertaken, it seemed unlikely that these problems would go away.

Implementation Strategies

In any political system, there may be a dominant style of policy implementation determined by the nature of the political system and its objectives. This usually occurs when there is a concentration of executive power and societal influences on policy implementation are limited. In turbulent times, disparate influences affect policy implementation and governments may be thankful for any successful means of achieving their goals. The style of policy implementation that

---

13. Yip, N. M. (2020, 1 May). Solving Hong Kong's housing affordability problem. *East Asia Forum*. https://www.eastasiaforum.org/2020/05/01/solving-hong-kongs-housing-affordability-problem/
14. Luk (2014) op. cit.
15. Jackson, L., & O'Leary, T. (2019). Education and the Hong Kong Umbrella Movement. *Educational Philosophy and Theory, 51*(2), 157–162.
16. Cheung, A. B. L. (2007b). Policy capacity in Hong Kong: Constrained institutions facing a crowding and differentiated polity. *Asia Pacific Journal of Public Administration, 29*(1), 51–75; Scott, I. (2007). Legitimacy, governance and public policy in post-handover Hong Kong. *Asia Pacific Journal of Public Administration, 29*(1), 29–49; Wong, M. Y. H. (2017). Discussing without deciding, deciding without acting: Veto players in Hong Kong, and Beijing's response. *Asian Journal of Comparative Politics, 2*(4), 347–361.
17. Hansard, 27 February 2019, 7244–7246.

a government adopts may also be influenced by the type of policy and historical experience. Implementing social policy, for example, requires rather different structures and political skills than implementing infrastructural or innovation policies. Government departments also build up knowledge about the best ways to deal with problems. Reliance on structures and methods that have produced positive results is an important consideration and routine policies that have been established over many years may continue to be implemented incrementally.

In post-handover Hong Kong, a mix of implementation strategies has been tried. Table 9.1 lists strategies that have been adopted, either solely or in combination, together with the conditions under which the government may feel that a particular strategy has more likelihood of success.

Top-Down

The post-handover government inherited the colonial top-down implementation strategy where success was often achieved through hierarchically organised departments by strong vertical coordination. Orders transmitted from the apex of the organisational pyramid were expected to be implemented without question by those at the base of the pyramid, often with limited or no communication and consultation with those affected by the decision or policy. If implementation required non-governmental or private sector providers, the government could bring them into line through regulations and funding arrangements. The government structure did not change substantially after the handover. Where policies have been in place for many years and if the policy is technical or not controversial, top-down implementation remains a characteristic of the system.

The disciplinary services retain strictly hierarchical structures which enable their objectives to be more easily achieved using a top-down strategy. The Police Force, particularly since the protests, announces and implements new law and order policies and regulations, usually without public consultation. Programme management and its strategic directions are set and controlled by the Commissioner of Police and his three deputies.[18] There is little feedback within the organisation or, seemingly, from other parts of the Hong Kong government. The provisions of the national security law provisions, enacted by the Chinese government for Hong Kong in June 2020, legalised a PRC agency to act in the HKSAR on security issues in conjunction with the Police Force.[19]

Other disciplined services (Correctional Services, Customs and Excise, Fire Services, and Immigration) often also issue regulations that are often refinements or

---

18. Hong Kong Police Force (2022). Hong Kong Police – About us. https://www.police.gov.hk/ppp_en/01_about_us/os.html
19. Government of the People's Republic of China (2020). *The Law of the People's Republic of China on safeguarding national security in the Hong Kong Special Administrative Region* (Ch. V). https://www.elegislation.gov.hk/doc/hk/a406/eng_translation_(a406)_en.pdf

Table 9.1 *A Typology of Policy Implementation Styles*

Type	Conditions	Examples	Advantages	Deficiencies
Top-down	Hierarchical and centralised departments insulated from popular pressures.	Policies devised by the disciplined services or in technical areas.	Strong vertical coordination with little external consultation enables speedy implementation.	Poor horizontal coordination with other departments and absence of a popular mandate.
Rational/ Consultative	Policies devised using rational techniques followed by public consultation.	Review of the statutory minimum wage rate.	If a consensus can be reached, implementation may be easier.	Consultation is time-consuming and there may be no consensus.
Incremental	Focuses on an aspect of policy that may be implemented by marginal changes.	The public housing Tenants Purchase Scheme.	May help avoid friction over the larger policy problem by offering temporary solutions to smaller problems.	Ignores larger problems associated with the same policy. May result in incremental drift with service delivery gradually becoming worse.
Symbolic	Government states goals, but lacks political and/or financial capacity to implement them.	Government's commitment to 70% home ownership by 2008 (yet to be implemented).	Deflects immediate opposition to government policy by making a future commitment.	Raises public expectations, but failure to deliver reduces government credibility.
Displacement	Government makes policy in areas where it is easiest to implement.	Innovation policies, cash handouts.	Reduced political friction in the chosen policy area means that government can give the impression that it is taking decisive action.	Expenditure comes with opportunity cost. Funds spent cannot be used to address more contentious policy problems.

Source: Author.

extensions of long-established, existing policies. These modifications may require consultation or negotiation with other parts of the Hong Kong or Mainland governments, but they are not usually a matter for public debate. In 2015, for example, the Immigration Department announced plans to extend the admission arrangements for talented mainland Chinese residents to Hong Kong without wide consultation.[20] Similarly, under the Free Trade Agreement Transhipment Scheme, the Custom and Excise Department frequently announces new measures for the facilitation of trade through Hong Kong to mainland China.[21] There is some consultation with industry, which pays for the scheme, and, presumably, with the Chinese authorities but none with the public.

Within the rest of the Hong Kong civil service, there is a continuing culture that sees top-down implementation as an appropriate way to achieve policy goals. Where there is little need for interaction with the public, the department may simply formulate the policy and then implement it through the hierarchy. As a consequence, top-down implementation often results in a sub-optimised perspective. It maximises one value—the strength of the focused, vertical organisation—at the expense of another value—horizontal coordination between different parts of the civil service in pursuit of common goals. Left to its own devices, the system would result in minimal consultation with other departments. In the traditional colonial civil service, this was not problematic because the functions of government were limited. Once social policies were introduced and government became one of the providers, horizontal coordination became much more important.

The weakness of horizontal coordination has led to some major problems and various ad hoc attempts to resolve the difficulties that this creates for implementation. The government's response to the SARS crisis in 2003, for example, led to three investigations on whether the outbreak could have been better handled.[22] Each dealt with matters that related to the coordination and delineation of responsibilities between the relevant bureaus, departments, and statutory bodies. The inadequate coordination between the government and the Hospital Authority received a good deal of critical attention. The Hospital Authority Review Panel described the situation as one in which there was an "absence of a clear chain of command" and "no central decision-making body".[23] There were also problems of communication

---

20. Immigration Department (2015, 28 April). Immigration Department to implement pilot admission scheme for 2nd generation Chinese HK residents to talent admission arrangements. https://www.info.gov.hk/gia/general/201504/28/P201504280699.htm
21. Customs and Excise Department (2015, 18 December). Hong Kong Customs Free Trade Agreement Transhipment Facilities Scheme. https://www.info.gov.hk/gia/general/201512/18/P201512180330.htm
22. Hospital Authority Review Panel (2003, September). *Report of the Hospital Authority Review Panel on the SARS outbreak*. Hong Kong: The Authority; Legislative Council (2004). *Report of the Select Committee into the Handling of the Severe Acute Respiratory Syndrome Outbreak by the Government and the Hospital Authority*. https://www.legco.gov.hk/yr03-04/english/sc/sc_sars/reports/sars_rpt.htm; SARS Expert Committee (2003). *SARS in Hong Kong: From experience to action: Report of the SARS Expert Committee*. https://www.sars-expertcom.gov.hk/english/reports/reports/reports_fullrpt.html
23. Hong Kong Government (2003, 16 October). *HWFB's statement on HA's SARS report* [Press release]. https://www.info.gov.hk/gia/general/200310/16/1016219.htm

between the policymaking body, the Health, Welfare and Food Bureau, and the Department of Health and the Hospital Authority. The bureau's initial response was to allow the Hospital Authority to solve the problem. As the crisis worsened, the Secretary, and eventually the Chief Executive, began to play more active roles, but there remained "a lack of common understanding".[24] These problems may be endemic to the relationship between the government and the statutory bodies, such as the Hospital Authority, but they impeded a coordinated response to the SARS crisis.

The difficulty of horizontal coordination in strongly hierarchically organised bureaucracies is that important issues can easily fall between jurisdictions delaying action because departments may think that responsibility does not lie with them. Eventually, the magnitude of the SARS problem and the effect that it had on the community and the economy was such that the government was able to mobilise sufficient resources to deal with the crisis effectively. Lessons were learned, however. When the COVID-19 crisis emerged, the government was better prepared. Although its policy on combatting the virus was widely criticised, horizontal coordination worked much better than it had during the SARS crisis.[25] This remedial policymaking is one way in which strongly hierarchical systems can mitigate the effects of poor horizontal coordination. But it is an expensive means of organisational learning and remedial measures are not always easily introduced.

SARS was a major crisis and policy had to be devised and implemented as quickly and efficiently as possible. In many other instances, the absence of horizontal coordination within government leads to smaller problems that are not immediately resolved and cause continuing inconvenience to the public. In one case, a repaired 200-metre stretch of a road was not opened for 18 years because each of the departments involved thought that the other had the responsibility for making the announcement.[26] In other cases, there were disputes over such matters as departmental responsibilities for illegally constructed shops encroaching on a pavement and endangering pedestrians, jurisdiction for monitoring and managing trees, and the department responsible for cleaning up a beach after a typhoon.[27] Departments do not want to take responsibility for unfunded activities and consequently do not usually engage in collaborative activities with other departments unless they have budgetary backing. Even then, hierarchically organised departments are poor

---

24. SARS Expert Committee (2003) op. cit., p. 72.
25. Hartley & Jarvis (2020) op. cit.
26. Yeung, R. (2017, 31 October). Transport Department criticised after part of Kowloon road goes unused for years. *SCMP*. http://www.scmp.com/news/hong-kong/community/article/2117820/transport-department-criticised-after-kowloon-road-goes
27. Knott, K. (2018, 24 September). Shek O beach residents angry and fearful over Hong Kong officials' response to debris clean-up after Typhoon Mangkhut destruction. *SCMP*. https://www.scmp.com/news/hong-kong/health-environment/article/2165317/shek-o-beach-residents-angry-and-fearful-over-hong; Office of the Ombudsman (2013). *Annual report 2012–13* (pp. 90–91). *People, trees, harmony* (Ch. 2). https://www.devb.gov.hk/en/home/report_of_the_task_force_on_tree_management.pdf.

collaborators. They want to retain control over their own resources and handle only those issues that fall squarely within their jurisdictions.

Dealing with the water seepage problem is a case in point. In 2006, two departments, the Buildings Department (BD) and the Food and Environment Hygiene Department (FEHD), set up a joint office (JO) to deal with complaints about water seepage in private sector apartments.[28] Private owners can seek government assistance if their neighbours are not cooperating in solving a seepage problem or the source of the seepage is not clear.[29] Public housing complaints are dealt with by the Housing Authority which receives some 15,000 to 20,000 repair requests per year,[30] but there do not seem to have been major difficulties or delays in dealing with those problems. In the private sector, however, despite the JO, complaints about the handling of seepage problems rose by 70% from 17,405 in 2007 to 29,617 in 2015.[31]

Each of the departments has a separate role in rectifying problems. The FEHD makes the initial inspection and can issue nuisance notices to uncooperative neighbours. The BD supervises contractors employed to detect the source of the seepage with the Water Supplies Department on call to deal with leaking pipes. As the complaints about the process increased, the Ombudsman decided to conduct a direct investigation into the JO.[32] She found that the departments were in an "uneasy relationship"; neither department was able to exercise proper authority over staff or take responsibility for its performance. There was no acknowledged head of the JO with "formal authority and clear lines of command over staff secondment and office management".[33] Subsequent investigations revealed that there was friction between the departments over investigations on seepage and on follow-up measures. In 2016, the Director of Audit further investigated the issue, observing that success rates in determining seepage problems had declined from 46% in 2007 to 36% in 2015.[34] The time taken to resolve issues had not improved, there were anomalies in the classification of information between departments and the JO and its 19 district offices still did not collect information consistently. Between January 2016 and September 2018, the Ombudsman received 360 complaints about the JO for failing to handle water seepage problems properly and launched yet another direct investigation into its activities. The investigation found that the JO had a "huge backlog" of cases. In June 2020, of over 23,000 outstanding cases, one-third had been received before 2019. The report concluded that the BD and FEHD might be working in

---

28. Office of the Ombudsman (2008). *Report on handling of water seepage complaints* (p. 9). https://ofomb.ombudsman.hk/abc/files/3-2008-2.pdf
29. Ibid.
30. Legislative Council Panel on Housing (2014). *Enhanced means to tackle water seepage problems in public rental flats*. CB (1) 289/14-15(03). http://www.legco.gov.hk/yr14-15/english/panels/hg/papers/hg20141209cb1-289-3-e.pdf
31. Director of Audit (2016). *Joint-office operation on water seepage in buildings*. Report No. 67. https://www.aud.gov.hk/pdf_e/e67ch09.pdf
32. Office of the Ombudsman (2008) op. cit.
33. Ibid., p. 9.
34. Director of Audit (2016) op. cit., p. iii.

organisational silos that "lack coordination [and] determination to solve problems in the absence of a coherent management structure overseeing JO's operations".[35]

Coordination problems between government silos of this kind can be resolved either by creating an entirely new agency with powers to deal with the issue or by devolving powers to the head of the collaborative body.[36] In the seepage case, neither department was willing to relinquish control over its personnel or, presumably, to agree to the appointment of an independent head of the JO. The government may also have anticipated political difficulties with the bureaus involved and departments themselves if their jurisdiction had been reduced by creating an entirely new agency.

Effective horizontal coordination in silos-dominated systems can be achieved by political intervention, by remedial policymaking, and by informal coordination between professionals and administrative elites who owe allegiance to the centre rather than to individual departments. A strictly hierarchical structure is not appropriate for governments engaged in widespread provision of social services where horizontal coordination is important. Top-down implementation is an appropriate means of implementation only when certain conditions are met. These conditions include an ability to formulate policy largely within the confines of a single organisation, to deliver services from the organisation's resources, and to generate outcomes that do not result in large numbers of complaints or protests. When these conditions do not apply, it is often necessary to use other or supplemental means to implement decisions and policies successfully.

Rational/Consultative

Under colonialism, there was time and space for policymakers to consider whether or not to take action and to debate appropriate solutions to problems. In the classical traditions of rational policy formulation, this led to the assumption that, since policy had been so well considered, implementation would follow automatically. The underlying epistemocratic basis of authority, which attributed superior knowledge and vision to the "best and brightest" chosen as administrative officers and consequently as policymakers, and relatively autonomous departments with strong hierarchies reinforced the view that what was officially proclaimed would unquestionably be implemented. The government was disinclined to admit that its policies might have been misconceived and civil society was insufficiently developed to call it to account.

In the later colonial and early post-handover periods, top-down policy implementation was modified to pay more attention to planning, coordination, and

---

35. Office of the Ombudsman (2020). *Effectiveness of Joint Office: Investigation of water seepage complaints: Executive summary* (p. 6). https://ofomb.ombudsman.hk/abc/en-us/direct_investigations
36. Scott, I., & Gong, T. (2021). Coordinating government silos: challenges and opportunities. *Global Public Policy and Governance, 1*(1), 20–38.

cost-benefit analysis and to undertake more consultation. The government took care not to frame its policies so that they would upset its support and consulted with the business community and traditional Chinese elites on advisory committees and by less formal means.[37] By 1997, the society had become more pluralistic and, although business and traditional elites were still well entrenched, the Mainland government and civil society organisations were becoming increasingly important actors in the policy process. Coordination between departments and public consultation over social policy implementation, in particular, was time-consuming and slowed down decision-making.

Under the rational/consultative model, the civil service would initiate and carefully formulate policy, then consult the relevant stakeholders and finally return the modified proposal to the department for implementation. Although this model has remained an ideal and a means by which some policies are still implemented, the introduction of the POAS and increasingly unchannelled and disparate demands from the political executive, pressure groups, political parties, and the Legislative Council has disrupted it.

Harbour Fest, a public-private venture undertaken to raise spirits after the SARS outbreak, illustrates the problems involved. Poor management meant that the government was liable for $100 million of the losses incurred by the concerts.[38] The Director of Audit's report severely criticised the project implementation and provided guidelines that the government should have followed but did not. These included: conducting a feasibility study, conducting options analysis, drawing up a formal business plan, having greater transparency and accountability in the use of public money, taking effective action to monitor the project, assessing whether it could be completed in time, and ensuring that the performance targets of private sector partners were reliable.[39]

When Tsang became Chief Executive in 2005, he adopted a more cautious approach. The civil service regained some of its previous power over policy formulation and the government was less confrontational with civil society organisations on implementation issues. His strategy was based more on accommodation rather than on attempts to enforce the government's position. In 2008, for example, he announced that the old age living allowance would be raised to $1,000 per month but that it would be means-tested.[40] This resulted in protests from legislators and pressure groups and a 60% negative response rate to a government survey.[41] Within 10 days, the means test was dropped. The government's cautious approach to its

---

37. Cheung, P. T. Y. (2011). Civic engagement in the policy process in Hong Kong: Change and continuity. *Public Administration and Development*, 31(2), 113–121.
38. Hansard, 5 November 2003, 907.
39. Director of Audit (2004). *Report No. 42: Hong Kong Harbour Fest* (pp. 60–65). Hong Kong: Government Logistics Department.
40. Tsang, D. Y. K. (2008). *Embracing new challenges* (para 71). www.policyaddress.gov.hk/08-09/index.html
41. Hong Kong Government (2008, 24 October). *CE's remarks on the old age allowance* [Press release]. https://www.info.gov.hk/gia/general/200810/24/P200810240231.htm

dealings with civil society was also apparent in the collapse of Lehman Brothers, which left an estimated 40,000 investors with losses of $15.5 billion.[42] With the help of political parties and professional advice, the victims were soon very well organised. They claimed that Hong Kong banks had sold high-risk financial products as safe investments. They wanted the government to make the banks pay compensation, but the government was reluctant to intervene because of the precedent for its future relationships with the private sector. It also knew that no solution would satisfy angry investors and the banks. But eventually it agreed to negotiate with the banks to refund investors.

Tsang's strategy required consultation and bargaining with Legislative Councillors and civil society organisations to get policies accepted and to try to implement them. In 2007, the government decided to pull down the Star Ferry and Queen's Piers on Hong Kong Island. Young demonstrators chained themselves to the buildings, arguing that the government's action was a violation of Hong Kong's heritage. The event has subsequently come to be regarded as the origin of the social movement opposing government policies.[43] Carrie Lam, then Development Secretary, went to Queen's Pier to meet the demonstrators and later said that she was surrounded by them for five hours. She said that this experience had persuaded her that the government should use civic engagement as a means of negotiating with pressure groups opposed to its policies. Civic engagement was used with some success on the harbour reclamation project when the government compromised with the groups involved. On other issues, however, such as the redevelopment of the Kai Tak Airport site and the urban renewal strategy, the government had little success with civic engagement and it gradually ceased to be incorporated into the policy implementation process.

Despite growing popular dissent on many government policies, the rational/consultative mode continued to be the formal template for the way policy is made and implemented. Once a policy has been formulated, the government often puts it to the public as a consultation document with an invitation to comment on the proposals. Between 1999 and 2007, it has been estimated that approximately 20 consultation documents were issued per year.[44] More recently, there were 24 in 2017, 28 in 2018, and 19 in 2019 although this includes some consultative documents for which the consultation period stretched from one year to the next.[45]

---

42. Hong Kong Government (2008, 31 October). *Speech by the SFST at the 9th Hong Kong Forum* [Press release]. https://www.info.gov.hk/gia/general/200810/31/P200810310133.htm
43. Ku, A. S. (2012). Remaking places and fashioning an opposition discourse: Struggle over Star Ferry pier and Queen's pier in Hong Kong. *Environment and Planning D: Society and Space, 30,* 5–22; Pang, J. (2017, 6 August). In pictures: Demonstrations and demolition—10 years since the Queen's pier was pulled down. *HKFP.* https://hongkongfp.com/2017/08/06/pictures-demonstrations-demolition-10-years-since-queens-pier-pulled/
44. Cheung, P. T. Y. (2011) op. cit.
45. Hong Kong Government (2020). Consultation papers in archive. https://www.gov.hk/en/residents/government/publication/consultation/archives.htm; Cheung, K. C. (2018, 22 January). Shockingly low response rate to Hong Kong government public consultation received. *SCMP.* https://www.scmp.com/news/hong-kong/politics/article/2129903/shockingly-low-response-rate-hong-kong-government-public

The documents covered many subjects and attracted differing response rates. For the more technical documents or those that related to a small proportion of the population, response rates were very low. In 2017, for example, proposals to amend the *Chinese Medicine Ordinance* and to update standards of toys and children's products received only two responses each and 15 consultation documents received fewer than 100 responses.[46] In contrast, issues relating to access to information, raising the minimum wage, and gender recognition attracted many responses.[47] In December 2013, the government's proposals on constitutional reform generated some 124,700 responses, 90% of which were signature campaigns from pro-Beijing groups.[48] There has also been long-standing scepticism about whether the government pays much attention to the comments it receives. As a study of housing policy suggested "the consultation process . . . appears to operate primarily to provide a degree of legitimacy for the Hong Kong government's policy decisions [and] its impact on policy itself is very limited".[49]

Once the responses to the document have been received, the proposals return to the home bureau for selective modification. The changes that are made are not usually major concessions to what was put forward in the consultation document, but there are occasionally cases, such as the attempt to introduce a goods and services tax, of the government dropping its proposal. The December 2013 constitutional reform consultative document concerned the election of the Chief Executive, the issue that sparked the Umbrella Movement. The government did not withdraw its proposals but was eventually defeated on its proposals in the Legislative Council.

Despite the weaknesses of its approach, the rational/consultative mode remains a common formal means of policy implementation. It succeeds with technical issues or where the numbers or organisations involved are small. On larger policy questions, the consultative document has been used less frequently and public views have often been expressed on the streets rather than through official channels. Policymaking on major issues has tended to become more symbolic.

Incremental

Incrementalism is defined as marginal changes to an existing policy. As far as policy implementation is concerned, it has the advantage that smaller changes are usually more easily accepted. Proposals may be sold to the public with the claim that not much will change and that what will change will be an improvement. The desired outcome is that over time many small changes will lead to the attainment of a larger

---

46. Ibid.
47. Ibid.
48. Hong Kong Government (2013). *Methods for selecting the Chief Executive in 2017 and for forming the Legislative Council in 2016*. https://www.legco.gov.hk/yr13-14/english/panels/ca/papers/ca1209-cdoc20131204-e.pdf
49. Brewer, B., & La Grange, A. (2001). *Whose views matter? Reforming public housing policy in Hong Kong* (p. 32). Public and Social Administration Working Paper Series. Hong Kong: City University of Hong Kong.

goal. Unfortunately, this does not always happen.[50] Incremental changes can sometimes result in gradual deterioration. In post-handover Hong Kong, social policies have resulted in worse access to services than before the incremental changes were adopted.

Incrementalism may be a dominant feature of the policymaking system at different times and for different reasons. Under colonialism, incrementalism was consistent with a top-down system of implementation and the primary objectives of the regime. The government was usually too concerned about balancing its budget and maintaining law and order to undertake many new initiatives. Housing policy, the creation of the new towns, and the expanded social policies of the 1970s were exceptions. But most policies, once established, needed only minor fine-tuning and decisions were implemented in top-down style through the hierarchy without much public dissent. The government believed that it lacked the capacity to implement major new policies successfully and was concerned that, if it did, its relationship with the public might become more conflictual.

After 1984, a more demanding public and the impending retrocession of Hong Kong to China meant that incrementalism alone was not thought to be able to maintain stability. There were concerns about the future on many fronts. The government had become more confident of its capacity to achieve infrastructural objectives, if not always its social policy goals, and it imagined that large projects—the construction of a new airport and a new university, for example—would serve to illustrate its continuing commitment to the public interest. But the handover also constrained the development of policies that spanned 1997 on which the Chinese government often held strong views. In some policy areas, policy implementation was symbolic: the government simply stated its ideals but did little to implement them.

After the handover, Tung's attempts to implement policy often produced intense conflict with affected groups and led to the rapid rise of civil society organisations. Many policies had to be modified or abandoned with the consequence that the government lost credibility. In education, for example, government policy consisted of measures that provoked friction with parents, teachers, students, and unions. These included: curriculum reform, benchmarking the qualifications of teachers, reforming the primary one admission system, reforming the secondary schools allocation mechanism, reforming the university admission system, redesignating schools as mother language teaching schools, and improving public examinations.[51] Conflict between the government and the teachers arose over the decision to assess their

---

50. Béland, D., Rocco, P., & Wadden, A. (2016). Reassessing policy drift: Social policy change in the United States. *Social Policy and Administration*, 50(2), 201–218.
51. Education Commission (2000). *Learning for life, learning through life: Reform proposals for the education system in Hong Kong*. Hong Kong: Printing Department; Tung (1997) op. cit., pp. 29–35; Tung, C. H. (1999). *Quality people, quality home: Positioning people for the 21st Century* (pp. 19–26). Hong Kong: Printing Department; Tung, C. H. (2000). *Serving the community, sharing common goals* (pp. 17–25). Hong Kong: Printing Department; Ho, L. S., Morris. P., & Chung, Y. C. (Eds.) (2005). *Education reform and the quest for excellence: The Hong Kong story*. Hong Kong: Hong Kong University Press. Morris, P., & Scott, I. (2003). Educational reform and policy implementation in Hong Kong. *Journal of Education Policy*, 18(1), 71–84.

language proficiency, over attempts to merge the subjects of history and Chinese history and over redundancies resulting from upgrading teacher education.[52] The decision to reduce the number of English language schools provoked widespread criticism from teachers, parents, and pupils and the proposal was eventually amended to require fewer schools to change to Chinese language teaching.[53] Policy in many areas had to be remade after it was supposed to have been implemented, a waste of time and resources.

The Tsang administration retreated to a more incremental mode. Social policies began to follow more familiar paths although civil society organisations were not appeased and their numbers and the intensity of their protests gradually grew. In their survey of demonstrations, rallies, and petitions between 2007 and 2016, Chan and Chan found that the numbers rose from 241 in 2007 to a peak of 496 in 2014 before falling to 236 in 2016.[54] Labour, planning, and professional interests constituted the greatest proportion of policies causing friction between the demonstrators and the government, but the most serious confrontations occurred over education policy and constitutional issues. Significantly, however, protests on Hong Kong/China issues did not begin until 2011.[55]

On education policy, the long history of friction between the government and the churches, teachers, and parents came to a head in 2012 when the government tried to introduce a "moral and national" education programme.[56] Unions, parents, students, and other civil society organisations believed it was an attempt to brainwash pupils and large demonstrations forced the government to withdraw its proposal. There were further major constitutional and democracy protests in 2014 over the Chinese government's decision that a nominating committee would decide the candidates who could run in Chief Executive elections and, in 2019, over the Extradition Bill.

The problem for the government in developing an implementation strategy was that it did not know when, how, or on what issues it would face opposition from civil society organisations. Protests might occur either during the policy process or after the government had announced that a policy would be implemented. Consultation became even less meaningful: public responses to government consultation might show apparent support for a policy, but there was no guarantee that protesters would not be mobilised to oppose it after the consultation period

---

52. Lai, K. C., Kwok, K. W., & Cheung, E. L. M. (2005). Implementation of graduate teacher policy in Hong Kong primary schools: Promises and disillusionment. In Ho, Morris, & Chung (Eds.) op. cit., pp. 127–146; Morris & Scott (2003) op cit.; Vickers, E. (2003). *In search of an identity: The politics of history as a school subject in Hong Kong 1960s–2002*. New York: Routledge.
53. Chan, E. (2002). Beyond pedagogy: Language and identity in post-colonial Hong Kong. *British Journal of Sociology of Education*, 23(2), 271–285.
54. Chan, E., & Chan, J. (2017). Hong Kong 2007–2017: A backlash in civil society. *Asia Pacific Journal of Public Administration*, 39(2), Table 1.
55. Ibid.
56. Morris, P., & Vickers, E. (2015). Schooling, politics and the construction of identity in Hong Kong: The 2012 "moral and national education" crises in historical perspective. *Comparative Education*, 51(3), 305–326.

had ended. The effect was to disrupt rational/consultative policymaking because the government could not anticipate the kinds of difficulty that it would face. Incrementalism seemed the safer option even if it did not answer the issues that civil society organisations wanted to be addressed.

It was particularly difficult to introduce new policies or to fix the problems confronting social policies. Housing, health, and welfare policies were left to drift without appropriate solutions. Public rental housing waiting lists grew, access to health care became more difficult, and the numbers living below the poverty line increased to well over a million.[57] The government was well aware of the problems, but there was a disconnection between the increasing inadequacy of services and the solutions proposed to resolve them. All that the government could offer were more incremental adjustments or more commissions of inquiry.

Incrementalism works in times of stability when there is general satisfaction with policy. It is not as suited for more turbulent times—although it may be perceived to be the safest option—when there is a need for more imaginative policymaking and implementation. With a government under siege, the temptation was for officials to retreat behind the parapets on social policies, look for short-term incremental solutions to the spreading discontent, and try to implement the policies that the Chinese government saw as priorities for Hong Kong.

Symbolic

Symbolic policies involve a statement of ideals to which the government and, by implication, the community should aspire but which cannot be attained until some undefined point in the future. The policy problem itself is identified, often backed by a report from a commission of inquiry, a task force, or an advisory committee. The government then states that it will take action and introduces non-controversial incremental measures. The difference from a pure incremental strategy is that the proposed measures have no prospect of significantly reducing the size of the problem; there is little relationship between means and ends. Unlike pure incremental policymaking, the measures are not intended to achieve a goal by making small changes but rather to offer a short-term placebo for a contentious issue in turbulent times.

From the government's standpoint, symbolic policymaking coupled with incremental measures has the advantages that it can be presented as evidence that action is being taken and that no call is being made on the coercive power of the state. The government tries to avoid conflict over the potentially divisive initiatives that are needed to resolve major issues. Instead, it relies on decisions that cause incremental policy drift and a gradual worsening of the fundamental problem. The incremental

---

57. Oxfam (2018). *Hong Kong inequality report* (p. 8). https://www.oxfam.org.hk/en/f/news_and_publication/16372/Oxfam_inequality%20report_Eng_FINAL.pdf

decisions are often also supplemented by the creation of new organisations or structural changes that are supposed to resolve the larger problem but which, in the absence of effective policy reforms, rarely do so.

The use of symbolic policymaking in Hong Kong dates from the Sino-British agreement in 1984. Before the agreement, the government could implement policy using top-down methods and incremental changes where needed. After the agreement, it was less autonomous and more vulnerable to policy interventions from both the Chinese and British governments. Social policy initiatives also became more problematic because the government had already expanded the housing supply, increased the number of school places, and enhanced health care and social welfare provision. Demands were focused more on qualitative rather than quantitative improvements and the maintenance of existing benefits under threat. The weakened colonial government was less able to respond to these concerns than it was to its traditional, but non-controversial, commitment to building infrastructure, housing estates, and schools and hospitals efficiently and economically. Consequently, its approach became more cautious and it sought to establish that the values were widely shared before making policy and that policies would not generate conflicts that could potentially jeopardise political stability.

The lesson that Tung's successors drew from the failures of his initiatives was that the price of introducing major new policies was the risk of social unrest.[58] There was opposition to implementation and delays on many policies and projects—for example, health care financing,[59] the West Kowloon Cultural District project,[60] domestic violence legislation,[61] harbour reclamation,[62] and small class teaching.[63] The government retreated into symbolic policymaking which left the values associated with social policy, in particular, in abeyance. Was the government still committed to providing public rental housing for those who wanted it? What was the government's role in providing health care? What were the limits to its welfare provision? What was it going to do about those who were slipping into poverty? What kind of education did it believe should be provided to Hong Kong children?

The government's treatment of these potentially controversial questions often began with an implicit or explicit affirmation of traditional public policy values. If it had done otherwise, it would have had to introduce substantial new policies, involving different values that might well have resulted in conflict with business or

---

58. Scott, I. (2007) op. cit.
59. Goodstadt, L. F. (2013). *Poverty in the midst of affluence: How Hong Kong mismanaged its prosperity* (pp. 139–146). Hong Kong: Hong Kong University Press.
60. Hayllar, M. R. (2010). Public-private partnerships in Hong Kong: Good governance—the essential missing ingredient. *Australian Journal of Public Administration, 69*, supplement, S99–119.
61. Barrow, A., & Scully-Hill, A. (2016). Failure to implement CEDAW in Hong Kong: Why isn't anyone using the Domestic and Cohabitation Relationships Violence Ordinance? *International Journal of Law, Policy and the Family, 30*(1), 50–78.
62. Ng, M. K. (2006). World-city formation under an executive-led government: The politics of harbour reclamation in Hong Kong. *The Town Planning Review, 77*(3), 311–337.
63. Hansard, 2 December 2004, 2263–2361.

civil society organisations. In 2013, in his first policy address, for example, Leung Chun-yin reaffirmed that the government regarded housing as the "top priority" and that the policy objectives remained "to assist grass-roots families to secure public housing", to encourage the middle class to purchase apartments, and to develop the private property market.[64] But the means of achieving these objectives seemed unlikely to make much difference. The government promised to introduce short- and medium-term measures, which included raising stamp duty, seeking to increase land supply, advocating "Hong Kong property for Hong Kong people" and building youth hostels.[65] A Long-Term Housing Steering Committee was to consider future developments. Within a few years, the government had conceded that it could not meet its ambitious targets for the next decade because it had been unable to identify sufficient land to build public housing.[66] By the end of Leung's term in office, the public rental housing waiting list was at an 18-year high.[67] Leung was successful in supporting the private sector property market and it might be argued that was always the government's primary policy objective.[68]

In Carrie Lam's first policy address in 2017, the same housing themes were reiterated.[69] There was, she said, a serious shortage of supply and there was still a need to increase the amount of land available for housing. A task force was set up to examine the issue. There was a small home ownership scheme success to report that might be the way towards future easing of the problem but, by June 2020, there was little evidence that much had changed. There were still 259,700 applicants on the waiting list for public rental housing. The average waiting time for non-elderly applicants was 5.5 years while elderly one-person applicants could expect to wait three years.[70]

The crux of the housing problem has been the government's unwillingness to do more to provide affordable social housing. It has not released enough land for sufficient public housing to be built although it does reserve land for private sector housing.[71] The consequence has been that private sector housing targets are in line

---

64. Leung, C. Y. (2013). *Seek change, maintain stability, serve the people with pragmatism* (paras 56, 58). https://www.policyaddress.gov.hk/2013/eng/pdf/PA2013.pdf
65. Ibid.
66. Yau, C., & Siu, P. (2016, 20 December). Hong Kong government unlikely to reach target of 280,000 new public housing flats over the next decade. *SCMP*. https://www.scmp.com/news/hong-kong/economy/article/2056082/hong-kong-government-falls-short-public-housing-construction
67. Ng, N., & Su, X. (2018, 10 August). Waiting time for Hong Kong public housing flat longest in 18 years: Five years, three months. *SCMP*. https://www.scmp.com/news/hong-kong/community/article/2159237/waiting-time-hong-kong-public-housing-flat-longest-18-years
68. Goodstadt (2013) op. cit., pp. 87–110; Poon, A. (2011). *Land and the ruling class in Hong Kong* (2nd ed., p. 25). Singapore: Enrich Professional Publishing.
69. Lam, C. (2017). *We connect for hope and happiness* (paras 141–152). https://www.policyaddress.gov.hk/2017/eng/pdf/PA2017.pdf
70. Housing Authority (2020). Number of applicants and average waiting time for public rental housing. https://www.housingauthority.gov.hk/en/about-us/publications-and-statistics/prh-applications-average-waiting-time/index.html
71. Legislative Council Panel on Housing (2020). Minutes of a meeting on 6 January (pp. 7–8). https://www.legco.gov.hk/yr19-20/english/panels/hg/minutes/hg20200106.pdf

with expectations, whereas public housing targets have not been achieved.[72] A task force set up to examine the problem found that there was a shortfall in land for all purposes of about 1,200 hectares and recommended that this could be found in the short-term by redeveloping brownfield sites, resuming control over private agricultural land in the New Territories and taking over 32 hectares of the Fanling golf course.[73] In the longer term, it recommended, *inter alia*, land reclamation. The government accepted the recommendations but has still to decide on the uses to which the land will be put.[74] Unless it confronts the developers, the shortage of public rental housing and the astronomical price of private sector housing seem likely to continue.[75]

Implementation has been equally problematic in other policymaking areas. In health care, the traditional value, still reiterated by the government, is that "no one is denied adequate medical treatment due to lack of means".[76] The problem for the government is that it cannot afford to pay for this generous policy. If it were to introduce a full "user-pays" health care system or to tax more affluent Hong Kongers to pay for the system, it would face political difficulties and perhaps major conflict. The present system provides free access for some services but requires the patient to pay for treatment of a wide range of illnesses that many cannot afford. Government funding has failed to match public demand, staff shortages have not been properly addressed, the high attrition rate of doctors in the public sector to better-paid positions in the private sector continues, demand for hospital beds exceeds capacity and waiting times for surgery and appointments have skyrocketed.[77]

On welfare policy, the problem has been that inequalities in the society have been increasing and that the "wealth gap" has been growing.[78] Despite the reiteration of the traditional value that the government will supply a "safety net" to provide for the most vulnerable, more people have been dropping below the poverty line and welfare provision has been insufficient to prevent this. In 2019, 1.4 million people, 21.4% of the population, were living in poverty.[79] The government attributed the problem to the ageing demographic. But its long-standing premise that

---

72. Yau & Siu (2016, 20 December) op. cit.
73. Task Force on Land Supply (2018). *Striving for multi-pronged land supply: Report of the Task Force on land supply* (p. 14). https://www.devb.gov.hk/filemanager/en/content_1171/Report%20(Eng).pdf
74. Legislative Council Brief (2019). Government's response to the report of the Task Force on land supply. https://www.devb.gov.hk/filemanager/en/content_1051/LegCo_Brief_TFLS_Report.pdf
75. Chun, J. (2020). A Rawlsian model for land justice in Hong Kong. In B. Yung & K. P. Yu (Eds.), *Land and housing controversies in Hong Kong: Perspectives of justice and social values* (pp. 63–81). Singapore: Springer.
76. Food and Health Bureau (2020). Overview of the health care system in Hong Kong. https://www.gov.hk/en/residents/health/hosp/overview.htm
77. Cheung, E., & Tsang, E. (2019, 26 February). Hong Kong's health system is teetering. What is wrong with it, what can be done to fix it and will the budget provide some answers? *SCMP*. https://www.scmp.com/news/hong-kong/health-environment/article/2187630/hong-kongs-health-care-system-teetering-brink; Hansard, 13 November 2019, 1504–1513; Schoeb, V. (2016). Healthcare service in Hong Kong and its challenges. *China Perspectives*, 4, 51–58.
78. Oxfam (2018) op. cit.
79. Hong Kong Government (2020, 23 December). Poverty rate slightly increases. https://www.news.gov.hk/eng/2020/12/20201223/20201223_175016_820.html

welfare should be provided to return able recipients to work as soon as possible had been devised in the 1950s when the population was predominantly young. By the time Leung took office in 2012, the social security measures and pension provisions were inadequate to meet the needs of the growing number of elderly, most of whom could not expect to be re-employed. The government did fund the CSSA Scheme and recognised that this helped to lift people out of poverty, but provision was insufficient.[80] Research also showed that the availability of public rental housing was an important factor in enabling the elderly to avoid poverty.[81] But government efforts to resolve the problem have generally been ineffectual. The Commission on Poverty has had little success if the growing numbers of those below the poverty line are any indicator. The fundamental problem has not been addressed.

In 2019, the government admitted its failings in social policy implementation and attributed the protests to that failure. It described the protests as a "social incident" and said that it would remedy its policy shortcomings. Two points are important. First, it is not clear that policy failures are causally linked to the protests. The protesters did not focus their demands on social policy reform; they wanted democratic change and the protection of civil liberties. Second, although the government steadfastly took the view that the protests were a "social incident", it was not clear what this meant. The Chief Secretary for Administration said that there was a need to study the protests "to obtain an understanding of the deep-seated problems in society".[82] Yet the government still claimed credit for $20 billion of "helping measures" that were intended to alleviate problems. These included tax relief and targeted measures for industries and an increase in the child allowance intended to help reduce the "wealth gap".[83] Even if there was a link between inequalities, lack of social mobility for young people, social policy failures and the protests, the government's remedial measures showed a disconnection between what young people on the streets might have been complaining about and a meaningful effort to resolve their grievances. The government was making policy in symbolic mode: identify what you think is the problem (even if it isn't) and then introduce non-controversial incremental measures that may have little to do with the problem that you have identified.

Symbolic policymaking has developed as a mode of implementation because key groups cannot be alienated. Pro-Beijing and business groups provide support for a weak government that has no mandate and doubts its capacity to deal with the basic problems afflicting social policy. Even with the coercive powers provided by the national security law, implementation ultimately depends on those at the interface and the public carrying out decisions reached at the centre. Many professionals

---

80. Ibid.
81. Legislative Council Secretariat Research Office (2020). *The 2020–21 budget* (pp. 5–6). https://www.legco.gov.hk/research-publications/english/1920rb01-the-2020-2021-budget-20200403-e.pdf
82. Hansard, 13 November 2019, 1613.
83. Ibid., 1614.

have called for solutions that would require much more government expenditure to ameliorate the present perilous situations in public housing, health care, and welfare. In its current financial state, the government feels unable to provide such funding unless it cuts back significantly in policy areas to which the Chinese government is committed or redirects its expenditure from measures, such as cash handouts and the greatly increased police budget, that do little to improve social policy outputs. Symbolic policy implementation involves a reaffirmation of traditional values that promise a better world. Yet the gap between what is promised and what is likely to be attained seems set to grow. The means are inadequate and insufficiently related to the objectives.

Displacement

It should not be supposed from the preceding analysis that the Hong Kong government has no capacity to implement policy. Rather, while its capacity to implement policy in some areas is severely constrained, under some circumstances it does implement policy. Two conditions must be present. Either the decision or policy is seen to be easily implemented without the prospect of contention or the Chinese government requires that the Hong Kong government take action. Displacement is a style of policy implementation rather than a method. Its primary characteristic is that it privileges harmony or the absence of dissent above the rational calculation of opportunity cost.

Cash handouts are a prime example of the first condition. The Hong Kong government thought that a cash handout would not be contentious and would relieve the financial burden that people were suffering as a consequence of the protests and COVID-19. In his 2020 budget, the Financial Secretary announced a handout of $10,000 per resident at a cost of $71 billion and said that about seven million people were expected to benefit.[84] He also provided approximately $6 billion for a month's payment to CSSA recipients and a month's rent for lower-income public housing tenants.[85] Although political parties applauded the cash handout, some democrats saw it as the government's attempt to deflect public anger against the greatly increased police budget and the intention to introduce national security laws.[86] The other issue is opportunity cost: whether $71 billion might have been used in a more productive way to address pressing problems in housing, health, and welfare. The handout was disbursed to some people who did not need it, was not guaranteed to stimulate the economy as intended, and did not represent an investment in the

---

84. Financial Secretary (2020). *The 2020–21 budget* (para 36). https://www.budget.gov.hk/2020/eng/budget09.html
85. Ibid., para 33c, d.
86. Huang, C. (2020, 27 February). HK finance chief Paul Chan criticised for unfair handouts, police funding. *The Straits Times*. https://www.straitstimes.com/asia/east-asia/hong-kong-finance-chief-criticised-for-unfair-handouts-police-funding. Kwok, B. (2020, 24 June). Why HK$10000 isn't good enough. *ejinsight*. https://www.ejinsight.com/eji/article/id/2502658/20200624-Why-HK$10,000-isn%E2%80%99t-good-enough

future. Rather, it was a temporary solution to what the government thought was a problem. It did "nothing to bring enough public housing online, nothing to increase wages or job creation, nothing to cap rents".[87]

The Hong Kong government has little option but to implement Chinese government-backed policies. In the case of the Extradition Bill and the national security law in 2003, it did withdraw the bills, but the insistence of the Mainland government eventually meant that national security laws were enacted by the Chinese government itself. Other strongly backed Mainland government initiatives have been funded and implemented by the Hong Kong government. These include the high-speed rail link and the HMZB, the Belt and Road Initiative, and commitment to innovation policies in collaboration with cross-border Mainland organisations. Implementation of some projects has proved difficult due to political and legal delays, technical problems, and vague objectives contributing to substantial cost overruns. The high-speed rail link and the HMZB had specific objectives but were obstructed by legal challenges and vociferously opposed by protesters (see pp. 312–315). The Belt and Road Initiative and innovation policies have much vaguer objectives. The government argued that they would have long-term benefits and that innovation policies would transform southern China into an innovation hub.

Innovation policy in Hong Kong dates from the beginning of the Tung administration. From the outset, the government's formulation of the policy was rhetorical rather than strictly based on the innovation systems conceptual approach on which it was supposedly founded.[88] There were immediate problems with the statutory bodies and government companies that were intended to implement the policy. Cyberport, which was to fund and house technology start-up companies, had difficulty in finding suitable tenants.[89] The Applied Science and Technology Research Institute Company, whose projects were supposed to produce cutting-edge developments, was investigated by the Director of Audit, who found that over half of its 21 projects had returns of 5% or less and that its staff were overpaid.[90]

The government nonetheless has persisted with its innovation policy. Innovation policy has the advantage that it can be presented as government action to stimulate the economy. In 2019, for example, following very soon after the release of the Mainland government's outline plan for the Greater Bay area,[91] the Financial Secretary provided $50 billion for innovation and technology, arguing that it would bring "huge economic benefits for Hong Kong" from the generation and commercialisation of intellectual property and the creation of quality employment and by

---

87. Pesek, W. (2020, 2 March). Hong Kong's cash handouts ignore city's true problems. *Nikkei Asia*. https://asia.nikkei.com/Opinion/Hong-Kong-s-cash-handouts-ignore-city-s-true-problems
88. Sharif, N. (2010). Rhetoric of innovation policy making in Hong Kong using the innovation systems conceptual approach. *Science, Technology and Human Values*, 35(3), 408–434.
89. Ostrov, B. C. (2002). Hong Kong's Cyberport. *The Independent Review*, 7(2), 221–236.
90. Director of Audit (2007). *Report No. 48, Chapter 2* (p. 6). https://www.aud.gov.hk/pdf_e/e48ch02_sum.pdf
91. Government of the People's Republic of China (2019). *Outline development plan for the Guangdong-Hong Kong-Macao Greater Bay Area*. www.bayarea.gov.hk/filemanager/en/share/pdf/Outline_Development_Plan.pdf

enabling people to live more comfortably.[92] The government claims that the benefits of the policy will not be clear until it is fully implemented at some time in the indefinite future. In turbulent times, innovation policy is less likely to attract political criticism than would attempts to resolve more controversial policy problems. There was relatively little criticism of the Financial Secretary's decision to provide $50 billion for innovation and technology in 2019. Most critics focused on the vague objectives of the policy rather than on possible alternative ways of spending $50 billion. In that sense, the government was successful in following a displacement strategy; few questions were asked about opportunity cost and critical issues in housing, health, and welfare were left unattended.

Each of the five styles of policy implementation—top-down, rational/consultative, incremental, symbolic, and displacement—can be employed in combination with others and with each or all of the policy instruments that we have examined. There is no one best way to implement policy. In turbulent times, pragmatic considerations take priority and whatever works will tend to be adopted. There is much to be said for such an approach, but it is necessarily constrained by certain conditions. The government must first identify the problem and then commit itself to resolve or alleviate it. In the examples that we have considered, the Hong Kong government has quite often misidentified the problem or consigned it to the "too hard" basket or tried to deflect public attention from the central issue using symbolic policymaking or displacement to policies that are more easily implemented. The consequence has been that many other policies have reverted to incrementalism, leading to detrimental policy drift and a worsening of the situation. There is no doubt that the government has faced formidable obstacles from public pressures and the Mainland government on which policies may or may not be implemented. But, as a consequence of its failures, its governance and credibility have been called into question and the quality of life of its citizens has deteriorated.

Evaluation

If policy is carried out according to the intentions of the policymakers, is it necessarily a success? Comparing results with goals is usually an important part of evaluation, but it is not the only dimension.[93] A policy may be implemented successfully from the standpoint of the government but may still fail to meet the needs of those who are affected by it. To evaluate policy, then, we need to look at it from different perspectives. In this section, we consider three different types of evaluating policy outputs and outcomes: that of the government; that of the Audit Commission, the independent body which monitors public accounts and conducts "value for money" studies; and that of the population, expressed through surveys.

---

92. Financial Secretary (2019). *The 2019–20 budget* (para 64). https://www.budget.gov.hk/2019/eng/budget14.html
93. Vedung, E. (1997). *Public policy and program evaluation* (Ch. 1). New Brunswick, NJ: Transaction.

Government's Assessment of Its Policy Implementation

An important feature of formal evaluation is reporting actual performance against the targets that have been set. The post-handover government committed itself to managing by results and subscribed to the hoary (but inaccurate) old cliché that "what gets measured gets done", stressing quantification of outputs as the basis for evaluation. The major reporting mechanism on whether the government has achieved its policy goals is the report by the Controlling Officer of the bureau or department in the annual estimates which accompany the budget. There are guidelines issued by the Financial Services and Treasury Bureau that prescribe what a Controlling Officer may or may not include in the report. They include whether programmes have met their targets and whether operational objectives have been achieved; the effectiveness of operations; and the determination of key performance measures which best indicate the quality, economy, efficiency, and effectiveness of their programmes.[94] In 2005, the Audit Commission undertook a comprehensive study of bureaus and departments to see whether these guidelines had been met.[95] It found that only 30% of performance measures concentrated on targets while 70% were indicators that were not quantifiable.[96] Further, only 11% were concerned with effectiveness, the remainder dealing with workload, service quality, or efficiency.[97] The commission recommended that bureaus and departments should focus on setting targets and improving performance measures.[98]

On grounds of accountability and assessing whether bureaus and departments have achieved their goals, these are important recommendations. Yet, by 2020, little progress had been made in improving performance measures. In the 2020 budget estimates, the targets that most departments set were "soft" and relatively easily attained. Indicators were frequently either not quantifiable or not directly related to the policy goal.[99] The Environmental Protection Department, for example, has a good story to tell about its efforts to improve the quality of living. But it is not possible to obtain much information relevant to evaluation from its performance measures. The department's estimates provide a picture of what it is doing, but the main message is that the targets for previous years, as with all other Hong Kong government departments, have been achieved or very nearly achieved. The Air Quality Health Index, for example, is set at an hourly target of below 7 (low or moderate risk to health), but many parts of Hong Kong are usually below that figure.[100] The target is easily reached but could be lowered, which might give a better picture of the

---

94. Director of Audit (2005). *Report No. 45, Chapter 6* (p. 8). Hong Kong: Government Logistics Department. https://www.aud.gov.hk/pdf_e/e45ch06.pdf
95. Ibid.
96. Ibid., p. 10.
97. Ibid., p. 16.
98. Ibid., p. 36.
99. Financial Secretary (2020). *The 2020–21 budget estimates.* https://www.budget.gov.hk/2020/eng/estimates.html
100. Ibid., p. 211.

department's progress to improving air quality over time. Air pollution has slowly improved, but it is still estimated to be much higher than that of many other world cities and its worst effects in Hong Kong are correlated with areas of social deprivation.[101] The government is not, of course, unbiased when it undertakes assessments of its own performance and wants to paint a positive picture. But the Director of Audit's critical observations in 2005 still seem relevant to its treatment of performance measures.[102]

There are three major problems in improving reporting for evaluation purposes. First, in evaluating whether policy has been successfully implemented, the ultimate test is whether the intended outcome has been achieved. A difficulty, common to many policies, is in developing qualitative measures. It is possible, for example, to calculate the number of secondary school graduates quite precisely but not so easy to make a quantitative judgement on the quality of education that they have received. Second, the Audit Commission, in its review of government performance measures, raised the issue of the reliability of the information on which they were based. In many departments, there is no means of verifying whether the figures are accurate.[103] What is being measured is not necessarily being done. Finally, simple quantification of whether a goal has been achieved or not tells us very little about its impact on people, its relative importance in government's priorities, whether the aims were completely or only partially realised or whether government was simply formally reporting completion, what problems were encountered, and whether residual or contingent problems still needed attention. Policy implementation is a complex business in which many of the outcomes are often unintended, but this larger picture is largely absent from the government's efforts to evaluate its work.

The Audit Commission

The Audit Commission has two functions. It reports each year to the Legislative Council on the accounts of the Hong Kong government ("regularity" audits) and it conducts "value for money" studies to determine whether the government is spending money wisely. Strictly speaking, the Direct of Audit is not entitled to "comment on policy decisions of the Executive and Legislative Councils except their effect on the public purse".[104] The wide range of other responsibilities that the commission has under the *Audit Ordinance* and rules agreed with the Legislative Council in February 1998 means that the distinction between whether the Director of Audit is or is not commenting on policy is very finely drawn. Under the rules agreed with

---

101. Li, V. O. K., Yang, H., Lam, J. C. K., Zhu, Y., & Bacon-Shone, J. (2018). Air pollution and environmental injustice: Are the socially deprived exposed to more PM2.5 pollution in Hong Kong? *Environmental Science and Policy*, 80, 53–61.
102. Director of Audit (2005) op. cit.
103. Ibid., Part 3.
104. Audit Commission (2020). About us. https://www.aud.gov.hk/eng/aboutus/about_valm.htm

the Legislative Council, the Director of Audit is entitled to consider the authority under which the policy objectives have been determined, whether there are satisfactory arrangements for considering alternative options in implementation, whether goals have been implemented, whether there is any conflict between policy aims and objectives or between the means chosen to implement them, and whether aims and objectives have been translated into operational targets and performance measures.[105] In exercising these functions, the commission has little option but to provide at least implicit commentary on the success or failure of government policies.

In 2018, for example, the Audit Commission investigated the issue of integrated education. Integrated education is based on the principle that all educational establishments should provide equal education opportunities, including those for children with special education needs.[106] The commission found that there were weaknesses in policy implementation and made many different recommendations to improve service delivery. Some recommendations, such as the identification and admission of special needs students, might be seen as suggestions for managerial or administrative improvements, but other recommendations called for additional resources and enhanced training and professional support.[107] The implicit message was that the special needs education programme probably required an overhaul and perhaps a complete reassessment.

The Audit Commission plays an invaluable role in identifying problems of inefficiency and unnecessary expenditure in public policies. Over the years, it has saved the government billions of dollars in poorly implemented programmes. Yet the commission operates under important constraints. It can only draw attention to problems after they have occurred or, occasionally, to future predictions. It is also restricted to comments on particular programmes rather than to making wider recommendations on policy formulation. And it cannot comment on the political factors that are often at the root of the problems. Nonetheless, preserving its independence is vital to policy evaluation. The commission may sometimes be a thorn in the side of the administration, drawing attention to its inadequacies, but the benefits from its reports far outweigh the political costs.

Surveys

Public reactions to the impact of government policies are most commonly assessed by surveys. The government itself, through the Home Affairs Bureau, previously conducted periodic surveys, but it ceased to publish those reports after high levels of dissatisfaction were recorded in 2003.[108] Since 2009, the Efficiency Unit (later

---

105. Ibid.
106. Director of Audit (2018). *Report No 70, Chapter 3: Education Bureau: integrated education* (p. 1). https://www.aud.gov.hk/pdf_e/e70ch03.pdf
107. Ibid., p. 10.
108. Home Affairs Bureau (2003). *Report of the HAB Telephone Survey—August 2003*. https://www.hab.gov.hk/file_manager/en/documents/references/telephone_opinion_survey/ReportAug03E.pdf

the Efficiency Office) has tried to address the issue by employing an independent company to conduct surveys. It not clear what questions the survey asks, but the data are used to compile the annual Hong Kong Government Service Excellence Index. In 2018/2019, the satisfaction rate was 62.9%, which was the lowest figure for the previous decade and seems to contradict HKUPOP/PORI findings that show a much lower satisfaction rate.[109] The Census and Statistics Department also produces thematic surveys on topics such as health and housing. While the purpose of the department's surveys is not to evaluate policy, they may draw attention to areas that need attention or where existing provision or regulation is inadequate. The department's reports on the poverty situation and on conditions in subdivided housing units provide a platform for action.[110] Many government departments and statutory bodies conduct regular customer satisfaction surveys, but they have an interest in generating favourable results, particularly if they relate to the budgetary estimates, and consequently often fail to ask critical questions.

Some private organisations also conduct polls that relate to public policy evaluation. A polling organisation, the Public Opinion Research Institute (PORI), previously HKUPOP, has used telephone surveys of between 1,000 and 2,000 respondents to report levels of satisfaction with government performance (see Chapter 11, Figure 11.1) and to discern public attitudes on policies such as climate change and welfare provision. Some think tanks, such as the Bauhinia Foundation and the Our Hong Kong Foundation, have also commissioned surveys on issues of concern but their intention has usually been more towards advocating new policies rather than evaluating public attitudes towards existing policies.

An approach that matches results against goals, analyses costs against benefits, and asks people to report their satisfaction with outputs and outcomes probably offers the best prospect of obtaining an accurate picture of the effects of policy implementation. In Hong Kong, the weaknesses of evaluation have been: too great a reliance on formal evaluation, an Audit Commission, which, while it has performed its duties admirably, has limited resources, and official attempts to capture public attitudes that seem primarily designed to present the government in a favourable light. The Ombudsman has suggested that evaluation could be improved if political leaders and civil servants asked themselves three questions during the policy formulation and implementation process: "Is there adequate consultation with affected individuals and groups *all the way* before programme initiatives are planned, developed, modified where necessary, and implemented? Is this consultation done in a meaningful and timely way? Is the way in which the final decision will be made clear

---

109. Efficiency Office (2020). Hong Kong Government Service Index. https://www.effo.gov.hk/en/our-work/management-consultancy/performance-measurement.html
110. Census and Statistics Department (2020). *Hong Kong poverty situation report.* https://www.censtatd.gov.hk/en/EIndexbySubject.html?pcode=B9XX0005&scode=461; Census and Statistics Department (2016). *Housing conditions of sub-divided units in Hong Kong.* Thematic Household Survey Report No. 60. https://www.censtatd.gov.hk/en/EIndexbySubject.html?pcode=B1130201&scode=453

from the outset to the affected persons?"[111] It seems unlikely that such questions are often asked. And, although the questions might help to improve performance and result in more positive public reactions to policy implementation, they do not address what is often the fundamental cause of difficulties: the political tensions between the government and civil society.

Conclusions

Policy implementation has changed considerably since the handover. Although top-down implementation through the hierarchy still characterises some policies, many others are too complex and have too many stakeholders to allow the government to succeed with those methods. Although the post-handover government has tried to develop a rational and more consultative approach, the inability to confront fundamental problems in a fractious polity has meant that many policies have become symbolic and not fully implemented or have been displaced into areas where there is less opposition. The rhetoric of policy—the affirmation of previous values arrived at consensually—has become more significant than the resolution of pressing problems. While that may change with the regime in place since July 2020, successful policy implementation depends ultimately on public acceptance of outcomes and outputs.

The choice of policy instruments has remained largely unchanged although there have been experiments with other means of delivering goods and services. Immediately after the handover, there was a greater reliance on statutory bodies, NGOs, and the private sector. Since 2007, the government has recentralised, signalled by the expansion of the civil service establishment, and measures taken to ensure that service providers, such as subvented organisations, are firmly under government control. Government departments remain the most important means of implementing policies. Their approach is conditioned by caution and incrementalism within which framework they employ a mixture of carrots, sticks, and sermons to try to attain their objectives.

The evaluation of policies around the world has changed in character over the past three decades. Most governments have shifted their focus to attempts to assess outputs and outcomes. The Hong Kong government is now more interested in evaluating its performance than it once was and it expends some effort in assessing whether it is meeting its policy objectives. But this assessment tends to be quantitative and does not always reflect either the Director of Audit's judgements about the efficiency and cost-effectiveness of government programmes or the more qualitative views of Hong Kong citizens. The gap between these formal quantitative evaluations and those that involve the view of the stakeholders is illustrative of the

---

111. Office of the Ombudsman (2001). *Administrative fairness checklist* (3rd ed., p. 5). Hong Kong: Printing Department. My italics.

general malaise affecting policy implementation. The government may say that it has achieved its objectives and that it deserves the support of the public because of its efforts. But if there are high levels of dissatisfaction with the performance of the government and its policies, then formal success in achieving policy objectives is of little relevance. The gridlock in policy implementation in post-1997 Hong Kong is a reflection of the friction between the government and society.

10
The Chinese Government's Influence on Policy

The Chinese government is unquestionably the major influence on Hong Kong policy formulation and implementation. In some areas, such as defence, foreign affairs, national security (broadly interpreted), and constitutional affairs, it makes policy for Hong Kong. In others, such as cross-border infrastructural projects and innovation policies, the Hong Kong government has little alternative but to implement instructions from Beijing. For the remaining policies, the extent of the Hong Kong government's autonomy varies considerably, depending on the political importance of the issue. Even if Beijing permits autonomous Hong Kong government decisions in some policy areas, the Chinese government's Liaison Office in Hong Kong and its wide network of support groups may have their own ideas about what action should be taken. The effect of pressure at all levels has been to reduce the "high degree of autonomy" of the Hong Kong government promised in the Basic Law to little more than drafting proposals that require the consent of the Chinese government or the Liaison Office or, on occasion, key pro-Beijing groups in business and the professions. Each of these groups may exercise, or attempt to exercise, a veto over the proposal or suggest an alternative approach. When the decision is finally taken, the Hong Kong government is left with the often-difficult task of implementing an agreement reached directly with the Chinese government or with the Liaison Office and its support groups in Hong Kong.

All principal officials have to be endorsed by the Chinese government and serve in roles that may require them to formulate and implement policies according to the wishes of the central government. Pro-Beijing groups in Hong Kong may also make their views known in many different forums: through their appointment to the Executive Council, in the Legislative Council, and through the pro-Beijing media and united front organisations, for example. The pro-Beijing groups do not always speak for the same interests. In the Legislative Council, for example, there are representatives of a pro-Beijing political party, the Democratic Alliance for Betterment and Progress of Hong Kong (DAB), a union, the Hong Kong Federation of Trade Unions (HKFTU), and various Beijing-affiliated business organisations. If the central government or the Liaison Office in Hong Kong has no firm stance on an issue, divergent positions may be expressed. If there is strong direction from the

Mainland government or the Liaison Office, then these groups unite in support of the Hong Kong government, or one of its policies, and have previously acted as a counter-force to democratic politicians in the legislature or protesters on the streets.

In this chapter, the Chinese government's evolving influence on Hong Kong policy is examined in its historical context and in specific policy areas:

- building support for Mainland government policies in Hong Kong;
- social integration, particularly immigration and national education policies;
- economic integration, the Closer Economic Partnership Agreement (CEPA), infrastructural development, Belt and Road Initiative and innovation policies; and
- national security and constitutional issues.

These policy areas should be seen as related to each other as part of the Chinese government's strategy for integrating Hong Kong into the Mainland. The strategy has changed at times, but it remains the most important factor influencing policy formation and implementation in Hong Kong.

Building Support for the Chinese Government in Hong Kong: The Transitional Period, 1984–1997

After the signing of the Sino-British agreement in 1984, the Chinese government had achieved its primary objective of securing the return of Hong Kong to China. But it was also faced with the task of reassuring a nervous public of the viability of the agreement and of building support for its intended relationship with the HKSAR and the future integration of Hong Kong into China.[1] Formally, the drafting of the Basic Law was supposed to provide reassurance that "one country, two systems" and the guarantees on civil liberties contained in the Sino-British agreement would be fully respected. Yet even at this stage there were signs of a serious rift over the issue of democracy. When the leading democrats left the drafting committee and were subsequently expelled from it, the scene was set for continuing conflict over democracy and constitutional issues.

Immediately after the agreement was signed, the Chinese Communist Party set about the task of increasing its presence and strengthening its united front efforts in Hong Kong. The party had a branch in Hong Kong from 1947 and began supervising the activities of left-wing organisations from the 1950s onwards under the formal auspices of the New China News Agency.[2] After 1984, the structure put in place was much more comprehensive and was aimed at dealing with the growing challenge of

---

1. Wong, M. F. (1997). *China's resumption of sovereignty over Hong Kong*. Hong Kong: David C. Lam Institute for East-West Studies, Hong Kong Baptist University.
2. Burns, J. P. (1990). The structure of communist party control in Hong Kong. *Asian Survey, 30*(80), 748–765; Chu, C. Y. Y. (2011). The long history of united front activity in Hong Kong. *The Hong Kong Journal*. https://carnegieendowment.org/hkjournal/PDF/2011_fall/5.pdf

democrats in Hong Kong. The democrats did well in the 1991 Legislative Council elections, which were the first to permit some directly elected seats, and there were calls for constitutional change to introduce more democratic elections to the legislature. The last British Governor, Chris Patten, introduced some liberalising electoral reforms for the 1995 elections which were expected to result in a "through road" after the resumption of Chinese sovereignty. The Chinese government, however, rejected the reforms and instead set up a Provisional Legislative Council in 1997 that excluded the democrats.

To counter democratic claims, the Chinese government endorsed the creation of a political party, the DAB, in 1992.[3] The DAB's primary purpose was to provide support for the Chinese government. It has never had well-articulated policy goals of its own or a distinct policy direction. It was designed as a peak organisation to bring together pro-Beijing groups from across the economic spectrum and to assist in promoting the Communist Party's united front work in Hong Kong.[4] It was established in close alliance with the HKFTU, which in 1992 represented 36.5% of the trade union members in Hong Kong.[5]

During the transitional period, the Chinese government sought to woo Hong Kong business and moved to oust the traditional British *hongs*.[6] Business had provided solid support for the Hong Kong government under colonialism but, with a new regime in the offing, many in business chose to switch sides.[7] Most, but not all, believed that their future lay in good relations with mainland China and with the willingness of its government to continue to permit the capitalist system promised in the Basic Law. After 1978, and the opening up of China, the enormous expansion of business opportunities in the Pearl River Delta (PRD) (later called the Greater Bay Area) led many Hong Kong companies to establish businesses across the border.[8] The Chinese government also wanted to ensure that Mainland companies had a presence in the territory, which began to list on the Hong Kong Stock Exchange (HKEx) and to buy property along the waterfront.[9]

The success of the Chinese government's efforts to court Hong Kong business may be judged by the numbers who were recruited as members of the National

---

3. Leung, J. Y. H. (1999). *State and society: The emergence and marginalization of political parties in Hong Kong* (pp. 255–258) [Unpublished doctoral thesis]. The University of Hong Kong.
4. Lo, S. H. H., Hung, S. C. F., & Loo, J. H. C. (2019). The Democratic Alliance for the Betterment and Progress of Hong Kong as flagship for united front work. In Lo, S. S. H., Hung, S. C. F., & Loo, J. H. C. (Eds.), *China's new united front work in Hong Kong: Penetrative politics and its implications* (pp. 43–75). London: Palgrave Macmillan.
5. Ibid., p. 257.
6. Chu, C. Y. Y. (2010). *Chinese communists and Hong Kong capitalists* (pp. 95–112). New York: Palgrave Macmillan.
7. Goodstadt, L. F. (2005). *Uneasy partners: The conflict between public interest and private profit in Hong Kong* (pp. 121–126, 133). Hong Kong: Hong Kong University Press.
8. Yang, C. (2004). From market-led to institution-based economic integration: The case of the Pearl River Delta and Hong Kong. *Issues and Studies*, 4(2), 79–118.
9. Wang-Kaeding, H., & Kaeding, M. P. (2019). Red capital in Hong Kong. *Asian Education and Development Studies*, 8(2), 149–160.

People's Congress and the Chinese People's Consultative Committee and other committees set up with the specific task of implementing the transition to Chinese sovereignty. Of the 1,590 representatives on all committees, business and professional appointments accounted for 62%, the remainder drawn from political activists and community leaders.[10] The first Chief Executive, Tung Chee Hwa, was a businessman chosen and endorsed by the Chinese government but selected by a 400-member Hong Kong committee in which business was strongly represented.[11]

The Post-handover Period

In the post-handover period, there was a gradual acceleration of the influence of the Chinese government and the Communist Party on politics, public policy, and society in Hong Kong. Business had become more dependent on the good will of the Chinese government and consequently less politically powerful than it was before the handover. The passage of the national security law in June 2020 and the role of Mainland authorities in administering the law has meant that the impact of the Chinese government and its intentions for the HKSAR has been felt even more widely within the Hong Kong government and in society. In the following sections, the Chinese government and the Communist Party's efforts to win the hearts and minds of the Hong Kong people through the Liaison Office, the DAB, the HKFTU, and united front groups are described and analysed.

The Liaison Office

In 2000, the Chinese government set up a Liaison Office in Hong Kong to take over the functions of the New China News Agency. It is headed by a senior party official and reports to the Hong Kong and Macau Affairs Office in Beijing. Formally, it has a role in promoting educational and cultural coordination and exchanges, helping PRC government departments manage their affairs in Hong Kong, liaising with the People's Liberation Army garrison, and implementing central government directives in Hong Kong. In practice, it has a much larger remit and operates as the Chinese government's principal representative organisation in Hong Kong. In playing that role, it appears to exercise some degree of discretion over how best to implement the Mainland government's views on how Hong Kong should be run. The Liaison Office works closely with the DAB, pro-Beijing business groups, and some legislators representing the professions. In 2008, it expanded the number of bureaus within the Office from nine to 25, organised geographically to oversee Legislative and District Council constituencies.[12] It has continued and deepened

---

10. Goodstadt, L. F. (2000). China and the selection of Hong Kong's post-colonial political elite. *The China Quarterly, 163,* 721–741.
11. Chu (2010) op. cit., pp. 112–126.
12. Cheng, E. W. (2020). United front work and mechanisms of countermobilization in Hong Kong. *The China Journal, 83*(1), 1–33.

the supervision of united front work through the Hong Kong and Macau Works Committee which is part of the office. It controls some of the Mainland media in Hong Kong, including the *Wen Wei Po, Ta Kung Pao,* and *Hong Kong Commercial Daily* newspapers,[13] and manages its own extensive property investments in the HKSAR. It maintains close personal contact with leading business people and with senior Hong Kong government officials on a wide range of issues.[14] Youth exchanges with China, in which a Liaison Office official usually takes part, have been seen as an important element of its work.[15] Since the beginning of 2020 and the subsequent enactment of the national security law, the Liaison Office has become the pivotal institution in Hong Kong, exercising control over security matters but also over governance and other policy issues.

The DAB

The Liaison Office has a close relationship with the DAB and, directly or indirectly, helps to fund the party, which is much better resourced than all other Hong Kong political parties combined. In 2016, the party had a budget of $124 million, enabling it to provide extensive support for electoral activities, community gatherings, conferences, national events, and festivals.[16] It sustains a large permanent organisation with more than 200 local branches, which, together with affiliated organisations, offers "cradle to grave" daily activities.[17] It has an evident influence on the Hong Kong government and benefits from appointments to the Executive Council, from the selection of party members as principal officials and members of advisory boards, and from the Liaison Office's efforts to raise money from business on its behalf. At a fundraising dinner in 2016, for example, reportedly attended by Carrie Lam, then Chief Secretary for Administration, the Financial Secretary and the Secretary for Security, a piece of calligraphy by the Director of the Liaison Office was auctioned to an entrepreneur for $18 million with the proceeds going to the party.[18]

---

13. Hong Kong Journalists Association (2020). *Annual report: Freedom in danger* (p. 13). https://www.ifj.org/fileadmin/user_upload/HKJA_Annual_Report_2020_English.pdf; see also Chan, C. K. (2021). China's influence on the Hong Kong media: Subduing press freedom. In B. C. H. Fong, J. M. Wu, & A. J. Nathan (Eds.), *China's influence and the center-periphery tug of war in Hong Kong, Taiwan and the Indo-Pacific*. London: Routledge.
14. Fong, B. C. H. (2014). The partnership between the Chinese government and the Hong Kong's capitalist class: Implications for HKSAR governance. *The China Quarterly, 217,* 195–220; Lee, E. W. Y. (2020). United front, clientelism and indirect rule: Theorizing the role of the "Liaison Office" in Hong Kong. *Journal of Contemporary China, 29*(125), 763–775; Schmidt, B. (2020, 17 August). The publishing empire helping silence dissent in Hong Kong. *Bloomberg.* https://www.bloomberg.com/news/features/2020-08-17/the-publishing-empire-helping-china-silence-dissent-in-hong-kong
15. Lam, W. M., & Lam, K. C. Y. (2013). China's united front work in civil society: The case of Hong Kong. *International Journal of China Studies, 4*(3), 301–325.
16. Ibid.
17. Cheng (2020) op. cit.
18. Ng, E. (2016, 22 November). Pro-Beijing DAB party raises tens of millions of dollars at dinner attended by top officials. *HKFP.* https://hongkongfp.com/2016/11/22/pro-beijing-dab-party-raises-tens-millions-dollars-dinner-attended-top-officials/

In the post-handover period, the DAB was the largest single party in the Legislative Council. In 2020, it held 12 seats although its percentage of the vote declined from 28% in 2008 to under 17% in the 2016 election. On constitutional issues, however, until the disqualification of some democratic members in 2016, the lobby fell short of the two-thirds of members of the Legislative Council needed to secure changes. In the District Councils, the November 2019 elections resulted in a seismic upheaval when 17 of 18 councils changed from pro-Beijing to democratic control. DAB councillors lost 96 of their 117 seats and the HKFTU a further 21. The DAB reportedly turned to Mainland companies in Hong Kong to find jobs for those who had lost their seats.[19] The DAB chair, Starry Lee, offered her resignation but it was rejected. In the December 2021 "patriots-only" Legislative Council elections, the DAB won 19 seats, the HKFTU eight, and the Business and Professional Alliance seven. With other pro-establishment groups and independents, pro-Beijing members held 89 of the 90 seats.

The DAB is well entrenched within the higher echelons of the Hong Kong government and the party has been well served by the post-handover system. It had over 100 members of the 1,200-member Election Committee that selected the Chief Executive in 2017. The numbers theoretically dropped sharply after the democrats won the 2019 District Council elections and should have replaced DAB members on the Election Committee. However, once the national security law was promulgated, most democrats resigned or were removed from the councils. The Election Committee was re-constituted so that it was composed almost entirely of 1,500 pro-Beijing/pro-establishment members.

Many of the DAB's senior members hold or have previously held positions as Executive Councillors and as policy secretaries. In Carrie Lam's Executive Council, for example, three councillors were DAB members. There were also representatives of other pro-Beijing groups, but no democrats. Among policy secretaries appointed from the DAB, Elsie Leung Oi-sie served as Secretary for Justice from 1997 to 2005 and was a member of the preparatory committee that set up the party.[20] In April 2020, another member of the DAB, Christopher Hui, was appointed as Secretary for Financial Services and the Treasury. Since 2007, the Home Affairs portfolio has also been held by DAB members. The former chair of the party, Tsang Tok-sing, was in post until 2015 when he was replaced by a vice-chair, Lau Kong-wah. Caspar Tsui Ying-wai, a party member who had served as political assistant to the Secretary of Home Affairs between 2008 and 2017, was appointed as policy secretary in 2020. The Home Affairs Bureau is thought to be important for the DAB's efforts to build support for the pro-Beijing position because the bureau has wide-ranging responsibilities for civic education, youth policy, district and community relations, and

---

19. Chung, K. (2019, 30 December). Pro-Beijing party scrambling to find 200 jobs and restore morale of staff crushed in Hong Kong elections. *SCMP*. https://www.scmp.com/news/hong-kong/politics/article/3043831/pro-beijing-party-scrambling-find-200-jobs-and-restore
20. Leung (1999) op. cit., p. 258.

culture and the arts, and monitors the performance of many statutory bodies concerned with social affairs.[21] Judging by the Umbrella Movement, the 2019 protests, and the results of the 2019 District Council elections, control of the Home Affairs Bureau has not resulted in increased support for the pro-Beijing position among youth or electors.

Because the DAB does not have an independent policy stance and follows guidance provided by the Chinese and Hong Kong governments, its policies are expressed in very general terms. It favours such policies as "activating and stimulating the economy" and "opening new roads for young people by developing their potential" but there are few concrete proposals in its platform.[22] On specific issues, however, building its electoral support sometimes leads it to nudge the government to take policy action. In a meeting with the Chief Executive in 2020, for example, senior DAB officials submitted 31 proposals for inclusion in the annual policy address. Although the proposals were not disclosed in full, it was reported that the party wanted more cash handouts, a health code system to permit Hong Kong residents to see their relatives in China and vice-versa, a committee to review anti-epidemic work, and action on its claim that the courts were too lenient on protest-related cases.[23]

The DAB was deeply concerned by its loss of electoral support in the 2019 District Council elections and the prospect that it might lose more support in the Legislative Council election which was to be held in September 2020 but was subsequently postponed until December 2021, allegedly because of concerns about the pandemic.[24] But it still has a large base of support in community organisations across Hong Kong. With the Liaison Office as its guiding authority, the DAB at the district level supervises a formidable array of united front groups, associations, and hometown organisations that can be mobilised at election time and used to support pro-Beijing policy goals.[25] The HKFTU, claiming 420,000 members in 2020, is also important in providing material support for workers.[26] United front organisations operate, overtly or covertly, within many organisations in Hong Kong. In public organisations, such as universities, where there is a formal board or council, pro-Beijing figures are appointed to the governing body. In the New Territories, Kowloon, and Hong Kong Island, there are associations of societies comprising hundreds of organisations, often engaged in charitable work, and with

---

21. Home Affairs Bureau (2020). Policy responsibilities. https://www.hab.gov.hk/en/policy_responsibilities/policy.htm
22. Lo, Hung, & Loo (2019) op. cit., p. 69.
23. Huang, E. (2020, 10 September). DAB calls on gov't to roll out "down to earth" policies. *China Daily*. https://global.chinadaily.com.cn/a/202009/10/WS5f5a2984a310f55b25a81cf0.html
24. Vines, S. (2020, 31 July). The real reason for Hong Kong's election delay? The pro-China camp are scared to face the electorate. *HKFP*. https://hongkongfp.com/2020/07/31/the-reason-reason-for-hong-kongs-election-delay-the-pro-china-camp-are-scared-to-face-the-electorate/
25. Lo, Hung, & Loo (2019) op. cit.
26. Hong Kong Federation of Trade Unions (2020). Introduction. http://www.ftu.org.hk/en/about_us/introduction/

many hundreds of thousands of members. The associations have close links with the DAB and their members are mobilised for elections and pro-Beijing demonstrations. There are also hometown organisations, based on the members' place of origin in China. With the substantial growth in immigration from China to Hong Kong, membership in these organisations peaked in 2008 and 2009 and provided an important source of electoral support.[27]

The DAB's importance for Beijing is that it can express the Chinese government's views in public institutions and forums. Through its vast networks of connections sustained by patronage, it receives the reciprocal benefits of electoral support and the capacity to mobilise if policy issues are in question. Although the Chinese government has probably already expressed those same views privately to Hong Kong's political leaders, other than issues that are constitutionally within its jurisdiction, it was not able to make its specific policy positions known publicly without violating the "high degree of autonomy" and "one country, two systems" principles. Since 2020, the prelude to, and subsequent enactment of, the national security law has seen more public Chinese government interventions in Hong Kong affairs. The DAB remains useful, however, as the local means of legislating and supporting policies that may have been decided in China or developed by the Hong Kong government with Chinese government advice.

Business and Professionals

In the transitional period, the Chinese government's political contacts with business were mainly leading tycoons who were appointed to major Chinese committees preparing for the handover.[28] The Liberal Party, which represented business interests in the legislature, was increasingly supportive of the Chinese policies and critical of Patten's efforts to introduce more democratic elections in the last years of British rule.[29] After the handover, business was much more dependent on Mainland largesse than it had been before 1997. The rapid economic development of China meant that Hong Kong capital became relatively less important as foreign investment from elsewhere became more readily available. The expansion of united front organisations and the creation of the DAB also gave the Chinese government a local power base. The role that business had played in supporting Chinese government policy positions in the last few years of colonial rule was no longer necessary; the relationship was reversed as business sought help from the Chinese government to persuade the Hong Kong government to take desired measures.[30] Although the

---

27. Cheng (2020) op. cit.; Yuen, S. (2020). Native-place networks and political mobilization: The case of Hong Kong. *Modern China*, 47(5), 510–539.
28. Chan, D. S. W., & Pun, N. (2020). Economic power of the politically powerless in the 2019 Hong Kong pro-democracy movement. *Critical Asian Studies*, 52(1), 33–43.
29. Dimbleby, J. (1997). *The last governor: Chris Patten and the handover of Hong Kong* (p. 297). London: Little, Brown and Company.
30. Fong (2014) op. cit.

advice, philanthropy, and direct investments of business in China were still valued, they became increasingly less significant as Mainland companies assumed a domestic and sometimes global role.

Mainland companies began listing on the HKEx in the 1990s and have since become a major force in the HKSAR economy. Since 2013, 50% of companies listed on the HKEx have been from the Mainland.[31] A survey of 377 Mainland companies listed on the stock exchange between 1972 and 2017 found that 298 were state-owned enterprises (SOEs).[32] Not all of these, especially the local SOEs seeking capital investment in their provinces, necessarily act in tune with the Mainland government, but there are party cells in SOEs that presumably require compliance with what the government wants.[33] Mainland companies operating in Hong Kong have had an important impact on the property market and the price of housing. In 2012/2013, they held a relatively insignificant 5%–6% of land but, by 2015/2016, this had leapt to 29%, driving many local investors from the market.[34] The reason for the sudden increase was attributed to a Chinese government's clampdown on foreign property investment outside China. In 2020, the economic effect of the coronavirus led Mainland companies to sell some of their Hong Kong properties, leading to a sharp fall in housing prices.[35] The increasing integration of the Mainland and Hong Kong economies has reduced the influence of local business and brought in Mainland business interests that are closely aligned to the Chinese government.

The reduction in the political influence of Hong Kong business has been mirrored in its efforts to organise a dedicated pro-Being political party. The creation of the Hong Kong Progressive Alliance in 1994 was initiated by the New China News Agency, which wanted to bring disparate business groups together to fight the 1995 election. Eventually, rifts within the organisation led to the merger of the party with the DAB in 2005. The Liberal Party's experience has been similar to that of the Hong Kong Progressive Alliance. It lost seats in the 2008 Legislative Council elections, which led to a split among legislators on whether the party should concentrate on the functional constituencies or whether it should run candidates in both the functional and directly elected constituencies. Three of the party's seven legislators left the party.[36]

In 2012, the Business and Professionals Alliance was formed as the principal pro-Beijing business party. The Liberal Party did not join the alliance and

---

31. Wang-Kaeding & Kaeding (2019) op. cit.
32. Ibid.; Wang-Kaeding, H. (2020, 9 August). Red capital: How Chinese companies exert political influence over Hong Kong. *HKFP*. https://hongkongfp.com/2020/08/09/red-capital-how-chinese-companies-exert-political-influence-over-hong-kong/
33. Wang-Kaeding & Kaeding (2019) op. cit.
34. Wu, V., & Jim, C. (2017, 29 January). Mainland Chinese firms expand property footprint in Hong Kong, set to fuel price rises. *Reuters*. https://fr.reuters.com/article/us-hongkong-property-china-idUSKBN15B0XM
35. Lam, L. S. (2020, 18 April). Mainland Chinese investors are selling Hong Kong property after China reports first GDP contraction in four decades. *SCMP*. https://www.scmp.com/business/article/3080505/mainland-chinese-investors-are-selling-hong-kong-property-after-china
36. Lam, J. T. M. (2010). Party institutionalization in Hong Kong. *Asian Perspective*, 34(2), 53–82.

subsequently contested some functional constituencies, narrowly failing to unseat the leader of the alliance, Jeffrey Lam, in 2016. After the 2016 elections, the alliance was the second-largest party in the Legislative Council, holding eight seats, seven in the functional constituencies, and one in a directly elected seat. The party claims to represent the middle class and to support measures that improve their livelihood. It does not commit to broader policies but has made statements endorsing the government's anti-epidemic actions, calling for MTR fares to be slashed by 20%–30%, and condemning the political protests.[37]

In the wider context of Mainland influence on domestic politics and policymaking, it is evident that, since the handover, the Chinese government has deepened and strengthened not only its political control over Hong Kong but also its bases of support in the society. Its electoral impact is evident in the role that the Liaison Office has increasingly played in sponsoring and funding pro-Beijing political parties.[38] It is also clear that the Chinese government has used its economic influence to pursue political goals. Its direct influence on policymaking in the Hong Kong government is explored in the following sections.

Social Integration

The immediate aims of the Chinese government after 1997 were to enhance the social and economic integration of Hong Kong into the Mainland. Social integration was focused on increased immigration from the Mainland and promoting national education in Hong Kong schools. The Chinese government has control over who can or cannot settle in the HKSAR, but education was in the hands of the Hong Kong government, which had to deal with many pressure groups with an intense interest in the school curriculum. Tensions between the PRC on what citizenship meant, and the very different conception that many Hong Kong people held, was a factor contributing to political unrest from 2011 onwards.[39]

Migration from the Mainland

The post-handover period saw growing tensions between local Hong Kong people and Mainlanders over access to public goods and services, parallel trading in which Chinese nationals bought goods in bulk to sell at higher prices back on the Mainland, and tourists who were perceived to behave in ways that violated local social norms. Since 1980, there had been provision for legal migration to Hong Kong from the PRC. After 1997, those numbers increased. By 2017, there were about 2.3

---

37. Business and Professionals Association (2020). About us. https://en.bpahk.org/our-belief/
38. Ma, N. (2017). The China factor in Hong Kong elections, 1991–2016. *China Perspectives*, 3, 17–26.
39. Wong, J. K., & So, A. Y. (2020). The re-making of developmental citizenship in post-handover Hong Kong. *Citizenship Studies*, 24(7), 934–949.

million Mainland migrants who had lived in Hong Kong for more than a year.[40] This included people entering Hong Kong on one-way permits which, since 1995, have amounted to 150 migrants per day or about 55,000 per year.[41] These migrants, who are disproportionately female with low levels of education and skills, are selected solely by Mainland authorities.[42] The Hong Kong government may reject applicants but it does not usually appear to do so. There are also schemes to allow university students to study in Hong Kong, a Quality Migrant Admission Scheme, and a Capital Investment Entrant Scheme to attract Mainlanders with skills or money to the HKSAR.[43] Migrants can become permanent residents after seven years of being "ordinarily resident" in Hong Kong for that period.

Until the 2019 protests and COVID-19, growing numbers of Mainland tourists were visiting Hong Kong. The numbers reached a high of 51.04 million in 2018 but fell to 43.77 million in 2019 and dropped sharply during the protests with only 2.6 million tourists visiting the city between January and September 2020.[44] A common complaint against the influx of Mainland tourists was that Hong Kong did not have sufficient infrastructure to accommodate them. A senior Chinese government official responded by noting that tourists were helping Hong Kong's economy and that it was natural for Chinese citizens to want to visit their country.[45] Parallel traders were accused of causing shortages of supplies for Hong Kong citizens. Complaints gradually became a generalised attack on the activities of Mainlanders in Hong Kong. They were characterised as "locusts" that ate up Hong Kong resources and there were demonstrations against the provision of public schooling and health care to Mainlanders.[46] During the 2019 protests, Mainland and pro-Beijing Hong Kong businesses were targeted and vandalised.[47]

Antagonism to the Chinese government's migration policies, Mainland tourists, and parallel traders do not explain the widespread protests of 2019, but they helped to create an underlying division between those who saw themselves as part of China and those who did not. The influx of Mainlanders was a major factor in

---

40. Statista (2020). Number of immigrants from mainland China living in Hong Kong. https://www.statista.com/statistics/901381/number-of-immigrants-from-mainland-china-living-in-hong-kong/
41. Bauhinia Foundation (2014). *Hong Kong's future population and manpower needs to 2030* (p. 36). http://www.bauhinia.org/assets/document/doc173eng.pdf
42. Ibid., p. 37.
43. Immigration Department (2020). *Hong Kong: The facts: immigration*. https://www.gov.hk/en/about/abouthk/factsheets/docs/immigration.pdf.
44. Statista (2020). Number of visitor arrivals in Hong Kong from mainland China, 2013 to 2019. https://www.statista.com/statistics/1089267/hong-kong-number-of-visitor-arrivals-from-mainland-china/; PartnerNet (2020, September). Monthly report: Visitor arrival statistics. https://partnernet.hktb.com/filemanager/intranet/pm/VisitorArrivalStatistics/ViS_Stat_E/ViSE_2020/Tourism%20Statistics%2009%202020.pdf
45. Martina, M. (2013, 4 March). China rejects complaints mainland visitors are flooding Hong Kong. *Reuters*. https://br.reuters.com/article/uk-china-parliament-hongkong-idUKLNE92301K20130304
46. So, A. Y. C. (2017). A new wave of anti-mainland protests since 2012: Characteristics, socio-political origins, and political implications. *Asian Education and Development Studies*, 6(4), 333–342.
47. Chatterjee, S., & Roantree, A. M. (2019, 2 October). Mainland banks, pro-Beijing businesses caught in Hong Kong protest cross-hairs. *Reuters*. https://www.reuters.com/article/us-hongkong-protests-cleanup-idUSKBN1WH055

increasing awareness of Hong Kong identity because of the detrimental impact that "mainlandisation" was perceived to have on the local culture, economy, and way of life. There was a significant rise in those who identified themselves as Hong Kongers. A PORI poll in December 2020 found that 69% of respondents identified themselves as Hong Kongers "in a broad sense" while 29% thought of themselves as Chinese "in a broad sense".[48] This was the lowest percentage of those identifying themselves as Chinese since polls on the issue were first taken in 1997. There is moreover a link between increased perceptions of a Hong Kong identity and greater political participation[49] through the localist political groups that emerged to run in the 2016 Legislative Council elections and subsequently played key roles in the protests.[50]

Moral and National Education

The Chinese government has always aimed at fostering a sense of patriotism and cultural heritage, an ability to speak Putonghua, and support for the Communist Party, especially, in the schools. In colonial times, these efforts were restricted to what were called leftist (now patriotic) schools funded by the party apparatus in Hong Kong. Unlike the mainstream schools, the leftist schools provided regular trips to China for students, promoted nationalism and the study of politics, and included Chinese culture in the curriculum.[51] Since the handover, the Hong Kong government and some charitable institutions, such as the Jockey Club, have provided strong support for this agenda. In his first policy address, Tung Chee Hwa said that it was necessary for the community to get "to know Chinese history and culture, so as to achieve a sense of belonging".[52] He promised more resources and a new civic education course.[53] A Quality Education Fund and the Committee on the Promotion of Civic Education, which comes under the Home Affairs Bureau, took on responsibilities for funding and promoting national education. In 2010, Donald

---

48. PORI (2020, 7–10 December). POP releases survey on Hong Kong people's ethnic identity. https://www.pori.hk/press-release-en/2020-12-22-pm.html?lang=en; see also Steinhardt, H. C., Li, L. C., & Jiang, Y. (2018). The identity shift in Hong Kong since 1997: Measurement and explanation. *Journal of Contemporary China*, 27(110), 261–276.
49. Chan, N. K. M., Nachman, J., & Mok, C. W. J. (2020). A red flag for participation: The influence of Chinese mainlandization on political behaviour in Hong Kong. *Political Research Quarterly*. https://doi.org/10.1177/1065912920957413
50. Kaeding, M. P. (2017). The rise of "localism" in Hong Kong. *Journal of Democracy*, 28(1), 157–171; Kwong, Y. H. (2016). The growth of "localism" in Hong Kong. A new path for the democracy movement? *China Perspectives*, 3, 63–68; Ma, N. (2015). The rise of "anti-China" sentiments in Hong Kong and the 2012 Legislative Council elections. *The China Review*, 39–66; Veg, S. (2017). The rise of "localism" and civic identity in post-handover Hong Kong: Questioning the Chinese nation-state. *The China Quarterly*, 230, 323–347.
51. Lau, T. (2013). State formation and education in Hong Kong: Pro-Beijing schools and national education. *Asian Survey*, 53(4), 728–753.
52. Tung, C. H. (1997). *Building Hong Kong for a new era* (para 110). https://www.policyaddress.gov.hk/pa97/english/patext.htm
53. Ibid., para 112.

Tsang went further, increasing the study hours on the Basic Law and promising to introduce a separate mandatory subject on "moral and national" education which would replace the subject of civic education.[54]

After the curriculum guidelines were released in May 2011, opposition to the proposal began to grow. Secondary school students created a pressure group, Scholarism, calling for the withdrawal of the government's proposal. By the following year, a further 15 organisations, bringing together unions, teachers, and democratic politicians, had joined in an alliance with Scholarism. At the root of their objections to "moral and national" education was resistance to what they regarded as "brainwashing" into a Chinese national identity and support for the Chinese government and the Communist Party.[55] Since there was a civic education subject in place, the protesters thought that its replacement by a national education curriculum was unnecessary.[56] There were also serious concerns that the new curriculum was poorly developed, overlapping with other subjects, and ignoring critical events in Chinese history such as the Tiananmen Square incident.[57] It was revealed to have taken two pro-Beijing companies over six years to produce educational material for the curriculum, costing $72 million.[58] Parents also feared that an emphasis on national education and teaching Putonghua might come at the expense of teaching English, which they saw as essential for their children's future opportunities. Finally, there were concerns that the Chinese government was driving the agenda following the release of a PRC report in May 2011, stressing that national education in Hong Kong should be strengthened.[59]

Protests increased in June and July 2012. The Tiananmen Square commemoration was estimated to have been attended by about 180,000, larger than in previous years. A demonstration against the newly installed Chief Executive, Leung Chun-ying, on 1 July attracted some 400,000. At the end of July, many thousands of demonstrators took to the streets, specifically opposing the "moral and national education" curriculum. Some occupied government buildings and went on hunger strikes and a concert was held in support of the alliance. On 8 September, the day before the Legislative Council elections, the government withdrew the proposal. Shortly afterwards, the Education Bureau announced that the full implementation of "moral and national education" had been "abolished" and that it had taken "out

---

54. Tsang, D. Y. K. (2010). *Sharing prosperity for a caring society* (paras 161–162). https://www.policyaddress.gov.hk/10-11/eng/index.html
55. Morris, P., & Vickers, E. (2015). Schooling, politics and the construction of identity in Hong Kong: The 2012 "moral and national education" crises in historical perspective. *Comparative Education*, 51(3), 305–326.
56. Leung, Y. W., & Ng, H. Y. (2014). Delivering civic education in Hong Kong: Why is it not an independent subject? *Citizenship, Social and Economics Education*, 13(1), 2–15.
57. Fung, D. C. L., & Lui, W. M. (2017). *Education policy analysis: Liberal studies and national education in Hong Kong* (pp. 27–29). Singapore: Springer.
58. Cheung, T. (2012, 9 September). A history of how national education was introduced in Hong Kong. *SCMP*. https://www.scmp.com/news/hong-kong/article/1032512/history-how-national-education-was-introduced-hong-kong
59. Leung & Ng (2014) op. cit.

the parts on contemporary China".[60] Schools were given an option on whether or not they would introduce the remainder of the curriculum.

Pressure on the government to introduce changes to the curriculum did not decline after the government withdrew the "moral and national education" proposal. Following the Umbrella Movement in 2014, in which Scholarism was a leading force, pro-Beijing legislators and the Chinese state media focused their attention on liberal studies, a subject that had been introduced into the curriculum in 1992. Initially, the subject was regarded as a failure. Teachers were unhappy with the curriculum structure and less than 10% of students chose to take the subject. It was reintroduced as a compulsory subject in 2009 with an emphasis on more specific learning objectives, a tighter curriculum structure, and the aim of developing critical thinking.[61] Pro-Beijing legislators and the communist media thought that liberal studies was a cause of the rising dissent among youth and claimed that obtaining good marks in the subject required providing politically correct answers. In June 2019, nine pro-Beijing legislators issued a statement attacking the government for keeping liberal studies as a compulsory subject.[62] Tung Chee Hwa said that the subject was partly responsible for violent protests in the city.[63] In the following year, Carrie Lam reportedly said that students were being "poisoned" and fed "false and biased information".[64] The national security law provides that the HKSAR government should take "necessary measures to strengthen public communication, guidance, supervision, and regulation over matters concerning national security, including those relating to schools, universities, social organisations, the media, and the internet."[65]

Despite the criticism of liberal studies, a task force appointed by the government and reporting in September 2020 decided that liberal studies should be retained as a compulsory subject. Bending in the wind, it recommended that the content of the subject should be trimmed and that current issues were not suitable for enquiry because it was difficult to arrive at judgements on controversial

---

60. Education Bureau (2012, 12 September). Amendment to the policy on the "moral and national" education subject. https://applications.edb.gov.hk/circular/upload/EDBCM/EDBCM12135E.pdf
61. Fung, D. L., & Yip, W. Y. (2010). The policies of reintroducing liberal studies in Hong Kong secondary schools. *Educational Research for Policy and Practice*, 9(1), 17–40.
62. Chiu, P. (2019, 29 June). Pro-Beijing politicians rail against liberal studies, the Hong Kong school subject that "politicises teens". *SCMP*. https://www.scmp.com/news/hong-kong/education/article/3016582/pro-beijing-politicians-rail-against-liberal-studies-hong
63. Cheung, G. (2020, 23 September). Was liberal studies responsible for radicalising Hong Kong youth and should it be axed? *SCMP*. https://www.scmp.com/news/hong-kong/politics/article/3102585/has-liberal-studies-radicalised-hong-kongs-youth-do-they; China Global Television Network (2019, 20 August). Problems in schools' liberal studies teaching partly to blame, says former HKSAR chief exec. https://news.cgtn.com/news/2019-08-20/Problems-in-schools-liberal-studies-teaching-partly-to-blame-JjgPEcoqEE/index.html
64. Davidson, H., and agencies (2020, 11 May). Carrie Lam blames education system for fuelling protests. *The Guardian*. https://www.theguardian.com/world/2020/may/11/carrie-lam-blames-hong-kong-education-system-for-fuelling-protests
65. Government of the People's Republic of China (2020). *The Law of the People's Republic of China on safeguarding national security in the Hong Kong Special Administrative Region* (Article 9). https://www.elegislation.gov.hk/doc/hk/a406/eng_translation_(a406)_en.pdf

matters.[66] It also thought that there should be regular reviews of the curriculum, changed assessment rules, the vetting of textbooks, and enhanced teacher training.[67] There were some pro-establishment voices raised in favour of liberal studies, but many other pro-Beijing figures thought that it should be stripped of discussion of contentious political topics that, in their view, led to dissent and violence.[68] In her November 2020 policy address, Carrie Lam said that her government would reintroduce "moral and national education", encourage more student study tours, and cultivate a better understanding of the importance of national security.[69] She also promised to reform the liberal studies curriculum.[70] Later in the same month, the Secretary for Education said that the teaching manuals would be vetted by the Education Bureau, that there would be more China content, that students would be taught about national security issues, and that there would be less material on current affairs.[71]

Neither the Hong Kong government's support for substantial Mainland migration and tourism nor education policies aimed at developing a national identity have been successful in achieving their objectives. On the contrary, they have helped create a local Hong Kong identity that, in the eyes of the Chinese government and many of its supporters in Hong Kong, has led to antipathy towards the Mainland and political unrest. There appears to be a causal link between the policies aimed at social integration and the rise of "localism" although many other factors are also relevant in explaining the emergence of a divided polity. What is clear is that the implementation of social integration policies has been markedly unsuccessful.

Economic Integration

Economic integration of the Mainland with Hong Kong initially centred on a trade, tourist and services agreement, the CEPA, which sought to enhance cooperation and encourage Hong Kong investments in the PRC.[72] An accompanying policy was aimed at providing faster cross-border transport links. Construction began in 2010 on a high-speed rail link and was completed in 2018. At the same time, the contractors began to build the Hong Kong side of the HZMB, the longest sea bridge in the world, which was also completed in 2018. Hong Kong has also been involved in

---

66. Education Bureau Task Force on Review of School Curriculum (2020). *Optimise the curriculum for the future: Foster whole-person development and diverse talents* (p. 25). https://www.edb.gov.hk/en/curriculum-development/renewal/taskforce_cur.html
67. Ibid., pp. 26–27.
68. Cheung (2020) op. cit.
69. Lam, C. (2020). *Strive ahead with renewed perseverance* (para 152). https://www.policyaddress.gov.hk/2020/eng/policy.html
70. Ibid., paras 153–154.
71. Chau, C. (2020, 27 November). Hong Kong Liberal Studies to be renamed and reformed—more China content, less focus on current affairs. https://hongkongfp.com/2020/11/27/hong-kong-liberal-studies-to-be-renamed-and-reformed-more-china-content-less-focus-on-current-affairs/
72. Hong Kong Government (2003, 29 June). *Signing of the Mainland and Hong Kong Closer Economic Partnership Arrangement* [Press release].

China's Belt and Road projects, extending previous developments in such fields as trade, transport, and real estate and providing capital markets for joint ventures and other projects expected to enhance economic cooperation. The Chinese government's 2019 plan for the Greater Bay Area assumes increased economic integration and specifies the role the HKSAR will play in the development of an innovation hub in southern China.[73] Much of the Chief Executive's 2020 policy address, the first following the enactment of the national security law, was devoted to increasing economic integration with the Mainland.[74]

The Pearl River Delta and the Closer Economic Partnership Agreement

The PRD began to emerge as a dynamic region of economic growth following the inception of China's open-door policy in 1979. Developing the delta was a natural, complementary match for economic expansion on both sides of the border. The Chinese authorities wanted Hong Kong capital and entrepreneurial expertise. Hong Kong business wanted cheap labour and land. By the end of 1997, Hong Kong investment in China amounted to US$121 billion (about 55% of all foreign investment), of which US$48 billion (about 80% of all foreign investment) was estimated to be in Guangdong province.[75] Following the handover, there was exponential economic interaction and growth in the region. Hong Kong gradually became less important as a source of foreign investment and its manufacturing companies appeared to be less productive than were other foreign firms.[76] By 2015, Hong Kong manufacturers in the PRD employed 4.5 million workers, about half the number employed 10 years earlier.[77] The PRD had moved up-market into information technology, automotive production, robotics, and logistics and reduced the size of its workforce, bringing in greater automation.

The Hong Kong and Mainland and provincial Chinese governments were supportive of economic expansion in the region during the transitional period, but it was not until after the handover that a formal agreement enhancing economic cooperation was signed. After 1997, Hong Kong's severe recession led to business pressure on the Chief Executive to ask the Mainland authorities to reduce tariffs and grant easier access to Chinese markets.[78] The CEPA, which had a strong impact on

---

73. Government of the People's Republic of China (2019). *Outline development plan for the Guangdong-Hong Kong-Macao Greater Bay Area* (pp. 9–10). www.bayarea.gov.hk/filemanager/en/share/pdf/Outline_Development_Plan.pdf
74. Lam, C. (2020) op. cit., paras 26–82.
75. Hong Kong Government (1998). *Hong Kong—a new era* (p. 49). Hong Kong: Information Services Department.
76. Yeung, G. (2018). End of a chapter? Hong Kong manufacturers in the Pearl River Delta. In T. L. Lui, S. W. K. Chiu, & R. Yep (Eds.), *Routledge handbook of contemporary Hong Kong* (pp. 397–413, 400). London: Routledge.
77. Yang, C. (2020). The transformation of foreign investment-induced "exo(genous)-urbanisation" amidst industrial restructuring in the Pearl River Delta, China. *Urban Studies, 57*(3), 618–635.
78. Kong, Q. (2003). Closer economic partnership agreement between China and Hong Kong. *China: An International Journal, 1*(1), 133–143.

the economic integration of Hong Kong with the PRD, came into effect at the beginning of 2004, eliminating import tariffs on 374 products and giving preferential market access to Hong Kong companies in 18 service areas.[79] By 2008, supplements to the CEPA allowed 1,500 tariff-free Hong Kong products to enter the PRC and banks and insurance companies were given easier access to the Mainland market.[80] The Hong Kong government estimated that the agreement helped to create 36,000 jobs in the SAR in the first three years after it was signed.[81] On the Chinese side, allowing Mainland tourists to visit the SAR and abolishing the quota system for Mainland companies listing on the HKEx also increased economic integration.

The CEPA has provided a flexible framework for ironing out obstacles to economic integration and has led to greater Hong Kong investment on the Mainland. Its overall economic benefits have not been questioned although the floods of Mainland tourists that descended on Hong Kong have not always been welcome. The CEPA has been seen as a positive example of how the Mainland and Hong Kong can collaborate for their mutual benefit.[82] There have, however, been some practical difficulties and potential opportunities that have not been taken. One Hong Kong criticism has been that "large doors open, but small doors close",[83] meaning that, although the Chinese government was on board with the changes, provincial governments sometimes kept regulations in place that inhibited investment and productivity.

Infrastructural Developments

Unlike the CEPA, two massive developments, the high-speed rail link to Guangdong and the HZMB, were constructed largely because the Chinese government wanted them. The colonial government considered a rail link in the 1990s, but the decision was postponed because of the handover. Post-1997 discussion in Hong Kong focused on an improved rail connection but not necessarily a high-speed link. The Chinese government, meanwhile, was building rapid transit rail links throughout the country, including areas close to Hong Kong. The HKSAR government finally authorised a 26-kilometre link in 2009 to connect with Guangdong and the rest of the network. The high-speed rail link was, in many ways, a great planning disaster. The MTRC's construction of the link was plagued by delays, cost overruns, and hostile public demonstrations. Flooding of the tunnels and boring through complex

---

79. Hong Kong Government (2004). *Hong Kong 2003* (p. 115). Hong Kong: Information Services Department.
80. Chen, H., & Unteroberdoerster, O. (2008). Hong Kong SAR economic integration with the Pearl River Delta. IMF Working Paper WP/08/273.
81. Ibid.
82. Cheung, P. T. Y. (2015). Toward collaborative governance between Hong Kong and Mainland China. *Urban Studies, 52*(10), 1915–1933; Fung, C. (2020). The Guangdong-Hong Kong-Macao Greater Bay Area: Enhancing collaborative governance of the CEPA implementation and regional integration. *China: An International Journal, 18*(1), 171–191.
83. Quoted in Fung (2020) op. cit.

geological formations resulted in long delays and substantial increases in costs. The original estimate was $39.4 billion but, by 2018, when the railway was completed, this had ballooned to $84.4 billion. The project was three years overdue and took eight years to construct. At the time, the railway was the most expensive railway line in the world per kilometre.[84]

Political opposition to the project has a long history. On the streets, protests began in 2009 focusing on whether the link was necessary, its cost, the effect on the environment, and the eviction of New Territories villagers to facilitate construction.[85] It was also pointed that there was an existing line to Guangzhou. When the project was debated in the Legislative Council in January 2010, protesters surrounded the legislature, preventing members from leaving. Legislators continued to express concerns about delays and the effects of construction on the lives of New Territories villagers.[86] Once the project neared completion, the question of how border controls would be managed became a major issue. In July 2017, the government announced that there would be co-location controls with about 800 Mainland personnel stationed inside the West Kowloon terminus in Hong Kong.[87] There were demonstrations on the streets against the decision and concerns that such action would violate the Basic Law.[88] When the controls were set up, there were further protests. In October 2019, one illegal demonstration outside the terminus drew crowds that organisers estimated to be 230,000 strong, police putting the number at 56,000.[89] During the 2019 protests, the MTRC's subway stations were extensively damaged by protesters. The damage was attributed to the MTRC permitting police to accost protesters on the trains but also to its construction of the rail link.[90]

Whether the rail link has contributed to economic integration seems in serious doubt. Given the potential volume of traffic between Hong Kong and the Mainland, the project was worth consideration. But the initial concerns are very important as to how the link should be evaluated. Was it worth the cost? The journey to

---

84. Cheng, K. (2018). Cost overruns and constitutional debate: Hong Kong's controversial express rail link explained. *HKFP*. https://hongkongfp.com/2018/09/23/cost-overruns-constitutional-debate-hong-kongs-controversial-express-rail-link-explained/
85. Lam-Knott, S. (2018). Anti-hierarchical activism in Hong Kong: The post-80s youth. *Social Movement Studies*, 17(4), 464–470.
86. Legislative Council Panel on Transport (2017, 2 June). Updated background brief on the construction of the Hong Kong section of the Guangzhou-Shenzhen-Hong Kong express rail link. https://www.legco.gov.hk/yr16-17/english/panels/tp/tp_rdp/papers/tp_rdp20170602cb4-1099-4-e.pdf
87. Department of Justice, Transport and Housing Bureau and Security Bureau (2017, July). Customs, immigration and quarantine arrangements for the Hong Kong section of the Guangzhou-Shenzhen-Hong Kong express rail link. https://www.thb.gov.hk/eng/policy/transport/policy/colocation/Eng_XRL_LegCo_(Final).pdf
88. Cheung, A. Y. H. (2019, 10 January). The express rail co-location case: The Hong Kong judiciary's retreat. *LawFare*. https://www.lawfareblog.com/express-rail-co-location-case-hong-kong-judiciarys-retreat
89. Chan, H. (2019, 7 July). Hongkongers march to China express rail station to spread anti-extradition message to Mainland Hong Kong tourists. *HKFP*. https://hongkongfp.com/2019/07/07/just-hong-kongs-anti-extradition-law-protesters-march-china-express-rail-station-spread-message-mainlanders/
90. Berti, A. (2020, 14 April) Hong Kong protests: How has the MTR been affected? *Railway Technology*, https://www.railway-technology.com/features/hong-kong-protests-mtr/

Guangzhou was certainly shortened from nearly 2 hours to 48 minutes. But because of the delays and the consequent increase in expenditure, it is difficult to see how utilisation will justify the cost. By 2020, the number of users had dropped substantially because of the protests and COVID-19. If the numbers do grow in the future, the link perhaps could become a symbol of economic integration. But its troubled history suggests that it is more likely to remain as a bungle in Hong Kong's collective memory.

If anything, the HZMB was an even more unsuccessful venture. A Hong Kong business tycoon was the first to propose a bridge, but much of the preliminary construction was carried out in Zhuhai before the Hong Kong government had formally decided whether it would fund and undertake construction. Its ambivalence about the project lay in its cost and economic viability. Construction on the Hong Kong side of the bridge began in December 2009. But it was soon halted for nine months when a judicial review found in favour of a complainant who challenged the validity of the environmental assessment reports on air quality, arguing that they were not in compliance with the *Environmental Impact Assessment Ordinance*.[91] According to the government, the delay added a further $8.8 billion to the original estimated cost of $76.2 billion. There were continuing concerns over the effect the bridge would have on the breeding habits and health of rare white dolphins. Further problems resulted from technical issues affecting the artificial islands and the protective sea walls and there were safety and corruption issues. An estimated 19 people died in the construction of the bridge and many hundreds were reported to have been injured.[92] Twelve technicians were convicted on corruption charges for falsifying test results.[93] When the bridge was finally completed in 2018, two years beyond schedule, its cost had risen to $117.7 billion and came with a $2.5 billion annual maintenance charge.[94]

There have been numerous criticisms of the HZMB's failure to generate the kind of economic interaction that it was supposed to promote.[95] Present numbers of

---

91. Kwok, D. W. H. (2011). *The Hong Kong-Zhuhai-Macau Bridge: Summary of the case*. Hong Kong: Civic Exchange.
92. Cheng, K. (2018, 23 October). Explainer: Hong Kong's troubled mega-bridge—counting the human, environmental and financial cost. *HKFP*. https://hongkongfp.com/2018/10/23/explainer-hong-kongs-troubled-mega-bridge-counting-human-environmental-financial-cost/
93. Hong Kong Government (2017, 24 May). Government's response to ICAC's arrest of staff members of a CEDD outsourced laboratory for allegedly falsifying concrete test reports. https://www.info.gov.hk/gia/general/201705/24/P2017052301095.htm; Wong, B. (2019, 20 November) Technicians guilty of faking test results for Hong Kong-Macau-Zhuhai bridge costing taxpayers HK$58 million. *SCMP*. https://www.scmp.com/news/hong-kong/law-and-crime/article/3038574/technicians-guilty-faking-test-results-hong-kong
94. Cheng (2018) op. cit.; Leung, K. (2018, 19 October) World's longest sea-crossing is finally finished but Hong Kong-Zhuhai-Macau bridge has come at a high cost. *SCMP*. https://www.scmp.com/news/hong-kong/transport/article/2169199/decade-deaths-and-delays-worlds-longest-sea-crossing
95. Hale, E. (2018, 15 August). An impressive, unnecessary, multi-city bridge. *Bloomberg*. https://www.bloomberg.com/news/articles/2018-08-15/the-hong-kong-zhuhai-macau-bridge-nears-completion-with-little-fanfare; Sebena, M. (2018, 20 October). The Hong Kong-Zhuhai-Macau bridge: White elephant in the Pearl river. *The Diplomat*. https://thediplomat.com/2018/10/the-hong-kong-zhuhai-macau-bridge-white-elephant-in-the-pearl-river/

vehicles using the bridge mean that it is unlikely that it will ever justify the costs of its construction. One difficulty is that the three governments involved have placed restrictions on the number of vehicles that may use the bridge. To use the HZMB requires a permit, only 10,000 of which have been issued to Hong Kong residents. Those who apply must follow numerous rules and switch from driving on the left in Hong Kong to driving on the right in China. The effects of COVID-19 have reduced travel even further, restricting traffic to fewer than 400 vehicles per day in April and May 2020.[96] The Mainland government's 2019 outline plan calls for the region to make "better use of the Guangzhou-Shenzhen-Hong Kong Express Rail Link and the Hong Kong-Zhuhai-Macao Bridge"[97] but so far this has not happened. Both projects are symbolic representations of future Chinese government intentions to integrate the region economically rather than major contributors to that aim.

Belt and Road Initiative

According to the Hong Kong government, the SAR has particular strengths that it can bring to China's infrastructural and maritime Belt and Road Initiative.[98] In December 2019, without any evidence of irony, the government listed these advantages as the "one country, two systems" model, a robust common law system, a free and open market, a level playing field, and a deep understanding of the Mainland's culture and business operations.[99] Two years earlier, the government had signed an agreement to participate in the Belt and Road Initiative with the PRC's National Development and Reform Commission which, the Chief Executive said, would be "grounded on Hong Kong's strengths in finance, infrastructure, economic and trade, and professional services".[100] The agreement provided for enhanced communication and cooperation with the Mainland in "five areas of connectivity": policy coordination, facilities connectivity, unimpeded trade, financial integration, and people-to-people bond.[101]

What has Hong Kong accomplished in support of the Belt and Road Initiative? It is difficult to determine what it has been doing in these five areas of connectivity that have been significantly different as a result of the Belt and Road Initiative. It is conceivable that the HKSAR syndicated loan market has been important in financing Belt and Road projects elsewhere. But the official overwhelming emphasis so far is not on what has been accomplished but on future opportunities for development.

---

96. Gu, M. (2020, 26 October). Underutilized HZMB finds it difficult bridging the gap. *China Daily*. https://www.chinadaily.com.cn/a/202010/26/WS5f967d8aa31024ad0ba8101c.html
97. Government of the People's Republic of China (2019) op. cit., 22.
98. Hong Kong Government (2019). *The Belt and Road initiative*. https://www.brandhk.gov.hk/uploads/brandhk/files/factsheets/Hong_Kong_Themes/Belt%20and%20Road_E_Dec%202019.pdf
99. Ibid.
100. Hong Kong Government (2017, 14 December). *Agreement between the NRDC and HKSAR Government on advancing Hong Kong's full participation in and contribution to Belt and Road initiative* [Press release]. https://www.info.gov.hk/gia/general/201712/14/P2017121400551.htm
101. Ibid.

The Belt and Road Initiative first appeared as a significant item in the Chief Executive's policy address in 2016 and has appeared in every subsequent address.[102] In her 2020 policy address, the Chief Executive promised yet another forum to explore corporate governance, more exchange visits, and support for Hong Kong companies seeking to set up businesses in ASEAN economic trade and cooperation zones.[103] The tone is consistently upbeat, but there are no specific examples of what Hong Kong has actually contributed. The government points to the signing of free trade agreements, professional services support schemes, high-level business missions and forums on the Belt and Road Initiative and Trade Development Council platforms as means of aiding the Belt and Road Initiative, but whether they do has not seemingly been subject to any evaluation.[104] Similarly, in the outline plan for the Greater Bay Area, the Belt and Road Initiative is described as a focal point although building a more efficient infrastructure in the PRD, deepening market integration, and developing an innovation hub seems to be a more immediate priority.[105]

Mainland–Hong Kong Innovation Integration

The post-handover Hong Kong government has long stressed the importance of innovation.[106] For some years, integration with the rapid developments, particularly in information technology, happening across the border in Shenzhen has been seen as a natural fit for Hong Kong. On the Chinese side, the aim is to integrate nine major cities in the PRD into an innovation and technology hub in which each will have a designated role. The outline plan for the Greater Bay Area seeks to give some substance to bringing Hong Kong and Macau into closer cooperation with the Mainland, avoiding duplication, communicating research and developments findings more quickly, funding joint projects, and providing a cross-border labour market for talented and skilled personnel.[107] Hong Kong is given the task of supporting five research and development centres on logistics and supplies, textiles and apparel, information and communications, automotive parts and accessory systems, and nano and advanced materials.[108] The plan for an innovation and technology hub is to locate it within a more integrated PRD with expanded, fast communication links, an education hub, and a more developed service sector and marine economy.

---

102. See, for example, Leung, C. Y. (2016). *Innovate for the economy, improve livelihood, foster harmony, share prosperity* (paras 36–66). https://www.policyaddress.gov.hk/2016/eng/pdf/PA2016.pdf; see also Lam, C. K., Cai, C., Dai, J., & Lee, H. W. (Eds.) (2020). *Hong Kong in the Belt and Road initiative*. Hong Kong: The Chinese University of Hong Kong Press.
103. Lam (2020) op. cit., paras 61–62.
104. Hong Kong Government (2019) op. cit.
105. Government of the People's Republic of China (2019) op. cit., pp. 7, 47, 49.
106. Scott, I. (2020). Context and innovation in traditional bureaucracies: A Hong Kong study. *Public Administration and Development*. https://doi.org/10.1002/pad.1899
107. Ibid.
108. Ibid., p. 17.

The Hong Kong and Shenzhen Information and Technology Park, which is supported in the plan, perhaps provides something of a model for the kind of cooperation that is envisaged. It is situated in the Lok Ma Chau loop, a small piece of Mainland territory on the border that was transferred to Hong Kong jurisdiction in 2017. The park is a wholly owned subsidiary of the Hong Kong Science and Technology Parks Corporation, which received very generous funding from the Hong Kong government in the 2019 and 2020 budgets. The board of management has a Hong Kong chair and includes the Permanent Secretary of the Information and Technology Bureau, many representatives of Hong Kong and Mainland companies, and overseas participants and academics as its directors.[109] By 2020, the Hong Kong–Shenzhen Information and Technology Park claimed to have 890 technology companies from 23 countries and regions and to have attracted $29 billion in funding and to have helped create two "unicorns", Sensetime and Lalamove.[110]

Whether this particular venture works or not, the impetus for economic integration through innovation, and particularly information and technology innovation, seems likely to proceed. Although Hong Kong has a poor record on innovation,[111] the success of Mainland information and technological enterprises and the development of the PRD as a hub has been accorded high priority on the Chinese government's agenda. For Hong Kong, the question lies in whether it contributes anything unique to this effort. Its present contribution seems to consist primarily in providing funding for projects and research and development centres.

Economic integration between the Mainland and Hong Kong is a central plank in the Chinese government's plans for the future. In the case of CEPA, it has worked to the benefit of Hong Kong investors and cross-border workers, opening up opportunities and reducing bureaucratic hurdles to economic interaction. The high-speed rail link and the HZMB were expected to accelerate that process. To date, however, there is no evidence that the billions of dollars spent on these projects will ever be economically justified. They remain symbols of the aspiration for greater economic integration, but they come with a long history of opposition from Hong Kong activists, which serves as a reminder of the difficulty of policy implementation in an atmosphere of contentious politics. The Belt and Road Initiative and innovation policies have been less controversial, but they have not so far been fully implemented. In many respects, the component projects are less tangible than the rail link and the bridge and not as liable, especially since the enactment of the national security law, to protests and disruption. Implementation may still pose problems. Even if the performance of Hong Kong public organisations on matters relating to innovation can be improved, the optimum organisational structure for joint cross-border ventures remains in question. Despite the setbacks that have

---

109. Hong Kong and Shenzhen Innovation and Technology Park (2020). Board of directors. https://www.hkstp.org/about-us/the-board-committees/board-of-directors/
110. Ibid. https://www.hkstp.org/about-us/our-footprint/hsitp/
111. Scott, I. (2020) op. cit.

been experienced in trying to increase economic integration, it seems likely that the Mainland and Hong Kong governments will continue to look for opportunities to pursue closer interaction so that the Greater Bay Area becomes a single, fused economic metropolis.

National Security Policies

The Chinese government has overriding authority on both constitutional and security issues in Hong Kong, but the Legislative Council and the courts may play some role before a final decision is reached. The NPCSC has the right to interpret the Basic Law and consequently to decide on how constitutional changes will be implemented. Article 159 of the Basic Law, however, requires that amendments must receive the consent of two-thirds of all members of the Legislative Council, a provision that has meant that some previous constitutional proposals favoured by the Chinese and Hong Kong governments were not accepted. Hong Kong courts may adjudicate on other issues concerning the Basic Law, providing that they do not concern affairs that are the responsibility of the Chinese government (Article 158).

On national security policies, Article 23 obliges the Hong Kong government to enact laws "on its own" to prohibit any act of treason, secession, sedition, subversion against the Central People's Government" and to prevent the theft of state secrets and to prohibit political organisations from establishing ties with foreign organisations. The inability of the Hong Kong government to legislate Article 23 in 2003 in the face of mass demonstrations and opposition in the Legislative Council led to continuing pressure from the Chinese government to enact legislation. After the 2014 publication of a State Council document on "one country, two systems"[112] and the decision on Chief Executive elections,[113] the Chinese government increased its direct influence over policymaking. In 2017, in a speech marking the twentieth anniversary of Hong Kong's retrocession to China, Xi Jinping said that Hong Kong should:

> improve its systems to uphold national sovereignty, security and development interests. It needs to enhance education and raise public awareness of the history and culture of the Chinese nation. It is yet to build a public consensus on some major political and legal issues.[114]

---

112. State Council of the People's Republic of China (2014). *The practice of the one country, two systems policy in the Hong Kong Special Administrative Region*. http://english.www.gov.cn/archive/white_paper/2014/08/23/content_281474982986578.htm
113. Standing Committee of the National People's Congress (2014, 1 September). *NPC Standing Committee decision on Hong Kong 2017 election framework*. http://be.china-embassy.org/eng/sghd/201409/t20140901_2076170.htm
114. Xi Jingping (2017, 1 July). Speech at meeting marking HK's 20th return anniversary, inaugural ceremony of 5th term HKSAR gov't. *China Daily*. https://www.chinadaily.com.cn/china/hk20threturn/2017-07/01/content_29959860.htm

He went on to say that the concept of "one country, two systems" was devised "to realize and uphold national unity" and that any attempt to use Hong Kong to carry out infiltration and sabotage activities against the Mainland was "absolutely impermissible".[115] The extensive protests in opposition to the Extradition Bill, support for greater democratisation and the "localists" proved the last straw for the Chinese government. In June 2020, the National People's Congress enacted national security legislation without the involvement of the Legislative Council or the public and, seemingly, with very little consultation with the Hong Kong government.[116] Its enactment was the culmination of what one Chinese official has described as a "second return", representing a much stronger Chinese government line on national security and political dissent in Hong Kong.[117]

Following the implementation of the national security legislation, the need for vocal and legislative support from united front organisations, pro-Beijing and pro-establishment political groups declined, especially when the pro-democracy members resigned from the Legislative Council. The pro-Beijing groups may still have a role to play in rubber-stamping legislative proposals and lobbying both governments behind the scenes in support of their interests, but their importance has been diminished. The effect of the national security legislation was to reduce significantly the impact of the democrats and the pro-Beijing groups and the relevance of the legislative framework.

The Chinese government's Liaison Office appears to have become the central source of policy direction for the Hong Kong government. Until the 2019 protests, the Liaison Office was a highly influential voice at the shoulder of Hong Kong policymakers, but it did not make policy on all issues. In January 2020, the Director of the Liaison Office, Wang Zhimin, was replaced by Luo Huining, who wasted no time in telling the Chief Executive that she should implement a national security law and introduce a more effective national education programme.[118] In April 2020, the Liaison Office formalised its more interventionist role following a controversy over the interpretation of the Basic Law.[119] The office criticised democratic legislators for delaying the appointment of the chair of a Legislative Council committee. The legislators responded by claiming that the Liaison Office had violated Article 22 of the Basic Law, which states that no Chinese government department may

---

115. Ibid.
116. Hui, M. (2020, 23 June). The leader of Hong Kong is in the dark about the law that will change Hong Kong forever. *Quartz.* https://qz.com/1871988/carrie-lam-knows-little-about-hong-kongs-national-security-law/
117. Pepper, S. (2020, 25 June). National security law: A "second handover" for Hong Kong? *HKFP.* https://hongkongfp.com/2020/06/25/national-security-law-a-second-handover-for-hong-kong/; see also Cabestan, J-P., & Daziano, L. (2020). *Hong Kong: The second handover.* Paris: Fondation pour L'Innovation Politique; Scott, I. (2017). One country, two systems: The end of a legitimating ideology? *Asia Pacific Journal of Public Administration, 39*(2), 83–99.
118. Wong, N. (2020, 20 January). Citing President Xi Jingping, Beijing's Hong Kong envoy Luo Huining says lack of national security law allows 'sabotage'. *SCMP.* https://www.scmp.com/news/hong-kong/politics/article/3046821/citing-president-xi-jinping-beijings-envoy-luo-huining
119. Richburg, K. B. (2020, 28 April). Hong Kong's autonomy dying in full view. *The Strategist.* https://www.aspistrategist.org.au/hong-kongs-autonomy-dying-in-full-view/

interfere in the affairs of the HKSAR and that all Mainland departments operating in Hong Kong must obey Hong Kong laws. The Liaison Office then stated that it was not a central government department and that it was charged with implementing the Basic Law in Hong Kong. Although the Secretary of Justice subsequently confirmed that the Liaison Office was not a Mainland government department,[120] the Hong Kong Bar Association and other commentators argued that the office was a body that owed its existence to the Chinese government and that there was no legal support for its claim to supervise the implementation of the Basic Law in Hong Kong.[121]

If the Liaison Office's interpretation of Article 22 is accepted, it places the Hong Kong government in a subordinate relationship to the Liaison Office and undermines the notion that it has a "high degree of autonomy" in policy formulation and implementation. In April 2020, the Constitutional and Mainland Affairs Bureau did release a statement which failed to mention that the Liaison Office had the right to supervise the implementation of the Basic Law in Hong Kong. Within a few days, the Secretary for Constitutional and Mainland Affairs, Patrick Nip, had been transferred to another bureau and the press release had been amended.[122]

The controversy was a sign of things to come. At the end of June, the National People's Congress enacted the national security law. The law has a wide-ranging impact on governance and civil liberties in Hong Kong.[123] In addition to the investigation and prosecution of broadly defined offences relating to treason, secession, subversion, and terrorism,[124] it requires the Hong Kong government to promote awareness of the national security provisions in educational institutions and social organisations.[125] The law also affects how Hong Kong government departments are expected to work. A new PRC office, the Office for Safeguarding National Security of the Central People's Government in the HKSAR, was established to work in Hong Kong with a Mainland official appointed to take charge. The office has wide

---

120. Sum, L. K. (2020, 27 April). Basic Law's Article 22 'does not apply' to Beijing's liaison office, Hong Kong's justice secretary says. *SCMP*. https://www.scmp.com/news/hong-kong/politics/article/3081816/basic-laws-article-22-does-not-apply-beijings-liaison
121. Hong Kong Bar Association (2020, 20 April). Further statement of the Hong Kong Bar Association on Article 22 of the Basic Law. https://www.hkba.org/sites/default/files/20200420%20-%20HKBA%27s%20Further%20Statement%20on%20Article%2022%20of%20the%20Basic%20Law%20%28English%29.pdf; Chan, J. (2020, 20 April). A strained interpretation of the Basic Law. *HKU Legal Scholarship Blog*, http://researchblog.law.hku.hk/2020/04/a-strained-interpretation-of-basic-law.html
122. Hong Kong Government (2020, 18 April). Government responds to media enquiries on remarks by HKMAO and LOCPG. https://www.info.gov.hk/gia/general/202004/18/P2020041800802.htm; Ho, K. (2020, 19 April). Gov't edits press release after contradicting Beijing on constitutional status of its Hong Kong office. *HKFP*. https://hongkongfp.com/2020/04/19/govt-edits-press-release-overnight-after-contradicting-beijing-on-constitutional-status-of-its-hong-kong-office/
123. Cabestan & Daziano (2020) op. cit.; Davis, M. C., & Hui, V. T. B. (2020). Beijing's national security law brings repression to Hong Kong. *The Diplomat*. https://thediplomat.com/2020/07/beijings-national-security-law-brings-mainland-repression-to-hong-kong/
124. Government of the People's Republic of China (2020) op. cit., Ch. III, Pts 1–3, Article 62.
125. Ibid., Articles 9, 10.

powers. Office personnel are not subject to the jurisdiction of the HKSAR[126] and they can require any Hong Kong government department to provide information relating to national security.[127] The Police Force is required to set up a new department to deal with security, and the office has a say in who is appointed as its head.[128] The Department of Justice is required to establish a special prosecution division for safeguarding national security efforts in Hong Kong with hand-picked prosecutors appointed by a high-level committee.[129] The Director of the Liaison Office has been appointed as security adviser to the Chief Executive and as a member of the committee overseeing security.[130]

Many commentators see the national security law as regime change and a clear violation of the Sino-British agreement and promises of "one country, two systems" and a "high degree of autonomy" for the HKSAR.[131] The Chinese and Hong Kong governments saw the national security law as a means of re-establishing order and of dealing with what they thought was foreign incitement of the protesters and the consequential threat to national security. The implementation of the law to date gives little cause to suppose that there will be any restoration of independent decision-making on security issues to the Hong Kong government in the foreseeable future and, since security is defined so broadly, it could be used to justify intervention in any field of government activity. Nonetheless, some present aspects of the Hong Kong policymaking system have advantages for the Chinese government. It rewards pro-Beijing supporters, particularly business, provides the necessary delivery of goods and services, is corruption-free, and has significant economic and technical benefits for the Mainland government in support of policies such as economic integration, innovation, and the Belt and Road Initiative. There may be Hong Kong situations with which the Chinese government is unhappy, such as the education curriculum and university autonomy, and where it seems likely that it will insist on more regulation. But wholesale changes to policy formulation and implementation may result in poor outcomes that would be detrimental to any system of direct rule over Hong Kong. The more pressing issues, for which the law seems to be designed, are the suppression of dissent, limiting civil liberties such as freedom of expression and academic autonomy,[132] curbing the ability of the Hong Kong Police Force to deal with security issues without supervision from Mainland

---

126. Ibid., Article 60.
127. Ibid., Article 61.
128. Ibid., Article 16.
129. Ibid., Article 18.
130. Ibid., Article 15.
131. Cabestan & Daziano (2020) op. cit., pp. 33–37; Kuo, L., & Davidson, H. (2020, 28 September). Who runs Hong Kong: Party faithful shipped in to carry out Beijing's will. *The Guardian*. https://www.theguardian.com/world/2020/sep/28/who-runs-hong-kong-party-faithful-shipped-in-to-carry-out-beijing-will-security-law; Rogers, B., & Patterson, J. (2020, 1 July). The death of Hong Kong. *The Spectator*. https://www.spectator.co.uk/article/the-death-of-hong-kong
132. Wang, V. (2020, 7 November). As Hong Kong law goes after "black sheep", fear clouds universities. *New York Times*. https://www.nytimes.com/2020/11/07/world/asia/hong-kong-china-national-security-law-university.html

security agencies, restricting judicial independence on security cases, and ensuring that senior Mainland officials are present on the committees and organisations that make decisions on such matters.

Although the importance of pro-Beijing, pro-establishment and united front groups has been diminished by direct intervention and their institutional role is now less important than it was, the maintenance of the structure may still be important to feed policy ideas and the public mood to the Liaison Office. The groups serve to provide a facile front to legitimise the legislative process and avoid government by decree and to maintain the Chinese government's position that it is still abiding by the Sino-British agreement and its promise of a high degree of autonomy for Hong Kong.

Conclusions

The major thrust of Chinese government policy on Hong Kong has been aimed at integrating the HKSAR with the Mainland. Efforts to increase social integration through more migration, tourism, cultural exchanges, and the attempt to introduce a compulsory "moral and national education" curriculum have met with strong resistance which appears to have led to greater identification with Hong Kong rather than with China and the rise of "localism" in politics. Economic integration with China has presented major advantages for Hong Kong business people and has generally been welcomed by them. For localists, however, the growth of Mainland economic influence in the city and the construction of expensive and uneconomic rail and bridge links have been seen as a threat to autonomy, an environmental degradation, and a waste of money. The Chinese government's intervention to enact national security legislation to counter the rise of localism and the 2019/2020 protests has reduced the Hong Kong government's already compromised autonomy to make policy even further. Whether the security provisions will determine policy formulation in every policy domain or whether some autonomy will be permitted in non-controversial areas remains to be seen.

Since the handover, policymaking in Hong Kong has undergone significant changes. The Hong Kong government entered the post-handover period confident in its ability to formulate policies to deal with a backlog of problems and to introduce innovative new developments. But implementation problems worsened under successive administrations. The rise of opposition focused on the need for democratic change further impaired implementation and presented the government with new challenges in dealing with security problems on the streets. Caught between the growing democratic opposition and a Chinese government intent on greater integration and political stability, the Hong Kong government was unable to introduce major new policies. Policy became hostage to an increasingly conflictual political situation in which the Chinese government eventually became the major actor. After the enactment of the national security law, the sharp further decline in its autonomy and a budget in long-term deficit, it is difficult to see how the Hong Kong government can begin to address the major economic and social problems that have been neglected over the past decade.

Part IV

The Government and the People

11
Efficiency, Responsiveness, and Transparency

What do people expect of their government? How does the government seek to meet those expectations? For any government that is not solely based on the coercive power of the state, these are important questions. In Hong Kong, where the government cannot be removed by elections and where there are few other justifications for its continuing rule, the ability to respond to people's needs and expectations is critical. Both the colonial and the post-handover regimes have rested their claims to rule on performance legitimacy, the belief that, if the government delivers the public goods and services that people want, then *ipso facto* it will also have political support and a rationale for exercising its authority. There are two critical assumptions underlying this claim: that the government can determine what those expectations are and that it has the capacity to meet them. If demands are relatively simple, then this may not be problematic. But if they are complex, expensive, or conflicting, then the government's ability to deliver may be in question. In Hong Kong, low capacity to implement policy has meant that the government has had difficulty in introducing new policies even when there are clear demands for them. The government has aimed at increasing efficiency not only because this accords with its traditional beliefs, such as "value for money" and fiscal frugality, but also because an efficient government, at least in its own eyes, is a legitimate government.

Although the government has always believed that efficiency is central to meeting people's expectations, it has not been the only value that it has sought to promote. A non-democratic government might still win popular support and reduce its legitimacy deficit if it acted responsibly and responsively. If relations between government and the public could be conducted courteously, quickly, and with attention to specific needs and if the government was able to assess public demands for policy changes and was transparent about its intentions, then it might benefit from increased political support. In this ideal world, efficiency, responsiveness, and transparency might be regarded as compatible values. If, for example, a department can make clear to its clients what its requirements and their entitlements are and serve them quickly and pleasantly, it may be acting transparently, efficiently, and responsively. But it is also possible that the values may be incompatible. A department that tells people what it is going to do, and why, is acting transparently, but if it fails to deliver, it loses credibility. A department that spends too much time looking after the diverse needs of citizens might be responsive without being efficient. Conversely, a department may deliver services efficiently but without much regard to the views or needs of its clients.

The balance between efficiency, responsiveness, and transparency is difficult to achieve. For the most part, the Hong Kong government has regarded efficiency as the overriding legitimating value. The argument that government should be cost-effective and efficient has usually won out over the view that it should listen to what people want and then deliver services appropriately, if perhaps less cost-effectively. At times, however, responsiveness has been seen as an alternative means of legitimation. In the last years of colonial rule, it was central to the government's objective of changing the culture of the civil service and "re-legitimating" the bureaucratic polity.[1] After 1997, this approach fell out of favour because Tung's initial stress was on the importance of managerialism, efficiency, and "executive-led" government. The mass demonstration against the national security legislation in 2003 persuaded the government that it should be more concerned about "people-based governance"[2] and more responsive to their policy demands. But this was essentially a formal commitment and did not lead to many new ways of improving its relationships with the public. The growing impasse in policymaking reflected the fact that, although the government provided its citizens with extensive information on its activities and its civil servants were often responsive and efficient, there were no easy ways to convert public expectations into policy outputs. In this chapter, we examine the attempt to use efficiency, responsiveness, and transparency to reduce the legitimacy deficit.

Performance Legitimacy and Efficiency

The legitimacy of a government (as distinct from that of a state) may rest on all or some of four measures: process (input) legitimacy; performance (output) legitimacy; shared beliefs; and international recognition.[3] In the Hong Kong context, three of these measures are either missing or have been compromised. Process legitimacy involves citizens' determination of how a government exercises power, often expressed through elected governments and the right to vote.[4] In Hong Kong, it has foundered on the failure to introduce direct elections for the Chief Executive and the legislature as provided for in the Basic Law. Legitimacy may also rest on

---

1. Cheung, A. B. L. (1996). Public sector reform and the re-legitimation of public bureaucratic power: The case of Hong Kong. *International Journal of Public Sector Management*, 9(5/6), 37–50.
2. Tsang, D. Y. K. (2005). *Strong governance for the people*. Hong Kong: Government Logistics Department; Tung, C. H. (2004). *Seizing opportunities for development, promoting people-based governance* (pp. 22–24). Hong Kong: Government Logistics Department; Tung, C. H. (2005). *Working together for economic development and social harmony* (pp. 9–10). Hong Kong: Government Logistics Department.
3. Dagher, R. (2018). Legitimacy and post-conflict state-building: The undervalued role of performance legitimacy. *Conflict, Security and Development*, 18(2), 85–111.
4. Beetham, D. (2013). *The legitimation of power* (2nd ed.). Basingstoke: Macmillan.

an assumption about shared values and beliefs: that those of the government are congruent with those of the people and that therefore it has a legitimate right to rule. The attempts to promote shared values with the Mainland through the education system, however, have not succeeded in attaining this objective and may have helped spark protests that represented a very different set of values. International recognition is not relevant since Hong Kong was previously a British colony and is now part of the People's Republic of China.

That leaves performance legitimacy as the basis for the Hong Kong government to seek to legitimise its rule. Performance legitimacy may be defined as the provision of desired and delivered goods and services in exchange for citizens' recognition of the government's right to exercise power.[5] If a government can meet citizens' daily needs, especially health, housing, education, welfare, and transport, then it may be recognised as a legitimate provider of desired goods and services. But two caveats are important. First, perceived needs may change over time. Expectations may rise and change and new demands may become more salient. The government must have sufficient capacity and flexibility to accommodate both gradual change within well-established parameters and the delivery of new goods and services that may require imaginative policy responses. Second, access is an important element of performance legitimacy. The presumption is that the whole population will benefit from good performance. But if access to public goods and services is unequal or compromised by poor delivery, the division between the beneficiaries and the excluded may have adverse political consequences.

In the absence of democratic legitimation, performance legitimacy has taken on important political as well as administrative significance. Lui observes that the credibility of the colonial government hinged almost entirely on bureaucratic performance; inefficiency was not simply administratively undesirable, it also threatened the political authority of unaccountable civil servants.[6] In the post-handover era, the POAS was expected, *inter alia*, to improve the government's ability to deliver goods and services more efficiently. Efficiency has remained politically important because the government has been unable to supplement its right to exercise power with other forms of legitimation.

Efficiency relates to at least three aspects of administrative performance. First, costs should be kept under control and new expenditure should meet the criterion of the greatest output for the least resources expended. Governments must be careful that what they deliver does not fall too far below citizens' expectations. The cheapest goods and services are not necessarily always the solution to the problem. Second, efficiency means rapid decision-making. Since the McKinsey recommendations, the disaggregation of the Government Secretariat into discrete policy bureaus

---

5. Dagher (2018) op. cit.
6. Lui, T. T. (1994). Efficiency as a political concept in the Hong Kong government: Issues and problems. In J. P. Burns (Ed.), *Asian civil service systems: Improving efficiency and productivity* (p. 18). Singapore: Times Academic Press.

and the decentralisation of some functions to the departments have allowed more decisions to be taken at a relatively lower level.[7] In post-handover Hong Kong, the problem has not been a lack of efficiency in responding to demands within existing programmes as much as securing support for new programmes that address pressing issues. Third, efficiency involves delivering services through an appropriate structure with qualified personnel. The government's hierarchical structure means that it can deliver some services efficiently. With the expansion of the education system, it has not been short of qualified personnel except in some professional areas where salaries in the private sector far exceed those in the public sector.

The idea that the government can acquire legitimacy through the efficient delivery of services is a thread that runs through Hong Kong's history, but there are significant differences between its earlier and later forms. In the 1970s, the government based its right to rule on the provision of much-expanded services, such as public housing, education, health care, welfare, and transport, and took credit for the territory's economic prosperity. This success encouraged the belief, particularly held by business and pro-Beijing groups, that Hong Kong people would be satisfied with any government that provided such goods and services, regardless of how it was selected. From this perspective, regime legitimacy was subsumed under the managerialist assumption that outcomes and ends, not means or process, mattered in securing political support. If this were so, then the only problem for a government was whether it could deliver what the people wanted. Tacit support would obviate the need for expressed consent. In both the transitional and post-handover periods, the evidence suggests that this approach oversimplifies the legitimacy problem, underestimating the complex support required to maintain consent and the legal and moral authority necessary to rule in a non-democratic system.

During the transitional period, the government was able to maintain its established record for service delivery. However, the Sino-British negotiations and the realisation that the British and Chinese governments would determine the fate of Hong Kong reduced the authority of the colonial administration. The retrocession to China also sparked demands for the protection of civil liberties and the rule of law after 1997, which neither the British government nor the colonial administration could guarantee. There were growing demands for representative government and pressure groups began to lobby for qualitatively better social policy outputs. As civil organisations gathered momentum, the predominance of a paternalistic civil service elite declined[8] even though senior civil servants themselves continued to believe that what the people wanted was best determined by the bureaucracy.[9]

---

7. McKinsey and Company (May 1973). *The machinery of government: A new framework for expanding services* (p. 5). Hong Kong: mimeo.
8. Painter, M. (2005). Transforming the administrative state: Reform in Hong Kong and the future of the developmental state. *Public Administration Review*, 65(3), 335–346.
9. Burns, J. P. & Li, W. (2015). The impact of external change on civil service values in post-colonial Hong Kong. *The China Quarterly*, 222, 522–546.

Towards the end of the colonial administration, some difficult decisions were postponed although the government still attempted to maintain stability by expanding social policy outputs. There were efforts to increase health care services and expand public housing.[10] To answer demands for qualitatively better social policies, the government set up an Environmental Protection Department, tried to reform the social welfare system, to resolve transport problems, and to improve teaching practices and learning.[11] A science and technology university was established to help meet demands for more tertiary-level education.

In 1995, the Efficiency Unit produced a document, *Serving the community*, which formally remains a template for government objectives.[12] The government committed itself to protecting individual rights and freedoms, maintaining the rule of law, improving the quality of life, fostering stability and prosperity, and encouraging participation in the community. The document also contained a section on efficiency, which provided for reviews of departmental programmes, advice on how departments were to be managed, "value for money" studies, and the promotion of new technology to improve services.[13]

In October 1997, Tung delivered the first post-handover policy address. There were promises of an even greater expansion of social policy outputs and rail and road services. Tung said his administration would increase the supply of land and ensure the construction of 85,000 public housing flats per year and the sale of 250,000 units. There were additional CSSA payments, more hospital beds, a new $5 billion Quality Education Fund, another review of health care, and more elderly care centres, all aimed at improving the quality of life. It proved impossible to deliver on the promise of 85,000 flats per year and other initiatives were affected by the Asian financial crisis and the subsequent economic recession.[14] Yet, like his predecessors, Tung was committed to legitimising his government by performance legitimacy and ensuring that his administration was efficient.

Although he praised the civil service in the policy address, Tung's view was that it needed substantial reform to make it more innovative, more attuned to business practices, and more cost-effective. Tung's public sector reforms were not successful (see Chapter 5), but they did temporarily reduce the size of the civil service and may have laid the foundation for a more professional civil service because the disproportionately large numbers of workers and labourers on the Model Scale 1 pay scale

---

10. Hutcheon, R. (1999). *Bedside manner: Hospital and health care in Hong Kong* (Ch. 3 & 4). Hong Kong: The Chinese University of Hong Kong Press; La Grange, A. (2007). Housing (1997–2007). In J. Y. S. Cheng (Ed.), *The Hong Kong Special Administrative Region in its first decade* (p. 701). Hong Kong: The City University of Hong Kong Press.
11. Bray, M. (1997). Education and colonial transition: The Hong Kong experience in comparative perspective. *Comparative Education*, 33(2), 157–169; Working Party on Social Welfare Policies and Services (1990). *Social welfare into the 1990s and beyond*. Hong Kong: Government Printer.
12. Efficiency Unit (1995). *Serving the community* (p. 5). Hong Kong: Government Printer.
13. Ibid., p. 47.
14. Tsang, C. K. (1999). The Hong Kong economy: Opportunities out of the crisis? *Journal of Contemporary China*, 8(20), 29–45.

were gradually replaced with more skilled and qualified personnel. In 1997, 12.3% (22,883) of the strength of the civil service was on Model Scale 1; by 2020, this had been reduced to 4.1% (7,432).[15] Although the government gradually increased its capacity, deploying resources to introduce major new programmes proved difficult. Success in basing legitimacy on performance and output was much more constrained by a contentious environment than it had been under colonialism.

The colonial government successfully addressed the task of meeting pent-up demands for basic goods and services. But it had several advantages: a balanced budget backed by substantial and usually increasing reserves, almost no opposition to its proposals, and an efficient, cost-effective, and expanding civil service. The converse applied in the post-handover period. Demands for services grew and were more complex, the budget was at times in deficit, and although, after 2007, the civil service expanded, its cost eventually became unsustainable. The government gradually became weaker and less credible, caught between Mainland government influence over its policies and democratic opposition in the legislature and on the streets.

The failure to satisfy demand on many issues led to dissatisfaction with government performance. Figure 11.1 shows HKUPOP/PORI survey responses to the question "Are you satisfied with the performance of the HKSAR government?" over the period 1997 to 2020. At only two points over those years does satisfaction with the performance of the government rise above 50%: in 1997 and at the start of the Tsang administration in 2005/2006. The percentages in Figure 11.1 for the satisfied and dissatisfied respondents conflate the views of the "very satisfied"/ "satisfied" and those who were "very dissatisfied"/ "dissatisfied" and represent the average of two polls taken annually. The number of respondents who were "very satisfied/ positive" ranged from a low of 0.7% in 1999 to a high of 7.7% in 2017.[16] Those who were "very dissatisfied"/ "dissatisfied" ranged from 1.9% in 1997 to 59.9% in 2019; on a single poll in 2019, the number who were "very dissatisfied" or "dissatisfied" reached 75.8%.[17] A government cannot base its right to rule on performance legitimacy with numbers like these.

Responses to HKUPOP/PORI polls show that, if the government is viewed unfavourably on the political dimension, it will be perceived to have performed unfavourably on all other dimensions.[18] A PORI question, for example, on the sufficiency of social welfare provision showed a sharp drop in levels of satisfaction with government performance once the 2019 protests began. Access to social services could also be an important factor in determining satisfaction. In a study of over

---

15. Civil Service Bureau (1997). *Civil service personnel statistics 1997* (p. 15). Hong Kong: Government Printer; Civil Service Bureau (2020). Strength of the civil service (as at 30 June 2020). https://www.csb.gov.hk/english/stat/quarterly/541.html
16. PORI (2020). People's satisfaction with the HKSAR government. https://www.pori.hk/pop-poll/government-en/h001.html?lang=en
17. Ibid.
18. Ibid.; Wong, M. Y. H. (2020). Welfare or politics? A survey experiment of political discontent and support for redistribution in Hong Kong. *Politics*, 40(1), 70–89.

Efficiency, Responsiveness, and Transparency 333

Figure 11.1 *Are You Satisfied with the Performance of the HKSAR Government? 1997–2020*

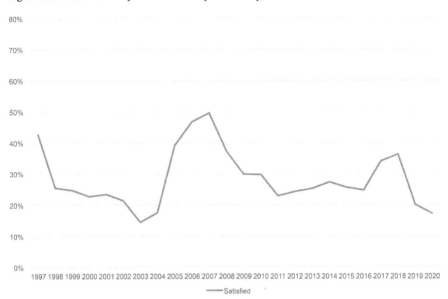

Source: Adapted from Hong Kong Public Opinion Research Institute (PORI) (2020) People's satisfaction with the HKSAR government, op. cit.

5,000 hospital patients, researchers found that 80% of respondents rated the care they received as good or better than good.[19] Yet another large study suggests that there was also considerable dissatisfaction with hospital waiting times.[20] A survey of public housing tenants found that they were dissatisfied with the lack of privacy, with noise, and with the size of their apartments but may still have been pleased to have a roof over their heads.[21] People with access to services may be satisfied with government performance because it usually delivers services reasonably efficiently. People without access or very slow access are likely to be aggrieved. The problem for the government has been accommodating new demands in a gridlocked political system with resource limitations.

Performance legitimacy is one means of securing consent to rule, but it has serious limitations in a developed economy. At best, it is often only a temporary fix

---

19. Wong, E. Y. L., Coulter, A., Cheung, A. W. L., Yam, C. H. K., Yeh, E. K., & Griffiths, S. M. (2012). Patient experiences with public hospital care: First benchmark study in Hong Kong. *Hong Kong Medical Journal*, 18(5), 371–380.
20. Siu, P. (2019, 19 May). Just one-third of Hong Kong residents satisfied with public hospital services as long waiting times and lack of care top list of gripes. *SCMP*. https://www.scmp.com/news/hong-kong/health-environment/article/3010839/just-one-third-hong-kong-residents-satisfied
21. Gou, Z., Xie, X., Lu, Y., & Khoshbakht, M. (2018). Quality of Life (QoL) survey in Hong Kong: Understanding the importance of housing environment and needs of residents from different housing sectors. *International Journal of Environmental Research and Public Health*, 15(2), 219.

and supplemental to other means of addressing a legitimacy deficit. In the 1970s, the colonial regime manufactured consent by providing highly desired public goods and then supplemented that provision by supporting the upward mobility of the younger generation. Performance legitimacy with the intent of buying political support usually has a limited shelf life. When basic needs are satisfied, they are likely to spark rising expectations for better quality and more specialised goods and services that are not realised as easily as basic provision and that will eventually come up against the constraint of finite financial resources. After the 1970s, a better educated, more prosperous community was inclined to look for justifications to exercise power in a more lasting resolution of the problem of consent and the protection of civil liberties and the rule of law. Performance legitimacy, defined in terms of efficiency, became a hygiene factor, a necessary condition for acceptable governance but insufficient to legitimise the government.

In the post-handover period, the government's credibility was often at stake. It was unable to resolve seemingly intractable and persistent problems such as the supply of land for public housing and the funding of the health care system. In the light of the failure to solve major policy problems, services ticked over, much as they always had, run by an efficient civil service and subvented voluntary agencies but without much prospect of reform and increasingly stretched to meet demand. Large cash handouts to the public in 2011 and 2020 signified a government that had lost direction and could not think of more productive ways to spend money to improve people's livelihood. It was no longer possible to match government claims about its performance with the reality of the human condition in Hong Kong although some of its alleviative measures do seem to have off-set the effects of a severe recession in 2020.[22]

Responsiveness

Responsiveness describes efforts to build a trusting relationship between the government and the people in which public officials make a positive effort to provide courteous help and services to citizens within the legal confines of their responsibilities.[23] How citizens receive services may help to reduce a legitimacy deficit and increase trust, but it must be seen to apply equally to all citizens and not used selectively to aid some but not others. How a responsive government should position itself is also an issue. Where does helpful service provision cease and the search for answers to citizens' demands begin?[24]

---

22. Census and Statistics Department (2021). *Hong Kong poverty situation report*. https://www.censtatd.gov.hk/en/data/stat_report/product/B9XX0005/att/B9XX0005E2020AN20E0100.pdf
23. OECD (2020). Trust in government—responsiveness. http://www.oecd.org/gov/trust-responsiveness.htm
24. Liao, Y. (2018). Towards a pragmatic model of public responsiveness: Implications for enhancing public administrators' responsiveness to citizen demands. *International Journal of Public Administration*, 41(2), 159–169.

When Patten assumed office in 1992, the possibility of legitimating the post-handover polity by democratic means had already disappeared. The Basic Law precluded the possibility of an elected government, and the Chinese government made it clear that it would overturn the minor changes made for the 1995 election as soon as it gained control of Hong Kong. Patten sought to bolster trust in his administration by other means. Aided by some reform-minded senior public servants and legislators, he made operational and legal changes to relationships between the civil service and the public.[25] The idea was to transform the public service from a colonial bureaucracy into an organisation that was more responsive, accountable, and open, and enhanced citizens' rights to information, data protection, freedom from discrimination, and legal aid. The reforms addressed the need to reduce the regime's legitimacy deficit,[26] strengthened the institutional stability of the civil service, and provided some assurance that a future government might still respond positively to citizens' needs.

Responsiveness, defined as a "culture of service" to the public, was a key value. The idea took some of its intellectual substance from British practice and from the OECD. It was predicated on assumptions about relationships between the government and the people: that the public should be able to readily understand how government worked, that citizens should be encouraged to participate in policymaking, and that government should satisfy their needs and be accessible.[27] At the heart of the idea was the accountability of civil servants to the public. The government still adhered, of course, to the potentially conflicting value of efficiency to which the government remained committed.[28]

Patten believed, however, that efficiency was not sufficient to meet public expectations:

> Good government is about much more than simply finding the wherewithal to upgrade our programmes, to improve our social services or enhance our infrastructure. An increasingly prosperous and sophisticated community quite rightly demands greater openness and accountability from the public sector . . . and an official attitude of mind that regards the public as *clients* not supplicants.[29]

The reforms initially focused on efforts to improve communication between civil servants and the public. Civil servants were required to identify themselves by name; interim replies to correspondence were to be received within 10 days; government forms were to be simplified and abolished if they were found to be unnecessary; and civil servants were to receive training to attain new standards of courtesy and

---

25. Patten, C. (1992). *Our next five years: The agenda for Hong Kong* (p. 26). Hong Kong: Government Printer; Patten, C. (1998). *East and West* (p. 46). London: Macmillan; Efficiency Unit (1995) op. cit.
26. Cheung (1996) op. cit.
27. OECD (1987). *Administration as service: The public as client* (p. 131). Paris: OECD.
28. Efficiency Unit (1995), op cit., p. 7; Hong Kong Government (1995, 10 February). *The Hong Kong Government serving the community* (p. 4). Hong Kong: Government Printer.
29. Patten (1992) op. cit., p. 26.

helpfulness.[30] These were seen as basic and preliminary measures. The broader aim was to introduce performance pledges which were to be adopted in all government departments providing services to the public.

Performance Pledges

The idea of performance pledges was drawn from the Citizen's Charter in Britain, which sets out the standards that the public has a right to expect from government departments. In Hong Kong, they were first introduced in departments that had the most contact with the public: the Department of Health and the Hospital Authority, the Police Force, fire and ambulance emergency services, immigration control points, the Inland Revenue Department, and Transport Department officials who dealt with vehicle and driving licences.[31] Departments were encouraged to set up customer liaison groups to provide feedback on services and to reflect consumer preferences.

The pledges were initially greeted with some suspicion in the civil service. The Finance Branch thought that there might be increases in operating expenses, which there were, and some departments thought that the standards might be unattainable, which proved not to be the case. By October 1993, 30 of the 50 government departments had produced performance pledges, 20 had created user or customer liaison groups, over 4,400 government forms had been reviewed and 800 had been abolished, and over 30,000 civil servants had attended training courses to improve their skills in dealing with members of the public.[32] By the following year, all civil service departments and many statutory bodies, such as the Hospital Authority, the Mass Transit Railway, and the Kowloon-Canton Railway, had produced performance pledges. Commitments to the public were prominently displayed in government offices throughout the territory; "service to the community" became the new public sector credo. Since the handover, the performance pledge has remained a feature of every department and most statutory bodies.[33]

The initial emphasis of performance pledges was on providing a "culture of service" reflecting the value of responsiveness. Performance pledges were to serve the functions of improving relationships with customers, imparting a customer focus to staff, acting as a management tool in daily operations, providing performance standards for staff, and creating a mechanism for reporting performance to customers and the community.[34] By 2020, however, there was much less empha-

---

30. Ibid., pp. 26–27.
31. Ibid.
32. Patten, C. (1993). *Hong Kong: Today's successes, tomorrow's challenges* (p. 29). Hong Kong: Government Printer.
33. Hong Kong Government (2019). Performance pledges@gov. https://www.serviceexcellence.gov.hk/en/performance-pledges/index.html
34. Efficiency Unit (1996). *The service imperative*. Hong Kong: Government Printer; Efficiency Unit (2001). Performance pledges. Hong Kong: Government Printer.

sis on responsiveness; the focus of performance pledges was largely on "targets, achievements, monitoring and communication".[35] There are nonetheless important differences in how departments construct their pledges. Some may be a consequence of their specific administrative functions; others seem designed to protect the departmental image and to provide an escape hatch if performance is not up to expectations.

A department may or may not choose to mention its culture of service in its performance pledge, but all are expected to demonstrate their efficiency in meeting quantifiable targets (key performance indicators, KPI). The Social Welfare Department, for example, pledges that its civil servants will be courteous, fair, respect confidentiality, respect privacy, process requests promptly, and have regard for personal circumstances.[36] The department also has KPI, achieving all but one of its 17 targets in 2019/2020. KPI are the most important element in the performance pledge for most departments, defining and assessing how efficient they have been in delivering services, not in how courteously, fairly, or impartially they have dealt with citizens. In some departments, this is a consequence of their functions. The Fire Services Department, for example, assesses its performance on how quickly it responds to fire alarms and how swiftly the injured are transported to hospital.[37] Although it runs an emergency ambulance service, its dealings with the public do not usually leave much room for social niceties.

Even departments in contact with the public in sometimes less difficult circumstances, such as the Police Force, the Housing Authority, the Water Supplies Department, and the Trade and Industry Department, have chosen to emphasise KPI in their performance pledges rather than values.[38] Targets are important because they can be presented as justifications of performance and the need for future funding in the budget estimates. But there is also potential conflict with responsiveness. The Social Welfare Department stresses responsiveness, which might not always be efficient, while many other departments have underlined their commitment to efficiency, which might not always be responsive. Since 1997, this tension between responsiveness and efficiency has been increasingly resolved in favour of efficiency with the values of the bureau or department expressed in mission and vision statements. Performance rather than responsiveness has become the criterion by which departments expect to be judged.

Performance pledges often set soft targets which are relatively easily achieved. In some departments, these are supplemented by further separate instructions on how civil servants should deal with the public. The Labour Department, for

---

35. Hong Kong Government (2019) op. cit.
36. Social Welfare Department (2021). Performance pledge. https://www.swd.gov.hk/en/index/site_aboutus/page_performanc/
37. Fire Services Department (2021). Performance pledge. https://www.hkfsd.gov.hk/eng/aboutus/performance.html
38. Hong Kong Government (2021). Performance pledges@gov.hk. https://www.serviceexcellence.gov.hk/en/performance-pledges/index.html

example, has issued internal guidelines on standards of service which are intended to make the staff more responsive. They include instructions to be patient, courteous, and flexible, to wear a pleasant smile, and to use name badges. There are also directions on how to maintain the office and to ensure that queuing systems are efficient and fair. Office managers are also expected to display complaint procedures prominently and to deploy staff effectively to meet changes in demand. The department's performance pledge, however, says very little about the standard of service that the public should expect.[39]

After their initial suspicions about the culture of service and performance pledges, civil servants' reactions to the changes gradually became more favourable. Offices were painted, counters were redesigned to make information more easily available and to facilitate interaction with clients and most departments introduced projects to motivate their staff to provide better service. These included a competition for the friendliest clinic in the Department of Health, a competition for the best counter service in the Immigration Department, and a staff quiz on the work of the Trade and Industry Department. In the Labour Department, all local employment service offices were involved in a contest for the best customer service. In 1999, a survey of 414 executive officers, who serve as middle managers across government departments, found that 75% of respondents thought that performance pledges had made a difference to their work, especially in departments that were dealing directly with the public.[40] Respondents who were critical of performance pledges mentioned soft targets and claimed that there had been little change to the culture of the civil service. There was generally more sympathy for reforms that increased responsiveness than for those that were seen as managerialist or aimed at improving efficiency.[41]

Commitment to a culture of service and performance pledges may have helped to reduce the legitimacy deficit, enhance responsiveness, improve the public image and morale of civil servants, and meet public expectations of better service.[42] After 1997, the increased stress on performance and the rise of contentious politics eroded some of these gains. Agencies in direct contact with citizens, such as the Police Force, the Housing Authority, and the Hospital Authority, inevitably receive more public attention than others if standards drop. In the following sections, we examine how responsiveness as a value has been affected in those agencies.

---

39. Labour Department (2021). Performance pledge. https://www.labour.gov.hk/eng/perform/pledge.htm
40. Scott, I. (2000). Public sector reform and middle managers in Hong Kong. *Asian Journal of Public Administration* 22(2), 107–134.
41. Ibid.
42. Cheung (1996) op. cit.

Responsiveness in Key Government Agencies

Responsiveness in the Police Force

As 1997 approached, the government and some senior police officers felt that there was a need to shift the focus of the force from its former paramilitary role to more community policing.[43] After a review of the organisational structure and role of the force, a Service Quality Wing (SQW) was established under an Assistant Commissioner of Police in May 1994. In March 1995, the SQW produced a policy document on Force Strategy on Quality of Service, which was based on the private sector notion of Total Quality Management and on the practices of the British police forces. The strategy aimed at developing a culture throughout the force that would be effective, efficient, and economical and would meet the expectations of the public, using periodic opinion polls and customer satisfaction surveys.[44]

The first customer satisfaction survey was conducted in December 1995.[45] It found satisfaction levels with force performance at 78%; only 3% of respondents regarded the police performance as poor although 19% gave unsolicited adverse comments on the service manners of police officers. The survey and a consultation process within the force and with the public were used to produce a *Vision and Statement of Common Purpose and Values*.[46] The document committed the force to core values such as fairness, impartiality and compassion, acceptance of responsibility and accountability, professionalism, dedication to quality service, responsiveness to change, and effective communication inside and outside the force. Two further surveys found that the public regarded police performance positively. In the first survey, 69% of respondents thought that the police were courteous and rated this as the best aspect of their performance while their speed and efficiency received the lowest rating.[47] Respondents to the second survey believed that the force was professional and efficient but was neither accountable nor transparent. Only 35% were satisfied with the police community relations effort and only half of the respondents were satisfied with how the police conducted their business.[48]

To address such concerns, the force spent considerable time and effort in developing a sophisticated programme aimed at communicating what their core values meant in practice and how this might make officers more responsive to public

---

43. Lo, C. W. H., & Cheuk, A. C. Y. (2004). Community policing in Hong Kong: Development, performance and constraints. *Policing: An International Journal of Police Strategies and Management, 27*(1), 97–127; So, B. K. T. (1999). *The Hong Kong Police as a new paradigm of policing in a post-colonial city: An analysis of reform achievement* [Unpublished master's thesis] (p. 49). The University of Hong Kong.
44. So (1999) op. cit., p. 51.
45. MDR Technology Ltd. (1998). *Opinion survey on the quality of police services: A report*. Hong Kong: The Company.
46. Hong Kong Police Force (1996). *Vision and statement of common purpose and values*. Hong Kong: mimeo.
47. Provisional Legislative Council Panel on Security (1997). *Customer satisfaction survey of the Police Force* (pp. 1–2). https://www.pori.hk/pop-poll/disciplinary-force-en/x001.html?lang=en
48. Social Science Research Centre (1999). *Public opinion survey on the public image of the Hong Kong Police Force: Survey report* (pp. 18, 22). Hong Kong: The Centre.

needs. The reforms involved changes in induction courses and in-service training in the Police College and new and well-designed programmes run by the SQW.[49] These included the Living the Values programme, an annual exercise in which the force would concentrate on one value and explore its meaning through workshops, videos, and competitions; the Healthy Lifestyle programme; the Lifelong Learning programme to promote further education; a volunteer service corps for charity work; and various kinds of development and ethical training. As a counterpoint to the community policing values programmes, it should also be mentioned that all police officers are required to serve for a period in the anti-riot Police Tactical Unit.[50] It may be surmised that the unit's values have not been primarily focused on community policing and responsiveness.

In 2013–2014, our research team assessed the impact that the Living the Values programme had on police attitudes towards their ethical responsibilities and community relations.[51] We surveyed 788 junior police constables, conducted eight focus groups of junior police officers from regional and divisional groups with 62 participants, and interviewed senior officers from the SQW and the Police College. The survey showed that young recruits were mostly committed to community policing although perhaps not to the same degree as the officers in the SQW and the Police College. The focus groups revealed differences in attitudes within the force. While young constables often accepted the value-based approach, they had doubts about whether it could be put into practice in their everyday duties.

In some cases, even if young police officers were acting in contradiction of rules and values promoted by the SQW and the Police College, standing against entrenched practices meant disrupting the local police organisation.[52] Nonetheless, there were occasional converts to community policing from among the more experienced officers. A veteran junior police officer told this story to a focus group:

> I followed my seniors to handle a case in which a mother complained that her son was unwilling to do homework. My seniors berated this mother for abuse of police manpower. After some years, when I became a senior, I handled a similar case with a newly graduated colleague. After the mediation, the newly graduated colleague said, "Thanks, Mrs Chan. We won't bother you again." I was very surprised and asked, "Is it necessary to be polite?" The newly graduated colleague responded, "It is what the Police College taught." Nevertheless, that mother appreciated it very

---

49. Cheung, K. C. (2011). The generational gap: Values and culture in the Hong Kong police force. In M. R. Haberfeld, C. A. Clarke, & D. L. Sheehan (Eds.), *Police organization and training* (pp. 137–152). New York: Springer; Hong Kong Police Force (2012). *Quality manual: Living the values workshops*. Hong Kong: mimeo.
50. Ho, L. K. K. (2020). Legitimization & de-legitimization of police: In British colonial & Chinese SAR Hong Kong. *Journal of Inter-regional Studies and Global Perspectives, 3*, 2–12.
51. Brewer, B., Leung J. Y. H., & Scott, I. (2015). *An assessment of the impact of value-based integrity programmes on the Hong Kong Police Force*. Hong Kong: Department of Public Policy, City University of Hong Kong; Brewer, B., Leung, J. Y. H., & Scott, I. (2015). Value-based integrity management and bureaucratic organizations: Changing the mix. *International Public Management Journal, 18*(3), 390–410.
52. Martin, J. T., & Chan, W. W. L. (2014). Hong Kong-style community policing: A study of the Yau Ma Tei fruit market. *Crime, Law and Social Change, 61*, 401–416.

much. Then I began to think that I needed to change my mind-set: "Well, I am just an employee. I don't need to be so angry."

Many uniformed police officers gained job satisfaction from community policing. A young policewoman recounted her experience with a potential suicide case:

> I handled a case in which a wife found her husband had extramarital affairs. She cried loudly and wanted to commit suicide. Her two daughters also cried loudly ... I spent more than an hour to appease the children as well as that mother. Finally, the event can be settled because I can persuade the mother to waive the thought of committing suicide. Then we can send them to the hospital. A few months later ... someone caught my arm suddenly. I found that it's the daughter I met on the case. She said thanks to me and told me that their current life is decent. I found the meaning of being a policewoman at this moment.

Such views were not shared by veteran officers or the criminal investigation division. As a veteran junior police officer put it:

> Most of us [veteran policemen] are waiting for retirement and receiving the pension. Frankly speaking, it's very hard to convert us totally. These Force values are tailor-made for uniformed branch colleagues because they have to face the public more frequently. For CID, we seldom use this approach to deal with our targets. We just arrest criminals. We would not mention providing services to them.

Another told us: "you don't think about human rights when you are breaking down a door wearing a bullet-proof vest." There was also resistance to playing what some regarded as an inappropriate role:

> A Police Force should be semi-military. We are not boy scouts, not social workers, and like a senior said, "it doesn't mean when the water drips, you come to find us."

After the Occupy Central/Umbrella Movement in 2014, junior police officers thought that it had become more difficult to undertake normal policing duties. Citizens were more abusive and did not follow police directions. Socially, young police officers found that some of their friends had defriended them on Facebook.

Until the Occupy Central/Umbrella Movement, community policing helped to improve the public image of the police. By the end of 2007, according to a HKUPOP poll, satisfaction with police performance stood at an all-time high of 81%.[53] Thereafter, there was a gradual fall in the satisfaction rate to just over 50% in July 2019.[54] From then on, public satisfaction with the Police Force went into rapid decline. Chinese University of Hong Kong surveys, held in August, September, and October 2019, found that 68%, 72%, and 69% of respondents respectively agreed

---

53. PORI (2022). *Hong Kong Police Force*. https://www.pori.hk/pop-poll/disciplinary-force-en/x001.html?lang=en
54. Ibid.

that the police had used excessive force during the protests.[55] By November 2019, a PORI poll showed that public satisfaction with the Police Force had declined precipitously to 27%, by far the lowest since these polls were first taken in 1997.[56] Of the respondents, 40% gave the police a zero rating.[57] As a former police officer observed, the Police Force had moved from "a situation of widespread public acceptance and support to one of public distrust and even hatred".[58]

It would be incorrect to suggest that the death of community policing meant that no police officers continued to subscribe to its values. But they were unable to express their views within the force because to do so would have seemed akin to treachery. The new norm was police solidarity to attempt to re-establish public order and maintain national security at whatever cost.[59] In the process, the force alienated a majority of the public and lost most of its carefully acquired responsiveness. Perhaps appropriately in the light of its changing values, in November 2019, the force decided to adopt a new slogan. Instead of "We serve with pride and care", the slogan was "Serving Hong Kong people with honour, duty and loyalty".[60]

Responsiveness in the Hospital Authority

Private health care in Hong Kong has always been very expensive. Eventually, the colonial government recognised that it had to make provision for those who could not afford medical care. Public health care was then offered at minimal levels in a top-down style over which doctors exercised almost total control.[61] Responsiveness improved after the creation of the Hospital Authority in 1990, but three issues remained critical: the question of patients' rights; how resources were allocated and whether patients should pay for services; and the extent to which doctors should monopolise decision-making.

There were expectations that the Hospital Authority would be more responsive to patients' rights.[62] Backed by the government and the Hong Kong Medical

---

55. Lee, F. L. K. (2019, 16 October). Our research in Hong Kong reveals what people really think of the protesters—and the police. *The Independent*. https://www.independent.co.uk/voices/hong-kong-protests-police-violence-public-opinion-polling-support-a9158061.html
56. PORI (2020, 8 December). POP releases popularity figures of Hong Kong forces and the PLA garrison. https://www.pori.hk/press-release-en/2020-12-08-pm.html?lang=en
57. Ibid.
58. Purbeck, M. (2019). A report of the 2019 protests. *Asian Affairs*, 50(4), 465–487.
59. Bradford, B., & Yesberg, J. (2019). *A report on the current attitudes and experiences of Hong Kong police officers*. https://www.ipcc.gov.hk/doc/en/report/thematic_report/research/attitudes/A%20report%20on%20the%20current%20attitudes%20and%20experiences%20of%20Hong%20Kong%20police%20officers.pdf
    This report was commissioned and managed by the IPCC. It notes that there was strong bonding within the police. Only a minority of officers were uncomfortable with the level of force used against protesters.
60. *Offbeat* (2019). Hong Kong Police Force new motto "Serving Hong Kong with honour, duty and loyalty." Issue 1149. https://www.police.gov.hk/offbeat/1149/eng/8331.html
61. Schoeb, V. (2016). Healthcare service in Hong Kong and its challenges. *China Perspectives*, 4, 51–58.
62. Chan, I. & Benitez, M. A. (2006). Changing patient expectations. In G. M. Leung & J. Bacon-Shone (Eds.), *Hong Kong's health system: Reflections, perspectives and visions* (pp. 81–94). Hong Kong: Hong Kong University Press.

Association, the authority chose to focus on the concept of "patient-centred" health and to involve the community as a "partner in health". A logical outcome of this approach was the introduction of a patients' charter in 1999. The charter provides for five major categories of rights: the right to medical treatment; the right to information; the right to a second opinion, to accept or refuse medication or treatments and to take part in medical research; the right to privacy, confidentiality, and respect for religious beliefs; and the right to complain.[63]

The charter was drafted without major input from patients or groups representing their interests and was primarily a codification of the principles which the Medical Association and the government thought should form the basis of doctor-patient relations. It is not legally enforceable. Although the charter is an improvement over the pre-1999 situation, the impetus for better health care treatment depends largely on the Hospital Authority and pressure from medical practitioners to bring about reform. The Hospital Authority runs focus groups with patients to canvass them for suggestions on such matters as the provision of inpatient, specialist outpatient, and accident and emergency services.[64] There are two patients' alliances that are consulted by the Hospital Authority when changes to practice are anticipated. One of these, the Hong Kong Patients' Rights Association, supported public health staff in their strike against the Hospital Authority in February 2020.[65] The Legislative Council Panel on Health Services monitors complaints against the health care system but, aside from some governance reforms to the Medical Council, has not endorsed any recent major changes.[66]

Both the Hospital Authority and the Department of Health, which is responsible for various outpatient services and public health information, focus principally on KPI in their pledges, relying on vision and mission statements to specify their values.[67] The Hospital Authority has an extensive vision statement committing itself to be a "people-first organization" which has a "caring heart", stressing teamwork and professionalism, and listening to patients through "two-way communication";[68] the Department of Health's vision is to build "a healthy Hong Kong".[69]

---

63. Hospital Authority (2021). Patients' rights and responsibilities. https://www3.ha.org.hk/pwh/content/comm/charterpamphlet_e.html
64. Hospital Authority (2020). Hospital Authority community focus group. https://www.ha.org.hk/visitor/ha_visitor_index.asp?Content_ID=10224&Lang=ENG&Dimension=100&Parent_ID=10160
65. Gnews (2020, 26 February). Hong Kong Patients' Rights Association disagrees with pro-Beijing camp for condemning medical staff on strike. https://gnews.org/123920/
66. Legislative Council Panel on Health Services (2016–2021). Healthcare complaints handling mechanism. https://www.legco.gov.hk/yr19-20/english/panels/hs/papers/hs_d.htm
67. Food and Health Bureau (2015). *Report of the steering committee on review of the Hospital Authority* (Appendix 8). https://www.fhb.gov.hk/download/committees/harsc/report/en_full_report.pdf; Department of Health (2020). Performance pledge. https://www.dh.gov.hk/english/aboutus/aboutus_pp/aboutus_pp.html
68. Hospital Authority (2021). Vision, mission and values. https://www.ha.org.hk/visitor/ha_visitor_index.asp?Content_ID=10009&Lang=ENG&Dimension=100
69. Department of Health (2022). Main service areas. https://www.dh.gov.hk/english/main/main_chp/health.html

A perennial complaint has been the length of waiting times for medical attention.[70] Studies show that the public is very satisfied with the health care system once they receive attention but are not satisfied with the level of access.[71] There have also been concerns over the way that the government handled the SARS and COVID-19 crises (see pp. 273–274) and survey evidence of a lower level of responsiveness for ethnic groups compared with local Chinese.[72]

A second controversial question is whether the public health care system allocates resources efficiently and is appropriately financed to meet citizens' needs. Decades of commissions and consultants have failed to resolve the issue.[73] The conventional view is that health care, as a former Hospital Authority chair put it, is a "black hole" in which a government on a limited budget seeks to meet increasing demand and puts pressure on medical personnel and facilities.[74] From this standpoint, the logical solution is to charge for services. The government has canvassed various proposals to maintain health services while attempting to persuade some of its patients to pay for them. Not surprisingly, reactions have been highly unfavourable and the government, concerned about the political consequences, has shelved them. An alternative view, advanced by Tsui and Fong, is that the allocation of resources within the Hospital Authority might partly cause the overloaded system.[75] They argue that 90% of resources are allocated to the treatment of disease and hospital services and that more primary care provision as a percentage of the current budget would reduce pressure on the hospitals and long waiting times. The government has also introduced a voluntary insurance scheme to try to wean people away from the public system. But disenchantment with private insurers and the cost of private health care has led instead to some migration from the private to the public system.[76]

A third problem that has affected responsiveness has been the location of power within the Hospital Authority and the Department of Health. Doctors have

---

70. Food and Health Bureau (2015) op. cit., p. 75.
71. He, A. J. (2018). Public satisfaction with the health system and Hong Kong popular support for state involvement in an East Asian welfare system: Health policy legitimacy of Hong Kong. *Social Policy and Administration*, 52(3), 750–770; Siu (2019) op. cit.; Tsui, Y. T., & Fong, B. Y. F. (2018). Waiting times in public hospitals: Case study of total joint replacement in Hong Kong. *Public Administration and Policy*, 21(2), 120–133; Wong, E. Y. L. et al. (2012) op. cit.
72. Vandan, N., Wong, J. Y. H., Gong, W. J., Yip, P. S. F., & Fong, D. Y. T. (2020). Health system responsiveness in Hong Kong: A comparison between South Asian and Chinese patients' experience. *Public Health*, 182 (May), 81–87.
73. Harvard Team (1999). *Improving Hong Kong's health care system: Why and for whom?* Hong Kong: Printing Department; Food and Health Bureau (2008). *Your health, your life.* Hong Kong: Government Logistics Bureau; Food and Health Bureau (2015) op. cit.
74. Leong, C. H. (2018). *The triumph of rationality: From surgical practice to public service* (p. 65). Hong Kong: Commercial Press.
75. Tsui & Fong (2018) op. cit.
76. Benitez, M. A. (2018, 4 July). Hong Kong's plan to steer 1.5 million people to private health sector will be "challenging". *SCMP*. https://www.scmp.com/news/hong-kong/health-environment/article/2153647/hong-kongs-plan-steer-15-million-towards-private

dominated the system to the virtual exclusion of any other interested parties.[77] Not only have they been in charge of the hospitals, but they have also held most of the senior positions in the Department of Health. The argument against this domination, which the government in principle supports, is that to be more responsive the health care system has to reflect the wider views of the community. Pressure group demands for more representation on key committees and boards have not been addressed. In 2020, of the 23 non-official members on the 28-member Hospital Authority board, only one was a representative of a patients' organisation.[78] The non-official membership of the board and the Food and Health Bureau's numerous advisory committees on health draw largely on professional and business advice. Non-medical representation on the Hospital Authority board or on the governing committees of the hospitals seems mostly window dressing with key decisions taken elsewhere in the Bureau or the Hospital Authority.

Responsiveness in the Housing Authority

The government is, by far, Hong Kong's largest landlord with about 42% of the population in public housing. In March 2021, 2.11 million people lived in 189 public rental housing estates.[79] The government conceives of housing policy as "a ladder" in which the aim is to ascend to home ownership.[80] Public rental housing is the lowest rung on the ladder. In September 2021, there was a waiting time of 5.9 years for a flat, the longest for many years; 153,000 applicants were on the waiting list and there were a further 100,000 non-elderly, one-person applications under the quota and points system.[81] Although the numbers living in public rental housing have declined, the Housing Authority has not been able to build enough flats to meet demand because land supply, some of which is held in land banks by private developers, has been inadequate.[82] There are problems at the top end of the ladder as well. Making the transition from public housing to private housing is difficult because of the very high prices of flats in private developments. How the government responds to the community's housing needs and how it deals with private developers means that its policies have an impact on virtually everyone in Hong Kong.

---

77. Schoeb (2016) op. cit.
78. Hospital Authority (2019). *Annual report, 2018–2019* (pp. 3–7). https://www.ha.org.hk/visitor/ha_visitor_index.asp?Content_ID=253826&Lang=ENG
79. Housing Authority (2020). *Annual report 2020/21.* Key figures. https://www.housingauthority.gov.hk/minisite/haar2021/en/common/pdf/1_Key_Figures_ENTC.pdf
80. Legislative Council Panel on Housing (2019). Housing-related initiatives in the Chief Executive's policy address and policy address supplement (pp. 6–8). https://www.legco.gov.hk/yr19-20/english/panels/hg/papers/hg20191108cb1-32-1-e.pdf
81. Housing Authority (2021). Number of applications and average waiting time for public rental housing. https://www.housingauthority.gov.hk/en/about-us/publications-and-statistics/prh-applications-average-waiting-time/
82. Task Force on Land Supply (2018). *Striving for multi-pronged land supply: Report of the Task Force on land supply* (pp. 14–18). https://www.devb.gov.hk/filemanager/en/content_1171/Report%20(Eng).pdf

At the housing estate management level, responsiveness is an issue of landlord-tenant relationships. Since the inception of the public housing policy in 1954, the government has maintained strict control over the conditions governing eligibility for public housing and the behaviour of its tenants. They may be evicted or prosecuted for failure to occupy the premises, subleasing a flat, using it for commercial purposes, failing to pay the rent, or engaging in illicit activities.[83] In the 1970s, tenants were encouraged to form mutual aid committees which were expected to provide the Housing Authority estate management with suggestions for improvements. In 1995, the government decided to set up estate management committees, which were composed of Housing Authority representatives, the chairs of mutual aid committees in the estates, representatives of commercial tenants, and elected District Council members. There has not been much enthusiasm for this form of participatory management among the tenants or their children.[84] The Housing Authority continues to dominate landlord-tenant relationships with the critical issues of rent increases and maintenance beyond the remit of the estate management advisory committees.[85]

The politics of housing revolve around long-standing intractable problems and it has been difficult to make inroads into entrenched practices. The Housing Authority argues that decisions are taken in association with the tenants, but the evidence suggests that it has been largely a top-down process. For some, even public rental housing seems an unachievable short-term goal. For those who have public rental housing, the government's schemes do not provide an easy upward path towards the difficult goal of home ownership. Dissatisfaction over access is reflected at various pressure points in the system.

Responsiveness was adversely affected by the 2019 protests and by government and police reactions to them. Surveys show a decline in trust across government, a necessary commodity if responsiveness is to be maintained or improved.[86] For the Police Force, the loss of trust has been even sharper than for the rest of the government and has spelt the end of community policing.[87] In the Hospital and Housing Authorities, there has been little change in their *modus operandi* over the past decade. Their services continue to be largely provided in top-down style with only marginal acknowledgement of the views of patients and tenants. There is evi-

---

83. Housing Authority (2021). Tenancy matters. https://www.housingauthority.gov.hk/en/public-housing/tenancy-matters/index.html
84. Forrest, R., & Xian, S. (2018). Accommodating discontent: Youth, conflict and the housing question in Hong Kong. *Housing Studies*, 33(1), 1–17; Yau, Y. (2011). Collectivism and activism in housing management in Hong Kong. *Habitat International*, 35(2), 327–334; Yip, N. M. (2001). Tenant participation and the management of public housing—The Estate Management Advisory Committee of Hong Kong. *Property Management*, 19(1), 10–18.
85. Housing Authority (2022). Responsibilities. https://www.housingauthority.gov.hk/en/public-housing/estate-management/estate-management-advisory-committee/responsibilities/index.html
86. PORI (2022). People's trust in the HKSAR government. https://www.pori.hk/pop-poll/government-en/k001.html?lang=en
87. PORI (2019) op. cit.

dence of satisfaction with medical services, and some sympathy for the pressures on public health personnel, but waiting times for attention and access to specialists have resulted in frustration. Public housing remains a critical, and worsening, problem. If the waiting list continues to grow, the numbers in squalid substandard housing, estimated at about 2% of the population, will increase. Access to public housing has been a major problem for decades and there is no immediate solution in sight. Sitting tenants have limited means of expressing their views and consultation mechanisms have not improved significantly since estate management committees were established in 1995. The responsiveness of the government in these three key agencies has, at best, remained the same and, at worst, has deteriorated considerably.

Redefining Efficiency and Responsiveness

In good governance terms, three values were broadly represented in the late colonial period and immediate post-handover administrations: efficiency as an indicator of service to the public, responsive relationships between civil servants and citizens, and openness and transparency. If these values had been fully realised, it might be argued that the government's accountability would have increased and that the legitimacy deficit might have decreased.

In post-1997 Hong Kong, these values have been reinterpreted, sometimes conflated and confused, sometimes defined in very different ways. Efficiency remains the overriding value; responsiveness is regarded as desirable but subject to the dictates of "executive-led" government; and transparency has been badly damaged by the government's attitude towards dissent. The government has assumed that, if it can implement policies that people want, its efforts will be valued and improvements to its responsiveness will become less relevant. Technology has become the preferred means of improving efficiency, which the government hopes will lead to more responsiveness, defined as the citizens' ability to lead more comfortable and convenient lives in a "smart" city.[88] Responsiveness has become conflated with efficiency.

E-government

A major thrust of the post-handover government's efforts to improve efficiency was the use of information communication technology and e-government. Although the digital strategy dates from the late colonial period, the creation of the government portal in 2006 signalled a commitment to provide a wide range of services online and to develop the "smart" city. The government portal has received international

---

88. Lam, C. (2017). *We connect for hope and happiness* (para 9). https://www.policyaddress.gov.hk/2017/eng/pdf/PA2017.pdf

recognition as a model of its kind[89] and aims to achieve a "citizen-centric mode of service delivery emphasising customer engagement [with integrated] services across government bureaux, departments and agencies".[90] There are expected to be efficiency gains, increasingly effective service delivery, and a platform for a knowledge-based society.[91]

The government's stress on technology is part of its attempt to position Hong Kong as an integral part of the southern China technology hub (see pp. 316–318). Financial contributions to the development of the hub have run into hundreds of billions of dollars with significant resources deployed to expand the use of technology in the civil service.[92] In 2012, the government proposed to set up a new Information and Technology Bureau, but opposition from the pan-democrats meant that the bureau was not established until 2015. Under Carrie Lam, the bureau was expanded to oversee four divisions: the Information and Technology Branch, the Information and Technology Commission, The Office of the Government Chief Information Officer (OGCIO), and the Efficiency Office (formerly the Efficiency Unit). Of these, the OGCIO and the Efficiency Office manage major programmes designed to expand the use of information communication and technology to improve efficiency.

By 2020, the OGCIO had five major initiatives in place: electronic information management, which covered content, records, and knowledge management with the aim of sharing services across bureaux and departments; a human resource management service also aimed at sharing services, but which, to date, has only been adopted by 11 bureaux and departments; "smart" identity cards, issued to all Hong Kong residents since 2003, which can be used at border checks and for various other purposes; the release of free public sector information in digital format to promote innovation and create business opportunities; and the installation of 400 "smart" lamp posts to collect data on such matters as air pollution and traffic flows.[93]

The Efficiency Office describes itself as a change agent for improving the management and delivery of services. It provides a management consultancy service for bureaux and departments and runs a "one-stop" shop, the Integrated Call Centre, for public complaints and inquiries (see pp. 380–381); a youth-related centre which supplies information on further study, careers, entrepreneurial opportunities, and cultural activities; and a social innovation fund, which seeks to alleviate poverty by funding innovative projects.[94]

---

89. Manoharan, A. P., Ingrams, A., Kang, D., & Zhao, H. (2021). Globalization and worldwide best practice in e-government. *International Journal of Public Administration*, 44(6), 465–476.
90. Commerce and Economic Development Bureau (2007). *2008 Digital 21 strategy* (p. 8). https://www.ogcio.gov.hk/en/news/publications/doc/2008D21S-booklet.pdf
91. Ibid., pp. 52, 64–70.
92. Scott, I. (2020). Context and innovation in a traditional bureaucracy: A Hong Kong study. *Public Administration and Development*, 41(1), 12–22.
93. Office of the Government Chief Information Officer (2020). Strategic and government IT initiatives. https://www.ogcio.gov.hk/en/our_work/strategies/
94. Efficiency Office (2020). Our work. https://www.effo.gov.hk/en/index.html

The public value of expenditure on innovation and technology in the civil service rests entirely on its ability to improve efficiency and productivity and to facilitate speedier and more responsive interactions with citizens. Two perennial problems have undermined the achievement of these goals. First, bureaus and departments have not always been enthusiastic about adopting the facilities that have been developed, preferring instead to run their own systems. That means some duplication of functions. If the systems had been broadly adopted, then there should have been cost savings; instead, the size of the civil service has ballooned and recurrent expenditure has increased exponentially. Second, a successful digital strategy depends on the willingness of the public to use the services. In 2017, the Director of Audit assessed the OGCIO's efforts to promote digital social inclusivity in four areas: an internet learning programme to support low-income families; increased use of the internet by the elderly; the use of digital inclusion mobile applications; and a Web/Mobil App Accessibility programme.[95] In none of those areas between 2013 and 2017 did the OGCIO register a success. The take-up for the internet learning programme and the apps was "lukewarm" and, although computer usage among the elderly increased to 31%, it was well below the OGCSIO's expectation of 50%.[96] It is evident that e-government is not a complete solution to the problem of responsiveness and that some developments provoke suspicion. During the 2019 protests, the "smart" lamp posts were attacked and damaged because protesters thought that the police were using them to collect information on their movements.

The relationship between e-government and efficiency and responsiveness remains fundamentally problematic. E-government is an impersonal activity that may be convenient and appreciated by those who use it, but which may also raise the hackles of those frustrated by poorly informed operators, recalcitrant electronic forms, and attempts to resolve issues involving multiple departments. Efficiency is a hygiene factor—people expect their government to be efficient—not a motivator of support for the political system. Responsiveness as a value is more about enhancing trust than about enabling citizens to deal with government efficiently. If the Hong Kong government still believes it can engender trust by being more efficient, it has probably misidentified its principal problem.

Transparency and Freedom of Information and Expression

If reducing the legitimacy deficit through responsive policymaking is ever to be realised, then transparency and trust are essential prerequisites. It is difficult to fault the Hong Kong government on its formal commitment to provide information to its citizens. The government website is a mine of information about what the Hong Kong government is doing about anything and everything. Right of access

---

95. Director of Audit (2018). *Report No. 70* (Ch. 6, pp. 11–35). https://www.aud.gov.hk/pdf_e/e70ch06.pdf
96. Ibid.

to information is provided for in the Bill of Rights and there is a code that permits citizens to make requests for information.[97] The government also produces consultation documents on proposed new policies and monitors the views of the public through consumer surveys and the hundreds of advisory boards that have been set up to keep bureaus and departments in touch with changing political, social, legal, and technological developments.

Although the government does make extensive information available to the public on its activities, its actions often seemed to contradict its formal commitment to transparency, adversely affecting its ability to win public trust. There is often suspicion that the information provided is less than the full story, that sensitive information has been withheld or manipulated, or that it has been presented in such a way that it is difficult to form a judgement. Even more damaging is the suppression of opinions based on the information that has been provided. The environment in which information is processed, discussed, and from which conclusions are drawn and expressed must also be free to promote transparency and trust. Even before the passage of the national security legislation suppressed dissent, the post-handover government had taken measures that were inimical to freedom of information and expression. Three important areas in which the government has adversely affected freedom of information and expression—academic autonomy; the independence of the government broadcaster, Radio Television Hong Kong and the participation of democrats in the legislature—are examined in greater detail.

Academic Freedom

Academic freedom is formally protected under the *Bill of Rights Ordinance* (Article 16), under the Basic Law (Articles 27 and 34), and by the International Covenant on Civil and Political Rights, to which Hong Kong subscribes. Academic freedom has been under threat almost since the post-handover government took office.

In July 2000, Robert Chung Ting-yiu, the director of the University of Hong Kong Public Opinion Programme (HKUPOP), alleged that he had been given a clear message from Tung Chee Hwa that his polling activities were unwelcome. Among many other subjects, the polls showed the Chief Executive's low levels of popularity and high levels of dissatisfaction with his government's performance. The university's council then set up an independent panel to investigate the allegations and found that one of the Chief Executive's senior aides had approached the vice-chancellor. A pro vice-chancellor passed on the message that the research would not be funded and that Chung should discontinue his polling work.[98] The vice-chancellor and a pro-vice-chancellor resigned after the findings were published.

---

97. Hong Kong Government (2020). *Code on access to information*. https://www.access.gov.hk/en/home/index.html
98. Currie, J., Petersen, C. J., & Mok, K. H. (2006). *Academic freedom in Hong Kong* (Ch. 3). Lanham, MD: Lexington Books.

In 2007, the Commission of Inquiry into the allegations concerning the Hong Kong Institute of Education (see pp. 86–88) found that the Education Bureau's Permanent Secretary had been at fault in trying to prevent the publication of articles by members of staff that were critical of the government's educational reforms.[99] The commission did not find that the Secretary of Education and Manpower, Arthur Li Kwok-cheung, had improperly interfered with the institutional autonomy of the Hong Kong Institute of Education.[100] In the following years, the government began appointing its supporters to the governing councils of the universities. At some universities, such as the City University of Hong Kong, the Chief Executive appoints a majority of the council. At the University of Hong Kong, the Chief Executive only appoints seven of 24 members but that includes the chair. In 2015, despite strong opposition from staff and students, Leung Chun-yin appointed Li to the council and six months later to the chair.[101]

In December 2014, Johannes Chan, a renowned scholar and former Dean of the Faculty of Law at the University of Hong Kong, was unanimously recommended by a search committee for appointment as a pro-vice-chancellor. The issue soon became a political controversy.[102] Chan, a democrat, was repeatedly attacked in the pro-Beijing press on his links with his colleague Benny Tai, one of the founders of the Occupy Central Movement.[103] In January, the University Council delayed the appointment of the pro-vice-chancellor, a decision that was re-confirmed at a closed meeting in July 2015. Student activists then broke into the meeting, reportedly injuring a member of the council.[104] On 1 September, the alumni association, which had no formal role in the process, passed a motion, by 7,821 votes to 1,371, supporting Chan's appointment.[105] However, on 30 September, when the issue came before the council once more, Chan's appointment was rejected by 12 votes to eight.[106] The reasons for his rejection were leaked by a student representative and

---

99. Morris, P. (2010). Academic freedom, university governance and the state: The Commission of Inquiry into the Hong Kong Institute of Education. *Journal of Education Policy*, 25(5), 587–563; Yeung, C. K., & Lee, J. P. (2007). *Report of the commission of inquiry on allegations relating to the Hong Kong Institute of Education* (pp. 91–97). Hong Kong: Government Logistics Department.
100. Ibid., p. 106.
101. Cheng, K. (2015, 31 December). CY ally Arthur Li appointed HKU council chairman despite strong opposition. *HKFP*. https://hongkongfp.com/2015/12/31/cy-ally-arthur-li-appointed-hku-council-chairman-amid-strong-opposition/
102. Burns, J. P. (2020). The state and higher education in Hong Kong. *The China Quarterly*, 244, 1031–1055. Chan, J. M. M., & Kerr, D. (2016). Academic freedom, political interference and public accountability: The Hong Kong experience. *Journal of Academic Freedom*, 7, 1–21; Law, W. W. (2019). *Politics, managerialism, and university governance: Lessons from Hong Kong under China's rule since 1997* (p. 195). Singapore: Springer.
103. Chan & Kerr (2016) op. cit.
104. Cheng, K. (2015, 30 September). The HKU Council debacle. *HKFP*. https://hongkongfp.com/2015/09/30/explainer-hku-council-rejects-johannes-chan-appointment-to-pro-vice-chancellor/
105. Ibid.
106. Cheng, K. (2015, 29 September). Johannes Chan appointment to HKU key position rejected, 12 votes to 8. *HKFP*. https://hongkongfp.com/2015/09/29/johannes-chan-appointment-to-hku-key-position-rejected/

a recording of the debate later surfaced.[107] The pro-government members argued that Chan should have a doctorate and that his publications were insufficiently recognised although neither requirement was part of the job description for the position. Benny Tai was later dismissed by the council, allegedly because he had been sentenced to 16 months for conspiracy to cause and incite public nuisance.[108] He was on bail pending an appeal at the time of his dismissal.

An academic freedom index published in March 2020 shows sharp declines in academic freedom in Hong Kong on four dimensions: freedom to research, freedom of academic research and dissemination, campus integrity, and freedom of academic and cultural expression.[109] Since the passage of the national security law, academic freedom—and with it the loss of transparency and trust—has declined even further.[110]

The Government and Radio Television Hong Kong (RTHK)

Freedom of the media to criticise government has become increasingly restricted since the handover. Reporters without Borders ranked Hong Kong 18th in press freedom in 2002, 69th in 2016, and 80th of 140 countries and places in 2020.[111] The decline may partly result from Mainland companies' takeovers of Hong Kong news outlets (see pp. 57–58), self-censorship, and the attitude of the government towards adverse critical comment. Radio Television Hong Kong (RTHK) is a public broadcaster and a government department under the Commerce and Economic Development Bureau. For many years, it has had an uneasy relationship with the bureau and the government, principally because it is an independent broadcaster, modelled on the BBC, rather than the government's public relations organisation. In 2018, the Director of Audit issued a report on RTHK which recommended that action should be taken on, *inter alia*, the decrease in staff productivity, high production costs for school educational programmes, low ratings for some programmes, and failure to meet 10 of 21 performance pledges.[112] It was beyond the Director of Audit's remit to comment on RTHK policies, but an appendix contained a list of its

---

107. Cheung, K. (2015, 29 September). Student leader reveals members' reasons for blocking Johannes Chan appointment. *HKFP*. https://hongkongfp.com/2015/09/30/student-leader-reveals-hku-council-members-reasons/
108. BBC (2020, 28 July). Benny Tai: Hong Kong university fires professor who led protests. https://www.bbc.com/news/world-asia-china-53567333
109. Kinzelbach, K., Saliba, I., Spannagel, J., & Quinn, R. (2020). *Free universities: Putting the academic freedom index into action*. Global Public Policy Institute (Figure 4). https://www.gppi.net/2020/03/26/free-universities
110. Cook, S. (2020, 23 November). Hong Kong academic freedom withers under national security law. *Freedom House*. https://freedomhouse.org/article/hong-kongs-academic-freedom-withers-under-national-security-law
111. Reporters without Borders (2020). Rankings. https://rsf.org/en/ranking
112. Director of Audit (2018). *Report No. 71: Radio Television Hong Kong: Provision of programmes* (pp. 93, 96, 101). https://www.aud.gov.hk/pdf_e/e71ch05.pdf

purposes, one of which was to provide "an open platform for the free exchange of views without fear or favour".[113]

During the 2019/2020 protests, RTHK produced some programmes that provoked ire among pro-establishment politicians and the government. The Communications Authority claimed that a 2019 television programme, *Pentaprism*, on the siege of the Hong Kong Polytechnic University, presented the police in a bad light and gave them no opportunity to respond. Subsequently, the authority said that other programmes on the force were also "biased and insulted the police".[114] In February 2020, the programme *Headliner*, which had been satirising politicians for the previous 31 years, ran a skit on the Police Force. Following complaints about the skit from, among others, the Police Commissioner, the programme was terminated in June 2020.[115] The Commerce and Economic Development Bureau, meanwhile, had announced that it intended to set up an internal review of RTHK based on "public concerns over its programmes, governance and management" and the slow implementation of the Director of Audit's recommendations.[116]

In the following months, the concept of RTHK as an independent broadcaster came under serious threat from the government. In June 2020, the acting director resigned.[117] In July, RTHK ran an award-winning programme "Who owns the truth?" on the Yuen Long attacks.[118] In November, one of the producers of the programme was arrested and subsequently convicted on a charge of violating the *Road Traffic Ordinance* by using registration numbers to contact the owners of vehicles parked in the area where the attacks took place.[119] Her contract with RTHK was not renewed. After pointedly questioning the Chief Executive, the police and the pro-Beijing Legislative Councillor Junius Ho on the Yuen Long attacks, another RTHK reporter had her probationary contract extended for a further 120 days and was then terminated.[120]

---

113. Ibid., Appendix A.
114. Chan J. (2021, 3 May). Timeline: Two months of turmoil at Hong Kong public broadcaster RTHK. *China Digital Times*. https://chinadigitaltimes.net/2021/05/timeline-two-months-of-turmoil-at-hong-kong-public-broadcaster-rthk/
115. Su, X. (2020, 22 September). Curtain falls on Hong Kong's oldest satirical TV show. *HKFP*. https://hongkongfp.com/2020/06/21/curtain-falls-on-hong-kongs-oldest-satirical-tv-show/
116. Hong Kong Government (2020, 28 May) RTHK review team to be set up. https://www.news.gov.hk/eng/2020/05/20200528/20200528_130224_926.html
117. Creery, J. (2020, 11 June). Public broadcaster acting deputy resigns citing health reasons, amid row over Hong Kong security law programming. *HKFP*. https://hongkongfp.com/2020/06/11/public-broadcasters-acting-deputy-resigns-citing-health-reasons-amid-row-over-hong-kong-security-law-programming/
118. RTHK (2020), Hong Kong Connection 7.21: Who owns the truth? [Video]. YouTube. https://www.youtube.com/watch?v=qdk0BhizyNw
119. *Hong Kong Special Administrative Region v Bao Choy Yuk-ling* (2021, July). Clooney Foundation for Justice: TrialWatch Initiative. https://cfj.org/wp-content/uploads/2021/07/Bao-Choy_July-2021_Fairness-Report.pdf
120. Kwan, R. (2020, 29 September). Hong Kong's Carrie Lam side-steps row over treatment of RTHK journalist, as union claims "political persecution". *HKFP*. https://hongkongfp.com/2020/09/29/hong-kongs-carrielam-side-steps-row-over-treatment-of-rthk-journalist-as-union-claims-political-persecution/

In February 2021, the government announced the appointment of Patrick Li Pak-chuen, former Deputy Secretary of Home Affairs, who had no previous media experience, as Director of Broadcasting and consequently as Editor-in-chief of RTHK.[121] At the same time, the Commerce and Economic Development Bureau released its internal review of RTHK, promising major organisational changes and stressing the core values of editorial independence, impartiality, and service to the public.[122] Li then announced that he would vet all programmes personally, then axed many programmes which he and his advisory committee regarded as potentially contentious, and introduced a new show featuring the Chief Executive talking about the December 2021 Legislative Council elections.[123] In May 2021, RTHK programmes more than one year old and its archival news service began to be removed from the internet.[124] Pro-Beijing legislators praised Li's work, but many others saw it as an attack on freedom of expression that devalued the credibility of the information that the broadcaster provided to the public.[125]

The Participation of Localists and Democrats in the Legislative Council

The Hong Kong electoral system is strongly biased in favour of pro-establishment and pro-Beijing parties (see Chapter 10) but, until the rise of localism, there was no major Hong Kong or Chinese government interference with the election of democratically elected legislators or their right to sit in the legislature. In 2016, the Electoral Affairs Commission introduced a nomination form that required all candidates to declare that Hong Kong was an inalienable part of China and that it came under the authority of the Chinese government. Six candidates were denied the right to stand, but the provision was not applied consistently, leaving the impression that the commission was using its discretion to decide whether a candidate should be permitted to contest an election.[126] The nomination form was only one means of preventing localists from running for office. Other methods came into play following the election. Six candidates who won seats in the 2016 Legislative Council election were disqualified for failing to take the oath of office properly and for insulting China.[127] In 2018, the Secretary for Security, using the *Societies Ordinance*, banned

---

121. Hong Kong Government (2021, 19 February). *Senior appointment* [Press release]. https://www.info.gov.hk/gia/general/202102/19/P2021021900209.htm
122. Commerce and Economic Development Bureau (2021). *The governance and management of Radio Television Hong Kong*. https://www.cedb.gov.hk/ccib/en/consultations-and-publications/reports/rthkreview.pdf
123. Chan, J. (2021, 3 May) op. cit.; Tsoi G. (2021, 27 May). How authorities cracked down on Hong Kong's only public broadcaster. *BBC*. https://www.bbc.com/news/world-asia-china-57253030; Yeung, C. (2021). The director's cuts. *Index on Censorship*, 50(1), pp.64–65. See also Legislative Council Panel on Information and Technology (2021, 25 May).The governance and management of Radio Television Hong Kong review report. https://www.legco.gov.hk/yr20-21/english/panels/itb/papers/itb20210525cb1-927-1-e.pdf
124. Chan, J. (2021, 3 May) op. cit.
125. Tsoi (2021) op. cit; Yeung (2021) op. cit.
126. Law (2019) op. cit., pp. 133–134.
127. Kaeding, M. P. (2017). The rise of "localism" in Hong Kong. *Journal of Democracy*, 28(1), 157–172.

the Hong Kong National Party, which advocated independence for Hong Kong and the expulsion of all mainlanders.[128]

After the 2019–2020 protests, it became increasingly evident that the target was not only localists advocating independence but the pan-democratic movement and perhaps anyone else who expressed dissent. In July 2020, the government prevented 12 localist and pan-democratic candidates from running in the then-scheduled September Legislative Council elections on grounds that included advocating independence, "objecting in principle" to the imposition of the national security law on Hong Kong, intending to vote down "indiscriminately" any future Hong Kong government legislative proposals and soliciting intervention by foreign governments in Hong Kong affairs.[129] The government later postponed the 2020 Legislative Council elections for a year, giving COVID-19 as the reason. In November, the NPCSC passed a resolution that disqualified Legislative Councillors:

> if the member advocates or supports "Hong Kong independence", refuses to recognise the People's Republic of China's sovereignty over Hong Kong and the exercise of sovereignty, solicits intervention by foreign or external forces in the HKSAR's affairs or carries out other activities endangering national security.[130]

The Hong Kong government then disqualified four sitting legislators. The remaining 15 pan-democrats resigned, leaving only two opposition members in the chamber.[131]

None of the four disqualified sitting members had advocated independence so the measures were evidently a much wider attack on the democrats and dissent. The Chinese government nonetheless said that the democrats who had resigned were abandoning their constituents. Whether the democrats will be permitted to stand again (or whether they would want to) remains to be seen, but democratic voices in the legislature will certainly be much more muted and critical appraisal of government bills will decline.

In each of these areas—academic freedom, the independence of the public broadcaster, and the disqualification of candidates and sitting members of the legislature—transparency and freedom of information have been adversely affected. Whether the Hong Kong government will continue to provide the same level of information without pressure from the media, legislators, and academia is not

---

128. Secretary for Security (2018, 24 September). *Transcript of remarks by Secretary for Security on exercising power under the Societies Ordinance* [Press release]. www.info.gov.hk/gia/general/201809/24/P2018092400678.htm
129. BBC (2020, 30 July). Hong Kong bars 12 opposition candidates from election. https://www.bbc.com/news/world-asia-china-53593187; Wong, R. (2020, 5 August). Explainer: How Hong Kong banned 12 democrats from legislative election. *HKFP*. https://hongkongfp.com/2020/08/05/explainer-how-hong-kong-banned-12-democrats-from-the-legislative-election/
130. Hong Kong Government (2020, 11 November). *HKSAR government announces disqualification of legislators concerned in accordance with NPCSC's decision on qualification of HKSAR legislators* [Press release]. https://www.info.gov.hk/gia/general/202011/11/P2020111100779.htm
131. Chan, H. (2020, 16 November). End of the road for Hong Kong's opposition camp? *The Interpreter*. https://www.lowyinstitute.org/the-interpreter/end-road-hong-kong-s-opposition-camp

certain. Even if it remains committed to keeping the public informed, generating new and critical information in much more restrictive circumstances means that the government will exercise a monopoly over information that reaches the public. At worst, there may be no alternative viewpoints or significant sources of other information in sensitive areas. The government looks likely to become less accountable, less transparent, and a major impediment to the free flow of information and expression.

Conclusions

Efficiency, responsiveness, and transparency assume particular significance in political systems suffering from legitimacy deficits. If a government can build trust and credibility through the interactions between the people and the administration and enhance those interactions by creating an efficient and responsive environment, it will go some way towards mitigating shortcomings in the legitimation of power. The post-1997 Hong Kong government redefined the late colonial emphasis on responsiveness with a heightened quest for efficiency. It assumed that a more efficient government would necessarily be a more responsive one and that e-government and new technology would win over an appreciative public. But it was always unlikely that efficiency alone would resolve the problem of legitimating a non-democratic regime. Overall and judged by standards elsewhere, the Hong Kong government in recent times has never been particularly inefficient. Fundamentally, the difficulty is not with efficiency and performance; it is with a political system that does not permit adequate and meaningful consultation on critical issues and with a government that has passed up the opportunity to ameliorate the situation by increasing responsiveness. Responsiveness, and the larger consideration of accountability to citizens, have become afterthoughts, rationalisations for courses of action, policies, and decisions which the government intends to take.

It used to be said that, although Hong Kong people did not have a democratically elected government, they did have civil liberties and were free to speak their minds. That has become increasingly untrue and has further detrimentally affected transparency and trust in government. The Hong Kong government has been responsible for the gradual erosion of freedom of expression. The national security law represents the culmination of a process that has been detrimental to the free flow of information and aimed at the suppression of dissent.

12
Rights, Complaints, and Redress

Regimes with legitimacy deficits may ease their problems by entrenching the rights to citizens to protect against the government's arbitrary use of coercive powers and by providing channels for the redress of complaints about unfair, unlawful, or corrupt administrative decisions. If recognition of citizens' rights and redress systems becomes an institutionalised part of the political system, they may help compensate for the absence of other forms of legitimation. If citizens have individual freedom, they may be more willing to tolerate, if not to approve, the government's unilateral decisions in matters that only indirectly affect their rights. Their liberties depend on the surety that rights will be protected and that the complaints and the individual grievances of citizens will be properly, fairly, and impartially handled. If rights are ignored and the complaints and redress systems are not credible, grievances may fester and contribute to more mistrust of the government.

In this chapter, we examine the contention over rights in Hong Kong and the attitudes of the post-1997 government towards protecting them, the evolution of complaint-handling bodies and how their work is perceived, and the development of the redress system and the problems that it has encountered. We distinguish between:

- **rights**: civil liberties, belonging to individuals rather than groups, which are protected by the legal system and possibly by other specific institutions;[1]
- **complaints**: relating to systemic or policy deficiencies; and
- **redress**: remedies for arbitrary, unfair or negligent administrative action against individuals, pursued through institutions established to decide whether the grievance is justified.

These distinctions are not self-contained. A person seeking redress through the Ombudsman, for example, is making an individual complaint but is also exercising a civil liberty and may be contributing to better governance. The distinction does enable us, however, to focus on the extent to which public institutions designed for these purposes have met their objectives.

---
1. Wesley-Smith, P. (1988). The method of protecting civil liberties in Hong Kong. In R. Wacks (Ed.), *Civil liberties in Hong Kong* (p. 11). Hong Kong: Oxford University Press.

Rights

Until 1984, the protection of civil liberties rested almost entirely on the rule of law and the legal system and on conventions about how the government would or would not use its power. Under such a system, civil liberties were residual and were not entrenched in domestic legislation; as one commentator observes, they were what was left over after the law had taken away.[2] With the change of sovereignty, there was public concern that civil liberties would be disregarded by the incoming regime. The Joint Declaration on the future of the territory addressed that concern and promised that the post-1997 government would honour

> the rights and freedom as provided for by the laws previously in force in Hong Kong, including freedom of the person, of speech, of the press, of assembly, of association, to form and join trade unions, of correspondence, of travel, of movement, of strike, of demonstration, of choice of occupation, of academic research, of belief, inviolability of the home, the freedom to marry and the right to raise a family freely.[3]

Every person should "have the right to challenge the actions of the executive in the courts"; religious freedom was guaranteed; and the provisions of the International Covenant on Civil and Political Rights and the International Covenant on Economic, Social and Cultural Rights, as they then applied to Hong Kong, were to remain in force.[4] The covenants themselves contain many specific rights and freedoms. However, the British government reserved some clauses, which includes Article 1 that states that people have the right of self-determination, that do not apply to Hong Kong.[5]

The Basic Law incorporates the civil liberties outlined in the Joint Declaration and specifies that the International Covenants shall apply in Hong Kong (Article 39). The promulgation of the Basic Law took place shortly after the Tiananmen Square incident in 1989. In its attempts to calm anxieties, the Hong Kong government promised to introduce a Bill of Rights that would have the effect of implementing the covenants. The Bill of Rights was passed in 1991, but the Chinese government claimed that it detracted from the pre-eminence of the Basic Law and might conflict with some of its provisions.[6] The debate rumbled on throughout the 1990s with various threats to make the Bill of Rights inoperative after 1997. It was

---

2. Merry, M. (1988). Freedom of expression: Defamation and contempt. In Wacks, op. cit., p. 186.
3. *Joint Declaration of the Government of the United Kingdom of Great Britain and Northern Ireland and the Government of the People's Republic of China on the Question of Hong Kong* (Section XIII) (1984). Hong Kong: Government Printer.
4. Ibid.
5. Ghai, Y. (1999). *Hong Kong's new constitutional order: The resumption of Chinese sovereignty and the Basic Law* (2nd ed., p. 406). Hong Kong: Hong Kong University Press; Constitutional and Mainland Affairs Bureau (2022). *Text of the covenant: application to the Hong Kong Special Administrative Region*. https://www.cmab.gov.hk/en/press/reports_human.htm#s2
6. Yeung, C. (1990, 22 May). Alarm at fate of laws under Bill of Rights. *SCMP*.

amended so that it did not apply to the private sector,[7] but the Chinese government was still unhappy. In February 1997, the NPCSC announced that three sections of the *Bill of Rights Ordinance* relating to the International Covenant on Civil and Political Rights would not be adopted after the handover, measures to which the outgoing colonial government objected.[8]

In the 1990s, the government had passed legislative measures that were designed to increase civil liberties or at least to reduce the coercive powers of the government. The *Societies Ordinance*, which had been used under colonial rule to control politically unacceptable organisations, was amended to provide better protection for societies from arbitrary action. In 1994, the government announced proposals to implement the United Nations conventions on the rights of the child and the elimination of all forms of discrimination against women, the establishment of an Equal Opportunities Commission and legislation to prevent discrimination, the introduction of a Code of Access to Information, legislation to protect personal privacy, and improved legal aid.[9] In 1995, the *Public Order Ordinance* was amended to replace the Commissioner of Police's power to license demonstrations and protests by a system of notification which required the Commissioner, when banning a demonstration, to comply with Article 21 of the International Covenant on Civil and Political Rights. In February 1997, the NPCSC made it clear that the major amendments to the *Societies Ordinance* and the *Public Order Ordinance* would not be adopted as SAR laws after the handover. The future Chief Executive's Office produced a consultation document that provided amendments that were acceptable to the Mainland government but to which the departing colonial government continued to object.[10]

After 1997, the increasing conflict between authoritarian and liberal values meant that civil liberties became a central issue.[11] In 2003, the government's attempt to legislate a security law under Article 23 of the Basic Law provoked widespread concern that personal liberties and freedom of the press would be adversely affected. Although the government backed down on its proposals, there was lasting suspicion that it was trying to modify or nullify the guarantees on civil liberties promised in the Basic Law. Civil society organisations and political parties used judicial review to challenge government policies and were quick to protest against perceived violations of rights. The situation continued to deteriorate. During the Umbrella Movement in 2014, the police, for the first time, used tear gas and pepper

---

7. Loh, C. (1996). Human rights—in a time warp. In M. K. Ngaw & S. M. Li (Eds.), *The other Hong Kong report* (pp. 99–100). Hong Kong: Chinese University Press.
8. Chief Executive's Office (1997). *Civil liberties and social order: Consultation document* (p. 2). Hong Kong: The Office; Hong Kong Government (1997). *Commentary on civil liberties and social order consultation document* (p. 3). Hong Kong: mimeo.
9. City and New Territories Administration (1993). *Green Paper on equal opportunities for women and men.* Hong Kong: Government Printer.
10. Chief Executive's Office (1997) op. cit, pp. 10–17; Hong Kong Government (1997), op. cit., pp. 4–7.
11. Chan, C. (2019). Thirty years from Tiananmen: China, Hong Kong, and the ongoing experiment to preserve liberal values in an authoritarian state. *International Journal of Constitutional Law, 17*(2), 439–452.

spray against protesters and in effect abandoned the community policing practices that had previously been used to control peaceful protesters. In 2016, Mainland security forces abducted five Hong Kong booksellers to China, raising further fears about freedom of the person and the rule of law and providing a platform for opposition to the government's proposed Extradition Bill in 2019.[12]

During the 2019 protests, violent protests and alleged police brutality led to demands for an independent inquiry and took the issue of rights into new and critical domains.[13] The failure of the government to control the Police Force and the apparent absence of any effective means of holding it accountable was a factor contributing to public sympathy and support for the protesters. In June 2020, when the Chinese government decided to legislate the national security law for Hong Kong, many of its provisions reduced the civil liberties guaranteed in the Basic Law and were so vaguely worded that they could be widely interpreted. Although the government continued to maintain that civil liberties were protected, the evidence that they had been very seriously damaged was evident in restrictions on freedom of expression, the disqualification of elected legislators, the decline in judicial independence and the rule of law, academic freedom, and institutional autonomy.

The gradual erosion of civil liberties has also had an impact on the specific institutions designed to protect or promote rights. We consider three areas in which reforms were introduced in the 1990s and the extent to which they have been supported by the post-1997 government: the right to information and the *Code on Access to Information*; the right to privacy and data protection under the Office of the Privacy Commissioner; and the right to equality administered by the Equal Opportunities Commission.

The Code on Access to Information

The *Code on Access to Information* was introduced in March 1995. The government recognises the value of access to information so that the public is "well informed about the Government, the services it provides and the basis for policies and decisions that affect individuals and the community".[14] The code promises that departments will publish details of their organisation annually, information on the services they provide, their performance pledges and whether they had been met, a list of their records, and a list of information either published or otherwise

---

12. Chou, O., & Siu, P. (2016). One year on: Hong Kong bookseller saga leaves too many questions unanswered. *SCMP*. https://www.scmp.com/news/hong-kong/politics/article/2058000/one-year-hong-kong-bookseller-saga-leaves-too-many-questions
13. Amnesty International (2020). *Hong Kong: Missing truth, missing justice; the case and international legal framework for the establishment of a commission of inquiry into the 2019 protests*. London: Amnesty International.
14. Hong Kong Government (2020). *Code on Access to Information* (Introduction). https://www.access.gov.hk/en/codeonacctoinfo/index.html

made available.[15] Responses to requests for information are supposed to be given quickly, ideally within 10 days. The government reserves many areas where it is not required to disclose information. These include: defence and security, external affairs, nationality, immigration and consular matters, public service management, internal discussion and advice, public employment, information potentially leading to improper gain, incomplete research, analysis or statistics, third-party information (unless the third party's consent has been obtained), and individual privacy.[16]

The code is administered by the information officer in each department. It is not legally enforceable. Efforts to make it so by enacting an ordinance have not so far been successful. In May 2013, the Secretary for Justice and the Chief Justice asked the Law Reform Commission to review the system. In the following year, the Ombudsman produced a direct investigation report in which he argued that there should be an *Access to Information Ordinance* because, unlike other jurisdictions, the Hong Kong system does not provide binding decisions by an adjudicating body or sanctions for non-compliance.[17] In 2018, after 48 meetings, the Law Reform Commission issued a consultation document that put forward proposals to strengthen access to information.[18] It endorsed the Ombudsman's view that access to information should be legally entrenched and recommended that a new ordinance be enforced by the Ombudsman. In December 2019, the government said that it would wait for the Law Reform Commission's final report before responding.[19] The situation has become more complicated since the enactment of the national security legislation in June 2020, which potentially widens the scope of what is excluded under the reservations in the code.

The code has been subject to many different criticisms since it came into force. Between 1995 and 2014, journalists were highly critical of its operation.[20] In 1999, as a consequence of their dissatisfaction, the Journalists Association started a campaign for open government.[21] In 2007, there were 15 complaints to the Ombudsman about the administration of the code. The Ombudsman criticised the government's attitude towards the provision of information, noting that departments had refused requests for information either without reason or for reasons not specified in the code and that departmental information officers were sometimes not aware of the provisions of the code.[22] In 2014, in addition to recommending legally enforceable access to information, the Ombudsman criticised the limited application of the code

---

15. Ibid., Section 1.4.
16. Ibid., Part 2.
17. The Ombudsman (2014). *The access to information regime in Hong Kong* (p. 2). https://ofomb.ombudsman.hk/abc/files/DI238_full_E-20_3_2014_with_Appendix_1.pdf
18. Law Reform Commission Access to Information Sub-Committee (2018). *Consultation paper: Access to information*. https://www.hkreform.gov.hk/en/docs/accesstoinfo_e.pdf
19. Hansard, 4 December 2019, 2671–2676.
20. Hong Kong Journalists Association (1999). *HKJA launches campaign for open government*. Hong Kong: The Association.
21. Ibid.
22. Office of the Ombudsman (2008). *Annual Report 2007/2008* (p. 5). www.ombudsman.gov.hk

to public organisations other than bureaus and departments, the spirit in which it was applied, the inadequate appeal process against a decision, poor promotion of the right to information, and the large number of requests for information that were not monitored.[23] In 2019, a Legislative Councillor reiterated complaints that the code allowed too much discretion to officials to keep information confidential and that there were often untenable justifications for refusing to release information.[24]

The government claims that the vast majority of requests are met. In the first quarter of 2020, it reported that 2,377 requests for information were received, of which 255 were withdrawn. Of the remainder, 1,924 (91%) were answered in full, 131 (6%) were answered in part, and 67 (3%) were refused.[25] On average, the departments that receive the largest number of requests for information are Inland Revenue, Buildings, Food and Environmental Hygiene, Water Supplies, and the Police Force. Sometimes, however, specific events inflate numbers. Between April and June 2019, the Housing Department (569) and the Police Force (537) received the largest number of requests, over three times their usual number. In the case of the Police Force, the increase in requests seems to relate mainly to the use of tear gas, pepper spray, and rubber bullets in a violent demonstration on 12 June 2019.[26] Of the 537 requests for information from the Police Force, 475 were refused.

Under more normal circumstances, many requests for information are routine and can be divulged without transgressing the categories of reserved information. There is still, however, a strong belief reflected in the Ombudsman's 2014 report and widely held among journalists and academics that the government's preference is to withhold information rather than to make it available. The system needs reform, but little progress has been made and the government has shown no inclination to speed up the process.

The Privacy Commissioner

The *Personal Data (Privacy) Ordinance* came into effect in 1996 to protect the rights of individuals providing data to government. The legislation, which created the Office of Privacy Commissioner to enforce its provisions, was intended to ensure that individuals were protected from misuse of personal data provided to the government and to allay fears that sensitive information on individuals might be passed to the Chinese government. Subsequently, through amending legislation, the Commissioner's powers have been strengthened and the office has taken on the wider remit of "securing the privacy of individuals . . . through monitoring and supervision of compliance with the Ordinance and the enforcement and promotion

---

23. The Ombudsman (2014) op. cit.
24. Hansard, 4 December 2019, 2671.
25. Hong Kong Government (2020) op. cit., statistics.
26. AccessInfo (2019). Request regarding the HK police during the 2019 HK protests. https://accessinfo.hk/en/request/request_regarding_hk_police_duri_2?unfold=1; see also Office of the Ombudsman (2020). *Annual report 2019/2020* (pp. 62, 67–68). https://ofomb.ombudsman.hk/doc/yr32/ar2020.pdf

of the culture of protecting and respecting personal data".[27] The Commissioner is also given authority to issue codes of practice on data protection and has done so in respect to identity cards, human resource management, consumer credit cards, and data privacy at work.[28]

In 2010, the government proposed to amend the ordinance to introduce more regulation on the use of data.[29] In 2008, there had been serious leaks of personal data held by the police, immigration, health authorities, and the Civil Service Bureau, stemming mainly from the loss of USB storage devices or inadvertent loading of material on to the internet. The records of 46,000 people had been leaked by government and other public sector bodies over the previous three years.[30] There was public concern about the protections in place and the Privacy Commissioner himself thought that the ordinance was outdated. Some Legislative Councillors saw the amending proposals as a restriction on business while others, especially the pan-democrats, were in favour of stronger measures to protect personal data. The proposed amendments did not reach the Legislative Council until July 2011 and it was another year before they were passed.

Although the amendments strengthened the powers of the office and provided more regulation, particularly in the areas of marketing and sale of personal information, the government did not allow the Commissioner to initiate prosecutions, as he had suggested. There are still major weaknesses in the legislation compared with other jurisdictions. When the Constitutional and Mainland Affairs Bureau conducted a further review of the ordinance in January 2020, it was pointed out that there is no specific legislation to prosecute hackers.[31] Yet *Apple Daily* newspaper, the HKEx, and Cathay Airlines had all experienced major cyberattacks. The Commissioner refers suspected cybercrimes to the police, which has a Cyber Security and Crime Bureau and may prosecute on grounds of damage to property. There have been relatively few prosecutions on cyber matters; most prosecutions have been concerned with commercial issues.

Under the ordinance, the Commissioner has responsibilities for dealing with requests from individuals who want to find out what information data users hold on them and with complaints about what data users might do with their personal information.[32] If, on receiving a complaint, the Commissioner believes that there

---

27. Office of the Privacy Commissioner for Personal Data (2021). About PCPD. https://www.pcpd.org.hk/english/about_pcpd/commissioner/commissioner.html
28. Ibid., Codes of Practice/Guidelines. https://www.pcpd.org.hk/english/data_privacy_law/code_of_practices/code.html
29. Constitutional and Mainland Affairs Bureau (2010). *Report on public consultation on review of the Personal Data (Privacy) Ordinance*. https://www.cmab.gov.hk/doc/issues/PCPO_report_en.pdf
30. Butt, J., & Wong, M. (2008, 11 May). Privacy chief gets tough on data leaks. *Sunday Morning Post*; Butt, J. (2008, 29 May). Data of 46,000 leaked over three years. *SCMP*.
31. Legislative Council Panel on Constitutional Affairs (2020). *Background brief: Review of Personal Data (Privacy) Ordinance*. https://www.legco.gov.hk/yr19-20/english/panels/ca/papers/ca20200120cb2-512-4-e.pdf
32. *Personal Data (Privacy) Ordinance*, Cap 486, S.18.

may have been a breach of the ordinance, the office may conduct an investigation.[33] In 2018, for example, the Commissioner found that Cathay Pacific and Hong Kong Dragon Airlines had breached the ordinance in ways that affected the privacy of 9.4 million passengers. Cathay Pacific did not notify the office until seven months after the breach had occurred and was under no legal obligation to do so. The Commissioner issued an enforcement notice requiring the airlines to revise their practices on handling the personal data of passengers but could not proscribe any penalty. The British Information Commissioner's Office subsequently fined the airline £500,000 for the data breach, but the Hong Kong Privacy Commissioner had no such powers.

In 2019/2020, the Privacy Commissioner received a record number of 11,220 complaints. Many were doxxing complaints arising from the political protests and were referred to the police since the Commissioner had no powers to deal with those offences. There were still 3,848 complaints that were unrelated to the protests, a rise of 105% from the previous year.[34] The Commissioner reported that a telecommunications company had leaked data on 380,000 customers and a government department had lost data on 8,100 voters.[35] The office has little power to deal with such cases apart from enforcement notices and the Commissioner was sufficiently frustrated that he recommended changes that would amend the ordinance to bring it into line with best practice elsewhere. The changes included the regulation of data processors, vesting investigation and prosecution powers in the office for offences such as doxing, giving the Commissioner power to impose fines, and introducing a mandatory breach notification system.[36]

In the following year, the number of complaints dropped sharply, by 71%, to 3,157. This was attributed largely to the decrease in doxxing cases which fell from 4,707 to 957.[37] The government promised to criminalise doxxing and to grant the Privacy Commissioner statutory powers to deal with such cases. It also made some preliminary responses to the Commissioner's request for reform, making data breach notifications mandatory and allowing the Commissioner to impose administrative fines for breaches of the Ordinance.[38] These changes do strengthen the role of the office, but whether they will bring its powers to the level of those exercised elsewhere remains to be seen. The national security law and Mainland Chinese provisions on privacy may affect the way in which any changes are implemented.[39]

---

33. Ibid., S.38.
34. Office of the Privacy Commissioner (2020). *Annual report 2019/20* (p. 3). https://www.pcpd.org.hk/english/resources_centre/publications/annual_report/files/anreport20_full.pdf
35. Ibid., p. 3.
36. Ibid., p. 7.
37. Office of the Privacy Commissioner (2021). *Annual report 2020/2021* (p. 60). https://www.pcpd.org.hk/english/resources_centre/publications/annual_report/annualreport2021.html
38. Ibid., 11.
39. Government of the People's Republic of China (2020). *The Law of the People's Republic of China on safeguarding national security in the Hong Kong Special Administrative Region* (Article 62). https://www.elegislation.gov.hk/doc/hk/a406/eng_translation_(a406)_en.pdf

The Equal Opportunities Commission (EOC)

In May 1996, the government established an Equal Opportunities Commission to administer two ordinances, the *Sex Discrimination Ordinance* and the *Disability Discrimination Ordinance*. The ordinances make it unlawful to discriminate on the grounds of sex, marital status, pregnancy, and disability. The commission also administers the *Family Status Discrimination Ordinance*, which was passed into law in November 1997. The ordinance makes it illegal to discriminate against anyone who has responsibility for the care of an immediate family member. In 2008, the *Race Discrimination Ordinance*, aimed at preventing discrimination, harassment, or vilification on grounds of race, was passed by the Legislative Council with the EOC as the administering authority. No major legislation concerning equal opportunities has been introduced since 2008. Between 2017 and 2019, the EOC itself undertook a review of its governance, management structure, and complaint-handling process.[40] Although most of the recommendations were for administrative reform and could be implemented immediately by the EOC, some required law reform. There is no evidence of any government urgency in attempting to bring these proposals into effect.

Much of the commission's work is concerned with complaints about alleged violations of the ordinances. In its early years, the commission was very forceful in championing allegations of discrimination. Between April 2001 and March 2002, the EOC received 832 complaints about the Secondary School Places Allocation System (SSPA) and sought a judicial review of the government's practices.[41] In June 2001, the court ruled that the system was sex discriminatory and unlawful.[42] The commission's work on the SSPA[43] and in other court cases where the government actively resisted the commission's attempts to enforce the laws gave the EOC a positive public image.[44] In 2003, the government did not renew the term of its chair, Anna Wu Hung-yuk, who had been instrumental in ensuring that the commission fought hard to make all organisations, including the government, comply with the laws against discrimination.[45]

The new chair, a former judge, Michael Wong Kin-chow, had previously been head of the Administrative Appeals Board. One of his first administrative acts was to rescind the appointment of a senior official, Patrick Yu Chung-yin, who had received an offer of employment but who had not yet taken up his position.[46] Wong's

---

40. Equal Opportunities Commission (2019). *Report of the review of the Equal Opportunities Commission: Governance, management structure and complaint-handling process*. https://www.eoc.org.hk/EOC/Upload/UserFiles/File/Process_Review/EOCs_Review_Report_E.pdf
41. EOC (2003). *Annual report 2002/2003* (p. 4). https://www.eoc.org.hk/en/AnnualReport/Detail/18
42. Ibid., p. 9; Petersen, C. J. (2001). The right to equality in the public sector: An assessment of post-colonial Hong Kong. *Hong Kong Law Journal, 32*(1), 103–134.
43. EOC (2003) op. cit., p. 9.
44. Petersen (2001) op. cit.
45. Hansard, 2 July 2003, 7960–7961.
46. Shamdasani, R. (2003, 23 October). New rights official is sacked before he starts work. *SCMP*.

decision, which was apparently triggered by an interview Yu gave to the press, caused a storm of protest. Thirteen pressure groups called on the Ombudsman to investigate his action and the Chair of the Society for Community Organisation called for his dismissal.[47] The matter was further complicated by allegations that Wong had received gifts of airline tickets from a property developer while still a judge, that he was living in a house that the developer had allegedly given to his daughter, and that he had received special permission from the Chief Executive to receive his pension as a judge and his salary as chair while he held the position.[48] The Legislative Council's Panel on Home Affairs decided that it wanted to interview Wong over the dismissal of Yu. On the day before the meeting, Wong resigned.

Under pressure from the Legislative Council, the government set up an Independent Panel of Inquiry into the incidents surrounding the termination of Yu's appointment, Wong's resignation, and Anna Wu's allegations that she had been subject to a smear campaign by the government and several members of the EOC.[49] The panel concluded that Yu had been properly appointed and terminated and that there was no truth in the allegation that government officials and EOC members had been involved in drafting a defamatory statement against Anna Wu at a private meeting the night before Wong resigned.[50] The Secretary for Home Affairs, who was at that meeting although not for its entirety, claimed that no one was smeared.

After 2003, the EOC became less active and fewer cases went to court. Wong had been quoted as saying that he intended "to downsize the EOC".[51] Had he stayed in office, it seems likely that there would have much less of the crusading spirit that Anna Wu had displayed. As it was, public confidence in the EOC dropped after the controversies. Complaints fell from 1,032 in 2003 to 595 in 2004.[52] The government appeared to want a quieter life. The Home Affairs Bureau picked up on a recommendation of the Panel of Inquiry to separate the position of chair from that of the chief executive officer.[53] Although the action was rationalised as being in line with practice in other non-departmental public bodies, it could also have been interpreted as the government constraining the powers of the head of the EOC. The passage of the *Race Discrimination Ordinance* in 2008 also suggested that the

---

47. Shamdasani, R. (2003, 24 October). Watchdog faces pressure to resign. *SCMP*.
48. Shamdasani, R., & Lee, S. (2003, 31 October). EOC chief faces "gifts" enquiry. *SCMP*; Hansard, 26 November, 2003, 1737.
49. Legislative Council Independent Panel of Inquiry (2005). *Report of the Independent Panel of Inquiry on the incidents relating to the Equal Opportunities Commission.* https://www.legco.gov.hk/yr04-05/english/panels/ha/papers/ha0321eoc_report_e.pdf; Legislative Council Secretariat (2005). Background brief: Termination of the employment of the Director (Operations) Designate by the Equal Opportunities Commission and other related Incidents. https://www.legco.gov.hk/yr04-05/english/panels/ha/papers/ha0321cb2-1003-1e.pdf
50. Legislative Council Independent Panel of Inquiry (2005) op. cit., II, III; Legislative Council Secretariat (2005) op. cit, p. 10.
51. Hansard, 26 November 2003, 1791.
52. Legislative Council Secretariat (2005) op. cit., p. 8.
53. Home Affairs Bureau (2006). *Interim Report No. 15—Review of the corporate governance of the Equal Opportunities Commission.* https://www.legco.gov.hk/yr05-06/english/panels/ha/papers/ha0113cb2-786-2e.pdf

government had no wish to find itself in court pitted against one of its statutory bodies. The ordinance provides that the government will be bound by its provisions, but there are important exclusions such as immigration law and policy.[54]

In 2018 and 2019, complaints and enquiries to the EOC suddenly increased dramatically, but then declined by 23% in 2020/2021.[55] The commission divides enquiries into general enquiries, mainly about procedures and events, and specific enquiries relating to particular ordinances and jurisdiction that may lead to complaints. In 2019/2020, there were 6,593 specific enquiries, a record number, and 1,526 complaints.[56] In 2020/2021, there were 1,179 complaints handled; the number of enquiries reached 24,303, but this was distorted by over 14,000 emails about a single incident from a largely similar template.[57] The commission attributed the rise in complaints and enquiries to greater awareness of the anti-discriminatory legislation and to the 2019 protests. About 58% of complaints handled in 2019/2020 and 65% in 2020/2021 were concerned with allegations of discrimination in employment.[58] The commission has generally sought to resolve complaints by conciliation, claiming a success rate of about 70% in 2018 and 2019 rising to 84% in 2020/2021.[59] If settlement cannot be reached, a complainant has the right to apply for legal assistance and to bring proceedings before the District Court. The EOC 2019 review suggests that the commission should adopt a more proactive "victim-centred" approach.[60]

The post-1997 experience of the *Code on Access to Information*, of the Privacy Commissioner, and the EOC has been rather different. The code has become part of civil service practice but its provisions are not strong enough to enforce its provisions in the courts. The protection of data is required by law, but its provisions are not sufficiently punitive, in the view of the Privacy Commissioner among others, to deal with changing circumstances. The EOC experience raises quite separate issues, calling into question the government's commitment to the protection of civil liberties. The perception that it is at best a lukewarm supporter of civil liberties has not been improved by its attempts to make organisational changes to reduce the impact of the EOC and by its inability to introduce reforms speedily. The government's predispositions towards civil liberties and the national security legislation prevent it from adopting a proactive position on civil liberties. Civil liberties will remain a key area of public concern.

---

54. *Race Discrimination Ordinance*, S.3, 55, 56.
55. EOC (2019). *Annual report 2018/2019* (p. 34). https://www.eoc.org.hk/EOC/Upload/AnnualReport/201819/EOC_annual%20report_2018-19.pdf; EOC (2020). *Annual report, 2019/2020* (p. 30). https://www.eoc.org.hk/EOC/Upload/AnnualReport/201920/EOC_AR_201920.pdf; EOC (2021). *Annual report 2020/2021* (p. 43). https://www.eoc.org.hk/en/AnnualReport/Detail/49
56. EOC (2020) op. cit., p. 29.
57. EOC (2021) op. cit., p. 42.
58. Calculated from EOC (2020) op. cit., p. 30 and EOC (2021) op. cit., p. 44.
59. EOC (2019) op. cit., p. 36; EOC (2020) op. cit., p. 32; EOC (2021) op. cit., p. 20.
60. EOC (2019). *Report of the review* op. cit., pp. 46–48.

Complaints

In the introduction to this chapter, we drew a distinction between complaints, which may have policy or systemic implications, and individual grievances. This section assesses the work of two institutions whose role in handling individual complaints is less significant than their contributions to the correction of policy problems and to the maintenance of systemic values. The Legislative Council has a role in redressing individual grievances, but its role has been diminished as other complaint-handling institutions have been created and as legislators themselves have sought to meet with groups with grievances rather than individuals.

The ICAC, similarly, has a systemic role. Complainants may or may not be personally affected by the corrupt behaviour which they report to the ICAC. But even if the report constitutes an individual grievance, it has wider significance as a call to investigate corruption, an alleged violation of one of the core values of the system. If citizens have the assurance that major problems can be resolved, and if core values are seen to be supported, this increases public trust in government.

The Legislative Council Redress System

In 1969, the colonial administration rejected the idea of an Ombudsman in favour of strengthening the representative function of Legislative Councillors.[61] The Unofficial Members of the Executive and Legislative Council (UMELCO) system that was introduced was fundamentally defective as a complaints-handling system. Civil servants were charged with the task of reporting and making recommendations on the alleged misdemeanours of other civil servants and complaints were consequently contained within the bureaucratic system without troubling Legislative Council members in most instances.

UMELCO became increasingly less relevant to the complaint-handling process as other avenues for complainants were created. A Consumer Council was established in 1974 and regularly received more complaints than the Legislative Council complaints division did.[62] The ICAC, which also came into operation in 1974, was soon well respected and received many complaints that had nothing to do with graft. The Urban Council and the District Boards provided other channels for redress for aggrieved members of the public. In 1989, the government established a weak ombudsman system, the Commissioner for Administrative Complaints. The Legislative Council had become one among a number of channels for redress and often not the most effective means of resolving problems.

With the introduction of some directly elected members to the Legislative Council in 1991, there was some reorganisation of the system. Councillors believed that "the primary target of the redress system should be towards representations

---

61. Hansard, 1 October 1969, 11; 8 October 1969, 95.
62. Hong Kong Government (1990). *Hong Kong 1989* (p. 91). Hong Kong: Government Printer.

that raise wide policy issues and matters of public concern".[63] Their role in handling individual complainants remained because they were required, under the Basic Law (Article 73(8)), to "receive and handle complaints from Hong Kong residents".

By that stage, the public was well aware that it had other speedier and more convenient avenues for redress. In a Census and Statistics Department survey in 2008, the Legislative Council did not even feature as a preferred channel of complaint. Most of those surveyed preferred to go directly to the department or public body concerned (35.5%), to the District Council (30.5%), to the Ombudsman (15.5%), or to the media (13.9%).[64] Many complaints directed to the Legislative Council Secretariat are now referred to other institutions or are dealt with by the Secretariat itself. Members work in groups of seven and take turns to be on duty each week although the same group of members usually handle complaints on the same issue. If members do have a representative function on behalf of their constituents, it is performed through their own offices rather than through the Legislative Council redress system.

In 2017/2018, Legislative Councillors received 294 group representations and 1,405 individual complaints.[65] In the following year, the number of individual complaints rose to 2,354 and there were 141 group representations.[66] These numbers are higher than the average number of individual complaints for the previous decade. The Legislative Council figures may reflect the beginnings of widespread discontent, but no statistics are available after mid-2019. Complaints, whether brought by individuals or deputations, provide a barometer of issues troubling the public. The management of the public housing estates, for example, has been a perennial source of complaints, deputations, and requests for assistance. In any given year, specific issues may trigger a spate of complaints. In 2002/2003, immigration and right of abode matters generated by far the most complaints.[67] In 2014/2015, the largest number of complaints was about the Security Bureau and, in the wake of the Umbrella Movement, there was a spike in complaints about the Police Force.[68] In 2017/2018, most complaints were about the Food and Health Bureau; in 2018/2019, transport issues headed the list.[69]

The surges in complaints in specific areas mirror the intent of the Legislative Council redress system. The principal aim is to resolve immediate policy issues

---

63. Legislative Council (1994). *Legislative Council annual report 1993–1994*. Hong Kong: Government Printer.
64. Census and Statistics Department (2008). *Thematic household survey: Report No. 33* (pp. 27–28). Hong Kong: Government Logistics Department.
65. Legislative Council (2018). *Annual report 2017/2018* (p. 121). https://www.legco.gov.hk/en/about-legco/annual-reports-of-legislative-council.html
66. Legislative Council (2019). *Annual report 2017/2018* (p. 115). https://www.legco.gov.hk/en/about-legco/annual-reports-of-legislative-council.html
67. Legislative Council (2003). *Legislative Council annual report 2002–2003* (p. 59). https://www.legco.gov.hk/en/about-legco/annual-reports-of-legislative-council.html
68. Legislative Council (2015). *Legislative Council annual report 2014–2015* (p. 111). https://www.legco.gov.hk/en/about-legco/annual-reports-of-legislative-council.html
69. Legislative Council (2018) op. cit., p. 124; Legislative Council (2019) op. cit., p. 119.

stemming from poor and/or contentious policy implementation, to deal with inadequate provision, and to remedy the causes of the problem. The system does not seek to address directly the problem of maladministration. Complaints are described as "resolved". Although the complaints may represent a bureaucratic mistake, the redress system is focused on mediation and improving the procedures and issues that are causing inconvenience. Legislative Councillors are primarily concerned with ensuring that complainants are mollified and that the policy problem does not reoccur. This may be achieved through discussion or written referrals to the bureaus or department concerned or by referring the case to another complaint-handling institution.

Within their remit, Legislative Councillors have been able to make improvements to policy implementation through the redress system. In 2018/2019, for example, the annual report highlighted four cases where the council had been able to secure remedial measures for complainants.[70] In two cases—objections to the design of a bus terminus and electricity charges in subdivided units—Councillors met with a deputation of the complainants. In another case involving damaged or fallen trees after a typhoon, the council received many complaints and was able to persuade government to act more swiftly. In the final case, a damaged drainpipe, which generated many complaints to the government, was not fixed until the council's intervention.

The Legislative Council seems to serve as a final channel of appeal for those with grievances whose representations to government complaint-handling institutions fall on deaf ears. It may not always be able to persuade the government to remedy a problem or to change its position, but it does provide a barometer for social problems, a forum for the expression of views and publicity for complainants' demands, and a role as a mediator between the society and the government. Despite these strengths, it is not the most appropriate channel for relatively minor complaints because the council sees its role as supplementary to the Ombudsman and other departmental complaint-handling units rather than as a focal point for those with grievances.

The Independent Commission Against Corruption (ICAC)

Corruption is a form of maladministration that may badly damage the performance of a public service. In colonial Hong Kong, syndicated police corruption and other corrupt practices in the civil service also seriously tarnished the reputation of the government and contributed to the legitimacy problem. When the ICAC was created in 1974, it assumed the mantle of a crusader for clean government and public sector morality using its strong powers under *The Prevention of Bribery Ordinance* (see Chapter 5). Despite some setbacks in its efforts to win public confidence, especially

---

70. Ibid., pp. 124–125.

immediately after November 1977 when there was a short-lived amnesty for police officers suspected of corruption offences, it has been able to retain high levels of public support. There has been some decline in belief in its effectiveness since about 2015 although levels of trust remain higher than in other institutions concerned with law and order.[71] The ICAC did not lose as much support as other agencies during the 2019 protests, but it was still affected by the perception that the government had handled the protests poorly. In a telephone survey of 1,885 respondents conducted in June 2020, 47% said that their view of the Hong Kong government had changed "a great deal" because of its handling of the protests whereas only 16% said that their view of the ICAC had been so affected.[72] When asked if they believed that the ICAC was trustworthy and/or effective, 60% said that they thought it was, but 26% thought it was neither. A majority of respondents (52%) believed that ICAC had once been effective but was no longer; 39% thought that it had "always been effective". Only 4% thought that the ICAC had never been effective.

The ICAC's non-election corruption reports (which may contain more than one complaint) declined slowly over the decade 2010–2019.[73] In 2011, there was a decade high of 4,619 reports. Thereafter, the number of reports declined, which was attributable at least in part to the investigation of the former Commissioner, Timothy Tong Hin-ming, on the issues of overspending on duty visits, gifts, and entertainment.[74] In 2019, the ICAC received only 2,297 reports, some 14% below its 2018 figures and the lowest figure for the decade.[75] Throughout its history, the ICAC has always regarded declining corruption reports not as an indication of less corruption but as a sign of a potential decrease in public trust and confidence. While the number of 2019 reports is not conclusive evidence of a decline in trust and effectiveness, it seems likely that there has been some spin-off effect on the willingness of the public to report corruption.

For most of its existence, the ICAC has been able to maintain qualities that engender support for institutions concerned with civil liberties, complaints, and redress: integrity, independence from government, and the willingness and ability to investigate complaints without fear or favour. Part of that success is the public perception that, if corruption is discovered, the ICAC will fully investigate it and wrongdoers will be punished. The commission's report-handling system represents

---

71. Scott, I. & Gong, T. (2019). *Corruption prevention and governance in Hong Kong*. Abingdon: Routledge; Bauhinia Foundation (2019). *Public perceptions towards the rule of law in Hong Kong—An opinion survey* (conducted for the Bauhinia Foundation by the Hong Kong Institute of Asia Pacific Studies, The Chinese University of Hong Kong). http://www.bauhinia.org/index.php/english/research/106
72. Gong, T., Scott, I., & Xiao, H. (2020). *Survey of institutional trust and perceptions of effectiveness in corruption prevention in Hong Kong*. Hong Kong: mimeo. The survey was conducted by the Social Science Research Centre, University of Hong Kong under the direction of Professor John Bacon-Shone.
73. ICAC (2011–2021). *Annual reports 2010–2020*. https://www.icac.org.hk/en/about/report/annual/index.html
74. Legislative Council (2014). *Report on matters relating to Mr Timothy Tong's duty visits, entertainment, and bestowing and receipt of gifts during his tenure as Commissioner of the Independent Commission Against Corruption*. https://www.legco.gov.hk/yr13-14/english/counmtg/papers/cm0709-ttong-members-rpt-e.pdf
75. ICAC (2020). *Annual report 2019* (p. 10). https://www.icac.org.hk/icac/annual-report/2019/

best practice and has served as a model for anti-corruption agencies around the world. The Operations Department, which is the largest of the agency's departments and is responsible for processing and investigating corruption reports, runs a 24-hour report centre.[76] Senior officers in the department classify the reports received daily. Some are not pursuable or are referred to other complaint-handling institutions. Those that are pursued may then be assigned to specialised teams and offenders may be prosecuted, cautioned, or referred to the Public Service Commission for disciplinary action. In election years, the ICAC usually also deals with numerous reports about violations of the electoral regulations; in 2019, there were 623 election-related complaints.[77]

In 2019, 157 persons were prosecuted, of whom 13 were public servants, 11 were private individuals with alleged illegal dealings with public servants, eight were from public bodies, and 125 were from the private sector.[78] The ICAC has a high conviction rate, normally above 75%. In 2019, of those prosecuted, 50 were convicted, 10 acquitted, and the remaining cases were pending.[79] The numbers prosecuted represent a normal distribution between the public and private sectors over time. There is no evidence of a significant increase in corruption in the civil service compared with the figures for the previous decade. In 2019, the total number prosecuted or cautioned in both public and private sectors was the lowest in the ICAC's history.[80]

Although its brief does not extend beyond investigating corruption, the ICAC does receive some non-corruption reports. In the colonial period, when there were few complaint-handling institutions and none with the reputation for independence and integrity of the ICAC, non-corruption reports ranged from 46% to 76% of all reports between 1974 and 1987, usually outnumbering corruption complaints.[81] Surveys revealed that many complainants were well aware that the ICAC was only responsible for investigating corruption reports and did not have a role in handling other complaints. There was nonetheless a widely held perception that the ICAC was fair and helpful, that its officers had high integrity, and that it might serve as an "unofficial court of appeal".[82] As other complaint-handling institutions became more institutionalised, non-corruption reports to the ICAC dropped. By 2019, the report centre received only 219 non-corruption reports, referring them to relevant departments and monitoring progress in investigations but taking no further part in the process.[83]

---

76. Scott & Gong (2019) op. cit., p. 77.
77. Ibid., p. 11.
78. ICAC (2020) op. cit., p. 43.
79. Ibid., Appendix 7.
80. Ibid., Appendix 6.
81. Ma Man, P. S. L. (1988). *A study of the ICAC's role in handling non-corruption complaints* [Unpublished master's thesis] (p. 19). The University of Hong Kong.
82. Ibid., pp. 89, 96.
83. ICAC (2020) op. cit., p. 11.

The ICAC has a "universal", zero-tolerance approach to corruption prevention, which means that it does not simply react to reports but attempts to stop corruption from occurring.[84] Two smaller departments focus on preventing corruption at its source. The Community Relations Department has a presence at the district level and helps organise anti-corruption community functions. There is also a Corruption Prevention Department which makes recommendations, particularly to government departments but also to public bodies and some private organisations, about the best procedures to prevent corruption in their organisation. The "universal" approach partly explains why the ICAC is one of the largest anti-corruption agencies in the world. In 2019, it had a strength of 1,413: 1,029 in the Operations Department, 165 in Community Relations, 75 in Corruption Prevention, and 154 in the Administration Branch.[85]

As a defender of public morality and the core value of clean government, the ICAC has been critical to good governance and to reducing the legitimacy deficit. Trust in the agency has been remarkably strong and has been sustained by the belief that it is a necessary feature of Hong Kong's institutional landscape. If that belief is undermined because of the government's handling of the protests or perceptions that the agency is unable to operate effectively or both, it will result in growing fears of corruption in the public service and lasting damage to the social fabric.

Redress

An effective redress system that deals impartially with individual complaints about unfair, arbitrary, or illegal government decisions and recommends remedies and improvements in procedures can be an important means of reducing a legitimacy deficit. Redress institutions provide avenues for appeal and means of obtaining explanations for official action. In non-democratic systems, they may be one of the few ways that citizens can object to unacceptable behaviour by public officials. In Hong Kong, the redress institutions—the Ombudsman, the departmental complaint-handling bodies, and administrative tribunals—were created because the colonial government wanted to present itself in a good light. The redress system has gradually won more respect from the public for its impartiality. But there remain areas, particularly the handling of complaints against the police and the procedures of some administrative tribunals, which do not follow best practice. There are also perennial issues about how redress institutions will be staffed, how their financial dependence on government affects their autonomy, and their willingness to press for justice.

Until the 1990s, the colonial administration believed that the rule of law and an impartial court system was sufficient to resolve any disputes that citizens might

---

84. Heilbrunn, J. R. (2004). *Anti-corruption commissions: Panacea or real medicine to fight corruption?* Washington, DC: World Bank.
85. Ibid., p. 22.

have with their government. But this conveniently ignored the practicalities of cost and the fact that courts consider the legality of a decision rather than whether it is fair or reasonable. Applications for judicial review of administrative decisions suffer from other problems. Unlike other court proceedings, judicial review focuses on the fairness of the process, "whether a decision-making authority has exceeded its powers, committed an error of law, committed a breach of the rules of natural justice, reached a decision which no reasonable tribunal could have reached or abused its powers."[86] The courts do not decide on the merits of the decision and they may not accept applications for judicial review if there is another avenue of appeal available. Finally, complaints that people have against their government, important as they are to the individual, are often not matters of sufficient significance for the courts and may be better resolved through other institutions which have procedures for conciliation or investigation into the causes of the complaint.

The Ombudsman

The rule of law and the Legislative Council redress system were never going to be sufficient to satisfy the mounting political pressure for independent channels of redress. The colonial government was anxious to reduce friction between the administration and the public in what were expected to be tension-filled years in the transition to Chinese sovereignty. And so, in the mid-1980s, the proposal to create an Ombudsman, which the Governor and the Colonial Secretary had killed 15 years earlier, was revisited. The government was still ambivalent about creating an institution that might uncover inequities and embarrass its senior officials and its consultative document on the redress of grievances, in 1986, reflected this caution.[87] After a self-congratulatory review of existing complaint-handling institutions and the possibility that no changes were required, the government suggested that an ombudsman system or a commissioner for administrative complaints might be considered.

The Commission for Administrative Complaints was established on 1 March 1989. From the outset, it suffered from the problems that had afflicted the British Parliamentary Commissioner system, on which it was based. A Legislative Councillor had to refer a complaint to the Commissioner for investigation. Relatively few complaints were referred: only 71 in 1989, 167 in 1990, 197 in 1991, and 150 in 1992.[88] Complaints that were substantiated were mostly concerned with small administrative mistakes. In 1992, when the Legislative Council reviewed the

---

86. Law, K. S., & Yue, S. Y. (1998). *The channels for redressing grievances in Hong Kong and in overseas countries* (p. 4). Hong Kong: Research and Library Services Division, Legislative Council Secretariat.
87. Hong Kong Government (1986). *Consultative document: Redress of grievances* (p. 7). Hong Kong: Government Printer.
88. Commissioner for Administrative Complaints (1989–1992). *Annual reports of the Commissioner for Administrative Complaints 1989–1992*. Appendix E (1989), Appendix D (1990–1992). Hong Kong: Government Printer.

system, the Commissioner made recommendations for change and the Governor soon announced that the powers of the office would be enhanced. The reforms resulted in a much more effective system. Complaints rose to 1,211 in 1994/1995 and could now be made directly to the Commissioner; publicity for individual cases was permitted; statutory bodies were included in the Commissioner's jurisdiction; and the Commissioner could conduct direct investigations of complaints with wide public significance.[89] The Commissioner's powers now more closely resembled those of a classical ombudsman. In 1996, the office was renamed the Office of the Ombudsman.

Although the Ombudsman's legal powers had increased, they were necessary, but not sufficient, conditions for effective performance. Much depended on how the Ombudsman interpreted the role and how the performance of the office was judged by the public and the departments against which complaints were lodged. The Office describes its functions as investigating complaints about maladministration and conducting direct investigations into areas of suspected maladministration, identifying administrative deficiencies, and recommending remedial measures.[90] Its jurisdiction presently covers 100 organisations including government departments, statutory bodies, and the court and tribunal registries, and administrative offices. Exclusions from the its jurisdiction include the police, the auxiliary police, the ICAC, and the Secretariat of the Public Service Commission, except for complaints relating to the *Code on Access to Information*. Security, defence and international relations, court proceedings, civil service personnel matters, any action taken personally by the Chief Executive, honours and awards, contracts (excluding procedures affecting tenders), investigation of crimes, any action taken relating to the code on takeovers and mergers, and decisions concerning "the imposition or variation of any condition of granting, extending or renewing any interest in Government land" are also excluded.[91]

In fulfilling its functions, the Ombudsman's Office must be seen to possess qualities that place its integrity beyond doubt. Investigation of the complaint must be thorough, decisions must be seen to be fair, complaints should be confidential, and its independence from government interference should be unquestioned.[92] Impartiality is also an essential quality for effective performance. For that reason, selecting an Ombudsman who has had a career in a profession that demands probity provides some public assurance that the office will be fair and above board. The power to appoint the Ombudsman in Hong Kong lies with the Chief Executive[93] although, in 2019, the appointment was made on the recommendation

---

89. Scott, I. (1994). Reforming the Ombudsman: The evolution of the Commissioner of Administrative Complaints Office in Hong Kong. *Public Law*, Spring, 27–38.
90. Office of the Ombudsman (2020) op. cit., p. 14.
91. *Ombudsman Ordinance*, Cap 397, Schedule 2.
92. Gottehrer, D., & Hostina, M. (1998). *Essential characteristics of a classical ombudsman*. United States Ombudsman Association. https://www.usombudsman.org/essential-characteristics-of-a-classical-ombudsman/
93. *Ombudsman Ordinance* op. cit., S.3 (3).

of a four-person selection board. A government is often a judge in its own cause: there is a case for the Legislative Council to make the appointment because the Ombudsman is investigating complaints against arbitrary executive action.

Of the six Ombudsmen who have held the office since 1989, the first was a former judge, the second was a former schoolteacher and previously an appointed member of the Legislative Council, the third and fourth were former senior civil servants, the fifth was a former Chief Executive Officer of the Consumer Council, and the sixth, Winnie Chiu, was a former Deputy Commissioner of Police. While there is no reason to suppose that former civil servants may not act independently and impartially as Ombudsmen, there is the possibility of a conflict of interest because they may be called upon to pass judgement on their previous decisions. There is also the prospect that the public might see such an appointment as civil servants investigating civil servants. On her appointment in 2019, Chiu said that she would recuse herself in cases involving the police.[94]

The Ombudsman's independence from government would mean very little if it were not accompanied by significant powers to investigate complaints. Under the ordinance, the Ombudsman may investigate a complaint if it is made by an aggrieved individual within 24 months of the event and it is not possible to appeal through the Chief Executive, the Chief Executive in Council, tribunals, or the court system.[95] There is an obligation to keep information relating to the complainant confidential; information cannot be shared with another complaint-handling institution without the consent of the complainant.[96] If the investigation proceeds further, the organisation concerned may be required to provide any information or documents the Ombudsman needs and officials may be interviewed. These are substantial powers, but most complaints are relatively minor and can be resolved without detailed investigation.

Figure 12.1 shows the number of complaints and enquiries received by the Ombudsman between 2007 and 2020. The number shows a steady "normal" range of complaints from a high of 6,572 complaints in 2013/2014 to a low of 4,642 complaints in 2017/2018. This was followed by an explosion of "topical" complaints in 2019/2020 when there were 19,767 complaints, of which 15,034 were topical complaints.[97] Topical complaints were mainly concerned with allowing domestic free television broadcasters to drop RTHK's programmes, the handling of the outbreak of COVID-19, inaction against unauthorised building works of a TV broadcasting company, and the Extradition Bill.[98] In 2020/2021, the number of complaints

---

94. Ting, V. (2019, 25 April). Hong Kong's new ombudsman tells government to get a move on with "freedom of information" law her office recommended. *SCMP*. https://www.scmp.com/news/hong-kong/politics/article/3007703/hong-kongs-new-ombudsman-tells-government-get-move-freedom
95. *Ombudsman Ordinance* op. cit., S.10.
96. Ibid., S. 15(1).
97. Office of the Ombudsman (2020) op. cit., p. 38.
98. Ibid., p. 32, Annex 3.

Figure 12.1 *Complaints and Enquiries to the Ombudsman 2016–2021*

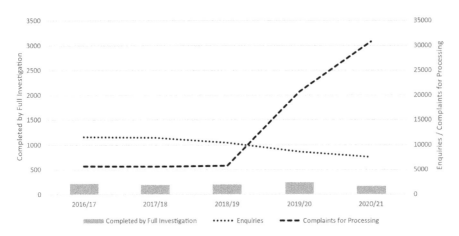

Source: Office of the Ombudsman (2021). *Annual report 2020/21* (Annex 3). https://ofomb.ombudsman.hk/doc/yr33/ar2021.pdf

rose even more dramatically to 29,814.[99] The ombudsman attributed the increase to complaints about government inaction on a tomb on government land, the handling of the pandemic and public service disruptions because of COVID-19.

In 2020/2021, 27,195 complaints were closed after assessment either because there were insufficient grounds to investigate (1,295 complaints) or because they were ultra vires (25,900 complaints).[100] Of the remaining cases, 2,480 were resolved by preliminary enquiry when information is sought from the organisation concerned without conducting a full investigation. A further 167 complaints were fully investigated, a procedure which involves notifying the organisation, asking for the comments of its head, visiting sites, calling witnesses and requesting documentation. Full investigations also potentially involve "issues of principle, serious maladministration, gross injustice, systemic flaws or procedural deficiencies . . .".[101] The remaining 179 cases were mediated, a process that requires the consent of the complainant and the organisation concerned and is used for minor complaints.[102] The Ombudsman's office acts as a facilitator.

Of the complaints that were fully investigated in 2020/2021, 7% were substantiated, 34% were partially substantiated, 7% were unsubstantiated but other inadequacies were found, 50% were unsubstantiated and the remainder were inconclusive

---

99. Office of the Ombudsman (2021). *Annual report 2020/2021*. https://ofomb.ombudsman.hk/doc/yr33/ar2021.pdf
100. Ibid., Annex 3.
101. Ibid., p. 40, Annex 6.
102. Ibid., pp. 60–61.

or withdrawn.[103] These figures show significant variations from 2019/2020 when nearly 13% of complaints were substantiated, 9% were partially substantiated, 42% were unsubstantiated but other inadequacies were found, and 34% were unsubstantiated.[104] The major reasons for substantiated complaints in 2020/2021 were error or wrong advice, faulty procedures, delay and negligence.[105] Substantiated complaints send a message to civil servants that they will not escape censure if they do not treat citizens legally, fairly, and properly. The Ombudsman also makes recommendations for improvements for future administration to prevent cases from reoccurring.

The departments about which the ombudsman received the most complaints in 2019/2020 and in 2020/2021, were Food and Environment Hygiene Department (FEHD), the Buildings Department (BD), the Lands Department, Home Affairs and the Police Force. The focus of complaints can change quickly, however, if topical issues attract public attention. In 2019/2020, the future of RTHK (see pp. 352–354), the handling of the pandemic and government action on the political protests increased the number of complaints about some departments. In 2020/2021, there were over 12,000 complaints each about the Lands Department and the Home Affairs Department, far above their usual levels. The BD and the FEHD have consistently been a focus of complaints over the years. The BD has responsibility for building inspections and, with the FEHD, for water seepage problems.[106] Aside from the COVID-19 issue, the FEHD usually also has a high number of complaints because some of its activities, such as hawker control and the inspection of commercial premises to check on hygiene standards, have the potential to provoke friction. Other departments that receive a large number of complaints in normal times are the Housing Department, the Lands Department, Immigration, Social Welfare, and Transport. Most complaints against the Police Force would have been not pursuable or *ultra vires*, but the Ombudsman did investigate nine allegations of breach of the *Code of Access to Information* against the force in 2019/2020, finding five cases to be substantiated, one partially substantiated, and three unsubstantiated but with other problems.[107] There were 280 complaints against the Police Force in 2020/2021 compared with 1,548 in 2019/2020.[108]

The Ombudsman has the power to conduct direct investigations where there is alleged maladministration in areas of significant social concerns or repeated complaints about the same issue.[109] The issue should not be an individual grievance and not normally subject to the jurisdiction of a court or tribunal. Issues have included many important matters such as dealing with seepage problems, the performance

---

103. Ibid., p. 41, Annex 6.
104. Office of the Ombudsman (2020) op. cit., p. 39.
105. Office of the Ombudsman (2021) op. cit., p. 41.
106. Office of the Ombudsman (2020). *Effectiveness of Joint Office for investigation of water seepage complaints in handling water seepage reports: Executive summary*. https://ofomb.ombudsman.hk/abc/en-us/direct_investigations
107. Office of the Ombudsman (2020) op. cit., pp. 103–104.
108. Ibid., Appendix 5.
109. Ibid., p. 20.

of the Integrated Call Centre, the Social Welfare Department's monitoring of residential care homes for the elderly, the regulation of Chinese medicine, controls over illegal burials, and problems relating to the fire safety regulations.[110]

Direct investigations results are reported at media conferences, which puts pressure on the government to address the problem and accept the recommendations. It was originally thought that there would only be a few direct investigations, but the average annual number more than doubled over the decade 2011–2020.[111] Between 2015 and 2021, the Ombudsman conducted 62 direct investigations. The office has also developed a partial direct investigation assessment system which is useful in identifying maladministration and other administrative problems.[112]

In their assessment of the performance of the Ombudsman, Chan and Wong observe that it displays the characteristics of the classical ombudsman, such as independence from government, impartiality, and confidentiality, and that it is widely respected.[113] The dramatic increase in the number of complaints in 2020 and 2021 (see Figure 12.1) attests to the public perception that the office is believed to deal with complaints fairly. Yet, as Chan and Wong also observe, its ability to continue to provide this function depends on the socio-political environment. Any decline in its independence from government will adversely affect its ability to fulfil its present functions.

Departmental Complaint-handling Units

In 2009, the Efficiency Unit laid down principles designed to attain consistency across government departments in the handling of complaints. Aside from the requirement, which has been in force since 1979, that complaints should be handled at the lowest level possible, the unit said that best practice should involve viewing matters from the complainant's perspective, solving the problem rather than allowing issues of departmental jurisdiction to cause delays, maintaining accurate and retrievable records, showing an awareness of value for money and effectiveness, and being accountable for outsourced services.[114] The unit's own experience in attempting to set up a call centre revealed that many departments fell well short of best practice.

---

110. Office of the Ombudsman (2020). Direct investigations. https://ofomb.ombudsman.hk/abc/en-us/direct_investigations
111. Office of the Ombudsman (2020) Direct investigations, op. cit.
112. Chan, J., & Wong, V. (2018). The politics of the ombudsman: The Hong Kong experience. In M. Hertogh & R. Kirkham (Eds.), *Research handbook on the ombudsman* (pp. 91–112). Cheltenham: Edward Elgar.
113. Ibid.
114. Efficiency Unit (2009). *A guide to complaint-handling and public enquiries* (p. 4). https://www.effo.gov.hk/en/reference/publications/A_Guide_to_Complaints_Handling_and_Public_Enquiries.pdf

The Integrated Call Centre

In 2001, the Efficiency Unit established the Integrated Call Centre (ICC) to answer queries and complaints concerning 12 departments. The public was able to use a single-number hotline for a one-stop, round-the-clock service. The new system was expected to be more responsive and more efficient because departments had previously passed callers from one officer to another and the delays had caused frustration. Although a customer satisfaction survey found that respondents saw merit in the ICC, there were 173 complaints to the Ombudsman between July 2001 and May 2003 which led to a direct investigation.[115] The report acknowledged that the ICC was an improvement over previous arrangements but also discovered many shortcomings: delays and lack of response, problems with the transmission of complaints and outdated information, and the maintenance of personal data privacy. The ICC's organisational culture was "more task- than people-oriented" and there were tensions between the ICC and the participating departments. It recommended that other departments should not be pressured to join the system.[116]

Despite her recommendations for change, the Ombudsman continued to receive complaints about the ICC and launched a further investigation of the service.[117] By that stage, the use of ICC services had climbed from 1.8 million in 2004 to 3.1 million in 2007.[118] But there were still some major problems. The service was patchy; there were difficulties in dealing with cross-departmental issues; some departments were considering dropping out of the system; and coverage was still limited to 20 departments, "far from its ultimate goal of an integrated call centre."[119] The Ombudsman found that the ICC was used as a shield when multiple departments were involved in areas such as illegal waste disposal, traffic, slope safety, and vegetation management and that they preferred to communicate with each other through the ICC rather than making direct contact with complainants.[120] Six departments wanted to join the ICC but could not because it was operating at full capacity; six other major departments—the Police Force, Housing, Home Affairs, Fire Services, Environmental Protection, and the Water Supplies Department—remained outside the system.[121]

The ICC has subsequently resolved some of its problems. Since 2011, a mobile application can be downloaded to make a complaint and receive a response from the departments although phone calls are still the most popular means of making a

---

115. Office of the Ombudsman (2003). *Report of investigation into the operation of the Integrated Call Centre.* https://ofomb.ombudsman.hk/abc/en-us/direct_investigations
116. Ibid., pp. 52–53.
117. Office of the Ombudsman (2008b). *Direct investigation on the effectiveness of the Integrated Call Centre in handling complaints.* https://ofomb.ombudsman.hk/abc/en-us/direct_investigations
118. Ibid., Executive Summary, p. 5.
119. Ibid., Executive Summary, p. 8.
120. Ibid., Ch. 3, p. 22.
121. Ibid., Ch. 2, p. 5.

complaint or enquiry.[122] By 2015, there were 22 participating departments, and the ICC was receiving over four million enquiries and complaints annually. By 2018, 4.8 million people were thought to be aware of mobile e-government services, a number that more than doubled between 2012 and 2018.[123] Major departments are still not part of the system and the service now seems to emphasise its role in answering enquiries rather than in handling complaints. It provides information on how to obtain a driving licence, how to track mail delivery, and the requirements of the home ownership scheme.[124] While these are useful services, complex problems and complaints still require human interaction.

Other Department Complaint-Handling Units

Some departments choose to keep their own complaint-handling units and do so for reasons that may include the ICC's lack of capacity, their ability to deal quickly with most complaints, or their view that the existing process is satisfactory and well established. The Transport Complaints Unit was established in 1980 and has received a growing number of complaints over the years. It has some features characteristic of successful complaint-handling bodies. First, it is independent. It is monitored by a subcommittee of the Transport Advisory Committee, which is composed of non-civil servants and does not come under the Transport Department. Second, it is very easy to make a complaint; most complaints are made through the unit's telephone hotline with the remainder received by e-mail, fax, or mail. Third, complainants can expect their grievances to be treated sympathetically. A majority of complaints—some 77% of 10,344 complaints and suggestions in the third quarter of 2021—were found to be substantiated.[125] Fourth, the Transport Complaints Units relays its statistics to the Transport Department to help solve persistent problems and refers reports of serious infractions to the police. Finally, the unit is inexpensive and the number of officers involved is small, considering the number of complaints received. There have been criticisms that investigations are superficial and that the complainants are usually only fleetingly concerned about the issue. Conversely, the complaint can be rectified or explained quickly in many cases and there is no need for a more extensive investigation. Similar types of complaint-handling mechanism have been established in the Inland Revenue and Water Supplies Departments, both of which also receive a large number of complaints.

---

122. Chan, B. (2016, 29 January). How 1823 app has made complaining to the Hong Kong government easier. *SCMP*. https://www.scmp.com/lifestyle/article/1906431/how-1823-app-makes-complaining-hong-kong-government-easier
123. Statista (2020). Number of people who are aware of the mobile e-government services in Hong Kong 2012 to 2018. https://www.statista.com/statistics/940934/hong-kong-number-of-people-aware-of-mobile-e-government-services/
124. Efficiency Office (2020). The story of 1823. https://www.effo.gov.hk/en/our-work/citizen-centric-services/1823.html
125. Hong Kong Government (2021, 21 December). TCU's third quarterly report of 2021 released. https://www.info.gov.hk/gia/general/202112/21/P2021122100324.htm

Complaints about professionals raise more difficult problems because they are often regulated by the professional body rather than by a government department. Complaints against doctors, for example, are regulated by the Medical Council. Since the Legislative Council amendment to the *Medical Registration Ordinance* in 2017, the investigating committee is now composed of 24 doctors and eight lay members (four appointed by the Chief Executive, three by patients' organisations, and one nominated by the Consumer Council).[126] For serious allegations, the first step is to establish a committee that makes a recommendation on whether or not the case should be investigated by an inquiry panel composed of three medical practitioners and two lay members. In 2018, the Medical Council received 639 complaints.[127] Two years later, the number had risen very sharply to 3,356, mainly relating to issues of professional responsibility to patients.[128] Preliminary investigative committees referred 105 cases to the panel of which 77 were dismissed, 21 were referred to a disciplinary panel and seven were recommended for no disciplinary investigation.[129] A further 32 cases were also referred for disciplinary investigation resulting from changes in complaint-handling procedures. For those found guilty of an offence, penalties are generally light unless the doctor has been convicted on a criminal charge. In 2020, most substantiated cases resulted in temporary suspension from the medical register for short periods or reprimands or warnings.[130]

The government's proposal to amend the *Medical Registration Ordinance* in 2016 was controversial, not so much because of the relatively minor changes that were proposed but because it raised questions about how the redress system worked. The Legislative Council had previously debated, and rejected, setting up an independent medical complaints council, but there were still calls for a Health Services Ombudsman.[131] There were also doubts about whether the new system would have much effect on the average length of time to process a complaint, which one legislator claimed was 59 months.[132] Others complained about the lack of public consultation and argued that the amendments were an attempt by the government to control the Medical Council.[133]

The dominant position of professional elites within the Hong Kong political system has made it difficult to reform bodies that traditionally have been self-regulating. But a more critical public, and several scandals, led some professional bodies, such as the legal and surveying professions, to examine their practices more closely. While the complaint-handling processes remain opaque, slow and controlled by the

---

126. *Medical Registration Ordinance*, Cap 161, Section 3.
127. Medical Council (2019). *Annual report 2018* (pp. 10, 35). https://www.mchk.org.hk/english/publications/index.html
128. Medical Council (2021). *Annual report 2020* (p. 9). https://www.mchk.org.hk/files/annual/files/2020/Annual_Report_2020_Eng.pdf
129. Ibid.
130. Ibid., 36–37.
131. Hansard, 7 July 2016, 13125.
132. Hansard, 7 July 2016, 13115.
133. Hansard, 6 July 2016, 13087.

professional body, there is little likelihood that they will win the public support that the Ombudsman and the ICAC have been able to achieve.

Complaints against the Police

The Complaints Against the Police Office (CAPO) was established in 1974 and has always been staffed by police officers seconded from other parts of the force. Attempts to monitor the work of CAPO date from 1977. The Independent Police Complaints Council (IPCC) was established in 1994 as a body that would review CAPO decisions, but periodic controversies have plagued its existence. In 1997, the government withdrew its bill after the Legislative Council amended proposed legislation to allow the IPCC to investigate complaints against the police. Ten years later, the Legislative Council passed revised legislation, *The Independent Police Complaints Council Ordinance*, which made the IPCC a statutory body and slightly increased its powers. However, the democrats still voted against the ordinance.[134] Other critics—human rights groups, the Bar Association and, in 2019, its own appointed international experts—wanted stronger controls over CAPO and more powers and resources for the IPPC to investigate cases.[135] Neither the government nor the Police Force has ever been willing to concede that power.

The ordinance provides that the IPCC may "observe, monitor and review the handling of reportable complaints", identify faults and deficiencies in practice and procedure, and may interview any person connected with a case.[136] Very few interviews are actually conducted and the IPCC is largely dependent on CAPO for its information. Before CAPO proceeds with an investigation, the complainant can express dissatisfaction with police behaviour without lodging a formal complaint.[137] If the complainant decides to make a reportable complaint, which must not be "vexatious or frivolous" and must be made "in good faith",[138] there is still the possibility of seeking informal resolution or withdrawing the complaint. In consequence, not all complaints are fully investigated.

In 2019/2020, CAPO received 1,293 reportable complaints, a decrease of 15.3% over the previous year despite the 2019 protests.[139] The reportable complaints pro-

---

134. *The Independent Police Complaints Council Ordinance*, Cap 604.
135. Hong Kong Human Rights Monitor (2007). Submission of Human Rights Monitor on Independent Police Complaints Council Bill. https://www.legco.gov.hk/yr06-07/english/bc/bc63/papers/bc631206cb2-499-2-e.pdf; Hong Kong Bar Association (2007). Independent Police Complaints Council Bill. https://www.legco.gov.hk/yr06-07/english/bc/bc63/papers/bc63cb2-649-1-e.pdf; Lum, A. (2019, 10 November). Hong Kong police watchdog does not have the powers and resources to cope with scale of protests, say IPCC's expert advisers. *SCMP*. https://www.scmp.com/news/hong-kong/politics/article/3037080/hong-kong-police-watchdog-does-not-have-powers-and
136. *The Independent Police Complaints Council Ordinance*, op. cit., Section 8.
137. Hong Kong Police Force (2020). *Complaints Against Police Office: A guide for complainants*. https://www.police.gov.hk/info/doc/pol/en/Pol_679.pdf
138. *The Independent Police Complaints Council Ordinance*, op. cit., Section 11.
139. IPCC (2020). *Report 2019/20* (p. 38). https://www.ipcc.gov.hk/en/publications/annual_report/2019.html

duced 2,209 allegations of misconduct, 202 of which were informally resolved, 462 were withdrawn, and 748 were not pursuable.[140] Of the 797 allegations that were fully investigated, 57 were substantiated, 19 were substantiated other than reported, and two were not fully substantiated.[141] Substantiated complaints mostly relate to minor offences. Of the 80 officers against whom disciplinary action was taken, two were subject to disciplinary review, 53 were given advice, and 25 received warnings.[142] The other 719 allegations were unsubstantiated, "no fault", or false.[143] Between mid-2015 and mid-2020, only one criminal proceeding was lodged against an officer as a result of a complaint.[144]

Table 12.1 shows the results of allegations of serious complaints against police officers. Assault is the most serious offence but, as Table 12.1 shows, between mid-2015 and mid-2021, only two of the 218 fully investigated complaints of assault were found to be substantiated.[145] Although during this period the political protests were at their height and there were many allegations of excessive use of force and

Table 12.1 *Substantiated and Reportable Allegations against the Police 2015–2021*

Allegations	2015/2016	2016/17	2017/2018	2018/2019	2019/2020	2020/2021
Assault	1/50	0/39	1/41	0/31	0/35	0/22
Neglect of Duty	120/718	71/493	90/563	57/344	58/424	70/396
Misconduct/ Improper Manner/ Abusive Language	8/309	12/297	16/307	14/204	15/268	17/226
Unnecessary Use of Authority	6/61	5/53	5/54	1/27	1/36	3/40
Threat	2/21	0/17	0/15	0/3	0/10	0/3

Sources: Compiled from https://www.ipcc.gov.hk/en/publications/annual_report/2016.html, 44–45; IPCC (2019). *Report 2018/2019*. https://www.ipcc.gov.hk/en/publications/annual_report/2018.html, 44–45. IPCC (2020). *Report 2019/2020*. https://www.ipcc.gov.hk/en/publications/annual_report/2019.html. IPCC (2021). *Report 2020/2021*. https://www.ipcc.gov.hk/en/publications/annual_report/2020.html

Notes:
1. The first number in the table is the total number of "substantiated" and "substantiated other than reported" allegations. The second number is the total number of reportable allegations.
2. The allegations cited relate to the most serious and common complaints against police behaviour. They do not include allegations against other forms of unacceptable police behaviour.

---

140. Ibid., p. 41.
141. Ibid.
142. Ibid., p. 44.
143. Ibid., p. 41.
144. IPCC (2017–2021). *Reports*. https://www.ipcc.gov.hk/en/publications/annual_report/2019.html
145. Ibid.

independent witnesses and credible evidence of events, nothing convinced CAPO that any police officer had assaulted any protesters or bystanders.[146]

CAPO's view is that every officer is entitled to be presumed innocent of a crime or misconduct unless the contrary is proven beyond reasonable doubt. It follows, according to police logic, that complaints are not necessarily without foundation but that, in one-on-one situations, when versions of events are irreconcilable, it is not always possible to reach a definitive conclusion and that the accused should be given benefit of the doubt. Historically, this concern with procedural rather than substantive justice has pervaded the entire complaint-handling process and is one reason why the public has little confidence in CAPO or the IPCC. After the 2019 protests, confidence even in procedural justice seems to have declined much further.[147]

Three conclusions may be drawn about the Police Force's complaint-handling process. The first is that, whether or not CAPO conducts investigations fairly, public perception is more important than actual practice. And that perception is that CAPO is not impartial. The police argue that only they know how to investigate cases properly. But this was the original argument against ICAC corruption investigations and it has not held up. A related argument that an independent body would adversely affect police morale has also been largely discredited by the ICAC experience, whose independence from the government has increased public confidence in the agency.

A second conclusion is that to win greater confidence in the complaint-handling process the police should take a less procedural and more substantive view of justice. The presumption of innocence for police officers who are accused of misconduct does accord with legal practice under the common law. But CAPO is not a court and many of the aggrieved—the young people and blue-collar workers who make up the bulk of complainants—may have little experience of what constitutes evidence or of how to present a case. To apply strict procedural guidelines under such circumstances is inappropriate. In a court of law, both procedural and substantive justice should be seen to be done. In an institution concerned with redress, the balance should be tilted more towards substantive justice. The playing field on complaints against the police in Hong Kong is not level.

A third conclusion is that the monitoring role of the IPCC has been ineffectual. On their joint resignation in December 2019, the panel of experts, which had been assisting the IPCC in its investigation of whether the police had used excessive force against the protesters, concluded that the council had neither the powers nor the

---

146. Amnesty International (2020) op. cit.; Stott, C., Ho, L., Radburn, M., Chan, Y. Y., Kyprianides, K., & Morales, P. S. (2020). Patterns of "disorder" during the 2019 protests in Hong Kong: Policing, social identity, intergroup dynamics and radicalization. *Policing: A Journal of Policy and Practice.* https://doi.org/10.1093/police/paaa073
147. Wan, C. (2020, 5 December). Calls grow for police accountability in Hong Kong. VOA. https://www.voanews.com/a/east-asia-pacific_calls-grow-police-accountability-hong-kong/6199209.html

resources to conduct the investigation.[148] The same comments apply to the relationship between the IPCC and CAPO. The IPCC has no independent means of checking whether the information that CAPO provides is accurate. While it may query that information, its inability to conduct an independent investigation is a critical weakness. In May 2020, that weakness became even more apparent when the IPCC produced its report on police handling of the protests.[149] Parts of the report seemed to fly in the face of what was widely known and had been reported about police behaviour by many reliable sources during the protests (see p. 63).

The purpose of redress is to assure the public that wrongs will be righted. The police complaint-handling process has never come near to attaining that objective.

Administrative Tribunals

Administrative tribunals have been established to serve a variety of purposes. They may resolve disputes, hear appeals against government decisions, act as commissions of inquiry, or make policy decisions on behalf of the government. These functions are not necessarily performed exclusively by bodies primarily designated as administrative tribunals. The Executive Council, for example, could be regarded as an administrative tribunal because some ordinances permit appeals to be made to it. With the range of laws and institutions involved, it is scarcely surprising that the practices of administrative tribunals have varied considerably and have sometimes been criticised. Do complainants have the right of appeal against the findings of the tribunal? Are the powers of the tribunal sufficiently publicised? Should procedures meet standards and rules of evidence that might apply in a court of law or should they be more informal? Should tribunals provide reasons for their decisions? Do those who hear the cases have appropriate qualifications? These questions have become increasingly pressing because there has been little by way of major reform to improve the practices and procedures of tribunals over many years.[150]

One criticism of tribunals is that no appeals are allowed against their decisions except for judicial review, which is at the discretion of the courts and may not deal with the substance of the complaint. Many tribunals hear appeals from individuals against a government action that has detrimentally affected them but that might not even be considered by other complaint-handling institutions. The Ombudsman, for example, cannot consider a complaint if there is "a right of appeal or an objection to the Chief Executive, the Chief Executive in Council, any tribunal constituted by or under any ordinance, or any board or other authority so constituted."[151] The

---

148. AFP (2019, 11 December). Int'l experts to quit Hong Kong investigation into police handling of protests. *HKFP*. https://hongkongfp.com/2019/12/11/breaking-international-experts-quit-hong-kong-investigation-police-handling-protests/
149. IPCC (2020) op. cit.
150. Thomson, S. (2017). Clutter and cobwebs: How administrative tribunals in Hong Kong can learn from the UK. *Civil Justice Quarterly*, 36(3), 363–386.
151. *Ombudsman Ordinance*, Cap 397, S.10.

complainant may have no choice about who hears the case and there may be no appeal against its decision.

Yet many of the matters that come before tribunals are extremely important. They concern people's liberties on matters such as the right of residence, commitment to a mental hospital, addiction treatment, and the possibility of torture if they are returned to their country of origin. In the commercial field, tribunals may decide on whether to issue licences, how fair competition is managed, and how violations of rules should be penalised. Many boards and tribunals are also appellate bodies. No reasons need be given for their decisions, which are often final and, if no reasons are given for a decision, it is difficult to question its reasonableness in court. Where procedures are defective, there is also concern that the complainant's natural justice will be affected. To create greater confidence in their work, tribunals must be seen to be fair, the procedures for lodging an application must be clear, and the process should be transparent, preferably with open hearings and easy access to written decisions.

Too often boards and tribunals in Hong Kong fall short on these counts. The Director of Immigration, for example, may issue orders deporting refugees to their country of origin (legally described as the rejection of a non-refoulement claim). Hong Kong is a signatory to the United Nations Convention against Torture. Refugees who allege that, if they are forced to return to their home country, they may suffer torture can appeal against the director's decision to the Torture Claims Appeal Board. If their claim is accepted, they are permitted to remain in Hong Kong. But chances of success are very low. In the first quarter of 2020, the board concluded 652 cases, of which 11 were allowed.[152] In 2017 and 2018, thousands of non-refoulement claimants also applied for leave for judicial review but met with a similar lack of success (see Chapter 2, Table 2.2). The Torture Claims Appeal Board, in common with other tribunals concerned with personal liberties which come under the Security Bureau, is not sufficiently transparent. Information on its caseload, for example, has to be obtained by making an application under the *Code on Access to Information*.

By contrast, the Labour Tribunal, which was created in 1973 "to provide a quick, informal and inexpensive means to settle monetary disputes between employees and employers", is much more of a conventional complaint-handling institution.[153] It stresses informal mediation that is facilitated initially by the Labour Department and then taken to the tribunal if no resolution is reached. The tribunal does not permit legal representation although some companies used to send along their lawyers to represent them, a practice which placed the worker at a considerable

---

152. Li, R. (2020). Torture Claims Appeal Board—Question 1–2020. https://accessinfo.hk/en/request/torture_claims_appeal_board_q1_2_3?utm_campaign=alaveteli-experiments-87&utm_content=sidebar_similar_requests&utm_medium=link&utm_source=accessinfo.hk
153. Hong Kong Judiciary (2022). *Labour Tribunal*. https://www.judiciary.hk/en/court_services_facilities/labour.html

disadvantage.[154] There were also complaints from employers, who found the practices of the tribunal to be cumbersome and time-consuming. In 2004, a review made recommendations that extended the tribunal's jurisdiction, improved its conciliation and settlement processes, and tightened other procedures.[155] Since then, there has been a marked improvement in waiting times for cases to be heard and settled. In 2020, the tribunal disposed of 3,172 of 3,731 cases and on average was able to deal with cases from appointment to first hearing in just under three months.[156]

The Labour Tribunal, together with the Lands Tribunal, the Obscene Articles Tribunal, the Small Claims Tribunal, and the Competition Tribunal, falls under the Judiciary. There are considerable variations in procedures between these tribunals because each has a specialised purpose. In contrast to the Labour Tribunal, the Competition Tribunal operates in effect as a court because all of its members are judges of the Court of First Instance. Cases may be appealed to the tribunal from the decisions of the Competition Commission. The commission is responsible for "agreements, practices and conduct that prevent, restrict or distort competition and ... mergers that substantially lessen competition in Hong Kong."[157] The commission only began work in 2015 and investigations are long and complex. By 2020, only three cases had been completed.[158] Enforcement is key to the commission's credibility and the tribunal's task is to ensure that its decisions and orders are sound. Any person or undertaking mentioned in the commission's findings may apply to the tribunal for redress but, for their case to be heard, it must have a reasonable prospect of success or be in the interests of justice.[159] It seems unlikely that the tribunal will be flooded with cases.

The Administrative Appeals Board meets the criterion that practices should be standardised in the interests of fair play. It was established in 1994 by the *Administrative Appeals Board Ordinance*. It allows the right of appeal against some administrative decisions under 77 ordinances and has the power to reverse the original administrative decision.[160] The board draws on legal expertise for its membership, its sessions are public, the appellant has the right to attend and to be represented, and the board is required to state its reasons for a decision in writing. Despite these positive elements, the board seems little known as an avenue for redress and there is almost no publicity for its activities. The board received 27 appeals in 2019 and 35 in 2020; three appeals were allowed in 2019 and one in 2020

---

154. Moir, J. (2003, 13 September). Combatants want to sort out redress mess. *SCMP*.
155. Hong Kong Judiciary (2004). *Report of the working party on the review of the Labour Tribunal.* https://www.judiciary.hk/doc/en/publications/lt_review_report-final.pdf
156. Hong Kong Judiciary (2021). *Annual report 2020*. https://www.judiciary.hk/en/publications./annu_rept_2020r/txteng/report.html
157. Competition Commission (2021). *Annual report 2020/2021* (p. 2). https://www.compcomm.hk/en/media/reports_publications/files/2020_21_CC_Annual_Report.pdf
158. Hong Kong Judiciary (2021). *Competition Tribunal.* https://www.judiciary.hk/en/publications./annu_rept_2020r/txteng/report.html
159. *Competition Ordinance*, Cap 619, Section 84.
160. *Administrative Appeals Board Ordinance*, Cap 442, Schedule.

although 15 cases lodged in 2020 are pending.[161] Since the tribunal has the potential to expand into a major institution for redressing grievances against administrative decisions, as it has in other countries such as Australia, its present, more limited, role seems to be a wasted opportunity.

Conclusions

Each type of complaint-handling institution that we have considered—those that protect civil liberties, those that can make systemic improvements by remedying problems, and those that redress individual grievances—can play a significant role in helping to reduce a legitimacy deficit. The Hong Kong government starts with the disadvantage in dealing with these organisations that it is likely to be seen as the principal cause of inadequate protection of civil liberties, the source of policy weaknesses or the reason for insufficient corruption controls, or the perpetrator of arbitrary, unfair, or illegal administrative decisions. Hong Kong's civil society has been deeply and continually concerned about the preservation of civil liberties and a free press. The government gains no immediate political benefit from ensuring that institutions that protect civil liberties or deal with complaints function well. If these institutions perform to a high standard, they receive credit from the public; if they do not, the government's numerous critics identify shortcomings where the institutions have proved deficient. What complaint-handling institutions may do over time, if they function successfully, is to reduce the legitimacy deficit and increase trust by reinforcing values that support recourse to justice after arbitrary, illegal, or corrupt action by public officials.

The question, then, is whether the government's actions have promoted the protection of the citizen against the arbitrary exercise of power. The answer to that question is at best mixed. The government has been moderately supportive of these institutions although less so in recent years. It has formally endorsed the principal values of the redress system: impartiality, fairness, and thoroughness of the investigative process. Some organisations, such as the ICAC and the Ombudsman, have become institutionalised and a valued part of the system. The government has recognised their role and, although there have been questions about the appointment of senior civil servants as Commissioner of the ICAC and to the position of Ombudsman, there has been no suggestion that this has affected their investigative procedures.

For other organisations, critical problems have not been resolved. There have been long-standing calls for an independent complaint-handling organisation to replace CAPO and the weak and ineffectual IPCC. Under the present circumstances, it seems unlikely that reforms will be introduced. There is also a case for a Health Services Ombudsman, independent of the Medical Council. Some administrative

---

161. Personal communication, Secretary, Administrative Appeals Board, 3 February 2021.

tribunals function well, but many others could benefit from review and reform. The Administrative Appeals Board could usefully publicise its role and serve more effectively as a redress institution. The government has been intent on maintaining the quiet, but often unsatisfactory, routine operation of these institutions. It has missed their potential for ameliorating tensions in an "executive-led" system where there is no prospect of changing the government and where other checks and balances have not been fully developed.

13
The Public Sector in Its Political Setting

This concluding chapter is an assessment of how contested values in a changing political environment have affected the public sector, particularly its accountability, policy formulation and implementation, and legitimacy. While there have not been many major changes to structure or procedures in the public sector since the handover, there has been a gradual shift away from traditional values accompanied by a decline in the authority and accountability of the Hong Kong government. A significant change in the location of power has sharply reduced the government's autonomy from Beijing and its capacity to make and implement public policy has been diminished by prolonged contention with civil society. Values have been at the centre of this conflict. The perception that civil liberties and the rule of law are in jeopardy has fuelled huge street protests and has been coupled with calls for a future democratic Hong Kong based on very different values from those on offer from the Chinese government.

It is possible to trace these changes over five sequential periods in which the common thread is a Hong Kong government increasingly caught between a disaffected public and a Chinese government intent on asserting greater control over the affairs of the SAR. At stake have been the protection of civil liberties and the extent to which constitutional reform could meet the democratic claims of civil society organisations. In the event, the assertion of the Chinese government's view of what the Joint Declaration and the Basic Law meant and the decision to enact national security legislation for Hong Kong saw the eclipse of traditional values and the inception of a new political order. In the following sections, these developments are analysed in greater detail.

The Transitional Period (1984–1997)

The critical feature of colonial administration in Hong Kong was that it was coterminous with the state. The integration of administrative and political functions, the absence of direct control from London, and public acceptance of the bureaucratic order meant that it was possible to create a system that developed in ways that were unique to Hong Kong and quite different from the usual constitutional evolution of British colonies. By the time negotiations took place with the Chinese government on the future of the territory, it was possible to envisage that the change of sovereignty might not lead to a change of system. On the Chinese side, the concept of "one country, two systems" gave recognition to the importance of capitalism to Hong Kong but also to the political, administrative, and legal supports that made such a system possible. On the British side, there was a clear intention to write into the Joint Declaration the essential values which gave Hong Kong, as the British Foreign Office diplomats saw it, freedom without democracy, executive government without the embarrassment of many legislative controls, and the continuing dominance of an efficient civil service. The Chinese government was willing to write those provisions into the Basic Law. Colonial political and administrative arrangements had the backing of the business community and could be changed after 1997 if they proved to be inappropriate. The consequence was that the political framework laid down in the Basic Law, except for some vague concessions to future democratic development, strongly resembled the pre-1997 political order.

There were three problems. The first was that the population had become much more politicised as a result of the agreement and subsequent developments, such as the Tiananmen Square incident, and began to demand more representative government and more protection for their civil liberties. Just before the retrocession in 1997, Patten observed that whenever there was a fair test of public opinion "approaching two-thirds of the electorate support a democratic agenda".[1] Every subsequent poll has shown that a majority of Hong Kong people were not happy with the existing system and that they had declining levels of trust in their government.[2] The measures introduced in the latter stages of the transitional period to the handover in 1997 were, in part, responses to that dissatisfaction. And, although the electoral reforms introduced in 1995 did not survive the retrocession, and the measures designed to protect civil liberties were seen to be fragile, they created expectations of progress towards a more representative system. When the incoming post-handover government dissolved the Legislative Council and announced more restrictive electoral procedures, support for the new political order, which appeared to be more autocratic than the departed colonial administration, was eroded from the outset.

A second problem was that the position of Chief Executive did not equate as easily with the position of Governor as had been anticipated. In colonial Hong Kong, the Governor tended to meld with the civil service rather to stand apart from it. There were, it is true, Governors, such as MacLehose, who sought to bring about fundamental change, but they tended to be the exception rather than the rule. When Tung came to office in 1997, there was little doubt that he wanted to bring about major changes. Some of his problems were inherited from the transitional period

---

1. Patten, C. (1996). *Hong Kong: Transition*. Hong Kong: Government Printer.
2. PORI (2020). On the whole, do you trust the HKSAR? https://develo.pori.hk/pop-poll/government-en/k001.html?lang=en

where difficult decisions were sometimes postponed to avoid political unrest, but most of the impetus for change probably came from his desire to stamp his imprint on the administration and from the Chinese government. Whatever the cause, there was tension between Tung and his senior civil servants, especially when his policies could not be implemented. This may have set the political stage for public sector reform. Even if the unreformed colonial system had been a model for the post-1997 government, it was no longer seen as appropriate for the public service that Tung wanted to create.

A third problem was that the values that underpinned the civil service, critical as they were, were not formalised into the constitutional arrangements. Neither the Joint Declaration nor the Basic Law captures the intricate relationship between the values which the civil service held dear and the construction of its dominant position within the polity. There is no mention in the Basic Law of such values as the public service vocation, meritocracy, and political neutrality. A civil service that exercises political power, such as that in colonial Hong Kong, requires a justification for its right to do so. The colonial administration had continuing problems justifying its right to rule although it did claim to have the consent of the people. What evidence supported that claim? How could consent be justified in a system which provided no means of democratic legitimation? The colonial administration offered several elaborate answers to those questions, including its performance, its efficiency, and various other values, such as meritocracy and political neutrality, none of which were entirely convincing. Perhaps the most pressing of its claims was that it had the right to rule because its most senior civil servants were the best and most able people available and because they also were imbued with a public service ethos which meant that the decisions that they took, as far as they were able to ensure, were in the best interests of the people of Hong Kong.

The importance of the public service ethos is a recurring theme in the memoirs and speeches of Hong Kong's senior civil servants. In a farewell speech, for example, Anson Chan said that as a young administrative officer she had been told that:

> you have joined a very special service which has an excellent reputation built up by the people who have gone before you. Your obligations as an administrative officer are simple. You must serve the people well and you must serve them with honour.[3]

It was, she said, advice that she passed on to her younger colleagues. When her successor, Donald Tsang Yam-kuen, was asked about the differences between him and Anson Chan, he stressed instead their common commitment to the people.[4] A host of other senior civil servants have testified to the importance of the public service ethos as a value that received constant stress within the government, served as a

---

3. Chan, A. (2001, 19 April). *Speech by the Chief Secretary of Administration at an Asia Society luncheon* [Press release].
4. Hong Kong Government (2001, 3 May). *Transcript of Chief Secretary for Administration's media session (Part 2)* [Press release].

bond between administrators, and created public expectations about the role that civil servants would play in the community. In the Civil Service Training Centre, as it then was, new graduates on the first day of their induction course were asked why bright young men and women such as them were prepared to work for a colonial regime.[5] In the embarrassed silence that usually followed, the instructor provided the answer: they were not there to serve a colonial regime; they were there to serve the people of Hong Kong.

To be overly cynical about such professions of the importance of the public service ethos misses a critical point. In any Weberian system of public administration, public service as a vocation, meritocratic recruitment, and political neutrality are central values. But in most Weberian systems, such values did not by themselves legitimate the exercise of power because there was also normally a political order, often democratically legitimated, which gave elected representatives a mandate to decide on what was in the best interests of the people. In Hong Kong, if civil servants were to exercise power, they needed legitimating principles to justify what they were doing. Public service as a vocation provided one such justification. Nor should we be surprised that this justification proved successful. Although it may be argued that Hong Kong's pre-1997 political system was unique, the ideas on which it was based had a long pedigree. Confucius and Plato would both have approved of a system in which able new recruits to the civil service were socialised and trained in a commitment to public service and where popular influence on government was restricted.

Despite the importance of these bureaucratic supports for the system, they were not sufficient to prevent the colonial administration from suffering from periodic crises of legitimacy and from an enduring legitimacy deficit. There remained major problems of consent and of legal and moral authority which the colonial administration could attempt to reduce but could never entirely resolve. The absence of alternative forms of legitimation became even more evident when it became clear that Hong Kong's democratic development was about to be curtailed. The authority of the post-1997 system was undermined by the dissolution of the Legislative Council and it was to be further compromised by the blame that the government received for its handling of the economy and for its policy failures. The question was which values, if any, might replace those of the colonial order.

The Post-handover Government: Political Control and Failed Changes (1997–2005)

The answer to that question was not immediately obvious. If Tung Chee Hwa had assumed the mantle of a colonial governor and defended his civil service against

---

5. Hayes, J. (1996). *Friends and teachers: Hong Kong and its people 1953–87*. Hong Kong: Hong University Press; Sinn, E. (Ed.) (2001). *Hong Kong: British crown colony revisited* (pp. 7, 126–127). Hong Kong: The University of Hong Kong.

the criticisms of his supporters in the business world, and if the Chinese government had refrained from interfering in the Hong Kong system, as it initially seemed inclined to do, then it is possible that the bureaucratic polity might have continued for some time. But the life of the bureaucratic polity was essentially limited by the political pressures from Tung, his supporters, and the Chinese government, on the one hand, and from the democrats, on the other. There was declining public support for a system based on rule by civil servants. The Tung administration wanted a new order which asserted political control over the civil service. It wanted to bring to government what it regarded as the virtues of private sector practices. The relative autonomy that the civil service had previously exercised in its decisions affecting the business community was diminished. The democrats were looking for a more accountable system, especially following the tensions between the Legislative Council and senior civil servants in the immediate aftermath of the retrocession.[6]

To fill the void, the government proposed two solutions. The first was the introduction of managerialist reforms that either reinterpreted the meaning of old values, such as efficiency, responsiveness, and eventually political neutrality, or sought to establish new values within the civil service that undermined the traditional norm of public service as a vocation. The emphasis was on downsizing, pay reductions, and the ability to implement bright ideas and politically determined ends rather than the notion of the public service ethos. The reforms, introduced in 1999, brought managerialist values to the forefront of future civil service practice,[7] proposing the introduction of more contractual conditions of employment, renewal of contracts to be determined by performance, the use of performance pay as a motivator, performance as the main determinant of promotion, and harsher sanctions for failure to meet minimal standards.

To pursue such an agenda is difficult enough under normal conditions. In Hong Kong, the government introduced its reforms at a time when it was suffering from a significant budget deficit. This was attributed in part to high recurrent expenditure for the civil service which Tung, and many in the business community, believed was too large and too well paid. The post-1999 reform initiatives soon became synonymous with downsizing and salary cuts. It was proposed that employment in the civil service as a lifetime career, an "iron rice bowl", should be replaced with programmes that brought in new recruits on short-term contracts and offered voluntary retirement to longer-serving officials. As salaries were cut and public and political criticism of the civil service increased, morale in the civil service declined alarmingly.[8] The key values, to which Anson Chan had referred, seemed increasingly under

---

6. Scott, I. (2000). The disarticulation of Hong Kong's post-handover political system. *The China Journal*, 43, 29–53.
7. Civil Service Bureau (1999). *Civil service reform: Consultation document: Civil service into the 21st century*. Hong Kong: Printing Department.
8. Cheng, J. (2003, 26 October). Team sprit lacking in demoralized civil service. *SCMP*; Cheung, J. (2003, 30 June). Civil servants' morale in dramatic fall since handover. *SCMP*; Yeung, C. (2002, 16 December). Observer. *SCMP*.

threat. And there was nothing to replace them once Tung's managerialist reforms failed except for the government's vague expectation that increased productivity and efficiency would result from a leaner civil service.

The second measure taken to reduce the power of senior civil servants was to shift political control to a new hand-picked political executive under the POAS arrangements. Tung's diagnosis of the problem was probably correct. There were demands for greater accountability after scandals relating to the handling of the avian flu issue, the opening of the airport, and the faulty construction of housing projects. But the POAS did not resolve the problem. Its fundamental weakness was that the principal officials were only accountable to the Chief Executive because only he and the NPCSC could appoint and remove them. To legitimise the system would have required a role for the Legislative Council in the appointment process, but that was not possible under the Basic Law and would not have been approved by the Chinese government even if it had been feasible.

Another weakness was that the POAS was seen as an attempt to undermine the concept of political neutrality. In reiterating the importance of political neutrality, the government shifted ground from the emphasis that Anson Chan had placed on "speaking truth to power" and acting in the public interest to the notion that the civil service should be loyal, first and foremost, to the government in power. The difficulty was that the government itself did not have express consent to exercise power and that the source of its authority, which was the Basic Law, had never been approved by the people of Hong Kong. Yet another weakness was that principal officials had policy and personal scandals with which to contend. Tung contributed to the problem by failing to ask for their resignations, which gave the impression that the system was no more accountable than its predecessor. A final weakness was that some senior civil servants had to choose between becoming principal officials under the new system or remaining as civil servants. The senior civil service was divided into those who were willing to make a political commitment to the government and those who continued to see themselves as career civil servants albeit with reduced powers.

Neither the managerialist reforms nor the POAS answered the problem of providing new values for those that were being discarded. Rather, they contributed to the further disarticulation of the political system. The Basic Law does not specify sufficiently how coordination between the executive, legislature, and civil service will occur; the emphasis is on the powers and duties of the institutions, not on their relationships with one another. It may be surmised that the drafters thought that coordination would probably occur much as it had done in the past: that an "executive-led" government would ensure that other institutions were brought into line and that policy formulation and implementation would consequently be unproblematic. This was a reasonable assumption at the time that the Basic Law was drafted. But it became less plausible as the Legislative Council became more critical of government action, as parties and pressure groups began to emerge, and as senior civil servants found that they had to play a more proactive political role to get their policies accepted.

After the handover, some senior civil servants did attempt to return to less political roles, which they were entitled to do under the provisions of the Basic Law. Relations between the government and the Legislative Council deteriorated as a consequence and, on the part of the democrats, became more hostile as they called for Tung's resignation. The right of abode issue and its impact on the relationship between the government and the Judiciary brought the issue of the rule of law and the judicial independence to centre stage. The failed attempt to legislate national security legislation under Article 23, when the population's commitment to civil liberties was very clearly expressed, further widened the distance between the government and the people. This was already a volatile mix. Added to that mix were the effects of the public sector reform programme and increased political control over the civil service. Bureaucratic dominance came to an end, but the cost was a more fragmented polity and greater disarticulation of its principal institutions. Faced with increasing public discontent and in the wake of the massive demonstrations against his attempt to introduce national security legislation, Tung resigned in March 2005.

The Policy Conundrum and Constitutional Development (2005–2013)

When Donald Tsang Yam-kuen, the former Chief Secretary for Administration, succeeded Tung as Chief Executive, his principal aim seemed to be to calm the waters that had been troubled by his predecessor. His natural inclination not to introduce controversial policies was reinforced by the disarticulated political system, the difficulty of gaining acceptance for policies in the Legislative Council and their sometimes-unanticipated public reception even if they had been approved by the council. Under the Basic Law, the Legislative Council had been expected to act largely as a rubber stamp, as it had done before 1984. Although hampered by their weak powers, Councillors made the best of what they had and were able to draw public attention to perceived deficiencies.

The government faced problems in attempting to persuade the legislature to adopt its proposals because it did not have a majority government party in the Legislative Council although it could normally rely on the DAB and the Liberal Party. Eventually, the polarisation of the polity was reflected in a rigid divide between pro-establishment/pro-Beijing legislators and the democrats. The democrats began to use filibusters to obstruct government proposals and had enough seats to prevent the government from reaching the two-thirds majority required for constitutional change. Many experienced legislators also employed their knowledge of council procedures to grill principal officials and senior civil servants on their proposals and sought to hold the government to account. Policies took longer to formulate and often became bogged down in committees.

Even if a policy proposal passed the scrutiny of the Legislative Council, there was no guarantee that it would not meet with a hostile reception on the streets, in the media, and even in the courts. Many smaller pressure groups were organised to respond to policies. These were new political actors, not the "usual suspects" but young activists, who were campaigning at "a higher, smarter level", using such means as judicial review to bring the government to book.[9] These groups proved difficult to deal with because they were excluded from the consultative framework either because government chose not to consult them or because they did not exist before the announcement of the policy. Their methods included thorough research of policy issues and possible alternative courses of action and knowledge of "how to campaign and get media attention".[10] Their strategies often involved coalitions of pressure groups, which created problems for the government. The opposition was hydra-headed, and concessions to one group did not necessarily satisfy another. Policy created its own politics. The colonial administration had controlled the timing, presentation, and politics of the policy process, but in the disarticulated, polyarchic system of post-1997 Hong Kong, opposition to government policy proposals could come from anywhere.

Major social policy issues were shelved because the government thought they would be too controversial. Social welfare had already been cut under Tung. Housing policy had been refocused from the provision of public housing to the provision of more private housing. Health policy reforms would have required asking the public to pay for services. The number of people below the poverty line increased. There were major protests over the decision to build an express rail link to the Mainland and over the government's ill-fated attempt, possibly under pressure from the Chinese government, to introduce "moral and national education" as a compulsory part of the curriculum. Thousands of students, parents, teachers, and unionists demonstrated against the proposal, eventually forcing the government to withdraw it. The demonstrations served as a training ground for activists who later took part in the Umbrella Movement.

Tsang did reverse some of Tung's changes in the relationships of senior civil servants with each other and the timing of the annual policy address, but the morale of the civil service continued to be affected. In 2012, the former Chief Secretary for Administration, Rafael Hui Si-yan, was arrested and subsequently convicted and sentenced to seven and a half years in prison on charges of misconduct in public office. Tsang himself was also later charged with misconduct in public office and served a custodial sentence before his conviction was quashed. In 2013, the former ICAC Commissioner, Timothy Tong Hin-ming, faced a Legislative Council Select Committee to explain allegations of excessive expenditure on gifts and expenses.

---

9. Loh, C. (2003, 25 September). Christine Loh's newsletter. *Civic Exchange*.
10. Ibid.

Leung Chun-ying, who succeeded Tsang as Chief Executive in 2012, was embroiled for much of his term in office in a controversy over payments made to him following the sale of his company. For many civil servants, the values that had sustained the service during Anson Chan's era had been subverted. The *Civil Service Code*, promulgated in 2009, confirmed that political neutrality now meant loyalty to the government.

As the community became increasingly polarised, democratic political activists began to focus on the constitutional question, particularly if, when, and how the Chief Executive was going to be directly elected. The Chinese government's parameters for its relationships with Hong Kong have been clear and consistent since 2004 when Tung was told that:

- "One country, two systems" meant the supremacy of the Chinese constitution: without one country, there would not be a second system;
- "Hong Kong people running Hong Kong" meant that patriots, defined as those who would not harm their country, must form the main body that runs the SAR;
- "a high degree of autonomy" meant that autonomy is only exercised under authorisation by the Central Government;
- "executive-led" government: constitutional development in Hong Kong should not deviate from this principle;
- "balanced participation" meant regard for the interests of all sectors of the society; and
- "gradual and orderly" progress and the "actual situation" should be reflected in constitutional development.[11]

In stark contrast, the democrats believed that the autonomy of Hong Kong was guaranteed in the Joint Declaration and the Basic Law, not by the Chinese government; that the Basic Law provided for the direct elections of the Chief Executive and the Legislative Council; and that participation should be egalitarian and not disproportionately biased in favour of business, pro-establishment, and pro-Beijing groups.

By December 2007, the NPCSC had decided that Hong Kong might be permitted to elect its Chief Executive by universal suffrage in 2017.[12] Two restrictions were not stressed in the announcement. The first was the Basic Law provision that the Chinese government must approve the appointment. The Chinese government had previously indicated that it did not regard this power as a formality.[13] The second restriction, which was also a Basic Law provision, was that a vetting committee

---

11. Tung, C. H. (2004, 15 March). *CE addresses Basic Law seminar* [Press release]. https://www.info.gov.hk/gia/general/200403/15/0315229.htm
12. National People's Congress of the People's Republic of China (2007, 29 December). *Full text of NPC's decision on Hong Kong constitutional development*. https://www.mfa.gov.cn/ce/cohk/eng/syzx/tyflsw/t944943.htm
13. Hong Kong Government (2007). *Green paper on constitutional development* (p. 8). https://www.legco.gov.hk/yr06-07/english/panels/ca/papers/ca0716-gppr200707-e.pdf

should approve the candidates who were permitted to run for office. The democrats saw this as a means of prohibiting their candidates from standing and began to organise demonstrations in support of universal suffrage for the election of the Chief Executive but with free choice in the selection of candidates. The annual July 1st demonstrations affirmed support for universal suffrage and reflected specific criticisms of government policies.

By the end of Tsang's term, Hong Kong's civil society organisations were much more organised and militant. The government had lost its bearings, retreating into its bunker on many social policy issues and subject to the Chinese government on constitutional reform and in other policy areas. The civil service, although still efficient, was less motivated than before and disinclined to take new initiatives.

The Umbrella Movement and Increasing Chinese Government Intervention in Hong Kong

In 2014, the Chinese government brought the constitutional issue to a head by publishing two documents, a definitive account of its interpretation of "one country, two systems" and proposals for the election of the Chief Executive in 2017. Neither contained surprises because they formalised what Tung had been told in 2004 and what the Hong Kong and Chinese governments had long said about the need for a nominating committee to determine who could stand for the office of Chief Executive. This time, however, they were presented as authoritative decisions with no room for negotiation. On "one country, two systems", the State Council said that any degree of autonomy enjoyed by the Hong Kong government was delegated by the Chinese government and could be rescinded.[14] On the 2017 elections, the NPCSC stated that a candidate for Chief Executive must "love the country and love Hong Kong" and that a nominating committee would select two or three candidates who must each have the support of more than half of the committee.[15] The announcements triggered the Occupy Central/Umbrella Movement in support of direct elections for the Chief Executive without the nominating committee. Parts of Hong Kong Island and Kowloon were occupied for 79 days.

The Umbrella Movement had a significant impact on public perceptions of the government. The police used tear gas in their initial confrontations with the mainly young protesters and were met with angry responses not only from the protesters but also from their parents. Community policing which had been successfully employed since the handover was seen to have been abandoned. According to one

---

14. State Council of the People's Republic of China (2014, 15 March). *The practice of the one country, two systems policy in the Hong Kong Special Administrative Region.* http://english.www.gov.cn/archive/white_paper/2014/08/23/content_281474982986578.htm
15. Standing Committee of the National People's Congress (2014, 1 September). *NPC Standing Committee decision on Hong Kong 2017 election framework.* http://be.china-embassy.org/eng/sghd/201409/t20140901_2076170.htm

poll, those who were quite or very dissatisfied with the performance of the Police Force increased from 13% in 2013 to 19% just before the Umbrella Movement to 27% once the occupation had taken place.[16] The dilemma for the government was that it was likely to lose public support and damage its credibility whatever it did. If the government had used the police to remove the protesters, it would have increased the numbers dissatisfied with their performance. If, as happened, the government let the protesters continue their occupation, it was perceived not to have the capacity or will to act. In a poll conducted in October 2014, almost half of the respondents were dissatisfied with the performance of the Hong Kong government and almost 45% did not trust it, both figures representing significant declines in satisfaction and trust from the previous year's figures.[17]

In the wake of the Umbrella Movement, the Hong Kong and Chinese governments faced fresh challenges posed by the difficulty of passing the Chinese model for electing the Chief Executive in the Legislative Council and the formation of localist political groups. Despite the Hong Kong government's campaign for the Chinese model,[18] the democratic parties remained staunchly opposed to it. The proposal needed a two-thirds majority in the Legislative Council to pass but was rejected by a much larger majority of those voting after a mix-up in the pro-establishment camp. The government's credibility was again damaged.

The localist parties were created with the intention of running candidates in the 2016 Legislative Council elections.[19] The growing sense of Hong Kong, as opposed to Chinese, identity that fuelled the Umbrella Movement continued to be a factor in electoral support for localist parties. Some parties called for the independence of Hong Kong; all of them stood for a much faster pace of constitutional reform and universal suffrage for both the Chief Executive and Legislative Council elections. After a localist won a by-election in February 2016, the Hong Kong government refused to register one localist party and the Electoral Affairs Commission introduced a regulation requiring all candidates to declare that Hong Kong was an inalienable part of China.[20] On that basis, it denied six candidates the right to contest the election. Despite these restrictions, five localist candidates were successful in the 2016 elections. When two of those elected chose to unfurl a banner reading "Hong Kong is not China" and pledged their loyalty to Hong Kong and insulted

---

16. PORI (2014). Hong Kong Police Force. https://www.pori.hk/pop-poll/disciplinary-force-en/x001.html?lang=en
17. PORI (2014). People's satisfaction with the HKSAR government. https://www.pori.hk/pop-poll/government-en/h001.html?lang=en; PORI (2020) op. cit.
18. Hong Kong Government (2015). *Methods for selecting the Chief Executive by universal suffrage.* http://www.2017.gov.hk/filemanager/template/en/doc/report_2nd/consultation_report_2nd.pdf
19. Ma, N. (2017). The China factor in Hong Kong elections, 1991–2016. *China Perspectives, 3,* 17–26.
20. Wong, H. (2016, 29 March). Newly formed pro-independence Hong Kong National Party denied registration by Companies Registry. *HKFP.* https://hongkongfp.com/2016/03/29/hong-kong-national-party-denied-registration-to-companies-registry/; Reuters (2016). Hong Kong election candidates must issue China pledge by law, says electoral commission. https://www.abc.net.au/news/2016-07-20/hk-election-candidates-must-issue-china-pledge-by-law-electoral/7645420

China, the Legislative Council Secretary-General refused to accept their oaths and the matter went to the High Court.[21] Before the High Court judge could announce his decision, however, the NPCSC said that it had considered the issue and that the two activists were disqualified from taking their seats. After the ruling, the judge said that he had reached the same decision as the Standing Committee.[22] The Hong Kong Bar Association said that the decision gave the impression that the Standing Committee was legislating for Hong Kong.[23]

By this stage, the values that were supposed to support Hong Kong and its public service were under serious threat. The intervention of the Standing Committee in the oath-taking case raised the issue of judicial independence and the rule of law. In its 2014 document, the State Council had said that there was no separation of powers in the Basic Law and that judges should be "administrators and patriots".[24] During the Umbrella Movement, the Hong Kong government had argued that the protesters were breaking the rule of law. The protesters claimed, to the contrary, that they were only breaking the law to achieve a better form of political and social justice. If judicial independence was compromised, then there was no fair arbitrator on whether the law was being violated. The consequences for civil liberties and ultimately for the economy, which required impartial judges to decide on the legal obligations of companies, was clear.

Other values came under equal stress. Freedom of the person was in question after five booksellers were thought to have been abducted from Hong Kong to the Mainland.[25] Freedom of the press was in doubt as Mainland companies took over many media organisations. Freedom of speech and of the right to stand for political office became an issue after the government prevented candidates from contesting the 2016 elections. Academic autonomy was also at stake with the governing councils of the universities increasingly dominated by the Chief Executive's appointees.

The government wanted to bolster its fading support by using public policy to supply more desired goods and services, but it was caught, once more, between opposing forces. If it tried to address the major issues of housing, health, and the growing numbers below the poverty line, it risked alienating its business base of

---

21. Cheung, T., Ng, J., & Lau, S. (2016, 16 October). Three rejections and multiple deviations mark Hong Kong Legislative Council swearing-in. *SCMP*. https://www.scmp.com/news/hong-kong/politics/article/2027413/three-rejections-and-four-deviations-mark-hong-kong
22. Ng, J. Y, Lau, C., Lam, J., & Cheung, T. (2016, 16 November). Barred Hong Kong localists vow to keep fighting after High Court decision. *SCMP*. http://www.scmp.com/news/hong-kong/politics/article/2046162/hong-kong-court-rules-localistlawmakers-must-vacate-legco
23. Hong Kong Bar Association (2016, 7 November). The Hong Kong Bar Association's statement concerning the interpretation made by the National People's Congress Standing Committee of Article 104 of the Basic Law. https://www.hkba.org/sites/default/files/20161107%20-%20Statement%20re%20NPCSC%20interpretration%20BL104%20%28Eng%20Version-web%29.pdf
24. State Council (2014) op. cit.
25. Palmer, A. W. (2018, 3 April). The case of Hong Kong's missing booksellers. *New York Times Magazine*. https://www.nytimes.com/2018/04/03/magazine/the-case-of-hong-kongs-missing-booksellers.html

support and possibly causing greater unrest by charging more for services. It was also under pressure to comply with Chinese government policies promoting Hong Kong's greater integration into China. By the end of this period, the express rail link and the HZMB had almost been completed and major initiatives were in train to support the Chinese government's development of a technology hub in Guangdong. One consequence was that social policies did not receive the funding needed to resolve the persistent problems that they faced. By 2016, 53% of respondents to a survey were not satisfied with the Chief Executive's policy direction while 25% were satisfied; only 4% were very satisfied while 30% were very dissatisfied.[26]

There was a gradual deterioration of public confidence and trust in the government during Leung Chun-ying's term in office. There was no longer a belief that the government would support the civil liberties promised under the Basic Law. Judicial independence and the rule of law which provided the best protection for those liberties were themselves under threat. Social policy problems continued to grow and the number of protests, some of which were violent, increased.

Carrie Lam and the 2019 Protests (2017–2020)

Carrie Lam produced her first policy address as Chief Executive, which she wrote herself, in October 2017.[27] The address was more favourably received than any policy addresses delivered by her predecessor.[28] It showed that Lam had an awareness of the major problems facing Hong Kong and there was some expectation that her lengthy experience in government and as Leung Chun-ying's Chief Secretary for Administration would enable her to do something about them. She also came into office with the apparent intent to assert the autonomy of the Hong Kong government from the Chinese government. "I am no puppet of Beijing" she proclaimed.[29] Yet, in less than two years, she was the central focus of widespread and continuous popular dissent. There was condemnation of her handling of the protests, particularly her failure to control the Police Force, and calls for her resignation. As the Chinese government began to assert even greater control over Hong Kong, the autonomy of the government declined still further. In June 2020, the national security legislation reduced civil liberties and provided the Chinese government with a presence inside the Hong Kong government's decision-making apparatus. By that stage, Carrie Lam had the lowest popularity (approval) rating of any Governor or Chief Executive

---

26. PORI (2021). Satisfaction with Chief Executive's policy address. https://www.pori.hk/pop-poll/policy-address-en/pa-overallsat.html?lang=en
27. Lam, C. (2017). *We connect for hope and happiness*. https://www.policyaddress.gov.hk/2017/eng/pdf/PA2017.pdf
28. PORI (2021) op. cit.
29. BBC (2017, 21 June). Hong Kong's Carrie Lam: "I am no puppet of Beijing." https://www.bbc.com/news/world-asia-china-40349611

since polls began in 1992; only 13% of respondents were satisfied with her policy address.[30]

With the introduction of the Extradition Bill in early 2019, the Hong Kong government started a process which, in hindsight, piled mistake upon mistake. On 16 June 2019, a mainly peaceful protest, estimated to be nearly two million strong, demonstrated against the Extradition Bill.[31] Most governments faced with a demonstration of an approximate size of 25% of their population, arguing that the proposed legislation violated their civil liberties, would have withdrawn the bill or made major concessions. But the Hong Kong government, apparently because it needed the consent of the Chinese government, chose not to do so. The protests continued, gradually becoming more violent, but the government did little to restrain the police force and make them accountable to the government and the public. The bill was finally withdrawn at the beginning of September. By then, the grievances had widened beyond the Extradition Bill to include calls for greater democratisation, the resignation of Carrie Lam, and an enquiry into alleged police brutality.

The government did not recognise the validity of these demands and originally constructed an explanation of why the protests had occurred based on its own social policy failures. The protests, according to this claim, were a "social incident" that could only be addressed by public policy action.[32] Bureaus and departments all subsequently blamed the extraordinary stresses that they had faced on the "social incident". The protests were a "social incident" in the sense that they touched communities and families across Hong Kong, but the causal link between the protests and social policy failures is difficult to establish. The protesters did not complain at all about the government's social policy deficiencies. Their grievances were focused on five demands that were manifestly political, questioning the government's right to rule and the alleged brutality of its police force. Subsequent government explanations of the causes of the protest based on foreign incitement and the damaging effects of the liberal studies programme on the minds of young people in the secondary schools seemed implausible.

A final mistake in the government's strategy was its decision to hold the November 2019 District Council elections. The elections might have been postponed on the grounds that the protests were in full swing. The government probably thought that it would win the election and then could claim that it was following policies with which most voters agreed. Unlike other Hong Kong elections, District

---

30. PORI (2021). Comparisons between Chris Patten, Tung Chee Hwa, Donald Tsang Yam-kuen, Leung Chun-ying and Carrie Lam. https://www.pori.hk/pop-poll/chief-executive-en/a-rating-combined.html?lang=en; PORI (2021). Satisfaction with the Chief Executive's policy address, op. cit.
31. BBC (2019, 17 June). Hong Kong protest: "Nearly two million" join demonstration. https://www.bbc.com/news/world-asia-china-48656471. Police estimates, always significantly lower than other estimates, put the number at 338,000.
32. *China Daily* (2019, 13 October). HK gov't seeks LegCo's assistance to address socio-economic issues. https://www.chinadaily.com.cn/a/201910/13/WS5da3180da310cf3e35570345.html

Council elections are held on a first-past-the-post system. Democrats and localist parties were well-organised and there was a high turnout. The democrats won control of 17 out of 18 District Councils and a clear majority of the popular vote. The government could not hide the fact that it had lost popular support and was out of touch with public sentiment.[33]

The government's poor handling of the protests meant that it had no room for manoeuvre when the Chinese government began to intervene even more directly in SAR affairs. The Basic Law (Article 22) prevents Chinese government departments from interfering in Hong Kong affairs, but the Chinese Liaison Office in Hong Kong claimed that the law did not apply to its activities. For many years, the Liaison Office intervened in Hong Kong elections and many other matters, but it now began to assert a public role as an alternative, and potentially superior, decision-making body. The stage was set for the introduction of national security legislation that could override the provisions of the Basic Law and provide the authority for Chinese government organisations in Hong Kong to provide advice and direction to the Hong Kong authorities.

When the Chinese government announced that the National People's Congress would pass national security legislation for Hong Kong, there were understandable concerns about how this would relate to the existing arrangements under the Basic Law. The Hong Kong Bar Association doubted whether the process was legal because Article 23 of the Basic Law states that Hong Kong should pass national security legislation "on its own", because the National People's Congress jurisdiction over Hong Kong is restricted to defence and foreign affairs, and because it does not conform with the International Covenant on Civil and Political Rights entrenched in the Basic Law.[34] The Chinese government's view was that, if the Hong Kong government could not pass national security legislation, then the National People's Congress would do so. The national security law provides that it shall prevail where provisions of the HKSAR laws are inconsistent with it (Article 62). Human rights and the rule of law are to be observed in the implementation of the law (Articles 4, 5), but its relationship to the rights and provisions of the Basic Law, and Article 62 of the law, implies that the national security legislation is the superior law. The HKSAR is still required to pass its own national security legislation (Article 7).

In July 2020, 12 democrats were barred from running in the (later-postponed) 2020 Legislative Council election on the grounds that they had promoted independence or self-determination, sought intervention from foreign governments, objected in principle to national security laws or were intent on voting down the

---

33. Delaney, M. (2019, 25 November). What just happened in Hong Kong elections? *Foreign Policy*. https://foreignpolicy.com/2019/11/25/what-happened-hong-kong-elections/
34. Hong Kong Bar Association (2020, 25 May). Statement of Hong Kong Bar Association on proposal of the National People's Congress to enact National Security Law for Hong Kong. https://www.hkba.org/sites/default/files/20200525%20-%20Proposal%20of%20National%20People's%20Congress%20to%20enact%20National%20Security%20Law%20in%20Hong%20Kong%20(E).pdf

budget.[35] Six months later, 55 pro-democracy figures were arrested under the national security legislation.[36] The Secretary for Security said that the organisers of a primary in July 2020 to choose candidates to contest the Legislative Council elections had planned to win 35 or more seats to secure a majority in the council. They then planned to vote down the budget, forcing the Chief Executive to resign.[37] This process is perfectly legal under the Basic Law (Article 52) but is, apparently, considered a crime under the national security legislation because, according to the Secretary for Security, it involves "overthrowing or interfering, seriously destroying the Hong Kong Government's legal execution of its duties".[38] If this does constitute a crime, freedom of speech may be considered more restricted than before the introduction of the national security law.

A problem with the national security legislation is that crimes are broadly, not precisely, defined and can be applied in many different situations.[39] This is contrary to the common law conception of criminal offences, which are defined as precisely possible. The Secretary of Justice has said that it would be "impractical and unreasonable" for the national security legislation to look like a Hong Kong statute,[40] but the importation of a Chinese-style law into the Hong Kong common law comes at a high cost, especially if the law has superior status within the common law and a determining impact on how an offence is defined. The offences that have warranted arrest show the broad scope of the law.[41] Many have been arrested for possessing independence flags or liberate Hong Kong signs, some for alleged collusion with foreign forces, others for inciting hatred and contempt against the government, some for advocating secession, the pro-democracy leaders for allegedly trying to overthrow the government, and one on a charge of terrorism.[42] Those arrested cover the spectrum of society from a 15-year-old girl found with an independence flag,

---

35. Ho, K., Grundy, T., & Creery, J. (2020, 30 July). Hong Kong bans Joshua Wong and 11 other pro-democracy figures from legislative election. *HKFP*. https://hongkongfp.com/2020/07/30/breaking-hong-kong-bans-8-pro-democracy-figures-from-legislative-election/
36. Davidson, H. (2021, 6 January). Dozens of pro-democracy figures arrested in sweeping crackdown. *The Guardian*. https://www.theguardian.com/world/2021/jan/06/dozens-of-hong-kong-pro-democracy-figures-arrested-in-sweeping-crackdown
37. Hong Kong Government (2021, 6 January). *S for S speaks on police arrest of people on suspicion of subversion* [Press release]. https://www.info.gov.hk/gia/general/202101/06/P2021010600580.htm
38. Ibid.
39. Hong Kong Bar Association (2020, 1 July). *Statement of the Hong Kong Bar Association on the Law of the People's Republic of China on safeguarding national security in the Hong Kong Special Administrative Region*, Section 15. (Press release). https://www.hkba.org/events-publication/press-releases-coverage
40. Creery, J. (2020, 15 June). Beijing's security law for Hong Kong won't be compatible with city's common law system, says Justice Sec. *HKFP*. https://hongkongfp.com/2020/06/15/beijings-security-law-for-hong-kong-wont-be-compatible-with-citys-common-law-system-says-justice-sec/
41. Wong L. & Kellogg, T. (2021 3 May). New data show Hong Kong's national security arrest follow a pattern. *ChinaFile*. https://www.chinafile.com/reporting-opinion/features/new-data-show-hong-kongs-national-security-arrests-follow-pattern
42. Davidson, H., & Ball, A. (2020, 29 September). The arrested Hongkongers caught up in Beijing's national security law. *The Guardian*. https://www.theguardian.com/world/ng-interactive/2020/sep/29/the-hong-kong-arrested

to young activists and political leaders, to the many professionals and academics in the democracy movement, to Jimmy Lai, the pro-democracy business tycoon, and his two sons, one on a charge of conspiracy to defraud, the other on suspicion of collusion with foreign forces.[43]

The national security law has led to major changes in the electoral system, effectively eliminating democrats from the Legislative Council and the District Councils. The government has encouraged democrats to run in elections provided they are "patriots", but it is difficult to see how they could mount an effective campaign when many of their leaders are in detention and their organisations have either been wound up or banned. Even if democrats were elected, their voices would be muted given the disqualification rules and the pre-ponderance of Election Committee and functional constituency members in the Legislative Council. This poses problems for the legitimacy of the Hong Kong government and diminishes debate in the legislature and on the councils. The government argues that the new system is more efficient. It may well be that decisions are taken more quickly and that there is no prospect of obstruction in the legislature. But the question in the longer run is whether those decisions can be effectively implemented without broader representation of public opinion in the legislature.

The impact of the national security law on the public sector and policy implementation has probably yet to be fully felt. The Office for Safeguarding National Safeguarding National Security of the Central Government in the HKSAR established under the law has broad powers and is not subject to Hong Kong law (Article 60). Mainland criminal law procedures, including investigation, trial, prosecution, and penalties, apply in cases where there are foreign or external forces involved, where the HKSAR government cannot enforce the law, or where there is a major and imminent threat to national security (Articles 55, 57). The newly created Police Force security department is expected to work in collaboration with Mainland security forces in Hong Kong.[44] The law also has implications for the Judiciary, for its prosecutions under the law, and for the Education Bureau, which has been required to revise the curriculum to teach students about the national security legislation. Other bureaus and departments may also be affected depending on how the office defines its tasks and whether it requests information and assistance from any Hong Kong governmental body in its work. The Director of the Liaison Office is now the Chief Executive's security adviser.

This review of the public sector in its political setting over the past two decades is a sad tale of the decline of a once confident and relatively autonomous government that oversaw the loss of its core values, of its autonomy, of the confidence and

---

43. International Press Institute (2021, 1 April). Hong Kong publisher Jimmy Lai found guilty. https://ipi.media/hong-kong-publisher-jimmy-lai-found-guilty/
44. Meagher, D. (2020, 14 July). Has Hong Kong national security law created secret police with Chinese characteristics? *The Strategist*. https://www.aspistrategist.org.au/has-hong-kongs-national-security-law-created-secret-police-with-chinese-characteristics/

trust of a significant proportion of its population, and a reduction in its capacity to make and implement policy. In the concluding sections, we consider the effects of these developments on themes that have run through this book: accountability, appropriate policymaking, and legitimacy.

Accountability

Public confidence and trust in governments can be greatly strengthened if governments are held accountable for their actions. Article 64 of the Basic Law stipulates that the Hong Kong government shall be accountable to the Legislative Council. In practice, principal officials are only accountable to the Chief Executive and to the Chinese government. They are answerable to the council but, even if it were to pass a vote of no confidence in a principal official, it has no power to require his or her resignation. Legislators do ask questions on critical issues and address matters raised in proposed legislation. But the government has usually been reluctant to give Councillors, especially democrats, ammunition that might be used against it; responses are sometimes less than transparent. Under the present arrangements, since democratic voices in the chamber have been silenced and the council is less representative, the system is more "executive-led" and the political accountability of the government to the legislature even further removed.

Most civil servants, by contrast, are bureaucratically accountable. They are held accountable through the hierarchy, disciplinary regulations, and their oath to "be responsible" to the government and by the external oversight of the Director of Audit, the ICAC, and the Ombudsman. Each of these institutions, the Integrated Call Centre, and some departmental complaint-handling units have performed well over the past two decades and have contributed to a clean and still mostly efficient civil service. The introduction of ethics officers to cover conflicts of interest has been largely successful. But the traditional values of the public service have also been seriously undermined. Loyalty to the government has become the defining characteristic of a "good" civil servant as far as the government is concerned.

The Police Force is an exception to the bureaucratic accountability of the rest of the civil service. It was accused of excessive use of force against the protesters during the Umbrella Movement and the 2019 protests. The only effective external check on the Police Force is the ICAC. Notionally, the Police Force is part of, and accountable to, the Hong Kong government, but it has often given the impression, especially during the 2019 protests, that it acts solely on the instructions of the Commissioner and his officers. Senior police officers have made clear that they are strongly opposed to any commission of inquiry into the force's activities. The IPCC is supposed to monitor complaints against the police which are processed through the force's ineffectual complaint-handling unit, the CAPO. As international experts have pointed out, the council has neither the power nor the resources to monitor the force properly.[45] The national security legislation places the Police Force under the scrutiny of Mainland authorities as far as security issues are concerned and its lack of accountability to the Hong Kong government may increase.

Another problematic area has been the accountability of public bodies to the Hong Kong government. The Director of Audit has gradually increased the number of audits of public bodies because of problems with their financial management, organisation, and performance. Some, such as the Tourism Board,[46] have been required to make changes in their relationship with the government as a result of the Audit Commission's findings. The MTR has been strongly criticised for both excessive expenditure and construction failures on the express rail link project and the Shatin-Central link and because of poor communication with the Hong Kong government about its problems. The government's difficulty in holding most public bodies accountable is that it believes that they need a degree of autonomy to complete their work but only discovers their problems long after they have occurred.

Overall, political accountability has diminished over the past two decades, particularly since Leung Chun-ying and Carrie Lam's terms in office. Bureaucratic accountability, except in the Police Force, remains much as it always has been but with some additional checks and controls over performance and behaviour. But it has seen its core values in the colonial period—public service as a vocation and political neutrality—largely replaced with an emphasis on loyalty to a political executive that is not itself accountable to the people. Public bodies present difficult problems: some are accountable and regularly report on their performance, but others have continuing problems that may only be resolved by tighter controls over their organisations.

Policy

Policy is appropriate when it addresses and provides remedial measures for perceived problems or facilitates new opportunities aimed at achieving carefully defined ends. It is not appropriate when the chosen policy instruments do not address or provide remedies for perceived problems or where the ends are only vaguely specified. Traditionally, the Hong Kong Financial Secretary released funding only grudgingly after long discussions about how and for what purpose the money was being used. When Tung came to office, he loosened the purse strings and gave his principal officials more discretion in the use of funds. One consequence was that some bright ideas were funded without proper consideration of their costs. A second

---

45. Kuo, L. (2019, 11 December). Foreign experts quit Hong Kong police brutality enquiry over lack of powers. *The Guardian*. https://www.theguardian.com/world/2019/dec/11/foreign-experts-quit-hong-kong-police-brutality-inquiry-over-lack-of-powers
46. Director of Audit (2020). *Report No. 75: Hong Kong Tourism Board: Corporate governance and administrative issues*. https://www.aud.gov.hk/eng/pubpr_arpt/aud_HonTou.htm

consequence was that the system, as Tung eventually conceded, did not sufficiently reflect public opinion and perceived problems.[47]

Tsang put the financial controls back in place, but he inherited the problem of a more demanding civil society, often highly critical of government policy proposals and able to cause government to reverse its policy proposals (the 2003 national security legislation, the 2011 "moral and national education" proposal, and the 2019 Extradition Bill, among others). Under Tsang, new initiatives in social policy were reduced and the government contented itself with administering the policies that were already in place. Pressure on the domestic front was matched by pressure from the Mainland government to commit to funding prestige projects, the express rail link to Guangdong and the local side of the HKZMB. The government's inability to put public money to productive use has been evident in its cash handouts in 2011 and 2020. Usually, the economic aim of a cash handout is to stimulate domestic consumption. In the Hong Kong case, it seemed to be in the vague hope that it would increase political support. In the event, it resulted in yet more protests against government policy.[48]

Under Leung and Lam, the disjunction between perceived policy problems and what the government was doing about them widened. Waiting lists for public housing lengthened and, not unrelated, more people fell below the poverty line. But there were opportunities for public expenditure elsewhere. The Chinese government was strongly supportive of attempts to build a technology hub in Guangdong and wanted Hong Kong to play a role in its development with the political aim of bringing about greater integration with the Mainland. The government ploughed billions of dollars into innovation policy, but the outcomes and the benefits for Hong Kong have been unclear and, at best, some distance in the future. Expenditure on innovation policy, cash handouts, and excessive recurrent expenditure led to a situation where the budget was unbalanced, in long-term deficit, and still failed to provide sufficient funding to resolve persistent social policy problems. The government has readily admitted its policy failings, arguing without much evidence that they were the cause of the 2019 protests.

There has been a wider systemic political problem. Caught between the vetoes exercised on policy implementation by civil society and the obstruction of the democrats in the Legislative Council, on the one hand, and Chinese government demands, on the other, policy became hostage to conflicting political forces. A weak government was unable to set a definitive course. Policymaking was ad hoc, aimed at appeasing political allies, winning public support, or meeting the Chinese government's goals. After the introduction of the national security legislation, the

---

47. Tung, C. H. (2005). *Working together for economic development and social harmony* (para 18). https://www.policyaddress.gov.hk/2005/eng/pdf/speech.pdf
48. Kwong, B. K. K. (2013). A comparative analysis of the cash handout policy of Hong Kong and Macau. *Journal of Current Chinese Affairs, 42*(3), 87–100.

influence of civil society on policy was sharply reduced, but it remains to be seen whether implementation becomes any easier.

Legitimacy

Legitimacy problems occur when political arrangements do not have the consent of the people and where there are serious doubts about the government's legal and moral authority to exercise power.[49] Legitimacy should not be confused with political stability. A regime may preside over long periods of stability and still suffer from a legitimacy deficit; colonial Hong Kong is a case in point. Regimes suffering from legitimacy deficits will usually attempt to compensate by attempting to win public support by good performance and the efficient delivery of desired goods and services. Such support is often short lived and systemic problems may build into a legitimacy crisis unless the fundamental issues of consent and legal and moral authority are addressed.

The Chinese government bases its right to rule in Hong Kong on its sovereignty and on the ethnic identity of most of the population (Basic Law, Preamble). It follows from this that power may be delegated to administer Hong Kong, but not devolved, and that there is no residual right of Hong Kong citizens to determine who will constitute their government. The concepts of "one country, two systems", "a high degree of autonomy" and "Hong Kong people administering (previously ruling) Hong Kong" are granted at the discretion of the Chinese government and may be amended or revoked at any time.[50] Under Article 5 of the Basic Law, the current political arrangements are essentially transitional until Hong Kong is fully integrated into China in 2047. Mainland government policies promoting greater economic integration and the national security law have speeded up that process.

Democrats and localists have taken a very different view on the right to rule Hong Kong. Their premise was that the provisions in the Joint Declaration and the Basic Law stipulating that the Chief Executive and the Legislative Council should be elected by universal suffrage. They argued that these documents provided entrenched political rights and civil liberties and that they represented a contract with the Hong Kong people that may not be revoked unilaterally by the Chinese government.[51] Democrats and localists differed on the future political order. Most democratic parties believed that the future lay within China while many localists advocated independence or self-determination. Both groups sought democratic legitimation of the right to rule Hong Kong.

The conflict between these irreconcilable values has been at the heart of political protests and debates about the future since the Sino-British Declaration was

---
49. Beetham, D. (2013). *The legitimation of power* (2nd ed.). Basingstoke: Macmillan.
50. Tung (2004) op. cit.; State Council of the People's Republic of China (2014) op. cit.
51. Scott, I. (2017). One country, two systems: The end of a legitimating ideology? *Asia Pacific Journal of Public Administration, 39*(2), 83–99.

promulgated in 1984. Weakened by the political strife, the Hong Kong government has tried to meet its legitimacy crisis by bolstering performance legitimacy. Even assuming successful policies can be formulated and implemented, something the post-handover Hong Kong government has never been able to achieve, increased legitimacy may not be the outcome. Performance legitimacy has a limited shelf life and can spark more expensive and unattainable demands. The necessary solution for the Hong Kong government's legitimacy crisis is political and constitutional reform, but that is entirely in the hands of a Chinese government unwilling to compromise on its monopoly of power.

For the public service, the resolution of the legitimacy issue is important to help it perform more efficiently and effectively. That it has not performed to expectations since 1997 is not the result of a sudden decline in the abilities of civil servants or the efficiency of the civil service. Rather, it is a consequence of the political conflict within which the civil service has tried to implement policy. Yet, even if the national security legislation extinguishes political opposition, there is no guarantee that the performance of the public sector will improve. The political conflict has created division within the public sector. Thousands of civil servants supported the protests but have been required to take an oath of allegiance to the HKSAR and to uphold the Basic Law or risk losing their jobs. If national security becomes the most pressing issue on the domestic agenda, their morale may be even more adversely affected and their appetite for new initiatives may be further reduced.

The civil service requires reform. It needs, among other improvements, better horizontal coordination and communication between bureaus and departments, increased investment in the policymaking system, improved consultative mechanisms with the population, and greater accountability of public bodies. But the portents are unfavourable. Until the relationship between the government and its people is fully addressed, until there is evidence that the problems of consent and of legal and moral authority have been accommodated within a political framework in which executive authority is properly accountable, the public sector in Hong Kong will continue to face major problems in providing good governance and successful policies.

Selected Bibliography

Primary Sources

Constitutional Documents and Commentaries

The Basic Law of the Hong Kong Special Administrative Region of the People's Republic of China (2020). https://www.basiclaw.gov.hk/en/basiclawtext/images/basiclaw_full_text_en.pdf

Chief Executive (2003, 27 June). *Responsibilities of the Financial Secretary and the Secretary for Financial Services and the Treasury*. https://www.fso.gov.hk/pdf/fs-sfst_e.pdf

Chief Executive Election Ordinance, Cap 569.

Civil Service Bureau (2002, 28 June). *Circular setting out the working relationship between civil servants and principal officials under the accountability system*. LC Paper CB (2) 2467/01-02 (01). https://www.legco.gov.hk/yr01-02/english/hc/sub_com/hs51/papers/hs51cb-2467-e1.pdf

Civil Service Bureau (2009). *The Civil Service Code*. https://www.csb.gov.hk/english/admin/conduct/files/CSCode_e.pdf#page=3

Constitutional Affairs Bureau (2002). *Legislative Council paper: Accountability system for principal officials*. https://www.legco.gov.hk/yr01-02/english/panels/ca/papers/ca0418cb2-paper-e.pdf

Constitutional and Mainland Affairs Bureau (2007). *Report on the further development of the political appointment system*. https://www.cmab.gov.hk/doc/issues/report_en.pdf

Constitutional and Mainland Affairs Bureau (2022). *Text of the covenant: application to the Hong Kong Special Administrative Region*. https://www.cmab.gov.hk/en/press/reports_human.htm#s2

Constitutional Development Task Force (2004). *The first report of the Constitutional Development Task Force: Issues of the legislative process in the Basic Law relating to constitutional development*. https://www.legco.gov.hk/yr03-04/english/panels/ca/papers/ca0331cb2-report-e.pdf

Constitutional Development Task Force (2004). *The second report of the Constitutional Development Task Force: Issues of principle in the Basic Law relating to constitutional development*. https://www.legco.gov.hk/yr03-04/english/panels/ca/papers/ca0416cb2-report2-e.pdf

Constitutional Development Task Force (2004, May). *The third report of the Constitutional Development Task Force: Areas which may be considered for amendment in respect of the methods for the selecting of the Chief Executive in 2007 and for forming the Legislative Council in 2008*. https://www.info.gov.hk/archive/consult/2004/cabreview-e.pdf

Government of the People's Republic of China (1994). Facts about a few important aspects of Sino-British talks on electoral arrangements in Hong Kong. *Chinese Law & Government*, 29(1), 21–49.

Government of the People's Republic of China (2020). *The Law of the People's Republic of China on safeguarding national security in the Hong Kong Special Administrative Region.* https://www.elegislation.gov.hk/doc/hk/a406/eng_translation_(a406)_en.pdf

Hong Kong Bar Association (2002). Response to the consultation document on the proposals to implement Article 23 of the Basic Law. https://www.hkba.org/sites/default/files/20021209-art23.pdf

Hong Kong Bar Association (2019, 2 April). Observation of the Hong Kong Bar Association (HKBA) on the Fugitive Offenders and Mutual Legal Assistance in criminal matters legislation. https://www.hkba.org/sites/default/files/HKBA%20Observations%20on%20FOMLACM%20Bill%202019%20%28Final%29.pdf

Hong Kong Bar Association (2020, 20 April). Further statement of the Hong Kong Bar Association on Article 22 of the Basic Law. https://www.hkba.org/sites/default/files/20200420%20-%20HKBA%27s%20Further%20Statement%20on%20Article%2022%20of%20the%20Basic%20Law%20%28English%29.pdf

Hong Kong Bar Association (2020, 25 May). Statement of Hong Kong Bar Association on proposal of the National People's Congress to enact National Security Law for Hong Kong. https://www.hkba.org/sites/default/files/20200525%20-%20Proposal%20of%20National%20People%27s%20Congress%20to%20enact%20National%20Security%20Law%20in%20Hong%20Kong%20%28E%29.pdf

Hong Kong Bill of Rights Ordinance, Cap. 383.

Hong Kong Government (1994, February). *Representative government in Hong Kong.* Hong Kong: Government Printer.

Hong Kong Government (2002). *Proposals to implement Article 23 of the Basic Law.* Hong Kong: Security Bureau.

Hong Kong Government (2007). *Green paper on constitutional development.* https://www.legco.gov.hk/yr06-07/english/panels/ca/papers/ca0716-gppr200707-e.pdf

Hong Kong Government (2013). *Methods for selecting the Chief Executive in 2017 and for forming the Legislative Council in 2016.* https://www.legco.gov.hk/yr13-14/english/panels/ca/papers/ca1209-cdoc20131204-e.pdf

Hong Kong Government (2015). *Methods for selecting the Chief Executive by universal suffrage.* http://www.2017.gov.hk/filemanager/template/en/doc/report_2nd/consultation_report_2nd.pdf

Hong Kong Government (2019, 3 August). Civil service neutrality restated. https://www.news.gov.hk/eng/2019/08/20190803/20190803_205232_873.html

Joint Declaration of the Government of the United Kingdom of Great Britain and Northern Ireland and the Government of the People's Republic of China on the Question of Hong Kong (1984). https://www.elegislation.gov.hk/hk/capA301

Legislative Council Panel on Constitutional Affairs (2003). *Review and public consultation on constitutional development after 2007.* LC Paper No CB (2) 119/03-04. https://www.legco.gov.hk/yr03-04/english/panels/ca/papers/ca1020cb2-119e02.pdf

Legislative Council Secretariat (2012). Re-organization of the Government Secretariat. https://www.legco.gov.hk/yr11-12/english/sec/library/1112in25-e.pdf

Ministry of Foreign Affairs of the People's Republic of China (2020, 30 June). Foreign Ministry spokesperson's remarks on the passage of the law safeguarding national security in

Hong Kong by the NPC Standing Committee. https://www.fmprc.gov.cn/mfa_eng/xwfw_665399/s2510_665401/2535_665405/t1793446.shtml

National People's Congress of the People's Republic of China (2007, 29 December). *Full text of NPC's decision on Hong Kong constitutional development.* http://www.npc.gov.cn/english-npc/c2762/200712/afc9a8b60cd6449b8a388568d5177ff2.shtm

NPC Observer (2020, 11 November). NPCSC clarifies "allegiance" requirements for Hong Kong legislators, disqualifies pro-democracy legislators. https://npcobserver.com/2020/11/11/npcsc-clarifies-allegiance-requirements-for-hong-kong-legislators-disqualifies-pro-democracy-legislators

NPC Observer (2021, 11 March). *Decision of the National People's Congress on improving the electoral system of the Hong Kong Special Administrative Region.* https://npcobserver.com/2021/03/11/2021-npc-session-npcs-hong-kong-electoral-overhaul-decision-explained/

Preliminary Working Committee (1995, 8 December). *Some views of the Preliminary Working Committee of the HKSAR Preparatory Committee on maintaining the stability of the Hong Kong Civil Service and its system.* Hong Kong: mimeo.

Secretary for Constitutional Affairs (2003). *Twelve-month report on implementation of the accountability system for principal officials.* https://www.cmab.gov.hk/upload/20040219153857/12mthreport-e.pdf

Security Bureau (2003). *Legislative Council brief: National Security (Legislative Provisions) Bill.* https://www.basiclaw23.gov.hk/english/resources/legco/legco_article/article9.htm

Standing Committee of the National People's Congress (2004). *Decision of the Standing Committee of the National People's Congress on issues relating to the methods for selecting the Chief Executive of the Hong Kong Special Administrative Region in the year 2007 and for forming the Legislative Council of the Hong Kong Special Administrative Region in the year 2008.* https://www.elegislation.gov.hk/hk/capA208

Standing Committee of the National People's Congress (2014, 1 September). *NPC Standing Committee decision on Hong Kong 2017 election framework.* SCMP. http://be.china-embassy.org/eng/sghd/201409/t20140901_2076170.htm

State Council of the People's Republic of China (2014, 15 March). *The practice of the one country, two systems policy in the Hong Kong Special Administrative Region.* http://english.www.gov.cn/archive/white_paper/2014/08/23/content_281474982986578.htm

State Council Information Office of the People's Republic of China (2021). *Hong Kong democratic progress under the framework of one country, two systems.* http://english.scio.gov.cn/node_8027477.html

Tung, C. H. (2004, 15 March). *CE addresses Basic Law seminar* [Press release]. https://www.info.gov.hk/gia/general/200403/15/0315229.htm

Policy Addresses by the Governor/Chief Executive

Lam, C. (2017). *We connect for hope and happiness.* https://www.policyaddress.gov.hk/2017/eng/pdf/PA2017.pdf

Lam, C. (2020). *Strive ahead with renewed perseverance.* https://www.policyaddress.gov.hk/2020/eng/policy.html

Leung, C. Y. (2013). *Seek change, maintain stability, serve the people with pragmatism.* https://www.policyaddress.gov.hk/2013/eng/pdf/PA2013.pdf

Leung, C. Y. (2016). *Innovate for the economy, improve livelihood, foster harmony, share prosperity.* https://www.policyaddress.gov.hk/2016/eng/pdf/PA2016.pdf
Patten, C. (1992). *Our next five years: The agenda for Hong Kong.* https://www.legco.gov.hk/yr92-93/english/lc_sitg/hansard/h921007.pdf
Patten, C. (1996). *Hong Kong: Transition.* https://www.legco.gov.hk/yr96-97/english/lc_sitg/hansard/han0210.htm
Tsang, D. Y. K. (2005). *Strong governance for the people.* https://www.policyaddress.gov.hk/05-06/eng/index.htm
Tsang, D. Y. K. (2007). *A new direction for Hong Kong.* https://www.policyaddress.gov.hk/07-08/eng/docs/policy.pdf
Tsang, D. Y. K. (2008). *Embracing new challenges.* www.policyaddress.gov.hk/08-09/index.html
Tung, C. H. (1997). *Building Hong Kong for a new era.* https://www.policyaddress.gov.hk/pa97/english/patext.htm
Tung, C. H. (1999). *Quality people, quality home: Positioning people for the 21st century.* https://www.policyaddress.gov.hk/pa99/english/speech.htm
Tung, C. H. (2004). *Seizing opportunities for development, promoting people-based governance.* Hong Kong: Government Logistics Department. https://www.policyaddress.gov.hk/pa04/eng/index.htm
Tung, C. H. (2005). *Working together for economic development and social harmony.* https://www.policyaddress.gov.hk/2005/eng/p23.htm

Legislative Council Debates and Background Papers

Legislative Council (1999). *Report of the Select Committee to inquire into the circumstances surrounding the commencement of the operation of the new Hong Kong International Airport at Chek Lap Kok since 6 July 1998 and related issues.* Vol. 1. https://www.legco.gov.hk/yr98-99/english/sc/sc01/papers/report.htm
Legislative Council (2004). *Report of the Select Committee into the handling of the Severe Acute Respiratory Syndrome outbreak by the government and the Hospital Authority.* https://www.legco.gov.hk/yr03-04/english/sc/sc_sars/reports/sars_rpt.htm
Legislative Council (2007). *Bills Committee on Independent Police Complaints Council Bill.* LC Paper No. CB (2) 184/07/08(1). https://www.legco.gov.hk/yr06-07/english/bills/brief/b34_brf.pdf
Legislative Council (2014). *Report on matters relating to Mr Timothy Tong's duty visits, entertainment, and bestowing and receipt of gifts during his tenure as Commissioner of the Independent Commission Against Corruption.* https://www.legco.gov.hk/yr13-14/english/counmtg/papers/cm0709-ttong-members-rpt-e.pdf
Legislative Council (2016). *A companion to the history, rules and practices of the Legislative Council of the Hong Kong Special Administrative Region.* https://www.legco.gov.hk/general/english/procedur/companion/main_toc.htm
Legislative Council Independent Panel of Inquiry (2005). *Report of the Independent Panel of Inquiry on the incidents relating to the Equal Opportunities Commission.* https://www.legco.gov.hk/yr04-05/english/panels/ha/papers/ha0321eoc_report_e.pdf
Legislative Council Panel on Constitutional Affairs (2020). *Background brief: Review of Personal Data (Privacy) Ordinance.* https://www.legco.gov.hk/yr19-20/english/panels/ca/papers/ca20200120cb2-512-4-e.pdf

Legislative Council Panel on Home Affairs (2005). *Progress report on review of advisory and statutory bodies.* https://www.legco.gov.hk/yr04-05/english/panels/ha/papers/ha0513cb2-1488-1e.pdf

Legislative Council Panel on Home Affairs (2005). *Review of advisory and statutory bodies: Interim report No. 14—Review of the classification system of advisory and statutory bodies in the public sector.* https://www.legco.gov.hk/yr04-05/english/panels/ha/papers/ha0708cb2-2176-4e.pdf

Legislative Council Panel on Home Affairs (2006). *Interim report No. 15—Review of the corporate governance of the Equal Opportunities Commission.* https://www.legco.gov.hk/yr05-06/english/panels/ha/papers/ha0113cb2-786-2e.pdf

Legislative Council Panel on Public Service (2005). Arrangements governing the taking up of outside work by directorate civil servants after ceasing active service. LC Paper No. CB (1)295/05-06(03). https://www.legco.gov.hk/yr05-06/english/panels/ps/papers/ps1121cb1-295-3e.pdf

Legislative Council Panel on Public Service (2008). Background brief on civil service recruitment policy. LC Paper No. CB (1)974/07-08. https://www.legco.gov.hk/yr07-08/english/panels/ps/papers/ps0311cb1-974-e.pdf

Legislative Council Panel on Public Service (2014). Updated background brief on integrity enhancement initiatives for civil servants. LC Paper No. CB (4)932/13-14(15). https://www.legco.gov.hk/yr13-14/english/panels/ps/papers/ps0721cb4-932-15-e.pdf

Legislative Council Panel on Public Service (2019, 16 December). Updated background brief on employment situation of non-contract staff. LC Paper No. CB (4)177/19-20(07). https://www.legco.gov.hk/yr19-20/english/panels/ps/papers/ps20191216cb4-177-7-e.pdf

Legislative Council Panel on Public Service (2020, 4 May). An overview of training and development for civil servants. https://www.legco.gov.hk/yr19-20/english/panels/ps/papers/ps20200504cb4-506-5-e.pdf

Legislative Council Panel on Public Service (2020). Updated background brief on 2020–2021 civil service pay adjustment. https://www.legco.gov.hk/yr19-20/english/panels/ps/papers/ps20200619cb4-699-3-e.pdf

Legislative Council Panel on Public Service (2021, 17 May). An overview of the civil service: es-tablishment, strength, retirement, age profile and gender profile. LC Paper No. CB(4) 986/20-21(03).

Legislative Council Panel on Public Service (2022, 9 February). Policy measures of the Civil Service Bureau in 2021 policy address. LC Paper No. CB(4) 57/2022(01).

Legislative Council Panel on Security (2002). Background paper prepared by the Legislative Council Secretariat: Independent Police Complaints Council. https://www.legco.gov.hk/yr01-02/english/panels/se/papers/se0704cb2-2433-4e.pdf

Legislative Council Panel on Transport (2008). Background brief on fare increase applications by franchised bus companies. LC Paper No. CB (1) 829/07-08. https://www.legco.gov.hk/yr07-08/english/panels/tp/papers/tp0222cb1-829-e.pdf

Legislative Council Panel on Welfare Services (2008). Lump sum grant subvention system. LC Paper No. CB (2) 1875/07-08(03). https://www.legco.gov.hk/yr07-08/english/panels/ws/papers/ws0516cb2-1875-3-e.pdf

Legislative Council Secretariat (2005). Background brief: Termination of the employment of the Director (Operations) Designate by the Equal Opportunities Commission and other related Incidents. https://www.legco.gov.hk/yr04-05/english/panels/ha/papers/ha0321cb2-1003-1e.pdf

Legislative Council Secretariat (2018). Women's participation in public affairs in Hong Kong. https://www.legco.gov.hk/research-publications/english/1819issf02-womens-participation-in-public-affairs-in-hong-kong-20181016-e.pdf

Legislative Council Secretariat (2019). Background brief on supplements and special grants under the Comprehensive Social Security Assistance Scheme. LC Paper No. CB (2)743/18-19(07) https://www.legco.gov.hk/yr18-19/english/panels/ws/papers/ws20190211cb2-743-7-e.pdf

Legislative Council Secretariat (2020). *Handbook on services provided for members by the Legislative Council Secretariat.* https://www.legco.gov.hk/general/english/sec/corg_ser/handbook/handbook-for-members.html

Legislative Council Secretariat Research Office (2019). Recruitment and turnover of civil servants. https://www.legco.gov.hk/research-publications/english/1920issh10-recruitment-and-turnover-of-civil-servants-20191111-e.pdf

Legislative Council Subcommittee on the West Kowloon Cultural District Development (2008). *Financial assessment of the West Kowloon Cultural District project.* https://www.legco.gov.hk/yr04-05/english/hc/sub_com/hs02/papers/hs020530wkcd-548-e.pdf

Official Proceedings of the Hong Kong Legislative Council (Hansard) (1973–2022).

Consultation Documents; Reports on Consultation Documents

Antiquities Advisory Board (2014). *Respecting our heritage while looking ahead: Policy on conservation of built heritage: Consultation paper.* https://www.gov.hk/en/residents/government/publication/consultation/docs/2014/CBH.pdf

Chief Executive's Office (1997). *Civil liberties and social order: Consultation document.* Hong Kong: The Office.

Civil Service Bureau (1999). *Civil service reform: Consultation document: Civil service into the 21st century.* https://www.info.gov.hk/archive/consult/1999/reforme.pdf

Civil Service Bureau (2018, February). *Consultation paper: Extension of service of civil servants who joined the government between 1 June 2000 and 31 May 2015.* https://www.csb.gov.hk/english/publication/files/Consultation_Paper_2018_Eng.pdf

Commerce and Economic Development Bureau (2013). *Public consultation on 2014 digital 21 strategy: Smarter Hong Kong, smarter living.* https://www.ogcio.gov.hk/en/news/consultations/d21_submission_2013/doc/2014D21S-booklet.pdf

Constitutional Affairs Bureau (1998). *Review of district organizations: Consultation report.* Hong Kong: Printing Department.

Economic Development and Labour Bureau (2004). *Consultation document on partial privatization of the Airport Authority.* https://www.thb.gov.hk/eng/psp/publications/transport/consultation/air01/Full%20paper.pdf

Economic Development and Labour Bureau (2005). *Report on public consultation on partial privatisation of the Airport Authority.* https://www.thb.gov.hk/eng/psp/publications/transport/consultation/air01/report.pdf

Education Bureau (2019). *Task force on review of school curriculum: Consultation document.* https://www.edb.gov.hk/attachment/en/about-edb/press/consultation/TF_Curriculum Review_Consultation_e.pdf

Education Bureau Task Force on Review of School Curriculum (2020). *Optimise the curriculum for the future: Foster whole-person development and diverse talents.* https://

www.edb.gov.hk/attachment/en/curriculum-development/renewal/taskforce_cur/TF_CurriculumReview_FinalReport_e.pdf
Environment Bureau (2019). *2025 air quality objectives review: Public consultation.* https://www.gov.hk/en/residents/government/publication/consultation/docs/2019/Air-Quality.pdf
Financial Services and Treasury Bureau (2006). *Broadening the tax base: Ensuring our future prosperity: What's the best option for Hong Kong?* https://www.taxreform.gov.hk/eng/doc_and_leaflet.htm
Financial Services and Treasury Bureau (2007). *Public consultation on tax reform: Final report.* https://www.taxreform.gov.hk/eng/pdf/finalreport.pdf
Food and Health Bureau (2010). *My health, my life: Healthcare reform second stage consultation document.* https://www.myhealthmychoice.gov.hk/pdf/consultation_full_eng.pdf
Home Affairs Bureau (2003). *Review of the role and functions of public sector advisory and statutory bodies: Consultation paper.* https://www.hab.gov.hk/file_manager/en/documents/whats_new/advisory_and_statutory_bodies/ASBmempaper.pdf
Hong Kong Housing Authority (2014). *Long-term housing strategy: Report on public consultation.* https://www.legco.gov.hk/yr13-14/english/panels/hg/hg_lths/papers/hg_lthscb1-915-1-e.pdf
Law Reform Commission Access to Information Sub-Committee (2018*). Consultation paper: Access to information.* https://www.hkreform.gov.hk/en/docs/accesstoinfo_e.pdf
Social Welfare Advisory Committee (2010). *Long-term social welfare planning in Hong Kong: Consultation paper.* https://www.gov.hk/en/theme/bf/pdf/SWAC_Consultation_Paper.pdf
Social Welfare Advisory Committee (2011). *Report on long-term social welfare planning in Hong Kong.* https://www.lwb.gov.hk/files/download/committees/swac/SWAC_consultation_report_Eng.pdf
Transport and Housing Bureau (2016*). Public consultation on the review of the MTR fare adjustment mechanism.* https://www.thb.gov.hk/eng/policy/transport/policy/consultation/FAM%20-%20Consultation%20paper%20-%20E%20-%20final.pdf

Commissions of Inquiry; Select Committees; Task Forces; Consultants' Reports

Chan, H. W. A., & Lai, A. N. (2015). *Report of the Commission of Inquiry into excess lead found in drinking water.* https://www.coi-drinkingwater.gov.hk/eng/report.html
Cheng, M. M. C., & Stevenson, B. (2004). *Report of the independent inquiry on the Harbour Fest.* https://www.gov.hk/en/residents/government/policy/government_reports/reports/docs/harbourfest.pdf
Committee on Review of Outside Work for Civil Servants (2009). *Report on review of outside work for directorate civil servants.* https://www.gov.hk/en/residents/government/policy/government_reports/reports/docs/RPOWDCS.pdf
Creative Commons (2019). *Statutory powers and monitoring of the HKPF: Investigation report.* LG 2019/002. https://docs.google.com/document/d/19Nl3_RPi5yfG-nzTjdF-WEt2mawtLZS9MwkVQhbCCS4/edit#
Equal Opportunities Commission (2019). *Report of the review of the Equal Opportunities Commission: Governance, management structure and complaint-handling process.* https://

www.eoc.org.hk/eoc/graphicsfolder/showcontent.aspx?content=our%20work-what%20is%20eoc

Financial Services and the Treasury Bureau (2015). *Report of the working group on long-term fiscal planning (phase one)*. https://www.fstb.gov.hk/tb/en/report-of-the-working-group-on-longterm-fiscal-planning-phase1.htm

Food and Health Bureau (2015). *Report of the steering committee review of the Hospital Authority*. https://www.fhb.gov.hk/download/committees/harsc/report/en_full_report.pdf

Harvard Team (1999). *Improving Hong Kong's health care system: Why and for whom?* https://www.fhb.gov.hk/en/press_and_publications/consultation/HCS.HTM#MAIN%20REPORT

Hong Kong Government (1999). *Report of the Commission of Inquiry on the New Airport*. https://www.gov.hk/en/residents/government/policy/government_reports/reports/docs/new_airport_report.pdf

Hong Kong Judiciary (2004). *Report of the working party on the review of the Labour Tribunal*. https://www.judiciary.hk/doc/en/publications/lt_review_report-final.pdf

Independent Investigation Panel (2000). *Report to the Council of the University of Hong Kong*. www.hku.hk/reportip

Kotewall, R. G., & Kwong, G. C. K. (2002). *Report of the panel of inquiry on the penny stocks incident*. https://www.info.gov.hk/info/pennystock-e.htm

Lump Sum Grant Independent Review Committee (2008). *Review report of the Lump Sum Grant Subvention System*. https://www.swd.gov.hk/doc/ngo/Report-eng.pdf

McKinsey and Company (1973). *The machinery of government: A new framework for expanding services*. Hong Kong: mimeo.

Office of the Ombudsman (2008). *Direct investigation report: Effectiveness of the Integrated Call Centre in handling complaints*. https://ofomb.ombudsman.hk/abc/files/6-2008-1.pdf

Office of the Ombudsman (2020). *Effectiveness of Joint Office for investigation of water seepage complaints: Executive summary*. https://ofomb.ombudsman.hk/abc/en-us/direct_investigations

SARS Expert Committee (2003). *SARS in Hong Kong: From experience to action: Report of the SARS expert committee*. https://www.sars-expertcom.gov.hk/english/reports/reports/reports_fullrpt.html

Task Force on Land Supply (2018). *Striving for multi-pronged land supply: Report of the Task Force on land supply*. https://www.devb.gov.hk/filemanager/en/content_1171/Report%20(Eng).pdf

Yeung, C. K., & Lee, J. P. (2007). *Report of the Commission of Inquiry on allegations relating to the Hong Kong Institute of Education*. https://www.gov.hk/en/residents/government/policy/government_reports/reports/docs/HKIEd.pdf

Annual Reports

Airport Authority (2020). *Annual report 2019/2020*. https://www.hongkongairport.com/en/airport-authority/publications/annual-interim-reports/annual2019

Competition Commission (2021). *Annual report 2020/2021*. https://www.compcomm.hk/en/media/reports_publications/files/2020_21_CC_Annual_Report.pdf

Environment Protection Department (2020). *Environment Hong Kong 2020*. https://www.epd.gov.hk/epd/misc/ehk20/en/pdf1/web/EHK_2020AR_EN.pdf

Selected Bibliography   421

Equal Opportunities Commission (2003). *Annual report 2002/2003.* https://www.eoc.org.hk/eoc/graphicsfolder/inforcenter/annual/default.aspx?Year=2002&IsContent
Equal Opportunities Commission (2021). *Annual report 2020/2021.* https://www.eoc.org.hk/en/AnnualReport/Detail/49
Hong Kong Government (2021). *Hong Kong yearbook 2020.* https://www.yearbook.gov.hk/2020/en/
Hong Kong Judiciary (2022). *Annual report 2021.* https://www.judiciary.hk/en/publications/annu_rept_2021r/index.htm
Hong Kong Monetary Authority (2021). *Annual report 2020.* https://www.hkma.gov.hk/eng/data-publications-and-research/publications/annual-report/2020/
Hong Kong Police Force (2021). *Hong Kong Police Review 2020.* https://www.police.gov.hk/info/review/2020/en/index.html
Hospital Authority (2021). *Annual report 2020–2021.* https://www.ha.org.hk/haho/ho/cc/HA_Annual_Report_2020-21_en.pdf
Housing Authority (2021). *Annual report 2020–2021.* https://www.housingauthority.gov.hk/mini-site/haar2021/en/index.html
Independent Commission Against Corruption (2011–2021). *Annual reports 2010–2020.* https://www.icac.org.hk/en/about/report/annual/index.html
Independent Police Complaints Council (2021). *2020/2021 report.* https://www.ipcc.gov.hk/en/home/index.html
Labour Department (2021). *Annual report 2020.* https://www.labour.gov.hk/eng/public/iprd/2020/index.html
Legislative Council (1993–2020). *Legislative Council annual reports.* Hong Kong: Government Printer 1993–1998. https://www.legco.gov.hk/en/about-legco/annual-reports-of-legislative-council.html
Office of the Ombudsman (2004–2021). *Annual reports of the Ombudsman.* https://www.ombudsman.hk/en-us/publications/annual_reports.html
Office of the Privacy Commissioner (2021). *Annual report 2020/2021.* https://www.pcpd.org.hk/english/resources_centre/publications/annual_report/annualreport2021.html
Public Service Commission (2001–2020) *Annual reports.* https://www.psc.gov.hk/eng/ann_rep/index.php
Social Welfare Department (2019). *SWD review 2017–2018 & 2018–2019.* https://www.swd.gov.hk/en/index/site_pubpress/page_swdarep/ [The Social Welfare department has not produced an annual report since 2019 but updates its statistics and "highlights" annually on its webpages.]
Transport Advisory Committee (2021, 21 December). TCU's third quarterly report of 2021 released. https://www.info.gov.hk/gia/general/202112/21/P2021122100324.htm
Transport Department (2020). *Annual transport digest 2021.* https://www.td.gov.hk/mini_site/atd/2021/en/index.html

Government Statistical Material and Surveys

Census and Statistics Department (2016). *Housing conditions of sub-divided units in Hong Kong. Thematic Household Survey Report No. 60.* https://www.statistics.gov.hk/pub/B11302602016XXXXB0100.pdf.
Census and Statistics Department (2021). *Hong Kong poverty situation report.* https://www.censtatd.gov.hk/en/EIndexbySubject.html?pcode=B9XX0005&scode=461

Census and Statistics Department (2021). *Hong Kong Annual Digest of Statistics*. 2020 edition. https://www.censtatd.gov.hk/en/EIndexbySubject.html?pcode=B1010003&scode=460

Civil Service Bureau (1974–2020). *Civil service personnel statistics*. Hong Kong: The Branch, 1974–1996; Printing Department, 1997–2001; The Bureau, 2002–2008; Civil Service Bureau (2020). Annually updated civil service personnel statistics. https://www.csb.gov.hk/english/stat/annually/546.html

Independent Commission Against Corruption (2020). *Annual survey 2020*. https://www.icac.org.hk/en/survey/finding/index.html

Labour Department (2020). *Annual statistical report of trade unions in Hong Kong 2019*. https://www.labour.gov.hk/tc/public/pdf/rtu/ASR2019.pdf

Public Opinion Research Institute (2020). https://develo.pori.hk/?lang=en

Other Government Reports, Documents, and Speeches

Central Policy Unit (2015). *A study on the role and functions of Hong Kong under the "one belt, one road" strategy*. https://www.pico.gov.hk/doc/en/research_reports/CPU_research_report-the_role_and_functions_of_hong_kong_under_the_one_belt_one_road_strategy_eng.pdf

Central Policy Unit (2016). *A study on "civic values" and engagement of "post-90s" in Hong Kong*. https://www.pico.gov.hk/doc/en/research_reports/CPU_research_report-civic_values_and_engagement_of_post90s_in_hong_kong.pdf

Civil Service Bureau (2003). *Development of an improved pay adjustment mechanism for the civil service*. https://www.csb.gov.hk/english/admin/pay/1570.htmlwww.csb.gov.hk

Civil Service Bureau (2013). Circular 6/2013: Performance management in the civil service. http://www.agtso.org/update/download/c201306e.pdf

Commerce and Economic Development Bureau (2021). *The governance and management of Radio Television Hong Kong*. https://www.cedb.gov.hk/ccib/en/consultations-and-publications/reports/rthkreview.pdf

Director of Audit (2004). *Report No. 42: Hong Kong Harbour Fest*. https://www.aud.gov.hk/pdf_e/e42ch04.pdf

Director of Audit (2007). *Report No. 48: Administration of Hong Kong Applied Science and Technology Research Institute Company Limited*. https://www.aud.gov.hk/pdf_e/e48ch02.pdf

Director of Audit (2007). *Report No. 49: Hong Kong Tourism Board: Corporate governance and administrative issues*. https://www.aud.gov.hk/pdf_e/e49ch05.pdf

Director of Audit (2013). *Report No. 60: Preventive education and enlisting support against corruption*. https://www.aud.gov.hk/pdf_e/e60ch07.pdf

Director of Audit (2018). *Report No. 71: Radio Television Hong Kong: Provision of programmes*. https://www.aud.gov.hk/pdf_e/e71ch05.pdf

Director of Audit (2019). *Report No. 73: Procurement of goods and services by the Immigration Department*. https://www.aud.gov.hk/pdf_e/e73ch08.pdf

Director of Audit (2020). *Report No. 75: Hong Kong Tourism Board: Corporate governance and administrative issues*. https://www.aud.gov.hk/pdf_e/e75ch07.pdf

Efficiency Unit (2007). *Serving the community by using the private sector: Policy and practice* (2nd ed.). https://www.effo.gov.hk/en/reference/publications/PolicyPractice2007.pdf

Efficiency Unit (2008). *Serving the community by using the private sector: An introductory guide to public-private partnerships* (2nd ed.). https://www.effo.gov.hk/en/reference/publications/ppp_guide_2008.pdf

Efficiency Unit (2008). *Serving the community by using the private sector: A general guide to outsourcing* (3rd ed.). https://www.effo.gov.hk/en/reference/publications/guide_to_outsourcing_200803.pdf

Efficiency Unit (2009). *A guide to complaint-handling and public enquiries.* https://www.effo.gov.hk/en/reference/publications/A_Guide_to_Complaints_Handling_and_Public_Enquiries.pdf

Environment Bureau (2017). *Hong Kong's climate action plan 2030.* https://www.climateready.gov.hk/files/report/en/HK_Climate_Action_Plan_2030+_booklet_En.pdf

Financial Secretary (2020). *The 2020–21 budget.* https://www.budget.gov.hk/2020/eng/speech.html

Financial Secretary (2021). *The 2021/22 budget.* https://www.budget.gov.hk/2021/eng/pdf/Budget2021_eng.pdf

Financial Secretary (2022). *The 2022–23 budget.* https://www.budget.gov.hk/2022/eng/speech.html

Financial Secretary (2022). *The 2022–23 budget estimates.* https://www.budget.gov.hk/2022/eng/estimates.html

Food and Health Bureau (2015). *Report of the steering committee on review of Hospital Authority.* https://www.fhb.gov.hk/download/committees/harsc/report/en_full_report.pdf

Government of the People's Republic of China (2019). *Outline development plan for the Guangdong-Hong Kong-Macao Greater Bay Area.* www.bayarea.gov.hk/filemanager/en/share/pdf/Outline_Development_Plan

Hong Kong Government (1995). *Serving the community.* Hong Kong: Government Printer.

Hong Kong Government (2003, 29 June). *Signing of the Mainland and Hong Kong Closer Economic Partnership Arrangement* [Press release].

Hong Kong Government (2018). *Organisation chart of the Government of the Hong Kong Special Administrative Region.* https://www.gov.hk/en/about/govdirectory/govchart/index.htm

Hong Kong Government (2020). *CJ's speech at ceremonial opening of the legal year 2020* (13 January). https://www.info.gov.hk/gia/general/202001/13/P2020011300622.htm

Hong Kong Government (2020). *Code on access to information.* https://www.access.gov.hk/en/home/index.html

Independent Commission against Corruption and Civil Service Bureau (2007). *Ethical leadership in action: Handbook for senior managers in the civil service.* https://www.csb.gov.hk/english/publication/files/Ethical_Leadership_in_Action_Handbook_2008_extract.pdf

Standing Commission on Civil Service Salaries and Conditions of Service (1979). *Report No. 1: First report on principles and practice governing civil service pay.* https://www.jsscs.gov.hk/reports/en/01/index.htm

Standing Commission on Civil Service Salaries and Conditions of Service (1980). *Report No. 4: Consultative machinery in the civil service.* https://www.jsscs.gov.hk/reports/en/04/index.htm

Standing Commission on Civil Service Salaries and Conditions of Service (2018). *Report No. 59: Review on civil service pay level survey and starting salaries.* https://www.jsscs.gov.hk/reports/en/59/pls&sssindex.html

Standing Committee on the Disciplined Services Salaries and Conditions of Service (2021, June). *Report on the grade review of the disciplined services grades.* https://www.jsscs.gov.hk/reports/en/scds_gsr_2021_eng.pdf

Transport and Housing Bureau (2014). *Long-term housing strategy.* https://www.thb.gov.hk/eng/policy/housing/policy/lths/LTHS201412.pdf

Secondary Sources

Amnesty International (2020). *Hong Kong: Missing truth, missing justice; the case and international legal framework for the establishment of a commission of inquiry into the 2019 protests*. London: Amnesty International.
Barrow, A., & Scully-Hill, A. (2016). Failure to implement CEDAW in Hong Kong: Why isn't anyone using the Domestic and Cohabitation Relationships Violence Ordinance? *International Journal of Law, Policy and the Family, 30*(1), 50–78.
Bauhinia Foundation (2019). *Public perceptions towards the rule of law in Hong Kong—An opinion survey* (conducted for the Bauhinia Foundation by the Hong Kong Institute of Asia Pacific Studies, The Chinese University of Hong Kong). http://www.bauhinia.org/index.php/english/research
Beetham, D. (2013). *The legitimation of power* (2nd ed.). Basingstoke: Macmillan.
Bray, D. (2001). *Hong Kong metamorphosis*. Hong Kong: Hong Kong University Press.
Brewer, B. (2003). The impact of differentiation and differential on Hong Kong's career civil service. *International Review of Administrative Sciences, 60*, 219–233.
Brewer, B., Leung, J. Y. H., & Scott, I. (2014). Values in perspective: Administrative ethics and the Hong Kong public servant revisited. *Administration & Society, 46*(8), 908–928.
Brewer, B., Leung, J. Y. H., & Scott, I. (2015). Value-based integrity management and bureaucratic organizations: Changing the mix. *International Public Management Journal, 18*(3), 390–410.
Burns, J. P. (2004). *Government capacity and the Hong Kong civil service*. Hong Kong: Oxford University Press.
Burns, J. P. (2004). The policy process in the HKSAR. In A. Nakamura (Ed.), *Public reform, policy change and new public management: From the Asia and Pacific perspective*. Tokyo: EROPA Local Government Center.
Burns, J. P. (2020). The state and higher education in Hong Kong. *The China Quarterly, 244*, 1031–1055.
Burns, J. P., & Li, W. (2015). The impact of external change on civil service values in postcolonial Hong Kong. *The China Quarterly, 222*, 522–546.
Burns, J. P., Li, W., & Peters, B. G. (2013). Changing governance structures and the evolution of public service bargains in Hong Kong. *International Review of Administrative Sciences, 79*(1), 131–148.
Bush, R. C. (2016). *Hong Kong in the shadow of China: Living with the Leviathan*. Washington, DC: Brookings Institution Press.
Cabestan, J-P., & Daziano, L. (2020). *Hong Kong: The second handover*. Paris: Fondation pour L'Innovation Politique.
Capano, G., & Howlett, M. (2020). The knowns and unknowns of policy instrument analysis: Policy tools and the current research agenda on policy mixes. *Sage Open*, 1–13.
Carroll, J. M. (2007). *A concise history of Hong Kong*. Hong Kong: Hong Kong University Press.
Caulfield, J., & Liu, A. (2006). Shifting concepts of autonomy in the Hong Kong Hospital Authority. *Public Organization Review, 6*(3), 203–219.
Chan, A. (2001). Public administration in Hong Kong: Challenges and reform. *Public Administration and Policy, 10*(2), 175–178.
Chan, A. (2001, 19 April). *Speech by the Chief Secretary of Administration at an Asia Society luncheon* [Press release].

Chan, C. (2019). Thirty years from Tiananmen: China, Hong Kong, and the ongoing experiment to preserve liberal values in an authoritarian state. *International Journal of Constitutional Law, 17*(2), 439–452.

Chan, C., & de Londras, F. (Eds.) (2020). *China's national security: Endangering Hong Kong's rule of law.* Oxford: Hart Publishing.

Chan, D. S. W., & Pun, N. (2020). Economic power of the politically powerless in the 2019 Hong Kong pro-democracy movement. *Critical Asian Studies, 52*(1), 33–43.

Chan, E. (2002). Beyond pedagogy: Language and identity in post-colonial Hong Kong. *British Journal of Sociology of Education, 23*(2), 271–285.

Chan, E., & Chan, J. (2007). The first ten years of the HKSAR: Civil society comes of age. *Asia Pacific Journal of Public Administration, 29*(1), 77–99.

Chan, E., & Chan, J. (2014). Liberal patriotism in Hong Kong. *Journal of Contemporary China, 23*(89), 952–970.

Chan, E., & Chan, J. (2017). Hong Kong 2007–2017: A backlash in civil society. *Asia Pacific Journal of Public Administration, 39*(2), 135–152.

Chan, J., & Chan, E. (2006, March/April). Perceptions of universal suffrage and functional representation in Hong Kong: A confused public? *Asian Survey, XLVI* (2), 257–274.

Chan, J., & Chan, E. (2006). Charting the state of social cohesion in Hong Kong. *The China Quarterly, 187,* 635–658.

Chan, J. M. M., & Kerr, D. (2016). Academic freedom, political interference and public accountability: The Hong Kong experience. *Journal of Academic Freedom, 7,* 1–21.

Chan, J., & Wong, V. (2018). The politics of the ombudsman: The Hong Kong experience. In M. Hertogh & R. Kirkham (Eds.), *Research handbook on the ombudsman* (pp. 91–112). Cheltenham: Edward Elgar.

Chan, N. K. M., Nachman, J., & Mok, C. W. J. (2020). A red flag for participation: The influence of Chinese mainlandization on political behaviour in Hong Kong. *Political Research Quarterly.* https://doi.org/10.1177/1065912920957413

Chan, R. K. H. (2020). Politics matters: The attempts and failure of health finance reform in Hong Kong. In M. M. Merviö (Ed.), *Recent social, environmental and cultural issues in East Asian Societies* (pp. 188–198). Hershey, PA: IGI Global.

Chau, K. L., & Wong, C. K. (2002). The social welfare reform: A way to reduce public burden? In S. K. Lau (Ed.), *The First Tung Chee-hwa Administration* (pp. 201–236). Hong Kong: The Chinese University of Hong Kong Press.

Cheng, E. W. (2016). Street politics in a hybrid regime: The diffusion of political activism in post-colonial Hong Kong. *The China Quarterly, 226,* 383–406.

Cheng, E. W. (2020). United front work and mechanisms of countermobilization in Hong Kong. *The China Journal, 83*(1), 1–33.

Cheng, E. W. L. (2019). Public–private partnerships for critical infrastructure development: The Hong Kong experience. In R. M. Clarke & S. Hakim (Eds.), *Public private partnerships* (pp. 207–232). Cham: Springer.

Cheng, J. Y. S. (Ed.) (2005). *The July 1 protest rally: Interpreting a historic event.* Hong Kong: City University of Hong Kong Press.

Cheng, J. Y. S. (Ed.) (2007). *The Hong Kong Special Administrative Region in its first decade.* Hong Kong: City University of Hong Kong Press.

Cheng, J. Y. S. (Ed.) (2014). *New trends of political participation in Hong Kong.* Hong Kong: City University Press.

Cheung, A. B. L. (1996). Performance pledges—Power to the consumer or a quagmire in public service legitimation? *International Journal of Public Administration, 19*(2), 233–260.

Cheung, A. B. L. (1996). Public sector reform and the re-legitimation of public bureaucratic power: The case of Hong Kong. *International Journal of Public Sector Management, 9*(5/6), 37–50.

Cheung, A. B. L. (1997). Reform in search of politics: The case of Hong Kong's aborted attempt to corporatise public broadcasting. *Asian Journal of Public Administration, 19*(2), 276–302.

Cheung, A. B. L. (2001). Civil service reform in post-1997 Hong Kong: Political challenges, managerial responses? *International Journal of Public Administration, 24*(9), 929–50.

Cheung, A. B. L. (2006). How autonomous are public corporations in Hong Kong? The case of the Airport Authority. *Public Organization Review, 6*(3), 221–236.

Cheung, A. B. L. (2006). Judicial review and policy making in Hong Kong: Changing interface between the legal and the political. *Asia Pacific Journal of Public Administration, 28*(2), 117–141.

Cheung, A. B. L. (2007). Executive-led governance or executive power: "Hollowed-out"—The political quagmire of Hong Kong. *Asian Journal of Political Science, 15*(1), 17–38.

Cheung, A. B. L. (2007). Policy capacity in post-1997 Hong Kong: Constrained institutions facing a crowded and differentiated polity. *Asia Pacific Journal of Public Administration, 29*(1), 51–75.

Cheung, A. B. L. (2016). NPM in Asian countries. In T. Christensen & P. Lægreid (Eds.), *The Ashgate research companion to new public management* (pp. 132–144). New York: Routledge.

Cheung, A. B. L., & Lee, J. C. Y. (Eds.) (2001). *Public sector reform in Hong Kong: Into the 21st century*. Hong Kong: The Chinese University of Hong Kong Press.

Cheung, A. B. L., & Scott, I. (2003). Governance and public sector reforms in Asia: Paradigms, paradoxes and dilemmas. In A. B. L. Cheung & I. Scott (Eds.), *Governance and public sector reform in Asia: Paradigm shifts or business as usual?* (pp. 1–24). London: RoutledgeCurzon.

Cheung, C. Y. (2003). The quest for good governance: Hong Kong's Principal Officials Accountability System. *China: An International Journal 1*(2), 249–272.

Cheung, K. C. (2011). The generational gap: Values and culture in the Hong Kong police force. In M. R. Haberfeld, C. A. Clarke, & D. L. Sheehan (Eds.), *Police organization and training* (pp. 137–152). New York: Springer.

Cheung, P. T. Y. (2011). Civic engagement in the policy process in Hong Kong. *Public Administration and Development, 31*(2), 113–121.

Cheung, P. T. Y. (2015). Toward collaborative governance between Hong Kong and Mainland China. *Urban Studies, 52*(10), 1915–1933.

Chu, C. Y. Y. (2010). *Chinese communists and Hong Kong capitalists*. New York: Palgrave Macmillan.

Chung, R. Y., & Wong, S. Y. S. (2015). Health inequality in Hong Kong. *China Review, 15*(2), 91–118.

Civicus (2006). *The HKSAR: A vibrant but loosely organised civil society*. Hong Kong: Hong Kong Council of Social Service.

Cohen, J. A. (2022). Hong Kong's transformed criminal justice system: Instrument of fear. *Academia Sinica Law Journal*. 2022 special issue, 1–20.

Cooper, T. L., & Lui, T. T. (1990). Democracy and the administrative state: The case of Hong Kong. *Public Administration Review, 50*(3), 332–344.

Currie, J., Petersen, C. J., & Mok, K. H. (2006). *Academic freedom in Hong Kong*. Lanham, MD: Lexington Books.

Dagher, R. (2018). Legitimacy and post-conflict state-building: The undervalued role of performance legitimacy. *Conflict, Security and Development, 18*(2), 85–111.

Delaney, M. (2019, 25 November). What just happened in Hong Kong elections? *Foreign Policy*. https://foreignpolicy.com/2019/11/25/what-happened-hong-kong-elections/

Dimbleby, J. (1997). *The last governor: Chris Patten and the handover of Hong Kong*. London: Little, Brown and Company.

Fong, B. C. H. (2013). State-society conflicts under Hong Kong's hybrid regime: Governing coalition building and civil society challenges. *Asia Survey, 13*(5), 854–882.

Fong, B. C. H. (2014). The partnership between the Chinese government and Hong Kong's capitalist class: Implications for HKSAR governance, 1997–2012. *China Quarterly, 217*, 195–220.

Fong, B. C. H. (2017). One country, two nationalisms: Centre-periphery relations between Mainland China and Hong Kong. *Modern China, 43*(5), 523–556.

Fong, B. C. H. (2022). *Hong Kong public budgeting*. Singapore: Palgrave Macmillan.

Fong, B. C. H., Wu, J. M., & Nathan, A. J. (Eds.) (2021). *China's influence and the center-periphery tug of war in Hong Kong, Taiwan and the Indo-Pacific*. London: Routledge.

Forrest, R., & Xian, S. (2018). Accommodating discontent: Youth, conflict and the housing question in Hong Kong. *Housing Studies, 33*(1), 1–17.

Fu, H. (2001). The national security factor: Putting Article 23 of the Basic Law in perspective. In S. Tsang (Ed.), Judicial *independence and the rule of law in Hong Kong* (pp. 73–98). Basingstoke: Palgrave.

Fung, D. C. L., & Lui, W. M. (2017). *Education policy analysis: Liberal studies and national education in Hong Kong*. Singapore: Springer.

Ghai, Y. (1999). *Hong Kong's new constitutional order: The resumption of Chinese sovereignty and the Basic Law* (2nd ed.). Hong Kong: Hong Kong University Press.

Ghai, Y. (2007). The legal foundations of Hong Kong's autonomy: Building on sand. *Asia Pacific Journal of Public Administration 29*(1), 3–28.

Gong, T., & Scott, I. (2016). Conflicts of interest and ethical decision-making: Mainland China and Hong Kong comparisons. In A. Lawton, Z. Van Der Wal, & L. Huberts (Eds.), *Ethics in public policy and management: A global research companion* (pp. 257–276). Abingdon: Routledge.

Gong, T., Wang, S., & Ren, J. (2015). Corruption in the eye of the beholder: Survey evidence from Mainland China and Hong Kong. *International Public Management Journal, 18*(3), 458–482.

Gong, T., & Xiao, H. (2017). Socially embedded anti-corruption governance: Evidence from Hong Kong. *Public Administration and Development, 37*(3), 176–190.

Goodstadt, L. F. (2000, September). China and the selection of Hong Kong's post-colonial political elite. *The China Quarterly, 163*, 721–741.

Goodstadt, L. F. (2005). *Uneasy partners: The conflict between public interest and private profit in Hong Kong*. Hong Kong: Hong Kong University Press.

Goodstadt, L. F. (2014). *Poverty in the midst of affluence: How Hong Kong mismanaged its prosperity* (Rev. ed.). Hong Kong: Hong Kong University Press.

Goodstadt, L. F. (2018). *A city mismanaged: Hong Kong's struggle for survival*. Hong Kong: Hong Kong University Press.

Gu, M. (2020, 26 October). Underutilized HZMB finds it difficult bridging the gap. *China Daily*. https://www.chinadaily.com.cn/a/202010/26/WS5f967d8aa31024ad0ba8101c.html

Haddon-Cave, P. (1984). The making of some aspects of public policy in Hong Kong. In D. Lethbridge (Ed.), *The business environment in Hong Kong* (2nd ed.). Hong Kong: Oxford University Press.

Hartley, K., & Jarvis, D. S. L. (2020). Policymaking in a low-trust state: Legitimacy, state capacity and responses to COVID-19 in Hong Kong. *Policy and Society, 39*(3), 403–423.

Hase, P. (2001). The district office. In E. Sinn (Ed.), *Hong Kong, British Crown Colony, revisited* (pp. 123–145). Hong Kong: Centre of Asian Studies, University of Hong Kong.

Hayes, J. (1996). *Friends and teachers: Hong Kong and its people 1953-87*. Hong Kong: Hong Kong University Press.

Hayllar, M. R. (2007). Governance and community engagement in managing SARS in Hong Kong. *Asian Journal of Political Science, 15*(1), 39–47.

Hayllar, M. R. (2010). Public-private partnerships in Hong Kong: Good governance—The essential missing ingredient. *Australian Journal of Public Administration, 69*, supplement, S99–S119.

He, A. J. (2018). Public satisfaction with the health system and Hong Kong popular support for state involvement in an East Asian welfare system: Health policy legitimacy of Hong Kong. *Social Policy and Administration, 52*(3), 750–770.

Higgins, C. D., & Huque, A. S. (2015). Public money and Mickey Mouse: Evaluating performance and accountability in the Hong Kong Disneyland joint venture public-private partnership. *Public Management Review, 17*(8), 1103–1123.

Ho, E. P. (2005). *Times of change: A memoir of Hong Kong's governance 1950-1991*. Hong Kong: Hong Kong University Press.

Ho, L. K. K. (2020). Legitimization & de-legitimization of police: In British colonial & Chinese SAR Hong Kong. *Journal of Inter-regional Studies and Global Perspectives, 3*, 2–12.

Ho, L. S., Morris, P., & Chung, Y. P. (Eds.) (2005). *Education reform and the quest for excellence: The Hong Kong story*. Hong Kong: Hong Kong University Press.

Ho, P. Y. (2004). *The administrative history of the Hong Kong government agencies 1841-2002*. Hong Kong: Hong Kong University Press.

Holliday, I., Ma, N., & Yep, R. (2002). A high degree of autonomy? Hong Kong Special Administrative Region, 1997-2002. *The Political Quarterly, 73*(4), 455–464.

Hui, D. L. H., & Au, R. C. Y. (2014). Police legitimacy and protest policing: A case study of Hong Kong. *Asian Education and Development Studies, 3*(3), 223–234.

Huque, A. S., & Lee, G. O. M. (2000). *Managing public services: Crises and lessons from Hong Kong* Aldershot: Ashgate.

Huque, A. S., Lee, G. O. M., & Cheung, A. B. L. (1998). *The civil service in Hong Kong: Continuity and change*. Hong Kong: Hong Kong University Press.

Ibrahim, Z., & Lam, J. (Eds.) (2020). *Rebel city: Hong Kong's year of water and fire*. Hong Kong: SCMP.

Jackson, L., & O'Leary, T. (2019). Education and the Hong Kong Umbrella Movement. *Educational Philosophy and Theory, 51*(2), 157–162.

Jao, Y. C. (2001). *The Asian financial crisis and the ordeal of Hong Kong*. Westport, CT: Quorum Books.

Jones, C. A. (2015). *Lost in China: Law, culture and identity in post-1997 Hong Kong*. Cambridge: Cambridge University Press.

Kaeding, M. P. (2017). The rise of "localism" in Hong Kong. *Journal of Democracy, 28*(1), 157–172.

King, A. Y. C. (1981). Administrative absorption of politics in Hong Kong: Emphasis on the grassroots level. In A. Y. C. King & R. P. L. Lee (Eds.), *Social life and development in Hong Kong* (pp. 127–146). Hong Kong: The Chinese University of Hong Kong Press.

Kingdon, J. W. (1995). *Agendas, alternatives and public policies* (2nd ed.). New York: Harper Collins.

Ku, A. S. (2001). The "public" up against the state: Narrative cracks and credibility crisis in postcolonial Hong Kong. *Theory, Culture and Society, 18*(1), 121–144.

Ku, A. S. (2012). Remaking places and fashioning an opposition discourse: Struggle over Star Ferry Pier and Queen's Pier in Hong Kong. *Environment and Planning D: Society and Space, 30*, 5–22.

Kuan, H. C., & Lau, S. K. (2002). Between liberal autocracy and democracy: Democratic legitimacy in Hong Kong. *Democratization, 9*(4), 58–76.

Kwok, D. W. H. (2011). *The Hong Kong-Zhuhai-Macau Bridge: Summary of the case.* Hong Kong: Civic Exchange.

Kwong, B. K. K. (2013). A comparative analysis of the cash handout policy of Hong Kong and Macau. *Journal of Current Chinese Affairs, 42*(3), 87–100.

Kwong, Y. H. (2016). The growth of "localism" in Hong Kong: A new path for the democracy movement? *China Perspectives, 3*, 63–68.

La Grange, A. (2007). Housing (1997–2007). In J. Y. S. Cheng (Ed.), *The Hong Kong Special Administrative Region in its first decade* (pp. 699–728). Hong Kong: City University of Hong Kong Press.

Lai, Y. H. (2019). Lady justice or the golden calf? The China factor in Hong Kong's legal system. *Social Transformations in Chinese Societies, 15*(2), 178–196.

Lam, J. T. M. (2015). Political decay in Hong Kong after the Occupy Central movement. *Asian Affairs: An American Review, 42*(2), 99–121.

Lam W. M. (2005). Depoliticization, citizenship, and the politics of community in Hong Kong. *Citizenship Studies, 9*(3), 309–322.

Lam, W. M. (2020). Belief in the rule of law and its resilience in the Hong Kong political identity. In C. Chan & F. de Londras (Eds.), *China's national security: Endangering Hong Kong's rule of law* (pp. 62–86). Oxford: Hart Publishing.

Lam, W. M., & Lam, K. C. Y. (2013). China's united front work in civil society: The case of Hong Kong. *International Journal of China Studies, 4*(3), 301–325.

Lam, W. M., Lui, P. L. T., & Wong, W. (Eds.) (2012). *Contemporary Hong Kong government and politics* (expanded 2nd ed.). Hong Kong: Hong Kong University Press.

Lam-Knott, S. (2018). Anti-hierarchical activism in Hong Kong: The post-80s youth. *Social Movement Studies, 17*(4), 464–470.

Lau, M., Pantakis, C., Gordon, D., Lai, L., & Sutton, E. (2015). Poverty in Hong Kong. *The China Review, 15*(2), 23–58.

Lau, S. K. (Ed.) (2002). *The first Tung Chee-hwa Administration: The first five years of the Hong Kong Special Administrative Region.* Hong Kong: The Chinese University of Hong Kong Press.

Lau, S. K., & Kuan, H. C. (2002). Hong Kong's stunted party system. *The China Quarterly, 172*, 1010–1028.

Law, W. W. (2019). *Politics, managerialism, and university governance: Lessons from Hong Kong under China's rule since 1997.* Singapore: Springer.

Lee, E. W. Y. (2020). United front, clientelism and indirect rule: Theorizing the role of the "Liaison Office" in Hong Kong. *Journal of Contemporary China, 29*(125), 763–775.

Lee, E. W. Y., Chan, E. Y. M., Chan, J. C. W., Cheung, P. T. Y., Lam, W. F., & Lam, W. M. (Eds.) (2013). *Public policymaking in Hong Kong: Civic engagement and state-society relations in a semi-democracy.* Abingdon: Routledge.

Lee, E. W. Y., & Haque, M. S. (2006). The new public management reform and governance in Asian NICS: A comparison of Hong Kong and Singapore. *Governance 19*(4), 605–626.

Lee, F. L. F., & Chan, J. M. (2011). *Media, social mobilisation and mass protests in post-colonial Hong Kong: The power of a critical event*. New York: Routledge.
Lee, F. L. F., Tang, G. K. Y., Yuen, S., & Cheng, E. W. (2020). Five demands (and not quite) beyond: Claim making and ideology in Hong Kong's anti-extradition bill movement. *Communist and Post-Communist Studies, 53*(4), 22–40.
Lee, J. (1999). *Housing, home ownership and social change in Hong Kong*. Aldershot: Ashgate.
Lethbridge, H. J. (1978). *Hong Kong: Stability and change*. Hong Kong: Oxford University Press.
Lethbridge, H. J. (1985). *Hard graft in Hong Kong*. Hong Kong: Oxford University Press.
Leung, G. M., & Bacon-Shone, J. (Eds.) (2006). *Hong Kong's health system: Reflections, perspectives and visions*. Hong Kong: Hong Kong University Press.
Leung, J. C. B. (2002). The advent of managerialism in social welfare: The case of Hong Kong. *The Hong Kong Journal of Social Work, 36*(1/2), 61–81.
Leung, J. Y. H. (1999). *State and society: The emergence and marginalization of political parties in Hong Kong* [Unpublished doctoral thesis] (pp. 255–258). The University of Hong Kong.
Leung, J. Y. H., & Chan, H. M. (2001). The school management reform in Hong Kong: Administrative control in a new cloak of managerialism. In A. B. L. Cheung & J. C. Y. Lee (Eds.), *Public sector reform in Hong Kong: Into the 21st Century* (pp. 229–259). Hong Kong: The Chinese University of Hong Kong Press.
Litton, H. (2019). *Is the Hong Kong judiciary sleepwalking to 2047?* Hong Kong: Sheriff Books.
Liu, H. K. (2019). The impact of transition from British to Chinese rule on social delivery systems. *Policy and Politics, 47*(2), 331–352.
Lo, P. Y., & Chen, A. H. Y. (2018). The judicial perspective of separation of powers in the Hong Kong Special Administrative Region of the People's Republic of China. *Journal of International and Comparative Law, 5*(2), 337–362.
Lo, S. S. H. (2001). *Governing Hong Kong: Legitimacy, communication and political decay*. New York: Nova Science Publishers.
Lo, S. S. H., Hung, S. C. F., & Loo, J. H. C. (Eds.) (2019). *China's new united front work in Hong Kong: Penetrative politics and its implications*. London: Palgrave Macmillan.
Loh, C. (2002). *Accountability without democracy? The Principal Officials Accountability System in Hong Kong*. Hong Kong: Civic Exchange.
Loh, C. (2003). Civil society and democratic development in Hong Kong. In C. Loh & Civic Exchange (Eds.), *Building democracy: Creating good government for Hong Kong* (pp. 127–135). Hong Kong: Hong Kong University Press.
Loh, C. (Ed.) (2006). *Functional constituencies: A unique feature of the Hong Kong Legislative Council*. Hong Kong: Hong Kong University Press.
Loh, C. (2018). *Underground front: The Chinese Communist Party in Hong Kong* (2nd ed.). Hong Kong: Hong Kong University Press.
Lowe, C. J. G. (1980). How the government in Hong Kong makes policy. *Hong Kong Journal of Public Administration 2*(2), 63–79.
Lui, T. T. (1994). Efficiency as a political concept in the Hong Kong government: Issues and problems. In J. P. Burns (Ed.), *Asian civil service systems: Improving efficiency and productivity* (pp. 17–58). Singapore: Times Academic Press.
Lui, T. T., & Cooper, T. L. (1996). Bureaucracy, democracy and administrative ethics: A study of public service values in Hong Kong. *International Review of Administrative Sciences, 62*(2), 177–196.
Lui, T. T., & Scott, I. (2001). Administrative ethics in a Chinese society. In T. L. Cooper (Ed.), *Handbook of administrative ethics* (2nd ed., pp. 649–669). New York: Marcel Dekker.

Luk, S. C. Y. (2014). The politics of health care financing reforms in Hong Kong. *Public Administration and Policy, 17*(1), 15–31.

Ma, N. (2007). *Political development in Hong Kong: State, political society, and civil society.* Hong Kong: Hong Kong University Press.

Ma, N. (2015). The rise of "anti-China" sentiments in Hong Kong and the 2012 Legislative Council elections. *China Review, 15*(1), 39–66.

Ma, N. (2017). The China factor in Hong Kong elections, 1991–2016. *China Perspectives, 3,* 17–26.

Ma, N., & Cheng, E. W. (Eds.) (2020). *The Umbrella Movement: Civil resistance and contentious space in Hong Kong* (rev. ed.). Amsterdam: Amsterdam University Press.

Manion, M. (2004). *Corruption by design: Building clean government in Mainland China and Hong Kong.* Cambridge, MA: Harvard University Press.

Martin, J. T., & Chan, W. W. L. (2014). Hong Kong-style community policing: A study of the Yau Ma Tei fruit market. *Crime, Law and Social Change, 61,* 401–416.

McWalters, I., & Bruce, A. (2019). *Bribery and corruption law in Hong Kong* (4th ed.). Hong Kong: LexisNexis.

Miners, N. J. (1987). *Hong Kong under imperial rule 1912–1941.* Hong Kong: Oxford University Press.

Miners, N. J. (1998). *The government and politics of Hong Kong* (5th ed.), with post-handover update by J. T. H. Tang. Hong Kong: Oxford University Press.

Miners, N. J. (1998). Executive-legislative relations. In I. Scott (Ed.), *Institutional change and the political transition in Hong Kong.* Basingstoke: Macmillan.

Morris, P. (2010). Academic freedom, university governance and the state: The Commission of Inquiry into the Hong Kong Institute of Education. *Journal of Education Policy, 25*(5), 587–563.

Morris, P., & Scott, I. (2003). Educational reform and policy implementation in Hong Kong. *Journal of Education Policy, 18*(1), 71–84.

Morris, P., & Vickers, E. (2015). Schooling, politics and the construction of identity in Hong Kong: The 2012 "moral and national education" crises in historical perspective. *Comparative Education, 51*(3), 305–326.

Ng, M. K. (2006). World-city formation under an executive-led government: The politics of harbour reclamation in Hong Kong. *The Town Planning Review, 77*(3), 311–337.

Ngan, R., & Li, M. K. Y. (2007). Responding to poverty, income inequality and social welfare: The neo-liberalist government versus a social investment state. In J. Y. S. Cheng (Ed.), *The Hong Kong Special Administrative Region in its first decade* (pp. 535–563). Hong Kong: City University Press.

Oxfam (2018). *Hong Kong inequality report.* https://www.oxfam.org.hk/en/f/news_and_publication/16372/Oxfam_inequality%20report_Eng_FINAL.pdf

Painter, M. (2005). Transforming the administrative state: Reform in Hong Kong and the future of the developmental state. *Public Administration Review, 65*(3), 335–346.

Painter, M. (2012). Hong Kong. In K. Verhoest, S. Van Thiel, G. Bouckaert, & P. Lægreid (Eds.), *Government agencies: Practices and lessons from 30 countries* (pp. 342–352). Basingstoke: Palgrave Macmillan.

Painter, M., & Yee, W. H. (2012). Agencies and policy in an administrative state: The case of Hong Kong. *Policy and Society, 31*(3), 223–235.

Palmer, A. W. (2018, 3 April). The case of Hong Kong's missing booksellers. *New York Times Magazine.* https://www.nytimes.com/2018/04/03/magazine/the-case-of-hong-kongs-missing-booksellers.html

Patten, C. (1998). *East and West*. London: Macmillan.
Pepper, S. (2008). *Keeping democracy at bay: Hong Kong and the challenge of Chinese political reform*. Lanham, MD: Rowan and Littlefield.
Petersen, C. J. (2001). The right to equality in the public sector: An assessment of post-colonial Hong Kong. *Hong Kong Law Journal, 32*(1), 103–134.
Poon, A. (2011). *Land and the ruling class in Hong Kong* (2nd ed.). Singapore: Enrich Professional Publishing.
Public Opinion Research Institute (2019). *Anti-extradition bill: People's public sentiment report*. https://static1.squarespace.com/static/5cfd1ba6a7117c000170d7aa/t/5df3158f04b7db043c7da1bd/1576211867361/PCF_Anti_Extradition_Bill_Stage+3_rpt_2019dec13_first+edition.pdf
Purbrick, M. (2019). A report of the 2019 protests. *Asian Affairs, 50*(4), 465–487.
Rabushka, A. (1979). *Hong Kong: A study in economic freedom*. Chicago: University of Chicago Press.
Rao, G., & Wan, Z. (2007). Hong Kong's "one country, two systems" experience under the Basic Law: Two perspectives from Chinese legal scholars. *Journal of Contemporary China 16*(2), 341–358.
Richburg, K. B. (2020, 28 April). Hong Kong's autonomy dying in full view. *The Strategist*. https://www.aspistrategist.org.au/hong-kongs-autonomy-dying-in-full-view/
Rowse, M. (2009). *No minister and no, minister: The true story of HarbourFest*. Hong Kong: Treloar Enterprises.
Schoeb, V. (2016). Healthcare service in Hong Kong and its challenges. *China Perspectives, 4*, 51–58.
Scott, I. (1987). Policy implementation in Hong Kong. *Southeast Asian Journal of Social Science, 15*(2), 1–19.
Scott, I. (1989). *Political change and the crisis of legitimacy in Hong Kong*. London: Hurst.
Scott, I. (1996). Civil service neutrality in Hong Kong. In H. K. Asmeron & E. P. Reis (Eds.), *Democratization and bureaucratic neutrality* (pp. 277–293). Basingstoke: Macmillan.
Scott, I. (2000). The disarticulation of Hong Kong's post-handover political system. *The China Journal, 43*, 29–53.
Scott, I. (2003). Organizations in the public sector in Hong Kong: Core government, quasi-government and private bodies with public functions. *Public Organization Review 3*(3), 247–267.
Scott, I. (2005). *Public administration in Hong Kong: Regime change and its impact on the public sector*. Singapore: Marshall Cavendish.
Scott, I. (2006). The government and statutory boards in Hong Kong: Centralization and autonomy. *Public Organization Review 6*(3), 185–202.
Scott, I. (2007). Legitimacy, governance and public policy in post-handover Hong Kong. *Asia Pacific Journal of Public Administration, 29*(1), 29–49.
Scott, I. (2014). Political scandals and the accountability of the Chief Executive in Hong Kong. *Asian Survey, 54*(5), 966–986.
Scott, I. (2017). One country, two systems: The end of a legitimating ideology? *Asia Pacific Journal of Public Administration, 39*(2), 83–99.
Scott, I. (2020). Context and innovation in traditional bureaucracies: A Hong Kong study. *Public Administration and Development. 41*(1), 12–22.
Scott, I., & Gong, T. (2015). Evidence-based policy-making for corruption prevention in Hong Kong: A bottom-up approach. *Asia Pacific Journal of Public Administration, 37*(2), 87–101.

Scott, I., & Gong, T. (2019). *Corruption prevention and governance in Hong Kong*. Abingdon: Routledge.
Shek, D. T. (2020). Protests in Hong Kong (2019–2020): A perspective based on quality of life and well-being. *Applied Research in Quality of Life, 15*(3), 611–635.
Sinn, E. (1989). *Power and charity: The early history of the Tung Wah Hospital*. Hong Kong: Oxford University Press.
Smart, A. (2006). *The Shek Kip Mei myth: Squatters, fires and colonial rule in Hong Kong 1950–1963*. Hong Kong: Hong Kong University Press.
Smart, A. (2018). The unbearable discretion of street-level bureaucrats: Corruption and collusion in Hong Kong. *Current Anthropology, 59* (supplement 18), S37–S47.
So, A. Y. C. (2017). A new wave of anti-mainland protests since 2012: Characteristics, sociopolitical origins, and political implications. *Asian Education and Development Studies, 6*(4), 333–342.
Steinhardt, H. C., Li, L. C., & Jiang, Y. (2018). The identity shift in Hong Kong since 1997: Measurement and explanation. *Journal of Contemporary China, 27*(110), 261–276.
Stott, C., Ho, L., Radburn, M., Chan, Y. Y., Kyprianides, K., & Morales, P. S. (2020). Patterns of "disorder" during the 2019 protests in Hong Kong: Policing, social identity, intergroup dynamics and radicalization. *Policing: A Journal of Policy and Practice*. https://doi.org/10.1093/police/paaa073
Tai, B. (2019). 30 years after Tiananmen: Hong Kong remembers. *Journal of Democracy, 30*(2), 64–69.
Tai, B., Veitch, S., Fu, H., & Cullen, R. (2020). Pursuing democracy in an authoritarian state: Protest and the rule of law in Hong Kong. *Social and Legal Studies, 29*(1), 1–39.
Thomson, S. (2017). Clutter and cobwebs: How administrative tribunals in Hong Kong can learn from the UK. *Civil Justice Quarterly, 36*(3), 363–386.
Thynne, I. (1998). Autonomy and integration. In I. Scott (Ed.), *Institutional change and the political transition in Hong Kong* (pp. 234–247). Basingstoke: Macmillan.
Thynne, I. (2006). Statutory bodies as instruments of government in Hong Kong: Review beginnings and analytical challenges ahead. *Public Administration and Development, 26*(1), 45–53.
Thynne, I. (2018). Fundamentals of government structure: Alignments of organizations at and beyond the center of power. In W. R. Thompson (Ed.), *Oxford research encyclopedia of politics*. New York: Oxford University Press. https://oxfordre.com/politics/view/10.1093/acrefore/9780190228637.001.0001/acrefore-9780190228637-e-128
Thynne, I., & Goldring, J. (1987). *Accountability and control: Government officials and the exercise of power*. Sydney: Law Book Company.
Tsang, S. Y. S. (Ed.) (2001). *Judicial independence and the rule of law in Hong Kong*. Basingstoke: Palgrave.
Tsang, S. Y. S. (2007). *Governing Hong Kong: Administrative officers from the nineteenth century to the handover to China, 1862–1997*. London: IB Taurus.
Tse, H., & Mak, M. C. F. (2022). Value dynamics in support to social movement: Hong Kong civil servants in the anti-extradition bill movement. *Social Transformations in Chinese Societies*. https://doi.org/10.1108/STICS-04-2021-0007
Turner, M. (1996). *60s/90s: Dissolving the people*. Hong Kong: Hong Kong Arts Centre.
Ure, G. (2012). *Governors, politics and the Colonial Office: Public policy in Hong Kong, 1918–58*. Hong Kong: Hong Kong University Press.
Veg, S. (2017). The rise of "localism" and civic identity in post-handover Hong Kong: Questioning the Chinese nation-state. *The China Quarterly, 230*, 323–347.

Wang-Kaeding, H., & Kaeding, M. P. (2019). Red capital in Hong Kong. *Asian Education and Development Studies*, 8(2), 149–160.

Wang, Z. (2008, April). The significance of China's decision on universal suffrage. *The Hong Kong Journal, 10*. www.hkjournal.org

Wong, C. K. (2008). Squaring the welfare circle in Hong Kong: Lessons for governance in social policy. *Asian Survey*, 48(2), 323–342.

Wong, E. Y. L., Coulter, A., Cheung, A. W. L., Yam, C. H. K., Yeh, E. K., & Griffiths, S. M. (2012). Patient experiences with public hospital care: First benchmark study in Hong Kong. *Hong Kong Medical Journal*, 18(5), 371–380.

Wong, J. K., & So, A. Y. (2020). The re-making of developmental citizenship in post-handover Hong Kong. *Citizenship Studies*, 24(7), 934–949.

Wong, J. S. C. (2017). The role of government in poverty alleviation in Hong Kong: Part 1—dynamics of policy attention, choice and change. *Asia Pacific Journal of Public Administration*, 39(4), 238–257.

Wong, J. S. C. (2018). The role of government in poverty alleviation in Hong Kong: Part II—diversity of instrument choice. *Asia Pacific Journal of Public Administration*, 40(1), 23–42.

Wong, K. T. W., Zheng, V., & Wan, P. S. (2021). Local versus national identity in Hong Kong 1998–2017. *Journal of Contemporary Asia*, 51(5), 803–827.

Wong, L., Kellogg, T. E., & Lai, E.Y. H. (2021, 28 June). Hong Kong's national security law and the right to fair trial: A GCAL briefing paper. https://www.law.georgetown.edu/law-asia/wp-content/uploads/sites/31/2021/06/HongKongNSLRightToFairTrial.pdf

Wong, M. Y. H. (2017). Discussing without deciding, deciding without acting: Veto players in Hong Kong, and Beijing's response. *Asian Journal of Comparative Politics*, 2(4), 347–361.

Wong, M. Y. H. (2020). Welfare or politics? A survey experiment of political discontent and support for redistribution in Hong Kong. *Politics*, 40(1), 70–89.

Wong, S. H. W. (2015). *Electoral politics in post-1997 Hong Kong*. Singapore: Springer.

Wong, S. H. W. (2019). Gerrymandering in elected autocracies: Evidence from Hong Kong. *British Journal of Political Science*, 49(2), 579–610.

Wong, S. H. W., Ma, N., & Lam, W. M. (2016). Migrants and democratization: The political economy of Chinese immigrants in Hong Kong. *Contemporary Chinese Political Economy and Strategic Relations*, 2(2), 909–940.

Wong, W., & Xiao, H. (2018). Twenty years of Hong Kong and Macao under Chinese rule: Being absorbed under "one country, two systems". *Public Policy and Management*, 38(6), 411–418.

Xiao, H., Wang, H., & Liu, C. (2020). Budgetary punctuations: A fiscal management perspective. *Policy Studies Journal*, 48(4), 896–925.

Xiao, W. (2001). *One country, two systems: An account of the drafting of the Hong Kong Basic Law*. Beijing: Peking University Press.

Yeung, G. (2018). End of a chapter? Hong Kong manufacturers in the Pearl River Delta. In T. L. Lui, S. W. K. Chiu, & R. Yep (Eds.), *Routledge handbook of contemporary Hong Kong* (pp. 397–413). London: Routledge.

Yeung, R. (2008). *Moving millions: The commercial and political controversies of Hong Kong's railways*. Hong Kong: Hong Kong University Press.

Yeung, R. L. K., Li, A. H. F., & Hung, S. K. (2015). Monetising social and environmental costs in infrastructure evaluation: The case of Hong Kong's third international airport runway. *Asia Pacific Journal of Public Administration*, 37(3), 207–215.

Young, S. N. M., & Cullen, R. (2010). *Electing Hong Kong's Chief Executive*. Hong Kong: Hong Kong University Press.

Yuen, S. (2021). Native-place networks and political mobilization: The case of post-handover Hong Kong. *Modern China*, 47(5), 510–539.

Yung, B., & Yu, K. P. (Eds.) (2020). *Land and housing controversies in Hong Kong: Perspectives of justice and social values*. Singapore: Springer.

Index

academic freedom, 87–8, 321, 350–2, 355, 360
accountability, 7, 10, 14–17, 22, 31–3, 37–99, 139, 159, 164, 167–8, 172, 175, 179, 186–7, 190, 193, 198, 230, 277, 290, 335, 339, 347, 356, 391, 396, 408–9, 412; civil servants, 9–10, 159, 164, 339, 408–9; Hong Kong government, 31–2, 37–66, 74, 94–6, 356, 396, 408. *See also* Basic Law; Chief Executive; elections; judicial review; Legislative Council; Police Force; political appointments system; POAS; public bodies
Administrative Appeals Board, 365, 388–9
administrative grade, 8, 17, 28, 86, 93, 103, 106–7, 113–19, 120; policymaking 17, 115, 117–19, 157, 244, 276, 389; Chinese government's attitude towards, 115–16, 117; criticism of the government, 118; promotion, 115, 116; recruitment, 113, 115, 276; values, 119, 389. *See also* civil service; policy; POAS
administrative tribunals, 373, 386–9
advisory boards, 173, 175, 187, 196–8, 300, 350; "6 plus 6" rule, 196; appointments, 196, 198, 296. *See also* consultation
Airport Authority, 1, 171–3, 176, 181; opening of the airport, 16, 78, 171, 187, 190, 396. *See also* privatisation
Air Quality Health Index, 290
Alliance for True Democracy, 49
American Chamber of Commerce, 84, 85, 173, 260
Apple Daily, 43, 363
Applied Science and Technology Research Institute (ASTRI), 173–4, 197, 288
Article 23. *See* national security legislation, 2003; national security legislation, 2020

Asian financial crisis, 16, 18, 127, 138, 172, 205, 213, 331
Audit Commission, 2–3, 14, 103, 105, 174, 192–3, 194, 196, 198, 289–93. *See also* Director of Audit
autonomy, 1–3, 6–8, 17, 23–4, 28, 30, 32, 37, 42, 52, 57, 65, 68, 71, 72–4, 87, 107, 110, 115, 121, 122, 167–8, 173, 176, 184, 186, 198, 206–7, 237, 254, 261, 264, 296, 320–3, 350, 351, 373, 391, 395, 399, 400, 402, 403, 407; bureaucratic autonomy, 1–3, 8, 17, 94, 107, 110, 132, 167–8, 175–6, 184, 186, 198, 395, 409; "high degree of autonomy", 6, 37, 39, 57, 71, 72–4, 296, 303, 320–2, 399, 400, 411; relative, 6, 189, 237, 254, 395. *See also* Basic Law; Joint Declaration
Avian flu, 76, 78, 396

Banking Ordinance, 171
Basic Law, 4, 6–7, 10, 14–15, 18, 20, 22–3, 29, 31, 37–74, 75, 76, 78, 79, 87, 89, 92, 93, 94, 116–17, 121, 127, 133, 139–41, 151, 156, 157–8, 163, 177, 178, 208, 220, 230, 254, 296–8, 308, 313, 318–20, 328, 335, 350, 358–9, 360, 369, 391–3, 395–6, 396–7, 399, 402–3, 405–6, 408, 411, 412; accountability, 39–44, 75, 220, 230, 408; civil liberties, 25, 53–65, 74, 94, 133, 358–60, 389; constitutional development, 22–4, 85, 397–400; deficiencies, 48–50, 254; executive-led government, 40, 42, 45, 78, 84, 328, 347, 390, 396, 399, 408; interpretation, 22–3, 25, 39, 43, 65–72, 318–19, 360, 366, 400, 402; promulgation, 40, 358; separation of powers, 20, 45, 69, 402; universal suffrage, 22–4, 48–50, 58, 73, 74, 117, 399–400. *See also* accountability; Chief Executive; Chinese government; civil liberties; civil service; Joint Declaration; Legislative

Council; national security legislation, 2003; national security legislation, 2020; "one country, two systems"
Basic Law Consultative Committee, 40
Basic Law Drafting Committee, 40
Bauhinia Foundation, 30, 255, 293
Beetham, David, 22
Belt and Road Initiative, 288, 297, 311, 315–17, 321
Bill of Rights, 10, 45, 65, 141, 246, 350, 358–9
booksellers' case, 53, 58–9, 259, 360, 402
British government 9, 40, 42, 44, 65, 116, 168, 206, 242–3, 283, 330. *See also* Joint Declaration
British National Overseas passports, 65
budget, 4–6, 9, 12, 18, 21, 42, 82, 85, 110, 125, 126, 127–8, 131–2, 136, 166, 168, 172, 179, 184, 203–35, 241, 250–2, 266, 274, 280, 287, 290, 293, 300, 317, 323, 332, 337, 344, 395, 406, 410; and the Chinese government, 218–19, 220, 287, 317, 410; Appropriations Bill, 222, 227, 230; balanced, 125, 128, 132, 168, 206–8, 210–11, 213, 220, 332; bonds, 217; cash handouts, 132, 212, 219, 227, 230, 232–3, 235, 270, 287, 302, 334, 410; consolidated account, 208, 211, 213; deficits, 5–6, 9, 18, 118, 125, 127, 136, 166, 205–6, 208, 209–11, 215, 217, 219, 221, 223, 224, 227, 251, 323, 332, 395, 410; expenditure, 4–6, 9, 20–1, 41, 86, 106, 107, 125, 127–8, 131–2, 168, 181–2, 184–5, 190, 205–13, 215–35, 249–50, 263–5, 270, 287, 292, 329, 349, 395, 409; land sales, 9, 208, 213–14, 217, 234; Medium Range Forecast (MRF), 211, 213, 221–4; operating account, 208, 210–11; principles, 206–11, 213–20; reserves, 20, 125, 203, 207–8, 210, 214, 217, 220, 221, 332; resource allocation exercise, 221–3; revenue, 9, 41, 127, 131, 172, 178, 184, 205–9, 210–11, 213–18, 220, 221, 223, 226, 241; Star Chamber, 86, 221–5; surpluses, 9, 18, 125, 126, 207, 209, 211, 216–17, 219, 221–4, 241; Task Force on public finances, 215. *See also* civil service pay; CSSA; Express rail link; HZMB; policy; poverty; taxes
Buildings Department, 111, 275, 378
business, 11, 16, 31, 38, 41, 50, 57, 59, 74, 91, 92, 127, 128, 129, 135, 138, 172, 207, 209, 215–16, 220–1, 237–8, 240, 241, 244–5, 253, 254–5, 260–2, 264, 270, 277, 283, 286, 291, 296, 298–300, 303–5, 311, 314,
315–16, 321, 322, 330, 331, 339, 363, 392, 395, 399, 402; and the Chinese government, 303–4, 311–13; and the Hong Kong government, 16, 59, 128, 215, 257, 296; Mainland businesses in Hong Kong, 57, 301, 304–5, 312, 317, 352, 402; political representation, 38, 74, 277, 304–5, 399. *See also* Business and Professionals Alliance; Hong Kong Stock Exchange; PRD
Business and Professionals Alliance, 304

Catholic Church, 69, 133
Census and Statistics Department, 111, 258, 293, 369
Central Policy Unit, 109, 226, 255. *See also* Policy Innovation and Coordination Unit
centralisation, 8–9, 15, 38, 45, 78, 105–6, 110, 115, 118, 121–2, 124, 125–6, 135, 167, 170, 186, 198, 242–3, 247, 294
Chan, Johannes, 351
Chan Mo-po, Paul, 210
Chan On-sang, Anson, 92, 117, 120, 159, 165, 190, 393, 395, 396, 399
Chan Pak-fong, Peter, 119
Chan Tong-kai, 259
Cheung Kin-chung, Matthew, 212. *See also* Chief Secretary for Administration
Chief Executive, 10, 15–17, 22–5, 27, 31, 39, 40–2, 43, 48–50, 53, 56, 59–60, 62, 68, 72–4, 77, 78–80, 82–5, 88, 91–3, 103, 107, 109, 117–19, 120, 131, 135, 138, 140, 161–3, 179, 187–8, 189, 204, 222, 225, 230, 315–16, 321, 350–1, 354, 366, 375–6, 382, 386, 392, 396, 399, 400–6, 408, 411; accountability, 17, 31–2, 39, 88, 409; appointment, 72; election, 22–25, 27, 29–30, 39, 48–50, 72, 77, 89, 109, 258, 279, 281, 301, 318, 328, 399–400; Election Committee, 23, 48, 49, 301; impeachment, 41–2; powers, 36–40, 60, 72–4, 77, 88, 94, 107, 163, 187–9, 277. *See also* Lam, Carrie; Leung Chun-ying; Tsang, Yam-kuen; Tung Chee Hwa
Chief Executive's Office, 78, 91, 227, 359
Chief Justice, 41, 70, 73, 361
Chief Secretary for Administration, 21, 86, 107, 111, 117, 118, 119, 139, 223, 270, 286. *See also* Chan On-sang, Anson; Cheung Kin-chung, Matthew; Hui Si-yan, Rafael; Lam, Carrie; Tsang Yam-kuen, Donald
Child Development Fund, 177, 180

Index

China Motor Bus Company, 185
Chinese Communist Party, 106, 126, 168, 297–9, 307–8
Chinese government, 6–7, 10, 14–15, 17–19, 22–4, 27, 31, 37–57, 64, 76, 79, 83, 85, 88–9, 94, 98, 115, 116, 117, 119, 121, 124, 127, 131, 133, 135, 153, 157, 170–1, 173, 174, 176, 198, 204, 205–6, 209, 220, 234, 235, 237, 239, 240, 242, 244, 245, 255, 256, 258, 259, 264–5, 270, 271, 280, 287–8, 296–323, 330, 335, 354, 358, 360, 391–3, 395–401, 403–5, 408, 410–12; and the Basic Law, 22–3, 31–2, 37–57, 64–5, 72–4, 76, 79, 83, 85, 88–9, 98, 117–19, 296, 318–20, 358–60, 391–2, 393, 396, 397, 399, 405, 408, 411; on democracy, 6, 23, 27, 46–7, 240, 281, 297; economic integration of Hong Kong, 231, 297, 310–18; Hong Kong and Macau Affairs Office, 73, 83, 299; Liaison Office, 17, 72–3, 89, 192, 254, 296–7, 299–300, 302, 319–22, 405, 407; political integration of Hong Kong, 6–7, 15, 17–19, 22–27, 37, 160, 212, 288, 297–305, 318–22, 391, 403, 410; social integration of Hong Kong, 74, 297, 305–22, 398; united front groups, 54, 57, 117, 254, 260, 296–300, 302–3, 319, 322. *See also* administrative grade; Belt and Road Initiative; budget; business; CEPA; CPP; DAB; elections; Hong Kong and Macau Affairs Office; national security legislation, 2003; national security legislation, 2020; New China News Agency; NPC; NPCSC; PRD; State Council
Chinese Medicine Ordinance, 289
Chinese University of Hong Kong, 86–7, 133, 257, 341
Chung Lai-kwok, Elaine, 162
Chung Ting-yiu, Robert, 350
Citizen's Charter, 336
civic engagement, 19, 258, 278
Civic Exchange, 255
Civil Human Rights Front, 56
civil liberties, 6, 10, 18, 22–6, 35, 37, 45, 47, 53–59, 64, 65, 73–4, 94, 133, 170, 242, 246, 254, 261, 263, 286, 297, 320–1, 330, 334, 356, 357–60, 367, 371, 389, 391–2, 397, 402–4, 411. *See also* Basic Law; Bill of Rights; Extradition Bill; International Covenant on Civil and Political Rights; International Covenant on Economic, Social and Cultural Rights; Joint Declaration; judicial review; national security legislation, 2003; national security legislation, 2020; press: freedom
civil service, 1–2, 7–17, 20–1, 28–30, 44–5, 78–80, 85, 86, 89, 92, 103–66, 167, 169–70, 194–5, 198, 204–6, 210, 219, 220, 223, 241–4, 249, 255–6, 273, 277, 328, 330–2, 335–6, 338, 348–9, 363, 367, 370, 372, 392–7, 400, 408, 412; anti-government protests, 10, 27–30, 120, 410; bureaus, 1, 8, 17, 21, 76, 78, 85, 86, 90–3–4, 103, 107–9, 110–13, 115–17, 121–4, 129, 140, 154, 167, 176, 178, 180, 221–6, 228, 230, 276, 290, 348–50, 370, 404, 407; coordination, 8, 12, 17, 20–1, 45, 79, 83, 86, 91, 106, 113, 115, 123–4, 226, 231, 271–7, 315, 396, 412; cost, 123, 129, 131, 134–5, 143–5, 150–1, 153, 157, 165, 219–24, 255, 331; departments, 1, 8, 12, 15–17, 21, 28, 76, 77, 103–15, 121–4, 128, 134, 138–40, 154, 156–7, 160, 163, 173, 221–34, 247, 274–7, 290–4, 320–1, 328, 331, 336–8, 348–50, 361–3, 378, 380–1, 404, 407, 412; discipline, 8, 45, 98, 121, 158–65; disciplined services, 110, 112, 132, 140, 142–9, 157, 271–3; expatriates, 9, 44, 116, 138, 141–2; gender, 143, 190, 279; grades and ranks, 113–19, 128, 141, 143, 145, 146–5; localisation, 9, 116, 138, 141; non-civil service staff (NCSC), 128–9, 226; oath of allegiance, 21, 121, 412; organisation, 107–13; performance appraisal, 150, 152, 153–6; political neutrality, 7, 9–10, 44, 91, 103–4, 119–21, 135, 159, 393–6, 409; post-retirement, 162; recruitment, 5, 9, 16, 44–5, 116, 127–9, 140–6, 394; reform, 15–17, 105–108, 127, 137–56, 393–4, 412; regulations, 45, 159, 160, 161; retirement, 16, 128, 140–5, 155, 147–148n97, 195, 341, 395; size, 1, 9, 16, 110–2, 125–6, 127–8, 131, 135, 137, 143, 153, 165–6, 210, 241, 244, 294, 331–2; terms of appointment, 141–3; training, 96–7, 137, 153–8, 165, 292, 335–6, 340. *See also* administrative grade; budget; Civil Service Bureau; Civil Service Code; civil service staff associations; complaints; civil service pay, executive grade; Director of Audit; ICAC; ICC; McKinsey reforms; Ombudsman; outsourcing; POAS; public bodies; public–private partnerships
Civil Service Branch, 106, 138
Civil Service Bureau, 91, 113, 121, 138, 363
Civil Service Code, 10, 17, 29, 92, 120–1, 159, 399

civil service pay, 16, 44, 113, 122, 129–32, 137, 139, 146–53, 165, 395; Master Pay Scale, 142, 149; Model Scale 1, 147-8, 331–2; pay cuts, 127–8, 151; Pay Investigation Unit, 146; performance pay, 16, 151–1, 396; Police pay scale, 149; principles, 137; qualification groups, 147; salaries commissions, 146; Standing Commission on Civil Service Salaries and Conditions of Service (SCCSS), 146–52; Task Force on the pay policy and System, 150–3. *See also* civil service: terms of appointment; civil service staff associations; PSC

civil service staff associations, 130, 131, 139, 143, 146, 149–50, 155, 162

Civil Service Training and Development Institute, 156

civil society, 6, 19, 31, 47, 71, 85, 89, 205, 209, 237, 239–1, 258, 276–8, 280–4, 294, 359, 389, 391, 400, 410–11. *See also* Catholic church; political parties, pressure groups

Closer Economic Partnership Arrangement (CEPA), 297, 311–12

Code on Access to Information, 360–1, 367, 375, 387. *See also* press; Hong Kong Journalists Association; Law Reform Commission

colonial administration, 7–15, 105–6, 118, 125, 206, 208, 243, 247–8, 256, 330–1, 368, 373, 391–4, 398; Secretariat, 105–6. *See also* policy

Commerce and Economic Development Bureau, 352–3

Commissioner for Administrative Complaints. *See* Ombudsman

Commissioner for Resettlement, 169

Communications Authority, 353

Community Chest, 184

Companies Registry, 171

Competition Tribunal, 388

complaints, 11, 14, 41, 76, 93, 97–8, 123, 134, 154, 157, 170, 183, 193, 205, 275–6, 340, 343, 344, 348, 353, 357–83, 386, 387, 404. *See also* CAPO; ICC; IPCC, Ombudsman

Complaints Against Police Office (CAPO), 97–8, 383–6, 408. *See also* complaints; IPCC; Ombudsman

Comprehensive Social Security Assistance (CSSA), 225, 248–53, 269, 286, 331

Constitutional and Mainland Affairs Bureau, 51, 92, 320, 363

consultation, 12, 19, 40, 53–6, 60, 76–7, 80, 91, 103, 130, 138–9, 141–2, 152, 156, 196, 216, 222, 225, 226, 234, 236, 238–9, 242, 244–5, 246, 248, 256–9, 260, 263, 269, 270, 271–3, 276–9, 281–2, 293–4, 339, 347, 350, 356, 359, 361, 382; consultation documents, 19, 54, 76, 91, 138–9, 141–2, 156, 196, 216, 222, 226, 257, 260, 278–9, 350, 359, 361. *See also* advisory boards

Consumer Council, 368

Coopers and Lybrand, 94

core government, 2, 167, 175, 178–9. *See also* centralisation

Correctional Services Department, 8, 110–11, 271

corruption. *See* ICAC, integrity management

Court of Final Appeal (CFA), 43, 65–8

Court of First Instance, 66, 388

COVID-19, 26, 71, 121, 131, 153, 157, 205, 212, 217, 220, 225, 227, 230, 268, 274, 287, 306, 314, 315, 344, 353, 376–7

Cultural Revolution, 126

Cyberport, 173–4, 186, 257, 288

Democratic Alliance for Betterment of Hong Kong (DAB), 46, 78, 83, 88, 90, 296, 298–304, 397. *See also* Legislative Council; political parties

Democratic Party, 48, 50, 83, 93, 216

Director of Audit, 78, 85, 122, 173, 187, 191, 193, 275, 288–92, 294, 349, 352–3, 408. *See also* Audit Commission; Legislative Council: Public Accounts Committee

Director of Environmental Protection, 69

Director of Public Prosecutions, 193

District Boards, 76–7, 368

District Councils, 15, 27, 49, 77, 197, 301, 346, 369. *See also* elections

District Watch Committee, 13

Disneyland, 134, 173, 186, 257

Education Bureau, 69, 111, 112, 180, 232, 307–10, 351, 407; "moral and national education", 28, 133, 256, 281, 307–10, 322, 398, 410; secondary schools place allocation (SSPA), 365; university merger, 133. *See also* Catholic church, EOC; HKIEd; Li Kwok-cheung, Arthur; Morris, Paul; Ng, Hak-kim, Eddie; Scholarism

Efficiency Office/Unit, 109, 138, 331, 348, 379–80

efficiency, 2, 16, 44, 78, 98, 103, 114, 135, 138, 147, 155–6, 290, 292, 294, 327–30, 334–9, 343, 347, 356, 379, 397. See also Efficiency Office/Unit
e-government, 347–9, 356, 381
elections, 14, 18, 22–8, 39, 42, 46, 47, 48–53, 68, 76–7, 89, 109, 197, 245, 279, 298, 301–5, 307–8, 318, 327–8, 354, 399–402, 404–7. See also Chief Executive; District Councils; Electoral Affairs Commission; Legislative Council; Urban Council
Electoral Affairs Commission, 24, 354, 401
Electrical and Mechanical Services Department, 171
Environmental Protection Department, 69, 173, 290–1, 331, 380
Equal Opportunities Commission (EOC), 10, 170, 197, 359–60, 365–7
Examination and Assessment Authority, 176
Executive Council, 12, 41, 46, 56, 68, 78, 80, 82, 117, 149, 221, 237, 243–4, 247, 252, 255, 296, 300–1, 386
executive grade, 114–15, 338
express rail link, 19, 174, 183, 187, 194, 205, 211, 288, 310, 312–15, 317, 398, 403, 409–10. See also protests
Extradition Bill, 25, 28, 39, 45, 53, 58–60, 120, 259–65, 281, 288, 319, 360, 376, 404, 410

Falun Gong, 54–5
Fang, Christine, 251
Finance Branch, 126, 207, 244, 336
Financial Secretary, 21, 56, 78, 80–2, 85–6, 106–7, 111, 117–18, 125, 121, 135, 172, 174, 179, 207–9, 211, 213, 215–21, 222, 223, 224, 226–7, 229, 230, 232, 223, 243–3, 287–9, 300, 409. See also Chan Mo-po, Paul; Leung Kam-chung, Antony, Tsang Yam-kuen, Donald
Financial Services and the Treasury Bureau, 80, 216, 221, 222–4, 290
Fire Services Department, 8, 110, 271, 337, 380
Food and Environmental Hygiene Department, 76, 111, 362, 378
freedom of the press. See press
Free Trade Agreement Transhipment Scheme, 273
Friedman, Milton, 11
Fugitive Offenders Ordinance. See Extradition Bill
Future Fund, 210

Gini coefficient, 20, 211
governance issues, 10, 18, 22, 24, 28–30, 89, 117, 167, 192, 199, 265, 289, 300, 320, 328, 334, 343, 347, 353, 365, 373, 412
Greater Bay Area. See PRD
Gross Domestic Product (GDP), 4–6, 14, 208–9, 213, 221
Guangdong. See PRD

Harbour Fest, 84–5, 134, 173, 277
harbour reclamation, 69, 258, 278, 283
health care financing, 12, 205, 212, 216, 269, 283
Heung Yee Kuk, 49
Ho, Chun-yan, Albert, 48
Ho, Kwan-yiu, Junius, 353
Home Affairs Bureau, 109, 167, 196–7, 292, 301–2, 307, 366
Hong Kong Alliance in Support of the Patriotic Democratic Movement in China, 54
Hong Kong and Macau Affairs Office, 73, 83, 299
Hong Kong Bar Association, 54, 60, 68, 71, 261, 320, 383, 402, 405
Hong Kong Commercial Daily, 300
Hong Kong Confederation of Trade Unions, 130, 172
Hong Kong Council of Social Service, 168, 184, 249, 251
Hong Kong Federation of Students, 50
Hong Kong Federation of Trade Unions (HKFTU), 296, 298–9, 301–2
Hong Kong government. See accountability; budget; centralisation; core government; Chief Executive, civil service, Executive Council; judiciary; Lam, Carrie; Leung Chun-ying; Legislative Council; legitimacy; national security legislation, 2003, national security legislation 2020; Police Force; policy; public bodies; "small government"; Tsang Yam-kuen; Tung Chee Hwa
Hong Kong identity, 307–8, 310, 401. See also Extradition Bill; localists; protests
Hong Kong Institute of Education (HKIEd), 86–7, 351
Hong Kong Journalists Association, 57. See also press
Hong Kong Monetary Authority, 111, 179
Hong Kong Professional Teachers' Union, 87
Hong Kong Progressive Alliance, 304

Hong Kong Public Opinion Programme (HKUPOP). *See* Public Opinion Research Institute
Hong Kong Science and Technology Parks Corporation, 317
Hong Kong–Shenzhen Information and Technology Park, 317
Hong Kong Sports Development Board, 197
Hong Kong Stock Exchange, 80, 298
Hong Kong University of Science and Technology, 257
Hong Kong Watch, 61
Hong Kong–Zhuhai–Macau bridge (HZMB), 19, 69, 176, 205, 211, 258, 310, 312, 314–15, 317, 403
Hospital Authority, 1, 8, 83–4, 110, 167, 170, 176–7, 181, 182, 189, 197, 273–4, 336; responsiveness, 342–5. *See also* Department of Health; health care financing; Medical Council; patients' rights; SARS
Hospital Authority Review Panel, 83, 273
Housing Authority, 169–70, 173, 181–2, 189–90, 275, 337–8; estate management committees, 346–7; responsiveness, 345–6; waiting lists, 211, 282, 284, 410. *See also* Housing Department; housing policy; poverty
Housing Department, 16, 111, 135, 169, 362, 378
housing policy, 169–70, 181, 255, 278–81, 345–7, 398. *See also* Housing Authority
Hui Si-yan, Rafael, 86, 161, 164, 398
Hu Jintao, 56

Immigration Department, 8, 78, 103, 111, 140, 159, 273, 336, 338, 361, 363, 367, 369, 378, 387. *See also* right of abode
Independent Commission Against Corruption (ICAC), 11, 82, 87–8, 94, 98, 137, 146, 158–60, 161, 163, 176, 180, 192–3, 314, 368, 370–3, 375, 383, 389, 408; cases, 372; misconduct in public office, 158–61, 165, 193, 398; non-corruption complaints, 372; organization, 371–3; *Prevention of Bribery Ordinance*, 10–11, 158, 267, 370. *See also* integrity management
Independent Police Complaints Council (IPCC), 61, 63, 96, 98, 383–6, 389; criticism, 96–8, 383, 389; powers, 385. *See also* Extradition Bill; CAPO; Yuen Long attack
Inland Revenue Department, 111, 336, 362, 381
Innovation and Technology Bureau, 109

innovation policies, 15, 109, 158, 186, 226, 235, 255, 271, 288–9, 296, 297, 311, 316–18, 348–9, 410. *See also* e-government; Innovation and Technology Bureau
Integrated Call Centre (ICC), 348, 379–81. *See also* Efficiency Office/Unit; Ombudsman
integrity management, 156, 158–62, 164–6. *See also* Civil Service Bureau; ICAC; PSC
International Covenant on Civil and Political Rights, 45, 65, 69, 350, 358–9, 405
International Covenant on Economic, Social and Cultural Rights, 358
Interpretation and General Clauses Ordinance, 187
InvestHK, 84–5
Ip Suk-yee, Regina, 82

Jiang Zemin, 118
Jockey Club, 184, 307
Joint Declaration on the future of Hong Kong, 6–7, 14, 39, 73, 358, 391–3, 399, 411. *See also* Basic Law
judicial review, 19, 21, 43, 46, 59, 65–71, 73, 74, 88, 130, 314, 359, 365, 374, 386–7, 398
judiciary, 26, 42–4, 46, 65–72, 105, 146, 387, 397; judicial independence, 30, 39, 43, 68–9, 72–4, 261, 322, 360, 397, 402–3, 403. *See also* CFA; Chief Justice; judicial review; rule of law

key performance indicators, 337
Kingdon, J. W., 238, 253, 255, 263–4
Kowloon Canton Railway Corporation (KCRC), 3, 169, 173, 177, 182–3

Labour Department, 248, 337–8
Labour Tribunal, 387–8
Lai, Jimmy, 407
Lam, Carrie, 5, 28, 41, 60, 64, 73, 89, 96, 109, 122, 133, 153, 157–8, 165, 186, 197, 205, 212–13, 226, 248, 250–2, 257, 261, 263–5, 278, 284, 300, 309–10, 354, 403–4, 409; Extradition Bill, 58–62, 259–65, 404; social welfare cuts, 248–51. *See also* Chief Executive; CSSA; protests
Lam Cheuk-ting, 63
Lam, Jeffrey, 305
Lands Registry, 171
Lau, Kevin, 58
Lau Kong-wah, 301
Law Chiu-fun, Fanny, 87
Lee Cheuk-yan, 172

Index   443

Lee Chu-ming, Martin, 40
legal aid, 66, 335, 359
Legislative Council, 10, 12, 16–27, 29–30, 31, 37–42, 45–6, 48–52, 53, 55–6, 59–62, 64, 70–84, 88–93, 98, 109, 116, 122, 128, 130, 141, 149, 161, 178–81, 187–8, 190–6, 211–12, 215, 216, 220, 222–3, 226–30, 233, 237, 244, 245, 251, 253, 256, 260–1, 270, 277–9, 291–2, 296, 298, 301–2, 304, 305, 307–8, 313, 318–19, 354–5, 362–3, 366, 368–70, 376, 382, 383, 392, 394–9, 401–3, 405–8; elections, 18, 22–5, 39, 48, 49–50, 70, 301, 302, 304, 307–8, 354, 401, 405; filibusters, 19, 21, 109, 212, 256, 397; Finance Committee, 109, 113, 149, 179, 222, 223, 227, 230–8, 243; functional constituencies, 20, 38, 42, 50, 304–5; House Committee, 84, 262; oath-taking, 21, 70, 354; panels, 80–2, 91, 128, 179–80, 251, 260, 341, 343, 366; powers, 42, 397; Public Accounts Committee, 191–4, 199, 231; redress system, 368–70, 371, 373, 374; Research Office, 211; select committees, 82–4, 171, 192–3, 398. *See also* accountability; DAB; Democratic Party; Liberal Party, localists
legitimacy, 9, 13–15, 21–2, 25–8, 30, 32–3, 47, 71, 74, 117, 169–70, 239, 248, 279, 327–35, 338, 347, 349, 356, 357, 370, 389, 391, 394, 407–8; consent, 13, 22, 32, 47, 57, 244, 330, 393–4, 396, 411–12; defined, 22, 327; performance legitimacy, 22, 204, 327–9, 330–2, 412. *See also* colonial administration
Lehman Brothers, 278
Leisure and Cultural Services Department, 77, 112
Leung Chin-man, 162
Leung Chung-hang, 70
Leung Chun-ying, 28, 41, 50, 69, 72, 88–90, 109, 122, 131, 135, 153, 161, 164–5, 198, 205, 248, 255, 351, 399, 403, 409. *See also* Chief Executive
Leung Kam-chung, Antony, 83
Leung Ming-yin, 159
Leung Oi-sIe, Elsie, 301
Liberal Party, 56, 78, 129, 138–9, 261, 301, 303–4, 397
Li Kwok-cheung, Arthur, 87, 351
localists, 24, 48, 69, 310, 319, 322, 354–6, 401, 405, 411. *See also* Extradition Bill
Luo Huining, 73, 319

MacLehose, Sir Murray, 8, 94, 207, 239, 241, 244, 246, 392
Mak Chai-kwong, 89
Ma Si-hang, Frederick, 80–1
Mass Transit Railway Corporation (MTRC), 3, 169, 171, 173–4, 176, 182–3, 187–8, 189, 198, 312–4. *See also* KCRC
Ma Tao-li, Geoffrey, 70
McKinsey reforms, 8, 106–7, 123, 243–4, 329–30
Media. *See* press; RTHK
Medical Council, 343, 382–3, 389
migration from mainland China, 303, 305–7
Ming Pao, 58
"moral and national education". *See* Education Bureau, Scholarism
Morris, Paul, 86

National People's Congress (NPC), 26, 40, 49, 52, 64, 66, 67, 121. *See also* national security legislation
national security legislation, 2003, 18, 37, 45, 53, 144, 242, 264, 288, 318, 356, 397, 409, 410. *See also* Basic Law; civil liberties; protests
national security legislation, 2020, 26, 37, 43, 45, 53, 64–5, 98, 121, 133, 157, 205, 212, 220, 271, 286–8, 299–300, 303, 309, 311, 318–22, 350, 352–3, 360, 361, 364, 391, 403–9, 410. *See also* Basic Law; civil liberties; Extradition Bill; NPC; protests
New China News Agency, 297, 299, 304
New Territories, 8, 11, 105, 285, 302, 313
New World First Bus Company, 185
Ng, Hak-kim, Eddie, 89
Ng Ka-ling v Director of Immigration, 66
NPC Standing Committee (NPCSC), 22–3, 25, 43, 48, 50, 66–8, 82, 318, 355, 359, 396, 399–400, 402. *See also* judiciary: judicial independence; right of abode

Occupy Central, 24, 49–50, 341, 351, 400. *See also* Umbrella Movement
Office of the Government Chief Information Officer, 348
Office of the Telecommunication Authority, 171
Official Secrets Ordinance, 54
Ombudsman, 2–3, 10, 14, 123, 159, 275–6, 293–4, 357, 361–2, 366, 368–9, 373, 374–9, 380, 383, 386, 389, 408

Organisation for Economic Co-operation and Development (OECD), 20, 335
"one country, two systems", 23, 37, 39, 64, 71, 255, 297, 303, 315, 318–19, 321, 392, 399, 400, 411
One Country Two Systems Research Institute, 255
Our Hong Kong Foundation, 255
outsourcing, 122, 124, 128, 134, 135, 143, 171, 185–6
Oxfam, 20

parallel traders, 57, 306
patients' rights, 342
Patten, Chris, 14, 242, 245, 298, 303, 335, 392
Pearl River Delta (PRD), 298, 311–12, 316, 317
penny stocks incident, 81, 122
People Power, 24
People's Liberation Army, 64, 299
performance pledges, 14, 336–8, 352, 360
Personal Data (Privacy) Ordinance, 362–4
Po Leung Kuk, 13, 178, 185
Police Force, 5, 8–11, 13–14, 24–6, 30, 44, 50, 55, 58, 60–4, 69, 75, 93–9, 103, 105, 110–13, 119, 129, 132, 138–41, 143–5, 147–9, 160, 163–4, 212, 224, 227, 228, 233, 241, 260, 263, 271, 313, 321, 336, 338–42, 346, 349, 353, 359–60, 362–3, 369–70, 370, 373, 375, 376, 378, 380, 400–1, 403–4, 407–9; accountability, 61, 93–9, 339, 360, 404, 408; allegations of excessive use of force, 26, 61, 95, 163, 342, 347, 384–5, 408; budget, 110, 132, 219, 227–9, 233, 241, 287; Commissioner of Police, 62, 78, 94–6, 113, 119, 140, 271, 339, 353, 359; complaints, *see* CAPO; IPCC; community policing, 24, 95–9, 339–42, 346, 360, 400; corruption, 10, 370; criminal investigation division, 95, 341; dissatisfaction with, 30, 97, 339, 341–2, 383, 401; expatriates, 9, 138, 141; "Living the Values", 97, 340; organization, 8, 113, 339; performance pledge, 337; Police College, 97, 340; responsiveness, 339–42; selective enforcement, 26, 62; size, 5, 110–11, 217. *See also* Extradition Bill; *Public Order Ordinance*; protests; Umbrella Movement
Police Force Council, 147
policy, 2, 11–13, 17, 45, 93, 112–13, 115, 117, 176, 203–6, 231–323, 327, 334, 410, 412; Chinese government's influence, 297–323; colonial policymaking, 11–13, 105–6, 125–7, 234–5; content, 246–53, 266; coordination, *see* civil service: coordination; definitions, 231, 236–7, 267–8; displacement, 272, 287–9; evaluation, 289–94; formulation, 12, 17–18, 31, 79, 91, 93, 98–9, 112–13, 203–5, 236–8, 240–1, 243–4, 252, 257, 263–5, 273, 276–8, 288, 292, 296, 320–2, 391, 396; implementation, 8, 11–13, 15, 18–21, 30, 32–3, 66, 79, 90–1, 93, 112, 117, 123–4, 170, 172, 201, 205, 231, 236–40, 243, 263–5, 266–92, 294, 317, 396–7, 407, 410; incremental, 110, 124, 205, 218, 220, 227, 231, 258, 270, 272, 279–83, 286, 289; instruments, 266–9; rational, 203–5, 236, 238–53, 265, 266, 276–9, 282, 287, 294; symbolic, 239, 242, 245–6, 265, 272, 279, 280, 282–7, 289; top-down, 8, 12, 115, 256–7, 271–6, 280, 283, 342, 346. *See also* housing policy; innovation policies; values
Policy Innovation and Coordination Office, 109, 255
political appointments system, 17, 75, 91–3, 99
political neutrality. *See* civil service
political parties, 6, 46–7, 204–5, 216–17, 220–1, 234, 237–8, 241, 244, 251–2, 277–8, 287, 300, 305, 359. *See also* Business and Professionals Alliance, DAB, Democratic Party; Hong Kong Progressive Alliance; Liberal Party
Post Office, 171, 173
poverty, 20, 205, 211–12, 228, 249, 257–8, 282–3, 285–6, 293, 334, 348, 398, 402, 410. *See also* Gini coefficient; Oxfam
Preliminary Working Committee, 44
press, 55, 57–8, 192, 268, 300, 351; freedom, 55, 57–8, 194, 352, 358–9, 389. *See also* civil liberties; Hong Kong Journalists Association; RTHK
pressure groups, 19, 47, 55, 204–6, 234, 237, 241, 244–5, 251–3, 255–6, 270, 277–8, 305, 330, 345, 366, 396. *See also* civil society
Prevention of Bribery Ordinance. See ICAC
Principal Officials Accountability System (POAS) 16–17, 20–1, 33, 75, 78–91, 98, 106–7, 115, 117–18, 121, 135, 139, 255–6, 277, 329, 396; accountability, 17, 78–91, 98, 121; appointment, 17, 32, 41, 75, 78–9, 86, 117, 296, 300–1, 399; Code of Practice, 82, 88; criticisms, 89–92, 98; dismissal, 82, 90, 399. *See also* Chief Executive
Privacy Commissioner, 10, 362, 362–4, 366
privatisation, 110, 128, 135, 167, 171–2, 176

Index 445

Productivity Commission, 176
property prices, 18, 57, 284, 304
protests, 7, 24–9, 30–2, 47, 50, 53, 56–8, 71, 73, 96, 99, 120, 131–2, 153, 205, 212–13, 217, 219, 227–8, 244, 254, 262–3, 264, 271, 276–7, 281, 286–7, 302, 305–7, 308–9, 313–14, 317, 319–20, 332, 342, 346, 349, 353, 355, 359–60, 364, 366, 371, 378, 383–6, 391, 398, 403–5, 408, 410–12; 2003 protests, 18–19, 47, 56, 239, 318, 397, 328; 2014 protests, 24, 49–50, 95, 302, 341, 400; 2019 protests, 25, 27–8, 42, 53–7, 114, 248–54, 303, 337, 347, 389–91; against the express rail link, 19, 179–80, 248, 278, 303, 384, 394–5; against "moral and national education", 126–7, 245, 271, 297–300, 312, 384, 395; others, 10, 19, 27–8, 42, 53, 114, 124, 126, 260, 270–1, 273, 292, 296, 298, 303, 384, 386. See also civil society; Extradition Bill; localists; pressure groups, Umbrella Movement
Provisional Legislative Council (PLC), 20, 66, 298
public bodies, 1–3, 7–10, 13, 15, 45, 75, 103, 110, 116, 122–3, 127, 158, 167–99, 208, 231, 269, 288, 294, 302, 336, 363, 409, 412; accountability, 122, 167–8, 172, 175–6, 179–80, 186–9, 409, 412; public corporations, 1–2, 169, 171–6, 177, 181–2, 185, 191, 194–5; statutory bodies, 1, 8, 10, 15, 45, 75, 115, 122, 127, 167, 170–1, 173–6, 180, 187–8, 192, 194–8, 273–4, 288, 293–4, 302, 336, 367, 375; subvented, 9, 171, 174, 177–8, 180–6, 190, 192, 195, 198, 209, 231, 269, 294, 334. See also ASTRI; MTRC; Tourism Board; voluntary welfare organizations
Public Opinion Research Institute (PORI), 30, 71, 293, 296–7, 332–1, 342–3
Public Order Ordinance, 359
public-private partnerships, 134–5, 167, 171, 173, 185, 198, 269. See also outsourcing
Public Service (Administration) Order, 45, 107, 155, 163
Public Service Commission (PSC), 9, 106, 140, 143, 154, 156, 164, 372, 375
Public Service (Disciplinary)Regulations, 107
Public Works Department, 105, 160

Qian Qichen, 117
Qiao Xiaoyang, 47
Quality Education Fund, 177, 180

Radio Television Hong Kong (RTHK), 170, 350, 352–4, 376, 378
Regional Council, 15, 69, 75, 77, 98
Regional Services Department, 76–7
responsiveness, 97, 142, 327–8, 334–47, 356, 395
right of abode, 66–8, 369, 397. See also CFA; judiciary
rights. See civil liberties
Rowse, Mike, 85
rule of law, 7, 10, 24, 30, 39, 42–3, 57, 62, 68, 71–2, 74, 104, 137, 158, 330–1, 334, 358, 360, 373–4, 391, 397, 402–3, 405. See also judiciary: judicial independence

Scholarism, 24, 50, 308–9
Secretary for the Civil Service, 29, 80, 131, 139, 149, 150, 159, 162, 219
Secretary for Constitutional and Mainland Affairs, 320
Secretary for Education and Manpower, 87–8
Secretary for Health, Welfare and Food, 84, 88, 252
Secretary for Home Affairs, 366
Secretary for Justice, 43, 55, 78, 107, 111, 117, 193, 301, 361
Secretary for Security, 55, 56, 82, 260, 262, 300, 354, 406
Secretary for Transport and Housing, 188
Securities and Futures Commission, 80
Security Bureau, 111, 113, 261, 369, 387
"Serving the Community", 14, 127, 331
severe acute respiratory syndrome (SARS), 18, 83–4, 88, 127, 213, 253, 273–4. See also civil service: coordination; Department of Health; Hospital Authority
Sewage Services, 171, 183
Shum Kwok-sher, 161
"small government", 4–6, 9, 104, 124–7, 131, 135, 171, 198, 207–8, 221, 254
Social Security Allowance (SSA), 225
Social Welfare Department, 111, 126, 133, 184–5, 190, 194, 198, 224, 228–9, 249, 251, 337, 379; lump sum grant scheme, 132, 183–4, 190, 194. See also CSSA; Lam, Carrie; SSA; poverty; SSA; voluntary welfare associations
Societies Ordinance, 178, 245–6, 354, 359
Society for Community Organisation, 366
squatters, 13, 126, 168–9
State Council (People's Republic of China), 23, 49, 69, 72, 120, 318, 400, 402

statutory bodies. *See* public bodies
Stott, Clifford, 61
SynergyNet, 256
Szeto Wah, 40

Ta Kung Pao, 300
Tai, Benny, 351
Taiwanese government, 260
tax, 1, 6, 9, 11, 19, 129, 168, 181, 193, 207, 213–17, 220–1, 230, 239, 241, 268, 286; company, 6, 9, 214; goods and services tax (GST), 215–16, 228, 239; income (salaries), 181, 213–15. *See also* budget
teachers, 28, 87, 133, 245, 256, 280–1, 308–9, 398
Telecommunications Ordinance, 69
Tiananmen Square, 10, 40, 170, 308, 392
Tien Pei-chun, James, 56, 129
Tong Hin-ming, Timothy, 192, 371, 398
Torture Claims Appeal Board, 387
Tourism Board, 174, 189, 192, 196, 409
tourists, 57, 305–6, 312, 322
Trade and Industry Department, 337
Trade Development Council, 176, 316
Trading Funds Ordinance, 170
transparency, 70, 85, 89–90, 134, 168, 191–6, 277, 327–8, 347, 349, 352
Transport Complaints Unit, 381
Transport Department, 336, 381
Tsang Chun-wah, John, 209
Tsang Yam-kuen, Donald, 4, 17, 21, 23, 41, 85, 92, 107, 109, 117, 122, 132, 135, 157, 160, 164, 172–3, 186, 196, 257–8, 277–8, 281, 307, 332, 393, 393–6, 397. *See also* Chief Executive
Tsui Ying-wai, Caspar, 301
Tung Chee Hwa, 16–17, 46, 48, 76, 91, 107, 118, 121–2, 127, 132–4, 138, 165, 171, 173–5, 185, 198, 239, 255, 257–8, 280, 283, 288, 299, 307, 309, 328, 331–2, 350, 378–86, 395. *See also* Chief Executive
Tung Wah group, 13, 185

Umbrella Movement, 24–5, 58, 69, 95, 97, 163, 279, 302, 309, 341, 359, 369, 398, 400–3, 408. *See also* Occupy Central; Police Force; protests
unemployment, 18, 126, 127, 172, 215–16, 225, 249–50
unions. *See* civil service staff associations; Hong Kong Confederation of Trade Unions; HKFTU

United Nations, 96, 359, 387
universal suffrage, 22–7, 39, 47–50, 58, 73–4, 117, 212, 263, 399–401, 411. *See also* Basic Law; Chinese government; localists; pan-democrats
University Grants Committee (UGC), 110, 177
University of Hong Kong, 350–1
Unofficial Members of the Executive and Legislative Councils (UMELCO), 368
Urban Council, 8, 75–77, 169, 368
Urban Renewal Authority, 188, 191, 195
Urban Services Department, 76, 112

values, 33, 37, 93, 96–8, 119, 135, 156, 159–60, 198, 221, 231, 236–42, 253–4, 327, 329, 339–41, 347, 368, 391, 402; bureaucratic, 31, 165, 181, 370, 394–7, 409; policy-making, 257; regime, 22, 117, 213, 215–16, 240–1, 357. *See also* civil service: political neutrality; efficiency; responsiveness; rule of law; transparency
voluntary welfare organizations, 175, 176, 183–5. *See also* Social Welfare Department

Wang Zhimin, 73, 319
water seepage problem, 123, 275–6, 378
Water Supplies Department, 111, 115, 275, 337, 362, 380
Wen Wei Po, 300
West Kowloon Cultural District, 134, 186, 283
Wilson, Sir David, 245
Women's Commission, 177
Wong Kin-chow, Michael, 365–6
Wu Hung-yuk, Anna, 365

Xia Baolong, 73
Xi Jinping, 259, 318
Xi Yang, 55
Xu Jiatun, 38

Yau Wai-ching, 70
Yeoh Eng-kiong, 83
Youde, Sir Edward, 245
Yu Chung-yin, Patrick, 365
Yuen Long attack, 62–4, 353

Zen Ze-kiun, Bishop, 133
Zhang Xiaoming, 72
Zhu Rongji, 239

Lightning Source UK Ltd.
Milton Keynes UK
UKHW031034181022
410673UK00010B/500